수능기출 전국연합 학력평가

하루 20분 30일 완성

미니 모의고사

고2 영어

KB212716

수능 모의고사 전문 출판
ing 입시플라이

하루 12문제·20분
영어 30일 완성

미니모의고사

가볍게 하루 12문제씩 20분을 학습하면 수능 실전 감각을 키워줄 뿐 아니라 '영어 1등급을 위한 나만의 학습 루틴(routine)'이 됩니다. [30일 완성 미니모의고사]는 수능 영어 전 유형을 매일 골고루 풀 수 있도록 7개년 수능 및 모의평가와 [고2 학력평가] 중 우수한 문제만을 엄선 후 난이도별로 배치했습니다. 학습 부담 없는 30일 완성 미니모의고사로 수능·내신 '1등급의 감각을 유지'하세요.

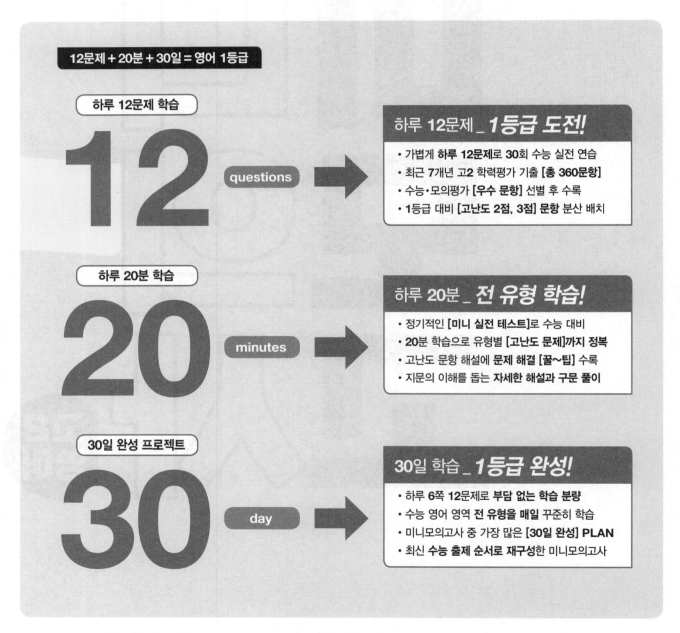

12문제 + 20분 + 30일 = 영어 1등급

하루 12문제 학습

12 questions →

하루 12문제 _ *1등급 도전!*
- 가볍게 **하루 12문제**로 30회 수능 실전 연습
- 최근 **7개년 고2 학력평가** 기출 [총 360문항]
- 수능·모의평가 [우수 문항] 선별 후 수록
- 1등급 대비 [고난도 2점, 3점] 문항 분산 배치

하루 20분 학습

20 minutes →

하루 20분 _ *전 유형 학습!*
- 정기적인 [미니 실전 테스트]로 수능 대비
- 20분 학습으로 유형별 [고난도 문제]까지 정복
- 고난도 문항 해설에 문제 해결 [꿀~팁] 수록
- 지문의 이해를 돕는 자세한 해설과 구문 풀이

30일 완성 프로젝트

30 day →

30일 학습 _ *1등급 완성!*
- 하루 6쪽 12문제로 부담 없는 학습 분량
- 수능 영어 영역 전 유형을 매일 꾸준히 학습
- 미니모의고사 중 가장 많은 [30일 완성] PLAN
- 최신 **수능 출제 순서로 재구성**한 미니모의고사

※ 미니모의고사가 수능에서 반드시 필요한 이유는 *대부분의 수험생들이 영어 과목을 주제(유형)별 위주로 학습하기 때문입니다*. 수능 영어 전 유형을 골고루 풀어 볼 수 있는 미니 모의고사로 하루 12문제씩 학습하면 '실전 감각도 함께 쌓을 수' 있습니다.

Contents &
30 Day planner

고2 영어

- 날짜별로 정해진 **학습 분량에 맞춰 공부**하고 학습 결과를 기록합니다.
- **planner**를 이용해 학습 일정을 계획하고 **자신의 성적을 체크**하면서 30일 완성으로 **목표**를 세우세요.
- 가볍게 매일 20분씩 꾸준하게 학습을 하세요. 주어진 목표 시간 안에 문제를 푸는 연습은 수능 실전에서 자신감까지 **UP**해 줍니다.

DAY 01

● 날짜 :   월   일 ● 시작 시각 :   시   분   초 ● 목표 시간 : 20분

※ 점수 표기가 없는 문항은 모두 **2점**입니다.

01

고2·2024년 3월 18번

다음 글의 목적으로 가장 적절한 것은?

Dear Art Crafts People of Greenville,

For the annual Crafts Fair on May 25 from 1 p.m. to 6 p.m., the Greenville Community Center is providing booth spaces to rent as in previous years. To reserve your space, please visit our website and complete a registration form by April 20. The rental fee is $50. All the money we receive from rental fees goes to support upcoming activities throughout the year. We expect all available spaces to be fully booked soon, so don't get left out. We hope to see you at the fair.

① 지역 예술가를 위한 정기 후원을 요청하려고
② 공예품 박람회의 부스 예약을 안내하려고
③ 대여 물품의 반환 방법을 설명하려고
④ 지역 예술가가 만든 물품을 홍보하려고
⑤ 지역 행사 일정의 변경 사항을 공지하려고

02

고2·2022년 9월 20번

다음 글에서 필자가 주장하는 바로 가장 적절한 것은?

We usually take time out only when we really need to switch off, and when this happens we are often overtired, sick, and in need of recuperation. Me time is complicated by negative associations with escapism, guilt, and regret as well as overwhelm, stress, and fatigue. All these negative connotations mean we tend to steer clear of it. Well, I am about to change your perception of the importance of me time, to persuade you that you should view it as vital for your health and wellbeing. Take this as permission to set aside some time for yourself! Our need for time in which to do what we choose is increasingly urgent in an overconnected, overwhelmed, and overstimulated world.

* recuperation: 회복

① 나를 위한 시간의 중요성을 인식해야 한다.
② 자신의 잘못을 성찰하는 자세를 가져야 한다.
③ 어려운 일이라고 해서 처음부터 회피해서는 안 된다.
④ 사회의 건강과 행복을 위하여 타인과 연대해야 한다.
⑤ 급변하는 사회에서 가치 판단을 신속하게 할 수 있어야 한다.

03

다음 글의 주제로 가장 적절한 것은? [3점]

An important advantage of disclosure, as opposed to more aggressive forms of regulation, is its flexibility and respect for the operation of free markets. Regulatory mandates are blunt swords; they tend to neglect diversity and may have serious unintended adverse effects. For example, energy efficiency requirements for appliances may produce goods that work less well or that have characteristics that consumers do not want. Information provision, by contrast, respects freedom of choice. If automobile manufacturers are required to measure and publicize the safety characteristics of cars, potential car purchasers can trade safety concerns against other attributes, such as price and styling. If restaurant customers are informed of the calories in their meals, those who want to lose weight can make use of the information, leaving those who are unconcerned about calories unaffected. Disclosure does not interfere with, and should even promote, the autonomy (and quality) of individual decision-making.

* mandate: 명령   ** adverse: 거스르는

*** autonomy: 자율성

① steps to make public information accessible to customers

② benefits of publicizing information to ensure free choices

③ strategies for companies to increase profits in a free market

④ necessities of identifying and analyzing current industry trends

⑤ effects of diversified markets on reasonable customer choices

04

Carol Ryrie Brink에 관한 다음 글의 내용과 일치하지 않는 것은?

Born in 1895, Carol Ryrie Brink was orphaned by age 8 and raised by her grandmother. Her grandmother's life and storytelling abilities inspired her writing. She married Raymond Woodard Brink, a young mathematics professor she had met in Moscow, Idaho many years before. After their son and daughter were born, early in her career, she started to write children's stories and edited a yearly collection of short stories. She and her husband spent several years living in France, and her first novel *Anything Can Happen on the River* was published in 1934. After that, she wrote more than thirty fiction and nonfiction books for children and adults. She received the Newbery Award in 1936 for *Caddie Woodlawn*.

① 할머니에 의해 길러졌다.

② Moscow에서 만났던 수학 교수와 결혼했다.

③ 자녀가 태어나기 전에 어린이 이야기를 쓰기 시작했다.

④ 1934년에 그녀의 첫 번째 소설이 출간되었다.

⑤ *Caddie Woodlawn*으로 Newbery 상을 받았다.

05

다음 글의 밑줄 친 부분 중, 어법상 틀린 것은? [3점]

Are cats liquid or solid? That's the kind of question that could win a scientist an Ig Nobel Prize, a parody of the Nobel Prize that honors research that "makes people laugh, then think." But it wasn't with this in mind ① that Marc-Antoine Fardin, a physicist at Paris Diderot University, set out to find out whether house cats flow. Fardin noticed that these furry pets can adapt to the shape of the container they sit in ② similarly to what fluids such as water do. So he applied rheology, the branch of physics that deals with the deformation of matter, to calculate the time ③ it takes for cats to take up the space of a vase or bathroom sink. The conclusion? Cats can be either liquid or solid, depending on the circumstances. A cat in a small box will behave like a fluid, ④ filled up all the space. But a cat in a bathtub full of water will try to minimize its contact with it and ⑤ behave very much like a solid.

06

다음 글의 밑줄 친 부분 중, 문맥상 낱말의 쓰임이 적절하지 않은 것은?

In order for us to be able to retain valuable pieces of information, our brain has to ① forget in a manner that is both targeted and controlled. Can you recall, for example, your very first day of school? You most likely have one or two noteworthy images in your head, such as putting your crayons and pencils into your pencil case. But that's probably the extent of the ② specifics. Those additional details that are apparently unimportant are actively deleted from your brain the more you go about remembering the situation. The reason for this is that the brain does not consider it ③ valuable to remember all of the details as long as it is able to convey the main message (i.e., your first day of school was great). In fact, studies have shown that the brain actively ④ strengthens regions responsible for insignificant or minor memory content that tends to disturb the main memory. Over time, the minor details vanish more and more, though this in turn serves to ⑤ sharpen the most important messages of the past.

07

다음 빈칸에 들어갈 말로 가장 적절한 것을 고르시오. [3점]

When is the right time for the predator to consume the fruit? The plant uses the color of the fruit to signal to predators that it is ripe, which means that the seed's hull has hardened — and therefore the sugar content is at its height. Incredibly, the plant has chosen to manufacture fructose, instead of glucose, as the sugar in the fruit. Glucose raises insulin levels in primates and humans, which initially raises levels of leptin, a hunger-blocking hormone — but fructose does not. As a result, the predator never receives the normal message that it is _____. That makes for a win-win for predator and prey. The animal obtains more calories, and because it keeps eating more and more fruit and therefore more seeds, the plant has a better chance of distributing more of its babies.

＊hull: 겉껍질 ＊＊primate: 영장류

① full   ② strong
③ tired   ④ dangerous
⑤ hungry

08 1등급 대비 고난도 3점 문제

다음 빈칸에 들어갈 말로 가장 적절한 것을 고르시오. [3점]

What is unusual about journalism as a profession is _____. In theory, practitioners in the classic professions, like medicine or the clergy, contain the means of production in their heads and hands, and therefore do not have to work for a company or an employer. They can draw their income directly from their clients or patients. Because the professionals hold knowledge, moreover, their clients are dependent on them. Journalists hold knowledge, but it is not theoretical in nature; one might argue that the public depends on journalists in the same way that patients depend on doctors, but in practice a journalist can serve the public usually only by working for a news organization, which can fire her or him at will. Journalists' income depends not on the public, but on the employing news organization, which often derives the large majority of its revenue from advertisers.

① its lack of independence
② the constant search for truth
③ the disregard of public opinion
④ its balance of income and faith
⑤ its overconfidence in its social influence

09

다음 글에서 전체 흐름과 관계 <u>없는</u> 문장은?

Nurses hold a pivotal position in the mental health care structure and are placed at the centre of the communication network, partly because of their high degree of contact with patients, but also because they have well-developed relationships with other professionals. ① Because of this, nurses play a crucial role in interdisciplinary communication. ② They have a mediating role between the various groups of professionals and the patient and carer. ③ Mental healthcare professionals are legally bound to protect the privacy of their patients, so they may be, rather than unwilling, unable to talk about care needs. ④ This involves translating communication between groups into language that is acceptable and comprehensible to people who have different ways of understanding mental health problems. ⑤ This is a highly sensitive and skilled task, requiring a high level of attention to alternative views and a high level of understanding of communication.

10 1등급 대비 고난도 2점 문제

주어진 글 다음에 이어질 글의 순서로 가장 적절한 것을 고르시오.

If you drive down a busy street, you will find many competing businesses, often right next to one another. For example, in most places a consumer in search of a quick meal has many choices, and more fast-food restaurants appear all the time.

(A) Yes, costs rise, but consumers also gain information to help make purchasing decisions. Consumers also benefit from added variety, and we all get a product that's pretty close to our vision of a perfect good — and no other market structure delivers that outcome.

(B) However, this misconception doesn't account for why firms advertise. In markets where competitors sell slightly differentiated products, advertising enables firms to inform their customers about new products and services.

(C) These competing firms advertise heavily. The temptation is to see advertising as driving up the price of a product without any benefit to the consumer.

① (A) − (C) − (B)　　② (B) − (A) − (C)
③ (B) − (C) − (A)　　④ (C) − (A) − (B)
⑤ (C) − (B) − (A)

[11 ~ 12] 다음 글을 읽고, 물음에 답하시오.

Being able to have a good fight doesn't just make us more civil; it also develops our creative muscles. In a classic study, highly creative architects were more likely than their technically competent but less original peers to come from homes with (a) plenty of friction. They often grew up in households that were "tense but secure," as psychologist Robert Albert notes: "The creative person-to-be comes from a family that is anything but (b) harmonious." The parents weren't physically or verbally abusive, but they didn't shy away from conflict, either. Instead of telling their children to be seen but not heard, they (c) encouraged them to stand up for themselves. The kids learned to dish it out — and take it. That's exactly what happened to Wilbur and Orville Wright, who invented the airplane.

When the Wright brothers said they thought together, what they really meant is that they fought together. When they were solving problems, they had arguments that lasted not just for hours but for weeks and months at a time. They didn't have such (d) ceaseless fights because they were angry. They kept quarreling because they enjoyed it and learned from the experience. "I like scrapping with Orv," Wilbur reflected. As you'll see, it was one of their most passionate and prolonged arguments that led them to (e) support a critical assumption that had prevented humans from soaring through the skies.

* dish it out: 남을 비판하다   ** scrap with: ~과 다투다

11

고2 · 2022년 3월 41번

윗글의 제목으로 가장 적절한 것은?

① The Power of Constructive Conflict
② Lighten Tense Moments with Humor
③ Strategies to Cope with Family Stress
④ Compromise: A Key to Resolving Conflict
⑤ Rivalry Between Brothers: A Serious Crisis

12 1등급 대비 고난도 3점 문제

고2 · 2022년 3월 42번

밑줄 친 (a) ~ (e) 중에서 문맥상 낱말의 쓰임이 적절하지 않은 것은? [3점]

① (a)   ② (b)   ③ (c)   ④ (d)   ⑤ (e)

DAY 02

수능기출 전국연합학력평가 **20분 미니 모의고사**

● 날짜 :   월   일 ● 시작 시각 :   시   분   초 ● 목표 시간 : 20분

※ 점수 표기가 없는 문항은 모두 **2점**입니다.

01

고2 · 2024년 6월 19번

다음 글에 드러난 Emma의 심경 변화로 가장 적절한 것은?

It was the championship race. Emma was the final runner on her relay team. She anxiously waited in her spot for her teammate to pass her the baton. Emma wasn't sure she could perform her role without making a mistake. Her hands shook as she thought, "What if I drop the baton?" She felt her heart rate increasing as her teammate approached. But as she started running, she received the baton smoothly. In the final 10 meters, she passed two other runners and crossed the finish line in first place! She raised her hands in the air, and a huge smile came across her face. As her teammates hugged her, she shouted, "We did it!" All of her hard training had been worth it.

① nervous → excited
② doubtful → regretful
③ confident → upset
④ hopeful → disappointed
⑤ indifferent → amused

02

고2 · 2021년 11월 22번

다음 글의 요지로 가장 적절한 것은?

Who is this person? This is the question all stories ask. It emerges first at the ignition point. When the initial change strikes, the protagonist overreacts or behaves in an otherwise unexpected way. We sit up, suddenly attentive. *Who is this person who behaves like this?* The question then re-emerges every time the protagonist is challenged by the plot and compelled to make a choice. Everywhere in the narrative that the question is present, the reader or viewer will likely be engaged. Where the question is absent, and the events of drama move out of its narrative beam, they are at risk of becoming detached — perhaps even bored. If there's a single secret to storytelling then I believe it's this. *Who is this person?* Or, from the perspective of the character, *Who am I?* It's the definition of drama. It is its electricity, its heartbeat, its fire.

* ignition: 발화 ** protagonist: 주인공

① 독자의 공감을 얻기 위해 구체적인 인물 묘사가 중요하다.
② 이야기의 줄거리를 단순화시키는 것이 독자의 이해를 높인다.
③ 거리를 두고 주인공의 상황을 객관적으로 바라볼 필요가 있다.
④ 주인공의 역경과 행복이 적절히 섞여야 이야기가 흥미로워진다.
⑤ 주인공에 대한 지속적인 궁금증 유발이 독자의 몰입을 도와준다.

03

다음 글의 제목으로 가장 적절한 것은? [3점]

From the earliest times, healthcare services have been recognized to have two equal aspects, namely clinical care and public healthcare. In classical Greek mythology, the god of medicine, Asklepios, had two daughters, Hygiea and Panacea. The former was the goddess of preventive health and wellness, or hygiene, and the latter the goddess of treatment and curing. In modern times, the societal ascendancy of medical professionalism has caused treatment of sick patients to overshadow those preventive healthcare services provided by the less heroic figures of sanitary engineers, biologists, and governmental public health officers. Nevertheless, the quality of health that human populations enjoy is attributable less to surgical dexterity, innovative pharmaceutical products, and bioengineered devices than to the availability of public sanitation, sewage management, and services which control the pollution of the air, drinking water, urban noise, and food for human consumption. The human right to the highest attainable standard of health depends on public healthcare services no less than on the skills and equipment of doctors and hospitals.

* ascendancy: 우세 ** dexterity: 기민함

① Public Healthcare: A Co-Star, Not a Supporting Actor
② The Historical Development of Medicine and Surgery
③ Clinical Care Controversies: What You Don't Know
④ The Massive Similarities Between Different Mythologies
⑤ Initiatives Opening up Health Innovation Around the World

04

Roselands Virtual Sports Day에 관한 다음 안내문의 내용과 일치하지 <u>않는</u> 것은?

Roselands Virtual Sports Day

Roselands Virtual Sports Day is an athletic competition that you can participate in from anywhere.

When: October 16th − 22nd, 2023

How the event works
• There are 10 challenges in total.
• You can see videos explaining each challenge on our school website.
• The more challenges you complete, the more points you will gain for your class.
• The class with the most points will get a prize.
• Parents and teachers can also participate.

How to submit your entry
• Email us videos of you completing the challenges at virtualsportsday@roselands.com.
• The size of the video file must not exceed 500MB.

① 10월 16일부터 22일까지 열린다.
② 총 10개의 도전 과제가 있다.
③ 학교 웹사이트에서 도전 과제를 설명하는 영상을 볼 수 있다.
④ 학부모와 교사는 참여할 수 없다.
⑤ 제출할 영상파일 용량이 500MB를 초과하면 안 된다.

05 1등급 대비 고난도 2점 문제

다음 글의 밑줄 친 부분 중, 어법상 틀린 것은?

Trends constantly suggest new opportunities for individuals to restage themselves, representing occasions for change. To understand how trends can ultimately give individuals power and freedom, one must first discuss fashion's importance as a basis for change. The most common explanation offered by my informants as to why fashion is so appealing is ① that it constitutes a kind of theatrical costumery. Clothes are part of how people present ② them to the world, and fashion locates them in the present, relative to what is happening in society and to fashion's own history. As a form of expression, fashion contains a host of ambiguities, enabling individuals to recreate the meanings ③ associated with specific pieces of clothing. Fashion is among the simplest and cheapest methods of self-expression: clothes can be ④ inexpensively purchased while making it easy to convey notions of wealth, intellectual stature, relaxation or environmental consciousness, even if none of these is true. Fashion can also strengthen agency in various ways, ⑤ opening up space for action.

* stature: 능력

06

(A), (B), (C)의 각 네모 안에서 문맥에 맞는 낱말로 가장 적절한 것은?

On projects in the built environment, people consider safety and functionality nonnegotiable. But the aesthetics of a new project — how it is *designed* — is too often considered (A) relevant / irrelevant. The question of how its design *affects* human beings is rarely asked. People think that design makes something highfalutin, called architecture, and that architecture differs from building, just as surely as the Washington National Cathedral differs from the local community church. This (B) connection / distinction between architecture and building — or more generally, between design and utility — couldn't be more wrong. More and more we are learning that the design of all our built environments matters so profoundly that safety and functionality must not be our only urgent priorities. All kinds of design elements influence people's experiences, not only of the environment but also of themselves. They (C) overlook / shape our cognitions, emotions, and actions, and even our well-being. They actually help constitute our very sense of identity.

* highfalutin: 허세를 부리는

	(A)		(B)		(C)
①	relevant	……	distinction	……	shape
②	relevant	……	connection	……	overlook
③	irrelevant	……	distinction	……	overlook
④	irrelevant	……	connection	……	overlook
⑤	irrelevant	……	distinction	……	shape

07 1등급 대비 고난도 3점 문제

다음 빈칸에 들어갈 말로 가장 적절한 것을 고르시오. [3점]

When he was dying, the contemporary Buddhist teacher Dainin Katagiri wrote a remarkable book called *Returning to Silence*. Life, he wrote, "is a dangerous situation." It is the weakness of life that makes it precious; his words are filled with the very fact of his own life passing away. "The china bowl is beautiful because sooner or later it will break.... The life of the bowl is always existing in a dangerous situation." Such is our struggle: this unstable beauty. This inevitable wound. We forget — how easily we forget — that love and loss are intimate companions, that we love the real flower so much more than the plastic one and love the cast of twilight across a mountainside lasting only a moment. It is this very _____ that opens our hearts.

① fragility
② stability
③ harmony
④ satisfaction
⑤ diversity

08 1등급 대비 고난도 2점 문제

글의 흐름으로 보아, 주어진 문장이 들어가기에 가장 적절한 곳을 고르시오.

> But the necessary and useful instinct to generalize can distort our world view.

Everyone automatically categorizes and generalizes all the time. Unconsciously. It is not a question of being prejudiced or enlightened. Categories are absolutely necessary for us to function. (①) They give structure to our thoughts. (②) Imagine if we saw every item and every scenario as truly unique — we would not even have a language to describe the world around us. (③) It can make us mistakenly group together things, or people, or countries that are actually very different. (④) It can make us assume everything or everyone in one category is similar. (⑤) And, maybe, most unfortunate of all, it can make us jump to conclusions about a whole category based on a few, or even just one, unusual example.

09

다음 글의 내용을 한 문장으로 요약하고자 한다. 빈칸 (A), (B)에 들어갈 말로 가장 적절한 것은?

Music is used to mold customer experience and behavior. A study was conducted that explored what impact it has on employees. Results from the study indicate that participants who listen to rhythmic music were inclined to cooperate more irrespective of factors like age, gender, and academic background, compared to those who listened to less rhythmic music. This positive boost in the participants' willingness to cooperate was induced regardless of whether they liked the music or not. When people are in a more positive state of mind, they tend to become more agreeable and creative, while those on the opposite spectrum tend to focus on their individual problems rather than giving attention to solving group problems. The rhythm of music has a strong pull on people's behavior. This is because when people listen to music with a steady pulse, they tend to match their actions to the beat. This translates to better teamwork when making decisions because everyone is following one tempo.

↓

According to the study, the music played in workplaces can lead employees to be _____ (A) _____ because the beat of the music creates a _____ (B) _____ for working.

	(A)		(B)
①	uncomfortable	......	competitive mood
②	cooperative	......	shared rhythm
③	distracted	......	shared rhythm
④	attentive	......	competitive mood
⑤	indifferent	......	disturbing pattern

[10 ~ 12] 다음 글을 읽고, 물음에 답하시오.

(A)

The basketball felt like it belonged in Chanel's hands even though it was only a practice game. She decided not to pass the ball to her twin sister, Vasha. Instead, (a) she stopped, jumped, and shot the ball toward the basket, but it bounced off the backboard. Chanel could see that her teammates were disappointed. The other team got the ball and soon scored, ending the game.

(B)

The next day, Chanel played in the championship game against a rival school. It was an intense game and the score was tied when Chanel was passed the ball by Vasha, with ten seconds left in the game. (b) She leaped into the air and shot the ball. It went straight into the basket! Chanel's last shot had made her team the champions. Vasha and all her other teammates cheered for her.

(C)

At first, Chanel did not like practicing with Vasha because every time Vasha shot the ball, it went in. But whenever it was Chanel's turn, she missed. (c) She got frustrated at not making a shot. "Don't give up!" Vasha shouted after each missed shot. After twelve misses in a row, her thirteenth shot went in and she screamed, "I finally did it!" Her twin said, "I knew (d) you could! Now let's keep practicing!"

(D)

When the practice game ended, Chanel felt her eyes sting with tears. "It's okay," Vasha said in a comforting voice. Chanel appreciated her, but Vasha wasn't making her feel any better. Vasha wanted to help her twin improve. She invited her twin to practice with (e) her. After school, they got their basketball and started practicing their basketball shots.

10

고2 · 2022년 11월 43번

주어진 글 (A)에 이어질 내용을 순서에 맞게 배열한 것으로 가장 적절한 것은?

① (B) − (D) − (C)   ② (C) − (B) − (D)
③ (C) − (D) − (B)   ④ (D) − (B) − (C)
⑤ (D) − (C) − (B)

11

고2 · 2022년 11월 44번

밑줄 친 (a)~(e) 중에서 가리키는 대상이 나머지 넷과 다른 것은?

① (a)   ② (b)   ③ (c)   ④ (d)   ⑤ (e)

12

고2 · 2022년 11월 45번

윗글의 Chanel에 관한 내용으로 적절하지 않은 것은?

① 연습 경기 중에 팀원들의 실망한 모습을 보았다.
② 라이벌 학교와의 챔피언십 경기에 출전했다.
③ 팀을 우승시키는 마지막 슛을 성공했다.
④ 슛 연습에서 연이은 실패 후에 12번째 슛이 들어갔다.
⑤ 방과 후에 농구 슛을 연습하기 시작했다.

DAY 02

학습 Check!

▶ 몰라서 틀린 문항 × 표기   ▶ 헷갈렸거나 찍은 문항 △ 표기   ▶ ×, △ 문항은 다시 풀고 ✔ 표기를 하세요.

종료 시각	시 분 초	문항 번호	01	02	03	04	05	06	07	08	09	10	11	12
소요 시간	분 초	채점 결과												
초과 시간	분 초	틀린 문항 복습												

DAY 03

수능기출
전국연합학력평가
20분 미니 모의고사

● 날짜 :   월   일 ● 시작 시각 :   시   분   초 ● 목표 시간 : 20분

※ 점수 표기가 없는 문항은 모두 **2점**입니다.

01

고3 · 2024학년도 수능 18번

다음 글의 목적으로 가장 적절한 것은?

I'm Charlie Reeves, manager of Toon Skills Company. If you're interested in new webtoon-making skills and techniques, this post is for you. This year, we've launched special online courses, which contain a variety of contents about webtoon production. Each course consists of ten units that help improve your drawing and story-telling skills. Moreover, these courses are designed to suit any level, from beginner to advanced. It costs $45 for one course, and you can watch your course as many times as you want for six months. Our courses with talented and experienced instructors will open up a new world of creativity for you. It's time to start creating your webtoon world at https://webtoonskills.com.

① 웹툰 제작 온라인 강좌를 홍보하려고
② 웹툰 작가 채용 정보를 제공하려고
③ 신작 웹툰 공개 일정을 공지하려고
④ 웹툰 창작 대회에 출품을 권유하려고
⑤ 기초적인 웹툰 제작 방법을 설명하려고

02

고2 · 2023년 3월 20번

다음 글에서 필자가 주장하는 바로 가장 적절한 것은?

The more people have to do unwanted things the more chances are that they create unpleasant environment for themselves and others. If you hate the thing you do but have to do it nonetheless, you have choice between hating the thing and accepting that it needs to be done. Either way you will do it. Doing it from place of hatred will develop hatred towards the self and others around you; doing it from the place of acceptance will create compassion towards the self and allow for opportunities to find a more suitable way of accomplishing the task. If you decide to accept the fact that your task has to be done, start from recognising that your situation is a gift from life; this will help you to see it as a lesson in acceptance.

① 창의력을 기르려면 익숙한 환경에서 벗어나야 한다.
② 상대방의 무리한 요구는 최대한 분명하게 거절해야 한다.
③ 주어진 과업을 정확하게 파악한 후에 일을 시작해야 한다.
④ 효율적으로 일을 처리하기 위해 좋아하는 일부터 해야 한다.
⑤ 원치 않는 일을 해야만 할 때 수용적인 태도를 갖춰야 한다.

03 1등급 대비 고난도 3점 문제

밑줄 친 <u>constantly wearing masks</u>가 다음 글에서 의미하는 바로 가장 적절한 것은? [3점]

Over the centuries various writers and thinkers, looking at humans from an outside perspective, have been struck by the theatrical quality of social life. The most famous quote expressing this comes from Shakespeare: "All the world's a stage, / And all the men and women merely players; / They have their exits and their entrances, / And one man in his time plays many parts." If the theater and actors were traditionally represented by the image of masks, writers such as Shakespeare are implying that all of us are <u>constantly wearing masks</u>. Some people are better actors than others. Evil types such as Iago in the play *Othello* are able to conceal their hostile intentions behind a friendly smile. Others are able to act with more confidence and bravado — they often become leaders. People with excellent acting skills can better navigate our complex social environments and get ahead.

* bravado: 허세

① protecting our faces from harmful external forces
② performing on stage to show off our acting skills
③ feeling confident by beating others in competition
④ doing completely the opposite of what others expect
⑤ adjusting our behavior based on the social context given

04

다음 도표의 내용과 일치하지 <u>않는</u> 것은?

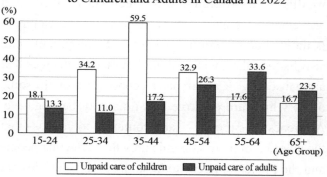

Proportion of People Who Provide Unpaid Care to Children and Adults in Canada in 2022

The graph above shows the percentage of people who provided unpaid care to children and adults by age group in Canada in 2022. ① Notably, the 35−44 group had the highest percentage of individuals providing unpaid care to children, reaching 59.5%. ② However, the highest percentage of individuals providing unpaid care to adults was found in the 55−64 group. ③ Compared to the 25−34 group, the 15−24 group had a lower percentage of individuals providing unpaid care to children and a higher percentage of individuals providing unpaid care to adults. ④ The percentage of people providing unpaid care to adults in the 45−54 group was more than twice as high as that in the 35−44 group. ⑤ The 55−64 group and the 65 and older group showed a similar percentage of individuals providing unpaid care to children, with a difference of less than 1 percentage point.

05

다음 글의 밑줄 친 부분 중, 어법상 틀린 것은? [3점]

Even though institutions like the World Bank use wealth ① to differentiate between "developed" and "developing" countries, they also agree that development is more than economic growth. "Development" can also include the social and environmental changes that are caused by or accompany economic growth, some of ② which are positive and thus may be negative. Awareness has grown — and continues to grow — that the question of how economic growth is affecting people and the planet ③ needs to be addressed. Countries are slowly learning that it is cheaper and causes ④ much less suffering to try to reduce the harmful effects of an economic activity or project at the beginning, when it is planned, than after the damage appears. To do this is not easy and is always imperfect. But an awareness of the need for such an effort indicates a greater understanding and moral concern than ⑤ was the previous widespread attitude that focused only on creating new products and services.

06

(A), (B), (C)의 각 네모 안에서 어법에 맞는 표현으로 가장 적절한 것은?

English speakers have one of the simplest systems for describing familial relationships. Many African language speakers would consider it absurd to use a single word like "cousin" to describe both male and female relatives, or not to distinguish whether the person (A) described / describing is related by blood to the speaker's father or to his mother. To be unable to distinguish a brother-in-law as the brother of one's wife or the husband of one's sister would seem confusing within the structure of personal relationships existing in many cultures. Similarly, how is it possible to make sense of a situation (B) which / in which a single word "uncle" applies to the brother of one's father and to the brother of one's mother? The Hawaiian language uses the same term to refer to one's father and to the father's brother. People of Northern Burma, who think in the Jinghpaw language, (C) has / have eighteen basic terms for describing their kin. Not one of them can be directly translated into English.

	(A)	(B)	(C)
①	described	which	have
②	described	in which	has
③	described	in which	have
④	describing	which	has
⑤	describing	in which	has

07

다음 빈칸에 들어갈 말로 가장 적절한 것을 고르시오. [3점]

Even the most respectable of all musical institutions, the symphony orchestra, carries inside its DNA the legacy of the _____. The various instruments in the orchestra can be traced back to these primitive origins — their earliest forms were made either from the animal (horn, hide, gut, bone) or the weapons employed in bringing the animal under control (stick, bow). Are we wrong to hear this history in the music itself, in the formidable aggression and awe-inspiring assertiveness of those monumental symphonies that remain the core repertoire of the world's leading orchestras? Listening to Beethoven, Brahms, Mahler, Bruckner, Berlioz, Tchaikovsky, Shostakovich, and other great composers, I can easily summon up images of bands of men starting to chase animals, using sound as a source and symbol of dominance, an expression of the will to predatory power.

* legacy: 유산 ** formidable: 강력한

① hunt
② law
③ charity
④ remedy
⑤ dance

08 1등급 대비 고난도 2점 문제

다음 빈칸에 들어갈 말로 가장 적절한 것을 고르시오.

There are several reasons why support may not be effective. One possible reason is that receiving help could be a blow to self-esteem. A recent study by Christopher Burke and Jessica Goren at Lehigh University examined this possibility. According to the threat to self-esteem model, help can be perceived as supportive and loving, or it can be seen as threatening if that help is interpreted as implying incompetence. According to Burke and Goren, support is especially likely to be seen as threatening if it is in an area that is self-relevant or self-defining — that is, in an area where your own success and achievement are especially important. Receiving help with a self-relevant task can _____, and this can undermine the potential positive effects of the help. For example, if your self-concept rests, in part, on your great cooking ability, it may be a blow to your ego when a friend helps you prepare a meal for guests because it suggests that you're not the master chef you thought you were.

① make you feel bad about yourself
② improve your ability to deal with challenges
③ be seen as a way of asking for another favor
④ trick you into thinking that you were successful
⑤ discourage the person trying to model your behavior

DAY 03

09

다음 글에서 전체 흐름과 관계 <u>없는</u> 문장은?

As far back as the seventeenth century, hair had a special spiritual significance in Africa. Many African cultures saw the head as the center of control, communication, and identity in the body. ① Hair was regarded as a source of power that personified the individual and could be used for spiritual purposes or even to cast a spell. ② Since it rests on the highest point on the body, hair itself was a means to communicate with divine spirits and it was treated in ways that were thought to bring good luck or protect against evil. ③ People had the opportunity to socialize while styling each other's hair, and the shared tradition of hair was passed down. ④ According to authors Ayana Byrd and Lori Tharps, "communication from the gods and spirits was thought to pass through the hair to get to the soul." ⑤ In Cameroon, for example, medicine men attached hair to containers that held their healing potions in order to protect the potions and enhance their effectiveness.

* potion: (마법의) 물약

10 [1등급 대비 고난도 2점 문제]

주어진 글 다음에 이어질 글의 순서로 가장 적절한 것을 고르시오.

The right to be forgotten is a right distinct from but related to a right to privacy. The right to privacy is, among other things, the right for information traditionally regarded as protected or personal not to be revealed.

(A) One motivation for such a right is to allow individuals to move on with their lives and not be defined by a specific event or period in their lives. For example, it has long been recognized in some countries, such as the UK and France, that even past criminal convictions should eventually be "spent" and not continue to affect a person's life.

(B) The right to be forgotten, in contrast, can be applied to information that has been in the public domain. The right to be forgotten broadly includes the right of an individual not to be forever defined by information from a specific point in time.

(C) Despite the reason for supporting the right to be forgotten, the right to be forgotten can sometimes come into conflict with other rights. For example, formal exceptions are sometimes made for security or public health reasons.

① (A) − (C) − (B)　　　② (B) − (A) − (C)
③ (B) − (C) − (A)　　　④ (C) − (A) − (B)
⑤ (C) − (B) − (A)

[11 ~ 12] 다음 글을 읽고, 물음에 답하시오.

Paralysis by analysis is a state of overthinking and analyzing a particular problem, but you still end up not making a decision. One famous ancient fable of the fox and the cat explains this situation of paralysis by analysis in the simplest way. In the story, the fox and the cat discuss how many ways they have to escape their hunters. Cat quickly climbs a tree. Fox, on the other hand, begins to analyze all the ways to escape that he knows. But unable to decide which one would be the best, he (a) fails to act and gets caught by the dogs. This story perfectly illustrates the analysis paralysis phenomenon: the (b) inability to act or decide due to overthinking about available alternatives. People experience that although they start with a good intention to find a solution to a problem, they often analyze indefinitely about various factors that might lead to wrong decisions. They don't feel satisfied with the available information and think they still need (c) more data to perfect their decision. Most often this situation of paralysis by analysis (d) arises when somebody is afraid of making an erroneous decision that can lead to potential catastrophic consequences: it might impact their careers or their organizations' productivity. So that's why people are generally (e) confident in making decisions that involve huge stakes.

* paralysis: 마비
** stakes: (계획·행동 등의 성공 여부에) 걸려 있는 것

11

고2 · 2021년 6월 41번

윗글의 제목으로 가장 적절한 것은?

① Best Ways to Keep You from Overthinking
② Overthinking or Overdoing: Which Is Worse?
③ Costs and Benefits of Having Various Alternatives
④ Overthinking: A Barrier to Effective Decision-making
⑤ Trapped in Moral Dilemma: Harmful for Your Survival

12

고2 · 2021년 6월 42번

밑줄 친 (a) ~ (e) 중에서 문맥상 낱말의 쓰임이 적절하지 않은 것은? [3점]

① (a)　　② (b)　　③ (c)　　④ (d)　　⑤ (e)

DAY 03

학습 Check!　　▶ 몰라서 틀린 문항 × 표기　▶ 헷갈렸거나 찍은 문항 △ 표기　▶ ×, △ 문항은 다시 풀고 ✔ 표기를 하세요.

종료 시각	시 　 분 　 초	문항 번호	01	02	03	04	05	06	07	08	09	10	11	12
소요 시간	분 　 초	채점 결과												
초과 시간	분 　 초	틀린 문항 복습												

[Day 03] 미니 모의고사　021

DAY 04

수능기출 전국연합학력평가 **20분 미니 모의고사**

● 날짜 : 　월　 일 　● 시작 시각 : 　시 　분 　초 　● 목표 시간 : 20분 　　　　　　　　 ※ 점수 표기가 없는 문항은 모두 2점입니다.

01
고2 • 2023년 9월 22번

다음 글의 요지로 가장 적절한 것은?

It's remarkable that positive fantasies help us relax to such an extent that it shows up in physiological tests. If you want to unwind, you can take some deep breaths, get a massage, or go for a walk — but you can also try simply closing your eyes and fantasizing about some future outcome that you might enjoy. But what about when your objective is to make your wish a reality? The *last* thing you want to be is relaxed. You want to be energized enough to get off the couch and lose those pounds or find that job or study for that test, and you want to be motivated enough to stay engaged even when the inevitable obstacles or challenges arise. The principle of "Dream it. Wish it. Do it." does not hold true, and now we know why: in dreaming it, you undercut the energy you need to do it. You put yourself in a temporary state of complete happiness, calmness — and inactivity.

* physiological: 생리학적인

① 과도한 목표 지향적 태도는 삶의 만족감을 떨어뜨린다.
② 긍정적 자세로 역경을 극복할 때 잠재 능력이 발휘된다.
③ 편안함을 느끼는 상황에서 자기 개선에 대한 동기가 생긴다.
④ 낙관적인 상상은 소망을 실현하는 데 필요한 동력을 약화시킨다.
⑤ 막연한 목표보다는 명확하고 구체적인 목표가 실현 가능성이 크다.

02
고2 • 2022년 3월 24번

다음 글의 제목으로 가장 적절한 것은?

The realization of human domination over the environment began in the late 1700s with the industrial revolution. Advances in manufacturing transformed societies and economies while producing significant impacts on the environment. American society became structured on multiple industries' capitalistic goals as the development of the steam engine led to the mechanized production of goods in mass quantities. Rural agricultural communities with economies based on handmade goods and agriculture were abandoned for life in urban cities with large factories based on an economy of industrialized manufacturing. Innovations in the production of textiles, iron, and steel provided increased profits to private companies. Simultaneously, those industries exerted authority over the environment and began dumping hazardous by-products in public lands and waterways.

① Strategies for Industrial Innovations
② Urbanization: A Road to a Better Life
③ Industrial Development Hurt the Environment
④ Technology: A Key to Sustainable Development
⑤ The Driving Force of Capitalism Was Not Greed

03

Charles H. Townes에 관한 다음 글의 내용과 일치하지 <u>않는</u> 것은?

Charles H. Townes, one of the most influential American physicists, was born in South Carolina. In his childhood, he grew up on a farm, studying the stars in the sky. He earned his doctoral degree from the California Institute of Technology in 1939, and then he took a job at Bell Labs in New York City. After World War II, he became an associate professor of physics at Columbia University. In 1958, Townes and his co-researcher proposed the concept of the laser. Laser technology won quick acceptance in industry and research. He received the Nobel Prize in Physics in 1964. He was also involved in Project Apollo, the moon landing project. His contribution is priceless because the Internet and all digital media would be unimaginable without the laser.

① 어린 시절에 농장에서 성장하였다.
② 박사 학위를 받기 전에 Bell Labs에서 일했다.
③ 1958년에 레이저의 개념을 제안하였다.
④ 1964년에 노벨 물리학상을 수상하였다.
⑤ 달 착륙 프로젝트에 관여하였다.

04

다음 글의 밑줄 친 부분 중, 어법상 틀린 것은? [3점]

Organisms living in the deep sea have adapted to the high pressure by storing water in their bodies, some ① consisting almost entirely of water. Most deep-sea organisms lack gas bladders. They are cold-blooded organisms that adjust their body temperature to their environment, allowing them ② to survive in the cold water while maintaining a low metabolism. Many species lower their metabolism so much that they are able to survive without food for long periods of time, as finding the sparse food ③ that is available expends a lot of energy. Many predatory fish of the deep sea are equipped with enormous mouths and sharp teeth, enabling them to hold on to prey and overpower ④ it. Some predators hunting in the residual light zone of the ocean ⑤ has excellent visual capabilities, while others are able to create their own light to attract prey or a mating partner.

* bladder: (물고기의) 부레

05

다음 글의 밑줄 친 부분 중, 문맥상 낱말의 쓰임이 적절하지 <u>않은</u> 것은? [3점]

Let's return to a time in which photographs were not in living color. During that period, people referred to pictures as "photographs" rather than "black-and-white photographs" as we do today. The possibility of color did not exist, so it was ① <u>unnecessary</u> to insert the adjective "black-and-white." However, suppose we did include the phrase "black-and-white" before the existence of color photography. By ② <u>highlighting</u> that reality, we become conscious of current limitations and thus open our minds to new possibilities and potential opportunities. World War I was given that name only ③ <u>after</u> we were deeply embattled in World War II. Before that horrific period of the 1940s, World War I was simply called "The Great War" or, even worse, "The War to End All Wars." What if we had called it "World War I" back in 1918? Such a label might have made the possibility of a second worldwide conflict an ④ <u>unpredictable</u> reality for governments and individuals. We become conscious of issues when we explicitly ⑤ <u>identify</u> them.

06

다음 빈칸에 들어갈 말로 가장 적절한 것을 고르시오.

In the course of his research on business strategy and the environment, Michael Porter noticed a peculiar pattern: Businesses seemed to be profiting from regulation. He also discovered that the stricter regulations were prompting more _____ than the weaker ones. The Dutch flower industry provides an illustration. For many years, the companies producing Holland's world-renowned tulips and other cut flowers were also contaminating the country's water and soil with fertilizers and pesticides. In 1991, the Dutch government adopted a policy designed to cut pesticide use in half by 2000 — a goal they ultimately achieved. Facing increasingly strict regulation, greenhouse growers realized they had to develop new methods if they were going to maintain product quality with fewer pesticides. In response, they shifted to a cultivation method that circulates water in closed-loop systems and grows flowers in a rock wool substrate. The new system not only reduced the pollution released into the environment; it also increased profits by giving companies greater control over growing conditions.

＊substrate: 배양판

① innovation   ② resistance
③ fairness   ④ neglect
⑤ unity

07 1등급 대비 고난도 3점 문제

다음 빈칸에 들어갈 말로 가장 적절한 것을 고르시오. [3점]

We might think that our gut instinct is just an inner feeling — a secret interior voice — but in fact it is shaped by a perception of something visible around us, such as a facial expression or a visual inconsistency so fleeting that often we're not even aware we've noticed it. Psychologists now think of this moment as a 'visual matching game'. So a stressed, rushed or tired person is more likely to resort to this visual matching. When they see a situation in front of them, they quickly match it to a sea of past experiences stored in a mental knowledge bank and then, based on a match, they assign meaning to the information in front of them. The brain then sends a signal to the gut, which has many hundreds of nerve cells. So the visceral feeling we get in the pit of our stomach and the butterflies we feel are a(n) _____.

* gut: 직감, 창자 ** visceral: 본능적인

① result of our cognitive processing system
② instance of discarding negative memories
③ mechanism of overcoming our internal conflicts
④ visual representation of our emotional vulnerability
⑤ concrete signal of miscommunication within the brain

08 1등급 대비 고난도 3점 문제

글의 흐름으로 보아, 주어진 문장이 들어가기에 가장 적절한 곳을 고르시오. [3점]

> When an overall silence appears on beats 4 and 13, it is not because each musician is thinking, "On beats 4 and 13, I will rest."

In the West, an individual composer writes the music long before it is performed. The patterns and melodies we hear are pre-planned and intended. (①) Some African tribal music, however, results from collaboration by the players on the spur of the moment. (②) The patterns heard, whether they are the silences when all players rest on a beat or the accented beats when all play together, are not planned but serendipitous. (③) Rather, it occurs randomly as the patterns of all the players converge upon a simultaneous rest. (④) The musicians are probably as surprised as their listeners to hear the silences at beats 4 and 13. (⑤) Surely that surprise is one of the joys tribal musicians experience in making their music.

* serendipitous: 우연히 얻은 ** converge: 한데 모아지다

09 1등급 대비 고난도 2점 문제

고2·2021년 3월 40번

다음 글의 내용을 한 문장으로 요약하고자 한다. 빈칸 (A), (B)에 들어갈 말로 가장 적절한 것은?

At the University of Iowa, students were briefly shown numbers that they had to memorize. Then they were offered the choice of either a fruit salad or a chocolate cake. When the number the students memorized was seven digits long, 63% of them chose the cake. When the number they were asked to remember had just two digits, however, 59% opted for the fruit salad. Our reflective brains know that the fruit salad is better for our health, but our reflexive brains desire that soft, fattening chocolate cake. If the reflective brain is busy figuring something else out — like trying to remember a seven-digit number — then impulse can easily win. On the other hand, if we're not thinking too hard about something else (with only a minor distraction like memorizing two digits), then the reflective system can deny the emotional impulse of the reflexive side.

＊reflective: 숙고하는 ＊＊reflexive: 반사적인

↓

According to the above experiment, the _____(A)_____ intellective load on the brain leads the reflexive side of the brain to become _____(B)_____ .

	(A)		(B)
①	limited	……	powerful
②	limited	……	divided
③	varied	……	passive
④	increased	……	dominant
⑤	increased	……	weakened

[10 ~ 12] 다음 글을 읽고, 물음에 답하시오.

(A)

There was a very wealthy man who was bothered by severe eye pain. He consulted many doctors and was treated by several of them. He did not stop consulting a galaxy of medical experts; he was heavily medicated and underwent hundreds of injections. However, the pain persisted and was worse than before. At last, (a) he heard about a monk who was famous for treating patients with his condition. Within a few days, the monk was called for by the suffering man.

＊monk: 수도사

(B)

In a few days everything around (b) that man was green. The wealthy man made sure that nothing around him could be any other colour. When the monk came to visit him after a few days, the wealthy man's servants ran with buckets of green paint and poured them all over him because he was wearing red clothes. (c) He asked the servants why they did that.

(C)

They replied, "We can't let our master see any other colour." Hearing this, the monk laughed and said "If only you had purchased a pair of green glasses for just a few dollars, you could have saved these walls, trees, pots, and everything else and you could have saved a large share of (d) his fortune. You cannot paint the whole world green."

(D)

The monk understood the wealthy man's problem and said that for some time (e) he should concentrate only on green colours and not let his eyes see any other colours. The wealthy man thought it was a strange prescription, but he was desperate and decided to try it. He got together a group of painters and purchased barrels of green paint and ordered that every object he was likely to see be painted green just as the monk had suggested.

10

주어진 글 (A)에 이어질 내용을 순서에 맞게 배열한 것으로 가장 적절한 것은?

① (B) – (D) – (C)   ② (C) – (B) – (D)
③ (C) – (D) – (B)   ④ (D) – (B) – (C)
⑤ (D) – (C) – (B)

12

윗글에 관한 내용으로 적절하지 <u>않은</u> 것은?

① 부자는 눈 통증으로 여러 명의 의사에게 치료받았다.
② 수도사는 붉은 옷을 입고 부자를 다시 찾아갔다.
③ 하인들은 녹색 안경을 구입했다.
④ 부자는 수도사의 처방이 이상하다고 생각했다.
⑤ 부자는 주변을 모두 녹색으로 칠하게 했다.

11

밑줄 친 (a)~(e) 중에서 가리키는 대상이 나머지 넷과 <u>다른</u> 것은?

① (a)   ② (b)   ③ (c)   ④ (d)   ⑤ (e)

학습 Check!

▶ 몰라서 틀린 문항 × 표기   ▶ 헷갈렸거나 찍은 문항 △ 표기   ▶ ×, △ 문항은 다시 풀고 ✔ 표기를 하세요.

종료 시각	시 분 초	문항 번호	01	02	03	04	05	06	07	08	09	10	11	12
소요 시간	분 초	채점 결과												
초과 시간	분 초	틀린 문항 복습												

DAY 05

수능기출
전국연합학력평가 **20분 미니 모의고사**

● 날짜 :　　월　　일 ● 시작 시각 :　　시　　분　　초 ● 목표 시간 : 20분　　　　　　※ 점수 표기가 없는 문항은 모두 2점입니다.

01

고3 · 2022학년도 수능 18번

다음 글의 목적으로 가장 적절한 것은?

Dear Ms. Green,

　My name is Donna Williams, a science teacher at Rogan High School. I am planning a special workshop for our science teachers. We are interested in learning how to teach online science classes. I have been impressed with your ideas about using internet platforms for science classes. Since you are an expert in online education, I would like to ask you to deliver a special lecture at the workshop scheduled for next month. I am sure the lecture will help our teachers manage successful online science classes, and I hope we can learn from your insights. I am looking forward to hearing from you.

Sincerely,
Donna Williams

① 과학 교육 정책 협의회 참여를 독려하려고
② 과학 교사 워크숍의 특강을 부탁하려고
③ 과학 교사 채용 계획을 공지하려고
④ 과학 교육 프로그램 개발을 요청하려고
⑤ 과학 교육 워크숍 일정의 변경을 안내하려고

02

고2 · 2022년 11월 20번

다음 글에서 필자가 주장하는 바로 가장 적절한 것은?

　Clarity in an organization keeps everyone working in one accord and energizes key leadership components like trust and transparency. No matter who or what is being assessed in your organization, what they are being assessed on must be clear and the people must be aware of it. If individuals in your organization are assessed without knowing what they are being assessed on, it can cause mistrust and move your organization away from clarity. For your organization to be productive, cohesive, and successful, trust is essential. Failure to have trust in your organization will have a negative effect on the results of any assessment. It will also significantly hinder the growth of your organization. To conduct accurate assessments, trust is a must — which comes through clarity. In turn, assessments help you see clearer, which then empowers your organization to reach optimal success.

① 조직이 구성원에게 제공하는 보상은 즉각적이어야 한다.
② 조직의 발전을 위해 구성원은 동료의 능력을 신뢰해야 한다.
③ 조직 내 구성원의 능력에 맞는 명확한 목표를 설정해야 한다.
④ 조직의 신뢰 형성을 위해 구성원에 대한 평가 요소가 명확해야 한다.
⑤ 구성원의 의견 수용을 위해 신뢰에 기반한 조직 문화가 구축되어야 한다.

03

고2 · 2021년 9월 23번

다음 글의 주제로 가장 적절한 것은?

Many marine species including oysters, marsh grasses, and fish were deliberately introduced for food or for erosion control, with little knowledge of the impacts they could have. Fish and shellfish have been intentionally introduced all over the world for aquaculture, providing food and jobs, but they can escape and become a threat to native species, ecosystem function, or livelihoods. Atlantic salmon are reared in ocean net-pens in Washington State and British Columbia. Many escape each year, and they have been recovered in both saltwater and freshwater in Washington State, British Columbia, and Alaska. Recreational fishing can also spread invasive species. Bait worms from Maine are popular throughout the country. They are commonly packed in seaweed which contains many other organisms. If the seaweed is discarded, it or the organisms on it can colonize new areas. Fishing boots, recreational boats, and trailers can pick up organisms at one location and move them elsewhere.

* aquaculture: 양식(업)

① benefits of recreational ocean fishing
② ways to maintain marine biodiversity
③ potential value of the ocean for ecotourism
④ contribution of ocean farming to food supply
⑤ human influence on the spread of invasive species

04

고2 · 2023년 3월 25번

다음 도표의 내용과 일치하지 <u>않는</u> 것은?

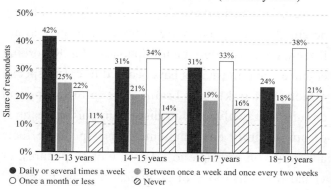

How Often Do You Read a Book? (Germany 2022)

Note: All percentages may not total 100% due to rounding.

The above graph shows how often German children and young adults read books in 2022 according to age groups. ① In each age group except 12 to 13-year-olds, those who said they read books once a month or less accounted for the largest proportion. ② Of the 12 to 13-year-old group, 42% stated they read daily or several times a week, which was the highest share within that group. ③ In the 14 to 15-year-old group, the percentage of teenagers who read daily or several times a week was three times higher than that of those who never read a book in the same age group. ④ In the 16 to 17-year-old group, those who read between once a week and once every two weeks were less than 20%. ⑤ More than one fifth of the age group of 18 to 19 years responded that they never read any book.

05

다음 글의 밑줄 친 부분 중, 어법상 틀린 것은? [3점]

There is a reason why so many of us are attracted to recorded music these days, especially considering personal music players are common and people are listening to music through headphones a lot. Recording engineers and musicians have learned to create special effects that tickle our brains by exploiting neural circuits that evolved ① to discern important features of our auditory environment. These special effects are similar in principle to 3-D art, motion pictures, or visual illusions, none of ② which have been around long enough for our brains to have evolved special mechanisms to perceive them. Rather, 3-D art, motion pictures, and visual illusions leverage perceptual systems that ③ are in place to accomplish other things. Because they use these neural circuits in novel ways, we find them especially ④ interested. The same is true of the way ⑤ that modern recordings are made.

* auditory: 청각의   ** leverage: 이용하다

06

다음 글의 밑줄 친 부분 중, 문맥상 낱말의 쓰임이 적절하지 않은 것은?

The "jolt" of caffeine does wear off. Caffeine is ① removed from your system by an enzyme within your liver, which gradually degrades it over time. Based in large part on genetics, some people have a more efficient version of the enzyme that degrades caffeine, ② allowing the liver to rapidly clear it from the bloodstream. These rare individuals can drink an espresso with dinner and fall fast asleep at midnight without a problem. Others, however, have a slower-acting version of the enzyme. It takes far ③ longer for their system to eliminate the same amount of caffeine. As a result, they are very ④ insensitive to caffeine's effects. One cup of tea or coffee in the morning will last much of the day, and should they have a second cup, even early in the afternoon, they will find it difficult to fall asleep in the evening. Aging also ⑤ alters the speed of caffeine clearance: the older we are, the longer it takes our brain and body to remove caffeine, and thus the more sensitive we become in later life to caffeine's sleep-disrupting influence.

* jolt: 충격   ** enzyme: 효소

07

다음 빈칸에 들어갈 말로 가장 적절한 것을 고르시오. [3점]

It is not the peasant's goal to produce the highest possible time-averaged crop yield, averaged over many years. If your time-averaged yield is marvelously high as a result of the combination of nine great years and one year of crop failure, you will still starve to death in that one year of crop failure before you can look back to congratulate yourself on your great time-averaged yield. Instead, the peasant's aim is to make sure to produce a yield above the starvation level in every single year, even though the time-averaged yield may not be highest. That's why _____ may make sense. If you have just one big field, no matter how good it is on the average, you will starve when the inevitable occasional year arrives in which your one field has a low yield. But if you have many different fields, varying independently of each other, then in any given year some of your fields will produce well even when your other fields are producing poorly.

① land leveling
② weed trimming
③ field scattering
④ organic farming
⑤ soil fertilization

08 1등급 대비 고난도 3점 문제

다음 빈칸에 들어갈 말로 가장 적절한 것을 고르시오. [3점]

The growing field of genetics is showing us what many scientists have suspected for years — _____ _____. This information helps us better understand that genes are under our control and not something we must obey. Consider identical twins; both individuals are given the same genes. In mid-life, one twin develops cancer, and the other lives a long healthy life without cancer. A specific gene instructed one twin to develop cancer, but in the other the same gene did not initiate the disease. One possibility is that the healthy twin had a diet that turned off the cancer gene — the same gene that instructed the other person to get sick. For many years, scientists have recognized other environmental factors, such as chemical toxins (tobacco for example), can contribute to cancer through their actions on genes. The notion that food has a specific influence on gene expression is relatively new.

① identical twins have the same genetic makeup
② our preference for food is influenced by genes
③ balanced diet is essential for our mental health
④ genetic engineering can cure some fatal diseases
⑤ foods can immediately influence the genetic blueprint

09

다음 글에서 전체 흐름과 관계 없는 문장은?

Before getting licensed to drive a cab in London, a person has to pass an incredibly difficult test with an intimidating name — "The Knowledge." ① The test involves memorizing the layout of more than 20,000 streets in the Greater London area — a feat that involves an incredible amount of memory resources. ② In fact, fewer than 50 percent of the people who sign up for taxi driver training pass the test, even after spending two or three years studying for it! ③ And as it turns out, the brains of London cabbies are different from non-cab-driving humans in ways that reflect their herculean memory efforts. ④ In other words, they must hold a full driving license, issued by the Driver and Vehicle Licensing Authority, for at least a year. ⑤ In fact, the part of the brain that has been most frequently associated with spatial memory, the tail of the sea horse-shaped brain region called the hippocampus, is *bigger* than average in these taxi drivers.

* herculean: 초인적인 ** hippocampus: 해마

10

주어진 글 다음에 이어질 글의 순서로 가장 적절한 것을 고르시오.
[3점]

Since we know we can't completely eliminate our biases, we need to try to limit the harmful impacts they can have on the objectivity and rationality of our decisions and judgments.

(A) If it did, we can move on and make an objective and informed decision. If it didn't, we can try the same strategy again or implement a new one until we are ready to make a rational judgment.

(B) Then we can choose an appropriate de-biasing strategy to combat it. After we have implemented a strategy, we should check in again to see if it worked in the way we had hoped.

(C) It is important that we are aware when one of our cognitive biases is activated and make a conscious choice to overcome that bias. We need to be aware of the impact the bias has on our decision making process and our life.

① (A) − (C) − (B)　　② (B) − (A) − (C)
③ (B) − (C) − (A)　　④ (C) − (A) − (B)
⑤ (C) − (B) − (A)

[11 ~ 12] 다음 글을 읽고, 물음에 답하시오.

One cannot take for granted that the findings of any given study will have validity. Consider a situation where an investigator is studying deviant behavior. In particular, she is investigating the extent to which cheating by college students occurs on exams. Reasoning that it is more (a) difficult for people monitoring an exam to keep students under surveillance in large classes than in smaller ones, she hypothesizes that a higher rate of cheating will occur on exams in large classes than in small. To test this hypothesis, she collects data on cheating in both large classes and small ones and then analyzes the data. Her results show that (b) more cheating per student occurs in the larger classes. Thus, the data apparently (c) reject the investigator's research hypothesis. A few days later, however, a colleague points out that all the large classes in her study used multiple-choice exams, whereas all the small classes used short answer and essay exams. The investigator immediately realizes that an extraneous variable (exam format) is interfering with the independent variable (class size) and may be operating as a (d) cause in her data. The apparent support for her research hypothesis may be nothing more than an artifact. Perhaps the true effect is that more cheating occurs on multiple-choice exams than on essay exams, regardless of class (e) size.

* validity: 타당도   ** surveillance: 감독
*** artifact: 가공물

11 1등급 대비 고난도 2점 문제   고2·2019년 6월 41번

윗글의 제목으로 가장 적절한 것은?

① Investigator's Attitude: Subjective vs. Objective
② Research Error from Wrong Experimental Design
③ Test Your Hypothesis to Obtain Academic Support
④ Limitations of Multiple-choice Exams in Large Classes
⑤ Is There Any Way to Discourage Students from Cheating?

12   고2·2019년 6월 42번

밑줄 친 (a) ~ (e) 중에서 문맥상 낱말의 쓰임이 적절하지 않은 것은?

① (a)   ② (b)   ③ (c)   ④ (d)   ⑤ (e)

DAY 05

학습 Check!   ▶ 몰라서 틀린 문항 × 표기   ▶ 헷갈렸거나 찍은 문항 △ 표기   ▶ ×, △ 문항은 다시 풀고 ✔ 표기를 하세요.

종료 시각	시 분 초	문항 번호	01	02	03	04	05	06	07	08	09	10	11	12
소요 시간	분 초	채점 결과												
초과 시간	분 초	틀린 문항 복습												

[Day 05] 미니 모의고사 033

DAY 06

수능기출
전국연합학력평가 **20분 미니 모의고사**

● 날짜 :   월   일 ● 시작 시각 :   시   분   초 ● 목표 시간 : 20분

※ 점수 표기가 없는 문항은 모두 **2점**입니다.

01

고3 · 2024학년도 수능 19번

다음 글에 드러난 David의 심경 변화로 가장 적절한 것은?

David was starting a new job in Vancouver, and he was waiting for his bus. He kept looking back and forth between his watch and the direction the bus would come from. He thought, "My bus isn't here yet. I can't be late on my first day." David couldn't feel at ease. When he looked up again, he saw a different bus coming that was going right to his work. The bus stopped in front of him and opened its door. He got on the bus thinking, "Phew! Luckily, this bus came just in time so I won't be late." He leaned back on an unoccupied seat in the bus and took a deep breath, finally able to relax.

① nervous → relieved
② lonely → hopeful
③ pleased → confused
④ indifferent → delighted
⑤ bored → thrilled

02

고2 · 2021년 9월 22번

다음 글의 요지로 가장 적절한 것은?

Too many officials in troubled cities wrongly imagine that they can lead their city back to its former glories with some massive construction project — a new stadium or light rail system, a convention center, or a housing project. With very few exceptions, no public policy can slow the tidal forces of urban change. We mustn't ignore the needs of the poor people who live in the Rust Belt, but public policy should help poor *people*, not poor places. Shiny new real estate may dress up a declining city, but it doesn't solve its underlying problems. The hallmark of declining cities is that they have *too much* housing and infrastructure relative to the strength of their economies. With all that supply of structure and so little demand, it makes no sense to use public money to build more supply. The folly of building-centric urban renewal reminds us that cities aren't structures; cities are people.

① 도시 재생을 위한 공공정책은 건설보다 사람에 중점을 두어야 한다.
② 대중 교통 이용이 편리하도록 도시 교통 체계를 구축해야 한다.
③ 사회기반시설 확충을 통해 지역 경제를 활성화해야 한다.
④ 에너지를 절감할 수 있는 친환경 건물을 설계해야 한다.
⑤ 문화유산 보존을 우선하는 도시 계획을 수립해야 한다.

03

고2·2021년 6월 24번

다음 글의 제목으로 가장 적절한 것은?

News reporters are taught to start their stories with the most important information. The first sentence, called the lead, contains the most essential elements of the story. A good lead can convey a lot of information. After the lead, information is presented in decreasing order of importance. Journalists call this the "inverted pyramid" structure — the most important information (the widest part of the pyramid) is at the top. The inverted pyramid is great for readers. No matter what the reader's attention span — whether she reads only the lead or the entire story — the inverted pyramid maximizes the information she gets. Think of the alternative: If news stories were written like mysteries with a dramatic payoff at the end, then readers who broke off in mid-story would miss the point. Imagine waiting until the last sentence of a story to find out who won the presidential election or the Super Bowl.

＊inverted: 거꾸로 된

① Inverted Pyramid: Logically Impossible Structure
② Curiosity Is What Makes Readers Keep Reading
③ Where to Put Key Points in News Writing
④ The More Information, the Less Attention
⑤ Readers, Tell the Facts from the Fakes!

04

고2·2022년 6월 26번

monarch butterfly에 관한 다음 글의 내용과 일치하지 않는 것은?

The monarch butterfly has lovely bright colors splashed on its wings. The wings have white spots on the outer margins. The hind wings are rounded, and they are lighter in color than the front wings. The body is black with white spots. The mother butterfly lays only one egg on the underside of milkweed leaves, which hatches about three to five days later. The monarch loves to fly around in the warm sunshine, from March through October, all across the United States. The monarch cannot survive the cold winter temperatures of the northern states. So, it very wisely migrates from the northern states to the south, and hibernates. The monarch is the only insect that can fly more than four thousand kilometers to a warmer climate.

＊hibernate: 동면하다

① 날개의 바깥 가장자리에 흰 점이 있다.
② 뒷날개는 앞날개보다 색이 더 밝다.
③ 알은 약 3일에서 5일 후에 부화한다.
④ 북부 주의 추운 겨울 기온에 잘 버틴다.
⑤ 4천 킬로미터 넘게 날 수 있다.

05 1등급 대비 고난도 3점 문제

다음 글의 밑줄 친 부분 중, 어법상 틀린 것은? [3점]

Research psychologists often work with *self-report data*, made up of participants' verbal accounts of their behavior. This is the case ① whenever questionnaires, interviews, or personality inventories are used to measure variables. Self-report methods can be quite useful. They take advantage of the fact that people have a unique opportunity to observe ② themselves full-time. However, self-reports can be plagued by several kinds of distortion. One of the most problematic of these distortions is the social desirability bias, which is a tendency to give ③ socially approved answers to questions about oneself. Subjects who are influenced by this bias work overtime trying to create a favorable impression, especially when subjects ④ ask about sensitive issues. For example, many survey respondents will report that they voted in an election or ⑤ gave to a charity when in fact it is possible to determine that they did not.

06

다음 글의 밑줄 친 부분 중, 문맥상 낱말의 쓰임이 적절하지 <u>않은</u> 것은? [3점]

Sudden success or winnings can be very dangerous. Neurologically, chemicals are released in the brain that give a powerful burst of excitement and energy, leading to the desire to ① repeat this experience. It can be the start of any kind of addiction or manic behavior. Also, when gains come quickly we tend to ② lose sight of the basic wisdom that true success, to really last, must come through hard work. We do not take into account the role that luck plays in such ③ hard-earned gains. We try again and again to recapture that high from winning so much money or attention. We acquire feelings of superiority. We become especially ④ resistant to anyone who tries to warn us — they don't understand, we tell ourselves. Because this cannot be sustained, we experience an inevitable ⑤ fall, which is all the more painful, leading to the depression part of the cycle. Although gamblers are the most prone to this, it equally applies to businesspeople during bubbles and to people who gain sudden attention from the public.

07 1등급 대비 고난도 2점 문제

다음 빈칸에 들어갈 말로 가장 적절한 것을 고르시오.

Free play is nature's means of teaching children that they are not _____. In play, away from adults, children really do have control and can practice asserting it. In free play, children learn to make their own decisions, solve their own problems, create and follow rules, and get along with others as equals rather than as obedient or rebellious subordinates. In active outdoor play, children deliberately dose themselves with moderate amounts of fear and they thereby learn how to control not only their bodies, but also their fear. In social play children learn how to negotiate with others, how to please others, and how to manage and overcome the anger that can arise from conflicts. None of these lessons can be taught through verbal means; they can be learned only through experience, which free play provides.

*rebellious: 반항적인

① noisy
② sociable
③ complicated
④ helpless
⑤ selective

08 1등급 대비 고난도 3점 문제

글의 흐름으로 보아, 주어진 문장이 들어가기에 가장 적절한 곳을 고르시오. [3점]

> But this is a short-lived effect, and in the long run, people find such sounds too bright.

Brightness of sounds means much energy in higher frequencies, which can be calculated from the sounds easily. A violin has many more overtones compared to a flute and sounds brighter. (①) An oboe is brighter than a classical guitar, and a crash cymbal brighter than a double bass. (②) This is obvious, and indeed people like brightness. (③) One reason is that it makes sound subjectively louder, which is part of the loudness war in modern electronic music, and in the classical music of the 19th century. (④) All sound engineers know that if they play back a track to a musician that just has recorded this track and add some higher frequencies, the musician will immediately like the track much better. (⑤) So it is wise not to play back such a track with too much brightness, as it normally takes quite some time to convince the musician that less brightness serves his music better in the end.

09

다음 글의 내용을 한 문장으로 요약하고자 한다. 빈칸 (A), (B)에 들어갈 말로 가장 적절한 것은? [3점]

Greenwashing involves misleading a consumer into thinking a good or service is more environmentally friendly than it really is. Greenwashing ranges from making environmental claims required by law, and therefore irrelevant (CFC-free for example), to puffery (exaggerating environmental claims) to fraud. Researchers have shown that claims on products are often too vague or misleading. Some products are labeled "chemical-free," when the fact is everything contains chemicals, including plants and animals. Products with the highest number of misleading or unverifiable claims were laundry detergents, household cleaners, and paints. Environmental advocates agree there is still a long way to go to ensure shoppers are adequately informed about the environmental impact of the products they buy. The most common reason for greenwashing is to attract environmentally conscious consumers. Many consumers do not find out about the false claims until after the purchase. Therefore, greenwashing may increase sales in the short term. However, this strategy can seriously backfire when consumers find out they are being deceived.

* CFC: 염화불화탄소 ** fraud: 사기

⬇

While greenwashing might bring a company profits ____(A)____ by deceiving environmentally conscious consumers, the company will face serious trouble when the consumers figure out they were ____(B)____.

	(A)		(B)
①	permanently	......	manipulated
②	temporarily	......	misinformed
③	momentarily	......	advocated
④	ultimately	......	underestimated
⑤	consistently	......	analyzed

[10 ~ 12] 다음 글을 읽고, 물음에 답하시오.

(A)

When Jack was a young man in his early twenties during the 1960s, he had tried to work in his father's insurance business, as was expected of him. His two older brothers fit in easily and seemed to enjoy their work. But Jack was bored with the insurance industry. "It was worse than being bored," he said. "I felt like I was dying inside." Jack felt drawn to hair styling and dreamed of owning a hair shop with a lively environment. He was sure that (a) he would enjoy the creative and social aspects of it and that he'd be successful.

(B)

Jack understood that his father feared adoption, in this case especially because the child was of a different racial background than their family. Jack and Michele risked rejection and went ahead with the adoption. It took years but eventually Jack's father loved the little girl and accepted (b) his son's independent choices. Jack realized that, although he often felt fear and still does, he has always had courage. In fact, courage was the scaffolding around which (c) he had built richness into his life.

* scaffolding: 발판

(C)

When he was twenty-six, Jack approached his father and expressed his intentions of leaving the business to become a hairstylist. As Jack anticipated, his father raged and accused Jack of being selfish, ungrateful, and unmanly. In the face of his father's fury, Jack felt confusion and fear. His resolve became weak. But then a force filled (d) his chest and he stood firm in his decision. In following his path, Jack not only ran three flourishing hair shops, but also helped his clients experience their inner beauty by listening and encouraging them when they faced dark times.

(D)

His love for his work led to donating time and talent at nursing homes, which in turn led to becoming a hospice volunteer, and eventually to starting fundraising efforts for the hospice program in his community. And all this laid a strong stepping stone for another courageous move in his life. When, after having two healthy children of their own, Jack and his wife, Michele, decided to bring an orphaned child into their family, (e) his father threatened to disown them.

10

고2 · 2023년 9월 43번

주어진 글 (A)에 이어질 내용을 순서에 맞게 배열한 것으로 가장 적절한 것은?

① (B) – (D) – (C)   ② (C) – (B) – (D)
③ (C) – (D) – (B)   ④ (D) – (B) – (C)
⑤ (D) – (C) – (B)

11

고2 · 2023년 9월 44번

밑줄 친 (a)~(e) 중에서 가리키는 대상이 나머지 넷과 다른 것은?

① (a)   ② (b)   ③ (c)   ④ (d)   ⑤ (e)

12

고2 · 2023년 9월 45번

윗글의 Jack에 관한 내용으로 적절하지 않은 것은?

① 두 형은 자신들의 일을 즐기는 것으로 보였다.
② 아버지의 반대로 입양을 포기했다.
③ 아버지에게 회사를 떠나겠다는 의사를 밝혔다.
④ 세 개의 번창하는 미용실을 운영했다.
⑤ 지역사회에서 모금 운동을 시작했다.

DAY 06

학습 Check!

▶ 몰라서 틀린 문항 ✕ 표기 ▶ 헷갈렸거나 찍은 문항 △ 표기 ▶ ✕, △ 문항은 다시 풀고 ✔ 표기를 하세요.

종료 시각	시	분	초	문항 번호	01	02	03	04	05	06	07	08	09	10	11	12
소요 시간		분	초	채점 결과												
초과 시간		분	초	틀린 문항 복습												

DAY 07

수능기출
전국연합학력평가 **20분 미니 모의고사**

● 날짜 :　　월　　일　● 시작 시각 :　　시　　분　　초　● 목표 시간 : 20분

※ 점수 표기가 없는 문항은 모두 2점입니다.

01

고2 · 2022년 3월 18번

다음 글의 목적으로 가장 적절한 것은?

As I explained on the telephone, I don't want to take my two children by myself on a train trip to visit my parents in Springfield this Saturday since it is the same day the Riverside Warriors will play the Greenville Trojans in the National Soccer Championship. I would really appreciate it, therefore, if you could change my tickets to the following weekend (April 23). I fully appreciate that the original, special-offer ticket was non-exchangeable, but I did not know about the soccer match when I booked the tickets and I would be really grateful if you could do this for me. Thank you in advance.

① 특가로 제공되는 기차표를 구매하려고
② 축구 경기 입장권의 환불을 요구하려고
③ 다른 날짜로 기차표 변경을 요청하려고
④ 기차표 예약이 가능한 날짜를 알아보려고
⑤ 축구 경기 날짜가 연기되었는지를 확인하려고

02

고3 · 2022학년도 수능 20번

다음 글에서 필자가 주장하는 바로 가장 적절한 것은?

One of the most common mistakes made by organizations when they first consider experimenting with social media is that they focus too much on social media tools and platforms and not enough on their business objectives. The reality of success in the social web for businesses is that creating a social media program begins not with insight into the latest social media tools and channels but with a thorough understanding of the organization's own goals and objectives. A social media program is not merely the fulfillment of a vague need to manage a "presence" on popular social networks because "everyone else is doing it." "Being in social media" serves no purpose in and of itself. In order to serve any purpose at all, a social media presence must either solve a problem for the organization and its customers or result in an improvement of some sort (preferably a measurable one). In all things, purpose drives success. The world of social media is no different.

① 기업 이미지에 부합하는 소셜 미디어를 직접 개발하여 운영해야 한다.
② 기업은 사회적 가치와 요구를 반영하여 사업 목표를 수립해야 한다.
③ 기업은 소셜 미디어를 활용할 때 사업 목표를 토대로 해야 한다.
④ 소셜 미디어로 제품을 홍보할 때는 구체적인 정보를 제공해야 한다.
⑤ 소비자의 의견을 수렴하기 위해 소셜 미디어를 적극 활용해야 한다.

03 1등급 대비 고난도 2점 문제

밑줄 친 the silent killers가 다음 글에서 의미하는 바로 가장 적절한 것은?

Author Elizabeth Gilbert tells the fable of a great saint who would lead his followers in meditation. Just as the followers were dropping into their zen moment, they would be disrupted by a cat that would walk through the temple meowing and bothering everyone. The saint came up with a simple solution: He began to tie the cat to a pole during meditation sessions. This solution quickly developed into a ritual: Tie the cat to the pole first, meditate second. When the cat eventually died of natural causes, a religious crisis followed. What were the followers supposed to do? How could they possibly meditate without tying the cat to the pole? This story illustrates what I call invisible rules. These are habits and behaviors that have unnecessarily rigidified into rules. Although written rules can be resistant to change, invisible ones are more stubborn. They're <u>the silent killers</u>.

* zen: (불교) 선(禪) ** rigidify: 굳게 하다

① hidden rules that govern our actions unconsciously
② noises that restrict one's level of concentration
③ surroundings that lead to the death of a cat
④ internal forces that slowly lower our self-esteem
⑤ experiences that discourage us from following rules

04

다음 글의 주제로 가장 적절한 것은?

A child whose behavior is out of control improves when clear limits on their behavior are set and enforced. However, parents must agree on where a limit will be set and how it will be enforced. The limit and the consequence of breaking the limit must be clearly presented to the child. Enforcement of the limit should be consistent and firm. Too many limits are difficult to learn and may spoil the normal development of autonomy. The limit must be reasonable in terms of the child's age, temperament, and developmental level. To be effective, both parents (and other adults in the home) must enforce limits. Otherwise, children may effectively split the parents and seek to test the limits with the more indulgent parent. In all situations, to be effective, punishment must be brief and linked directly to a behavior.

* indulgent: 멋대로 하게 하는

① ways of giving reward and punishment fairly
② considerations when placing limits on children's behavior
③ increasing necessity of parents' participation in discipline
④ impact of caregivers' personality on children's development
⑤ reasons for encouraging children to do socially right things

DAY 07

05

다음 글의 밑줄 친 부분 중, 어법상 틀린 것은? [3점]

All social interactions require some common ground upon which the involved parties can coordinate their behavior. In the interdependent groups ① in which humans and other primates live, individuals must have even greater common ground to establish and maintain social relationships. This common ground is morality. This is why morality often is defined as a shared set of standards for ② judging right and wrong in the conduct of social relationships. No matter how it is conceptualized — whether as trustworthiness, cooperation, justice, or caring — morality ③ to be always about the treatment of people in social relationships. This is likely why there is surprising agreement across a wide range of perspectives ④ that a shared sense of morality is necessary to social relations. Evolutionary biologists, sociologists, and philosophers all seem to agree with social psychologists that the interdependent relationships within groups that humans depend on ⑤ are not possible without a shared morality.

06

다음 글의 밑줄 친 부분 중, 문맥상 낱말의 쓰임이 적절하지 않은 것은? [3점]

The objective point of view is illustrated by John Ford's "philosophy of camera." Ford considered the camera to be a window and the audience to be ① outside the window viewing the people and events within. We are asked to watch the actions as if they were taking place at a distance, and we are not asked to participate. The objective point of view employs a static camera as much as possible in order to ② avoid this window effect, and it concentrates on the actors and the action without drawing attention to the camera. The objective camera suggests an emotional distance between camera and subject; the camera seems simply to be recording, as ③ straightforwardly as possible, the characters and actions of the story. For the most part, the director uses natural, normal types of camera positioning and camera angles. The objective camera does not comment on or ④ interpret the action but merely records it, letting it unfold. We see the action from the viewpoint of an impersonal observer. If the camera moves, it does so unnoticeably, calling as ⑤ little attention to itself as possible.

07

다음 빈칸에 들어갈 말로 가장 적절한 것을 고르시오.

Once we own something, we're far more likely to _____ it. In a study conducted at Duke University, students who won basketball tickets in an extremely onerous lottery (one that they had to wait in line to enter for more than a day) said they wouldn't sell their tickets for less than, on average, $2,400. But students who had waited and hadn't won said they would only pay, on average, $170 per ticket. Once a student owned the tickets, he or she saw them as being worth much more in the market than they were. In another example, during the housing market crash of 2008, a real estate website conducted a survey to see how homeowners felt the crash affected the price of their homes. 92% of respondents, aware of nearby foreclosures, asserted these had hurt the price of homes in their neighborhood. However, when asked about the price of their *own* home, 62% believed it had increased.

＊onerous: 성가신 ＊＊foreclosure: 압류

① overvalue
② exchange
③ disregard
④ conceal
⑤ share

08 1등급 대비 고난도 3점 문제

다음 빈칸에 들어갈 말로 가장 적절한 것을 고르시오. [3점]

In most of the world, capitalism and free markets are accepted today as constituting the best system for allocating economic resources and encouraging economic output. Nations have tried other systems, such as socialism and communism, but in many cases they have either switched wholesale to or adopted aspects of free markets. Despite the widespread acceptance of the free-market system, _____. Government involvement takes many forms, ranging from the enactment and enforcement of laws and regulations to direct participation in the economy through entities like the U.S.'s mortgage agencies. Perhaps the most important form of government involvement, however, comes in the attempts of central banks and national treasuries to control and affect the ups and downs of economic cycles.

＊enactment: (법률의) 제정 ＊＊entity: 실체

① markets are rarely left entirely free
② governments are reluctant to intervene
③ supply and demand are not always balanced
④ economic inequality continues to get worse
⑤ competition does not guarantee the maximum profit

DAY 07

09

다음 글에서 전체 흐름과 관계 <u>없는</u> 문장은?

Human processes differ from rational processes in their outcome. A process is *rational* if it always does the right thing based on the current information, given an ideal performance measure. In short, rational processes go by the book and assume that the book is actually correct. ① Human processes involve instinct, intuition, and other variables that don't necessarily reflect the book and may not even consider the existing data. ② As an example, the rational way to drive a car is to always follow the laws. ③ Likewise, pedestrian crossing signs vary depending on the country with differing appearances of a person crossing the street. ④ However, traffic isn't rational; if you follow the laws precisely, you end up stuck somewhere because other drivers aren't following the laws precisely. ⑤ To be successful, a self-driving car must therefore act humanly, rather than rationally.

10 1등급 대비 고난도 3점 문제

주어진 글 다음에 이어질 글의 순서로 가장 적절한 것을 고르시오.
[3점]

To an economist who succeeds in figuring out a person's preference structure — understanding whether the satisfaction gained from consuming one good is greater than that of another — explaining behavior in terms of changes in underlying likes and dislikes is usually highly problematic.

(A) When income rises, for example, people want more children (or, as you will see later, more satisfaction derived from children), even if their inherent desire for children stays the same.

(B) To argue, for instance, that the baby boom and then the baby bust resulted from an increase and then a decrease in the public's inherent taste for children, rather than a change in relative prices against a background of stable preferences, places a social scientist in an unsound position.

(C) In economics, such an argument about birth rates would be equivalent to saying that a rise and fall in mortality could be attributed to an increase in the inherent desire change for death. For an economist, changes in income and prices, rather than changes in tastes, affect birth rates.

① (A) − (C) − (B)　　② (B) − (A) − (C)
③ (B) − (C) − (A)　　④ (C) − (A) − (B)
⑤ (C) − (B) − (A)

[11 ~ 12] 다음 글을 읽고, 물음에 답하시오.

In this day and age, it is difficult to imagine our lives without email. But how often do we consider the environmental impact of these virtual messages? At first glance, digital messages appear to (a) save resources. Unlike traditional letters, no paper or stamps are needed; nothing has to be packaged or transported. Many of us tend to assume that using email requires little more than the electricity used to power our computers. It's easy to (b) overlook the invisible energy usage involved in running the network — particularly when it comes to sending and storing data.

Every single email in every single inbox in the world is stored on a server. The incredible quantity of data requires huge server farms — gigantic centres with millions of computers which store and transmit information. These servers consume (c) minimum amounts of energy, 24 hours a day, and require countless litres of water, or air conditioning systems, for cooling. The more messages we send, receive and store, the (d) more servers are needed — which means more energy consumed, and more carbon emissions. Clearly, sending and receiving electronic messages in an environmentally conscious manner is by no means enough to stop climate change. But with a few careful, mindful changes, (e) unnecessary CO_2 emissions can easily be avoided.

11
고2·2021년 9월 41번

윗글의 제목으로 가장 적절한 것은?

① Recycling Makes Your Life Even Better
② Eco-friendly Use of Email Saves the Earth
③ Traditional Letters: The Bridge Between Us
④ Email Servers: Records of Past and Present
⑤ Technicians Looking for Alternative Energy

12
고2·2021년 9월 42번

밑줄 친 (a) ~ (e) 중에서 문맥상 낱말의 쓰임이 적절하지 않은 것은?

① (a)　② (b)　③ (c)　④ (d)　⑤ (e)

DAY 08

● 날짜 :　　월　　일 ● 시작 시각 :　　시　　분　　초 ● 목표 시간 : 20분　　　　　　※ 점수 표기가 없는 문항은 모두 **2점**입니다.

01
고2 · 2022년 11월 19번

다음 글에 드러난 'I'의 심경 변화로 가장 적절한 것은?

　　Dan and I were supposed to make a presentation that day. Right after the class started, my phone buzzed. It was a text from Dan saying, "I can't make it on time. There's been a car accident on the road!" I almost fainted. 'What should I do?' Dan didn't show up before our turn, and soon I was standing in front of the whole class. I managed to finish my portion, and my mind went blank for a few seconds, wondering what to do. 'Hold yourself together!' I quickly came to my senses and worked through Dan's part of the presentation as best as I could. After a few moments, I finished the entire presentation on my own. Only then did the tension vanish. I could see our professor's beaming face.

① panicked　　→ relieved
② sorrowful　　→ indifferent
③ sympathetic → content
④ jealous　　　→ delighted
⑤ confused　　→ humiliated

02
고2 · 2022년 9월 22번

다음 글의 요지로 가장 적절한 것은?

　　Most parents think that if our child would just "behave," we could stay calm as parents. The truth is that managing our own emotions and actions is what allows us to feel peaceful as parents. Ultimately we can't control our children or the obstacles they will face — but we can always control our own actions. Parenting isn't about what our child does, but about how we respond. In fact, most of what we call parenting doesn't take place between a parent and child but within the parent. When a storm brews, a parent's response will either calm it or trigger a full-scale tsunami. Staying calm enough to respond constructively to all that childish behavior — and the stormy emotions behind it — requires that we grow, too. If we can use those times when our buttons get pushed to reflect, not just react, we can notice when we lose equilibrium and steer ourselves back on track. This inner growth is the hardest work there is, but it's what enables you to become a more peaceful parent, one day at a time.

① 자녀의 행동 변화를 위해 부모의 즉각적인 반응이 필요하다.
② 부모의 내적 성장을 통한 평정심 유지가 양육에 중요하다.
③ 부모는 자녀가 감정을 다스릴 수 있게 도와주어야 한다.
④ 부모와 자녀는 건설적인 의견을 나눌 수 있어야 한다.
⑤ 바람직한 양육은 자녀에게 모범을 보이는 것이다.

03

고3 • 2024학년도 수능 24번

다음 글의 제목으로 가장 적절한 것은? [3점]

The concept of overtourism rests on a particular assumption about people and places common in tourism studies and the social sciences in general. Both are seen as clearly defined and demarcated. People are framed as bounded social actors either playing the role of hosts or guests. Places, in a similar way, are treated as stable containers with clear boundaries. Hence, places can be full of tourists and thus suffer from overtourism. But what does it mean for a place to be full of people? Indeed, there are examples of particular attractions that have limited capacity and where there is actually no room for more visitors. This is not least the case with some man-made constructions such as the Eiffel Tower. However, with places such as cities, regions or even whole countries being promoted as destinations and described as victims of overtourism, things become more complex. What is excessive or out of proportion is highly relative and might be more related to other aspects than physical capacity, such as natural degradation and economic leakages (not to mention politics and local power dynamics).

* demarcate: 경계를 정하다

① The Solutions to Overtourism: From Complex to Simple
② What Makes Popular Destinations Attractive to Visitors?
③ Are Tourist Attractions Winners or Losers of Overtourism?
④ The Severity of Overtourism: Much Worse than Imagined
⑤ Overtourism: Not Simply a Matter of People and Places

04

고2 • 2022년 6월 28번

EZ Portable Photo Printer 사용에 관한 다음 안내문의 내용과 일치하는 것은?

EZ Portable Photo Printer
User Manual

Note on LED Indicator

• White: Power on
• Red: Battery charging

How to Operate

• Press the power button to turn the printer on.
• Press the power button twice to turn the printer off.
• To charge the battery, connect the cable to the USB port. It takes 60 − 90 minutes for a full charge.
• To connect to the printer wirelessly, download the 'EZ Printer App' on your mobile device.

How to Load Photo Paper

• Lift the printer's top cover.
• Insert the photo paper with any logos facing downward.

---

① LED 표시기의 흰색은 충전 중임을 나타낸다.
② 전원 버튼을 한 번 누르면 전원이 꺼진다.
③ 배터리가 완전히 충전되는 데 2시간 이상 걸린다.
④ 무선 연결을 위해 앱을 다운로드해야 한다.
⑤ 인화지를 로고가 위로 향하도록 넣어야 한다.

05 1등급 대비 고난도 2점 문제

고2·2021년 3월 29번

다음 글의 밑줄 친 부분 중, 어법상 틀린 것은?

While reflecting on the needs of organizations, leaders, and families today, we realize that one of the unique characteristics ① is inclusivity. Why? Because inclusivity supports ② what everyone ultimately wants from their relationships: collaboration. Yet the majority of leaders, organizations, and families are still using the language of the old paradigm in which one person — typically the oldest, most educated, and/or wealthiest — makes all the decisions, and their decisions rule with little discussion or inclusion of others, ③ resulting in exclusivity. Today, this person could be a director, CEO, or other senior leader of an organization. There is no need for others to present their ideas because they are considered ④ inadequate. Yet research shows that exclusivity in problem solving, even with a genius, is not as effective as inclusivity, ⑤ which everyone's ideas are heard and a solution is developed through collaboration.

06

고2·2017년 11월 29번

(A), (B), (C)의 각 네모 안에서 문맥에 맞는 낱말로 가장 적절한 것은?

A lot of people find that physical movement can sometimes dispel negative feelings. If we are feeling negative, it can be very easy for us to stop wanting to stay (A) active / inactive in our everyday life. This is why many people who suffer from depression are also found sleeping in and having no motivation to go outside or exercise. Unfortunately, this (B) excess / lack of exercise can actually compound many negative emotions. Exercise and movement is a great way for us to start getting rid of negative energies. Many people find that when they are angry, they go into a state where they want to exercise or clean. This is actually a very healthy and positive thing for you to do and a great way for you to begin to (C) deconstruct / intensify your negative emotions so that they no longer affect your life and harm your relationships.

	(A)	(B)	(C)
①	active	excess	deconstruct
②	active	lack	intensify
③	active	lack	deconstruct
④	inactive	lack	intensify
⑤	inactive	excess	intensify

07 1등급 대비 고난도 3점 문제

다음 빈칸에 들어갈 말로 가장 적절한 것을 고르시오. [3점]

While leaders often face enormous pressures to make decisions quickly, premature decisions are the leading cause of decision failure. This is primarily because leaders respond to the superficial issue of a decision rather than taking the time to explore the underlying issues. Bob Carlson is a good example of a leader _____ in the face of diverse issues. In the economic downturn of early 2001, Reell Precision Manufacturing faced a 30 percent drop in revenues. Some members of the senior leadership team favored layoffs and some favored salary reductions. While it would have been easy to push for a decision or call for a vote in order to ease the tension of the economic pressures, as co-CEO, Bob Carlson helped the team work together and examine all of the issues. The team finally agreed on salary reductions, knowing that, to the best of their ability, they had thoroughly examined the implications of both possible decisions.

*revenue: 총수입 **implication: 영향

① justifying layoffs
② exercising patience
③ increasing employment
④ sticking to his opinions
⑤ training unskilled members

08 1등급 대비 고난도 3점 문제

글의 흐름으로 보아, 주어진 문장이 들어가기에 가장 적절한 곳을 고르시오. [3점]

> There isn't really a way for us to pick up smaller pieces of debris such as bits of paint and metal.

The United Nations asks that all companies remove their satellites from orbit within 25 years after the end of their mission. This is tricky to enforce, though, because satellites can (and often do) fail. (①) To tackle this problem, several companies around the world have come up with novel solutions. (②) These include removing dead satellites from orbit and dragging them back into the atmosphere, where they will burn up. (③) Ways we could do this include using a harpoon to grab a satellite, catching it in a huge net, using magnets to grab it, or even firing lasers to heat up the satellite, increasing its atmospheric drag so that it falls out of orbit. (④) However, these methods are only useful for large satellites orbiting Earth. (⑤) We just have to wait for them to naturally re-enter Earth's atmosphere.

*harpoon: 작살

09

다음 글의 내용을 한 문장으로 요약하고자 한다. 빈칸 (A), (B)에 들어갈 말로 가장 적절한 것은?

In 2011, Micah Edelson and his colleagues conducted an interesting experiment about external factors of memory manipulation. In their experiment, participants were shown a two minute documentary film and then asked a series of questions about the video. Directly after viewing the videos, participants made few errors in their responses and were correctly able to recall the details. Four days later, they could still remember the details and didn't allow their memories to be swayed when they were presented with any false information about the film. This changed, however, when participants were shown fake responses about the film made by other participants. Upon seeing the incorrect answers of others, participants were also drawn toward the wrong answers themselves. Even after they found out that the other answers had been fabricated and didn't have anything to do with the documentary, it was too late. The participants were no longer able to distinguish between truth and fiction. They had already modified their memories to fit the group.

↓

According to the experiment, when participants were given false information itself, their memories remained ____(A)____, but their memories were ____(B)____ when they were exposed to other participants' fake responses.

	(A)		(B)
①	stable	······	falsified
②	fragile	······	modified
③	stable	······	intensified
④	fragile	······	solidified
⑤	concrete	······	maintained

[10 ~ 12] 다음 글을 읽고, 물음에 답하시오.

(A)

Henrietta is one of the greatest "queens of song." She had to go through a severe struggle before (a) she attained the enviable position as the greatest singer Germany had produced. At the beginning of her career she was hissed off a Vienna stage by the friends of her rival, Amelia. But in spite of this defeat, Henrietta endured until all Europe was at her feet.

* hiss off: 야유하여 쫓아내다

(B)

The answer was, "That's my mother, Amelia Steininger. She used to be a great singer, but she lost her voice, and she cried so much about it that now (b) she can't see anymore." Henrietta inquired their address and then told the child, "Tell your mother an old acquaintance will call on her this afternoon." She searched out their place and undertook the care of both mother and daughter. At her request, a skilled doctor tried to restore Amelia's sight, but it was in vain.

(C)

But Henrietta's kindness to (c) her former rival did not stop here. The next week she gave a benefit concert for the poor woman, and it was said that on that occasion Henrietta sang as (d) she had never sung before. And who can doubt that with the applause of that vast audience there was mingled the applause of the angels in heaven who rejoice over the good deeds of those below?

(D)

Many years later, when Henrietta was at the height of her fame, one day she was riding through the streets of Berlin. Soon she came across a little girl leading a blind woman. She was touched by the woman's helplessness, and she impulsively beckoned the child to (e) her, saying "Come here, my child. Who is that you are leading by the hand?"

10

주어진 글 (A)에 이어질 내용을 순서에 맞게 배열한 것으로 가장 적절한 것은?

① (B) − (D) − (C)   ② (C) − (B) − (D)
③ (C) − (D) − (B)   ④ (D) − (B) − (C)
⑤ (D) − (C) − (B)

11

밑줄 친 (a) ~ (e) 중에서 가리키는 대상이 나머지 넷과 다른 것은?

① (a)   ② (b)   ③ (c)   ④ (d)   ⑤ (e)

12

윗글에 관한 내용으로 적절하지 않은 것은?

① Amelia와 Henrietta는 라이벌 관계였다.
② Henrietta는 모녀의 거처를 찾아내서 그들을 돌보았다.
③ 숙련된 의사가 Amelia의 시력을 회복시켰다.
④ 불쌍한 여성을 위해 Henrietta는 자선 콘서트를 열었다.
⑤ Henrietta는 눈먼 여성을 데리고 가는 여자 아이와 마주쳤다.

DAY 08

DAY 09

● 날짜 :   월   일   ● 시작 시각 :   시   분   초   ● 목표 시간 : 20분

※ 점수 표기가 없는 문항은 모두 2점입니다.

01

고2 · 2021년 9월 18번

다음 글의 목적으로 가장 적절한 것은?

Dear parents and students of Douglas School,

As you know, our school was built over 150 years ago. While we are proud of our school's history, the facilities are not exactly what they should be for modern schooling. Thanks to a generous donation to the school foundation, we will be able to start renovating those parts of our campus that have become outdated. We hope this will help provide our students with the best education possible. I'm writing to inform you that the auditorium will be the first building closed for repairs. Students will not be able to use the auditorium for about one month while the repairs are taking place. We hope that you will understand how this brief inconvenience will encourage community-wide benefits for years to come.

Sincerely,
Vice Principal Kyla Andrews

① 수리로 인한 강당 폐쇄를 안내하려고
② 캠퍼스 투어 프로그램 일정을 조정하려고
③ 강당 사용을 위한 신청 방법을 공지하려고
④ 강당 신축을 위한 기금 모금 행사를 홍보하려고
⑤ 집짓기 행사에 참여할 자원 봉사자를 모집하려고

02

고2 · 2022년 6월 20번

다음 글에서 필자가 주장하는 바로 가장 적절한 것은?

In the rush towards individual achievement and recognition, the majority of those who make it forget their humble beginnings. They often forget those who helped them on their way up. If you forget where you came from, if you neglect those who were there for you when things were tough and slow, then your success is valueless. No one can make it up there without the help of others. There are parents, friends, advisers, and coaches that help. You need to be grateful to all of those who helped you. Gratitude is the glue that keeps you connected to others. It is the bridge that keeps you connected with those who were there for you in the past and who are likely to be there in the end. Relationships and the way you treat others determine your real success.

① 원만한 인간관계를 위하여 사고의 유연성을 길러야 한다.
② 성공에 도움을 준 사람들에게 감사하는 마음을 가져야 한다.
③ 자신의 분야에서 성공하기 위해서는 경험의 폭을 넓혀야 한다.
④ 원하는 직업을 갖기 위해서는 다른 사람의 조언을 경청해야 한다.
⑤ 타인의 시선을 의식하지 않고 부단히 새로운 일에 도전해야 한다.

03

밑줄 친 make oneself public to oneself가 다음 글에서 의미하는 바로 가장 적절한 것은? [3점]

Coming of age in the 18th and 19th centuries, the personal diary became a centerpiece in the construction of a modern subjectivity, at the heart of which is the application of reason and critique to the understanding of world and self, which allowed the creation of a new kind of knowledge. Diaries were central media through which enlightened and free subjects could be constructed. They provided a space where one could write daily about her whereabouts, feelings, and thoughts. Over time and with rereading, disparate entries, events, and happenstances could be rendered into insights and narratives about the self, and allowed for the formation of subjectivity. It is in that context that the idea of "the self [as] both made and explored with words" emerges. Diaries were personal and private; one would write for oneself, or, in Habermas's formulation, one would make oneself public to oneself. By making the self public in a private sphere, the self also became an object for self-inspection and self-critique.

* disparate: 이질적인 ** render: 만들다

① use writing as a means of reflecting on oneself
② build one's identity by reading others' diaries
③ exchange feedback in the process of writing
④ create an alternate ego to present to others
⑤ develop topics for writing about selfhood

04

다음 글의 주제로 가장 적절한 것은?

Native Americans often sang and danced in preparation for launching an attack. The emotional and neurochemical excitement that resulted from this preparatory singing gave them stamina to carry out their attacks. What may have begun as an unconscious, uncontrolled act — rushing their victims with singing and beating drums in a frenzy — could have become a strategy as the victors saw firsthand the effect their actions had on those they were attacking. Although war dances risk warning an enemy of an upcoming attack, the arousal and synchronizing benefits for the attackers may compensate for the loss of surprise. Humans who sang, danced, and marched may have enjoyed a strong advantage on the battlefield as well as intimidated enemies who witnessed such a spectacle. Nineteenth-and twentieth-century Germans feared no one more than the Scots — the bagpipes and drums were disturbing in their sheer loudness and visual spectacle.

* frenzy: 격분 ** synchronize: 동시에 움직이게 하다

① cultural differences in honoring war victims
② benefits of utilizing sound and motion in warfare
③ functions of music in preventing or resolving conflicts
④ strategies of analyzing an enemy's vulnerable points in war
⑤ effects of religious dances on lowering anxiety on the battlefield

05

다음 글의 밑줄 친 부분 중, 어법상 틀린 것은? [3점]

Despite abundant warnings that we shouldn't measure ourselves against others, most of us still do. We're not only meaning-seeking creatures but social ① ones as well, constantly making interpersonal comparisons to evaluate ourselves, improve our standing, and enhance our self-esteem. But the problem with social comparison is that it often backfires. When comparing ourselves to someone who's doing better than we are, we often feel ② inadequate for not doing as well. This sometimes leads to what psychologists call *malignant envy*, the desire for someone ③ to meet with misfortune ("I wish she didn't have what she has"). Also, comparing ourselves with someone who's doing worse than we are ④ risk scorn, the feeling that others are something undeserving of our beneficence ("She's beneath my notice"). Then again, comparing ourselves to others can also lead to *benign envy*, the longing to reproduce someone else's accomplishments without wishing them ill ("I wish I had what she has"), ⑤ which has been shown in some circumstances to inspire and motivate us to increase our efforts in spite of a recent failure.

* backfire: 역효과를 내다 ** scorn: 경멸

06 [1등급 대비 고난도 *2*점 문제]

다음 글의 밑줄 친 부분 중, 문맥상 낱말의 쓰임이 적절하지 않은 것은?

Adam Smith pointed out that specialization, where each of us focuses on one specific skill, leads to a general improvement of everybody's well-being. The idea is simple and powerful. By specializing in just one activity — such as food raising, clothing production, or home construction — each worker gains ① mastery over the particular activity. Specialization makes sense, however, only if the specialist can subsequently ② trade his or her output with the output of specialists in other lines of activity. It would make no sense to produce more food than a household needs unless there is a market outlet to exchange that ③ scarce food for clothing, shelter, and so forth. At the same time, without the ability to buy food on the market, it would not be possible to be a specialist home builder or clothing maker, since it would be ④ necessary to farm for one's own survival. Thus Smith realized that the division of labor is ⑤ limited by the extent of the market, whereas the extent of the market is determined by the degree of specialization.

07

다음 빈칸에 들어갈 말로 가장 적절한 것을 고르시오. [3점]

A good many scientists and artists have noticed the _____ of creativity. At the Sixteenth Nobel Conference, held in 1980, scientists, musicians, and philosophers all agreed, to quote Freeman Dyson, that "the analogies between science and art are very good as long as you are talking about the creation and the performance. The creation is certainly very analogous. The aesthetic pleasure of the craftsmanship of performance is also very strong in science." A few years later, at another multidisciplinary conference, physicist Murray Gell-Mann found that "everybody agrees on where ideas come from. We had a seminar here, about ten years ago, including several painters, a poet, a couple of writers, and the physicists. Everybody agrees on how it works. All of these people, whether they are doing artistic work or scientific work, are trying to solve a problem."

① formality   ② objectivity
③ complexity   ④ universality
⑤ uncertainty

08 1등급 대비 고난도 3점 문제

다음 빈칸에 들어갈 말로 가장 적절한 것을 고르시오. [3점]

Sociologists have proven that people bring their own views and values to the culture they encounter; books, TV programs, movies, and music may affect everyone, but they affect different people in different ways. In a study, Neil Vidmar and Milton Rokeach showed episodes of the sitcom *All in the Family* to viewers with a range of different views on race. The show centers on a character named Archie Bunker, an intolerant bigot who often gets into fights with his more progressive family members. Vidmar and Rokeach found that viewers who didn't share Archie Bunker's views thought the show was very funny in the way it made fun of Archie's absurd racism — in fact, this was the producers' intention. On the other hand, though, viewers who were themselves bigots thought Archie Bunker was the hero of the show and that the producers meant to make fun of his foolish family! This demonstrates why it's a mistake to assume that a certain cultural product _____ .

* bigot: 고집쟁이

① can provide many valuable views
② reflects the idea of the sociologists
③ forms prejudices to certain characters
④ will have the same effect on everyone
⑤ might resolve social conflicts among people

DAY **09**

09

다음 글에서 전체 흐름과 관계 없는 문장은?

There is a pervasive idea in Western culture that humans are essentially rational, skillfully sorting fact from fiction, and, ultimately, arriving at timeless truths about the world. ① This line of thinking holds that humans follow the rules of logic, calculate probabilities accurately, and make decisions about the world that are perfectly informed by all available information. ② Conversely, failures to make effective and well-informed decisions are often attributed to failures of human reasoning — resulting, say, from psychological disorders or cognitive biases. ③ In this picture, whether we succeed or fail turns out to be a matter of whether individual humans are rational and intelligent. ④ Our ability to make a reasonable decision has more to do with our social interactions than our individual psychology. ⑤ And so, if we want to achieve better outcomes — truer beliefs, better decisions — we need to focus on improving individual human reasoning.

* pervasive: 널리 스며 있는

10 *1등급* 대비 고난도 *3점* 문제

글의 흐름으로 보아, 주어진 문장이 들어가기에 가장 적절한 곳을 고르시오. [3점]

> However, when a bill was introduced in Congress to outlaw such rules, the credit card lobby turned its attention to language.

Framing matters in many domains. (①) When credit cards started to become popular forms of payment in the 1970s, some retail merchants wanted to charge different prices to their cash and credit card customers. (②) To prevent this, credit card companies adopted rules that forbade their retailers from charging different prices to cash and credit customers. (③) Its preference was that if a company charged different prices to cash and credit customers, the credit price should be considered the "normal" (default) price and the cash price a discount — rather than the alternative of making the cash price the usual price and charging a surcharge to credit card customers. (④) The credit card companies had a good intuitive understanding of what psychologists would come to call "framing." (⑤) The idea is that choices depend, in part, on the way in which problems are stated.

[11 ~ 12] 다음 글을 읽고, 물음에 답하시오.

Events or experiences that are out of ordinary tend to be remembered better because there is nothing competing with them when your brain tries to access them from its storehouse of remembered events. In other words, the reason it can be (a) difficult to remember what you ate for breakfast two Thursdays ago is that there was probably nothing special about that Thursday or that particular breakfast — consequently, all your breakfast memories combine together into a sort of generic impression of a breakfast. Your memory (b) merges similar events not only because it's more efficient to do so, but also because this is fundamental to how we learn things — our brains extract abstract rules that tie experiences together.

This is especially true for things that are (c) routine. If your breakfast is always the same — cereal with milk, a glass of orange juice, and a cup of coffee for instance — there is no easy way for your brain to extract the details from one particular breakfast. Ironically, then, for behaviors that are routinized, you can remember the generic content of the behavior (such as the things you ate, since you always eat the same thing), but (d) particulars to that one instance can be very difficult to call up (such as the sound of a garbage truck going by or a bird that passed by your window) *unless* they were especially distinctive. On the other hand, if you did something unique that broke your routine — perhaps you had leftover pizza for breakfast and spilled tomato sauce on your dress shirt — you are (e) less likely to remember it.

11

고2·2023년 6월 41번

윗글의 제목으로 가장 적절한 것은?

① Repetition Makes Your Memory Sharp!
② How Does Your Memory Get Distorted?
③ What to Consider in Routinizing Your Work
④ Merging Experiences: Key to Remembering Details
⑤ The More Unique Events, the More Vivid Recollection

12

고2·2023년 6월 42번

밑줄 친 (a) ~ (e) 중에서 문맥상 낱말의 쓰임이 적절하지 <u>않은</u> 것은?

① (a)　　② (b)　　③ (c)　　④ (d)　　⑤ (e)

DAY 09

학습 Check!　　　▶ 몰라서 틀린 문항 × 표기　▶ 헷갈렸거나 찍은 문항 △ 표기　▶ ×, △ 문항은 다시 풀고 ✔ 표기를 하세요.

종료 시각	시 분 초	문항 번호	01	02	03	04	05	06	07	08	09	10	11	12
소요 시간	분 초	채점 결과												
초과 시간	분 초	틀린 문항 복습												

DAY 10

수능기출 전국연합학력평가 20분 미니 모의고사

● 날짜 :   월   일 ● 시작 시각 :   시   분   초 ● 목표 시간 : 20분

※ 점수 표기가 없는 문항은 모두 2점입니다.

01

고3 · 2023학년도 수능 19번

다음 글에 드러난 Jamie의 심경 변화로 가장 적절한 것은?

Putting all of her energy into her last steps of the running race, Jamie crossed the finish line. To her disappointment, she had failed to beat her personal best time, again. Jamie had pushed herself for months to finally break her record, but it was all for nothing. Recognizing how she felt about her failure, Ken, her teammate, approached her and said, "Jamie, even though you didn't set a personal best time today, your performances have improved dramatically. Your running skills have progressed so much! You'll definitely break your personal best time in the next race!" After hearing his comments, she felt confident about herself. Jamie, now motivated to keep pushing for her goal, replied with a smile. "You're right! Next race, I'll beat my best time for sure!"

① indifferent → regretful
② pleased → bored
③ frustrated → encouraged
④ nervous → fearful
⑤ calm → excited

02

고2 · 2023년 3월 22번

다음 글의 요지로 가장 적절한 것은?

Brands that fail to grow and develop lose their relevance. Think about the person you knew who was once on the fast track at your company, who is either no longer with the firm or, worse yet, appears to have hit a plateau in his or her career. Assuming he or she did not make an ambitious move, more often than not, this individual is a victim of having failed to stay relevant and embrace the advances in his or her industry. Think about the impact personal computing technology had on the first wave of executive leadership exposed to the technology. Those who embraced the technology were able to integrate it into their work styles and excel. Those who were resistant many times found few opportunities to advance their careers and in many cases were ultimately let go through early retirement for failure to stay relevant and update their skills.

*hit a plateau: 정체기에 들다

① 다양한 업종의 경력이 있으면 구직 활동에 유리하다.
② 직원의 다양한 능력을 활용하면 업계를 주도할 수 있다.
③ 기술이 발전함에 따라 단순 반복 업무가 사라지고 있다.
④ 자신의 약점을 인정하면 동료들로부터 도움을 얻기 쉽다.
⑤ 변화를 받아들이지 못하면 업계에서의 적합성을 잃게 된다.

03

다음 글의 제목으로 가장 적절한 것은?

The free market has liberated people in a way that Marxism never could. What is more, as A. O. Hirschman, the Harvard economic historian, showed in his classic study *The Passions and the Interests*, the market was seen by Enlightenment thinkers Adam Smith, David Hume, and Montesquieu as a powerful solution to one of humanity's greatest traditional weaknesses: violence. When two nations meet, said Montesquieu, they can do one of two things: they can wage war or they can trade. If they wage war, both are likely to lose in the long run. If they trade, both will gain. That, of course, was the logic behind the establishment of the European Union: to lock together the destinies of its nations, especially France and Germany, in such a way that they would have an overwhelming interest not to wage war again as they had done to such devastating cost in the first half of the twentieth century.

＊Marxism: 마르크스주의

① Trade War: A Reflection of Human's Innate Violence
② Free Market: Winning Together over Losing Together
③ New Economic Framework Stabilizes the Free Market
④ Violence Is the Invisible Hand That Disrupts Capitalism!
⑤ How Are Governments Involved in Controlling the Market?

04

Carl-Gustaf Rossby에 관한 다음 글의 내용과 일치하지 <u>않는</u> 것은?

Carl-Gustaf Rossby was one of a group of notable Scandinavian researchers who worked with the Norwegian meteorologist Vilhelm Bjerknes at the University of Bergen. While growing up in Stockholm, Rossby received a traditional education. He earned a degree in mathematical physics at the University of Stockholm in 1918, but after hearing a lecture by Bjerknes, and apparently bored with Stockholm, he moved to the newly established Geophysical Institute in Bergen. In 1925, Rossby received a scholarship from the Sweden-America Foundation to go to the United States, where he joined the United States Weather Bureau. Based in part on his practical experience in weather forecasting, Rossby had become a supporter of the "polar front theory," which explains the cyclonic circulation that develops at the boundary between warm and cold air masses. In 1947, Rossby accepted the chair of the Institute of Meteorology, which had been set up for him at the University of Stockholm, where he remained until his death ten years later.

① Stockholm에서 성장하면서 전통적인 교육을 받았다.
② University of Stockholm에서 수리 물리학 학위를 받았다.
③ 1925년에 장학금을 받았다.
④ polar front theory를 지지했다.
⑤ University of Stockholm에 마련된 직책을 거절했다.

DAY 10

05 [1등급 대비 고난도 3점 문제]

고2 · 2021년 6월 29번

다음 글의 밑줄 친 부분 중, 어법상 틀린 것은? [3점]

While working as a research fellow at Harvard, B. F. Skinner carried out a series of experiments on rats, using an invention that later became known as a "Skinner box." A rat was placed in one of these boxes, ① which had a special bar fitted on the inside. Every time the rat pressed this bar, it was presented with food. The rate of bar-pressing was ② automatically recorded. Initially, the rat might press the bar accidentally, or simply out of curiosity, and as a consequence ③ receive some food. Over time, the rat learned that food appeared whenever the bar was pressed, and began to press ④ it purposefully in order to be fed. Comparing results from rats ⑤ gives the "positive reinforcement" of food for their bar-pressing behavior with those that were not, or were presented with food at different rates, it became clear that when food appeared as a consequence of the rat's actions, this influenced its future behavior.

06 [1등급 대비 고난도 2점 문제]

고2 · 2020년 9월 30번

다음 글의 밑줄 친 부분 중, 문맥상 낱말의 쓰임이 적절하지 않은 것은?

Spine-tingling ghost stories are fun to tell if they are really scary, and even more so if you claim that they are true. People get a ① thrill from passing on those stories. The same applies to miracle stories. If a rumor of a miracle gets written down in a book, the rumor becomes hard to ② believe, especially if the book is ancient. If a rumor is ③ old enough, it starts to be called a "tradition" instead, and then people believe it all the more. This is rather odd because you might think they would realize that older rumors have had more time to get ④ distorted than younger rumors that are close in time to the alleged events themselves. Elvis Presley and Michael Jackson lived too ⑤ recently for traditions to have grown up, so not many people believe stories like "Elvis seen on Mars."

07 [1등급 대비 고난도 3점 문제]

다음 빈칸에 들어갈 말로 가장 적절한 것을 고르시오. [3점]

Psychologists Leon Festinger, Stanley Schachter, and sociologist Kurt Back began to wonder how friendships form. Why do some strangers build lasting friendships, while others struggle to get past basic platitudes? Some experts explained that friendship formation could be traced to infancy, where children acquired the values, beliefs, and attitudes that would bind or separate them later in life. But Festinger, Schachter, and Back pursued a different theory. The researchers believed that _____ was the key to friendship formation; that "friendships are likely to develop on the basis of brief and passive contacts made going to and from home or walking about the neighborhood." In their view, it wasn't so much that people with similar attitudes became friends, but rather that people who passed each other during the day tended to become friends and so came to adopt similar attitudes over time.

* platitude: 상투적인 말

① shared value
② physical space
③ conscious effort
④ similar character
⑤ psychological support

08

글의 흐름으로 보아, 주어진 문장이 들어가기에 가장 적절한 곳을 고르시오. [3점]

> However, the rigidity of rock means that land rises and falls with the tides by a much smaller amount than water, which is why we notice only the ocean tides.

The difference in the Moon's gravitational pull on different parts of our planet effectively creates a "stretching force." (①) It makes our planet slightly stretched out along the line of sight to the Moon and slightly compressed along a line perpendicular to that. (②) The tidal stretching caused by the Moon's gravity affects our entire planet, including both land and water, inside and out. (③) The stretching also explains why there are generally *two* high tides (and two low tides) in the ocean each day. (④) Because Earth is stretched much like a rubber band, the oceans bulge out both on the side facing toward the Moon and on the side facing away from the Moon. (⑤) As Earth rotates, we are carried through both of these tidal bulges each day, so we have high tide when we are in each of the two bulges and low tide at the midpoints in between.

* rigidity: 단단함   ** perpendicular: 직각을 이루는
*** bulge: 팽창하다

09

고2·2023년 6월 40번

다음 글의 내용을 한 문장으로 요약하고자 한다. 빈칸 (A), (B)에 들어갈 말로 가장 적절한 것은?

People behave in highly predictable ways when they experience certain thoughts. When they agree, they nod their heads. So far, no surprise, but according to an area of research known as "proprioceptive psychology," the process also works in reverse. Get people to behave in a certain way and you cause them to have certain thoughts. The idea was initially controversial, but fortunately it was supported by a compelling experiment. Participants in a study were asked to fixate on various products moving across a large computer screen and then indicate whether the items appealed to them. Some of the items moved vertically (causing the participants to nod their heads while watching), and others moved horizontally (resulting in a side-to-side head movement). Participants preferred vertically moving products without being aware that their "yes" and "no" head movements had played a key role in their decisions.

↓

In one study, participants responded   (A)   to products on a computer screen when they moved their heads up and down, which showed that their decisions were unconsciously influenced by their   (B)   .

	(A)		(B)
①	favorably	⋯⋯	behavior
②	favorably	⋯⋯	instinct
③	unfavorably	⋯⋯	feeling
④	unfavorably	⋯⋯	gesture
⑤	irrationally	⋯⋯	prejudice

[10 ～ 12] 다음 글을 읽고, 물음에 답하시오.

(A)

A businessman boarded a flight. Arriving at his seat, he greeted his travel companions: a middle-aged woman sitting at the window, and a little boy sitting in the aisle seat. After putting his bag in the overhead bin, he took his place between them. After the flight took off, he began a conversation with the little boy. He appeared to be about the same age as (a) his son and was busy with a coloring book.

(B)

As the plane rose and fell several times, people got nervous and sat up in their seats. The man was also nervous and grabbing (b) his seat as tightly as he could. Meanwhile, the little boy was sitting quietly beside (c) him. His coloring book and crayons were put away neatly in the seat pocket in front of him, and his hands were calmly resting on his legs. Incredibly, he didn't seem worried at all.

(C)

Then, suddenly, the turbulence ended. The pilot apologized for the bumpy ride and announced that they would be landing soon. As the plane began its descent, the man said to the little boy, "You are just a little boy, but (d) I have never met a braver person in all my life! Tell me, how is it that you remained so calm while all of us adults were so afraid?" Looking him in the eyes, he said, "My father is the pilot, and he's taking me home."

＊turbulence: 난기류

(D)

He asked the boy a few usual questions, such as his age, his hobbies, as well as his favorite animal. He found it strange that such a young boy would be traveling alone, so he decided to keep an eye on (e) him to make sure he was okay. About an hour into the flight, the plane suddenly began experiencing turbulence. The pilot told everyone to fasten their seat belts and remain calm, as they had encountered rough weather.

10

고2 · 2022년 6월 43번

주어진 글 (A)에 이어질 내용을 순서에 맞게 배열한 것으로 가장 적절한 것은?

① (B) − (D) − (C) ② (C) − (B) − (D)
③ (C) − (D) − (B) ④ (D) − (B) − (C)
⑤ (D) − (C) − (B)

11

고2 · 2022년 6월 44번

밑줄 친 (a) ~ (e) 중에서 가리키는 대상이 나머지 넷과 <u>다른</u> 것은?

① (a)   ② (b)   ③ (c)   ④ (d)   ⑤ (e)

12

고2 · 2022년 6월 45번

윗글에 관한 내용으로 적절하지 <u>않은</u> 것은?

① 사업가는 중년 여성과 소년 사이에 앉았다.
② 비행기가 오르락내리락하자 사람들은 긴장했다.
③ 소년은 색칠 공부 책과 크레용을 가방에 넣었다.
④ 소년은 자신의 아버지가 조종사라고 말했다.
⑤ 조종사는 사람들에게 안전벨트를 매고 침착하라고 말했다.

DAY 10

DAY 11

수능기출
전국연합학력평가 **20분 미니 모의고사**

● 날짜 :　　　월　　　일 ● 시작 시각 :　　　시　　　분　　　초 ● 목표 시간 : 20분　　　　※ 점수 표기가 없는 문항은 모두 2점입니다.

01
고2 · 2021년 9월 20번

다음 글에서 필자가 주장하는 바로 가장 적절한 것은?

Without guidance from their teacher, students will not embark on a journey of personal development that recognizes the value of cooperation. Left to their own devices, they will instinctively become increasingly competitive with each other. They will compare scores, reports, and feedback within the classroom environment — just as they do in the sporting arena. We don't need to teach our students about winners and losers. The playground and the media do that for them. However, we do need to teach them that there is more to life than winning and about the skills they need for successful cooperation. A group working together successfully requires individuals with a multitude of social skills, as well as a high level of interpersonal awareness. While some students inherently bring a natural understanding of these skills with them, they are always in the minority. To bring cooperation between peers into your classroom, you need to teach these skills consciously and carefully, and nurture them continuously throughout the school years.

① 학생의 참여가 활발한 수업 방법을 개발해야 한다.
② 학생에게 성공적인 협동을 위한 기술을 가르쳐야 한다.
③ 학생의 의견을 존중하는 학교 분위기를 조성해야 한다.
④ 학생의 전인적 발달을 위해 체육활동을 강화해야 한다.
⑤ 정보를 올바르게 선별하도록 미디어 교육을 실시해야 한다.

02
고2 · 2022년 11월 22번

다음 글의 요지로 가장 적절한 것은?

In one study, when researchers suggested that a date was associated with a new beginning (such as "the first day of spring"), students viewed it as a more attractive time to kick-start goal pursuit than when researchers presented it as an unremarkable day (such as "the third Thursday in March"). Whether it was starting a new gym habit or spending less time on social media, when the date that researchers suggested was associated with a new beginning, more students wanted to begin changes right then. And more recent research by a different team found that similar benefits were achieved by showing goal seekers modified weekly calendars. When calendars depicted the current day (either Monday or Sunday) as the first day of the week, people reported feeling more motivated to make immediate progress on their goals.

① 새로운 시작을 하기 전에 장기적인 계획을 세우는 것이 바람직하다.
② 자신이 해야 할 일을 일정표에 표시하는 것이 목표 달성에 효과적이다.
③ 문제 행동을 개선하기 위해 원인이 되는 요소를 파악할 필요가 있다.
④ 날짜가 시작이라는 의미와 관련지어질 때 목표 추구에 강한 동기가 부여된다.
⑤ 상세한 일정표를 작성하는 것은 여러 목표를 동시에 달성하는 데 도움이 된다.

03

고3 · 2021학년도 수능 23번

다음 글의 주제로 가장 적절한 것은? [3점]

Difficulties arise when we do not think of people and machines as collaborative systems, but assign whatever tasks can be automated to the machines and leave the rest to people. This ends up requiring people to behave in machine-like fashion, in ways that differ from human capabilities. We expect people to monitor machines, which means keeping alert for long periods, something we are bad at. We require people to do repeated operations with the extreme precision and accuracy required by machines, again something we are not good at. When we divide up the machine and human components of a task in this way, we fail to take advantage of human strengths and capabilities but instead rely upon areas where we are genetically, biologically unsuited. Yet, when people fail, they are blamed.

① difficulties of overcoming human weaknesses to avoid failure

② benefits of allowing machines and humans to work together

③ issues of allocating unfit tasks to humans in automated systems

④ reasons why humans continue to pursue machine automation

⑤ influences of human actions on a machine's performance

04

고2 · 2019년 6월 29번

다음 글의 밑줄 친 부분 중, 어법상 틀린 것은?

Trying to produce everything yourself would mean you are using your time and resources to produce many things ① for which you are a high-cost provider. This would translate into lower production and income. For example, even though most doctors might be good at record keeping and arranging appointments, ② it is generally in their interest to hire someone to perform these services. The time doctors use to keep records is time they could have spent seeing patients. Because the time ③ spent with their patients is worth a lot, the opportunity cost of record keeping for doctors will be high. Thus, doctors will almost always find it ④ advantageous to hire someone else to keep and manage their records. Moreover, when the doctor specializes in the provision of physician services and ⑤ hiring someone who has a comparative advantage in record keeping, costs will be lower and joint output larger than would otherwise be achievable.

05 1등급 대비 고난도 3점 문제 고2·2023년 3월 30번

다음 글의 밑줄 친 부분 중, 문맥상 낱말의 쓰임이 적절하지 않은 것은? [3점]

Robert Blattberg and Steven Hoch noted that, in a changing environment, it is not clear that consistency is always a virtue and that one of the advantages of human judgment is the ability to detect change. Thus, in changing environments, it might be ① advantageous to combine human judgment and statistical models. Blattberg and Hoch examined this possibility by having supermarket managers forecast demand for certain products and then creating a composite forecast by averaging these judgments with the forecasts of statistical models based on ② past data. The logic was that statistical models ③ deny stable conditions and therefore cannot account for the effects on demand of novel events such as actions taken by competitors or the introduction of new products. Humans, however, can ④ incorporate these novel factors in their judgments. The composite — or average of human judgments and statistical models — proved to be more ⑤ accurate than either the statistical models or the managers working alone.

* composite: 종합적인; 종합된 것

06 1등급 대비 고난도 3점 문제 고2·2018년 9월 31번

다음 빈칸에 들어갈 말로 가장 적절한 것을 고르시오. [3점]

Online environments vary widely in how easily you can save whatever happens there, what I call its *recordability* and *preservability*. Even though the design, activities, and membership of social media might change over time, the content of what people posted usually remains intact. Email, video, audio, and text messages can be saved. When perfect preservation is possible, time has been suspended. Whenever you want, you can go back to reexamine those events from the past. In other situations, _____ slips between our fingers, even challenging our reality testing about whether something existed at all, as when an email that we seem to remember receiving mysteriously disappears from our inbox. The slightest accidental tap of the finger can send an otherwise everlasting document into nothingness.

① scarcity   ② creativity
③ acceleration   ④ permanency
⑤ mysteriousness

07

다음 빈칸에 들어갈 말로 가장 적절한 것을 고르시오.

Color is an interpretation of wavelengths, one that only exists internally. And it gets stranger, because the wavelengths we're talking about involve only what we call "visible light", a spectrum of wavelengths that runs from red to violet. But visible light constitutes only a tiny fraction of the electromagnetic spectrum — less than one ten-trillionth of it. All the rest of the spectrum — including radio waves, microwaves, X-rays, gamma rays, cell phone conversations, wi-fi, and so on — all of this is flowing through us right now, and we're completely unaware of it. This is because we don't have any specialized biological receptors to pick up on these signals from other parts of the spectrum. The slice of reality that we can see is _____.

* electromagnetic: 전자기의 ** receptor: 수용체

① hindered by other wavelengths
② derived from our imagination
③ perceived through all senses
④ filtered by our stereotypes
⑤ limited by our biology

08

다음 글에서 전체 흐름과 관계 없는 문장은?

Taking a stand is important because you become a beacon for those individuals who are your people, your tribe, and your audience. ① When you raise your viewpoint up like a flag, people know where to find you; it becomes a rallying point. ② Displaying your perspective lets prospective (and current) customers know that you don't just sell your products or services. ③ The best marketing is never just about selling a product or service, but about taking a stand — showing an audience why they should believe in what you're marketing enough to want it at any cost, simply because they agree with what you're doing. ④ If you want to retain your existing customers, you need to create ways that a customer can feel like another member of the team, participating in the process of product development. ⑤ Products can be changed or adjusted if they aren't functioning, but rallying points align with the values and meaning behind what you do.

* beacon: 횃불 ** rallying point: 집합 지점

09 1등급 대비 고난도 2점 문제

주어진 글 다음에 이어질 글의 순서로 가장 적절한 것을 고르시오.

There is no doubt that the length of some literary works is overwhelming. Reading or translating a work in class, hour after hour, week after week, can be such a boring experience that many students never want to open a foreign language book again.

(A) Moreover, there are some literary features that cannot be adequately illustrated by a short excerpt: the development of plot or character, for instance, with the gradual involvement of the reader that this implies; or the unfolding of a complex theme through the juxtaposition of contrasting views.

(B) Extracts provide one type of solution. The advantages are obvious: reading a series of passages from different works produces more variety in the classroom, so that the teacher has a greater chance of avoiding monotony, while still giving learners a taste at least of an author's special flavour.

(C) On the other hand, a student who is only exposed to 'bite-sized chunks' will never have the satisfaction of knowing the overall pattern of a book, which is after all the satisfaction most of us seek when we read something in our own language.

＊excerpt: 발췌 ＊＊juxtaposition: 병치

① (A) − (C) − (B)
② (B) − (A) − (C)
③ (B) − (C) − (A)
④ (C) − (A) − (B)
⑤ (C) − (B) − (A)

10

다음 글의 내용을 한 문장으로 요약하고자 한다. 빈칸 (A), (B)에 들어갈 말로 가장 적절한 것은?

Anne Thorndike, a primary care physician in Boston, had a crazy idea. She believed she could improve the eating habits of thousands of hospital staff and visitors without changing their willpower or motivation in the slightest way. In fact, she didn't plan on talking to them at all. Thorndike designed a study to alter the "choice architecture" of the hospital cafeteria. She started by changing how drinks were arranged in the room. Originally, the refrigerators located next to the cash registers in the cafeteria were filled with only soda. She added water as an option to each one. Additionally, she placed baskets of bottled water next to the food stations throughout the room. Soda was still in the primary refrigerators, but water was now available at all drink locations. Over the next three months, the number of soda sales at the hospital dropped by 11.4 percent. Meanwhile, sales of bottled water increased by 25.8 percent.

↓

The study performed by Thorndike showed that the ___(A)___ of drinks at the hospital cafeteria influenced the choices people made, which ___(B)___ the consumption of soda.

	(A)		(B)
①	placement	……	lowered
②	placement	……	boosted
③	price	……	lowered
④	price	……	boosted
⑤	flavor	……	maintained

[11 ~ 12] 다음 글을 읽고, 물음에 답하시오.

Evolutionary biologists believe sociability drove the evolution of our complex brains. Fossil evidence shows that as far back as 130,000 years ago, it was not (a) unusual for *Homo sapiens* to travel more than a hundred and fifty miles to trade, share food and, no doubt, gossip. Unlike the Neanderthals, their social groups extended far beyond their own families. Remembering all those (b) connections, who was related to whom, and where they lived required considerable processing power.

It also required wayfinding savvy. Imagine trying to (c) maintain a social network across tens or hundreds of square miles of Palaeolithic wilderness. You couldn't send a text message to your friends to find out where they were — you had to go out and visit them, remember where you last saw them or imagine where they might have gone. To do this, you needed navigation skills, spatial awareness, a sense of direction, the ability to store maps of the landscape in your mind and the motivation to travel around. Canadian anthropologist Ariane Burke believes that our ancestors (d) developed all these attributes while trying to keep in touch with their neighbours. Eventually, our brains became primed for wayfinding. Meanwhile the Neanderthals, who didn't travel as far, never fostered a spatial skill set; despite being sophisticated hunters, well adapted to the cold and able to see in the dark, they went extinct. In the prehistoric badlands, nothing was more (e) useless than a circle of friends.

* savvy: 요령, 지식　** Palaeolithic: 구석기 시대의

11

고2 · 2020년 11월 41번

윗글의 제목으로 가장 적절한 것은?

① Social Networks: An Evolutionary Advantage
② Our Brain Forced Us to Stay Close to Our Family!
③ How We Split from Our Way and Kept Going on My Way
④ Why Do Some People Have Difficulty in Social Relationships?
⑤ Being Connected to Each Other Leads to Communicative Skills

12

고2 · 2020년 11월 42번

밑줄 친 (a) ~ (e) 중에서 문맥상 낱말의 쓰임이 적절하지 않은 것은? [3점]

① (a)　② (b)　③ (c)　④ (d)　⑤ (e)

학습 Check!　▶ 몰라서 틀린 문항 × 표기　▶ 헷갈렸거나 찍은 문항 △ 표기　▶ ×, △ 문항은 다시 풀고 ✔ 표기를 하세요.

종료 시각	시	분	초	문항 번호	01	02	03	04	05	06	07	08	09	10	11	12
소요 시간		분	초	채점 결과												
초과 시간		분	초	틀린 문항 복습												

DAY 12

● 날짜 :   월   일 ● 시작 시각 :   시   분   초 ● 목표 시간 : 20분

※ 점수 표기가 없는 문항은 모두 2점입니다.

01

고2 · 2022년 11월 18번

다음 글의 목적으로 가장 적절한 것은?

Dear local business owners,

My name is Carol Williams, president of the student council at Yellowstone High School. We are hosting our annual quiz night on March 30 and plan to give prizes to the winning team. However, this event won't be possible without the support of local businesses who provide valuable products and services. Would you be willing to donate a gift certificate that we can use as a prize? We would be grateful for any amount on the certificate. In exchange for your generosity, we would place an advertisement for your business on our answer sheets. Thank you for taking time to read this letter and consider our request. If you'd like to donate or need more information, please call or email me. I look forward to hearing from you soon.

Carol Williams

① 행사 홍보물 게시가 가능한지를 문의하려고
② 학교 퀴즈 행사에 사용할 물품 제작을 의뢰하려고
③ 우승 상품으로 사용할 상품권을 기부해 줄 것을 요청하려고
④ 학교 행사로 예상되는 소음 발생에 대해 양해를 구하려고
⑤ 퀴즈 행사 개최를 위한 장소 사용 허가를 받으려고

02

고2 · 2022년 9월 21번

밑줄 친 the innocent messenger who falls before a firing line이 다음 글에서 의미하는 바로 가장 적절한 것은? [3점]

Perhaps worse than attempting to get the bad news out of the way is attempting to soften it or simply not address it at all. This "Mum Effect" — a term coined by psychologists Sidney Rosen and Abraham Tesser in the early 1970s — happens because people want to avoid becoming the target of others' negative emotions. We all have the opportunity to lead change, yet it often requires of us the courage to deliver bad news to our superiors. We don't want to be the innocent messenger who falls before a firing line. When our survival instincts kick in, they can override our courage until the truth of a situation gets watered down. "The Mum Effect and the resulting filtering can have devastating effects in a steep hierarchy," writes Robert Sutton, an organizational psychologist. "What starts out as bad news becomes happier and happier as it travels up the ranks — because after each boss hears the news from his or her subordinates, he or she makes it sound a bit less bad before passing it up the chain."

① the employee being criticized for being silent
② the peacemaker who pursues non-violent solutions
③ the negotiator who looks for a mutual understanding
④ the subordinate who wants to get attention from the boss
⑤ the person who gets the blame for reporting unpleasant news

03 1등급 대비 고난도 2점 문제   고3·2021학년도 수능 24번

다음 글의 제목으로 가장 적절한 것은?

People don't usually think of touch as a temporal phenomenon, but it is every bit as time-based as it is spatial. You can carry out an experiment to see for yourself. Ask a friend to cup his hand, palm face up, and close his eyes. Place a small ordinary object in his palm — a ring, an eraser, anything will do — and ask him to identify it without moving any part of his hand. He won't have a clue other than weight and maybe overall size. Then tell him to keep his eyes closed and move his fingers over the object. He'll most likely identify it at once. By allowing the fingers to move, you've added time to the sensory perception of touch. There's a direct analogy between the fovea at the center of your retina and your fingertips, both of which have high acuity. Your ability to make complex use of touch, such as buttoning your shirt or unlocking your front door in the dark, depends on continuous time-varying patterns of touch sensation.

* analogy: 유사 ** fovea: (망막의) 중심와(窩)
*** retina: 망막

① Touch and Movement: Two Major Elements of Humanity
② Time Does Matter: A Hidden Essence of Touch
③ How to Use the Five Senses in a Timely Manner
④ The Role of Touch in Forming the Concept of Time
⑤ The Surprising Function of Touch as a Booster of Knowledge

04   고2·2023년 6월 27번

Peace Marathon Festival에 관한 다음 안내문의 내용과 일치하지 <u>않는</u> 것은?

Peace Marathon Festival

The Peace Marathon Festival will be held to promote world peace and share compassion for people in need. Join us to enjoy running and make a better world.

When & Where
• Sunday, September 3, 2023
  (Start time: 10 a.m.)
• Civic Stadium

Participation Fee & Qualification
• Full & Half: $30 (20 years or older)
• 10 km & 5 km: $15 (No age limit)

Registration
• The number of participants is limited to 1,000.
  (First come, first served.)
• Online only at ipmarathon.com

Notes
• Souvenirs and medals will be given to all participants.
• Changing rooms will be available at no charge.
• Water will be provided every 2.5km and at the finish line.

① 출발 시각은 오전 10시이다.
② 5 킬로미터 코스는 참가에 나이 제한이 없다.
③ 참가자는 선착순 1,000명으로 제한된다.
④ 모든 참가자들에게 기념품과 메달이 주어진다.
⑤ 물은 결승선에서만 제공된다.

05 1등급 대비 고난도 3점 문제 〈고2·2021년 11월 29번〉

다음 글의 밑줄 친 부분 중, 어법상 틀린 것은? [3점]

Anchoring bias describes the cognitive error you make when you tend to give more weight to information arriving early in a situation ① compared to information arriving later — regardless of the relative quality or relevance of that initial information. Whatever data is presented to you first when you start to look at a situation can form an "anchor" and it becomes significantly more challenging ② to alter your mental course away from this anchor than it logically should be. A classic example of anchoring bias in emergency medicine is "triage bias," ③ where whatever the first impression you develop, or are given, about a patient tends to influence all subsequent providers seeing that patient. For example, imagine two patients presenting for emergency care with aching jaw pain that occasionally ④ extends down to their chest. Differences in how the intake providers label the chart — "jaw pain" vs. "chest pain," for example — ⑤ creating anchors that might result in significant differences in how the patients are treated.

＊triage: 부상자 분류　＊＊intake provider: 환자를 예진하는 의료 종사자

06 1등급 대비 고난도 3점 문제 〈고2·2019년 9월 30번〉

다음 글의 밑줄 친 부분 중, 문맥상 낱말의 쓰임이 적절하지 않은 것은? [3점]

A champion of free speech and religious toleration, Voltaire was a controversial figure. He is, for instance, supposed to have declared, "I hate what you say, but will defend to the death your right to say it," a powerful ① defense of the idea that even views that you despise deserve to be heard. In eighteenth-century Europe, however, the Catholic Church strictly ② controlled what could be published. Many of Voltaire's plays and books were censored and burned in public, and he was even imprisoned in the Bastille in Paris because he had ③ insulted a powerful aristocrat. But none of this stopped him challenging the prejudices and pretensions of those around him. In his short philosophical novel, *Candide*, he completely ④ supported the kind of religious optimism about humanity and the universe that other contemporary thinkers had expressed, and he did it in such an entertaining way that the book became an instant bestseller. Wisely, Voltaire left his name ⑤ off the title page, otherwise its publication would have landed him in prison again for making fun of religious beliefs.

07

고2 · 2017년 11월 31번

다음 빈칸에 들어갈 말로 가장 적절한 것을 고르시오. [3점]

What is the true nature of the brain? The brain is a slow-changing machine, and that's a good thing. If your brain could completely change overnight, you would be unstable. Let's just say that your norm is to wake up, read the paper with coffee and a bagel, walk your dog, and watch the news. This is your habitual routine. Then one night, you get a phone call at 3 a.m. and have to run outside in your underwear to check on your neighbors. What if your brain latched on to this new routine and you continued to run outside at 3 a.m. every night in your underwear? Nobody would want that, so it's a good thing our brains require more repetition than that! Let's accept and be thankful for the _____ our slow-changing brains provide us.

* latch on to: ~을 자기 것으로 하다

① stability
② maturity
③ curiosity
④ variability
⑤ productivity

08

고2 · 2021년 3월 38번

글의 흐름으로 보아, 주어진 문장이 들어가기에 가장 적절한 곳을 고르시오. [3점]

> However, some types of beliefs cannot be tested for truth because we cannot get external evidence in our lifetimes (such as a belief that the Earth will stop spinning on its axis by the year 9999 or that there is life on a planet 100-million light-years away).

Most beliefs — but not all — are open to tests of verification. This means that beliefs can be tested to see if they are correct or false. (①) Beliefs can be verified or falsified with objective criteria external to the person. (②) There are people who believe the Earth is flat and not a sphere. (③) Because we have objective evidence that the Earth is in fact a sphere, the flat Earth belief can be shown to be false. (④) Also, the belief that it will rain tomorrow can be tested for truth by waiting until tomorrow and seeing whether it rains or not. (⑤) Also, meta-physical beliefs (such as the existence and nature of a god) present considerable challenges in generating evidence that everyone is willing to use as a truth criterion.

* verification: 검증, 확인 ** falsify: 거짓임을 입증하다

09

다음 글의 내용을 한 문장으로 요약하고자 한다. 빈칸 (A), (B)에 들어갈 말로 가장 적절한 것은?

Why do we help? One widely held view is that self-interest underlies all human interactions, that our constant goal is to maximize rewards and minimize costs. Accountants call it *cost-benefit analysis*. Philosophers call it *utilitarianism*. Social psychologists call it social exchange theory. If you are considering whether to donate blood, you may weigh the costs of doing so (time, discomfort, and anxiety) against the benefits (reduced guilt, social approval, and good feelings). If the rewards exceed the costs, you will help. Others believe that we help because we have been socialized to do so, through norms that prescribe how we ought to behave. Through socialization, we learn the reciprocity norm: the expectation that we should return help, not harm, to those who have helped us. In our relations with others of similar status, the reciprocity norm compels us to give (in favors, gifts, or social invitations) about as much as we receive.

↓

People help because helping gives them ____(A)____, but also because they are socially learned to ____(B)____ what others have done for them.

	(A)		(B)
①	advantages	······	repay
②	patience	······	evaluate
③	wisdom	······	forget
④	advantages	······	accept
⑤	patience	······	appreciate

[10 ～ 12] 다음 글을 읽고, 물음에 답하시오.

(A)

John was a sensitive boy. Even his hair was ticklish. When breeze touched his hair he would burst out laughing. And when this ticklish laughter started, no one could make him stop. John's laughter was so contagious that when John started feeling ticklish, everyone ended up in endless laughter. He tried everything to control his ticklishness: wearing a thousand different hats, using ultra strong hairsprays, and shaving his head. But nothing worked. One day he met a clown in the street. The clown was very old and could hardly walk, but when he saw John in tears, he went to cheer (a) him up.

＊ticklish: 간지럼을 타는

(B)

All were full of children who were sick, or orphaned, children with very serious problems. But as soon as they saw the clown, their faces changed completely and lit up with a smile. That day was even more special, because in every show John's contagious laughter would end up making the kids laugh a lot. The old clown winked at (b) him and said "Now do you see what a serious job it is? That's why I can't retire, even at my age."

(C)

It didn't take long to make John laugh, and they started to talk. John told (c) him about his ticklish problem. Then he asked the clown how such an old man could carry on being a clown. "I have no one to replace me," said the clown, "and I have a very serious job to do." And then he took John to many hospitals, shelters, and schools.

(D)

And he added, "Not everyone could do it. He or she has to have a special gift for laughter." This said, the wind again set off John's ticklishness and (d) <u>his</u> laughter. After a while, John decided to replace the old clown. From that day onward, the fact that John was different actually made (e) <u>him</u> happy, thanks to his special gift.

10

고2 • 2022년 3월 43번

주어진 글 (A)에 이어질 내용을 순서에 맞게 배열한 것으로 가장 적절한 것은?

① (B) − (D) − (C)　　② (C) − (B) − (D)

③ (C) − (D) − (B)　　④ (D) − (B) − (C)

⑤ (D) − (C) − (B)

11

고2 • 2022년 3월 44번

밑줄 친 (a)∼(e) 중에서 가리키는 대상이 나머지 넷과 <u>다른</u> 것은?

① (a)　　② (b)　　③ (c)　　④ (d)　　⑤ (e)

12

고2 • 2022년 3월 45번

윗글의 John에 관한 내용으로 적절하지 <u>않은</u> 것은?

① 간지럼을 타지 않으려고 온갖 시도를 했다.

② 전염성 있는 웃음으로 아이들을 많이 웃게 했다.

③ 광대에게 그렇게 늙어서도 어떻게 계속 일할 수 있는지 물었다.

④ 광대와 함께 여러 병원과 보호 시설, 학교에 갔다.

⑤ 광대의 뒤를 잇지 않기로 했다.

▶ 몰라서 틀린 문항 × 표기　▶ 헷갈렸거나 찍은 문항 △ 표기　▶ ×, △ 문항은 다시 풀고 ✔ 표기를 하세요.

학습 Check!

종료 시각	시	분	초	문항 번호	01	02	03	04	05	06	07	08	09	10	11	12
소요 시간		분	초	채점 결과												
초과 시간		분	초	틀린 문항 복습												

[Day 12] 미니 모의고사　**075**

DAY 12

DAY 13

수능기출
전국연합학력평가 **20분 미니 모의고사**

● 날짜 :   월   일 ● 시작 시각 :   시   분   초 ● 목표 시간 : 20분

※ 점수 표기가 없는 문항은 모두 2점입니다.

01

고2 · 2023년 6월 19번

다음 글에 드러난 Ester의 심경 변화로 가장 적절한 것은?

Ester stood up as soon as she heard the hum of a hover engine outside. "Mail," she shouted and ran down the third set of stairs and swung open the door. It was pouring now, but she ran out into the rain. She was facing the mailbox. There was a single, unopened letter inside. She was sure this must be what she was eagerly waiting for. Without hesitation, she tore open the envelope. She pulled out the paper and unfolded it. The letter said, 'Thank you for applying to our company. We would like to invite you to our internship program. We look forward to seeing you soon.' She jumped up and down and looked down at the letter again. She couldn't wait to tell this news to her family.

① anticipating → excited
② confident → ashamed
③ curious → embarrassed
④ surprised → confused
⑤ indifferent → grateful

02

고2 · 2022년 3월 20번

다음 글에서 필자가 주장하는 바로 가장 적절한 것은?

Though we are marching toward a more global society, various ethnic groups traditionally do things quite differently, and a fresh perspective is valuable in creating an open-minded child. Extensive multicultural experience makes kids more creative (measured by how many ideas they can come up with and by association skills) and allows them to capture unconventional ideas from other cultures to expand on their own ideas. As a parent, you should expose your children to other cultures as often as possible. If you can, travel with your child to other countries; live there if possible. If neither is possible, there are lots of things you can do at home, such as exploring local festivals, borrowing library books about other cultures, and cooking foods from different cultures at your house.

① 자녀가 전통문화를 자랑스럽게 여기게 해야 한다.
② 자녀가 주어진 문제를 깊이 있게 탐구하도록 이끌어야 한다.
③ 자녀가 다른 문화를 가능한 한 자주 접할 수 있게 해야 한다.
④ 창의성 발달을 위해 자녀의 실수에 대해 너그러워야 한다.
⑤ 경험한 것을 돌이켜 볼 시간을 자녀에게 주어야 한다.

03

다음 글의 요지로 가장 적절한 것은?

The problem with simply adopting any popular method of parenting is that it ignores the most important variable in the equation: the uniqueness of your child. So, rather than insist that one style of parenting will work with every child, we might take a page from the gardener's handbook. Just as the gardener accepts, without question or resistance, the plant's requirements and provides the right conditions each plant needs to grow and flourish, so, too, do we parents need to custom-design our parenting to fit the natural needs of each individual child. Although that may seem difficult, it is possible. Once we understand who our children really are, we can begin to figure out how to make changes in our parenting style to be more positive and accepting of each child we've been blessed to parent.

* equation: 방정식

① 자녀의 특성에 맞는 개별화된 양육이 필요하다.
② 식물을 키우는 것이 자녀의 창의성 발달에 도움이 된다.
③ 정서적 교감은 자녀의 바람직한 인격 형성에 필수적이다.
④ 자녀에게 타인을 존중하는 태도를 가르치는 것이 중요하다.
⑤ 전문가에 의해 검증된 양육 방식을 따르는 것이 바람직하다.

04

다음 도표의 내용과 일치하지 <u>않는</u> 것은?

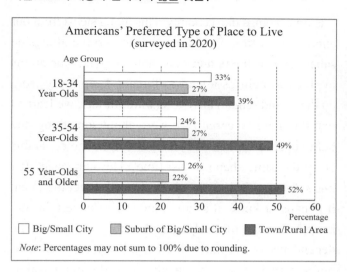

The above graph shows the percentages of Americans' preferred type of place to live by age group, based on a 2020 survey. ① In each of the three age groups, Town/Rural Area was the most preferred type of place to live. ② In the 18-34 year-olds group, the percentage of those who preferred Big/Small City was higher than that of those who preferred Suburb of Big/Small City. ③ In the 35-54 year-olds group, the percentage of those who preferred Suburb of Big/Small City exceeded that of those who preferred Big/Small City. ④ In the 55 year-olds and older group, the percentage of those who chose Big/Small City among the three preferred types of place to live was the lowest. ⑤ Each percentage of the three preferred types of place to live was higher than 20% across the three age groups.

05

다음 글의 밑줄 친 부분 중, 어법상 **틀린** 것은? [3점]

Human beings like certainty. This liking stems from our ancient ancestors ① who needed to survive alongside saber-toothed tigers and poisonous berries. Our brains evolved to help us attend to threats, keep away from ② them, and remain alive afterward. In fact, we learned that the more ③ certain we were about something, the better chance we had of making the right choice. Is this berry the same shape as last time? The same size? If I know for certain it ④ is, my brain will direct me to eat it because I know it's safe. And if I'm uncertain, my brain will send out a danger alert to protect me. The dependence on certainty all those millennia ago ensured our survival to the present day, and the danger-alert system continues to protect us. This is achieved by our brains labeling new, vague, or unpredictable everyday events and experiences as uncertain. Our brains then ⑤ generating sensations, thoughts, and action plans to keep us safe from the uncertain element, and we live to see another day.

* saber-toothed tiger: 검치호(검 모양의 송곳니를 가진 호랑이)

06

(A), (B), (C)의 각 네모 안에서 문맥에 맞는 낱말로 가장 적절한 것은? [3점]

A story is only as believable as the storyteller. For story to be effective, trust must be established. Yes, trust. Whenever someone stops to listen to you, an element of unspoken trust (A) exists / vanishes . Your listener unconsciously trusts you to say something worthwhile to him, something that will not waste his time. The few minutes of attention he is giving you is (B) deceptive / sacrificial . He could choose to spend his time elsewhere, yet he has stopped to respect your part in a conversation. This is where story comes in. Because a story illustrates points clearly and often bridges topics easily, trust can be established *quickly*, and recognizing this time element to story is essential to trust. (C) Respecting / Wasting your listener's time is the capital letter at the beginning of your sentence — it leads the conversation into a sentence worth listening to *if* trust is earned and not taken for granted.

	(A)		(B)		(C)
①	exists	……	deceptive	……	Respecting
②	exists	……	sacrificial	……	Respecting
③	exists	……	sacrificial	……	Wasting
④	vanishes	……	sacrificial	……	Respecting
⑤	vanishes	……	deceptive	……	Wasting

07

다음 빈칸에 들어갈 말로 가장 적절한 것을 고르시오.

No learning is possible without an error signal. Organisms only learn when events violate their expectations. In other words, surprise is one of the fundamental drivers of learning. Imagine hearing a series of identical notes, AAAAA. Each note draws out a response in the auditory areas of your brain — but as the notes repeat, those responses progressively decrease. This is called "adaptation," a deceptively simple phenomenon that shows that your brain is learning to anticipate the next event. Suddenly, the note changes: AAAAA#. Your primary auditory cortex immediately shows a strong surprise reaction: not only does the adaptation fade away, but additional neurons begin to vigorously fire in response to the unexpected sound. And it is not just repetition that leads to adaptation: what matters is whether the notes are _____. For instance, if you hear an alternating set of notes, such as ABABA, your brain gets used to this alternation, and the activity in your auditory areas again decreases. This time, however, it is an unexpected repetition, such as ABABB, that triggers a surprise response.

① audible　　　　　② predictable
③ objective　　　　④ countable
⑤ recorded

08 1등급 대비 고난도 3점 문제

다음 빈칸에 들어갈 말로 가장 적절한 것을 고르시오. [3점]

At the pharmaceutical giant Merck, CEO Kenneth Frazier decided to motivate his executives to take a more active role in leading innovation and change. He asked them to do something radical: generate ideas that would put Merck out of business. For the next two hours, the executives worked in groups, pretending to be one of Merck's top competitors. Energy soared as they developed ideas for drugs that would crush theirs and key markets they had missed. Then, their challenge was to reverse their roles and figure out how to defend against these threats. This "kill the company" exercise is powerful because _____. When deliberating about innovation opportunities, the leaders weren't inclined to take risks. When they considered how their competitors could put them out of business, they realized that it was a risk not to innovate. The urgency of innovation was apparent.

＊crush: 짓밟다　＊＊deliberate: 심사숙고하다

① the unknown is more helpful than the negative
② it highlights the progress they've already made
③ it is not irrational but is consumer-based practice
④ it reframes a gain-framed activity in terms of losses
⑤ they discuss how well it fits their profit-sharing plans

09 1등급 대비 고난도 2점 문제

고2·2023년 9월 35번

다음 글에서 전체 흐름과 관계 <u>없는</u> 문장은?

The irony of early democracy in Europe is that it thrived and prospered precisely because European rulers for a very long time were remarkably weak. ① For more than a millennium after the fall of Rome, European rulers lacked the ability to assess what their people were producing and to levy substantial taxes based on this. ② The most striking way to illustrate European weakness is to show how little revenue they collected. ③ For this reason, tax collectors in Europe were able to collect a huge amount of revenue and therefore had a great influence on how society should function. ④ Europeans would eventually develop strong systems of revenue collection, but it took them an awfully long time to do so. ⑤ In medieval times, and for part of the early modern era, Chinese emperors and Muslim caliphs were able to extract much more of economic production than any European ruler with the exception of small city-states.

＊levy: 부과하다   ＊＊caliph: 칼리프(과거 이슬람 국가의 통치자)

10 1등급 대비 고난도 3점 문제

고2·2020년 3월 37번

주어진 글 다음에 이어질 글의 순서로 가장 적절한 것을 고르시오. [3점]

Regardless of whether the people existing after agriculture were happier, healthier, or neither, it is undeniable that there were more of them. Agriculture both supports and requires more people to grow the crops that sustain them.

(A) And a larger population doesn't just mean increasing the size of everything, like buying a bigger box of cereal for a larger family. It brings qualitative changes in the way people live.

(B) Estimates vary, of course, but evidence points to an increase in the human population from 1-5 million people worldwide to a few hundred million once agriculture had become established.

(C) For example, more people means more kinds of diseases, particularly when those people are sedentary. Those groups of people can also store food for long periods, which creates a society with haves and have-nots.

＊sedentary: 한 곳에 정착해 있는

① (A) − (C) − (B) 　② (B) − (A) − (C)
③ (B) − (C) − (A) 　④ (C) − (A) − (B)
⑤ (C) − (B) − (A)

[11 ~ 12] 다음 글을 읽고, 물음에 답하시오.

An organization imported new machinery with the capacity to produce quality products at a lesser price. A manager was responsible for large quantities in a relatively short span of time. He started with the (a) full utilization of the new machinery. He operated it 24/7 at maximum capacity. He paid the least attention to downtime, recovery breaks or the general maintenance of the machinery. As the machinery was new, it continued to produce results and, therefore, the organization's profitability (b) soared and the manager was appreciated for his performance. Now after some time, this manager was promoted and transferred to a different location. A new manager came in his place to be in charge of running the manufacturing location. But this manager realized that with heavy utilization and without any downtime for maintenance, a lot of the parts of the machinery were significantly (c) worn and needed to be replaced or repaired. The new manager had to put significant time and effort into repair and maintenance of the machines, which resulted in lower production and thus a loss of profits. The earlier manager had only taken care of the goal of production and (d) ignored the machinery although he had short-term good results. But ultimately not giving attention to recovery and maintenance resulted in long-term (e) positive consequences.

11

고2 · 2020년 6월 41번

윗글의 제목으로 가장 적절한 것은?

① Why Are Quality Products Important?
② Give Machines a Break to Avoid Overuse
③ Providing Incentives to Maximize Workers' Abilities
④ Tip for Managers: The Right Man in the Right Place
⑤ Wars for High Productivity in a World of Competition

12

고2 · 2020년 6월 42번

밑줄 친 (a) ~ (e) 중에서 문맥상 낱말의 쓰임이 적절하지 않은 것은?

① (a)   ② (b)   ③ (c)   ④ (d)   ⑤ (e)

학습 Check!   ▶ 몰라서 틀린 문항 × 표기   ▶ 헷갈렸거나 찍은 문항 △ 표기   ▶ ×, △ 문항은 다시 풀고 ✔ 표기를 하세요.

종료 시각	시 분 초	문항 번호	01	02	03	04	05	06	07	08	09	10	11	12
소요 시간	분 초	채점 결과												
초과 시간	분 초	틀린 문항 복습												

[Day 13] 미니 모의고사   081

DAY 14

수능기출 전국연합학력평가 **20분 미니 모의고사**

● 날짜 :   월   일 ● 시작 시각 :   시   분   초 ● 목표 시간 : 20분

※ 점수 표기가 없는 문항은 모두 **2점**입니다.

01

고2 · 2023년 6월 18번

다음 글의 목적으로 가장 적절한 것은?

Dear parents,

Regular attendance at school is essential in maximizing student potential. Recently, we've become concerned about the number of unapproved absences across all grades. I would like to further clarify that your role as a parent is to approve any school absence. Parents must provide an explanation for absences to the school within 7 days from the first day of any period of absence. Where an explanation has not been received within the 7-day time frame, the school will record the absence as unjustified on the student's record. Please ensure that you go to the parent portal site and register the reason any time your child is absent. Please approve all absences, so that your child will not be at a disadvantage. Many thanks for your cooperation.

Sincerely,
Natalie Brown, Vice Principal

① 자녀의 결석 사유를 등록해 줄 것을 요청하려고
② 학교 홈페이지의 일시적 운영 중단을 공지하려고
③ 자녀가 지각하지 않도록 부모의 지도를 당부하려고
④ 방과 후 프로그램에 대한 부모의 관심을 독려하려고
⑤ 인정 결석은 최대 7일까지 허용된다는 것을 안내하려고

02

고3 · 2020학년도 수능 21번

밑줄 친 playing intellectual air guitar가 다음 글에서 의미하는 바로 가장 적절한 것은? [3점]

Any learning environment that deals with only the database instincts or only the improvisatory instincts ignores one half of our ability. It is bound to fail. It makes me think of jazz guitarists: They're not going to make it if they know a lot about music theory but don't know how to jam in a live concert. Some schools and workplaces emphasize a stable, rote-learned database. They ignore the improvisatory instincts drilled into us for millions of years. Creativity suffers. Others emphasize creative usage of a database, without installing a fund of knowledge in the first place. They ignore our need to obtain a deep understanding of a subject, which includes memorizing and storing a richly structured database. You get people who are great improvisers but don't have depth of knowledge. You may know someone like this where you work. They may look like jazz musicians and have the appearance of jamming, but in the end they know nothing. They're playing intellectual air guitar.

* rote-learned: 기계적으로 암기한

① acquiring necessary experience to enhance their creativity
② exhibiting artistic talent coupled with solid knowledge of music
③ posing as experts by demonstrating their in-depth knowledge
④ performing musical pieces to attract a highly educated audience
⑤ displaying seemingly creative ability not rooted in firm knowledge

03

고2 · 2022년 11월 24번

다음 글의 제목으로 가장 적절한 것은?

The recent "cycling as a lifestyle" craze has expressed itself in an increase in the number of active cyclists and in growth of cycling club membership in several European, American, Australian and Asian urban areas. It has also been accompanied by a symbolic reinterpretation of the bicycle. After the bicycle had been associated with poverty for many years, expensive recreational bicycles or recreationally-inspired commuting bicycles have suddenly become aspirational products in urban environments. In present times, cycling has become an activity which is also performed for its demonstrative value, its role in identity construction and its effectiveness in impressing others and signaling social status. To a certain extent, cycling has turned into a symbolic marker of the well-off. Obviously, value-laden consumption behavior is by no means limited to cycling. However, the link with identity construction and conspicuous consumption has become particularly manifest in the case of cycling.

* conspicuous: 눈에 잘 띄는

① Cycling Contributes to a City's Atmosphere and Identity
② The Rise of Cycling: A New Status Symbol of City Dwellers
③ Cycling Is Wealth-Building but Worsens Social Inequality
④ How to Encourage and Sustain the Bicycle Craze in Urban Areas
⑤ Expanding Bike Lane Networks Can Lead to More Inclusive Cities

04

고2 · 2023년 9월 26번

Camille Flammarion에 관한 다음 글의 내용과 일치하지 <u>않는</u> 것은?

Camille Flammarion was born at Montigny-le-Roi, France. He became interested in astronomy at an early age, and when he was only sixteen he wrote a book on the origin of the world. The manuscript was not published at the time, but it came to the attention of Urbain Le Verrier, the director of the Paris Observatory. He became an assistant to Le Verrier in 1858 and worked as a calculator. At nineteen, he wrote another book called *The Plurality of Inhabited Worlds*, in which he passionately claimed that life exists outside the planet Earth. His most successful work, *Popular Astronomy*, was published in 1880, and eventually sold 130,000 copies. With his own funds, he built an observatory at Juvisy and spent May to November of each year there. In 1887, he founded the French Astronomical Society and served as editor of its monthly publication.

* observatory: 천문대

① 어린 나이에 천문학에 흥미가 생겼다.
② 1858년에 Le Verrier의 조수가 되었다.
③ 19세에 쓴 책에서 외계 생명체의 존재를 부인했다.
④ 자신의 자금으로 Juvisy에 천문대를 세웠다.
⑤ French Astronomical Society를 설립했다.

05 1등급 대비 고난도 2점 문제

다음 글의 밑줄 친 부분 중, 어법상 틀린 것은?

Every farmer knows that the hard part is getting the field ① prepared. Inserting seeds and watching ② them grow is easy. In the case of science and industry, the community prepares the field, yet society tends to give all the credit to the individual who happens to plant a successful seed. Planting a seed does not necessarily require overwhelming intelligence; creating an environment that allows seeds to prosper ③ does. We need to give more credit to the community in science, politics, business, and daily life. Martin Luther King Jr. was a great man. Perhaps his greatest strength was his ability ④ to inspire people to work together to achieve, against all odds, revolutionary changes in society's perception of race and in the fairness of the law. But to really understand ⑤ that he accomplished requires looking beyond the man. Instead of treating him as the manifestation of everything great, we should appreciate his role in allowing America to show that it can be great.

* manifestation: 표명

06

다음 글의 밑줄 친 부분 중, 문맥상 낱말의 쓰임이 적절하지 않은 것은?

The overabundance of options in today's marketplace gives you more freedom of choice. However, there may be a price to pay in terms of happiness. According to research by psychologists David Myers and Robert Lane, all this choice often makes people ① depressed. Researchers gave some shoppers 24 choices of jams to taste and others only 6 choices. Those who had ② fewer choices were happier with the tasting. Even more surprisingly, the ones with a smaller selection purchased jam 31% of the time, while those with a wider range of choices only purchased jam 3% of the time. The ironic thing about this is that people nearly always say they want ③ more choices. Yet, the more options they have, the more ④ relieved they become. Savvy restaurant owners provide fewer choices. This allows customers to feel more relaxed, ⑤ prompting them to choose easily and leave more satisfied with their choices.

* savvy: 사리에 밝은

07 1등급 대비 고난도 2점 문제
고2·2021년 9월 32번

다음 빈칸에 들어갈 말로 가장 적절한 것을 고르시오.

Philosophical activity is based on the _____
_____. The philosopher's thirst for knowledge
is shown through attempts to find better answers to
questions even if those answers are never found. At the
same time, a philosopher also knows that being too sure
can hinder the discovery of other and better possibilities.
In a philosophical dialogue, the participants are aware
that there are things they do not know or understand.
The goal of the dialogue is to arrive at a conception
that one did not know or understand beforehand. In
traditional schools, where philosophy is not present,
students often work with factual questions, they learn
specific content listed in the curriculum, and they are
not required to solve philosophical problems. However,
we know that awareness of what one does not know
can be a good way to acquire knowledge. Knowledge
and understanding are developed through thinking
and talking. Putting things into words makes things
clearer. Therefore, students must not be afraid of saying
something wrong or talking without first being sure that
they are right.

① recognition of ignorance
② emphasis on self-assurance
③ conformity to established values
④ achievements of ancient thinkers
⑤ comprehension of natural phenomena

08 1등급 대비 고난도 3점 문제
고2·2020년 11월 39번

글의 흐름으로 보아, 주어진 문장이 들어가기에 가장 적절한 곳을
고르시오. [3점]

> However, according to Christakis and Fowler, we
> cannot transmit ideas and behaviours much beyond
> our friends' friends' friends (in other words, across
> just three degrees of separation).

In the late twentieth century, researchers sought
to measure how fast and how far news, rumours or
innovations moved. (①) More recent research
has shown that ideas — even emotional states and
conditions — can be transmitted through a social
network. (②) The evidence of this kind of contagion
is clear: 'Students with studious roommates become
more studious. Diners sitting next to heavy eaters eat
more food.' (③) This is because the transmission
and reception of an idea or behaviour requires a
stronger connection than the relaying of a letter or the
communication that a certain employment opportunity
exists. (④) Merely knowing people is not the same as
being able to influence them to study more or over-eat.
(⑤) Imitation is indeed the sincerest form of flattery,
even when it is unconscious.

＊flattery: 아첨

09

다음 글의 내용을 한 문장으로 요약하고자 한다. 빈칸 (A), (B)에 들어갈 말로 가장 적절한 것은?

The great irony of performance psychology is that it teaches each sportsman to believe, as far as he is able, that he will win. No man doubts. No man indulges his inner skepticism. That is the logic of sports psychology. But only one man *can* win. That is the logic of sport. Note the difference between a scientist and an athlete. Doubt is a scientist's stock in trade. Progress is made by focusing on the evidence that refutes a theory and by improving the theory accordingly. Skepticism is the rocket fuel of scientific advance. But doubt, to an athlete, is poison. Progress is made by ignoring the evidence; it is about creating a mindset that is immune to doubt and uncertainty. Just to reiterate: From a rational perspective, this is nothing less than crazy. Why should an athlete convince himself he will win when he knows that there is every possibility he will lose? Because, to win, one must proportion one's belief, not to the evidence, but to whatever the mind can usefully get away with.

* reiterate: 되풀이하다

↓

Unlike scientists whose ___(A)___ attitude is needed to make scientific progress, sports psychology says that to succeed, athletes must ___(B)___ feelings of uncertainty about whether they can win.

	(A)		(B)
①	confident	······	keep
②	skeptical	······	eliminate
③	arrogant	······	express
④	critical	······	keep
⑤	stubborn	······	eliminate

[10 ~ 12] 다음 글을 읽고, 물음에 답하시오.

(A)

It was a hot day in early fall. Wylder was heading to the school field for his first training. He had just joined the team with five other students after a successful tryout. Approaching the field, (a) he saw players getting ready, pulling up their socks and strapping on shin guards. But they weren't together. New players were sitting in the shade by the garage, while the others were standing in the sun by the right pole. Then Coach McGraw came and watched the players.

* shin: 정강이

(B)

'Wow,' thought Wylder. From his new location on the grass, he stretched out his legs. He liked what he was hearing. A new sense of team spirit came across (b) him, a deeper sense of connection. It was encouraging to hear Coach talk about this, to see him face the challenge head-on. Now his speech was over. The players got up and started walking on the field to warm up. "Good job, Coach. That was good," Wylder said to McGraw in a low voice as he walked past him, keeping (c) his eyes down out of respect.

(C)

McGraw continued to point, calling each player out, until he was satisfied with the rearrangement. "Okay, this is how it's going to be," he began. "We need to learn how to trust and work with each other. This is how a team plays. This is how I want you to be on and off the field: together." The players looked at each other. Almost immediately, McGraw noticed a change in their postures and faces. (d) He saw some of them starting to smile.

(D)

Coach McGraw, too, saw the pattern — new kids and others grouping separately. 'This has to change,' he thought. He wanted a winning team. To do that, he needed to build relationships. "I want you guys to come over here in the middle and sit," he called the players as he walked over. "You!" McGraw roared, pointing at Wylder. "Come here onto the field and sit. And Jonny! You sit over there!" He started pointing, making sure they mixed together. Wylder realized what Coach was trying to do, so (e) he hopped onto the field.

11

밑줄 친 (a) ~ (e) 중에서 가리키는 대상이 나머지 넷과 <u>다른</u> 것은?

① (a) ② (b) ③ (c) ④ (d) ⑤ (e)

10

주어진 글 (A)에 이어질 내용을 순서에 맞게 배열한 것으로 가장 적절한 것은?

① (B) − (D) − (C)   ② (C) − (B) − (D)
③ (C) − (D) − (B)   ④ (D) − (B) − (C)
⑤ (D) − (C) − (B)

12

윗글에 관한 내용으로 적절하지 <u>않은</u> 것은?

① Wylder는 다섯 명의 다른 학생과 팀에 합류했다.
② Wylder는 잔디 위의 새로운 자리에서 다리를 쭉 폈다.
③ McGraw는 재배열이 마음에 들 때까지 선수들을 불러 냈다.
④ McGraw는 선수들의 자세와 얼굴의 변화를 알아차렸다.
⑤ McGraw는 선수들에게 운동장 밖으로 나가라고 말했다.

DAY 15

수능기출 전국연합학력평가 **20분 미니 모의고사**

● 날짜 : 월 일 ● 시작 시각 : 시 분 초 ● 목표 시간 : 20분

※ 점수 표기가 없는 문항은 모두 2점입니다.

01

고2·2023년 3월 19번

다음 글에 드러난 Isabel의 심경 변화로 가장 적절한 것은?

On opening day, Isabel arrives at the cafe very early with nervous anticipation. She looks around the cafe, but she can't shake off the feeling that something is missing. As she sets out cups, spoons, and plates, Isabel's doubts grow. She looks around, trying to imagine what else she could do to make the cafe perfect, but nothing comes to mind. Then, in a sudden burst of inspiration, Isabel grabs her paintbrush and transforms the blank walls into landscapes, adding flowers and trees. As she paints, her doubts begin to fade. Looking at her handiwork, which is beautifully done, she is certain that the cafe will be a success. 'Now, success is not exactly guaranteed,' she thinks to herself, 'but I'll definitely get there.'

① calm → surprised
② doubtful → confident
③ envious → delighted
④ grateful → frightened
⑤ indifferent → uneasy

02

고2·2021년 3월 20번

다음 글에서 필자가 주장하는 바로 가장 적절한 것은?

No matter what your situation, whether you are an insider or an outsider, you need to become the voice that challenges yesterday's answers. Think about the characteristics that make outsiders valuable to an organization. They are the people who have the perspective to see problems that the insiders are too close to really notice. They are the ones who have the freedom to point out these problems and criticize them without risking their job or their career. Part of adopting an outsider mentality is forcing yourself to look around your organization with this disassociated, less emotional perspective. If you didn't know your coworkers and feel bonded to them by your shared experiences, what would you think of them? You may not have the job security or confidence to speak your mind to management, but you can make these "outsider" assessments of your organization on your own and use what you determine to advance your career.

① 조직 내의 의사소통이 원활한지 수시로 살피라.
② 외부자의 관점으로 자기 조직을 비판적으로 바라보라.
③ 관심사의 공유를 통해 직장 동료와의 관계를 개선하라.
④ 과거의 성공에 도취되어 자기 계발을 소홀히 하지 말라.
⑤ 동료의 실수를 비판하기보다는 먼저 이해하려고 노력하라.

03

다음 글의 요지로 가장 적절한 것은?

The psychology professor Dr. Kelly Lambert's research explains that keeping what she calls the "effort-driven rewards circuit" well engaged helps you deal with challenges in the environment around you or in your emotional life more effectively and efficiently. Doing hands-on activities that produce results you can see and touch — such as knitting a scarf, cooking from scratch, or tending a garden — fuels the reward circuit so that it functions optimally. She argues that the documented increase in depression among Americans may be directly correlated with the decline of purposeful physical activity. When we work with our hands, it increases the release of the neurochemicals dopamine and serotonin, both responsible for generating positive emotions. She also explains that working with our hands gives us a greater sense of control over our environment and more connection to the world around us. All of which contributes to a reduction in stress and anxiety and builds resilience against the onset of depression.

① 긍정적인 감정은 타인에게 쉽게 전이된다.
② 감정 조절은 대인 관계 능력의 핵심 요소이다.
③ 수작업 활동은 정신 건강에 도움을 줄 수 있다.
④ 과도한 신체활동은 호르몬 분비의 불균형을 초래한다.
⑤ 취미 활동을 통해 여러 분야의 사람들을 만날 수 있다.

04

Goldbeach SeaWorld Sleepovers에 관한 다음 안내문의 내용과 일치하는 것은?

Goldbeach SeaWorld Sleepovers

Do your children love marine animals? A sleepover at Goldbeach SeaWorld will surely be an exciting overnight experience for them. Join us for a magical underwater sleepover.

Participants
- Children ages 8 to 12
- Children must be accompanied by a guardian.

When: Saturdays 5 p.m. to Sundays 10 a.m. in May, 2022

Activities: guided tour, underwater show, and photo session with a mermaid

Participation Fee
- $50 per person (dinner and breakfast included)

Note
- Sleeping bags and other personal items will not be provided.
- All activities take place indoors.
- Taking photos is not allowed from 10 p.m. to 7 a.m.

For more information, you can visit our website at www.goldbeachseaworld.com.

① 7세 이하의 어린이가 참가할 수 있다.
② 평일에 진행된다.
③ 참가비에 아침 식사가 포함된다.
④ 모든 활동은 야외에서 진행된다.
⑤ 사진 촬영은 언제든지 할 수 있다.

05

다음 글의 밑줄 친 부분 중, 어법상 틀린 것은? [3점]

Pre-emption means that a strategy is designed to prevent a rival from starting some particular activity. In some case a pre-emptive move may simply be an announcement of some intent ① that might discourage rivals from doing the same. The idea of pre-emption implies that timing is sometimes very important — a decision or an action at one point in time might be much more rewarding than ② doing it at a different time point. Pre-emption may involve up-weighting advertising for a period before and during ③ when a new entrant launches into a market. The intent is to make it more difficult for the new entrant's advertising to make an impression on potential buyers. Product proliferation is another potential pre-emption strategy. The general idea is to launch a large variety of product variants so that there is very little in the way of market demand that ④ are not accommodated. Arguably, if a market is already filled with product variants it is more difficult for competitors to find ⑤ untapped pockets of market demand.

＊pre-emption: 선매 행위　＊＊proliferation: 확산

06

다음 글의 밑줄 친 부분 중, 문맥상 낱말의 쓰임이 적절하지 않은 것은? [3점]

Over the past several decades, there have been some agreements to reduce the debt of poor nations, but other economic challenges (like trade barriers) ① remain. Nontariff trade measures, such as quotas, subsidies, and restrictions on exports, are increasingly prevalent and may be enacted for policy reasons having nothing to do with trade. However, they have a ② discriminatory effect on exports from countries that lack the resources to comply with requirements of nontariff measures imposed by rich nations. For example, the huge subsidies that ③ poor nations give to their farmers make it very difficult for farmers in the rest of the world to compete with them. Another example would be domestic health or safety regulations, which, though not specifically targeting imports, could ④ impose significant costs on foreign manufacturers seeking to conform to the importer's market. Industries in developing markets may have more ⑤ difficulty absorbing these additional costs.

＊nontariff: 비관세의　＊＊subsidy: 보조금

07

다음 빈칸에 들어갈 말로 가장 적절한 것을 고르시오.

The tendency for one purchase to lead to another one has a name: the Diderot Effect. The Diderot Effect states that obtaining a new possession often creates a spiral of consumption that leads to additional purchases. You can spot this pattern everywhere. You buy a dress and have to get new shoes and earrings to match. You buy a toy for your child and soon find yourself purchasing all of the accessories that go with it. It's a chain reaction of purchases. Many human behaviors follow this cycle. You often decide what to do next based on what you have just finished doing. Going to the bathroom leads to washing and drying your hands, which reminds you that you need to put the dirty towels in the laundry, so you add laundry detergent to the shopping list, and so on. No behavior happens in _____. Each action becomes a cue that triggers the next behavior.

① isolation   ② comfort
③ observation   ④ fairness
⑤ harmony

08 [1등급 대비 고난도 3점 문제]

다음 빈칸에 들어갈 말로 가장 적절한 것을 고르시오. [3점]

Much of human thought is designed to screen out information and to sort the rest into a manageable condition. The inflow of data from our senses could create an overwhelming chaos, especially given the enormous amount of information available in culture and society. Out of all the sensory impressions and possible information, it is vital to find a small amount that is most relevant to our individual needs and to organize that into a usable stock of knowledge. Expectancies accomplish some of this work, helping to screen out information that is irrelevant to what is expected, and focusing our attention on clear contradictions. The processes of learning and memory _____. People notice only a part of the world around them. Then, only a fraction of what they notice gets processed and stored into memory. And only part of what gets committed to memory can be retrieved.

＊ retrieve: 생각해 내다

① tend to favor learners with great social skills
② are marked by a steady elimination of information
③ require an external aid to support our memory capacity
④ are determined by the accuracy of incoming information
⑤ are facilitated by embracing chaotic situations as they are

09

다음 글에서 전체 흐름과 관계 <u>없는</u> 문장은?

Today's "digital natives" have grown up immersed in digital technologies and possess the technical aptitude to utilize the powers of their devices fully. ① But although they know which apps to use or which websites to visit, they do not necessarily understand the workings behind the touch screen. ② People need technological literacy if they are to understand machines' mechanics and uses. ③ In much the same way as factory workers a hundred years ago needed to understand the basic structures of engines, we need to understand the elemental principles behind our devices. ④ The lifespan of devices depends on the quality of software operating them as well as the structure of hardware. ⑤ This empowers us to deploy software and hardware to their fullest utility, maximizing our powers to achieve and create.

* deploy: 사용하다

10

주어진 글 다음에 이어질 글의 순서로 가장 적절한 것을 고르시오.

> The lotus plant (a white water lily) grows in the dirty, muddy bottom of lakes and ponds, yet despite this, its leaves are always clean.

(A) As a result of this investigation, a German company produced a house paint. On the market in Europe and Asia, the product even came with a guarantee that it would stay clean for five years without detergents or sandblasting.

(B) That is because whenever the smallest particle of dust lands on the plant, it immediately waves the leaf, directing the dust particles to one particular spot. Raindrops falling on the leaves are sent to that same place, to thus wash the dirt away.

(C) This property of the lotus led researchers to design a new house paint. Researchers began working on how to develop paints that wash clean in the rain, in much the same way as lotus leaves do.

① (A) − (C) − (B)   ② (B) − (A) − (C)
③ (B) − (C) − (A)   ④ (C) − (A) − (B)
⑤ (C) − (B) − (A)

[11 ～ 12] 다음 글을 읽고, 물음에 답하시오.

Common sense suggests that discussion with others who express different opinions should produce more moderate attitudes for everyone in the group. Surprisingly, this is not always the case. In group polarization, a period of discussion pushes group members to take more extreme positions in the direction that they were already inclined to prefer. Group polarization does not (a) reverse the direction of attitudes, but rather accentuates the attitudes held at the beginning. Two pressures appear to push individuals to take more extreme positions following a group discussion. First, conformity and desire for affiliation contribute to group polarization. If the majority of a group is leaning in a particular direction, what could be a better way of fitting in than (b) agreeing with that majority, and maybe even taking its argument one step farther? There is also a tendency for like-minded people to affiliate with one another, which can provide (c) reinforcement for existing opinions, increase people's confidence in those opinions, lead to the discovery of new reasons for those opinions and counterarguments to opposing views, and reduce exposure to conflicting ideas. Second, exposure to discussion on a topic introduces new reasons for (d) changing an attitude. If you are already opposed to gun control and you listen to additional arguments supporting your position, you might end up more (e) opposed than you were originally.

* accentuate: 강화하다   ** affiliation: 소속

11 1등급 대비 고난도 2점 문제

윗글의 제목으로 가장 적절한 것은?

① Have More Companions and Perform Better!
② Group Competition: Not Necessarily Harmful
③ Exposure to New Ideas Weakens Group Identity
④ Sharing Ideas: The Surest Way to Foster Creativity
⑤ Black Gets Darker, White Gets Brighter in Group Discussion

12 1등급 대비 고난도 3점 문제

밑줄 친 (a) ～ (e) 중에서 문맥상 낱말의 쓰임이 적절하지 <u>않은</u> 것은? [3점]

① (a)   ② (b)   ③ (c)   ④ (d)   ⑤ (e)

학습 Check!   ▶ 몰라서 틀린 문항 × 표기 ▶ 헷갈렸거나 찍은 문항 △ 표기 ▶ ×, △ 문항은 다시 풀고 ✔ 표기를 하세요.

종료 시각	시 분 초	문항 번호	01	02	03	04	05	06	07	08	09	10	11	12
소요 시간	분 초	채점 결과												
초과 시간	분 초	틀린 문항 복습												

DAY 16

● 날짜 :　월　일　● 시작 시각 :　시　분　초　● 목표 시간 : 20분　　　　　※ 점수 표기가 없는 문항은 모두 2점입니다.

01
고2 · 2023년 9월 18번

다음 글의 목적으로 가장 적절한 것은?

To whom it may concern,

I would like to draw your attention to a problem that frequently occurs with the No. 35 buses. There is a bus stop about halfway along Fenny Road, at which the No. 35 buses are supposed to stop. It would appear, however, that some of your drivers are either unaware of this bus stop or for some reason choose to ignore it, driving past even though the buses are not full. I would be grateful if you could remind your drivers that this bus stop exists and that they should be prepared to stop at it. I look forward to seeing an improvement in this service soon.

Yours faithfully,
John Williams

① 버스 운전기사 채용 계획을 문의하려고
② 버스 정류장의 위치 변경을 요청하려고
③ 도로 공사로 인한 소음에 대해 항의하려고
④ 출퇴근 시간의 버스 배차 간격 단축을 제안하려고
⑤ 버스 정류장 무정차 통과에 대한 시정을 요구하려고

02 1등급 대비 고난도 3점 문제
고2 · 2020년 9월 21번

밑줄 친 got "colder"가 다음 글에서 의미하는 바로 가장 적절한 것은? [3점]

If creators knew when they were on their way to fashioning a masterpiece, their work would progress only forward: they would halt their idea-generation efforts as they struck gold. But in fact, they backtrack, returning to versions that they had earlier discarded as inadequate. In Beethoven's most celebrated work, the Fifth Symphony, he scrapped the conclusion of the first movement because it felt too short, only to come back to it later. Had Beethoven been able to distinguish an extraordinary from an ordinary work, he would have accepted his composition immediately as a hit. When Picasso was painting his famous *Guernica* in protest of fascism, he produced 79 different drawings. Many of the images in the painting were based on his early sketches, not the later variations. If Picasso could judge his creations as he produced them, he would get consistently "warmer" and use the later drawings. But in reality, it was just as common that he got "colder."

① moved away from the desired outcome
② lost his reputation due to public criticism
③ became unwilling to follow new art trends
④ appreciated others' artwork with less enthusiasm
⑤ imitated masters' styles rather than creating his own

03

다음 글의 제목으로 가장 적절한 것은?

A building is an inanimate object, but it is not an inarticulate one. Even the simplest house always makes a statement, one expressed in brick and stone, in wood and glass, rather than in words — but no less loud and obvious. When we see a rusting trailer surrounded by weeds and abandoned cars, or a brand-new mini-mansion with a high wall, we instantly get a message. In both of these cases, though in different accents, it is "Stay Out of Here." It is not only houses, of course, that communicate with us. All kinds of buildings — churches, museums, schools, hospitals, restaurants, and offices — speak to us silently. Sometimes the statement is deliberate. A store or restaurant can be designed so that it welcomes mostly low-income or high-income customers. Buildings tell us what to think and how to act, though we may not register their messages consciously.

* inarticulate: 표현을 제대로 하지 못하는

① Buildings Do Talk in Their Own Ways!
② Design of Buildings Starts from Nature
③ Language of Buildings: Too Vague to Grasp
④ Which Is More Important, Safety or Beauty?
⑤ How Do Architects Attach Emotions to Buildings?

04

Niklas Luhmann에 관한 다음 글의 내용과 일치하지 <u>않는</u> 것은?

Niklas Luhmann, a renowned sociologist of the twentieth century, was born in Lüneburg, Germany in 1927. After World War II, he studied law at the University of Freiburg until 1949. Early in his career, he worked for the State of Lower Saxony, where he was in charge of educational reform. In 1960-1961, Luhmann had the chance to study sociology at Harvard University, where he was influenced by Talcott Parsons, one of the most famous social system theorists. Later, Luhmann developed his own social system theory. In 1968, he became a professor of sociology at the University of Bielefeld. He researched a variety of subjects, including mass media and law. Although his books are known to be difficult to translate, they have in fact been widely translated into other languages.

① 제2차 세계 대전 이후에 법을 공부했다.
② State of Lower Saxony에서 교육 개혁을 담당했다.
③ Harvard University에 있을 때 Talcott Parsons의 영향을 받았다.
④ 다양한 주제에 관해 연구했다.
⑤ 그의 책은 번역하기가 쉽다고 알려져 있다.

05 1등급 대비 고난도 3점 문제

다음 글의 밑줄 친 부분 중, 어법상 틀린 것은? [3점]

One of the keys to insects' successful survival in the open air ① lies in their outer covering — a hard waxy layer that helps prevent their tiny bodies from dehydrating. To take oxygen from the air, they use narrow breathing holes in the body-segments, which take in air ② passively and can be opened and closed as needed. Instead of blood ③ containing in vessels, they have free-flowing hemolymph, which helps keep their bodies rigid, aids movement, and assists the transportation of nutrients and waste materials to the appropriate parts of the body. The nervous system is modular — in a sense, each of the body segments has ④ its own individual and autonomous brain — and some other body systems show a similar modularization. These are just a few of the many ways ⑤ in which insect bodies are structured and function completely differently from our own.

* hemolymph: 혈림프
** modular: 모듈식의(여러 개의 개별 단위로 되어 있는)

06

(A), (B), (C)의 각 네모 안에서 문맥에 맞는 낱말로 가장 적절한 것은? [3점]

Our culture is biased toward the fine arts — those creative products that have no function other than pleasure. Craft objects are less worthy; because they serve an everyday function, they're not purely (A) creative / practical . But this division is culturally and historically relative. Most contemporary high art began as some sort of craft. The composition and performance of what we now call "classical music" began as a form of craft music (B) ignoring / satisfying required functions in the Catholic mass, or the specific entertainment needs of royal patrons. For example, chamber music really was designed to be performed in chambers — small intimate rooms in wealthy homes — often as background music. The dances composed by famous composers from Bach to Chopin originally did indeed accompany dancing. But today, with the contexts and functions they were composed for (C) born / gone , we listen to these works as fine art.

* mass: 미사 ** patron: 후원자

	(A)	(B)	(C)
①	creative	satisfying	gone
②	creative	ignoring	gone
③	creative	satisfying	born
④	practical	ignoring	born
⑤	practical	satisfying	gone

07 1등급 대비 고난도 3점 문제

다음 빈칸에 들어갈 말로 가장 적절한 것을 고르시오. [3점]

Children develop the capacity for solitude in the presence of an attentive other. Consider the silences that fall when you take a young boy on a quiet walk in nature. The child comes to feel increasingly aware of what it is to be alone in nature, supported by being "with" someone who is introducing him to this experience. Gradually, the child takes walks alone. Or imagine a mother giving her two-year-old daughter a bath, allowing the girl's reverie with her bath toys as she makes up stories and learns to be alone with her thoughts, all the while knowing her mother is present and available to her. Gradually, the bath, taken alone, is a time when the child is comfortable with her imagination. _____ enables solitude.

＊reverie: 공상

① Hardship   ② Attachment
③ Creativity   ④ Compliment
⑤ Responsibility

08

글의 흐름으로 보아, 주어진 문장이 들어가기에 가장 적절한 곳을 고르시오.

> Rather, we have to create a situation that doesn't actually occur in the real world.

The fundamental nature of the experimental method is manipulation and control. Scientists manipulate a variable of interest, and see if there's a difference. At the same time, they attempt to control for the potential effects of all other variables. The importance of controlled experiments in identifying the underlying causes of events cannot be overstated. (①) In the real-uncontrolled-world, variables are often correlated. (②) For example, people who take vitamin supplements may have different eating and exercise habits than people who don't take vitamins. (③) As a result, if we want to study the health effects of vitamins, we can't merely observe the real world, since any of these factors (the vitamins, diet, or exercise) may affect health. (④) That's just what scientific experiments do. (⑤) They try to separate the naturally occurring relationship in the world by manipulating one specific variable at a time, while holding everything else constant.

09

다음 글의 내용을 한 문장으로 요약하고자 한다. 빈칸 (A), (B)에 들어갈 말로 가장 적절한 것은?

A young child may be puzzled when asked to distinguish between the directions of right and left. But that same child may have no difficulty in determining the directions of up and down or back and front. Scientists propose that this occurs because, although we experience three dimensions, only two had a strong influence on our evolution: the vertical dimension as defined by gravity and, in mobile species, the front/back dimension as defined by the positioning of sensory and feeding mechanisms. These influence our perception of vertical versus horizontal, far versus close, and the search for dangers from above (such as an eagle) or below (such as a snake). However, the left-right axis is not as relevant in nature. A bear is equally dangerous from its left or the right side, but not if it is upside down. In fact, when observing a scene containing plants, animals, and man-made objects such as cars or street signs, we can only tell when left and right have been inverted if we observe those artificial items.

* axis: 축

↓

Having affected the evolution of our ___(A)___ perception, vertical and front/back dimensions are easily perceived, but the left-right axis, which is not ___(B)___ in nature, doesn't come instantly to us.

	(A)		(B)
①	spatial	……	significant
②	spatial	……	scarce
③	auditory	……	different
④	cultural	……	accessible
⑤	cultural	……	desirable

[10 ～ 12] 다음 글을 읽고, 물음에 답하시오.

(A)

Jennifer was on her way home. She decided to stop at a gas station to get coffee. After she paid for her coffee, she got back into her car, but before she started it, she noticed a woman standing outside in front of the building. (a) She could tell that the woman was homeless by her appearance. Her clothes were worn and she was nothing but skin and bones. *She must have not had enough money to get something to eat.* Jennifer thought to herself, feeling pity for her.

(B)

Watching the scene changed Jennifer's life entirely. You see, that day was Mother's Day. It took a homeless woman to show (b) her what selfless giving and love is. From that day on, Jennifer has helped people in trouble, especially mothers struggling to raise children. The homeless woman made Jennifer a better person.

(C)

Jennifer sat in her car, looking at the dog. She noticed that people were walking by without paying attention to the dog. But (c) she still did not do anything. However, someone did. The homeless woman, who Jennifer thought did not have money to buy herself anything to eat, went into the store. And what she did brought tears to Jennifer's eyes. She had gone into the store, bought a can of dog food, and fed that dog. (d) She looked so happy to do it as well.

(D)

Suddenly, a dog walked up to the front of the building. Being a dog lover, Jennifer noticed that the dog was a German Shepherd. She could also tell that the dog was a mother, because anyone could notice that she had been feeding puppies. The dog was terribly in need of something to eat and (e) she felt so bad for her. She knew if the dog didn't eat soon, she and her puppies would not make it.

10

고2 · 2021년 11월 43번

주어진 글 (A)에 이어질 내용을 순서에 맞게 배열한 것으로 가장 적절한 것은?

① (B) – (D) – (C)
② (C) – (B) – (D)
③ (C) – (D) – (B)
④ (D) – (B) – (C)
⑤ (D) – (C) – (B)

12

고2 · 2021년 11월 45번

윗글에 관한 내용으로 적절하지 <u>않은</u> 것은?

① Jennifer는 커피를 사기 위해 주유소에 들렀다.
② 사건이 일어난 날은 어머니날이었다.
③ 지나가던 사람들은 개에게 관심을 보이지 않았다.
④ Jennifer는 가게에 들어가서 개의 먹이를 샀다.
⑤ Jennifer는 개가 어미 개라는 것을 알았다.

11

고2 · 2021년 11월 44번

밑줄 친 (a) ~ (e) 중에서 가리키는 대상이 나머지 넷과 <u>다른</u> 것은?

① (a)　　② (b)　　③ (c)　　④ (d)　　⑤ (e)

학습 Check!

▶ 몰라서 틀린 문항 × 표기　▶ 헷갈렸거나 찍은 문항 △ 표기　▶ ×, △ 문항은 다시 풀고 ✔ 표기를 하세요.

종료 시각	시	분	초	문항 번호	01	02	03	04	05	06	07	08	09	10	11	12
소요 시간		분	초	채점 결과												
초과 시간		분	초	틀린 문항 복습												

DAY 17

수능기출 전국연합학력평가 20분 미니 모의고사

● 날짜 :   월   일 ● 시작 시각 :   시   분   초 ● 목표 시간 : 20분

※ 점수 표기가 없는 문항은 모두 **2점**입니다.

01

고2 · 2023년 6월 20번

다음 글에서 필자가 주장하는 바로 가장 적절한 것은?

The introduction of new technologies clearly has both positive and negative impacts for sustainable development. Good management of technological resources needs to take them fully into account. Technological developments in sectors such as nuclear energy and agriculture provide examples of how not only environmental benefits but also risks to the environment or human health can accompany technological advances. New technologies have profound social impacts as well. Since the industrial revolution, technological advances have changed the nature of skills needed in workplaces, creating certain types of jobs and destroying others, with impacts on employment patterns. New technologies need to be assessed for their full potential impacts, both positive and negative.

① 기술 혁신을 저해하는 과도한 법률적 규제를 완화해야 한다.
② 기술의 도입으로 인한 잠재적인 영향들을 충분히 고려해야 한다.
③ 혁신적 농업 기술을 적용할 때는 환경적인 측면을 검토해야 한다.
④ 기술 진보가 가져온 일자리 위협에 대한 대비책을 마련해야 한다.
⑤ 기술 발전을 위해서는 혁신적 사고와 창의성이 뒷받침되어야 한다.

02

고2 · 2022년 3월 22번

다음 글의 요지로 가장 적절한 것은?

Advice from a friend or family member is the most well-meaning of all, but it's not the best way to match yourself with a new habit. While hot yoga may have changed your friend's life, does that mean it's the right practice for you? We all have friends who *swear* their new habit of getting up at 4:30 a.m. changed their lives and that we have to do it. I don't doubt that getting up super early changes people's lives, sometimes in good ways and sometimes not. But be cautious: You don't know if this habit will actually make your life better, especially if it means you get less sleep. So yes, you can try what worked for your friend, but don't beat yourself up if your friend's answer doesn't change you in the same way. All of these approaches involve guessing and chance. And that's not a good way to strive for change in your life.

① 한번 잘못 들인 습관은 바로잡기가 어렵다.
② 꾸준한 반복을 통해 올바른 습관을 들일 수 있다.
③ 친구나 가족의 조언은 항상 귀담아들을 필요가 있다.
④ 사소하더라도 좋은 습관을 들이면 인생이 바뀔 수 있다.
⑤ 타인에게 유익했던 습관이 자신에게는 효과가 없을 수 있다.

03

다음 글의 주제로 가장 적절한 것은?

In the movie *Groundhog Day*, a weatherman played by Bill Murray is forced to re-live a single day over and over again. Confronted with this seemingly endless loop, he eventually rebels against living through the same day the same way twice. He learns French, becomes a great pianist, befriends his neighbors, helps the poor. Why do we cheer him on? Because we don't want perfect predictability, even if what's on repeat is appealing. Surprise engages us. It allows us to escape autopilot. It keeps us awake to our experience. In fact, the neurotransmitter systems involved in reward are tied to the level of surprise: rewards delivered at regular, predictable times yield a lot less activity in the brain than the same rewards delivered at random unpredictable times. Surprise gratifies.

＊loop: 고리   ＊＊neurotransmitter: 신경전달물질

① considerations in learning foreign languages
② people's inclination towards unpredictability
③ hidden devices to make a movie plot unexpected
④ positive effects of routine on human brain function
⑤ danger of predicting the future based on the present

04

다음 도표의 내용과 일치하지 <u>않는</u> 것은?

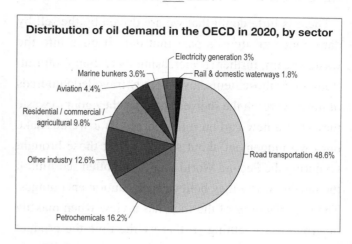

Distribution of oil demand in the OECD in 2020, by sector

Electricity generation 3%
Marine bunkers 3.6%
Rail & domestic waterways 1.8%
Aviation 4.4%
Residential / commercial / agricultural 9.8%
Road transportation 48.6%
Other industry 12.6%
Petrochemicals 16.2%

The above graph shows the distribution of oil demand by sector in the OECD in 2020. ① The Road transportation sector, which took up 48.6%, was the greatest oil demanding sector in the OECD member states. ② The percentage of oil demand in the Petrochemicals sector was one-third that of the Road transportation sector. ③ The difference in oil demand between the Other industry sector and the Petrochemicals sector was smaller than the difference in oil demand between the Aviation sector and the Electricity generation sector. ④ The oil demand in the Residential, commercial and agricultural sector took up 9.8% of all oil demand in the OECD, which was the fourth largest among all the sectors. ⑤ The percentage of oil demand in the Marine bunkers sector was twice that of the oil demand in the Rail & domestic waterways sector.

05

다음 글의 밑줄 친 부분 중, 어법상 틀린 것은?

There is little doubt that we are driven by the sell-by date. Once an item is past that date it goes into the waste stream, further ① increasing its carbon footprint. Remember those items have already travelled hundreds of miles ② reach the shelves and once they go into waste they start a new carbon mile journey. But we all make our own judgement about sell-by dates; those brought up during the Second World War ③ are often scornful of the terrible waste they believe such caution encourages. The manufacturer of the food has a view when making or growing something ④ that by the time the product reaches the shelves it has already been travelling for so many days and possibly many miles. The manufacturer then decides that a product can reasonably be consumed within say 90 days and 90 days minus so many days for travelling gives the sell-by date. But ⑤ whether it becomes toxic is something each individual can decide. It would seem to make sense not to buy large packs of perishable goods but non-perishable items may become cost-effective.

* sell-by date: 판매 유효 기한　** scornful: 경멸하는

06 　1등급 대비 고난도 2쩜 문제

다음 글의 밑줄 친 부분 중, 문맥상 낱말의 쓰임이 적절하지 않은 것은?

It has been suggested that "organic" methods, defined as those in which only natural products can be used as inputs, would be less damaging to the biosphere. Large-scale adoption of "organic" farming methods, however, would ① reduce yields and increase production costs for many major crops. Inorganic nitrogen supplies are ② essential for maintaining moderate to high levels of productivity for many of the non-leguminous crop species, because organic supplies of nitrogenous materials often are either limited or more expensive than inorganic nitrogen fertilizers. In addition, there are ③ benefits to the extensive use of either manure or legumes as "green manure" crops. In many cases, weed control can be very difficult or require much hand labor if chemicals cannot be used, and ④ fewer people are willing to do this work as societies become wealthier. Some methods used in "organic" farming, however, such as the sensible use of crop rotations and specific combinations of cropping and livestock enterprises, can make important ⑤ contributions to the sustainability of rural ecosystems.

* nitrogen fertilizer: 질소 비료　** manure: 거름
*** legume: 콩과(科) 식물

07

다음 빈칸에 들어갈 말로 가장 적절한 것을 고르시오. [3점]

Translating academic language into everyday language can be an essential tool for you as a writer to _____. For, as writing theorists often note, writing is generally not a process in which we start with a fully formed idea in our heads that we then simply transcribe in an unchanged state onto the page. On the contrary, writing is more often a means of discovery in which we use the writing process to figure out what our idea is. This is why writers are often surprised to find that what they end up with on the page is quite different from what they thought it would be when they started. What we are trying to say here is that everyday language is often crucial for this discovery process. Translating your ideas into more common, simpler terms can help you figure out what your ideas really are, as opposed to what you initially imagined they were.

＊transcribe: 옮겨 쓰다

① finish writing quickly
② reduce sentence errors
③ appeal to various readers
④ come up with creative ideas
⑤ clarify your ideas to yourself

08 1등급 대비 고난도 3점 문제

다음 빈칸에 들어갈 말로 가장 적절한 것을 고르시오. [3점]

One vivid example of how _____ _____ is given by Dan Ariely in his book *Predictably Irrational*. He tells the story of a day care center in Israel that decided to fine parents who arrived late to pick up their children, in the hope that this would discourage them from doing so. In fact, the exact opposite happened. Before the imposition of fines, parents felt guilty about arriving late, and guilt was effective in ensuring that only a few did so. Once a fine was introduced, it seems that in the minds of the parents the entire scenario was changed from a social contract to a market one. Essentially, they were paying for the center to look after their children after hours. Some parents thought it worth the price, and the rate of late arrivals increased. Significantly, once the center abandoned the fines and went back to the previous arrangement, late arrivals remained at the high level they had reached during the period of the fines.

① people can put aside their interests for the common good
② changing an existing agreement can cause a sense of guilt
③ imposing a fine can compensate for broken social contracts
④ social bonds can be insufficient to change people's behavior
⑤ a market mindset can transform and undermine an institution

DAY 17

09

다음 글에서 전체 흐름과 관계 없는 문장은?

An interesting phenomenon that arose from social media is the concept of *social proof*. It's easier for a person to accept new values or ideas when they see that others have already done so. ① If the person they see accepting the new idea happens to be a friend, then social proof has even more power by exerting peer pressure as well as relying on the trust that people put in the judgments of their close friends. ② For example, a video about some issue may be controversial on its own but more credible if it got thousands of *likes*. ③ When expressing feelings of liking to friends, you can express them using nonverbal cues such as facial expressions. ④ If a friend recommends the video to you, in many cases, the credibility of the idea it presents will rise in direct proportion to the trust you place in the friend recommending the video. ⑤ This is the power of social media and part of the reason why videos or "posts" can become "viral."

* exert: 발휘하다 ** viral: 바이러스성의, 입소문이 나는

10 1등급 대비 고난도 3점 문제

주어진 글 다음에 이어질 글의 순서로 가장 적절한 것을 고르시오.
[3점]

The online world is an artificial universe — entirely human-made and designed. The design of the underlying system shapes how we appear and what we see of other people.

(A) They determine whether we see each other's faces or instead know each other only by name. They can reveal the size and makeup of an audience, or provide the impression that one is writing intimately to only a few, even if millions are in fact reading.

(B) Architects, however, do not control how the residents of those buildings present themselves or see each other — but the designers of virtual spaces do, and they have far greater influence on the social experience of their users.

(C) It determines the structure of conversations and who has access to what information. Architects of physical cities determine the paths people will take and the sights they will see. They affect people's mood by creating cathedrals that inspire awe and schools that encourage playfulness.

* cathedral: 대성당

① (A) − (C) − (B) ② (B) − (A) − (C)
③ (B) − (C) − (A) ④ (C) − (A) − (B)
⑤ (C) − (B) − (A)

[11 ~ 12] 다음 글을 읽고, 물음에 답하시오.

A neuropsychologist, Michael Gazzaniga conducted a study that shows that our brains (a) excel at creating coherent (but not necessarily true) stories that deceive us. In the study, split-brain patients were shown an image such that it was visible to only their left eye and asked to select a related card with their left hand. Left-eye vision and left-side body movement are controlled by the right hemisphere. In a split-brain patient, the connection between the right and left hemispheres has been broken, meaning no information can cross from one hemisphere to the other. Therefore, in this experiment, the right hemisphere was doing all of the work, and the left hemisphere was (b) aware of what was happening.

Gazzaniga then asked participants why they chose the card that they did. Because language is processed and generated in the left hemisphere, the left hemisphere is required to respond. However, because of the experiment's design, only the right hemisphere knew why the participant selected the card. As a result, Gazzaniga expected the participants to be (c) silent when asked to answer the question. But instead, every subject fabricated a response. The left hemisphere was being asked to provide a (d) rationalization for a behavior done by the right hemisphere. The left hemisphere didn't know the answer. But that didn't keep it from fabricating an answer. That answer, however, had no basis in reality. Now if this study had been limited to split-brain patients, it would be interesting but not very (e) relevant to us. It turns out split-brain patients aren't the only ones who fabricate reasons. We all do it. We all need a coherent story about ourselves, and when information in that story is missing, our brains simply fill in the details.

* coherent: 일관성 있는

11

윗글의 제목으로 가장 적절한 것은?

① Which Side of the Brain Do We Tend to Use More?
② How Our Brain's Hemispheres Interact in Storytelling
③ The Deceptive Brain: Insights from a Split-Brain Patient Study
④ To Be Creative, Activate Both Hemispheres of Your Brain!
⑤ The Dominance of the Left Brain in Image Processing

12

밑줄 친 (a) ~ (e) 중에서 문맥상 낱말의 쓰임이 적절하지 않은 것은? [3점]

① (a) ② (b) ③ (c) ④ (d) ⑤ (e)

학습 Check! ▶ 몰라서 틀린 문항 × 표기 ▶ 헷갈렸거나 찍은 문항 △ 표기 ▶ ×, △ 문항은 다시 풀고 ✔ 표기를 하세요.

종료 시각	시 분 초	문항 번호	01	02	03	04	05	06	07	08	09	10	11	12
소요 시간	분 초	채점 결과												
초과 시간	분 초	틀린 문항 복습												

DAY 18

수능기출 전국연합학력평가 **20분 미니 모의고사**

● 날짜 : 월 일 ● 시작 시각 : 시 분 초 ● 목표 시간 : 20분

※ 점수 표기가 없는 문항은 모두 2점입니다.

01

고2 · 2022년 6월 18번

다음 글의 목적으로 가장 적절한 것은?

Dear Ms. Stevens,

My name is Peter Watson, and I'm the manager of the Springton Library. Our storytelling program has been so well-attended that we are planning to expand the program to 6 days each week. This means that we need to recruit more volunteers to read to the children. People still talk about the week you filled in for us when one of our volunteers couldn't come. You really brought those stories to life! So, would you be willing to read to the preschoolers for an hour, from 10 to 11 a.m. every Friday? I hope you will take this opportunity to let more children hear your voice. We are looking forward to your positive reply.

Best regards,
Peter Watson

---

① 도서관의 운영 시간 연장을 제안하려고
② 봉사 활동 시간이 변경된 것을 안내하려고
③ 독서 토론 수업에 참여할 아동을 모집하려고
④ 봉사 활동에 참여하지 못하게 된 것을 사과하려고
⑤ 책 읽어 주기 자원봉사에 참여해 줄 것을 요청하려고

02

고3 · 2020학년도 수능 23번

다음 글의 주제로 가장 적절한 것은?

Human beings do not enter the world as competent moral agents. Nor does everyone leave the world in that state. But somewhere in between, most people acquire a bit of decency that qualifies them for membership in the community of moral agents. Genes, development, and learning all contribute to the process of becoming a decent human being. The interaction between nature and nurture is, however, highly complex, and developmental biologists are only just beginning to grasp just how complex it is. Without the context provided by cells, organisms, social groups, and culture, DNA is inert. Anyone who says that people are "genetically programmed" to be moral has an oversimplified view of how genes work. Genes and environment interact in ways that make it nonsensical to think that the process of moral development in children, or any other developmental process, can be discussed in terms of nature *versus* nurture. Developmental biologists now know that it is really both, or nature *through* nurture. A complete scientific explanation of moral evolution and development in the human species is a very long way off.

＊decency: 예의 ＊＊inert: 비활성의

① evolution of human morality from a cultural perspective
② difficulties in studying the evolutionary process of genes
③ increasing necessity of educating children as moral agents
④ nature versus nurture controversies in developmental biology
⑤ complicated gene-environment interplay in moral development

03

다음 글의 제목으로 가장 적절한 것은?

New words and expressions emerge continually in response to new situations, ideas and feelings. *The Oxford English Dictionary* publishes supplements of new words and expressions that have entered the language. Some people deplore this kind of thing and see it as a drift from correct English. But it was only in the eighteenth century that any attempt was made to formalize spelling and punctuation of English at all. The language we speak in the twenty-first century would be virtually unintelligible to Shakespeare, and so would his way of speaking to us. Alvin Toffler estimated that Shakespeare would probably only understand about 250,000 of the 450,000 words in general use in the English language now. In other words, so to speak, if Shakespeare were to materialize in London today he would understand, on average, only five out of every nine words in our vocabulary.

* deplore: 한탄하다

① Original Meanings of Words Fade with Time
② Dictionary: A Gradual Continuation of the Past
③ Literature: The Driving Force Behind New Words
④ How Can We Bridge the Ever-Widening Language Gap?
⑤ Language Evolution Makes Even Shakespeare Semi-literate!

04

John Bowlby에 관한 다음 글의 내용과 일치하지 <u>않는</u> 것은?

John Bowlby, British developmental psychologist and psychiatrist, was born in 1907, to an upper-middle-class family. His father, who was a member of the King's medical staff, was often absent. Bowlby was cared for primarily by a nanny and did not spend much time with his mother, as was customary at that time for his class. Bowlby was sent to a boarding school at the age of seven. He later recalled this as being traumatic to his development. This experience, however, proved to have a large impact on Bowlby, whose work focused on children's development. Following his father's suggestion, Bowlby enrolled at Trinity College, Cambridge to study medicine, but by his third year, he changed his focus to psychology. During the 1950s, Bowlby briefly worked as a mental health consultant for the World Health Organization. His attachment theory has been described as the dominant approach to understanding early social development.

① 아버지는 왕의 의료진의 일원이었다.
② 어머니와 많은 시간을 보내지 못했다.
③ 기숙 학교로 보내진 것이 성장에 있어 충격적인 일이었다.
④ Trinity 대학에 심리학을 공부하기 위해 입학했다.
⑤ 세계 보건 기구에서 정신 건강 자문 위원으로 일했다.

05 1등급 대비 고난도 3점 문제

고2 · 2019년 9월 29번

다음 글의 밑줄 친 부분 중, 어법상 틀린 것은? [3점]

Not only are humans ① <u>unique</u> in the sense that they began to use an ever-widening tool set, we are also the only species on this planet that has constructed forms of complexity that use external energy sources. This was a fundamental new development, ② <u>which</u> there were no precedents in big history. This capacity may first have emerged between 1.5 and 0.5 million years ago, when humans began to control fire. From at least 50,000 years ago, some of the energy stored in air and water flows ③ <u>was</u> used for navigation and, much later, also for powering the first machines. Around 10,000 years ago, humans learned to cultivate plants and ④ <u>tame</u> animals and thus control these important matter and energy flows. Very soon, they also learned to use animal muscle power. About 250 years ago, fossil fuels began to be used on a large scale for powering machines of many different kinds, thereby ⑤ <u>creating</u> the virtually unlimited amounts of artificial complexity that we are familiar with today.

06

고2 · 2019년 3월 29번

다음 글의 밑줄 친 부분 중, 문맥상 낱말의 쓰임이 적절하지 <u>않은</u> 것은? [3점]

Painters have in principle an infinite range of colours at their disposal, especially in modern times with the chromatic ① <u>explosion</u> of synthetic chemistry. And yet painters don't use all the colours at once, and indeed many have used a remarkably ② <u>restrictive</u> selection. Mondrian limited himself mostly to the three primaries red, yellow and blue to fill his black-ruled grids, and Kasimir Malevich worked with similar self-imposed restrictions. For Yves Klein, one colour was ③ <u>enough</u>; Franz Kline's art was typically black on white. There was nothing ④ <u>new</u> in this: the Greeks and Romans tended to use just red, yellow, black and white. Why? It's impossible to generalize, but both in antiquity and modernity it seems likely that the ⑤ <u>expanded</u> palette aided clarity and comprehensibility, and helped to focus attention on the components that mattered: shape and form.

* chromatic: 유채색의 ** grid: 격자무늬

07 1등급 대비 고난도 3점 문제

고2·2018년 6월 32번

다음 빈칸에 들어갈 말로 가장 적절한 것을 고르시오. [3점]

"Survivorship bias" is a common logical fallacy. We're prone to listen to the success stories from survivors because the others aren't around to tell the tale. A dramatic example from history is the case of statistician Abraham Wald who, during World War Ⅱ, was hired by the U.S. Air Force to determine how to make their bomber planes safer. The planes that returned tended to have bullet holes along the wings, body, and tail, and commanders wanted to reinforce those areas because they seemed to get hit most often. Wald, however, saw that the important thing was that these bullet holes had not destroyed the planes, and what needed more protection were _____.
Those were the parts where, if a plane was struck by a bullet, it would never be seen again. His calculations based on that logic are still in use today, and they have saved many pilots.

＊fallacy: 오류

① the areas that were not hit
② high technologies to make airplanes
③ military plans for bombing the targets
④ the data that analyzed broken parts
⑤ the commanders of the army

08 1등급 대비 고난도 3점 문제

고2·2020년 6월 39번

글의 흐름으로 보아, 주어진 문장이 들어가기에 가장 적절한 곳을 고르시오. [3점]

> We have a continual desire to communicate our feelings and yet at the same time the need to conceal them for proper social functioning.

For hundreds of thousands of years our hunter-gatherer ancestors could survive only by constantly communicating with one another through nonverbal cues. Developed over so much time, before the invention of language, that is how the human face became so expressive, and gestures so elaborate. (①) With these counterforces battling inside us, we cannot completely control what we communicate. (②) Our real feelings continually leak out in the form of gestures, tones of voice, facial expressions, and posture. (③) We are not trained, however, to pay attention to people's nonverbal cues. (④) By sheer habit, we fixate on the words people say, while also thinking about what we'll say next. (⑤) What this means is that we are using only a small percentage of the potential social skills we all possess.

＊counterforce: 반대 세력 ＊＊sheer: 순전한

09

고2 · 2023년 9월 40번

다음 글의 내용을 한 문장으로 요약하고자 한다. 빈칸 (A), (B)에 들어갈 말로 가장 적절한 것은?

In 2006, researchers conducted a study on the motivations for helping after the September 11th terrorist attacks against the United States. In the study, they found that individuals who gave money, blood, goods, or other forms of assistance because of other-focused motives (giving to reduce another's discomfort) were almost four times more likely to still be giving support one year later than those whose original motivation was to reduce personal distress. This effect likely stems from differences in emotional arousal. The events of September 11th emotionally affected people throughout the United States. Those who gave to reduce their own distress reduced their emotional arousal with their initial gift, discharging that emotional distress. However, those who gave to reduce others' distress did not stop empathizing with victims who continued to struggle long after the attacks.

* distress: (정신적) 고통 ** arousal: 자극

↓

A study found that the act of giving was less likely to be ____(A)____ when driven by self-centered motives rather than by other-focused motives, possibly because of the ____(B)____ in emotional arousal.

	(A)		(B)
①	sustained	……	decline
②	sustained	……	maximization
③	indirect	……	variation
④	discouraged	……	reduction
⑤	discouraged	……	increase

[10 ~ 12] 다음 글을 읽고, 물음에 답하시오.

(A)

There once lived a girl named Melanie. She wanted to be a ballet dancer. One day, Melanie's mother saw her dancing with the flawless steps and enthusiasm of a ballerina. "Isn't it strange? Melanie is dancing so well without any formal training!" her mother said. "I must get (a) her professional lessons to help her polish her skill."

(B)

Disappointed, they returned home, tears rolling down Melanie's cheeks. With her confidence and ego hurt, Melanie never danced again. (b) She completed her studies and became a schoolteacher. One day, the ballet instructor at her school was running late, and Melanie was asked to keep an eye on the class so that they wouldn't roam around the school. Once inside the ballet room, she couldn't control herself. She taught the students some steps and kept on dancing for some time. Unaware of time or the people around her, (c) she was lost in her own little world of dancing.

(C)

Just then, the ballet instructor entered the classroom and was surprised to see Melanie's incredible skill. "What a performance!" the instructor said with a sparkle in her eyes. Melanie was embarrassed to see the instructor in front of her. "Sorry, Ma'am!" she said. "For what?" the instructor asked. "You are a true ballerina!" The instructor invited Melanie to accompany (d) her to a ballet training center, and Melanie has never stopped dancing since. Today, she is a world-renowned ballet dancer.

(D)

The following day, Melanie accompanied her mother to a local dance institute. Upon meeting the dance teacher, Mr. Edler, her mother requested to admit Melanie to his institute. The teacher asked Melanie to audition. (e) She was happy and showed him some of her favorite dance steps. However, he wasn't interested in her dance. He was busy with other tasks in the dance room. "You can leave now! The girl is just average. Don't let her waste her time aspiring to be a dancer," he said. Melanie and her mother were shocked to hear this.

10

고2 · 2021년 9월 43번

주어진 글 (A)에 이어질 내용을 순서에 맞게 배열한 것으로 가장 적절한 것은?

① (B) − (D) − (C)   ② (C) − (B) − (D)
③ (C) − (D) − (B)   ④ (D) − (B) − (C)
⑤ (D) − (C) − (B)

11

고2 · 2021년 9월 44번

밑줄 친 (a)~(e) 중에서 가리키는 대상이 나머지 넷과 다른 것은?

① (a)   ② (b)   ③ (c)   ④ (d)   ⑤ (e)

12

고2 · 2021년 9월 45번

윗글에 관한 내용으로 적절하지 않은 것은?

① 엄마는 Melanie가 발레리나의 열정을 가지고 춤추는 것을 보았다.
② Melanie는 학생들에게 스텝을 가르쳤다.
③ Melanie는 세계적으로 유명한 발레 댄서이다.
④ Melanie는 지역 댄스 학원에 엄마와 동행했다.
⑤ Mr. Edler는 Melanie의 춤에 관심을 보였다.

DAY 18

DAY 19

● 날짜 :　　월　　일　● 시작 시각 :　　시　　분　　초　● 목표 시간 : 20분　　　　　　　　　　※ 점수 표기가 없는 문항은 모두 2점입니다.

01

고2 · 2021년 6월 20번

다음 글에서 필자가 주장하는 바로 가장 적절한 것은?

Sibling rivalry is natural, especially between strong-willed kids. As parents, one of the dangers is comparing children unfavorably with each other, since they are always looking for a competitive advantage. The issue is not how fast a child can run, but who crosses the finish line first. A boy does not care how tall he is; he is vitally interested in who is tallest. Children systematically measure themselves against their peers on everything from skateboarding ability to who has the most friends. They are especially sensitive to any failure that is talked about openly within their own family. Accordingly, parents who want a little peace at home should guard against comparative comments that routinely favor one child over another. To violate this principle is to set up even greater rivalry between them.

＊sibling: 형제, 자매

① 아이를 칭찬할 때는 일관성 있게 하라.
② 자녀를 서로 비교하는 발언을 자제하라.
③ 아이의 발전을 위하여 경쟁을 활용하라.
④ 아이에게 실패를 두려워하지 말라고 가르쳐라.
⑤ 자녀가 구체적인 목표를 설정하도록 조언하라.

02

고2 · 2020년 6월 22번

다음 글의 요지로 가장 적절한 것은?

Personal blind spots are areas that are visible to others but not to you. The developmental challenge of blind spots is that you don't know what you don't know. Like that area in the side mirror of your car where you can't see that truck in the lane next to you, personal blind spots can easily be overlooked because you are completely unaware of their presence. They can be equally dangerous as well. That truck you don't see? It's really there! So are your blind spots. Just because you don't see them, doesn't mean they can't run you over. This is where you need to enlist the help of others. You have to develop a crew of special people, people who are willing to hold up that mirror, who not only know you well enough to see that truck, but who also care enough about you to let you know that it's there.

① 모르는 부분을 인정하고 질문하는 것이 중요하다.
② 폭넓은 인간관계는 성공에 결정적인 영향을 미친다.
③ 자기발전은 실수를 기회로 만드는 능력에서 비롯된다.
④ 주변에 관심을 가지고 타인을 도와주는 것이 바람직하다.
⑤ 자신의 맹점을 인지하도록 도와줄 수 있는 사람이 필요하다.

03

다음 글의 주제로 가장 적절한 것은?

If cooking is as central to human identity, biology, and culture as the biological anthropologist Richard Wrangham suggests, it stands to reason that the decline of cooking in our time would have serious consequences for modern life, and so it has. Are they all bad? Not at all. The outsourcing of much of the work of cooking to corporations has relieved women of what has traditionally been their exclusive responsibility for feeding the family, making it easier for them to work outside the home and have careers. It has headed off many of the domestic conflicts that such a large shift in gender roles and family dynamics was bound to spark. It has relieved other pressures in the household, including longer workdays and overscheduled children, and saved us time that we can now invest in other pursuits. It has also allowed us to diversify our diets substantially, making it possible even for people with no cooking skills and little money to enjoy a whole different cuisine. All that's required is a microwave.

① current trends in commercial cooking equipment
② environmental impacts of shifts in dietary patterns
③ cost-effective ways to cook healthy meals at home
④ reasons behind the decline of the food service industry
⑤ benefits of reduced domestic cooking duties through outsourcing

04

다음 도표의 내용과 일치하지 <u>않는</u> 것은?

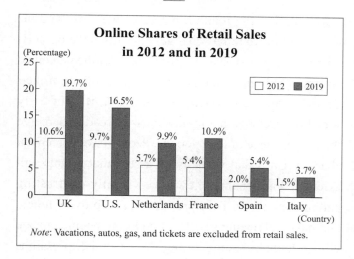

Note: Vacations, autos, gas, and tickets are excluded from retail sales.

The graph above shows the online shares of retail sales for each of six countries in 2012 and in 2019. The online share of retail sales refers to the percentage of retail sales conducted online in a given country. ① For each country, its online share of retail sales in 2019 was larger than that in 2012. ② Among the six countries, the UK owned the largest online share of retail sales with 19.7% in 2019. ③ In 2019, the U.S. had the second largest online share of retail sales with 16.5%. ④ In 2012, the online share of retail sales in the Netherlands was larger than that in France, whereas the reverse was true in 2019. ⑤ In the case of Spain and Italy, the online share of retail sales in each country was less than 5.0% both in 2012 and in 2019.

05

다음 글의 밑줄 친 부분 중, 어법상 틀린 것은? [3점]

By noticing the relation between their own actions and resultant external changes, infants develop self-efficacy, a sense ① that they are agents of the perceived changes. Although infants can notice the effect of their behavior on the physical environment, it is in early social interactions that infants most ② readily perceive the consequence of their actions. People have perceptual characteristics that virtually ③ assure that infants will orient toward them. They have visually contrasting and moving faces. They produce sound, provide touch, and have interesting smells. In addition, people engage with infants by exaggerating their facial expressions and inflecting their voices in ways that infants find ④ fascinated. But most importantly, these antics are responsive to infants' vocalizations, facial expressions, and gestures; people vary the pace and level of their behavior in response to infant actions. Consequentially, early social interactions provide a context ⑤ where infants can easily notice the effect of their behavior.

* inflect: (음성을) 조절하다 ** antics: 익살스러운 행동

06

(A), (B), (C)의 각 네모 안에서 문맥에 맞는 낱말로 가장 적절한 것은?

The ancient Egyptians and Mesopotamians were the Western world's philosophical forebears. In their concept of the world, nature was not an (A) assistant / opponent in life's struggles. Rather, man and nature were in the same boat, companions in the same story. Man thought of the natural world in the same terms as he thought of himself and other men. The natural world had thoughts, desires, and emotions, just like humans. Thus, the realms of man and nature were (B) distinguishable / indistinguishable and did not have to be understood in cognitively different ways. Natural phenomena were imagined in the same terms as human experience. These ancients of the Near East did (C) neglect / recognize the relation of cause and effect, but when speculating about it they came from a "who" rather than a "what" perspective. When the Nile rose, it was because the river wanted to, not because it had rained.

	(A)		(B)		(C)
①	assistant	⋯⋯	distinguishable	⋯⋯	neglect
②	assistant	⋯⋯	indistinguishable	⋯⋯	recognize
③	opponent	⋯⋯	distinguishable	⋯⋯	recognize
④	opponent	⋯⋯	indistinguishable	⋯⋯	neglect
⑤	opponent	⋯⋯	indistinguishable	⋯⋯	recognize

07

다음 빈칸에 들어갈 말로 가장 적절한 것을 고르시오.

_____ works as a general mechanism for the mind, in many ways and across many different areas of life. For example, Brian Wansink, author of *Mindless Eating*, showed that it can also affect our waistlines. We decide how much to eat not simply as a function of how much food we actually consume, but by a comparison to its alternatives. Say we have to choose between three burgers on a menu, at 8, 10, and 12 ounces. We are likely to pick the 10-ounce burger and be perfectly satisfied at the end of the meal. But if our options are instead 10, 12, and 14 ounces, we are likely again to choose the middle one, and again feel equally happy and satisfied with the 12-ounce burger at the end of the meal, even though we ate more, which we did not need in order to get our daily nourishment or in order to feel full.

① Originality
② Relativity
③ Visualization
④ Imitation
⑤ Forgetfulness

08 [1등급 대비 고난도 3점 문제]

다음 빈칸에 들어갈 말로 가장 적절한 것을 고르시오. [3점]

In the modern world, we look for certainty in uncertain places. We search for order in chaos, the right answer in ambiguity, and conviction in complexity. "We spend far more time and effort on trying to control the world," best-selling writer Yuval Noah Harari says, "than on trying to understand it." We look for the easy-to-follow formula. Over time, we _____.
Our approach reminds me of the classic story of the drunk man searching for his keys under a street lamp at night. He knows he lost his keys somewhere on the dark side of the street but looks for them underneath the lamp, because that's where the light is. Our yearning for certainty leads us to pursue seemingly safe solutions — by looking for our keys under street lamps. Instead of taking the risky walk into the dark, we stay within our current state, however inferior it may be.

① weigh the pros and cons of our actions
② develop the patience to bear ambiguity
③ enjoy adventure rather than settle down
④ gain insight from solving complex problems
⑤ lose our ability to interact with the unknown

09

다음 글에서 전체 흐름과 관계 <u>없는</u> 문장은?

Inflationary risk refers to uncertainty regarding the future real value of one's investments. Say, for instance, that you hold $100 in a bank account that has no fees and accrues no interest. If left untouched there will always be $100 in that bank account. ① If you keep that money in the bank for a year, during which inflation is 100 percent, you've still got $100. ② Only now, if you take it out and put it in your wallet, you'll only be able to purchase half the goods you could have bought a year ago. ③ In other words, if inflation increases faster than the amount of interest you are earning, this will decrease the purchasing power of your investments over time. ④ It would be very useful to know in advance what would happen to your firm's total revenue if you increased your product's price. ⑤ That's why we differentiate between nominal value and real value.

* accrue: 생기다 ** nominal: 명목의, 액면(상)의

10 [1등급 대비 고난도 3점 문제]

주어진 글 다음에 이어질 글의 순서로 가장 적절한 것을 고르시오.
[3점]

Like the physiological discoveries of the late nineteenth century, today's biological breakthrough has fundamentally altered our understanding of how the human organism works and will change medical practice fundamentally and thoroughly.

(A) Remember the scientific method, which you probably first learned about back in elementary school? It has a long and difficult process of observation, hypothesis, experiment, testing, modifying, retesting, and retesting again and again and again.

(B) That's how science works, and the breakthrough understanding of the relationship between our genes and chronic disease happened in just that way, building on the work of scientists from decades — even centuries — ago. In fact, it is still happening; the story continues to unfold as the research presses on.

(C) The word "breakthrough," however, seems to imply in many people's minds an amazing, unprecedented revelation that, in an instant, makes everything clear. Science doesn't actually work that way.

① (A) − (C) − (B)　　　② (B) − (A) − (C)
③ (B) − (C) − (A)　　　④ (C) − (A) − (B)
⑤ (C) − (B) − (A)

[11 ~ 12] 다음 글을 읽고, 물음에 답하시오.

Animal studies have dealt with the distances creatures may keep between themselves and members of other species. These distances determine the functioning of the so-called 'flight or fight' mechanism. As an animal senses what it considers to be a predator approaching within its 'flight' distance, it will quite simply run away. The distance at which this happens is amazingly (a) consistent, and Hediger, a Swiss biologist, claimed to have measured it remarkably precisely for some of the species that he studied. Naturally, it varies from species to species, and usually the larger the animal the (b) shorter its flight distance. I have had to use a long focus lens to take photographs of giraffes, which have very large flight distances. By contrast, I have several times nearly stepped on a squirrel in my garden before it drew attention to itself by suddenly escaping! We can only assume that this (c) variation in distance matches the animal's own assessment of its ability to accelerate and run.

The 'fight' distance is always (d) smaller than the flight distance. If a perceived predator approaches within the flight distance but the animal is trapped by obstacles or other predators and cannot (e) flee, it must stand its ground. Eventually, however, attack becomes the best form of defence, and so the trapped animal will turn and fight.

11

고2・2020년 3월 41번

윗글의 제목으로 가장 적절한 것은?

① How Animals Migrate Without Getting Lost
② Flight or Fight Mechanism: Still in Our Brain
③ Why the Size Matters in the Survival of Animals
④ Distances: A Determining Factor for Flight or Attack
⑤ Competition for Food Between Large and Small Animals

12 1등급 대비 고난도 2점 문제

고2・2020년 3월 42번

밑줄 친 (a) ~ (e) 중에서 문맥상 낱말의 쓰임이 적절하지 않은 것은?

① (a)　　② (b)　　③ (c)　　④ (d)　　⑤ (e)

DAY 19

학습 Check!

▶ 몰라서 틀린 문항 × 표기　▶ 헷갈렸거나 찍은 문항 △ 표기　▶ ×, △ 문항은 다시 풀고 ✔ 표기를 하세요.

종료 시각	시	분	초	문항 번호	01	02	03	04	05	06	07	08	09	10	11	12
소요 시간		분	초	채점 결과												
초과 시간		분	초	틀린 문항 복습												

DAY 20

● 날짜 :   월   일 ● 시작 시각 :   시   분   초 ● 목표 시간 : 20분

※ 점수 표기가 없는 문항은 모두 2점입니다.

01

고2 · 2022년 9월 18번

다음 글의 목적으로 가장 적절한 것은?

Dear Customer Service,

I am writing in regard to my magazine subscription. Currently, I have just over a year to go on my subscription to *Economy Tomorrow* and would like to continue my subscription as I have enjoyed the magazine for many years. Unfortunately, due to my bad eyesight, I have trouble reading your magazine. My doctor has told me that I need to look for large print magazines and books. I'd like to know whether there's a large print version of your magazine. Please contact me if this is something you offer. Thank you for your time. I look forward to hearing from you soon.

Sincerely,
Martin Gray

① 잡지 기삿거리를 제보하려고
② 구독 기간 변경을 신청하려고
③ 구독료 인상에 대해 항의하려고
④ 잡지의 큰 글자판이 있는지 문의하려고
⑤ 잡지 기사 내용에 대한 정정을 요구하려고

02 1등급 대비 고난도 2점 문제

고2 · 2019년 11월 21번

밑줄 친 the democratization of business financing이 다음 글에서 의미하는 바로 가장 적절한 것은?

Crowdfunding is a new and more collaborative way to secure funding for projects. It can be used in different ways such as requesting donations for a worthy cause anywhere in the world and generating funding for a project with the contributors then becoming partners in the project. In essence, crowdfunding is the fusion of social networking and venture capitalism. In just the same way as social networks have rewritten the conventional rules about how people communicate and interact with each other, crowdfunding in all its variations has the potential to rewrite the rules on how businesses and other projects get funded in the future. Crowdfunding can be viewed as the democratization of business financing. Instead of restricting capital sourcing and allocation to a relatively small and fixed minority, crowdfunding empowers everyone connected to the Internet to access both the collective wisdom and the pocket money of everyone else who connects to the Internet.

① More people can be involved in funding a business.
② More people will participate in developing new products.
③ Crowdfunding can reinforce the conventional way of financing.
④ Crowdfunding keeps social networking from facilitating funding.
⑤ The Internet helps employees of a company interact with each other.

03

고2 · 2020년 11월 24번

다음 글의 제목으로 가장 적절한 것은?

In government, in law, in culture, and in routine everyday interaction beyond family and immediate neighbours, a widely understood and clearly formulated language is a great aid to mutual confidence. When dealing with property, with contracts, or even just with the routine exchange of goods and services, concepts and descriptions need to be as precise and unambiguous as possible, otherwise misunderstandings will arise. If full communication with a potential counterparty in a deal is not possible, then uncertainty and probably a measure of distrust will remain. As economic life became more complex in the later Middle Ages, the need for fuller and more precise communication was accentuated. A shared language facilitated clarification and possibly settlement of any disputes. In international trade also the use of a precise and well-formulated language aided the process of translation. The Silk Road could only function at all because translators were always available at interchange points.

＊accentuate: 강조하다

① Earn Trust with Reliable Goods Rather Than with Words!
② Linguistic Precision: A Key to Successful Economic Transactions
③ Difficulties in Overcoming Language Barriers and Distrust in Trade
④ The More the Economy Grows, the More Complex the World Gets
⑤ Excessive Confidence: The Biggest Reason for Miscommunication

04

고2 · 2022년 11월 27번

2022 Strawberry Festival에 관한 다음 안내문의 내용과 일치하지 <u>않는</u> 것은?

2022 Strawberry Festival

Join us for a fun family festival. This year, we are back to hosting an in-person event in Berry Square!

□ **Date**: November 26, 2022 (11:00 a.m. − 5:00 p.m.)
□ **Tickets**: $20 per person
             (Children 6 and under are FREE.)

□ **Special Events**
• 11:00 a.m.: Baking Class for Kids
• 1:00 p.m.: Strawberry Pie-Eating Contest
• 3:00 p.m.: Strawberry Costume Contest

□ **Note**
• The parking fee is $5 and includes tram service to the ticket booth.
• If you are interested in volunteering, complete an application form and email it to manager@strawberryfestival.org.

---

① 올해는 대면 행사로 개최된다.
② 6세 이하의 어린이에게는 입장료를 받지 않는다.
③ 딸기파이 먹기 대회가 오후에 열린다.
④ 매표소로 가는 트램 서비스는 주차비에 포함되지 않는다.
⑤ 자원봉사에 관심이 있다면 신청서를 이메일로 보내야 한다.

05 1등급 대비 고난도 3점 문제   고3·2019학년도 수능 29번

다음 글의 밑줄 친 부분 중, 어법상 틀린 것은? [3점]

"Monumental" is a word that comes very close to ① expressing the basic characteristic of Egyptian art. Never before and never since has the quality of monumentality been achieved as fully as it ② did in Egypt. The reason for this is not the external size and massiveness of their works, although the Egyptians admittedly achieved some amazing things in this respect. Many modern structures exceed ③ those of Egypt in terms of purely physical size. But massiveness has nothing to do with monumentality. An Egyptian sculpture no bigger than a person's hand is more monumental than that gigantic pile of stones ④ that constitutes the war memorial in Leipzig, for instance. Monumentality is not a matter of external weight, but of "inner weight." This inner weight is the quality which Egyptian art possesses to such a degree that everything in it seems to be made of primeval stone, like a mountain range, even if it is only a few inches across or ⑤ carved in wood.

* gigantic: 거대한 ** primeval: 원시 시대의

06   고2·2022년 6월 30번

다음 글의 밑줄 친 부분 중, 문맥상 낱말의 쓰임이 적절하지 않은 것은?

The most advanced military jets are fly-by-wire: They are so unstable that they require an automated system that can sense and act more quickly than a human operator to maintain control. Our dependence on smart technology has led to a ① paradox. As technology improves, it becomes more reliable and more efficient, and human operators depend on it even more. Eventually they lose focus, become ② distracted, and check out, leaving the system to run on its own. In the most extreme case, piloting a massive airliner could become a ③ passive occupation, like watching TV. This is fine until something unexpected happens. The unexpected reveals the value of humans; what we bring to the table is the ④ flexibility to handle new situations. Machines aren't collaborating in pursuit of a joint goal; they are merely serving as tools. So when the human operator gives up oversight, the system is ⑤ less likely to have a serious accident.

* fly-by-wire: 전자식 비행 조종 장치

07 1등급 대비 고난도 2점 문제

다음 빈칸에 들어갈 말로 가장 적절한 것을 고르시오.

Would you expect the physical expression of pride to be biologically based or culturally specific? The psychologist Jessica Tracy has found that young children can recognize when a person feels pride. Moreover, she found that isolated populations with minimal Western contact also accurately identify the physical signs. These signs include a smiling face, raised arms, an expanded chest, and a pushed-out torso. Tracy and David Matsumoto examined pride responses among people competing in judo matches in the 2004 Olympic and Paralympic Games. Sighted and blind athletes from 37 nations competed. After victory, the behaviors displayed by sighted and blind athletes were very similar. These findings suggest that pride responses are _____.

① innate
② creative
③ unidentifiable
④ contradictory
⑤ offensive

08

글의 흐름으로 보아, 주어진 문장이 들어가기에 가장 적절한 곳을 고르시오. [3점]

> For others, whose creativity is more focused on methods and technique, creativity may lead to solutions that drastically reduce the work necessary to solve a problem.

Creativity can have an effect on productivity. Creativity leads some individuals to recognize problems that others do not see, but which may be very difficult. (①) Charles Darwin's approach to the speciation problem is a good example of this; he chose a very difficult and tangled problem, speciation, which led him into a long period of data collection and deliberation. (②) This choice of problem did not allow for a quick attack or a simple experiment. (③) In such cases creativity may actually decrease productivity (as measured by publication counts) because effort is focused on difficult problems. (④) We can see an example in the development of the polymerase chain reaction (PCR) which enables us to amplify small pieces of DNA in a short time. (⑤) This type of creativity might reduce the number of steps or substitute steps that are less likely to fail, thus increasing productivity.

* speciation: 종(種) 분화
** polymerase chain reaction: 중합 효소 연쇄 반응

DAY 20

09

다음 글의 내용을 한 문장으로 요약하고자 한다. 빈칸 (A), (B)에 들어갈 말로 가장 적절한 것은?

A primary school teacher is helping students to understand fractional parts by using what she thinks is a commonplace reference. "Today, we're going to talk about cutting up a Thanksgiving holiday favorite — pumpkin pie." She continues with an explanation of parts. Well into her discourse, a young African American boy, looking puzzled, asks, "What is pumpkin pie?" Most African Americans are likely to serve sweet potato pie for holiday dinners. In fact, one of the ways that African American parents explain pumpkin pie to their children is to say that it is something like sweet potato pie. For them, sweet potato pie is the common referent. Even the slight difference of being unfamiliar with pumpkin pie can serve as a source of interference for the student. Rather than be engaged actively in the lesson, he may have been preoccupied with trying to imagine pumpkin pie: What does it taste like? How does it smell? Is its texture chunky like apple or cherry pie? In the mind of a child, all of these questions can become more of the focus than the subject of fractions that the teacher is attempting to teach.

* fraction: 분수

↓

Even small differences in _____(A)_____ knowledge have the potential to affect students' _____(B)_____ .

	(A)		(B)
①	cultural	······	learning
②	cultural	······	responsibility
③	mathematical	······	imagination
④	mathematical	······	intelligence
⑤	nutritional	······	development

[10 ~ 12] 다음 글을 읽고, 물음에 답하시오.

(A)

Victor applied for the position of office cleaner at a very big company. The manager interviewed him, then gave him a test: cleaning, stocking, and supplying designated facility areas. After observing what (a) he was doing, the manager said, "You are hired. Give me your email address, and I'll send you some documents to fill out."

(B)

(b) He then sold the tomatoes in a door to door round. In two hours, he succeeded to double his capital. He repeated the operation three times and returned home with 60 dollars. Victor realized that he could survive by this way, and started to go every day earlier, and returned late. Thus, (c) his money doubled or tripled each day. Shortly later, he bought a cart, then a truck, and then he had his own fleet of delivery vehicles.

(C)

Victor replied, "I don't have a computer, nor an email." "I'm sorry," said the manager. And he added, "If you don't have an email, how do you intend to do this job? This job requires you to have an email address. I can't hire you." Victor left with no hope at all. (d) He didn't know what to do, with only 10 dollars in his pocket. He then decided to go to the supermarket and bought a 10kg box of tomatoes.

(D)

Several years later, Victor's company became the biggest food company in his city. He started to plan his family's future, and decided to get a life insurance. He called an insurance broker. When the conversation was concluded, (e) he asked him his email. Victor replied: "I don't have an email." The broker replied curiously, "You don't have an email, and yet have succeeded to build an empire. Do you imagine what you could have been if you had an email?" He thought for a while, and replied, "An office cleaner!"

10

고2 · 2021년 6월 43번

주어진 글 (A)에 이어질 내용을 순서에 맞게 배열한 것으로 가장 적절한 것은?

① (B) − (D) − (C)   ② (C) − (B) − (D)

③ (C) − (D) − (B)   ④ (D) − (B) − (C)

⑤ (D) − (C) − (B)

12

고2 · 2021년 6월 45번

윗글의 Victor에 관한 내용으로 적절하지 <u>않은</u> 것은?

① 사무실 청소부 자리에 지원하였다.

② 2시간 만에 자본금을 두 배로 만들었다.

③ 슈퍼마켓에 가서 토마토를 샀다.

④ 그의 회사는 도시에서 가장 큰 식품 회사가 되었다.

⑤ 이메일이 있다고 보험 중개인에게 답했다.

11

고2 · 2021년 6월 44번

밑줄 친 (a) ~ (e) 중에서 가리키는 대상이 나머지 넷과 <u>다른</u> 것은?

① (a)   ② (b)   ③ (c)   ④ (d)   ⑤ (e)

DAY 20

학습 Check!   ▶ 몰라서 틀린 문항 × 표기   ▶ 헷갈렸거나 찍은 문항 △ 표기   ▶ ×, △ 문항은 다시 풀고 ✔ 표기를 하세요.

종료 시각	시	분	초	문항 번호	01	02	03	04	05	06	07	08	09	10	11	12
소요 시간		분	초	채점 결과												
초과 시간		분	초	틀린 문항 복습												

DAY 21

● 날짜 : 월 일 ● 시작 시각 : 시 분 초 ● 목표 시간 : 20분

※ 점수 표기가 없는 문항은 모두 2점입니다.

01

고2 · 2020년 11월 20번

다음 글에서 필자가 주장하는 바로 가장 적절한 것은?

When trying to convince someone to change their mind, most people try to lay out a logical argument, or make a passionate plea as to why their view is right and the other person's opinion is wrong. But when you think about it, you'll realize that this doesn't often work. As soon as someone figures out that you are on a mission to change their mind, the metaphorical shutters go down. You'll have better luck if you ask well-chosen, open-ended questions that let someone challenge their own assumptions. We tend to approve of an idea if we thought of it first — or at least, if we *think* we thought of it first. Therefore, encouraging someone to question their own worldview will often yield better results than trying to force them into accepting your opinion as fact. Ask someone well-chosen questions to look at their own views from another angle, and this might trigger fresh insights.

① 타인의 신뢰를 얻기 위해서는 일관된 행동을 보여 주어라.

② 협상을 잘하기 위해 질문에 담긴 상대방의 의도를 파악하라.

③ 논쟁을 잘하려면 자신의 가치관에서 벗어나려는 시도를 하라.

④ 원만한 대인 관계를 유지하려면 상대를 배려하는 태도를 갖춰라.

⑤ 설득하고자 할 때 상대방이 스스로 관점을 돌아보게 하는 질문을 하라.

02

고3 · 2024학년도 수능 22번

다음 글의 요지로 가장 적절한 것은?

Being able to prioritize your responses allows you to connect more deeply with individual customers, be it a one-off interaction around a particularly delightful or upsetting experience, or the development of a longer-term relationship with a significantly influential individual within your customer base. If you've ever posted a favorable comment — or any comment, for that matter — about a brand, product or service, think about what it would feel like if you were personally acknowledged by the brand manager, for example, as a result. In general, people post because they have something to say — and because they want to be recognized for having said it. In particular, when people post positive comments they are expressions of appreciation for the experience that led to the post. While a compliment to the person standing next to you is typically answered with a response like "Thank You," the sad fact is that most brand compliments go unanswered. These are lost opportunities to understand what drove the compliments and create a solid fan based on them.

* compliment: 칭찬

① 고객과의 관계 증진을 위해 고객의 브랜드 칭찬에 응답하는 것은 중요하다.

② 고객의 피드백을 면밀히 분석함으로써 브랜드의 성공 가능성을 높일 수 있다.

③ 신속한 고객 응대를 통해서 고객의 긍정적인 반응을 이끌어 낼 수 있다.

④ 브랜드 매니저에게는 고객의 부정적인 의견을 수용하는 태도가 요구된다.

⑤ 고객의 의견을 경청하는 것은 브랜드의 새로운 이미지 창출에 도움이 된다.

03

고2 · 2022년 9월 23번

다음 글의 주제로 가장 적절한 것은?

We have already seen that learning is much more efficient when done at regular intervals: rather than cramming an entire lesson into one day, we are better off spreading out the learning. The reason is simple: every night, our brain consolidates what it has learned during the day. This is one of the most important neuroscience discoveries of the last thirty years: sleep is not just a period of inactivity or a garbage collection of the waste products that the brain accumulated while we were awake. Quite the contrary: while we sleep, our brain remains active; it runs a specific algorithm that replays the important events it recorded during the previous day and gradually transfers them into a more efficient compartment of our memory.

* consolidate: 통합 정리하다

① how to get an adequate amount of sleep
② the role that sleep plays in the learning process
③ a new method of stimulating engagement in learning
④ an effective way to keep your mind alert and active
⑤ the side effects of certain medications on brain function

04

고2 · 2023년 6월 28번

Out to Lunch에 관한 다음 안내문의 내용과 일치하는 것은?

Out to Lunch

Do you want to enjoy an afternoon with tasty food and great music? 'Out to Lunch' is the perfect event to meet your needs! Come and enjoy this event held in Caras Park in downtown Missoula!

Dates & Times
• Every Wednesday in June, 12 p.m. – 3 p.m.

Highlights
• 10% discount at all food trucks including Diamond Ice Cream
• Live music performance of the new group Cello Brigade
• Face-painting and water balloon fight for kids

Notices
• Bring your own lawn chairs and blankets.
• Dispose of your waste properly.
• Drinking alcoholic beverages is strictly banned.

① 일 년 내내 수요일마다 열리는 행사이다.
② 푸드 트럭에서는 가격을 20% 할인해 준다.
③ 라이브 음악 공연이 마련되어 있다.
④ 개인 의자와 담요를 가지고 올 수 없다.
⑤ 주류를 포함한 음료를 마실 수 있다.

05

다음 글의 밑줄 친 부분 중, 어법상 **틀린** 것은? [3점]

What comes to mind when we think about time? Let us go back to 4,000 B.C. in ancient China where some early clocks were invented. ① To demonstrate the idea of time to temple students, Chinese priests used to dangle a rope from the temple ceiling with knots representing the hours. They would light it with a flame from the bottom so that it burnt evenly, ② indicating the passage of time. Many temples burnt down in those days. The priests were obviously not too happy about that until someone invented a clock ③ was made of water buckets. It worked by punching holes in a large bucket ④ full of water, with markings representing the hours, to allow water to flow out at a constant rate. The temple students would then measure time by how fast the bucket drained. It was much better than burning ropes for sure, but more importantly, it taught the students ⑤ that once time was gone, it could never be recovered.

06 1등급 대비 고난도 2점 문제

(A), (B), (C)의 각 네모 안에서 문맥에 맞는 낱말로 가장 적절한 것은?

A phenomenon in social psychology, the Pratfall Effect states that an individual's perceived attractiveness increases or decreases after he or she makes a mistake — depending on the individual's (A) perceived / hidden competence. As celebrities are generally considered to be competent individuals, and often even presented as flawless or perfect in certain aspects, committing blunders will make one's humanness endearing to others. Basically, those who never make mistakes are perceived as being less attractive and "likable" than those who make occasional mistakes. Perfection, or the attribution of that quality to individuals, (B) creates / narrows a perceived distance that the general public cannot relate to — making those who never make mistakes perceived as being less attractive or likable. However, this can also have the opposite effect — if a perceived average or less than average competent person makes a mistake, he or she will be (C) more / less attractive and likable to others.

＊blunder: 부주의하거나 어리석은 실수

	(A)	(B)	(C)
①	perceived	creates	less
②	perceived	narrows	more
③	perceived	creates	more
④	hidden	creates	less
⑤	hidden	narrows	less

07 1등급 대비 고난도 3점 문제

다음 빈칸에 들어갈 말로 가장 적절한 것을 고르시오. [3점]

Do you advise your kids to keep away from strangers? That's a tall order for adults. After all, you expand your network of friends and create potential business partners by meeting strangers. Throughout this process, however, analyzing people to understand their personalities is not all about potential economic or social benefit. There is your safety to think about, as well as the safety of your loved ones. For that reason, Mary Ellen O'Toole, who is a retired FBI profiler, emphasizes the need to _____ in order to understand them. It is not safe, for instance, to assume that a stranger is a good neighbor, just because they're polite. Seeing them follow a routine of going out every morning well-dressed doesn't mean that's the whole story. In fact, O'Toole says that when you are dealing with a criminal, even your feelings may fail you. That's because criminals have perfected the art of manipulation and deceit.

* tall order: 무리한 요구

① narrow down your network in social media
② go beyond a person's superficial qualities
③ focus on intelligence rather than wealth
④ trust your first impressions of others
⑤ take advantage of criminals

08

다음 빈칸에 들어갈 말로 가장 적절한 것을 고르시오. [3점]

A typical soap opera creates an abstract world, in which a highly complex web of relationships connects fictional characters that exist first only in the minds of the program's creators and are then recreated in the minds of the viewer. If you were to think about how much human psychology, law, and even everyday physics the viewer must know in order to follow and speculate about the plot, you would discover it is considerable — at least as much as the knowledge required to follow and speculate about a piece of modern mathematics, and in most cases, much more. Yet viewers follow soap operas with ease. How are they able to cope with such abstraction? Because, of course, the abstraction _____. The characters in a soap opera and the relationships between them are very much like the real people and relationships we experience every day. The abstraction of a soap opera is only a step removed from the real world. The mental "training" required to follow a soap opera is provided by our everyday lives.

* soap opera: 드라마, 연속극

① is separated from the dramatic contents
② is a reflection of our unrealistic desires
③ demonstrates our poor taste in TV shows
④ is built on an extremely familiar framework
⑤ indicates that unnecessary details are hidden

09

다음 글에서 전체 흐름과 관계 <u>없는</u> 문장은?

Of all the human emotions, none is trickier or more elusive than envy. It is very difficult to actually discern the envy that motivates people's actions. ① The reason for this elusiveness is simple: we almost never directly express the envy we are feeling. ② Envy entails the admission to ourselves that we are inferior to another person in something we value. ③ Not only is it painful to admit this inferiority, but it is even worse for others to see that we are feeling this. ④ Envy can cause illness because people with envy can cast the "evil eye" on someone they envy, even unwittingly, or the envious person can become ill from the emotion. ⑤ And so almost as soon as we experience the initial feelings of envy, we are motivated to disguise it to ourselves — it is not envy we feel but unfairness at the distribution of goods or attention, resentment at this unfairness, even anger.

＊elusive: 이해하기 어려운

10

주어진 글 다음에 이어질 글의 순서로 가장 적절한 것을 고르시오. [3점]

A common but incorrect assumption is that we are creatures of reason when, in fact, we are creatures of both reason and emotion. We cannot get by on reason alone since any reason always eventually leads to a feeling. Should I get a wholegrain cereal or a chocolate cereal?

(A) These deep-seated values, feelings, and emotions we have are rarely a result of reasoning, but can certainly be influenced by reasoning. We have values, feelings, and emotions before we begin to reason and long before we begin to reason effectively.

(B) I can list all the reasons I want, but the reasons have to be based on something. For example, if my goal is to eat healthy, I can choose the wholegrain cereal, but what is my reason for wanting to be healthy?

(C) I can list more and more reasons such as wanting to live longer, spending more quality time with loved ones, etc., but what are the reasons for those reasons? You should be able to see by now that reasons are ultimately based on non-reason such as values, feelings, or emotions.

① (A) − (C) − (B) ② (B) − (A) − (C)
③ (B) − (C) − (A) ④ (C) − (A) − (B)
⑤ (C) − (B) − (A)

[11 ~ 12] 다음 글을 읽고, 물음에 답하시오.

Stories populate our lives. If you are not a fan of stories, you might imagine that the best world is a world without them, where we can only see the facts in front of us. But to do this is to (a) deny how our brains work, how they are *designed* to work. Evolution has given us minds that are alert to stories and suggestion because, through many hundreds of thousands of years of natural selection, minds that can attend to stories have been more (b) successful at passing on their owners' genes.

Think about what happens, for example, when animals face one another in conflict. They rarely plunge into battle right away. No, they first try to (c) signal in all kinds of ways what the *outcome* of the battle is going to be. They puff up their chests, they roar, and they bare their fangs. Animals evolved to attend to stories and signals because these turn out to be an efficient way to navigate the world. If you and I were a pair of lions on the Serengeti, and we were trying to decide the strongest lion, it would be most (d) sensible — for both of us — to plunge straight into a conflict. It is far better for each of us to make a show of strength, to tell *the story* of how our victory is inevitable. If one of those stories is much more (e) convincing than the other, we might be able to agree on the outcome without actually having the fight.

*fang: 송곳니

11

고2 · 2021년 11월 41번

윗글의 제목으로 가장 적절한 것은?

① The Light and Dark Sides of Storytelling
② How to Interpret Various Signals of Animals
③ Why Are We Built to Pay Attention to Stories?
④ Story: A Game Changer for Overturning a Losing Battle
⑤ Evolution: A History of Human's Coexistence with Animals

12 1등급 대비 고난도 2점 문제

고2 · 2021년 11월 42번

밑줄 친 (a) ~ (e) 중에서 문맥상 낱말의 쓰임이 적절하지 않은 것은?

① (a)　　② (b)　　③ (c)　　④ (d)　　⑤ (e)

학습 Check!　　▶ 몰라서 틀린 문항 ✕ 표기　▶ 헷갈렸거나 찍은 문항 △ 표기　▶ ✕, △ 문항은 다시 풀고 ✔ 표기를 하세요.

종료 시각	시	분	초	문항 번호	01	02	03	04	05	06	07	08	09	10	11	12
소요 시간		분	초	채점 결과												
초과 시간		분	초	틀린 문항 복습												

DAY 22

수능기출
전국연합학력평가 **20분 미니 모의고사**

● 날짜 :　　월　　일　 ● 시작 시각 :　　시　　분　　초　 ● 목표 시간 : 20분

※ 점수 표기가 없는 문항은 모두 **2점**입니다.

01

고2·2023년 3월 18번

다음 글의 목적으로 가장 적절한 것은?

It was a pleasure meeting you at your gallery last week. I appreciate your effort to select and exhibit diverse artwork. As I mentioned, I greatly admire Robert D. Parker's paintings, which emphasize the beauty of nature. Over the past few days, I have been researching and learning about Robert D. Parker's online viewing room through your gallery's website. I'm especially interested in purchasing the painting that depicts the horizon, titled *Sunrise*. I would like to know if the piece is still available for purchase. It would be a great pleasure to house this wonderful piece of art. I look forward to your reply to this inquiry.

① 좋아하는 화가와의 만남을 요청하려고
② 미술 작품의 구매 가능 여부를 문의하려고
③ 소장 중인 미술 작품의 감정을 의뢰하려고
④ 미술 작품의 소유자 변경 내역을 확인하려고
⑤ 기획 중인 전시회에 참여하는 화가를 홍보하려고

02

고2·2021년 11월 23번

다음 글의 주제로 가장 적절한 것은?

Shutter speed refers to the speed of a camera shutter. In behavior profiling, it refers to the speed of the eyelid. When we blink, we reveal more than just blink rate. Changes in the speed of the eyelid can indicate important information; shutter speed is a measurement of fear. Think of an animal that has a reputation for being fearful. A Chihuahua might come to mind. In mammals, because of evolution, our eyelids will speed up to minimize the amount of time that we can't see an approaching predator. The greater the degree of fear an animal is experiencing, the more the animal is concerned with an approaching predator. In an attempt to keep the eyes open as much as possible, the eyelids involuntarily speed up. Speed, when it comes to behavior, almost always equals fear. In humans, if we experience fear about something, our eyelids will do the same thing as the Chihuahua; they will close and open more quickly.

* eyelid: 눈꺼풀

① eye contact as a way to frighten others
② fast blinking as a symptom of eye fatigue
③ blink speed as a significant indicator of fear
④ fast eye movement as proof of predatory instinct
⑤ blink rate as a difference between humans and animals

03

고2·2023년 9월 24번

다음 글의 제목으로 가장 적절한 것은?

As you may already know, what and how you buy can be political. To whom do you want to give your money? Which companies and corporations do you value and respect? Be mindful about every purchase by carefully researching the corporations that are taking our money to decide if they deserve our support. Do they have a record of polluting the environment, or do they have fair-trade practices and an end-of-life plan for the products they make? Are they committed to bringing about good in the world? For instance, my family has found a company producing recycled, plastic-packaging-free toilet paper with a social conscience. They contribute 50 percent of their profits to the construction of toilets around the world, and we're genuinely happy to spend our money on this special toilet paper each month. Remember that the corporate world is built on consumers, so as a consumer you have the power to vote with your wallet and encourage companies to embrace healthier and more sustainable practices with every purchase you choose to make.

① Green Businesses: Are They Really Green?

② Fair Trade Does Not Always Appeal to Consumers

③ Buy Consciously, Make Companies Do the Right Things

④ Do Voters Have a Powerful Impact on Economic Policy?

⑤ The Secret to Saving Your Money: Record Your Spending

04

고3·2024학년도 수능 29번

다음 글의 밑줄 친 부분 중, 어법상 틀린 것은?

A number of studies provide substantial evidence of an innate human disposition to respond differentially to social stimuli. From birth, infants will orient preferentially towards the human face and voice, ① seeming to know that such stimuli are particularly meaningful for them. Moreover, they register this connection actively, imitating a variety of facial gestures that are presented to them — tongue protrusions, lip tightenings, mouth openings. They will even try to match gestures ② which they have some difficulty, experimenting with their own faces until they succeed. When they ③ do succeed, they show pleasure by a brightening of their eyes; when they fail, they show distress. In other words, they not only have an innate capacity for matching their own kinaesthetically experienced bodily movements with ④ those of others that are visually perceived; they have an innate drive to do so. That is, they seem to have an innate drive to imitate others whom they judge ⑤ to be 'like me'.

* innate: 타고난   ** disposition: 성향
*** kinaesthetically: 운동감각적으로

05

다음 글의 밑줄 친 부분 중, 문맥상 낱말의 쓰임이 적절하지 <u>않은</u> 것은?

Allowing people to influence each other reduces the ① <u>precision</u> of a group's estimate. To derive the most useful information from multiple sources of evidence, you should always try to make these sources ② <u>independent</u> of each other. This rule is part of good police procedure. When there are multiple witnesses to an event, they are not allowed to ③ <u>discuss</u> it before giving their testimony. The goal is not only to prevent collusion by hostile witnesses, it is also to prevent witnesses from influencing each other. Witnesses who exchange their experiences will tend to make similar errors in their testimony, ④ <u>improving</u> the total value of the information they provide. The standard practice of ⑤ <u>open</u> discussion gives too much weight to the opinions of those who speak early and confidently, causing others to line up behind them.

* testimony: 증언   ** collusion: 공모, 담합

06

다음 빈칸에 들어갈 말로 가장 적절한 것을 고르시오. [3점]

There are countless examples of scientific inventions that have been generated by accident. However, often this accident has required a person with above-average knowledge in the field to interpret it. One of the better-known examples of the cooperation between _____ _____ is the invention of penicillin. In 1928, Scottish biologist Alexander Fleming went on a vacation. As a slightly careless man, Fleming left some bacterial cultures on his desk. When he returned, he noticed mold in one of his cultures, with a bacteria-free zone around it. The mold was from the *penicillium notatum* species, which had killed the bacteria on the Petri dish. This was a lucky coincidence. For a person who does not have expert knowledge, the bacteria-free zone would not have had much significance, but Fleming understood the magical effect of the mold. The result was penicillin — a medication that has saved countless people on the planet.

* culture: (세균 등의) 배양균
** mold: 곰팡이

① trial and error
② idea and a critic
③ risk and stability
④ chance and a researcher
⑤ a professional and an amateur

07 1등급 대비 고난도 3점 문제

다음 빈칸에 들어갈 말로 가장 적절한 것을 고르시오. [3점]

The whole history of mathematics is one long sequence of taking the best ideas of the moment and finding new extensions, variations, and applications. Our lives today are totally different from the lives of people three hundred years ago, mostly owing to scientific and technological innovations that required the insights of calculus. Isaac Newton and Gottfried von Leibniz independently discovered calculus in the last half of the seventeenth century. But a study of the history reveals that mathematicians had thought of all the essential elements of calculus before Newton or Leibniz came along. Newton himself acknowledged this flowing reality when he wrote, "If I have seen farther than others it is because I have stood on the shoulders of giants." Newton and Leibniz came up with their brilliant insight at essentially the same time because _____. All creative people, even ones who are considered geniuses, start as nongeniuses and take baby steps from there.

* calculus: 미적분학

① calculus was considered to be the study of geniuses

② it was not a huge leap from what was already known

③ it was impossible to make a list of the uses of calculus

④ they pioneered a breakthrough in mathematic calculations

⑤ other mathematicians didn't accept the discovery as it was

08 1등급 대비 고난도 3점 문제

글의 흐름으로 보아, 주어진 문장이 들어가기에 가장 적절한 곳을 고르시오. [3점]

> In terms of the overall value of an automobile, you can't drive without tires, but you can drive without cup holders and a portable technology dock.

Some resources, decisions, or activities are *important* (highly valuable on average) while others are *pivotal* (small changes make a big difference). Consider how two components of a car relate to a consumer's purchase decision: tires and interior design. Which adds more value on average? The tires. (①) They are essential to the car's ability to move, and they impact both safety and performance. (②) Yet tires generally do not influence purchase decisions because safety standards guarantee that all tires will be very safe and reliable. (③) Differences in interior features — optimal sound system, portable technology docks, number and location of cup holders — likely have far more effect on the consumer's buying decision. (④) Interior features, however, clearly have a greater impact on the purchase decision. (⑤) In our language, the tires are important, but the interior design is pivotal.

09 1등급 대비 고난도 2점 문제 〔고2·2020년 3월 40번〕

다음 글의 내용을 한 문장으로 요약하고자 한다. 빈칸 (A), (B)에 들어갈 말로 가장 적절한 것은?

Some natural resource-rich developing countries tend to create an excessive dependence on their natural resources, which generates a lower productive diversification and a lower rate of growth. Resource abundance in itself need not do any harm: many countries have abundant natural resources and have managed to outgrow their dependence on them by diversifying their economic activity. That is the case of Canada, Australia, or the US, to name the most important ones. But some developing countries are trapped in their dependence on their large natural resources. They suffer from a series of problems since a heavy dependence on natural capital tends to exclude other types of capital and thereby interfere with economic growth.

↓

Relying on rich natural resources without _____(A)_____ economic activities can be a _____(B)_____ to economic growth.

	(A)		(B)
①	varying	……	barrier
②	varying	……	shortcut
③	limiting	……	challenge
④	limiting	……	barrier
⑤	connecting	……	shortcut

[10 ~ 12] 다음 글을 읽고, 물음에 답하시오.

(A)

Once upon a time there lived a poor but cheerful shoemaker. He was so happy, he sang all day long. The children loved to stand around his window to listen to (a) him. Next door to the shoemaker lived a rich man. He used to sit up all night to count his gold. In the morning, he went to bed, but he could not sleep because of the sound of the shoemaker's singing.

(B)

He could not sleep, or work, or sing — and, worst of all, the children no longer came to see (b) him. At last, the shoemaker felt so unhappy that he seized his bag of gold and ran next door to the rich man. "Please take back your gold," he said. "The worry of it is making me ill, and I have lost all of my friends. I would rather be a poor shoemaker, as I was before." And so the shoemaker was happy again and sang all day at his work.

(C)

There was so much there that the shoemaker was afraid to let it out of his sight. So he took it to bed with him. But he could not sleep for worrying about it. Very early in the morning, he got up and brought his gold down from the bedroom. He had decided to hide it up the chimney instead. But he was still uneasy, and in a little while he dug a hole in the garden and buried his bag of gold in it. It was no use trying to work. (c) He was too worried about the safety of his gold. And as for singing, he was too miserable to utter a note.

(D)

One day, (d) <u>he</u> thought of a way of stopping the singing. He wrote a letter to the shoemaker asking him to visit. The shoemaker came at once, and to his surprise the rich man gave him a bag of gold. When he got home again, the shoemaker opened the bag. (e) <u>He</u> had never seen so much gold before! When he sat down at his bench and began, carefully, to count it, the children watched through the window.

10

주어진 글 (A)에 이어질 내용을 순서에 맞게 배열한 것으로 가장 적절한 것은?

① (B) − (D) − (C)   ② (C) − (B) − (D)
③ (C) − (D) − (B)   ④ (D) − (B) − (C)
⑤ (D) − (C) − (B)

11

다음 밑줄 친 (a)~(e) 중에서 가리키는 대상이 나머지 넷과 <u>다른</u> 것은?

① (a)   ② (b)   ③ (c)   ④ (d)   ⑤ (e)

12

윗글의 shoemaker에 관한 내용으로 적절하지 <u>않은</u> 것은?

① 그의 노래로 인해 옆집 사람이 잠을 잘 수 없었다.
② 예전처럼 가난하게 살고 싶지 않다고 말했다.
③ 정원에 구멍을 파고 금화가 든 가방을 묻었다.
④ 부자가 보낸 편지에 즉시 그를 만나러 갔다.
⑤ 금화를 셀 때 아이들이 그 모습을 봤다.

DAY 23 수능기출 전국연합학력평가 **20분 미니 모의고사**

● 날짜 :   월   일 ● 시작 시각 :   시   분   초 ● 목표 시간 : 20분   ※ 점수 표기가 없는 문항은 모두 **2점**입니다.

01
고2 · 2022년 9월 19번

다음 글에 나타난 'I'의 심경 변화로 가장 적절한 것은?

There was no choice next morning but to turn in my private reminiscence of Belleville. Two days passed before Mr. Fleagle returned the graded papers, and he returned everyone's but mine. I was anxiously expecting for a command to report to Mr. Fleagle immediately after school for discipline when I saw him lift my paper from his desk and rap for the class's attention. "Now, boys," he said, "I want to read you an essay. This is titled 'The Art of Eating Spaghetti.'" And he started to read. My words! He was reading *my words* out loud to the entire class. What's more, the entire class was listening attentively. Then somebody laughed, then the entire class was laughing, and not in contempt and ridicule, but with openhearted enjoyment. I did my best to avoid showing pleasure, but what I was feeling was pure ecstasy at this startling demonstration that my words had the power to make people laugh.

* reminiscence: 회상

① relieved → scared
② nervous → delighted
③ bored → confident
④ satisfied → depressed
⑤ confused → ashamed

02
고2 · 2021년 11월 20번

다음 글에서 필자가 주장하는 바로 가장 적절한 것은?

In 2003, British Airways made an announcement that they would no longer be able to operate the London to New York Concorde flight twice a day because it was starting to prove uneconomical. Well, the sales for the flight on this route increased the very next day. There was nothing that changed about the route or the service offered by the airlines. Merely because it became a scarce resource, the demand for it increased. If you are interested in persuading people, then the principle of scarcity can be effectively used. If you are a salesperson trying to increase the sales of a certain product, then you must not merely point out the benefits the customer can derive from the said product, but also point out its uniqueness and what they will miss out on if they don't purchase the product soon. In selling, you should keep in mind that the more limited something is, the more desirable it becomes.

① 상품 판매 시 실현 가능한 판매 목표를 설정해야 한다.
② 판매를 촉진하기 위해서는 가격 경쟁력을 갖추어야 한다.
③ 효과적인 판매를 위해서는 상품의 희소성을 강조해야 한다.
④ 고객의 신뢰를 얻기 위해서는 일관된 태도를 유지해야 한다.
⑤ 고객의 특성에 맞춰 다양한 판매 전략을 수립하고 적용해야 한다.

03

다음 글의 요지로 가장 적절한 것은?

When it comes to the decision to get more exercise, you are setting goals that are similar to running a half marathon with very little training! You make a decision to buy a gym membership and decide to spend an hour at the gym every day. Well, you might stick to that for a day or two, but chances are you won't be able to continue to meet that commitment in the long term. If, however, you make a commitment to go jogging for a few minutes a day or add a few sit-ups to your daily routine before bed, then you are far more likely to stick to your decision and to create a habit that offers you long-term results. The key is to start small. Small habits lead to long-term success.

① 상황에 따른 유연한 태도가 목표 달성에 효과적이다.
② 올바른 식습관과 규칙적인 운동이 건강 유지에 도움이 된다.
③ 나쁜 습관을 고치기 위해서는 장기적인 계획이 필수적이다.
④ 꿈을 이루기 위해서는 원대한 목표를 세우는 것이 중요하다.
⑤ 장기적인 성공을 위해 작은 습관부터 시작하는 것이 필요하다.

04

다음 도표의 내용과 일치하지 <u>않는</u> 것은?

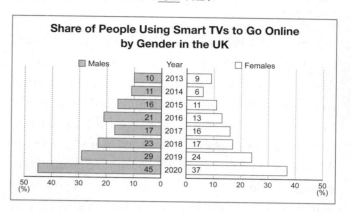

The graph above shows the findings of a survey on the use of smart TVs to go online in the UK from 2013 to 2020, by gender. ① In each year from 2013 to 2020, the percentage of male respondents who used smart TVs to access the Internet was higher than that of female respondents. ② The percentage gap between the two genders was the largest in 2016 and in 2020, which both had an 8 percentage point difference. ③ In 2020, the percentage of respondents who reported using smart TVs to go online was higher than 30% for both males and females. ④ For male respondents, 2017 was the only year that saw a decrease in the percentage of those accessing the Internet via smart TVs compared to the previous year, during the given period. ⑤ In 2014, the percentage of females using smart TVs to access the Internet was the lowest during the given period at 6%, and it was still below 10% in 2015.

DAY 23

05

(A), (B), (C)의 각 네모 안에서 어법에 맞는 표현으로 가장 적절한 것은? [3점]

Getting in the habit of asking questions (A) transform / transforms you into an active listener. This practice forces you to have a different inner life experience, since you will, in fact, be listening more effectively. You know that sometimes when you are supposed to be listening to someone, your mind starts to wander. All teachers know that this happens frequently with students in classes. It's what goes on inside your head that makes all the difference in how well you will convert (B) what / that you hear into something you learn. Listening is not enough. If you are constantly engaged in asking yourself questions about things you are hearing, you will find that even boring lecturers become a bit more (C) interesting / interested , because much of the interest will be coming from what you are generating rather than what the lecturer is offering. When someone else speaks, you need to be thought provoking!

* thought provoking: 생각을 불러일으키는

	(A)	(B)	(C)
①	transform	what	interesting
②	transform	that	interested
③	transforms	what	interesting
④	transforms	that	interesting
⑤	transforms	what	interested

06

다음 글의 밑줄 친 부분 중, 문맥상 낱말의 쓰임이 적절하지 <u>않은</u> 것은? [3점]

Everywhere we turn we hear about almighty "cyberspace"! The hype promises that we will leave our boring lives, put on goggles and body suits, and enter some metallic, three-dimensional, multimedia otherworld. When the Industrial Revolution arrived with its great innovation, the motor, we didn't leave our world to go to some ① <u>remote</u> motorspace! On the contrary, we brought the motors into our lives, as automobiles, refrigerators, drill presses, and pencil sharpeners. This ② <u>absorption</u> has been so complete that we refer to all these tools with names that declare their usage, not their "motorness." These innovations led to a major socioeconomic movement precisely because they entered and ③ <u>affected</u> profoundly our everyday lives. People have not changed fundamentally in thousands of years. Technology changes constantly. It's the one that must ④ <u>adapt</u> to us. That's exactly what will happen with information technology and its devices under human-centric computing. The longer we continue to believe that computers will take us to a magical new world, the longer we will ⑤ <u>maintain</u> their natural fusion with our lives, the hallmark of every major movement that aspires to be called a socioeconomic revolution.

* hype: 과대광고   ** hallmark: 특징

07 1등급 대비 고난도 3점 문제

고2 • 2017년 6월 32번

다음 빈칸에 들어갈 말로 가장 적절한 것을 고르시오. [3점]

Honeybees have evolved what we call "swarm intelligence," with up to 50,000 workers in a single colony coming together to make democratic decisions. When a hive gets too crowded in springtime, colonies send scouts to look for a new home. If any scouts disagree on where the colony should build its next hive, they argue their case the civilized way: through a dance-off. Each scout performs a "waggle dance" for other scouts in an attempt to convince them of their spot's merit. The more enthusiastic the dance is, the happier the scout is with his spot. The remainder of the colony _____, flying to the spot they prefer and joining in the dance until one potential hive overcomes all other dances of the neighborhood. It would be great if Congress settled their disagreements the same way.

＊colony: (개미, 벌 등의) 집단, 군집

① votes with their bodies
② invades other bees' hives
③ searches for more flowers
④ shows more concern for mates
⑤ improves their communication skills

08

고2 • 2020년 11월 32번

다음 빈칸에 들어갈 말로 가장 적절한 것을 고르시오.

One of the primary ways by which music is able to take on significance in our inner world is by the way it interacts with memory. Memories associated with important emotions tend to be more deeply embedded in our memory than other events. Emotional memories are more likely to be vividly remembered and are more likely to be recalled with the passing of time than neutral memories. Since music can be extremely emotionally evocative, key life events can be emotionally heightened by the presence of music, ensuring that memories of the event become deeply encoded. Retrieval of those memories is then enhanced by contextual effects, in which a recreation of a similar context to that in which the memories were encoded can facilitate their retrieval. Thus, _____ can activate intensely vivid memories of the event.

＊evocative: 불러일으키는 ＊＊retrieval: 회복

① analyzing memories of the event thoroughly
② increasing storage space for recalling the event
③ re-hearing the same music associated with the event
④ reconstructing the event in the absence of background music
⑤ enhancing musical competence to deliver emotional messages

09

다음 글에서 전체 흐름과 관계 없는 문장은?

Academics, politicians, marketers and others have in the past debated whether or not it is ethically correct to market products and services directly to young consumers. ① This is also a dilemma for psychologists who have questioned whether they ought to help advertisers manipulate children into purchasing more products they have seen advertised. ② Advertisers have admitted to taking advantage of the fact that it is easy to make children feel that they are losers if they do not own the 'right' products. ③ When products become more popular, more competitors enter the marketplace and marketers lower their marketing costs to remain competitive. ④ Clever advertising informs children that they will be viewed by their peers in an unfavorable way if they do not have the products that are advertised, thereby playing on their emotional vulnerabilities. ⑤ The constant feelings of inadequateness created by advertising have been suggested to contribute to children becoming fixated with instant gratification and beliefs that material possessions are important.

* fixated: 집착하는   ** gratification: 만족(감)

10

주어진 글 다음에 이어질 글의 순서로 가장 적절한 것을 고르시오.

When evaluating a policy, people tend to concentrate on how the policy will fix some particular problem while ignoring or downplaying other effects it may have. Economists often refer to this situation as *The Law of Unintended Consequences.*

(A) But an unintended consequence is that the jobs of some autoworkers will be lost to foreign competition. Why? The tariff that protects steelworkers raises the price of the steel that domestic automobile makers need to build their cars.

(B) For instance, suppose that you impose a tariff on imported steel in order to protect the jobs of domestic steelworkers. If you impose a high enough tariff, their jobs will indeed be protected from competition by foreign steel companies.

(C) As a result, domestic automobile manufacturers have to raise the prices of their cars, making them relatively less attractive than foreign cars. Raising prices tends to reduce domestic car sales, so some domestic autoworkers lose their jobs.

① (A) − (C) − (B)   ② (B) − (A) − (C)
③ (B) − (C) − (A)   ④ (C) − (A) − (B)
⑤ (C) − (B) − (A)

[11 ~ 12] 다음 글을 읽고, 물음에 답하시오.

Creative people aren't all cut from the same cloth. They have (a) varying levels of maturity and sensitivity. They have different approaches to work. And they're each motivated by different things. Managing people is about being aware of their unique personalities. It's also about empathy and adaptability, and knowing how the things you do and say will be interpreted and adapting accordingly. Who you are and what you say may not be the (b) same from one person to the next. For instance, if you're asking someone to work a second weekend in a row, or telling them they aren't getting that deserved promotion just yet, you need to bear in mind the (c) group. Vincent will have a very different reaction to the news than Emily, and they will each be more receptive to the news if it's bundled with different things. Perhaps that promotion news will land (d) easier if Vincent is given a few extra vacation days for the holidays, while you can promise Emily a bigger promotion a year from now. Consider each person's complex positive and negative personality traits, their life circumstances, and their mindset in the moment when deciding what to say and how to say it. Personal connection, compassion, and an individualized management style are (e) key to drawing consistent, rock star-level work out of everyone.

11 1등급 대비 고난도 2점 문제
고2·2023년 3월 41번

윗글의 제목으로 가장 적절한 것은?

① Know Each Person to Guarantee Best Performance
② Flexible Hours: An Appealing Working Condition
③ Talk to Employees More Often in Hard Times
④ How Empathy and Recognition Are Different
⑤ Why Creativity Suffers in Competition

12 1등급 대비 고난도 2점 문제
고2·2023년 3월 42번

밑줄 친 (a) ~ (e) 중에서 문맥상 낱말의 쓰임이 적절하지 않은 것은?

① (a)　　② (b)　　③ (c)　　④ (d)　　⑤ (e)

학습 Check!　　▶ 몰라서 틀린 문항 × 표기　▶ 헷갈렸거나 찍은 문항 △ 표기　▶ ×, △ 문항은 다시 풀고 ✔ 표기를 하세요.

종료 시각	시 분 초	문항 번호	01	02	03	04	05	06	07	08	09	10	11	12
소요 시간	분 초	채점 결과												
초과 시간	분 초	틀린 문항 복습												

[Day 23] 미니 모의고사　141

DAY 24

수능기출
전국연합학력평가 **20분 미니 모의고사**

● 날짜 :   월   일 ● 시작 시각 :   시   분   초 ● 목표 시간 : 20분

※ 점수 표기가 없는 문항은 모두 **2점**입니다.

01

고2 · 2023년 9월 20번

다음 글에서 필자가 주장하는 바로 가장 적절한 것은?

Managers frequently try to play psychologist, to "figure out" why an employee has acted in a certain way. Empathizing with employees in order to understand their point of view can be very helpful. However, when dealing with a problem area, in particular, remember that it is not the person who is bad, but the actions exhibited on the job. Avoid making suggestions to employees about personal traits they should change; instead suggest more acceptable ways of performing. For example, instead of focusing on a person's "unreliability," a manager might focus on the fact that the employee "has been late to work seven times this month." It is difficult for employees to change who they are; it is usually much easier for them to change how they act.

① 직원의 개인적 성향을 고려하여 업무를 배정하라.
② 업무 효율성 향상을 위해 직원의 자율성을 존중하라.
③ 조직의 안정을 위해 직원의 심리 상태를 수시로 확인하라.
④ 직원의 업무상 고충을 이해하기 위해 직원과 적극적으로 소통하라.
⑤ 문제를 보이는 직원에게 인격적 특성보다는 행동 방식에 대해 제안하라.

02 1등급 대비 고난도 2점 문제

고2 · 2022년 3월 23번

다음 글의 주제로 가장 적절한 것은?

Individual human beings differ from one another physically in a multitude of visible and invisible ways. If races — as most people define them — are real biological entities, then people of African ancestry would share a wide variety of traits while people of European ancestry would share a wide variety of *different* traits. But once we add traits that are less visible than skin coloration, hair texture, and the like, we find that the people we identify as "the same race" are less and less like one another and more and more like people we identify as "different races." Add to this point that the physical features used to identify a person as a representative of some race (e.g. skin coloration) are continuously variable, so that one cannot say where "brown skin" becomes "white skin." Although the physical differences themselves are real, the way we use physical differences to classify people into discrete races is a cultural construction.

＊entity: 실체 ＊＊discrete: 별개의

① causes of physical variations among different races
② cultural differences between various races
③ social policies to overcome racism
④ importance of environmental factors in evolution
⑤ misconception about race as a biological construct

03

다음 도표의 내용과 일치하지 <u>않는</u> 것은?

Second-Dose Measles Vaccinations among Children
by Region in 2000 and in 2020

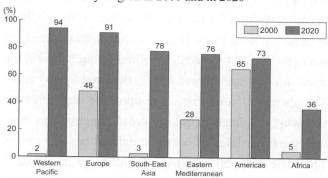

＊measles: 홍역

The graph above shows the percentage of children who received second-dose measles vaccinations in six regions in 2000 and in 2020. ① The percentage of vaccinated children in the Western Pacific was lower than that of Europe in 2000, but the vaccination percentage in 2020 of the Western Pacific exceeded that of Europe by 3 percentage points. ② Among all regions, South-East Asia achieved the second biggest increase in its percentage of vaccinated children over the two decades, and it ranked third in the percentage of vaccinated children among the six regions in 2020. ③ In the Eastern Mediterranean, the percentage of vaccinated children more than doubled from 2000 to 2020, but did not exceed that of the Americas in either year. ④ The percentage of vaccinated children in the Americas was the highest among the six regions in 2000, but it increased the least of all regions over the two decades. ⑤ In Africa, the percentage of children who received the vaccine in 2020 was more than seven times higher than in 2000, but was still the lowest among the six regions in 2020.

04

2022 Korean Speech Contest에 관한 다음 안내문의 내용과 일치하지 <u>않는</u> 것은?

2022 Korean Speech Contest

Are you a foreign student who wants to show off your Korean? Make your own video sharing your experiences in Korea.

- **Theme**: "My Experiences While Staying in Korea"
- **Video Submission Deadline**: September 5th
- **Prizes**
  – 1st place: $100 and traditional Korean tea
  – 2nd place: $50 and a traditional Korean doll
- **Details**
  – Your name must be mentioned at the beginning of the video.
  – Your video must be between 3 to 5 minutes.
  – Please email your video file to k-speech@kcontest.com.

① 한국에서 지내는 동안의 경험을 주제로 한다.
② 영상 제출 마감일은 9월 5일이다.
③ 1등에게는 상금과 한국 전통 인형이 주어진다.
④ 영상 도입부에 이름이 언급되어야 한다.
⑤ 이메일로 영상 파일을 보내야 한다.

05 [1등급 대비 고난도 3점 문제]

고3 · 2018학년도 수능 28번

다음 글의 밑줄 친 부분 중, 어법상 틀린 것은? [3점]

Psychologists who study giving behavior ① have noticed that some people give substantial amounts to one or two charities, while others give small amounts to many charities. Those who donate to one or two charities seek evidence about what the charity is doing and ② what it is really having a positive impact. If the evidence indicates that the charity is really helping others, they make a substantial donation. Those who give small amounts to many charities are not so interested in whether what they are ③ doing helps others — psychologists call them warm glow givers. Knowing that they are giving makes ④ them feel good, regardless of the impact of their donation. In many cases the donation is so small — $10 or less — that if they stopped ⑤ to think, they would realize that the cost of processing the donation is likely to exceed any benefit it brings to the charity.

06

고2 · 2020년 3월 30번

다음 글의 밑줄 친 부분 중, 문맥상 낱말의 쓰임이 적절하지 않은 것은? [3점]

I was sitting outside a restaurant in Spain one summer evening, waiting for dinner. The aroma of the kitchens excited my taste buds. My future meal was coming to me in the form of molecules drifting through the air, too small for my eyes to see but ① detected by my nose. The ancient Greeks first came upon the idea of atoms this way; the smell of baking bread suggested to them that small particles of bread ② existed beyond vision. The cycle of weather ③ disproved this idea: a puddle of water on the ground gradually dries out, disappears, and then falls later as rain. They reasoned that there must be particles of water that turn into steam, form clouds, and fall to earth, so that the water is ④ conserved even though the little particles are too small to see. My paella in Spain had inspired me, four thousand years too ⑤ late, to take the credit for atomic theory.

* taste bud: 미뢰(혀의 미각 기관) ** molecule: 분자
*** paella: 파에야(스페인 요리의 하나)

07 1등급 대비 고난도 2점 문제

다음 빈칸에 들어갈 말로 가장 적절한 것을 고르시오.

Most importantly, money needs to be _____ in a predictable way. Precious metals have been desirable as money across the millennia not only because they have intrinsic beauty but also because they exist in fixed quantities. Gold and silver enter society at the rate at which they are discovered and mined; additional precious metals cannot be produced, at least not cheaply. Commodities like rice and tobacco can be grown, but that still takes time and resources. A dictator like Zimbabwe's Robert Mugabe could not order the government to produce 100 trillion tons of rice. He was able to produce and distribute trillions of new Zimbabwe dollars, which is why they eventually became more valuable as toilet paper than currency.

* intrinsic: 내재적인

① invested
② scarce
③ transferred
④ divisible
⑤ deposited

08

글의 흐름으로 보아, 주어진 문장이 들어가기에 가장 적절한 곳을 고르시오. [3점]

Even though there may be a logically easy set of procedures to follow, it's still an emotional battle to change your habits and introduce new, uncomfortable behaviors that you are not used to.

Charisma is eminently learnable and teachable, and in many ways, it follows one of Newton's famed laws of motion: *For every action, there is an equal and opposite reaction.* (①) That is to say that all of charisma and human interaction is a set of signals and cues that lead to other signals and cues, and there is a science to deciphering which signals and cues work the most in your favor. (②) In other words, charisma can often be simplified as a checklist of what to do at what time. (③) However, it will require brief forays out of your comfort zone. (④) I like to say that it's just a matter of using muscles that have long been dormant. (⑤) It will take some time to warm them up, but it's only through practice and action that you will achieve your desired goal.

* decipher: 판독하다 ** foray: 시도
*** dormant: 활동을 중단한

09

고2 · 2020년 9월 40번

다음 글의 내용을 한 문장으로 요약하고자 한다. 빈칸 (A), (B)에 들어갈 말로 가장 적절한 것은?

Some researchers at Sheffield University recruited 129 hobbyists to look at how the time spent on their hobbies shaped their work life. To begin with, the team measured the seriousness of each participant's hobby, asking them to rate their agreement with statements like "I regularly train for this activity," and also assessed how similar the demands of their job and hobby were. Then, each month for seven months, participants recorded how many hours they had dedicated to their activity, and completed a scale measuring their belief in their ability to effectively do their job, or their "self-efficacy." The researchers found that when participants spent longer than normal doing their leisure activity, their belief in their ability to perform their job increased. But this was only the case when they had a serious hobby that was dissimilar to their job. When their hobby was both serious and similar to their job, then spending more time on it actually decreased their self-efficacy.

↓

Research suggests that spending more time on serious hobbies can boost ____(A)____ at work if the hobbies and the job are sufficiently ____(B)____.

	(A)		(B)
①	confidence	......	different
②	productivity	......	connected
③	relationships	......	balanced
④	creativity	......	separate
⑤	dedication	......	similar

[10~12] 다음 글을 읽고, 물음에 답하시오.

(A)

"You've been a very good girl this year, Emma. Tonight, Santa will drop by our house to leave you some presents." Martha told (a) her little girl, smiling. "And for you too, Fred," she added. She wanted to give her two children so much more, but this year had been especially hard for Martha. She had worked day and night to buy some Christmas gifts for her children.

(B)

Emma came running up to her mother the next morning. "Mommy, Santa really did come last night!" Martha smiled, thinking of the candies and cookies (b) she must have found in her socks. "Did you like his gifts?" "Yes, they are wonderful. Fred loves his toys, too." Martha was confused. She wondered how the candies and cookies had become toys overnight. Martha ran into Emma's room and saw a small red box that was half open. She knelt down and glanced inside to see its contents.

(C)

That night, after everyone had gone to bed, Emma slowly climbed out of bed. She took out a page from a notebook to write a letter to Santa. She whispered to herself as she wrote. "Dear Santa, will you send a few smiles and laughs for my mother? (c) She doesn't laugh much. And will you send a few toys for Fred as well? Thank you." Emma folded the letter twice and sealed it within an envelope. She left the envelope outside the front door and went back to sleep.

(D)

The box contained some toys, countless little candies and cookies. "Mommy, this is for you from Santa." Emma said holding out a card towards Martha. Puzzled, (d) she opened it. It said, "Dear Emma's mother. A very merry Christmas! Hi, I am Amelia. I found your child's letter blowing across the street last night. I was touched and couldn't help but respond. Please accept the gift as a Christmas greeting." Martha felt tears falling down (e) her cheeks. She slowly wiped them off and hugged her daughter. "Merry Christmas, Emma. Didn't I tell you Santa would come?"

10

주어진 글 (A)에 이어질 내용을 순서에 맞게 배열한 것으로 가장 적절한 것은?

① (B) − (D) − (C)　　② (C) − (B) − (D)
③ (C) − (D) − (B)　　④ (D) − (B) − (C)
⑤ (D) − (C) − (B)

11

밑줄 친 (a)~(e) 중에서 가리키는 대상이 나머지 넷과 다른 것은?

① (a)　　② (b)　　③ (c)　　④ (d)　　⑤ (e)

12

윗글에 관한 내용으로 적절하지 않은 것은?

① 올해는 Martha에게 힘든 한 해였다.
② Fred가 선물받은 장난감을 마음에 들어 했다.
③ Martha가 자신의 방에서 작은 빨간 상자를 보았다.
④ Emma가 산타에게 편지를 썼다.
⑤ Emma가 Martha에게 산타가 보냈다고 말하며 카드를 내밀었다.

● 날짜 : 월 일 ● 시작 시각 : 시 분 초 ● 목표 시간 : 20분　　　　※ 점수 표기가 없는 문항은 모두 2점입니다.

01
고3 · 2021학년도 수능 18번

다음 글의 목적으로 가장 적절한 것은?

Dear Friends,

Season's greetings. As some of you already know, we are starting the campus food drive. This is how you participate. You can bring your items for donation to our booths. Our donation booths are located in the lobbies of the campus libraries. Just drop off the items there during usual library hours from December 4 to 23. The donated food should be non-perishable like canned meats and canned fruits. Packaged goods such as jam and peanut butter are also good. We will distribute the food to our neighbors on Christmas Eve. We truly appreciate your help.

Many blessings,
Joanna at Campus Food Bank

① 음식 기부에 참여하는 방법을 안내하려고
② 음식 배달 자원봉사 참여에 감사하려고
③ 도서관 이용 시간 변경을 공지하려고
④ 음식물 낭비의 심각성을 알려 주려고
⑤ 크리스마스 행사 일정을 문의하려고

02
고2 · 2023년 6월 22번

다음 글의 요지로 가장 적절한 것은?

Perhaps, the advent of Artificial Intelligence (AI) in the workplace may bode well for Emotional Intelligence (EI). As AI gains momentum and replaces people in jobs at every level, predictions are, there will be a premium placed on people who have high ability in EI. The emotional messages people send and respond to while interacting are, at this point, far beyond the ability of AI programs to mimic. As we get further into the age of the smart machine, it is likely that sensing and managing emotions will remain one type of intelligence that puzzles AI. This means people and jobs involving EI are safe from being taken over by machines. In a survey, almost three out of four executives see EI as a "must-have" skill for the workplace in the future as the automatizing of routine tasks bumps up against the impossibility of creating effective AI for activities that require emotional skill.

* bode: ~의 징조가 되다　** momentum: 추진력

① 감성 지능의 결여는 직장 내 대인 관계 갈등을 심화시킨다.
② 미래의 직장에서는 감성 지능의 가치가 더욱 높아질 것이다.
③ 미래 사회에서는 감성 지능을 갖춘 기계가 보편화될 것이다.
④ 미래에는 대부분의 직장 업무를 인공 지능이 대신할 것이다.
⑤ 인간과 인공 지능 간의 상호 작용은 감성 지능의 발달을 저해한다.

03

Janaki Ammal에 관한 다음 글의 내용과 일치하지 <u>않는</u> 것은?

Janaki Ammal, one of India's most notable scientists, was born in 1897, and was expected to wed through an arranged marriage. Despite living at a time when literacy among women in India was less than one percent, she decided to reject tradition and attend college. In 1924, she went to the U.S. and eventually received a doctorate in botany from the University of Michigan. Ammal contributed to the development of the sweetest sugarcane variety in the world. She moved to England where she co-authored the *Chromosome Atlas of Cultivated Plants*. Following a series of famines, she returned to India to help increase food production at the request of the Prime Minister. However, Ammal disagreed with the deforestation taking place in an effort to grow more food. She became an advocate for the preservation of native plants and successfully saved the Silent Valley from the construction of a hydroelectric dam.

① 관습을 따르지 않고 대학에 입학하기로 결심했다.
② 세계에서 가장 단 사탕수수 품종 개발에 기여했다.
③ *Chromosome Atlas of Cultivated Plants*를 공동 집필했다.
④ 식량 생산을 증가시키는 데 도움을 주기 위해 인도로 돌아갔다.
⑤ 수력 발전 댐의 건설로부터 Silent Valley를 지키는 데 실패했다.

04

Plogging Event에 관한 다음 안내문의 내용과 일치하는 것은?

Plogging Event

Have you heard of Plogging? It comes from the Swedish word for pick up, "plocka upp" and is a combination of jogging and picking up litter. In 2016, it started in Sweden and has recently come to the UK, becoming a new movement for saving nature.

When & Where
- 9 a.m. on the first Monday of each month
- Outside the ETNA Centre, East Twickenham

What to Prepare
- Just bring your running shoes, and we will provide all the other equipment.
- There is no fee to participate, but you are welcome to donate toward our conservation work.

※ No reservations are necessary to participate.

For more information, visit www.environmenttrust.org.

① 2016년에 영국에서 시작되었다.
② 매달 첫 번째 일요일 오전 9시에 열린다.
③ 운동화를 포함한 장비들이 지급된다.
④ 참가비는 무료이다.
⑤ 참가하려면 예약이 필요하다.

05

다음 글의 밑줄 친 부분 중, 어법상 틀린 것은? [3점]

Why do we often feel that others are paying more attention to us than they really are? The spotlight effect means seeing ourselves at center stage, thus intuitively overestimating the extent ① to which others' attention is aimed at us. Timothy Lawson explored the spotlight effect by having college students ② change into a sweatshirt with a big popular logo on the front before meeting a group of peers. Nearly 40 percent of them ③ were sure the other students would remember what the shirt said, but only 10 percent actually did. Most observers did not even notice ④ that the students changed sweatshirts after leaving the room for a few minutes. In another experiment, even noticeable clothes, such as a T-shirt with singer Barry Manilow on it, ⑤ provoking only 23 percent of observers to notice — far fewer than the 50 percent estimated by the students sporting the 1970s soft rock singer on their chests.

* sport: 자랑해 보이다

06

밑줄 친 부분이 가리키는 대상이 나머지 넷과 다른 것은?

Jack stopped the cycle of perfectionism that ① his son Mark was developing. Mark could not stand to lose at games by the time he was eight years old. Jack was contributing to Mark's attitude by always letting him win at chess because ② he didn't like to see Mark get upset and cry. One day, Jack realized it was more important to allow Mark some experience with losing, so ③ he started winning at least half the games. Mark was upset at first, but soon began to win and lose with more grace. Jack felt a milestone had been reached one day when ④ he was playing catch with Mark and threw a bad ball. Instead of getting upset about missing the ball, Mark was able to use ⑤ his sense of humor and commented, "Nice throw, Dad. Lousy catch, Mark."

* milestone: 중대한 시점

07 1등급 대비 고난도 2점 문제

다음 빈칸에 들어갈 말로 가장 적절한 것을 고르시오.

Over 4.5 billion years ago, the Earth's primordial atmosphere was probably largely water vapour, carbon dioxide, sulfur dioxide and nitrogen. The appearance and subsequent evolution of exceedingly primitive living organisms (bacteria-like microbes and simple single-celled plants) began to change the atmosphere, liberating oxygen and breaking down carbon dioxide and sulfur dioxide. This made it possible for higher organisms to develop. When the earliest known plant cells with nuclei evolved about 2 billion years ago, the atmosphere seems to have had only about 1 percent of its present content of oxygen. With the emergence of the first land plants, about 500 million years ago, oxygen reached about one-third of its present concentration. It had risen to almost its present level by about 370 million years ago, when animals first spread on to land. Today's atmosphere is thus not just a requirement to sustain life as we know it — it is also _____.

　*primordial: 원시의　**sulfur dioxide: 이산화황

① a barrier to evolution
② a consequence of life
③ a record of primitive culture
④ a sign of the constancy of nature
⑤ a reason for cooperation among species

08

다음 빈칸에 들어갈 말로 가장 적절한 것을 고르시오.

We are often faced with high-level decisions, where we are unable to predict the results of those decisions. In such situations, most people end up quitting the option altogether, because the stakes are high and results are very unpredictable. But there is a solution for this. You should use the process of _____. In many situations, it's wise to dip your toe in the water rather than dive in headfirst. Recently, I was about to enroll in an expensive coaching program. But I was not fully convinced of how the outcome would be. Therefore, I used this process by enrolling in a low-cost mini course with the same instructor. This helped me understand his methodology, style, and content; and I was able to test it with a lower investment, and less time and effort before committing fully to the expensive program.

　*stakes: (계획·행동 등의 성공 여부에) 걸려 있는 것

① trying out what other people do
② erasing the least preferred options
③ testing the option on a smaller scale
④ sharing your plans with professionals
⑤ collecting as many examples as possible

DAY 25

09 1등급 대비 고난도 3점 문제

고2 · 2022년 9월 37번

주어진 글 다음에 이어질 글의 순서로 가장 적절한 것을 고르시오. [3점]

> One benefit of reasons and arguments is that they can foster humility. If two people disagree without arguing, all they do is yell at each other. No progress is made.

(A) That is one way to achieve humility — on one side at least. Another possibility is that neither argument is refuted. Both have a degree of reason on their side. Even if neither person involved is convinced by the other's argument, both can still come to appreciate the opposing view.

(B) Both still think that they are right. In contrast, if both sides give arguments that articulate reasons for their positions, then new possibilities open up. One of the arguments gets refuted — that is, it is shown to fail. In that case, the person who depended on the refuted argument learns that he needs to change his view.

(C) They also realize that, even if they have some truth, they do not have the whole truth. They can gain humility when they recognize and appreciate the reasons against their own view.

*humility: 겸손 **articulate: 분명히 말하다

① (A) − (C) − (B)
② (B) − (A) − (C)
③ (B) − (C) − (A)
④ (C) − (A) − (B)
⑤ (C) − (B) − (A)

10

고2 · 2022년 6월 39번

글의 흐름으로 보아, 주어진 문장이 들어가기에 가장 적절한 곳을 고르시오.

> But by the 1970s, psychologists realized there was no such thing as a general "creativity quotient."

The holy grail of the first wave of creativity research was a personality test to measure general creativity ability, in the same way that IQ measured general intelligence. (①) A person's creativity score should tell us his or her creative potential in any field of endeavor, just like an IQ score is not limited to physics, math, or literature. (②) Creative people aren't creative in a general, universal way; they're creative in a specific sphere of activity, a particular domain. (③) We don't expect a creative scientist to also be a gifted painter. (④) A creative violinist may not be a creative conductor, and a creative conductor may not be very good at composing new works. (⑤) Psychologists now know that creativity is domain specific.

*quotient: 지수 **holy grail: 궁극적 목표

[11 ~ 12] 다음 글을 읽고, 물음에 답하시오.

We're creatures who live and die by the energy stores we've built up in our bodies. Navigating the world is a difficult job that requires moving around and using a lot of brainpower — an energy-expensive endeavor. When we make correct (a) predictions, that saves energy. When you know that edible bugs can be found beneath certain types of rocks, it saves turning over *all* the rocks. The better we predict, the less energy it costs us. Repetition makes us more confident in our forecasts and more efficient in our actions. So there's something (b) appealing about predictability.

But if our brains are going to all this effort to make the world predictable, that begs the question: if we love predictability so much, why don't we, for example, just replace our televisions with machines that emit a rhythmic beep twenty-four hours a day, predictably? The answer is that there's a problem with a (c) lack of surprise. The better we understand something, the less effort we put into thinking about it. Familiarity (d) reduces indifference. Repetition suppression sets in and our attention diminishes. This is why — no matter how much you enjoyed watching the World Series — you aren't going to be satisfied watching that same game over and over. Although predictability is reassuring, the brain strives to (e) incorporate new facts into its model of the world. It always seeks novelty.

11

고2·2019년 11월 41번

윗글의 제목으로 가장 적절한 것은?

① Why Are Television Reruns Still Popular?
② Predictability Is Something Not to Be Feared!
③ What Really Satisfies Our Brain: Familiarity or Novelty
④ Repetition Gives Us Expertise at the Expense of Creativity
⑤ Our Hunter-Gatherer Ancestors Were Smart in Saving Energy

12 1등급 대비 고난도 3점 문제

고2·2019년 11월 42번

밑줄 친 (a) ~ (e) 중에서 문맥상 낱말의 쓰임이 적절하지 않은 것은? [3점]

① (a)   ② (b)   ③ (c)   ④ (d)   ⑤ (e)

학습 Check! ▶ 몰라서 틀린 문항 × 표기 ▶ 헷갈렸거나 찍은 문항 △ 표기 ▶ ×, △ 문항은 다시 풀고 ✔ 표기를 하세요.

종료 시각	시 분 초	문항 번호	01	02	03	04	05	06	07	08	09	10	11	12
소요 시간	분 초	채점 결과												
초과 시간	분 초	틀린 문항 복습												

DAY 26

수능기출
전국연합학력평가 **20분 미니 모의고사**

● 날짜 : 월 일 ● 시작 시각 : 시 분 초 ● 목표 시간 : 20분

※ 점수 표기가 없는 문항은 모두 **2점**입니다.

01

고2 · 2023년 9월 19번

다음 글에 드러난 'I'의 심경 변화로 가장 적절한 것은?

My 10-year-old appeared, in desperate need of a quarter. "A quarter? What on earth do you need a quarter for?" My tone bordered on irritation. I didn't want to be bothered with such a trivial demand. "There's a garage sale up the street, and there's something I just gotta have! It only costs a quarter. Please?" I placed a quarter in my son's hand. Moments later, a little voice said, "Here, Mommy, this is for you." I glanced down at the hands of my little son and saw a four-inch cream-colored statue of two small children hugging one another. Inscribed at their feet were words that read *It starts with 'L' ends with 'E' and in between are 'O' and 'V.'* As I watched him race back to the garage sale, I smiled with a heart full of happiness. That 25-cent garage sale purchase brought me a lot of joy.

* quarter: 25센트 동전 ** inscribe: 새기다

① annoyed → delighted
② ashamed → relieved
③ excited → confused
④ scared → confident
⑤ indifferent → jealous

02

고2 · 2022년 6월 21번

밑줄 친 'give away the house'가 다음 글에서 의미하는 바로 가장 적절한 것은? [3점]

For companies interested in delighting customers, exceptional value and service become part of the overall company culture. For example, year after year, Pazano ranks at or near the top of the hospitality industry in terms of customer satisfaction. The company's passion for satisfying customers is summed up in its credo, which promises that its luxury hotels will deliver a truly memorable experience. Although a customer-centered firm seeks to deliver high customer satisfaction relative to competitors, it does not attempt to *maximize* customer satisfaction. A company can always increase customer satisfaction by lowering its price or increasing its services. But this may result in lower profits. Thus, the purpose of marketing is to generate customer value profitably. This requires a very delicate balance: the marketer must continue to generate more customer value and satisfaction but not 'give away the house'.

* credo: 신조

① risk the company's profitability
② overlook a competitor's strengths
③ hurt the reputation of the company
④ generate more customer complaints
⑤ abandon customer-oriented marketing

03

다음 글의 제목으로 가장 적절한 것은?

Invasions of natural communities by non-indigenous species are currently rated as one of the most important global-scale environmental problems. The loss of biodiversity has generated concern over the consequences for ecosystem functioning and thus understanding the relationship between both has become a major focus in ecological research during the last two decades. The "biodiversity-invasibility hypothesis" by Elton suggests that high diversity increases the competitive environment of communities and makes them more difficult to invade. Numerous biodiversity experiments have been conducted since Elton's time and several mechanisms have been proposed to explain the often observed negative relationship between diversity and invasibility. Beside the decreased chance of empty ecological niches but the increased probability of competitors that prevent invasion success, diverse communities are assumed to use resources more completely and, therefore, limit the ability of invaders to establish. Further, more diverse communities are believed to be more stable because they use a broader range of niches than species-poor communities.

* indigenous: 토착의 ** niche: 생태적 지위

① Carve Out More Empty Ecological Spaces!
② Guardian of Ecology: Diversity Resists Invasion
③ Grasp All, Lose All: Necessity of Species-poor Ecology
④ Challenges in Testing Biodiversity-Invasibility Hypothesis
⑤ Diversity Dilemma: The More Competitive, the Less Secure

04

다음 글의 밑줄 친 부분 중, 어법상 틀린 것은? [3점]

The competition to sell manuscripts to publishers ① is fierce. I would estimate that less than one percent of the material ② sent to publishers is ever published. Since so much material is being written, publishers can be very selective. The material they choose to publish must not only have commercial value, but ③ being very competently written and free of editing and factual errors. Any manuscript that contains errors stands ④ little chance at being accepted for publication. Most publishers will not want to waste time with writers ⑤ whose material contains too many mistakes.

05

다음 글의 밑줄 친 부분 중, 문맥상 낱말의 쓰임이 적절하지 않은 것은? [3점]

Human innovation in agriculture has unlocked modifications in apples, tulips, and potatoes that never would have been realized through a plant's natural reproductive cycles. This cultivation process has created some of the recognizable vegetables and fruits consumers look for in their grocery stores. However, relying on only a few varieties of cultivated crops can leave humankind ① vulnerable to starvation and agricultural loss if a harvest is destroyed. For example, a million people died over the course of three years during the Irish potato famine because the Irish relied ② primarily on potatoes and milk to create a nutritionally balanced meal. In order to continue its symbiotic relationship with cultivated plants, humanity must allow for biodiversity and recognize the potential ③ benefits that monocultures of plants can introduce. Planting seeds of all kinds, even if they don't seem immediately useful or profitable, can ④ ensure the longevity of those plants for generations to come. A ⑤ balance must be struck between nature's capacity for wildness and humanity's desire for control.

*symbiotic: 공생의

06

다음 빈칸에 들어갈 말로 가장 적절한 것을 고르시오.

The elements any particular animal needs are relatively predictable. They are predictable based on the past: what an animal's ancestors needed is likely to be what that animal also needs. _____, therefore, can be hardwired. Consider sodium (Na). The bodies of terrestrial vertebrates, including those of mammals, tend to have a concentration of sodium nearly fifty times that of the primary producers on land, plants. This is, in part, because vertebrates evolved in the sea and so evolved cells dependent upon the ingredients that were common in the sea, including sodium. To remedy the difference between their needs for sodium and that available in plants, herbivores can eat fifty times more plant material than they otherwise need (and eliminate the excess). Or they can seek out other sources of sodium. The salt taste receptor rewards animals for doing the latter, seeking out salt in order to satisfy their great need.

*terrestrial: 육생의   **vertebrate: 척추동물
***herbivore: 초식 동물

① Taste preferences
② Hunting strategies
③ Migration patterns
④ Protective instincts
⑤ Periodic starvations

07 1등급 대비 고난도 3점 문제

다음 빈칸에 들어갈 말로 가장 적절한 것을 고르시오. [3점]

Early in the term, our art professor projected an image of a monk, his back to the viewer, standing on the shore, looking off into a blue sea and an enormous sky. The professor asked the class, "What do you see?" The darkened auditorium was silent. We looked and looked and thought and thought as hard as possible to unearth the hidden meaning, but came up with nothing — we must have missed it. With dramatic exasperation she answered her own question, "It's a painting of a monk! His back is to us! He is standing near the shore! There's a blue sea and enormous sky!" Hmm... why didn't we see it? So as not to bias us, she'd posed the question without revealing the artist or title of the work. In fact, it was Caspar David Friedrich's *The Monk by the Sea*. To better understand your world, _____ _____ rather than guess at what you think you are supposed to see.

* exasperation: 격분

① consciously acknowledge what you actually see
② accept different opinions with a broad mind
③ reflect on what you've already learned
④ personally experience even a small thing
⑤ analyze the answers from various perspectives

08

다음 글에서 전체 흐름과 관계 <u>없는</u> 문장은?

Cultural globalization has multiple centers in Asia like Bollywood movies made in India and Kung Fu movies made in Hong Kong. ① They are subtitled in as many as 17 languages and distributed to specific diasporas. ② These cultural spaces, which are dominated by languages like Hindi and Mandarin, ignore and challenge the spread of English. ③ Professor Vaish has shown how Chinese and Indian children in Singapore are networked into the pan-Chinese and pan-Indian culture through their engagement with Chinese pop music and Indian movies respectively. ④ As the world's two most populous nations, China is India's largest trading partner, with the size of trade between them valuing $71.5 billion. ⑤ She thus empirically challenges the idea that Asian youth are passive victims of cultural globalization, or "world culture" that comes out of the West.

* diaspora: 디아스포라(이주하여 해외에 사는 사람들 또는 그 집단)

09

고2・2017년 11월 40번

다음 글의 내용을 한 문장으로 요약하고자 한다. 빈칸 (A), (B)에 들어갈 말로 가장 적절한 것은? [3점]

Power distance is the term used to refer to how widely an unequal distribution of power is accepted by the members of a culture. It relates to the degree to which the less powerful members of a society accept their inequality in power and consider it the norm. In cultures with high acceptance of power distance (e.g., India, Brazil, Greece, Mexico, and the Philippines), people are not viewed as equals, and everyone has a clearly defined or allocated place in the social hierarchy. In cultures with low acceptance of power distance (e.g., Finland, Norway, New Zealand, and Israel), people believe inequality should be minimal, and a hierarchical division is viewed as one of convenience only. In these cultures, there is more fluidity within the social hierarchy, and it is relatively easy for individuals to move up the social hierarchy based on their individual efforts and achievements.

↓

Unlike cultures with high acceptance of power distance, where members are more _____(A)_____ to accept inequality, cultures with low acceptance of power distance allow more _____(B)_____ within the social hierarchy.

	(A)		(B)
①	willing	······	mobility
②	willing	······	assistance
③	reluctant	······	resistance
④	reluctant	······	flexibility
⑤	afraid	······	openness

[10 ～ 12] 다음 글을 읽고, 물음에 답하시오.

(A)

I was on a train in Switzerland. The train came to a stop, and the conductor's voice over the loudspeaker delivered a message in German, then Italian, then French. I had made the mistake of not learning any of those languages before my vacation. After the announcement, everyone started getting off the train, and an old woman saw I was confused and stressed. (a) She came up to me.

(B)

So we went from one train station to the next, getting to know each other along the way. It was a 2.5-hour journey in total, and when we finally made it to the destination, we got off and said our good-byes. I had made it just in time to catch my train to Rome, and she told me she had a train to catch too. I asked (b) her how much farther she had to go, and it turned out her home was two hours back the other way.

(C)

She spoke some English, and she told me that an accident had happened on the tracks. She asked me where I was trying to get to, then she got off the train and went to a woman in the ticket booth. The old woman got a rail map and timetable from (c) her and came back to tell me that we'd have to hop trains three or four times to get there. I was really glad (d) she was headed the same way because it would have been hopeless for me to figure it out on my own.

(D)

She had jumped from train to train and traveled the whole way just to make sure I made it. "You are the nicest person I've ever met," I said. She smiled gently and hugged me and told me I'd better hurry off so I wouldn't miss my train. This woman spent her entire day sitting on trains taking (e) her hours away from her home just to help out a confused tourist visiting her country. No matter how many countries I visit or sites I see, I always say the most beautiful country in the world is Switzerland.

10

주어진 글 (A)에 이어질 내용을 순서에 맞게 배열한 것으로 가장 적절한 것은?

① (B) − (D) − (C)   ② (C) − (B) − (D)
③ (C) − (D) − (B)   ④ (D) − (B) − (C)
⑤ (D) − (C) − (B)

11

밑줄 친 (a) ~ (e) 중에서 가리키는 대상이 나머지 넷과 다른 것은?

① (a)   ② (b)   ③ (c)   ④ (d)   ⑤ (e)

12

윗글에 관한 내용으로 적절하지 않은 것은?

① 안내 방송 후 모두가 기차에서 내리기 시작했다.
② 'I'는 로마로 가는 기차 시간에 맞춰 도착하지 못했다.
③ 노부인은 선로에서 사고가 발생했다고 말했다.
④ 노부인은 기차에서 내려 티켓 부스로 갔다.
⑤ 'I'는 세계에서 가장 아름다운 나라가 스위스라고 항상 말한다.

학습 Check!

▶ 몰라서 틀린 문항 × 표기   ▶ 헷갈렸거나 찍은 문항 △ 표기   ▶ ×, △ 문항은 다시 풀고 ✔ 표기를 하세요.

종료 시각	시	분	초	문항 번호	01	02	03	04	05	06	07	08	09	10	11	12
소요 시간		분	초	채점 결과												
초과 시간		분	초	틀린 문항 복습												

● 날짜 :   월   일 ● 시작 시각 :   시   분   초 ● 목표 시간 : 20분   ※ 점수 표기가 없는 문항은 모두 **2점**입니다.

01
고3 • 2024학년도 수능 20번

다음 글에서 필자가 주장하는 바로 가장 적절한 것은?

Values alone do not create and build culture. Living your values only some of the time does not contribute to the creation and maintenance of culture. Changing values into behaviors is only half the battle. Certainly, this is a step in the right direction, but those behaviors must then be shared and distributed widely throughout the organization, along with a clear and concise description of what is expected. It is not enough to simply talk about it. It is critical to have a visual representation of the specific behaviors that leaders and all people managers can use to coach their people. Just like a sports team has a playbook with specific plays designed to help them perform well and win, your company should have a playbook with the key shifts needed to transform your culture into action and turn your values into winning behaviors.

① 조직 문화 혁신을 위해서 모든 구성원이 공유할 핵심 가치를 정립해야 한다.
② 조직 구성원의 행동을 변화시키려면 지도자는 명확한 가치관을 가져야 한다.
③ 조직 내 문화가 공유되기 위해서 구성원의 자발적 행동이 뒷받침되어야 한다.
④ 조직의 핵심 가치 실현을 위해 구성원 간의 지속적인 의사소통이 필수적이다.
⑤ 조직의 문화 형성에는 가치를 반영한 행동의 공유를 위한 명시적 지침이 필요하다.

02
고2 • 2020년 11월 23번

다음 글의 주제로 가장 적절한 것은?

I was brought up to believe that if I get lost in a large forest, I will sooner or later end up where I started. Without knowing it, people who are lost will always walk in a circle. In the book *Finding Your Way Without Map or Compass*, author Harold Gatty confirms that this is true. We tend to walk in circles for several reasons. The most important is that virtually no human has two legs of the exact same length. One leg is always slightly longer than the other, and this causes us to turn without even noticing it. In addition, if you are hiking with a backpack on, the weight of that backpack will inevitably throw you off balance. Our dominant hand factors into the mix too. If you are right-handed, you will have a tendency to turn toward the right. And when you meet an obstacle, you will subconsciously decide to pass it on the right side.

① abilities to construct a mental map for walking
② factors that result in people walking in a circle
③ reasons why dominance exists in nature
④ instincts that help people return home
⑤ solutions to finding the right direction

03

고2 · 2020년 3월 25번

다음 도표의 내용과 일치하지 <u>않는</u> 것은?

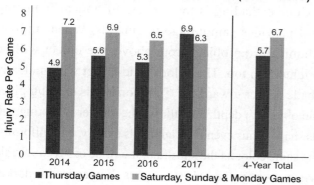

Injury Rate by Day of Game in NFL (2014–2017)

The above graph shows the injury rate by day of game in the National Football League (NFL) from 2014 to 2017. ① The injury rate of Thursday games was the lowest in 2014 and the highest in 2017. ② The injury rate of Saturday, Sunday and Monday games decreased steadily from 2014 to 2017. ③ In all the years except 2017, the injury rate of Thursday games was lower than that of Saturday, Sunday and Monday games. ④ The gap between the injury rate of Thursday games and that of Saturday, Sunday and Monday games was the largest in 2014 and the smallest in 2017. ⑤ In two years out of the four, the injury rate of Thursday games was higher than that of the 4-year total.

04

고2 · 2023년 6월 26번

John Ray에 관한 다음 글의 내용과 일치하지 <u>않는</u> 것은?

Born in 1627 in Black Notley, Essex, England, John Ray was the son of the village blacksmith. At 16, he went to Cambridge University, where he studied widely and lectured on topics from Greek to mathematics, before joining the priesthood in 1660. To recover from an illness in 1650, he had taken to nature walks and developed an interest in botany. Accompanied by his wealthy student and supporter Francis Willughby, Ray toured Britain and Europe in the 1660s, studying and collecting plants and animals. He married Margaret Oakley in 1673 and, after leaving Willughby's household, lived quietly in Black Notley to the age of 77. He spent his later years studying samples in order to assemble plant and animal catalogues. He wrote more than twenty works on theology and his travels, as well as on plants and their form and function.

＊theology: 신학

① 마을 대장장이의 아들이었다.
② 성직자의 길로 들어서기 전 Cambridge 대학에 다녔다.
③ 병에서 회복하기 위해 자연을 산책하기 시작했다.
④ Francis Willughby에게 후원받아 홀로 유럽을 여행하였다.
⑤ 동식물의 목록을 만들기 위해 표본을 연구하며 말년을 보냈다.

05 1등급 대비 고난도 3점 문제

다음 글의 밑줄 친 부분 중, 어법상 틀린 것은? [3점]

Cutting costs can improve profitability but only up to a point. If the manufacturer cuts costs so deeply ① that doing so harms the product's quality, then the increased profitability will be short-lived. A better approach is to improve productivity. If businesses can get more production from the same number of employees, they're ② basically tapping into free money. They get more product to sell, and the price of each product falls. As long as the machinery or employee training ③ needed for productivity improvements costs less than the value of the productivity gains, it's an easy investment for any business to make. Productivity improvements are as important to the economy as they ④ do to the individual business that's making them. Productivity improvements generally raise the standard of living for everyone and ⑤ are a good indication of a healthy economy.

06 1등급 대비 고난도 3점 문제

다음 글의 밑줄 친 부분 중, 문맥상 낱말의 쓰임이 적절하지 않은 것은? [3점]

Countershading is the process of optical flattening that provides camouflage to animals. When sunlight illuminates an object from above, the object will be brightest on top. The color of the object will gradually shade darker toward the ① bottom. This shading gives the object ② depth and allows the viewer to distinguish its shape. Thus even if an animal is exactly, but uniformly, the same color as the substrate, it will be easily ③ visible when illuminated. Most animals, however, are darker above than they are below. When they are illuminated from above, the darker back is lightened and the lighter belly is shaded. The animal thus appears to be a ④ single color and easily blends in with the substrate. This pattern of coloration, or countershading, ⑤ reinforces the visual impression of shape in the organism. It allows the animal to blend in with its background.

* camouflage: 위장 ** substrate: 밑바탕, 기질(基質)

07

다음 빈칸에 들어갈 말로 가장 적절한 것을 고르시오.

Firms in almost every industry tend to be clustered. Suppose you threw darts at random on a map of the United States. You'd find the holes left by the darts to be more or less evenly distributed across the map. But the real map of any given industry looks nothing like that; it looks more as if someone had thrown all the darts in the same place. This is probably in part because of reputation; buyers may be suspicious of a software firm in the middle of the cornfields. It would also be hard to recruit workers if every time you needed a new employee you had to persuade someone to move across the country, rather than just poach one from your neighbor. There are also regulatory reasons: zoning laws often try to concentrate dirty industries in one place and restaurants and bars in another. Finally, people in the same industry often have similar preferences (computer engineers like coffee, financiers show off with expensive bottles of wine). _____ makes it easier to provide the amenities they like.

* poach: (인력을) 빼내다

① Automation   ② Concentration
③ Transportation   ④ Globalization
⑤ Liberalization

08   **1등급 대비 고난도 3점 문제**

다음 빈칸에 들어갈 말로 가장 적절한 것을 고르시오. [3점]

Psychological research has shown that people naturally _____, often without thinking about it. Imagine you're cooking up a special dinner with a friend. You're a great cook, but your friend is the wine expert, an amateur sommelier. A neighbor drops by and starts telling you both about the terrific new wines being sold at the liquor store just down the street. There are many new wines, so there's a lot to remember. How hard are you going to try to remember what the neighbor has to say about which wines to buy? Why bother when the information would be better retained by the wine expert sitting next to you? If your friend wasn't around, you might try harder. After all, it would be good to know what a good wine would be for the evening's festivities. But your friend, the wine expert, is likely to remember the information without even trying.

① divide up cognitive labor
② try to avoid disagreements
③ seek people with similar tastes
④ like to share old wisdom
⑤ balance work and leisure

09

주어진 글 다음에 이어질 글의 순서로 가장 적절한 것을 고르시오.

> Touch receptors are spread over all parts of the body, but they are not spread evenly. Most of the touch receptors are found in your fingertips, tongue, and lips.

(A) But if the fingers are spread far apart, you can feel them individually. Yet if the person does the same thing on the back of your hand (with your eyes closed, so that you don't see how many fingers are being used), you probably will be able to tell easily, even when the fingers are close together.

(B) You can test this for yourself. Have someone poke you in the back with one, two, or three fingers and try to guess how many fingers the person used. If the fingers are close together, you will probably think it was only one.

(C) On the tip of each of your fingers, for example, there are about five thousand separate touch receptors. In other parts of the body there are far fewer. In the skin of your back, the touch receptors may be as much as 2 inches apart.

① (A) − (C) − (B)   ② (B) − (A) − (C)
③ (B) − (C) − (A)   ④ (C) − (A) − (B)
⑤ (C) − (B) − (A)

10

글의 흐름으로 보아, 주어진 문장이 들어가기에 가장 적절한 곳을 고르시오.

> For instance, the revolutionary ideas that earned Einstein his Nobel Prize — concerning the special theory of relativity and the photoelectric effect — appeared as papers in the *Annalen der Physik*.

In the early stages of modern science, scientists communicated their creative ideas largely by publishing books. (①) This modus operandi is illustrated not only by Newton's *Principia*, but also by Copernicus' *On the Revolutions of the Heavenly Spheres*, Kepler's *The Harmonies of the World*, and Galileo's *Dialogues Concerning the Two New Sciences*. (②) With the advent of scientific periodicals, such as the *Transactions of the Royal Society of London*, books gradually yielded ground to the technical journal article as the chief form of scientific communication. (③) Of course, books were not abandoned altogether, as Darwin's *Origin of Species* shows. (④) Even so, it eventually became possible for scientists to establish a reputation for their creative contributions without publishing a single book-length treatment of their ideas. (⑤) His status as one of the greatest scientists of all time does not depend on the publication of a single book.

* photoelectric effect: 광전 효과
** modus operandi: 작업 방식[절차]

[11 ~ 12] 다음 글을 읽고, 물음에 답하시오.

In England in the 1680s, it was unusual to live to the age of fifty. This was a period when knowledge was not spread (a) <u>widely</u>, there were few books and most people could not read. As a consequence, knowledge passed down through the oral traditions of stories and shared experiences. And since older people had accumulated more knowledge, the social norm was that to be over fifty was to be wise. This social perception of age began to shift with the advent of new technologies such as the printing press. Over time, as more books were printed, literacy (b) <u>increased</u>, and the oral traditions of knowledge transfer began to fade. With the fading of oral traditions, the wisdom of the old became less important and as a consequence being over fifty was no longer seen as (c) <u>signifying</u> wisdom.

We are living in a period when the gap between chronological and biological age is changing fast and where social norms are struggling to (d) <u>adapt</u>. In a video produced by the AARP (formerly the American Association of Retired Persons), young people were asked to do various activities 'just like an old person'. When older people joined them in the video, the gap between the stereotype and the older people's actual behaviour was (e) <u>unnoticeable</u>. It is clear that in today's world our social norms need to be updated quickly.

11

윗글의 제목으로 가장 적절한 것은?

① Our Social Norms on Aging: An Ongoing Evolution
② The Power of Oral Tradition in the Modern World
③ Generational Differences: Not As Big As You Think
④ There's More to Aging than What the Media Shows
⑤ How Well You Age Depends on Your Views of Aging

12

밑줄 친 (a) ~ (e) 중에서 문맥상 낱말의 쓰임이 적절하지 <u>않은</u> 것은?

① (a)   ② (b)   ③ (c)   ④ (d)   ⑤ (e)

학습 Check!

▶ 몰라서 틀린 문항 × 표기 ▶ 헷갈렸거나 찍은 문항 △ 표기 ▶ ×, △ 문항은 다시 풀고 ✔ 표기를 하세요.

종료 시각	시	분	초	문항 번호	01	02	03	04	05	06	07	08	09	10	11	12
소요 시간		분	초	채점 결과												
초과 시간		분	초	틀린 문항 복습												

DAY 28

수능기출
전국연합학력평가
20분 미니 모의고사

● 날짜 :   월   일 ● 시작 시각 :   시   분   초 ● 목표 시간 : 20분

※ 점수 표기가 없는 문항은 모두 **2점**입니다.

01

고2 · 2020년 11월 19번

다음 글에 드러난 Ryan의 심경 변화로 가장 적절한 것은?

Ryan, an eleven-year-old boy, ran home as fast as he could. Finally, summer break had started! When he entered the house, his mom was standing in front of the refrigerator, waiting for him. She told him to pack his bags. Ryan's heart soared like a balloon. *Pack for what? Are we going to Disneyland?* He couldn't remember the last time his parents had taken him on a vacation. His eyes beamed. "You're spending the summer with uncle Tim and aunt Gina." Ryan groaned. "The whole summer?" "Yes, t he who l e s ummer." The anticipation he had felt disappeared in a flash. For three whole miserable weeks, he would be on his aunt and uncle's farm. He sighed.

① excited → disappointed
② furious → regretful
③ irritated → satisfied
④ nervous → relaxed
⑤ pleased → jealous

02

고2 · 2021년 3월 24번

다음 글의 제목으로 가장 적절한 것은?

Some beginning researchers mistakenly believe that a good hypothesis is one that is guaranteed to be right (e.g., *alcohol will slow down reaction time*). However, if we already know your hypothesis is true before you test it, testing your hypothesis won't tell us anything new. Remember, research is supposed to produce *new* knowledge. To get new knowledge, you, as a researcher-explorer, need to leave the safety of the shore (established facts) and venture into uncharted waters (as Einstein said, "If we knew what we were doing, it would not be called research, would it?"). If your predictions about what will happen in these uncharted waters are wrong, that's okay: Scientists are allowed to make mistakes (as Bates said, "Research is the process of going up alleys to see if they are blind"). Indeed, scientists often learn more from predictions that do not turn out than from those that do.

＊uncharted waters: 미개척 영역

① Researchers, Don't Be Afraid to Be Wrong
② Hypotheses Are Different from Wild Guesses
③ Why Researchers Are Reluctant to Share Their Data
④ One Small Mistake Can Ruin Your Whole Research
⑤ Why Hard Facts Don't Change Our Minds

03

One Day Camp at Seattle Children's Museum에 관한 다음 안내문의 내용과 일치하지 <u>않는</u> 것은?

One Day Camp at Seattle Children's Museum

One Day Camp at Seattle Children's Museum is an experience that promises to inspire creativity in children. Join us on an amazing journey of discovery!

- **Date**: Thursday, July 8, 2021
- **Ages**: 5 – 10
- **Schedule**

Time	Activity
10:30 – 12:30	Arts &Crafts
12:30 – 13:30	Lunch
13:30 – 15:30	Music & Dance

- **Participation Fees**
  - Child: $30
  - Adult: $10

- **Notes**
  - All children must be accompanied by an adult.
  - The participation fee includes lunch and materials for the program.

---

① 7월 8일 목요일에 진행된다.

② 음악과 춤 활동이 있다.

③ 아이의 참가비는 30달러이다.

④ 모든 아이들은 어른과 동행해야 한다.

⑤ 점심 식사는 참가비에 포함되지 않는다.

04 1등급 대비 고난도 3점 문제

다음 글의 밑줄 친 부분 중, 어법상 틀린 것은? [3점]

Application of Buddhist-style mindfulness to Western psychology came primarily from the research of Jon Kabat-Zinn at the University of Massachusetts Medical Center. He initially took on the difficult task of treating chronic-pain patients, many of ① them had not responded well to traditional pain-management therapy. In many ways, such treatment seems completely ② paradoxical — you teach people to deal with pain by helping them to become more aware of it! However, the key is to help people let go of the constant tension that ③ accompanies their fighting of pain, a struggle that actually prolongs their awareness of pain. Mindfulness meditation allowed many of these people to increase their sense of well-being and ④ to experience a better quality of life. How so? Because such meditation is based on the principle that if we try to ignore or repress unpleasant thoughts or sensations, then we only end up ⑤ increasing their intensity.

05 1등급 대비 고난도 2점 문제   고3·2018학년도 수능 29번

다음 글의 밑줄 친 부분 중, 문맥상 낱말의 쓰임이 적절하지 <u>않은</u> 것은?

Some prominent journalists say that archaeologists should work with treasure hunters because treasure hunters have accumulated valuable historical artifacts that can reveal much about the past. But archaeologists are not asked to cooperate with tomb robbers, who also have valuable historical artifacts. The quest for profit and the search for knowledge cannot coexist in archaeology because of the ① <u>time</u> factor. Rather incredibly, one archaeologist employed by a treasure hunting firm said that as long as archaeologists are given six months to study shipwrecked artifacts before they are sold, no historical knowledge is ② <u>found</u>! On the contrary, archaeologists and assistants from the INA (Institute of Nautical Archaeology) needed more than a decade of year-round conservation before they could even ③ <u>catalog</u> all the finds from an eleventh-century AD wreck they had excavated. Then, to interpret those finds, they had to ④ <u>learn</u> Russian, Bulgarian, and Romanian, without which they would never have learned the true nature of the site. Could a "commercial archaeologist" have ⑤ <u>waited</u> more than a decade or so before selling the finds?

＊prominent: 저명한   ＊＊excavate: 발굴하다

06 1등급 대비 고난도 3점 문제   고2·2023년 9월 31번

다음 빈칸에 들어갈 말로 가장 적절한 것을 고르시오. [3점]

Rebels may think they're rebels, but clever marketers influence them just like the rest of us. Saying, "Everyone is doing it" may turn some people off from an idea. These people will look for alternatives, which (if cleverly planned) can be exactly what a marketer or persuader wants you to believe. If I want you to consider an idea, and know you strongly reject popular opinion in favor of maintaining your independence and uniqueness, I would present the majority option first, which you would reject in favor of my actual preference. We are often tricked when we try to maintain a position of defiance. People use this _____ to make us "independently" choose an option which suits their purposes. Some brands have taken full effect of our defiance towards the mainstream and positioned themselves as rebels; which has created even stronger brand loyalty.

＊defiance: 반항

① reversal   ② imitation
③ repetition   ④ conformity
⑤ collaboration

07

고2 · 2023년 3월 34번

다음 빈칸에 들어갈 말로 가장 적절한 것을 고르시오. [3점]

It seems natural to describe certain environmental conditions as 'extreme', 'harsh', 'benign' or 'stressful'. It may seem obvious when conditions are 'extreme': the midday heat of a desert, the cold of an Antarctic winter, the salinity of the Great Salt Lake. But this only means that these conditions are extreme *for us*, given our particular physiological characteristics and tolerances. To a cactus there is nothing extreme about the desert conditions in which cacti have evolved; nor are the icy lands of Antarctica an extreme environment for penguins. It is lazy and dangerous for the ecologist to assume that _____. Rather, the ecologist should try to gain a worm's-eye or plant's-eye view of the environment: to see the world as others see it. Emotive words like harsh and benign, even relativities such as hot and cold, should be used by ecologists only with care.

*benign: 온화한 **salinity: 염도

① complex organisms are superior to simple ones
② technologies help us survive extreme environments
③ ecological diversity is supported by extreme environments
④ all other organisms sense the environment in the way we do
⑤ species adapt to environmental changes in predictable ways

08

고2 · 2020년 6월 35번

다음 글에서 전체 흐름과 관계 <u>없는</u> 문장은?

Marketing management is concerned not only with finding and increasing demand but also with changing or even reducing it. For example, Uluru (Ayers Rock) might have too many tourists wanting to climb it, and Daintree National Park in North Queensland can become overcrowded in the tourist season. ① Power companies sometimes have trouble meeting demand during peak usage periods. ② In these and other cases of excess demand, the needed marketing task, called demarketing, is to reduce demand temporarily or permanently. ③ Efforts should be made to compensate for the losses caused by the increase in supply. ④ The aim of demarketing is not to completely destroy demand, but only to reduce or shift it to another time, or even another product. ⑤ Thus, marketing management seeks to affect the level, timing, and nature of demand in a way that helps the organisation achieve its objectives.

09

고2 · 2021년 11월 40번

다음 글의 내용을 한 문장으로 요약하고자 한다. 빈칸 (A), (B)에 들어갈 말로 가장 적절한 것은?

In a study, Guy Mayraz, a behavioral economist, showed his experimental subjects graphs of a price rising and falling over time. The graphs were actually of past changes in the stock market, but Mayraz told people that the graphs showed recent changes in the price of wheat. He asked each person to predict where the price would move next — and offered them a reward if their forecasts came true. But Mayraz had also divided his participants into two categories, "farmers" and "bakers". Farmers would be paid extra if wheat prices were high. Bakers would earn a bonus if wheat was cheap. So the subjects might earn two separate payments: one for an accurate forecast, and a bonus if the price of wheat moved in their direction. Mayraz found that the prospect of the bonus influenced the forecast itself. The farmers hoped and *predicted* that the price of wheat would rise. The bakers hoped for — and predicted — the opposite. They let their hopes influence their reasoning.

⬇

When participants were asked to predict the price change of wheat, their ___(A)___ for where the price would go, which was determined by the group they belonged to, ___(B)___ their predictions.

	(A)		(B)
①	wish	......	affected
②	wish	......	contradicted
③	disregard	......	restricted
④	disregard	......	changed
⑤	assurance	......	realized

[10 ~ 12] 다음 글을 읽고, 물음에 답하시오.

(A)

Bahati lived in a small village, where baking bread for a hungry passerby is a custom when one misses someone. She had an only son living far away and missed him a lot, so (a) she baked an extra loaf of bread and put it on the window sill every day, for anyone to take away. Every day, a poor old woman took away the bread, just muttering "The good you do, comes back to you!" instead of expressing gratitude.

(B)

This time, instead of being irritated, Bahati decided to offer a prayer. For years, she had got no news of her son. (b) She prayed for his safety. That night, there was a knock on the door. As she opened it, (c) she was surprised to find her son standing in the doorway. He had grown thin and lean. His clothes were torn. Crying and hugging her son, she gave him clothes to change into and some food.

(C)

"Not a word of gratitude," Bahati said to herself. One day, irritated, she was tempted to stop baking extra bread, but soon changed her mind. She baked an extra loaf and kept doing good because the words of the poor old woman kept coming back to her. (d) She placed the bread on the window sill. The poor old woman took away the loaf as usual, muttering the same words.

(D)

After taking some rest, Bahati's son said, "On my way home, I was so starved that I collapsed. I saw an old woman with a loaf of bread. I begged her for a small piece of bread. But (e) she gave me the whole loaf saying my need was greater than hers." It was then that Bahati finally realized the meaning of the words of the poor old woman: "The good you do, comes back to you!"

10

주어진 글 (A)에 이어질 내용을 순서에 맞게 배열한 것으로 가장 적절한 것은?

① (B) − (D) − (C) 　② (C) − (B) − (D)

③ (C) − (D) − (B) 　④ (D) − (B) − (C)

⑤ (D) − (C) − (B)

12

윗글의 Bahati에 관한 내용으로 적절하지 <u>않은</u> 것은?

① 멀리 살고 있는 아들을 몹시 그리워했다.

② 수년간 아들의 소식을 듣지 못했다.

③ 아들에게 갈아입을 옷과 음식을 주었다.

④ 여분의 빵을 굽는 일을 그만두었다.

⑤ 결국은 노파의 말의 의미를 깨달았다.

11

밑줄 친 (a)~(e) 중에서 가리키는 대상이 나머지 넷과 <u>다른</u> 것은?

① (a) 　② (b) 　③ (c) 　④ (d) 　⑤ (e)

DAY 28

종료 시각	시 분 초	문항 번호	01	02	03	04	05	06	07	08	09	10	11	12
소요 시간	분 초	채점 결과												
초과 시간	분 초	틀린 문항 복습												

DAY 29

● 날짜 :   월   일 ● 시작 시각 :   시   분   초 ● 목표 시간 : 20분

※ 점수 표기가 없는 문항은 모두 2점입니다.

01

고2 • 2020년 6월 18번

다음 글의 목적으로 가장 적절한 것은?

Dear Mr. Stanton:

  We at the Future Music School have been providing music education to talented children for 10 years. We hold an annual festival to give our students a chance to share their music with the community and we always invite a famous musician to perform in the opening event. Your reputation as a world-class violinist precedes you and the students consider you the musician who has influenced them the most. That's why we want to ask you to perform at the opening event of the festival. It would be an honor for them to watch one of the most famous violinists of all time play at the show. It would make the festival more colorful and splendid. We look forward to receiving a positive reply.

Sincerely,
Steven Forman

① 개막 행사에서 연주를 요청하려고
② 공연 스케줄 변경을 공지하려고
③ 학교 행사 취소를 통보하려고
④ 모금 행사 참여를 독려하려고
⑤ 올해의 음악가 상 수상을 축하하려고

02

고2 • 2020년 11월 21번

밑줄 친 turns the life stories of these scientists from lead to gold가 다음 글에서 의미하는 바로 가장 적절한 것은? [3점]

  In school, there's one curriculum, one right way to study science, and one right formula that spits out the correct answer on a standardized test. Textbooks with grand titles like *The Principles of Physics* magically reveal "the principles" in three hundred pages. An authority figure then steps up to the lectern to feed us "the truth." As theoretical physicist David Gross explained in his Nobel lecture, textbooks often ignore the many alternate paths that people wandered down, the many false clues they followed, the many misconceptions they had. We learn about Newton's "laws" — as if they arrived by a grand divine visitation or a stroke of genius — but not the years he spent exploring, revising, and changing them. The laws that Newton failed to establish — most notably his experiments in alchemy, which attempted, and spectacularly failed, to turn lead into gold — don't make the cut as part of the one-dimensional story told in physics classrooms. Instead, our education system <u>turns the life stories of these scientists from lead to gold</u>.

* lectern: 강의대 ** alchemy: 연금술

① discovers the valuable relationships between scientists
② emphasizes difficulties in establishing new scientific theories
③ mixes the various stories of great scientists across the world
④ focuses more on the scientists' work than their personal lives
⑤ reveals only the scientists' success ignoring their processes and errors

03

다음 글의 요지로 가장 적절한 것은?

If you're an expert, having a high follower count on your social media accounts enhances all the work you are doing in real life. A great example is a comedian. She spends hours each day working on her skill, but she keeps being asked about her Instagram following. This is because businesses are always looking for easier and cheaper ways to market their products. A comedian with 100,000 followers can promote her upcoming show and increase the chances that people will buy tickets to come see her. This reduces the amount of money the comedy club has to spend on promoting the show and makes the management more likely to choose her over another comedian. Plenty of people are upset that follower count seems to be more important than talent, but it's really about firing on all cylinders. In today's version of show business, the business part is happening online. You need to adapt, because those who don't adapt won't make it very far.

① 성공하는 데 소셜 미디어에서의 인기가 중요하다.
② 코미디언에게 인기에 대한 지나친 집착은 독이 된다.
③ 온라인 상황과 실제 상황을 구별하는 것이 필요하다.
④ 소비자의 성향을 파악하는 것이 마케팅의 효과를 높인다.
⑤ 공연을 완성하기 위해서는 다양한 분야의 협조가 필요하다.

04

다음 도표의 내용과 일치하지 <u>않는</u> 것은?

Travel and Tourism's Contribution to GDP

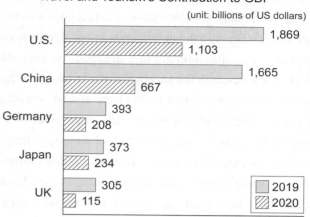

The above graph shows travel and tourism's contribution to GDP for each of the five countries in 2019 and in 2020. ① In all five countries, travel and tourism's contribution to GDP in 2020 decreased compared to the previous year. ② Both in 2019 and in 2020, the U.S. showed the largest contribution of travel and tourism to GDP among the five countries, followed by China. ③ In China, travel and tourism's contribution to GDP in 2020 was less than a third that in 2019. ④ In 2019, Germany showed a larger contribution of travel and tourism to GDP than Japan, whereas the reverse was true in 2020. ⑤ In 2020, the UK was the only country where the contribution of travel and tourism to GDP was less than $200 billion.

05 1등급 대비 고난도 2점 문제

고2·2019년 3월 28번

다음 글의 밑줄 친 부분 중, 어법상 틀린 것은?

If there's one thing koalas are good at, it's sleeping. For a long time many scientists suspected that koalas were so lethargic ① because the compounds in eucalyptus leaves kept the cute little animals in a drugged-out state. But more recent research has shown that the leaves are simply so low in nutrients ② that koalas have almost no energy. Therefore they tend to move as little as possible — and when they ③ do move, they often look as though they're in slow motion. They rest sixteen to eighteen hours a day and spend most of that unconscious. In fact, koalas spend little time thinking; their brains actually appear to ④ have shrunk over the last few centuries. The koala is the only known animal ⑤ its brain only fills half of its skull.

* lethargic: 무기력한   ** drugged-out: 몽롱한, 취한

06

고3·2021학년도 수능 30번

다음 글의 밑줄 친 부분 중, 문맥상 낱말의 쓰임이 적절하지 않은 것은?

How the bandwagon effect occurs is demonstrated by the history of measurements of the speed of light. Because this speed is the basis of the theory of relativity, it's one of the most frequently and carefully measured ① quantities in science. As far as we know, the speed hasn't changed over time. However, from 1870 to 1900, all the experiments found speeds that were too high. Then, from 1900 to 1950, the ② opposite happened — all the experiments found speeds that were too low! This kind of error, where results are always on one side of the real value, is called "bias." It probably happened because over time, experimenters subconsciously adjusted their results to ③ match what they expected to find. If a result fit what they expected, they kept it. If a result didn't fit, they threw it out. They weren't being intentionally dishonest, just ④ influenced by the conventional wisdom. The pattern only changed when someone ⑤ lacked the courage to report what was actually measured instead of what was expected.

* bandwagon effect: 편승 효과

07

다음 빈칸에 들어갈 말로 가장 적절한 것을 고르시오.

Much of the spread of fake news occurs through _____. A 2016 study from Columbia University in New York City and Inria, a French technology institute, found that 59 percent of the news from links shared on social media wasn't read first. People see an intriguing headline or photo in their news feed or on another website and then click the Share button to repost the item to their social media friends — without ever clicking through to the full article. Then they may be sharing fake news. To stop the spread of fake news, read stories before you share them. Respect your social media friends enough to know what information you are sending their way. You may discover, on close inspection, that an article you were about to share is obviously fraudulent, that it doesn't really say what the headline promises, or that you actually disagree with it.

*fraudulent: 속이는

① political campaigns
② irrational censorship
③ irresponsible sharing
④ overheated marketing
⑤ statistics manipulation

08 [1등급 대비 고난도 3점 문제]

다음 빈칸에 들어갈 말로 가장 적절한 것을 고르시오. [3점]

Deep-fried foods are tastier than bland foods, and children and adults develop a taste for such foods. Fatty foods cause the brain to release oxytocin, a powerful hormone with a calming, antistress, and relaxing influence, said to be the opposite of adrenaline, into the blood stream; hence the term "comfort foods." We may even be genetically programmed to eat too much. For thousands of years, food was very scarce. Food, along with salt, carbs, and fat, was hard to get, and the more you got, the better. All of these things are necessary nutrients in the human diet, and when their availability was limited, you could never get too much. People also had to hunt down animals or gather plants for their food, and that took a lot of calories. It's different these days. We have food at every turn — lots of those fast-food places and grocery stores with carry-out food. But that ingrained "caveman mentality" says that we can't ever get too much to eat. So craving for "unhealthy" food may _____.

① actually be our body's attempt to stay healthy
② ultimately lead to harm to the ecosystem
③ dramatically reduce our overall appetite
④ simply be the result of a modern lifestyle
⑤ partly strengthen our preference for fresh food

DAY 29

09 1등급 대비 고난도 2점 문제 고2 · 2021년 6월 36번

주어진 글 다음에 이어질 글의 순서로 가장 적절한 것을 고르시오.

Consider the story of two men quarreling in a library. One wants the window open and the other wants it closed. They argue back and forth about how much to leave it open: a crack, halfway, or three-quarters of the way.

(A) The librarian could not have invented the solution she did if she had focused only on the two men's stated positions of wanting the window open or closed. Instead, she looked to their underlying interests of fresh air and no draft.

(B) After thinking a minute, she opens wide a window in the next room, bringing in fresh air without a draft. This story is typical of many negotiations. Since the parties' problem appears to be a conflict of positions, they naturally tend to talk about positions — and often reach an impasse.

(C) No solution satisfies them both. Enter the librarian. She asks one why he wants the window open: "To get some fresh air." She asks the other why he wants it closed: "To avoid a draft."

* draft: 외풍 ** impasse: 막다름

① (A) − (C) − (B) 　② (B) − (A) − (C)
③ (B) − (C) − (A) 　④ (C) − (A) − (B)
⑤ (C) − (B) − (A)

10 고2 · 2022년 3월 39번

글의 흐름으로 보아, 주어진 문장이 들어가기에 가장 적절한 곳을 고르시오. [3점]

Although sport clubs and leagues may have a fixed supply schedule, it is possible to increase the number of consumers who watch.

A supply schedule refers to the ability of a business to change their production rates to meet the demand of consumers. Some businesses are able to increase their production level quickly in order to meet increased demand. However, sporting clubs have a fixed, or inflexible(inelastic) production capacity. (①) They have what is known as a fixed supply schedule. (②) It is worth noting that this is not the case for sales of clothing, equipment, memberships and memorabilia. (③) But clubs and teams can only play a certain number of times during their season. (④) If fans and members are unable to get into a venue, that revenue is lost forever. (⑤) For example, the supply of a sport product can be increased by providing more seats, changing the venue, extending the playing season or even through new television, radio or Internet distribution.

* memorabilia: 기념품 ** venue: 경기장

[11 ~ 12] 다음 글을 읽고, 물음에 답하시오.

U.S. commercial aviation has long had an extremely effective system for encouraging pilots to submit reports of errors. The program has resulted in numerous improvements to aviation safety. It wasn't easy to establish: pilots had severe self-induced social pressures against (a) admitting to errors. Moreover, to whom would they report them? Certainly not to their employers. Not even to the Federal Aviation Authority (FAA), for then they would probably be punished. The solution was to let the National Aeronautics and Space Administration (NASA) set up a (b) voluntary accident reporting system whereby pilots could submit semi-anonymous reports of errors they had made or observed in others.

Once NASA personnel had acquired the necessary information, they would (c) detach the contact information from the report and mail it back to the pilot. This meant that NASA no longer knew who had reported the error, which made it impossible for the airline companies or the FAA (which enforced penalties against errors) to find out who had (d) rejected the report. If the FAA had independently noticed the error and tried to invoke a civil penalty or certificate suspension, the receipt of self-report automatically exempted the pilot from punishment. When a sufficient number of similar errors had been collected, NASA would analyze them and issue reports and recommendations to the airlines and to the FAA. These reports also helped the pilots realize that their error reports were (e) valuable tools for increasing safety.

11

윗글의 제목으로 가장 적절한 것은?

① Aviation Safety Built on Anonymous Reports
② More Flexible Manuals Mean Ignored Safety
③ Great Inventions from Unexpected Mistakes
④ Controversies over New Safety Regulations
⑤ Who Is Innovating Technology in the Air?

12

밑줄 친 (a) ~ (e) 중에서 문맥상 낱말의 쓰임이 적절하지 않은 것은? [3점]

① (a)   ② (b)   ③ (c)   ④ (d)   ⑤ (e)

DAY 29

학습 Check!   ▶ 몰라서 틀린 문항 × 표기   ▶ 헷갈렸거나 찍은 문항 △ 표기   ▶ ×, △ 문항은 다시 풀고 ✔ 표기를 하세요.

종료 시각	시 분 초	문항 번호	01	02	03	04	05	06	07	08	09	10	11	12
소요 시간	분 초	채점 결과												
초과 시간	분 초	틀린 문항 복습												

[Day 29] 미니 모의고사 177

DAY 30

● 날짜 :   월   일 ● 시작 시각 :   시   분   초 ● 목표 시간 : 20분

※ 점수 표기가 없는 문항은 모두 2점입니다.

01

고2 · 2019년 11월 20번

다음 글에서 필자가 주장하는 바로 가장 적절한 것은?

Over the years, memory has been given a bad name. It has been associated with rote learning and cramming information into your brain. Educators have said that understanding is the key to learning, but how can you understand something if you can't remember it? We have all had this experience: we recognize and understand information but can't recall it when we need it. For example, how many jokes do you know? You've probably heard thousands, but you can only recall about four or five right now. There is a big difference between remembering your four jokes and recognizing or understanding thousands. Understanding doesn't create use: only when you can instantly recall what you understand, and practice using your remembered understanding, do you achieve mastery. Memory means storing what you have learned; otherwise, why would we bother learning in the first place?

① 창의력 신장을 학습 활동의 목표로 삼아야 한다.
② 배운 것을 활용하기 위해서는 내용을 기억해야 한다.
③ 기억력 저하를 예방하기 위해 자신의 일상을 기록해야 한다.
④ 자연스러운 분위기를 만들 수 있는 농담을 알고 있어야 한다.
⑤ 학습 의욕을 유지하기 위해서는 실천 가능한 계획을 세워야 한다.

02 1등급 대비 고난도 3점 문제

고2 · 2023년 6월 23번

다음 글의 주제로 가장 적절한 것은? [3점]

Education must focus on the trunk of the tree of knowledge, revealing the ways in which the branches, twigs, and leaves all emerge from a common core. Tools for thinking stem from this core, providing a common language with which practitioners in different fields may share their experience of the process of innovation and discover links between their creative activities. When the same terms are employed across the curriculum, students begin to link different subjects and classes. If they practice abstracting in writing class, if they work on abstracting in painting or drawing class, and if, in all cases, they call it abstracting, they begin to understand how to think beyond disciplinary boundaries. They see how to transform their thoughts from one mode of conception and expression to another. Linking the disciplines comes naturally when the terms and tools are presented as part of a universal imagination.

① difficulties in finding meaningful links between disciplines
② drawbacks of applying a common language to various fields
③ effects of diversifying the curriculum on students' creativity
④ necessity of using a common language to integrate the curriculum
⑤ usefulness of turning abstract thoughts into concrete expressions

03

Alice Coachman에 관한 다음 글의 내용과 일치하지 <u>않는</u> 것은?

Alice Coachman was born in 1923, in Albany, Georgia, U.S.A. Since she was unable to access athletic training facilities because of the racism of the time, she trained using what was available to her, running barefoot along the dirt roads near her home and using homemade equipment to practice her jumping. Her talent in track and field was noticeable as early as elementary school. Coachman kept practicing hard and gained attention with her achievements in several competitions during her time in high school and college. In the 1948 London Olympics, Coachman competed in the high jump, reaching 5 feet, 6.5 inches, setting both an Olympic and an American record. This accomplishment made her the first black woman to win an Olympic gold medal. She is in nine different Halls of Fame, including the U.S. Olympic Hall of Fame. Coachman died in 2014, at the age of 90 in Georgia after she had dedicated her life to education.

① 집 근처에서 맨발로 달리며 훈련했다.
② 육상 경기에서의 재능을 고등학교 때부터 보였다.
③ 런던 올림픽에서 높이뛰기 올림픽 기록과 미국 기록을 세웠다.
④ 흑인 여성 최초로 올림픽 금메달리스트가 되었다.
⑤ 9개의 명예의 전당에 올랐다.

04

다음 글의 밑줄 친 부분 중, 어법상 <u>틀린</u> 것은? [3점]

Regulations covering scientific experiments on human subjects are strict. Subjects must give their informed, written consent, and experimenters must submit their proposed experiments to thorough examination by overseeing bodies. Scientists who experiment on themselves can, functionally if not legally, avoid the restrictions ① <u>associated</u> with experimenting on other people. They can also sidestep most of the ethical issues involved: nobody, presumably, is more aware of an experiment's potential hazards than the scientist who devised ② <u>it</u>. Nonetheless, experimenting on oneself remains ③ <u>deeply</u> problematic. One obvious drawback is the danger involved; knowing that it exists ④ <u>does</u> nothing to reduce it. A less obvious drawback is the limited range of data that the experiment can generate. Human anatomy and physiology vary, in small but significant ways, according to gender, age, lifestyle, and other factors. Experimental results derived from a single subject are, therefore, of limited value; there is no way to know ⑤ <u>what</u> the subject's responses are typical or atypical of the response of humans as a group.

＊consent: 동의 ＊＊anatomy: (해부학적) 구조
＊＊＊physiology: 생리적 현상

05 1등급 대비 고난도 3점 문제

다음 글의 밑줄 친 부분 중, 문맥상 낱말의 쓰임이 적절하지 <u>않은</u> 것은? [3점]

What exactly does normal science involve? According to Thomas Kuhn it is primarily a matter of *puzzle-solving*. However successful a paradigm is, it will always ① <u>encounter</u> certain problems — phenomena which it cannot easily accommodate, or mismatches between the theory's predictions and the experimental facts. The job of the normal scientist is to try to ② <u>eliminate</u> these minor puzzles while making as few changes as possible to the paradigm. So normal science is a ③ <u>conservative</u> activity — its practitioners are not trying to make any earth-shattering discoveries, but rather just to develop and extend the existing paradigm. In Kuhn's words, 'normal science does not aim at novelties of fact or theory, and when successful finds none'. Above all, Kuhn stressed that normal scientists are not trying to *test* the paradigm. On the contrary, they accept the paradigm ④ <u>unquestioningly</u>, and conduct their research within the limits it sets. If a normal scientist gets an experimental result which ⑤ <u>corresponds</u> with the paradigm, they will usually assume that their experimental technique is faulty, not that the paradigm is wrong.

* practitioner: (어떤 일을) 실행하는 사람

06

다음 빈칸에 들어갈 말로 가장 적절한 것을 고르시오. [3점]

When Charles Darwin developed his theory of natural selection, he created a picture of the evolutionary process in which organismic adaptation was ultimately caused by competition for survival and reproduction. This biological "struggle for existence" bears considerable resemblance to the human struggle between businessmen who are striving for economic success in competitive markets. Long before Darwin published his work, social scientist Adam Smith had already considered that in business life, competition is the driving force behind economic efficiency and adaptation. It is indeed very striking how _____ the ideas are on which the founders of modern theory in evolutionary biology and economics based their main thoughts.

* organismic: 유기체의

① similar   ② confusing
③ unrealistic   ④ conventional
⑤ complex

07

다음 글에서 전체 흐름과 관계 <u>없는</u> 문장은?

The major oceans are all interconnected, so that their geographical boundaries are less clear than those of the continents. As a result, their biotas show fewer clear differences than those on land. ① The oceans themselves are continually moving because the water within each ocean basin slowly rotates. ② These moving waters carry marine organisms from place to place, and also help the dispersal of their young or larvae. ③ In other words, coastal ocean currents not only move animals much less often than expected, but they also trap animals within near-shore regions. ④ Furthermore, the gradients between the environments of different areas of ocean water mass are very gradual and often extend over wide areas that are inhabited by a great variety of organisms of differing ecological tolerances. ⑤ There are no firm boundaries within the open oceans although there may be barriers to the movement of organisms.

* biota: 생물 군집 ** gradient: 변화도

08 1등급 대비 고난도 2점 문제

글의 흐름으로 보아, 주어진 문장이 들어가기에 가장 적절한 곳을 고르시오.

> The illusion of relative movement works the other way, too.

You are in a train, standing at a station next to another train. Suddenly you seem to start moving. But then you realize that you aren't actually moving at all. (①) It is the second train that is moving in the opposite direction. (②) You think the other train has moved, only to discover that it is your own train that is moving. (③) It can be hard to tell the difference between apparent movement and real movement. (④) It's easy if your train starts with a jolt, of course, but not if your train moves very smoothly. (⑤) When your train overtakes a slightly slower train, you can sometimes fool yourself into thinking your train is still and the other train is moving slowly backwards.

* apparent: 외견상의 ** jolt: 덜컥하고 움직임

09

다음 글의 내용을 한 문장으로 요약하고자 한다. 빈칸 (A), (B)에 들어갈 말로 가장 적절한 것은?

When a child experiences painful, disappointing, or scary moments, it can be overwhelming, with intense emotions and bodily sensations flooding the right brain. When this happens, we as parents can help bring the left hemisphere into the picture so that the child can begin to understand what's happening. One of the best ways to promote this type of integration is to help retell the story of the frightening or painful experience. Bella, for instance, was nine years old when the toilet overflowed when she flushed, and the experience of watching the water rise and pour onto the floor left her unwilling to flush the toilet afterward. When Bella's father, Doug, learned about the "name it to tame it" technique, he sat down with his daughter and retold the story of the time the toilet overflowed. He allowed her to tell as much of the story as she could and helped to fill in the details. After retelling the story several times, Bella's fears lessened and eventually went away.

↓

We may enable a child to _____ (A) _____ their painful, frightening experience by having them _____ (B) _____ as much of the painful story as possible.

	(A)		(B)
①	recall	······	adapt
②	recall	······	repeat
③	overcome	······	erase
④	overcome	······	repeat
⑤	prevent	······	erase

[10~12] 다음 글을 읽고, 물음에 답하시오.

(A)

Maria Sutton was a social worker in a place where the average income was very low. Many of Maria's clients had lost their jobs when the coal industry in a nearby town collapsed. Every Christmas season, knowing how much children loved presents at Christmas, Maria tried to arrange a special visit from Santa Claus for one family. Alice, the seven-year-old daughter of Maria, was very enthusiastic about helping with (a) her mother's Christmas event.

(B)

On Christmas Eve, Maria and Alice visited Karen's house with Christmas gifts. When Karen opened the door, Maria and Alice wished the astonished woman a merry Christmas. Then Alice began to unload the gifts from the car, handing them to Karen one by one. Karen laughed in disbelief, and said she hoped she would one day be able to do something similar for someone else in need. On her way home, Maria said to Alice, "God multiplied (b) your gift."

(C)

This year's lucky family was a 25-year-old mother named Karen and her 3-year-old son, who she was raising by herself. However, things went wrong. Two weeks before Christmas Day, a representative from a local organization called Maria to say that the aid she had requested for Karen had fallen through. No Santa Claus. No presents. Maria saw the cheer disappear from Alice's face at the news. After hearing this, (c) she ran to her room.

(D)

When Alice returned, her face was set with determination. She counted out the coins from her piggy bank: $4.30. "Mom," she told Maria, "(d) I know it's not much. But maybe this will buy a present for the kid." Maria gave her daughter a lovely hug. The next day, Maria told her coworkers about her daughter's latest project. To (e) her surprise, staff members began to open their purses. The story of Alice's gift had spread beyond Maria's office, and Maria was able to raise $300 — plenty for a Christmas gift for Karen and her son.

10

주어진 글 (A)에 이어질 내용을 순서에 맞게 배열한 것으로 가장 적절한 것은?

① (B) − (D) − (C) ② (C) − (B) − (D)
③ (C) − (D) − (B) ④ (D) − (B) − (C)
⑤ (D) − (C) − (B)

11

밑줄 친 (a)~(e) 중에서 가리키는 대상이 나머지 넷과 다른 것은?

① (a)　② (b)　③ (c)　④ (d)　⑤ (e)

12

윗글에 관한 내용으로 적절하지 않은 것은?

① Maria는 평균 소득이 매우 낮은 지역의 사회복지사였다.
② 크리스마스 전날 Karen은 선물을 받았다.
③ Karen은 세 살 된 아들을 키우고 있었다.
④ Maria는 지역 단체 대표의 연락을 받지 못했다.
⑤ Maria는 300달러를 모금할 수 있었다.

MEMO

DAY 01
01② 02① 03② 04③ 05④ 06④
07① 08① 09③ 10⑤ 11① 12⑤

DAY 02
01① 02⑤ 03① 04④ 05② 06⑤
07① 08③ 09② 10⑤ 11⑤ 12④

DAY 03
01① 02⑤ 03⑤ 04④ 05⑤ 06③
07① 08① 09③ 10② 11④ 12⑤

DAY 04
01④ 02③ 03② 04⑤ 05④ 06①
07① 08③ 09④ 10④ 11③ 12④

DAY 05
01② 02④ 03⑤ 04③ 05④ 06④
07③ 08⑤ 09④ 10⑤ 11② 12④

DAY 06
01① 02① 03③ 04④ 05④ 06③
07④ 08⑤ 09② 10④ 11② 12②

DAY 07
01③ 02③ 03① 04③ 05③ 06②
07① 08① 09③ 10③ 11② 12③

DAY 08
01① 02② 03⑤ 04④ 05⑤ 06③
07② 08⑤ 09① 10④ 11② 12③

DAY 09
01① 02② 03① 04② 05④ 06③
07④ 08④ 09④ 10③ 11⑤ 12⑤

DAY 10
01③ 02⑤ 03② 04⑤ 05⑤ 06②
07② 08③ 09① 10④ 11⑤ 12③

DAY 11
01② 02④ 03③ 04⑤ 05③ 06④
07⑤ 08④ 09③ 10① 11① 12⑤

DAY 12
01③ 02⑤ 03② 04⑤ 05⑤ 06④
07① 08⑤ 09① 10② 11③ 12⑤

DAY 13
01① 02③ 03① 04④ 05⑤ 06②
07② 08④ 09③ 10② 11② 12⑤

DAY 14
01① 02⑤ 03② 04③ 05⑤ 06④
07① 08③ 09② 10⑤ 11④ 12⑤

DAY 15
01② 02② 03③ 04③ 05④ 06③
07① 08② 09④ 10③ 11⑤ 12④

DAY 16
01⑤ 02① 03① 04⑤ 05③ 06①
07② 08④ 09① 10⑤ 11④ 12④

DAY 17
01② 02⑤ 03② 04③ 05② 06③
07⑤ 08⑤ 09③ 10⑤ 11③ 12②

DAY 18
01⑤ 02⑤ 03⑤ 04④ 05② 06⑤
07① 08① 09① 10④ 11④ 12⑤

DAY 19
01② 02⑤ 03⑤ 04⑤ 05④ 06⑤
07② 08⑤ 09④ 10④ 11④ 12②

DAY 20
01④ 02① 03② 04④ 05② 06⑤
07① 08④ 09① 10② 11⑤ 12⑤

DAY 21
01⑤ 02① 03② 04③ 05③ 06①
07② 08④ 09④ 10③ 11③ 12④

DAY 22
01② 02③ 03③ 04② 05④ 06④
07② 08④ 09① 10⑤ 11④ 12②

DAY 23
01② 02③ 03⑤ 04⑤ 05③ 06⑤
07① 08③ 09③ 10② 11① 12⑤

DAY 24
01⑤ 02⑤ 03③ 04③ 05② 06③
07② 08④ 09① 10④ 11② 12③

DAY 25
01① 02② 03⑤ 04④ 05⑤ 06⑤
07① 08③ 09② 10② 11③ 12④

DAY 26
01① 02① 03③ 04③ 05③ 06①
07① 08④ 09① 10② 11③ 12②

DAY 27
01⑤ 02② 03⑤ 04④ 05④ 06⑤
07② 08① 09⑤ 10⑤ 11① 12⑤

DAY 28
01① 02① 03⑤ 04① 05② 06①
07④ 08③ 09① 10② 11⑤ 12④

DAY 29
01① 02⑤ 03① 04③ 05⑤ 06⑤
07③ 08① 09⑤ 10① 11① 12④

DAY 30
01② 02④ 03② 04⑤ 05⑤ 06①
07③ 08② 09④ 10③ 11⑤ 12④

수능기출 전국연합 학력평가
하루 20분 30일 완성

30 Days completed
2030
하루 20분   30일 완성

- 최신 **7개년 수능·모의평가** 및 **고2 학력평가** 문제 중 우수 문항 총 **360제** 수록
- 가볍게 하루 **12문제**를 **20분**씩 학습하는 [30일 완성] mini 모의고사
- 매일 영어 영역 [전 유형을 골고루] 풀 수 있는 체계적인 문항 배치
- 지문의 이해를 돕는 [구문 풀이와 자세한 해설] 및 고난도 문제 해결 꿀팁

고2
영어

해설편

수능 모의고사 전문 출판
입시플라이

DAY 01
01② 02① 03② 04③ 05④ 06④
07① 08① 09③ 10⑤ 11① 12⑤

DAY 02
01① 02⑤ 03① 04④ 05② 06⑤
07① 08③ 09② 10⑤ 11⑤ 12④

DAY 03
01① 02⑤ 03⑤ 04④ 05⑤ 06③
07① 08① 09③ 10② 11④ 12⑤

DAY 04
01④ 02③ 03② 04⑤ 05④ 06①
07① 08③ 09④ 10④ 11③ 12③

DAY 05
01② 02④ 03⑤ 04③ 05④ 06④
07③ 08⑤ 09④ 10⑤ 11② 12③

DAY 06
01① 02① 03③ 04④ 05④ 06③
07④ 08⑤ 09② 10③ 11② 12②

DAY 07
01③ 02③ 03① 04② 05③ 06②
07① 08① 09③ 10③ 11② 12③

DAY 08
01① 02② 03⑤ 04④ 05⑤ 06③
07② 08⑤ 09① 10④ 11② 12③

DAY 09
01① 02② 03① 04② 05④ 06③
07④ 08④ 09④ 10③ 11⑤ 12⑤

DAY 10
01③ 02⑤ 03② 04⑤ 05⑤ 06②
07② 08③ 09① 10④ 11⑤ 12③

DAY 11
01② 02④ 03③ 04⑤ 05③ 06④
07⑤ 08④ 09③ 10① 11① 12⑤

DAY 12
01③ 02⑤ 03② 04⑤ 05⑤ 06④
07① 08⑤ 09① 10② 11③ 12⑤

DAY 13
01① 02③ 03① 04④ 05⑤ 06②
07② 08④ 09③ 10② 11② 12⑤

DAY 14
01① 02⑤ 03② 04③ 05⑤ 06④
07① 08③ 09② 10⑤ 11④ 12⑤

DAY 15
01② 02② 03③ 04③ 05④ 06③
07① 08② 09④ 10③ 11⑤ 12④

DAY 16
01⑤ 02① 03① 04⑤ 05③ 06①
07② 08④ 09① 10⑤ 11④ 12④

DAY 17
01② 02⑤ 03② 04③ 05② 06③
07⑤ 08⑤ 09③ 10① 11③ 12②

DAY 18
01⑤ 02⑤ 03① 04④ 05② 06⑤
07① 08① 09① 10④ 11④ 12⑤

DAY 19
01② 02⑤ 03⑤ 04⑤ 05④ 06⑤
07② 08⑤ 09④ 10④ 11④ 12②

DAY 20
01④ 02① 03② 04④ 05② 06⑤
07① 08④ 09① 10② 11⑤ 12⑤

DAY 21
01⑤ 02① 03② 04③ 05③ 06①
07② 08④ 09④ 10③ 11③ 12④

DAY 22
01② 02③ 03③ 04② 05④ 06④
07② 08④ 09① 10⑤ 11④ 12②

DAY 23
01② 02③ 03⑤ 04⑤ 05③ 06⑤
07① 08③ 09③ 10② 11① 12⑤

DAY 24
01⑤ 02⑤ 03③ 04③ 05② 06③
07② 08④ 09① 10② 11② 12③

DAY 25
01① 02② 03⑤ 04④ 05⑤ 06⑤
07② 08③ 09② 10② 11③ 12④

DAY 26
01① 02① 03② 04③ 05③ 06①
07① 08④ 09① 10② 11③ 12②

DAY 27
01⑤ 02② 03⑤ 04④ 05④ 06⑤
07② 08① 09⑤ 10⑤ 11① 12⑤

DAY 28
01① 02① 03⑤ 04① 05② 06①
07④ 08③ 09① 10④ 11⑤ 12④

DAY 29
01① 02⑤ 03① 04③ 05⑤ 06⑤
07③ 체① 09⑤ 10⑤ 11① 12④

DAY 30
01② 02④ 03② 04⑤ 05⑤ 06①
07③ 08② 09④ 10③ 11⑤ 12④

하루 20분 30일 완성
미니모의고사 고2 영어
해설편

Contents

수록된 정답률은 실제와 차이가 있을
수 있습니다. 문제 난도를 파악하는데
참고용으로 활용하시기 바랍니다.

DAY 01 · 20분 미니 모의고사

01 ②	02 ①	03 ②	04 ③	05 ④
06 ④	07 ①	08 ①	09 ③	10 ⑤
11 ①	12 ⑤			

---

01 마을 공예가들에게 부스 대여 안내   정답률 85% | 정답 ②

다음 글의 목적으로 가장 적절한 것은?

① 지역 예술가를 위한 정기 후원을 요청하려고
☑ 공예품 박람회의 부스 예약을 안내하려고
③ 대여 물품의 반환 방법을 설명하려고
④ 지역 예술가가 만든 물품을 홍보하려고
⑤ 지역 행사 일정의 변경 사항을 공지하려고

[본문 해석]

친애하는 Greenville의 공예가들에게,
5월 25일 오후 1시부터 6시까지 열리는 연례 공예품 박람회를 위해서, Greenville 커뮤니티 센터에서는 지난 몇 년간처럼 대여 부스 공간을 제공합니다. 공간을 예약하기 위해서는 저희 웹사이트를 방문하여 4월 20일까지 신청서를 작성해 주세요. 대여 요금은 50달러입니다. 대여료로 받은 모든 돈은 연중 예정된 활동을 지원하는데 사용됩니다. 우리는 모든 이용할 수 있는 공간이 곧 모두 예약될 것으로 예상되니 놓치지 마세요. 박람회에서 뵙기를 희망합니다.

Why? 왜 정답일까?

마을 공예가에게 부스 대여와 함께 박람회를 홍보하는 내용(For the annual Crafts Fair on May 25 from 1 p.m. to 6 p.m., the Greenville Community Center is providing booth spaces to rent as in previous years.)이므로, 글의 목적으로 가장 적절한 것은 ② '공예품 박람회의 부스 예약을 안내하려고'이다.

- craft ⓝ 수공예품
- book ⓥ 예약하다
- reserve ⓥ 예약하다
- fair ⓝ 전시회

구문 풀이

5행 To reserve your space, please visit our website and complete
  to부정사(부사적) · 동사(병렬1) · 동사(병렬2)
a registration form by April 20.

---

02 자신을 위한 시간이 필요함을 느끼기   정답률 90% | 정답 ①

다음 글에서 필자가 주장하는 바로 가장 적절한 것은?

☑ 나를 위한 시간의 중요성을 인식해야 한다.
② 자신의 잘못을 성찰하는 자세를 가져야 한다.
③ 어려운 일이라고 해서 처음부터 회피해서는 안 된다.
④ 사회의 건강과 행복을 위하여 타인과 연대해야 한다.
⑤ 급변하는 사회에서 가치 판단을 신속하게 할 수 있어야 한다.

[본문 해석]

우리는 보통 정말로 신경을 꺼야 할 때만 휴식을 취하고, 이러한 상황이 발생할 때 우리는 종종 지나치게 피곤하거나 아프거나 회복해야 한다. 나를 위한 시간은 '압도감, 스트레스, 피로감' 뿐만 아니라 '현실 도피, 죄책감, 후회'와의 부정적인 연상에 의해 복잡해진다. 이러한 모든 부정적인 함축은 우리가 그것을 피하려는 경향이 있음을 의미한다. 나는 이제 나를 위한 시간의 중요성에 관한 당신의 인식을 바꾸고, 당신이 이것을 건강과 행복에 필수적인 것으로 간주해야 한다고 설득하고자 한다. 이것을 당신 자신을 위해 일부 시간을 할애하는 것에 대한 허락으로 받아 들여라! 우리가 선택하는 일을 할 시간이 필요하다는 것은 지나치게 연결되고 압도적이며 지나치게 자극적인 세상에서 점점 절박해지고 있다.

Why? 왜 정답일까?

'Well, I am about to change your perception of the importance of me time, to persuade you that you should view it as vital for your health and wellbeing.' 이후로 자신을 위한 시간이 부정적인 것이 아니라 건강과 행복에 실로 중요한 요소임을 깨달아야 한다는 내용이 이어지고 있다. 따라서 필자가 주장하는 바로 가장 적절한 것은 ① '나를 위한 시간의 중요성을 인식해야 한다.'이다.

- complicated ⓐ 복잡한
- regret ⓝ 후회, 유감
- set aside ~을 따로 두다, 마련하다
- escapism ⓝ 현실 도피
- steer clear of ~을 피하다, 가까이 가지 않다
- overstimulate ⓥ 과도하게 자극하다

구문 풀이

11행 Our need for time in which to do what we choose is
  주어 · = when · 동사(단수)
increasingly urgent in an overconnected, overwhelmed, and overstimulated world.

---

03 정보 공개의 중요한 이점   정답률 61% | 정답 ②

다음 글의 주제로 가장 적절한 것은? [3점]

① steps to make public information accessible to customers
  공공의 정보를 소비자가 이용할 수 있게 하는 절차
☑ benefits of publicizing information to ensure free choices
  자유로운 선택을 보장하기 위해 정보를 공개하는 것의 이점
③ strategies for companies to increase profits in a free market
  기업들이 자유 시장에서 이윤을 늘리는 전략들
④ necessities of identifying and analyzing current industry trends
  현재 산업 동향을 파악하고 분석할 필요성
⑤ effects of diversified markets on reasonable customer choices
  다양화된 시장이 합리적인 고객 선택에 미치는 영향

[본문 해석]

공개의 중요한 이점은 더 공세적인 형태의 규제와는 반대로 자유 시장의 작용에 대한 유연성과 존중이다. 규제하는 명령은 무딘 칼이어서, 그것들은 다양성을 무시하는 경향이 있으며, 의도하지 않은 심각한 역효과를 발생시킬 수도 있다. 예를 들어, 가전제품에 대한 에너지 효율 요건은 덜 잘 작동하거나 소비자가 원하지 않는 특성을 가진 제품을 만들어 낼 수도 있다. 반대로 정보 제공은 선택의 자유를 존중한다. 자동차 제조업체가 자동차의 안전 특성을 측정하고 공개해야 한다면, 잠재적인 자동차 구매자는 안전에 대한 우려를 가격과 스타일 같은 다른 속성과 맞바꿀 수 있다(가격과 스타일은 올라도 안전은 더 보장받을 수 있다). 식당 손님들에게 식사에 들어 있는 칼로리를 알려주면, 살을 빼고 싶은 사람들은 그 정보를 이용할 수 있고, 칼로리에 신경 쓰지 않는 사람들은 영향 받지 않은 채로 있게 된다. 공개는 개인 의사 결정의 자율성(과 품질)을 방해하지 않으며, 오히려 촉진할 것이다.

Why? 왜 정답일까?

첫 문장에서 언급하듯이 정보 공개의 이점을 설명하는 글이다. 글 중반부 이후로 정보 공개는 선택의 자유를 존중하며(Information provision ~ respects freedom of choice.), 그렇기에 개인 의사 결정의 자율성과 품질을 방해하지 않고 촉진할 수 있다(Disclosure does not interfere with, and should even promote, the autonomy (and quality) of individual decision-making.)는 내용이 제시된다. 따라서 글의 주제로 가장 적절한 것은 ② '자유로운 선택을 보장하기 위해 정보를 공개하는 것의 이점(benefits of publicizing information to ensure free choices)'이다.

- disclosure ⓝ 공개, 폭로
- regulation ⓝ 규제
- blunt ⓐ (끝이) 무딘
- adverse ⓐ 거스르는
- measure ⓥ 측정하다
- attribute ⓝ 특성, 속성
- unaffected ⓐ 영향받지 않는
- as opposed to ~와는 달리
- mandate ⓝ 명령
- neglect ⓥ 무시하다, 도외시하다
- requirement ⓝ (필수)요건
- safety concern 안전에 대한 우려
- lose weight 살을 빼다
- strategy ⓝ 전략

구문 풀이

13행 If restaurant customers are informed of the calories in their
  「A + be informed of + B : A에게 B를 알려주다」
meals, those who want to lose weight can make use of the information,
  ~한 사람들
leaving {those who are unconcerned about calories} unaffected.
  분사구문(그리고 ~하다) · 목적어 · 목적격 보어

---

04 Carol Ryrie Brink의 생애   정답률 93% | 정답 ③

Carol Ryrie Brink에 관한 다음 글의 내용과 일치하지 않는 것은?

① 할머니에 의해 길러졌다.
② Moscow에서 만났던 수학 교수와 결혼했다.

✔ 자녀가 태어나기 전에 어린이 이야기를 쓰기 시작했다.
④ 1934년에 그녀의 첫 번째 소설이 출간되었다.
⑤ *Caddie Woodlawn*으로 Newbery 상을 받았다.

[본문 해석]

「1895년에 태어난 Carol Ryrie Brink는 8살 때 고아가 되었고 할머니에 의해 길러졌다.」 그녀의 할머니의 삶과 스토리텔링 능력은 그녀의 글쓰기에 영감을 주었다. 「그녀는 수년 전 Idaho주 Moscow에서 만났던 젊은 수학 교수인 Raymond Woodard Brink와 결혼했다.」 그들의 아들과 딸이 태어난 후 경력 초기에 「그녀는 어린이 이야기를 쓰기 시작했고」, 연간 단편 소설집을 편집했다. 「그녀와 그녀의 남편은 프랑스에서 수년간 살았고」, 그녀의 첫 번째 소설인 *Anything Can Happen on the River*가 1934년에 출판되었다. 그 후, 그녀는 어린이들과 어른들을 위해 30권 이상의 소설과 논픽션을 썼다. 「그녀는 *Caddie Woodlawn*으로 1936년에 Newbery 상을 받았다.」 ──「：⑤의 근거 일치

Why? 왜 정답일까?

'After their son and daughter were born, early in her career, she started to write children's stories ~'에서 Carol Ryrie Brink는 아들과 딸이 태어난 이후 어린이 이야기를 쓰기 시작했다고 하므로, 내용과 일치하지 않는 것은 ③ '자녀가 태어나기 전에 어린이 이야기를 쓰기 시작했다.'이다.

Why? 왜 오답일까?

① '~ raised by her grandmother.'의 내용과 일치한다.
② 'She married Raymond Woodard Brink, a young mathematics professor she had met in Moscow, ~'의 내용과 일치한다.
④ '~ her first novel *Anything Can Happen on the River* was published in 1934.'의 내용과 일치한다.
⑤ 'She received the Newbery Award in 1936 for *Caddie Woodlawn*.'의 내용과 일치한다.

- **orphan** ⓥ 고아로 만들다 ⓝ 고아
- **professor** ⓝ 교수
- **spend A ~ing** ~하는 데 A를 쓰다
- **inspire** ⓥ 영감을 주다
- **edit** ⓥ (글 등을 발간할 수 있게) 수정하다
- **publish** ⓥ 출판하다

구문 풀이

3행 She married Raymond Woodard Brink, a young mathematics
〔동격(= Raymond Woodard Brink)〕
professor [(whom) she had met in Moscow, Idaho many years before].
생략(목적격 관·대)

05 고양이가 액체인가 고체인가에 관한 연구 정답률 49% | 정답 ④

다음 글의 밑줄 친 부분 중, 어법상 틀린 것은? [3점]

[본문 해석]

고양이는 액체일까 고체일까? 이는 '사람들을 웃긴 다음 생각을 하게 만드는' 연구에 경의를 표하는, 노벨상의 패러디인 이그노벨상을 과학자가 타게 할 수 있는 종류의 질문이다. 하지만 Paris Diderot 대학의 물리학자인 Marc-Antoine Fardin은 이를 염두에 두고서 집고양이가 액체처럼 흐물거리며 움직이는지를 알아내는 데 착수한 것은 아니었다. Fardin은 털로 덮인 이 애완동물이 물 같은 액체와 마찬가지로, 그들이 들어가 앉아 있는 용기의 모양에 맞게 조절할 수 있다는 것을 알아냈다. 그래서 그는 고양이가 꽃병 또는 욕조의 공간을 채우는 데 걸리는 시간을 계산하기 위해 물질의 변형을 다루는 물리학의 한 분야인 유동학을 적용했다. 결론은? 고양이는 환경에 따라 액체도 될 수 있고 고체도 될 수 있다. 작은 상자 안의 고양이는 그 모든 공간을 채우며 액체처럼 행동할 것이다. 하지만 물로 가득 찬 욕조의 고양이는 그것과의 접촉을 최소화하려고 노력하면서 고체와 매우 유사하게 움직일 것이다.

Why? 왜 정답일까?

앞에 주절이 나온 뒤 분사구문이 이어지고 있는데, 뒤에 all the space라는 목적어가 있고, 주어인 a cat이 용기를 '채우는' 주체이므로 능동을 나타내는 현재분사 filling을 써야 한다. 따라서 어법상 틀린 것은 ④이다.

Why? 왜 오답일까?

① 'it is ~ that' 강조구문의 that이다.
② 앞에 나온 동사 adapt to를 꾸미는 부사로서 similarly를 쓴 것은 어법상 맞다.
③ 'it takes + 시간 + 의미상 주어 + to부정사' 구문이다.

⑤ and 앞의 동사원형 try와 병렬을 이루는 말로서 동사원형인 behave를 쓴 것은 어법 상 맞다.

- **set out** 착수하다, 시작하다
- **adapt to** ~에 맞게 조절하다, 적응하다
- **fluid** ⓝ 유동체, 유체(액체·기체)
- **branch** ⓝ 분야
- **take up** (공간이나 시간을) 채우다, 차지하다
- **bathtub** ⓝ 욕조
- **furry** ⓐ 털로 뒤덮인
- **similarly to** ~와 마찬가지로
- **rheology** ⓝ 유동학
- **deformation** ⓝ 변형, 기형
- **circumstances** ⓝ 환경, 상황

구문 풀이

4행 But it wasn't with this in mind that Marc-Antoine Fardin,
「it is + 강조하는 말 + that + 나머지 문장 : 강조구문」 　주어
(a physicist at Paris Diderot University), set out to find out whether
( ) : 동격 　　　　　　　　　 동사 　　~인지 아닌지
house cats flow.

06 세부 사항의 망각 정답률 52% | 정답 ④

다음 글의 밑줄 친 부분 중, 문맥상 낱말의 쓰임이 적절하지 **않은** 것은?

[본문 해석]

우리가 가치 있는 정보의 조각들을 기억할 수 있기 위해서 우리의 뇌는 조준되면서도 통제된 방식으로 ① 잊어야만 한다. 예를 들어 여러분은 학교에서의 맨 첫날을 기억할 수 있는가? 여러분은 아마도 크레용과 연필을 필통에 넣는 것 같은 주목할 만한 심상 한두 개를 머릿속에 가지고 있을 것이다. 하지만 그것은 아마도 ② 세부 사항의 범위일 것이다. 명백히 중요하지 않은 그러한 추가적인 세부 사항들은 여러분이 그 상황을 계속 기억하려고 할수록 뇌에서 적극적으로 삭제된다. 이것의 이유는 뇌가 주요 메시지(가령, 학교 첫날이 좋았다)를 전달할 수 있는 한 모든 세부 사항을 기억하는 것을 ③ 가치 있다고 여기지 않기 때문이다. 사실 연구에 따르면 주기억을 저해하는 경향이 있는 중요하지 않거나 사소한 기억 내용을 담당하는 영역을 뇌가 적극적으로 ④ 강화한다(→ 억제한다)고 한다. 시간이 지나면서 그 사소한 세부 사항들은 점점 더 사라지지만, 그래도 이것은 결국 과거의 가장 중요한 메시지들을 ⑤ 선명하게 하는 데 도움이 된다.

Why? 왜 정답일까?

주기억에 도움이 되지 않는 세부 사항은 점점 적극적으로 잊혀 간다는 핵심 내용으로 보아, ④가 포함된 문장은 세부 사항에 대한 기억을 담당하는 뇌 영역이 '강화되기'보다는 더 '약해진다'는 의미를 나타내야 한다. 따라서 strengthens를 controls로 고쳐야 한다. 문맥상 낱말의 쓰임이 적절하지 않은 것은 ④이다.

- **retain** ⓥ 지니다, 보유하다
- **noteworthy** ⓐ 주목할 만한
- **specific** ⓝ 세부 사항, 구체적인 것
- **convey** ⓥ 전달하다
- **insignificant** ⓐ 중요하지 않은
- **sharpen** ⓥ 선명하게 하다, 연마하다
- **recall** ⓥ 기억하다, 회상하다
- **extent** ⓝ 정도, 범위
- **apparently** [ad] 명백히
- **responsible for** ~을 담당하는, 책임지는
- **disturb** ⓥ 저해하다, 방해하다

구문 풀이

10행 The reason for this is that the brain does not consider it
　　　　　　　　　　　　　　　　 5형식 동사 가목적어
valuable to remember all of the details as long as it is able to
목적격 보어 　진목적어 　　　　　　　　 접속사(~하는 한)
convey the main message (i.e., your first day of school was great).

07 과일이 당분으로 과당을 선택한 이유 정답률 48% | 정답 ①

다음 빈칸에 들어갈 말로 가장 적절한 것을 고르시오. [3점]

✔ full - 배가 부르다
② strong - 튼튼하다
③ tired - 피곤하다
④ dangerous - 위험하다
⑤ hungry - 배가 고프다

[본문 해석]

포식자가 과일을 섭취하기에 적절한 시기는 언제인가? 식물은 포식자에게 과일이 익었음을 알려주기 위해 과일의 색깔을 이용하며, 이는 씨의 껍질이 딱딱해졌음을, 그리하여 당도가 최고에 이르렀음을 의미한다. 놀랍게도, 식물은 과일의 당분으로서 포도당 대신 과당을 만들기로 선택해왔다. 포도당은 영장류와 인간의 인슐린 수치를 높여서, 처음에는 배고픔을 막는 호르몬인 렙틴의 수치를 높이지만, 과당은 그렇지 않다. 그 결과 포식자는 결코 배가 부르다는 일반

적인 메시지를 받지 못한다. 그것이 포식자와 먹이에게 상호 이익이 된다. 동물은 더 많은 열량을 얻고, 그것이 계속해서 더 많은 과일을, 따라서 더 많은 씨를 먹기 때문에 식물은 더 많은 후손을 퍼뜨릴 더 높은 가능성을 얻는다.

Why? 왜 정답일까?

'Glucose raises insulin levels in primates and humans, which initially raises levels of leptin, a hunger—blocking hormone—but fructose does not.'에서 포도당과는 달리 과당은 배고픔을 막는 호르몬 분비 증가를 유도하지 않는다고 설명하는 것으로 보아, 빈칸에는 동물이 이로 인해 '배부름'을 느끼지 못한다는 의미를 완성하는 ① '배가 부르다'가 들어가야 적절하다. 마지막 두 문장은 이로 인해 동물이 계속해서 과일을 먹고 결과적으로 과일의 씨도 더 많이 먹게 되므로 과일이 번식할 가능성을 높여준다는 결론을 제시하고 있다.

- predator ⓝ 포식자
- harden ⓥ 딱딱해지다
- at one's height 최고조에 이른
- manufacture ⓥ 생산하다
- glucose ⓝ 포도당
- distribute ⓥ 퍼뜨리다, 분포시키다
- ripe ⓐ (과일 등이) 다 익은
- content ⓝ 함량
- incredibly ⓐⓓ 놀랍게도, 믿기 힘들게도
- fructose ⓝ 과당
- initially ⓐⓓ 처음에는

구문 풀이

2행 The plant uses the color of the fruit to signal to predators
→ to signal의 목적어(선행사)   목적(~하기 위해)
that it is ripe, which means that the seed's hull has hardened — and
계속적 용법 접속사(~것)   주어1   동사1(현재완료)
therefore the sugar content is at its height.
주어2   동사2

★★★ 1등급 대비 고난도 3점 문제

08 일반 전문직과 저널리즘의 차이점   정답률 32% | 정답 ①

다음 빈칸에 들어갈 말로 가장 적절한 것을 고르시오. [3점]

✓① its lack of independence – 그것의 독립성의 부족
② the constant search for truth – 지속적인 진리 추구
③ the disregard of public opinion – 여론의 무시
④ its balance of income and faith – 수입과 신념의 균형
⑤ its overconfidence in its social influence – 사회적 영향에 대한 과신

[본문 해석]

직업으로서의 저널리즘에서 특이한 점은 그것의 독립성의 부족이다. 이론적으로, 의학이나 성직자처럼 고전적인 전문직에 종사하는 사람들은 머리와 손 안에 생산 수단을 지니고 있으므로, 회사나 고용주를 위해 일할 필요가 없다. 그들은 고객이나 환자로부터 직접 수입을 끌어낼 수 있다. 게다가, 전문직 종사자들은 지식을 보유하고 있기 때문에, 고객은 이들에게 의존한다. 언론인들은 지식을 보유하고 있지만, 그것은 본질적으로 이론적이지 않다. 어떤 사람들은 환자들이 의사들에게 의존하는 것과 같은 방식으로 대중이 언론인들에게 의존한다고 주장할지도 모르지만, 실제로 언론인은 일반적으로 뉴스 기관을 위해 일해야만 대중들에게 봉사할 수 있으며, 그 기관은 그 사람을 마음대로 해고할 수 있다. 언론인들의 수입은 대중이 아닌, 고용한 뉴스 기관에 의존하는데, 이 기관들은 종종 광고주들로부터 수익의 대부분을 얻는다.

Why? 왜 정답일까?

마지막 두 문장(~ but in practice a journalist can serve the public usually only by working for a news organization, which can fire her or him at will. Journalists' income depends not on the public, but on the employing news organization, ~)에서, 언론인은 고전적인 전문직과는 달리 지식을 보유하고 있어도 독립적이지 못한 채 자신을 고용한 뉴스 기관을 위해 일해야 한다고 설명한다. 따라서 빈칸에 들어갈 말로 가장 적절한 것은 ① '그것의 독립성의 부족'이다.

- practitioner ⓝ 전문직 종사자, 현역
- means of production 생산 수단
- theoretical ⓐ 이론적인
- at will 마음대로
- disregard ⓝ 무시
- clergy ⓝ 성직자
- draw A from B A를 B로부터 끌어내다
- in nature 본질적으로
- derive A from B A를 B로부터 얻다
- overconfidence ⓝ 과신

구문 풀이

1행 {What is unusual about journalism as a profession} is its
[ ] : 주어(명사절)   전치사(~로서) 동사(단수)
lack of independence.

★★ 문제 해결 꿀~팁 ★★

▶ 많이 틀린 이유는?
저널리스트를 설명하는 글 중후반부에 the public이 많이 등장하므로, 얼핏 보면 public이 포함된 ③이 정답처럼 보인다. 하지만 저널리스트들이 '대중의 의견을 무시'한다는 내용은 글 어디에도 없다.

▶ 문제 해결 방법은?
전문직과 저널리스트를 구별하는 부분을 잘 봐야 한다. 전문직은 자기 분야에 대한 전문성과 지식을 인정받기 때문에, 회사를 위해서 일할 필요가 없으며 의뢰인도 이들의 지식을 신뢰한다는 내용이 글 중반까지 나온다. 하지만 'Journalists hold knowledge, ~' 이후로는 저널리스트들의 상황이 '다르다'는 내용이 주를 이룬다. 이들은 회사에 '종속되어' 일하므로 '업무 독립성에 제약이 있다'는 것이다.

09 간호사들의 중간자적 역할   정답률 54% | 정답 ③

다음 글에서 전체 흐름과 관계 없는 문장은?

[본문 해석]

간호사들은 정신 건강 관리 체계에서 중추적인 역할을 맡고 있으며 의사소통망의 중심에 위치해 있는데, 부분적으로는 그들의 환자들과의 높은 접촉 정도뿐만 아니라 다른 전문직 종사자들과 잘 발달된 관계를 유지하기 때문이다. ① 이런 이유로 간호사들은 여러 학문 분야가 관련된 의사소통에서 중요한 역할을 한다. ② 그들은 다양한 전문직 종사자들 집단과 환자와 보호자 집단 사이에서 중개 역할을 한다. ③ 정신건강 관리 전문직 종사자들은 법적으로 자신의 환자의 사생활을 보호하기로 되어 있어, 그들은 치료에 필요한 것에 관해 말하기를 꺼린다기보다도, 말할 수 없는 것일지도 모른다. ④ 이것은 정신 건강 상의 문제를 이해하는 다양한 방식을 가진 사람들에게 납득 가능하고 이해 가능한 언어로 집단 간 의사소통을 번역하는 것을 포함한다. ⑤ 이것은 고도로 민감하고 숙련된 작업이며 대안적 시각에 대한 높은 수준의 관심과 높은 수준의 의사소통 이해를 요구한다.

Why? 왜 정답일까?

간호사들은 여러 분과 간의 소통, 의료인과 환자 간의 소통 등에서 중요한 역할을 한다는 내용의 글이다. ①, ②는 간호사들이 주로 중간자적 역할을 담당한다는 내용을, ④, ⑤는 그 역할의 구체적 내용을 제시하지만, ③은 환자의 사생활 보호에 관해 언급하며 주제에서 벗어난다. 따라서 전체 흐름과 관계 없는 문장은 ③이다.

- pivotal ⓐ 핵심적인
- communication ⓝ 의사소통
- well-developed 잘 발달된 [다듬어진]
- crucial ⓐ 중요한
- mediate ⓥ 중재하다
- be bound to ~하게 되어 있다
- translate ⓥ 번역하다
- comprehensible ⓐ 이해 가능한
- skilled ⓐ 숙련된, 노련한
- structure ⓝ 구조, 체계
- contact ⓝ 접촉, 연락
- professional ⓝ 전문직 종사자
- interdisciplinary ⓐ 여러 학문 분야가 관련된
- legally ⓐⓓ 법적으로
- unwilling ⓐ ~하려 하지 않는, 내키지 않는
- acceptable ⓐ 용인되는
- sensitive ⓐ 민감한, 예민한
- alternative ⓐ 대안이 되는

구문 풀이

12행 This involves translating communication between groups
동사   목적어(동명사)
into language [that is acceptable and comprehensible to people
선행사 주격 관·대   선행사
[who have different ways of understanding mental health problems]].
주격 관·대

★★★ 1등급 대비 고난도 2점 문제

10 광고를 하는 이유   정답률 33% | 정답 ⑤

주어진 글 다음에 이어질 글의 순서로 가장 적절한 것을 고르시오.

① (A) – (C) – (B)   ② (B) – (A) – (C)
③ (B) – (C) – (A)   ④ (C) – (A) – (B)
✓⑤ (C) – (B) – (A)

[본문 해석]

만약 여러분이 번화한 거리를 운전한다면, 여러분은 바로 서로 옆에서 경쟁하는 많은 업체들을 흔히 발견할 것이다. 예를 들어, 대부분의 장소에서 간단한 식사를 찾는 소비자에게는 선택권이 많고, 항상 여러 패스트푸드 식당들이 눈에 띈다.

(C) 이 경쟁 업체들은 광고를 많이 한다. 광고라고 하면 소비자에게 어떤 혜택도 없이 제품의 가격을 올린다고 보기 쉽다.

(B) 그러나 이러한 오해는 회사들이 광고하는 이유를 설명해주지 않는다. 경쟁사들이 약간씩 차별화된 제품들을 판매하는 시장에서, 광고는 회사들이 소비자들에게 새로운 제품과 서비스를 알릴 수 있게 해 준다.

(A) 물론 가격이 상승하기는 하지만, 소비자들은 구매 결정을 내리는 데 도움이 되는 정보도 얻는다. 또한 소비자들은 추가된 다양성으로 혜택을 얻고, 우리 모두는 완벽한 제품에 대한 우리의 상상에 매우 근접한 제품을 얻는데, 다른 어떤 시장 구조도 그러한 결과를 제공하지 않는다.

Why? 왜 정답일까?

주어진 글은 우리가 일상에서 경쟁 관계에 있는 업체들을 많이 볼 수 있다는 내용이고, (C)는 '이 업체들'이 살아남기 위해 광고를 한다는 내용이다. 특히 (C)의 후반부는 우리가 광고 때문에 제품 가격이 올라간다고 여기기 쉽다고 하는데, (B)는 이런 '오해'가 광고의 이유를 설명해주지 못한다면서 광고의 효과를 설명하기 시작한다. (A) 또한 (B)에 이어 광고의 이득과 효과를 언급하므로, 글의 순서로 가장 적절한 것은 ⑤ '(C) – (B) – (A)'이다.

- in search of ~을 찾아서
- benefit from ~에서 이득을 보다
- vision ⑩ 상상
- misconception ⑩ 오해
- advertise ⓥ 광고하다
- differentiate ⓥ 차별(화)하다, 구별하다
- temptation ⑩ 유혹
- quick meal 간단한 식사
- variety ⑩ 다양성, 품종
- deliver ⓥ (결과를) 내놓다, 산출하다
- account for ~을 설명하다
- slightly ⓐⅆ 약간
- heavily ⓐⅆ 많이, 심하게
- drive up (값 등을) 끌어올리다

구문 풀이

13행 In markets [where competitors sell slightly differentiated
　　　　　장소 선행사　　　　　　　관계부사절
products], advertising enables firms to inform their customers about
　　　　　　　　　　　「enable + 목적어 + to부정사 : ~이 …할 수 있게 해주다」
new products and services.

★★ 문제 해결 꿀~팁 ★★

▶ 많이 틀린 이유는?
(C)의 driving up the price of a product 다음에 (A)의 Yes, costs rise가 와도 자연스러워 보이지만, (A) 다음 (B)가 자연스럽지 않다. (A)에서 '오해'로 볼 만한 내용이 언급되지 않기 때문이다.

▶ 문제 해결 방법은?
(C)의 see advertising as driving up the price of a product without any benefit to the consumer가 (B)의 this misconception으로 연결되고, also가 포함된 (A)에서 광고의 이점에 대한 내용을 추가하는 흐름이다.

11-12 잘 싸우는 것의 이점

[본문 해석]

「잘 싸울 수 있다는 것은 우리를 더 정중하게 만들 뿐만 아니라 우리의 창의적 근력을 발달시킨다.」 고전적인 연구에 따르면, 매우 창의적인 건축가는 기술적으로 유능하지만 덜 독창적인 그들의 동료보다 충돌이 (a) 많은 가정에서 나올 가능성이 더 크다. 그들은 흔히 '긴장감이 있지만 안전한' 집안에서 자랐는데, 심리학자 Robert Albert는 "창의적인 사람이 될 사람은 전혀 (b) 화목하지 않은 가정에서 나온다."라고 언급한다. 그 부모들이 신체적으로나 언어적으로 학대한 것은 아니었지만 갈등을 피하지도 않았다. 그들은 자녀에게 눈앞에 있어 아무 말도 하지 말라고 말하는 대신 자신의 입장을 내세우라고 (c) 권장했다. 「그 자녀들은 남을 비판하고 비판을 받아들이는 것을 배웠다. 그것이 바로 비행기를 발명한 Wilbur와 Orville Wright 형제에게 일어난 일이었다.」 : 12번의 근거 Wright 형제가 자기들은 함께 생각한다고 말했을 때 그 말의 진짜 의미는 함께 싸웠다는 것이다. 그들이 문제를 풀고 있었을 때 그들은 한 번에 몇 시간 동안뿐만 아니라 몇 주, 몇 달 동안 지속된 논쟁을 했다. 그들이 화가 나서 그토록 (d) 끊임없는 싸움을 한 것은 아니었다. 그들은 그것을 즐기고 그 경험으로부터 배웠기 때문에 계속 싸웠다. "나는 Orv와 다투는 것을 좋아한다."라고 Wilbur는 회고했다. 보다시피, 바로 그들의 가장 열정이고 장기적인 논쟁 중 하나가 인간이 하늘로 날아오르지 못하게 했던 결정적 가정을 그들이 (e) 지지하도록 (→ 재고하도록) 이끌었다.

- civil ⓐ 정중한, 예의 바른
- technically ⓐⅆ 기술적으로
- friction ⑩ 마찰, 저항, 갈등
- anything but ~이 결코 아닌
- abusive ⓐ 학대하는
- stand up for ~을 대변하다, 옹호하다
- prolonged ⓐ 장기간의
- cope with ~에 대처하다
- architect ⑩ 건축가
- competent ⓐ 유능한
- secure ⓐ 안전한
- harmonious ⓐ 조화로운
- shy away from ~을 피하다
- ceaseless ⓐ 끊임없는
- soar ⓥ 솟구치다
- compromise ⑩ 타협, 절충 ⓥ 타협하다

구문 풀이

25행 As you'll see, it was one of their most passionate and
　　　　　　　　　　「it is[was] ~ that … 강조 구문 : …한 것은 바로 ~이다[였다]」
prolonged arguments that led them to rethink a critical assumption
　　　　　　　　　　　　　　　　　　　　　　　　　　선행사
[that had prevented humans from soaring through the skies].
「prevent + A + from + B : A가 B하지 못하게 막다」

11 제목 파악　　　　　　　정답률 54% | 정답 ①

윗글의 제목으로 가장 적절한 것은?

☑① The Power of Constructive Conflict – 건설적인 갈등의 힘
② Lighten Tense Moments with Humor – 유머로 긴장된 순간을 가볍게 하라
③ Strategies to Cope with Family Stress – 가족 스트레스에 대처하는 전략
④ Compromise: A Key to Resolving Conflict – 타협: 갈등 해결의 열쇠
⑤ Rivalry Between Brothers: A Serious Crisis – 형제 간의 경쟁: 심각한 위기

Why? 왜 정답일까?

주제문인 첫 문장에서 건설적인 갈등은 우리를 정중하게 만들 뿐 아니라 창의력도 길러준다(Being able to have a good fight doesn't just make us more civil; it also develops our creative muscles.)고 하므로, 글의 제목으로 가장 적절한 것은 ① '건설적인 갈등의 힘'이다.

★★★ 1등급 대비 고난도 3점 문제

12 어휘 추론　　　　　　　정답률 17% | 정답 ⑤

밑줄 친 (a) ~ (e) 중에서 문맥상 낱말의 쓰임이 적절하지 않은 것은? [3점]
① (a)　　② (b)　　③ (c)　　④ (d)　　☑⑤ (e)

Why? 왜 정답일까?

첫 단락의 마지막 두 문장에서 Wright 형제는 남을 비판하고 자신에 대한 비판도 받아들이는 법을 배웠으며, 그 결과 비행기의 발명이라는 창의적인 업적까지 이르렀다고 한다. 다시 말해, 이들 형제는 끝없이 서로 논쟁하는 과정에서 사람이 날지 못할 것이라는 믿음을 '지지하는' 대신 '다시 생각하고 비판하여' 사고의 성장을 이루었다는 것이므로, (e)의 support를 rethink로 고쳐야 문맥이 자연스럽다. 따라서 문맥상 낱말의 쓰임이 가장 적절하지 않은 것은 ⑤ '(e)'이다.

★★ 문제 해결 꿀~팁 ★★

▶ 많이 틀린 이유는?
밑줄 주변 문맥에 답의 근거가 있다. ④ '(d)' 바로 앞에서 Wright 형제는 문제를 해결하는 도중 몇 시간, 몇 주, 심지어 몇 달간 이어지는 싸움을 했다고 언급하는 것으로 보아, 싸움이 '끊임없었다'는 의미의 ceaseless는 적합하다.

▶ 문제 해결 방법은?
정답인 ⑤ '(e)'가 포함된 문장은 호흡이 길기 때문에 시간을 들여 정확하게 읽어야 한다. Wright 형제가 끊임없는 싸움과 문제 해결 과정을 통해 결국 비행에 '성공한' 인물임을 고려할 때, 기존에 비행을 좌절시켰던 생각을 이들이 '지지했다'는 설명은 적합하지 않다. 이들이 통념을 '깨려' 했기 때문에 남들이 하지 못한 창의적인 생각을 할 수 있었던 것이다.

DAY 02 — 20분 미니 모의고사

01 ①	02 ⑤	03 ①	04 ④	05 ②
06 ⑤	07 ①	08 ③	09 ②	10 ⑤
11 ⑤	12 ④			

---

01 계주 주자 Emma의 심경변화
정답률 95% | 정답 ①

다음 글에 드러난 Emma의 심경 변화로 가장 적절한 것은?

✓① nervous → excited
긴장한 → 신난
② doubtful → regretful
의심스러운 → 후회스러운
③ confident → upset
자신감 있는 → 화난
④ hopeful → disappointed
희망찬 → 실망한
⑤ indifferent → amused
무관심한 → 즐거운

[본문 해석]

결승전 경주였다. Emma는 그녀의 계주 팀의 마지막 주자였다. 그녀는 그녀의 자리에서 팀 동료가 그녀에게 바통을 건네주기를 초조하게 기다렸다. Emma는 그녀가 실수를 하지 않고 자신의 역할을 수행할 수 있을지 확신하지 못했다. "만약 내가 바통을 떨어뜨리면 어떡하지?" 라고 생각하면서 그녀의 손이 떨렸다. 그녀는 그녀의 팀 동료가 다가올수록 심박수가 증가하는 것을 느꼈다. 하지만 그녀가 달리기 시작했을 때, 그녀는 순조롭게 바통을 받았다. 마지막 10미터에서, 그녀는 두 명의 다른 주자를 제치고 나서 1위로 결승선을 통과했다! 그녀는 두 손을 하늘로 치켜들고, 얼굴에 큰 미소를 지었다. 팀 동료들이 그녀를 안아주자, 그녀는 "우리가 해냈어!"라고 소리쳤다. 그녀의 모든 힘든 훈련이 그럴만한 가치가 있었다.

Why? 왜 정답일까?

Emma는 바통을 받기 전에 바통을 떨어뜨릴까봐 걱정했지만, 바통을 순조롭게 받고 1위로 결승선을 통과했기 때문에 글에 드러난 Emma의 심경 변화로 가장 적절한 것은 ① '긴장한 → 신난'이다.

- **championship** ⓝ 챔피언십, 선수권 대회
- **anxiously** ⓐⓓ 걱정스럽게, 불안하게
- **smoothly** ⓐⓓ 원활하게
- **training** ⓝ 훈련, 연습
- **relay** ⓝ 계주, 릴레이
- **perform** ⓥ 수행하다, 공연하다
- **finish line** 결승선

구문 풀이

7행 But as she started running, she received the baton smoothly.
　　　전치사　　　　　　　　　동명사

---

02 독자 또는 시청자를 몰입하게 하는 요소
정답률 87% | 정답 ⑤

다음 글의 요지로 가장 적절한 것은?

① 독자의 공감을 얻기 위해 구체적인 인물 묘사가 중요하다.
② 이야기의 줄거리를 단순화시키는 것이 독자의 이해를 높인다.
③ 거리를 두고 주인공의 상황을 객관적으로 바라볼 필요가 있다.
④ 주인공의 역경과 행복이 적절히 섞여야 이야기가 흥미로워진다.
✓⑤ 주인공에 대한 지속적인 궁금증 유발이 독자의 몰입을 도와준다.

[본문 해석]

이 사람은 누구지? 이것은 모든 이야기가 물어보는 질문이다. 그것은 발화 지점에서 가장 먼저 나타난다. 처음 변화가 발생할 때 주인공은 과민 반응하거나 다른 예상치 못한 방식으로 행동한다. 우리는 일어나 앉아 갑자기 주의를 기울인다. *이렇게 행동하는 이 사람은 누구야?* 그리고 나서 그 질문은 주인공이 줄거리에 도전받고 선택을 하도록 강요받을 때마다 다시 나타난다. 그 질문이 존재하는 이야기의 모든 곳에서 독자 또는 시청자는 몰입하게 될 것이다. 그 질문이 부재하고 드라마의 사건들이 이야기의 빛줄기에서 벗어나는 곳에서 그들은 무심해지거나, 심지어는 지루해질 위험에 처할 수도 있다. 만약 스토리텔링에 한 가지 비밀이 있다면 나는 이것이 비밀이라 믿는다. *이 사람은 누구지?* 또는 등장인물의 관점에서 *나는 누구지?* 라는 질문 말이다. 그것이 드라마의 정의이다. 그것이 드라마의 전기이고 심장 박동이자 불이다.

Why? 왜 정답일까?

주인공이 누구인가에 대한 물음은 드라마 전체에 걸쳐 지속되며, 독자 또는 시청자를 몰

(우측 단 이어서)

입하게 만드는 원천(Everywhere in the narrative that the question is present, the reader or viewer will likely be engaged.)이라는 내용의 글이다. 따라서 글의 요지로 가장 적절한 것은 ⑤ '주인공에 대한 지속적인 궁금증 유발이 독자의 몰입을 도와준다.'이다.

- **emerge** ⓥ 나타나다, 출현하다
- **behave** ⓥ 행동하다
- **attentive** ⓐ 주의를 기울이는
- **engaged** ⓐ 몰입한
- **at risk of** ~할 위험에 처한
- **electricity** ⓝ 전기
- **overreact** ⓥ 과민 반응하다
- **otherwise** ⓐ 다른
- **compel** ⓥ 강요하다
- **absent** ⓐ 부재한
- **definition** ⓝ 정의
- **heartbeat** ⓝ 심장박동

구문 풀이

10행 Where the question is absent, and the events of drama move
　　　접속사(~한 곳에서, ~한 경우에)
out of its narrative beam, they are at risk of becoming detached —
　　　　　　　　　　　　　　주어　동사　　　보어
perhaps even bored.

---

03 병원 치료만큼 중요한 예방적 공공 보건 서비스
정답률 50% | 정답 ①

다음 글의 제목으로 가장 적절한 것은? [3점]

✓① Public Healthcare: A Co-Star, Not a Supporting Actor
공공 보건 서비스: 조연이 아닌 공동 주연
② The Historical Development of Medicine and Surgery
의학과 수술의 역사적 발달
③ Clinical Care Controversies: What You Don't Know
병원 치료의 논란: 여러분이 모르는 것
④ The Massive Similarities Between Different Mythologies
다양한 신화 간의 엄청나게 큰 유사성
⑤ Initiatives Opening up Health Innovation Around the World
전 세계 보건 혁신을 가능하게 하는 계획

[본문 해석]

가장 초기의 시대부터, 의료 서비스는 두 가지의 동등한 영역, 즉 병원 치료와 공공 보건을 포함하는 것으로 인식되어 왔다. 고대 그리스 신화에서 의료의 신 아스클레피오스에게는 하이기아와 파나시아라는 두 딸이 있었다. 전자는 예방적 건강과 건강 관리, 즉 위생의 여신이었고, 후자는 치료와 치유의 여신이었다. 현대 시대에, 의료 전문성에 대한 사회적 우세는 아픈 환자들의 치료로 인해 위생 공학자, 생물학자, 정부 공공 건강 관료와 같은 덜 영웅적인 인물들에 의해서 제공되는 그러한 예방적 보건 서비스가 빛을 잃게 만들었다. 그럼에도 불구하고, 인류가 향유하는 건강의 질은 공공 위생, 하수 관리, 그리고 대기 오염, 식수, 도시 소음, 인간이 소비하는 음식을 관리하는 서비스들의 이용 가능성에 비해 수술적 기민함, 혁신적 제약 제품, 그리고 생물 공학적 장비에 덜 바탕을 둔다. 달성 가능한 최고 수준의 건강에 대한 인간의 권리는 의사와 병원의 기술과 장비 못지 않게 공공 보건 서비스에 달려 있다.

Why? 왜 정답일까?

건강 수준을 높이기 위해서는 병원 치료뿐 아니라 위생과 관련된 예방적 공공 보건 서비스도 중요한 역할을 한다(The human right to the highest attainable standard of health depends on public healthcare services no less than on the skills and equipment of doctors and hospitals.)고 하므로, 글의 제목으로 가장 적절한 것은 ① '공공 보건 서비스: 조연이 아니라 공동 주연'이다.

- **healthcare service** 공공 보건 서비스
- **mythology** ⓝ 신화
- **wellness** ⓝ 건강
- **overshadow** ⓥ 빛을 잃게 하다, 가리다
- **be attributable to** ~에 기인하다
- **pharmaceutical** ⓐ 약학의
- **attainable** ⓐ 달성 가능한
- **co-star** ⓝ 공동 주연 ⓥ 공동 주연을 맡다
- **clinical care** 임상 진료
- **preventive** ⓐ 예방적인
- **hygiene** ⓝ 위생
- **heroic** ⓐ 영웅적인
- **surgical** ⓐ 수술적인
- **sewage** ⓝ 오물
- **no less than** ~에 못지 않게

구문 풀이

1행 From the earliest times, healthcare services have been
　　　　기간 부사구　　　　　　　　　　　　현재완료 수동태
recognized to have two equal aspects, namely clinical care and
public healthcare.

---

04 가상 운동회
정답률 95% | 정답 ④

Roselands Virtual Sports Day에 관한 다음 안내문의 내용과 일치하지 않는 것은?

① 10월 16일부터 22일까지 열린다.
② 총 10개의 도전 과제가 있다.
③ 학교 웹사이트에서 도전 과제를 설명하는 영상을 볼 수 있다.
☑ 학부모와 교사는 참여할 수 없다.
⑤ 제출할 영상파일 용량이 500MB를 초과하면 안 된다.

[본문 해석]

Roselands Virtual Sports Day
(Roselands 가상 운동회)

Roselands Virtual Sports Day는 여러분이 어디에서나 참여할 수 있는 운동 시합입니다.

「시기: 2023년 10월 16일 ~ 22일」──「」: ①의 근거 일치

행사 진행 방식
· 「총 10개의 도전 과제가 있습니다.」──「」: ②의 근거 일치
· 「여러분은 우리 학교 웹사이트에서 각 도전 과제를 설명하는 영상을 볼 수 있습니다.」──「」: ③의 근거 일치
· 여러분이 더 많은 도전 과제를 완수할수록, 학급을 위한 더 많은 점수를 얻을 수 있습니다.
· 가장 많은 점수를 얻은 학급은 상을 받을 것입니다.
· 「학부모와 교사도 참여할 수 있습니다.」──「」: ④의 근거 불일치

출품작 제출 방법
· 여러분이 도전 과제를 완수하는 영상을 virtualsportsday@roselands.com으로 이메일로 보내주세요.
· 「제출할 영상파일 용량은 500MB를 초과하면 안 됩니다.」──「」: ⑤의 근거 일치

Why? 왜 정답일까?
'Parents and teachers can also participate.'에서 학부모와 교사도 참가할 수 있다고 하므로, 안내문의 내용과 일치하지 않는 것은 ④ '학부모와 교사는 참여할 수 없다.'이다.

Why? 왜 오답일까?
① 'When: October 16th – 22nd, 2023'의 내용과 일치한다.
② 'There are 10 challenges in total.'의 내용과 일치한다.
③ 'You can see videos explaining each challenge on our school website.'의 내용과 일치한다.
⑤ 'The size of the video file must not exceed 500MB.'의 내용과 일치한다.

- virtual ⓐ 가상의
- participate in ~에 참여하다
- gain ⓥ 얻다, 따다
- exceed ⓥ 초과하다, 능가하다
- athletic ⓐ 운동의, 육상의
- complete ⓥ 완수하다 ⓐ 완수된
- entry ⓝ 출품, 입장

★★★ 1등급 대비 고난도 2점 문제

05 패션이 매력적인 이유   정답률 34% | 정답 ②

다음 글의 밑줄 친 부분 중, 어법상 틀린 것은?

[본문 해석]

유행은 사람들이 자신을 재조정할 새로운 기회를 끊임없이 제시하고, 변화의 때를 나타낸다. 유행이 궁극적으로 어떻게 개인에게 힘과 자유를 줄 수 있는지를 이해하기 위해서는 먼저 변화를 위한 기반으로서의 패션의 중요성에 대해 논의해야 한다. 왜 패션이 그렇게 매력적인지에 대해 나의 정보 제공자들이 준 가장 흔한 설명은 그것이 일종의 연극적인 의상을 구성한다는 것이다. 옷은 사람들이 자신을 세상에 보여주는 방식의 일부이고, 패션은 사회의 현재 상황과 패션 자체의 역사와 관련하여 그들을 현재에 위치시킨다. 표현 형태로서 패션은 많은 모호함을 담고 있어 개인이 특정한 옷과 연관된 의미를 재창조할 수 있게 한다. 패션은 자기표현의 가장 단순하고 값싼 방법 중 하나로, 옷은 저렴하게 구매할 수 있으며, 비록 다음 중 아무것도 해당되지 않을지라도 부, 지적 능력, 휴식 또는 환경 의식에 대한 개념 (등등)을 쉽게 전달할 수 있다. 패션은 또한 행동을 위한 공간을 열어주며 다양한 방법으로 행동력을 강화할 수 있다.

Why? 왜 정답일까?
문맥상 how가 이끄는 간접의문문의 주어인 people이 옷을 통해 '자기 자신'을 세상에 드러내는 것이므로, 목적어 자리에 them 대신 themselves를 써야 한다. 따라서 어법상 틀린 것은 ②이다.

Why? 왜 오답일까?
① 동사 is의 주격 보어로 완전한 문장이 연결되므로 접속사 that이 바르게 쓰였다.
③ the meanings가 '연관 짓는' 행위의 대상이므로 associated가 과거분사로 바르게 쓰였다.
④ can be purchased라는 동사구를 꾸미기 위해 부사 inexpensively가 중간에 삽입되었다.
⑤ 주절의 동사는 can also strengthen이고 뒤에 접속사가 없기 때문에 opening은 분사구문 자리가 맞다. 분사구문의 의미상 주어인 Fashion이 '열어주는' 주체이므로 opening이 현재분사로 바르게 쓰였다.

- opportunity ⓝ 기회
- occasion ⓝ 때, 경우
- basis ⓝ 기반, 근거
- as to ~에 관해
- theatrical ⓐ 연극의
- present ⓥ 보여주다, 제시하다 ⓐ 현재
- relative to ~와 관련해서, ~에 비해
- ambiguity ⓝ 모호함
- associated with ~와 관련된
- wealth ⓝ 부유함
- relaxation ⓝ 기분 전환, 오락
- represent ⓥ 표현하다, 나타내다, 대표하다
- ultimately ⓐⓓ 궁극적으로
- informant ⓝ 정보원, 정보 제공자
- appealing ⓐ 매력적인
- costumery ⓝ 의상, 복식
- locate A in B A를 B에 위치시키다
- a host of 많은, 다수의
- recreate ⓥ 재창조하다, 재현하다
- inexpensively ⓐⓓ 값싸게, 저렴하게
- stature ⓝ 능력, 위상
- agency ⓝ 행동력

구문 풀이

5행 The most common explanation offered by my informants
주어 ╱ 과거분사구
as to why fashion is so appealing is that it constitutes a kind of
~에 대해   동사 ╱ 접속사(~것)
theatrical costumery.

★★ 문제 해결 꿀~팁 ★★

▶ 많이 틀린 이유는?
오답 선택지 중에서도 ⑤는 '준동사 vs. 동사' 포인트를 다룬다. 콤마 앞에 완전한 절이 나오는데 콤마 뒤에 접속사가 없으므로 추가로 동사를 연결할 수 없어서 분사를 쓴 것이다. 분사이므로 '능동 vs. 수동' 판단이 중요한 이슈인데, 의미상 주어(= 문장의 주어)인 Fashion이 '행동 공간을 열어주는' 주체이다. 따라서 opening을 쓴 것은 종합적으로 적절하다. 큰 포인트를 판단한 후 추가 검토 사항을 챙기는 풀이 흐름을 숙지해두도록 한다.

▶ 문제 해결 방법은?
① 'that vs. what', ② '인칭대명사 vs. 재귀대명사', ③ '현재분사 vs. 과거분사', ④ '형용사 vs. 부사' 등 모든 선택지가 빈출 포인트를 다루고 있다. 특히 정답인 ②는 반드시 문맥을 봐야 해서 독해력까지 요구한다.

06 건축에서의 디자인과 실용성   정답률 53% | 정답 ⑤

(A), (B), (C)의 각 네모 안에서 문맥에 맞는 낱말로 가장 적절한 것은?

	(A)	(B)	(C)
①	relevant 관련 있는	distinction 구분	shape 형성한다
②	relevant 관련 있는	connection 연결	overlook 간과한다
③	irrelevant 무관하다	distinction 구분	overlook 간과한다
④	irrelevant 무관하다	connection 연결	overlook 간과한다
☑	irrelevant 무관하다	distinction 구분	shape 형성한다

[본문 해석]

건축 환경에서의 설계에 대해 사람들은 안전성과 기능성은 협상의 여지가 없다고 여긴다. 하지만 어떻게 그것이 *디자인*되어 있는지와 같은 새로운 설계의 미학은 너무 종종 (A) 무관하다고 여겨진다. 어떻게 그것의 디자인이 인간에게 *영향을 미치는지*에 대한 질문은 거의 하지 않는다. 사람들은 디자인이 (미학적) 건축물이라고 불리는, 허세를 부리는 것을 만들어 낸다고 생각하며, 워싱턴 국립 대성당이 지역 사회 교회와는 다른 것과 마찬가지로 분명하게 (미학적) 건축물은 (일반적) 건축물과 다르다고 생각한다. (미학적) 건축물과 (일반적) 건축물, 더 일반적으로는 디자인과 실용성 사이의 이러한 (B) 구분은 더할 나위 없이 잘못된 것이다. 우리의 모든 건축 환경의 디자인이 너무나도 대단히 중요해서 안전성과 기능성만이 우리의 시급한 우선순위여서는 안 된다는 것을 우리는 더욱더 알아가고 있다. 모든 종류의 디자인 요소들은 환경뿐 아니라 자신에 대한 사람들의 경험에도 영향을 미친다. 그것들은 우리의 인지, 감정, 행

동, 심지어 행복까지 (C) 형성한다. 그것들은 실제로 우리의 정체성까지 만들어 내도록 돕는다.

Why? 왜 정답일까?

(A) 'The question of how its design *affects* human beings is rarely asked.'에서 건물의 미학적 디자인이 어떻게 인간에게 영향을 미치는지에 관해서는 거의 질문이 제기되지 않는다고 언급하고 있다. 이를 토대로, 사람들은 건물의 안전성과 기능성에 대해서는 중요하게 생각하면서도 디자인은 '별 상관이 없다'고 여기고 있다는 내용을 추론할 수 있다. 따라서 (A)에는 irrelevant가 적절하다.

(B) 'People think ~ that architecture differs from building, ~'에서 사람들은 보통 디자인적 고려가 들어간 '건축물'이 일반 '빌딩'과는 다르다고 생각하는 경향이 있다고 언급한다. 이를 토대로, 건물의 디자인과 실용성에 대해서 일반적으로 '구분'이 이루어지고 있다는 내용을 유추할 수 있다. 따라서 (B)에는 distinction이 적절하다.

(C) 'All kinds of design elements influence people's experiences, not only of the environment but also of themselves.'에서 모든 디자인적 요소는 환경뿐 아니라 자신에 대한 사람들의 경험에도 영향을 미친다고 언급한다. 이를 근거로 할 때, 디자인적 요소는 사람들의 인지, 감정, 행동, 심지어 행동에도 두루 영향을 미친다는 의미가 되도록 (C)에는 shape가 들어가야 한다. 따라서 (A), (B), (C)의 각 네모 안에서 문맥에 맞는 낱말로 가장 적절한 것은 ⑤ '(A) irrelevant(무관하다) – (B) distinction (구분) – (C) shape(형성한다)'이다.

- **functionality** ⓝ 기능성
- **irrelevant** ⓐ 무관한
- **rarely** [ad] 드물게, 좀처럼 ~하지 않는
- **architecture** ⓝ 건축(물)
- **utility** ⓝ 실용성
- **urgent** ⓐ 긴박한, 시급한
- **shape** ⓥ 형성하다, 영향을 미치다
- **constitute** ⓥ 구성하다
- **nonnegotiable** ⓐ 협상의 여지가 없는
- **aesthetics** ⓝ 미학
- **highfalutin** ⓐ 허세를 부리는
- **distinction** ⓝ 구분
- **profoundly** [ad] 완전히, 깊이
- **overlook** ⓥ 간과하다
- **cognition** ⓝ 인지

구문 풀이

12행 More and more we are learning that the design of all our
　　　　　　　　 주어　　동사　　　　　　　　　　　　주어
built environments matters so profoundly that safety and functionality
　　　　　　　　 동사 「so ~ that … : 너무 ~해서 …하다」
must not be our only urgent priorities.

「비교급 + and + 비교급 : 점점 더 ~한/하게」 「접속사(~것)」

★★★ 1등급 대비 고난도 3편 문제

07 연약해서 아름다운 삶　　　　정답률 45% | 정답 ①

다음 빈칸에 들어갈 말로 가장 적절한 것을 고르시오. [3점]

☑ fragility – 연약함
② stability – 안정성
③ harmony – 조화
④ satisfaction – 만족감
⑤ diversity – 다양성

[본문 해석]

현대의 불교 스승인 Dainin Katagiri는 죽음을 앞두고 *침묵으로의 회귀*라는 경이로운 책을 집필했다. 그는 삶이란 "위험한 상황이다."라고 썼다. 삶을 소중하게 만드는 것은 바로 삶의 취약함이며, 그의 글은 자신의 삶이 끝나가고 있다는 바로 그 사실로 채워져 있다. "자기 그릇은 언젠가 깨질 것이기 때문에 아름답다…. 그 그릇의 생명은 늘 위험한 상황에 놓여 있다." 그런 것이 우리의 고행이다. 이 불안정한 아름다움. 이 피할 수 없는 상처. 우리는 사랑과 상실이 친밀한 동반자라는 것을, 우리가 진짜 꽃을 플라스틱 꽃보다 훨씬 더 사랑하고 산 중턱을 가로지르는 한 순간만 지속하는 황혼의 색조를 사랑한다는 것을 잊는다 — 그것도 너무나 쉽게 잊는다. 우리의 마음을 여는 것은 바로 이 연약함이다.

Why? 왜 정답일까?

'It is the weakness of life that makes it precious; ~'에서 Dainin Katagiri는 죽음을 앞두고 쓴 책에서 삶을 소중하게 만드는 것이 삶의 취약함이라고 기술했다는 내용이 나온다. 따라서 빈칸에 들어갈 말로 가장 적절한 것은 weakness의 동의어인 ① '연약함'이다.

- **contemporary** ⓐ 현대의
- **pass away** (존재하던 것이) 없어지다
- **unstable** ⓐ 불안정한
- **wound** ⓝ 상처 ⓥ 상처 입히다
- **companion** ⓝ 동반자
- **stability** ⓝ 안정성
- **remarkable** ⓐ 경이로운, 주목할 만한
- **sooner or later** 언젠가, 곧, 조만간
- **inevitable** ⓐ 피할 수 없는
- **intimate** ⓐ 친밀한
- **fragility** ⓝ 연약함

구문 풀이

10행 We forget — (how easily we forget) — that love and loss are
　　　　　　　 동사　　( ) : 삽입절　　　　　접속사1(~것)
intimate companions, that we love the real flower so much more than
　　　　　　　　　　　　 접속사2(~것)　　　　　　　　 비교급 강조
the plastic one and love the cast of twilight across a mountainside
　　　　　　　　　　　　　　　　　　　　　　　　 전명구
lasting only a moment.
현재분사구(twilight 꾸밈)

★★ 문제 해결 꿀~팁 ★★

▶ 많이 틀린 이유는?
삶은 언젠가 끝나기 마련인 특유의 연약함 때문에 아름답게 여겨진다는 내용의 글로, ②의 '안정성'은 주제와 반대된다. ③의 '조화', ④의 '만족감'은 글에서 언급되지 않았다.

▶ 문제 해결 방법은?
강조구문인 'It is the weakness of life ~'에서 삶의 연약함을, 도치 구문인 'Such is our struggle: this unstable beauty.'에서 삶의 불안정한 아름다움을 강조하고 있는 것으로 볼 때 ①이 답으로 적절하다.

★★★ 1등급 대비 고난도 2편 문제

08 일반화하려는 본능의 순기능과 역기능　　정답률 38% | 정답 ③

글의 흐름으로 보아, 주어진 문장이 들어가기에 가장 적절한 곳을 고르시오.

[본문 해석]

모든 사람들은 항상 자동적으로 분류하고 일반화한다. 무의식적으로 (그렇게 한다). 그것은 편견을 갖고 있다거나 계몽되어 있다는 것의 문제가 아니다. 범주는 우리가 제 기능을 하는 데 반드시 필요하다. ① 그것들은 우리의 사고에 체계를 준다. ② 만일 우리가 모든 품목과 모든 있을 법한 상황을 정말로 유일무이한 것으로 본다고 상상해 보라. 우리는 우리 주변의 세계를 설명할 언어조차 갖지 못할 것이다. ③ 그러나 필연적이고 유용한 일반화 본능은 우리의 세계관을 왜곡할 수 있다. 그것은 우리가 실제로는 아주 다른 사물들이나 사람들, 혹은 나라들을 하나로 잘못 묶게 만들 수 있다. ④ 그것은 우리가 하나의 범주 안에 있는 모든 것이나 모든 사람이 비슷하다고 가정하게 만들 수 있다. ⑤ 그리고 어쩌면 모든 것 중에서 가장 유감스러운 것은, 그것이 우리로 하여금 몇 가지, 또는 심지어 고작 하나의 특이한 사례를 바탕으로 전체 범주에 대해 성급하게 결론을 내리게 만들 수 있다는 것이다.

Why? 왜 정답일까?

③ 앞까지 인간은 대상을 무의식적으로 범주에 따라 분류하고 일반화하려는 경향이 있어, 이를 토대로 체계적인 사고를 해나갈 수 있다는 내용이 언급되고 있다. **But**으로 시작하는 주어진 문장은 이와 같은 흐름을 반전시키며 이러한 일반화 본능이 역으로 우리 세계관을 '왜곡할' 여지가 있음을 상기시키고 있다. ③ 뒤부터는 주어진 문장의 'the necessary and useful instinct'를 It으로 가리키며, 일반화 본능으로 인해 우리가 실제로 굉장히 다른 대상을 한 범주로 잘못 묶거나 한 범주 안의 개별적인 대상들을 비슷하다고 오해할 여지가 생긴다고 설명한다. 따라서 주어진 문장이 들어가기에 가장 적절한 곳은 ③이다.

- **instinct** ⓝ 본능
- **distort** ⓥ 왜곡하다
- **categorize** ⓥ (개개의 범주로) 분류하다
- **prejudice** ⓥ 편견을 갖게 하다
- **function** ⓥ (정상적으로) 활동하다
- **group together** ~을 하나로 묶다
- **jump to a conclusion** 성급한 결론을 내리다
- **generalize** ⓥ 일반화하다
- **automatically** [ad] 자동적으로, 저절로
- **unconsciously** [ad] 무의식적으로
- **enlighten** ⓥ 계몽하다
- **structure** ⓝ 체계
- **mistakenly** [ad] 잘못하여, 실수로

구문 풀이

7행 Imagine (that) if we saw every item and every scenario as
　　　　 생략　　「if + 주어 + 과거 동사 ~,
truly unique — we would not even have a language to describe the
　　　　　　　　　 주어 + 조동사 과거형 +　　　동사원형 ~ : 가정법 과거」 　형용사적 용법
world around us.

★★ 문제 해결 꿀~팁 ★★

▶ 많이 틀린 이유는?
④ 앞에서, 우리는 일반화 본능 때문에 실제로 서로 다른 대상을 한 가지 범주 안에 묶을지도 모르게 된다고 언급한다. 이어서 ④ 뒤의 문장에서는 '나아가' 우리가 한 범주 안의 대상이 다 비슷할 것이라고 잘못 가정할 수도 있다는 점을 언급한다. 즉 ④ 앞

뒤가 흐름 단절 없이 자연스럽게 서로 연결되므로, 주어진 문장이 ④에 들어가는 것은 적합하지 않다.

▶ 문제 해결 방법은?
③ 앞뒤의 논리적 공백을 포착해야 한다. ③ 앞에서는 우리가 일반화 본능 '덕분에' 주변 세계를 설명할 수 있다는 내용인 반면, ③ 뒤에서는 일반화 본능 '때문에' 우리가 서로 다른 대상을 하나로 잘못 묶을 수도 있다는 내용이 이어진다. 즉 '일반화 본능'이라는 한 가지 소재에 대해 ③ 앞은 긍정적 시각, ③ 뒤는 부정적 시각을 비치고 있기 때문에, ③ 앞뒤로 논리적 공백이 발생하고 있다.

09 음악에 영향을 받을 수 있는 협력성 정답률 76% | 정답 ②

다음 글의 내용을 한 문장으로 요약하고자 한다. 빈칸 (A), (B)에 들어갈 말로 가장 적절한 것은?

(A)	(B)
① uncomfortable 불편하게	competitive mood 경쟁적 분위기
✔ cooperative 협동적이게	shared rhythm 공유된 리듬
③ distracted 산만해지게	shared rhythm 공유된 리듬
④ attentive 주의 집중하게	competitive mood 경쟁적 분위기
⑤ indifferent 무관심하게	disturbing pattern 골치 아픈 패턴

[본문 해석]

음악은 고객의 경험과 행동을 형성하는 데 사용된다. 그것이 직원에게 어떤 영향을 끼치는지를 탐구하는 연구가 수행되었다. 연구 결과는 리듬감 있는 음악을 듣는 참가자가 리듬감이 덜 있는 음악을 듣는 참가자에 비해 나이, 성별, 학력과 같은 요인에 관계없이 더 협력하는 경향이 있다는 것을 보여준다. 이러한 참가자의 협력하려는 자발성의 긍정적인 촉진제는 그들이 음악을 좋아하는지 혹은 그렇지 않은지와 상관없이 야기되었다. 사람들이 좀 더 긍정적인 심리 상태에 있을 때, 그들은 더 기분이 좋고 창의적이 되는 경향이 있는 반면, 반대 스펙트럼에 있는 사람은 집단 문제 해결에 주의를 기울이기보다는 자신의 개별 문제에 초점을 두는 경향이 있다. 음악의 리듬은 사람들의 행동을 강하게 끌어당긴다. 이것은 사람이 일정한 박자로 음악을 들을 때, 자신의 행동을 박자에 맞추는 경향이 있기 때문이다. 이것은 모두가 한 박자를 따르고 있어 결정을 내릴 때 더 좋아지는 팀워크로 이해된다.

➡ 연구에 따르면 작업 동안 음악의 박자가 (B) 공유된 리듬을 만들기 때문에 직장에서 연주되는 음악은 직원이 (A) 협동적이게 이끌 수 있다.

Why? 왜 정답일까?

'Results from the study indicate that participants who listen to rhythmic music were inclined to cooperate more ~'에서 리듬이 있는 음악을 듣는 사람들은 리듬이 덜한 음악을 듣는 이들에 비해 더 협력적이라고 하는데, 마지막 두 문장에 따르면 이는 사람들이 듣고 있는 음악의 박자에 행동을 맞추는 경향이 있어 모두가 같은 박자를 따를 때 팀워크가 증진되는 현상과 관련이 있다. 따라서 요약문의 빈칸 (A), (B)에 들어갈 말로 적절한 것은 ② '(A) cooperative(협동적이게), (B) shared rhythm (공유된 리듬)'이다.

- mold ⓥ 형성하다, 빚다
- indicate ⓥ 보여주다
- be inclined to ~하는 경향이 있다
- academic background 학력
- willingness ⓝ (기꺼이) ~하려는 마음
- regardless of ~와 상관없이
- spectrum ⓝ 스펙트럼, 빛 띠
- steady ⓐ 고정적인, 한결같은
- beat ⓝ 박자, 운율
- tempo ⓝ 박자, 속도
- distracted ⓐ 산만해진

- employee ⓝ 직원
- rhythmic ⓐ 리드미컬한, 리듬감이 있는
- irrespective of ~와 관계없이
- boost ⓝ 증진
- induce ⓥ 유발하다
- agreeable ⓐ 기분 좋은, 선뜻 동의하는
- rhythm ⓝ 리듬
- pulse ⓝ 리듬, 맥박
- translate to ~로 이해되다, 해석되다
- workplace ⓝ 직장, 업무 현장
- disturbing ⓐ 골치 아픈, 불안감을 주는

구문 풀이

3행 Results from the study indicate that participants [who listen
　　　　　　　　　　　　　　　접속사(~것)　주어
to rhythmic music] were inclined to cooperate more irrespective of
　　　　　　　　　　　동사　　　　　　　　　　　　~와 관계없이
factors (like age, gender, and academic background), compared to
　　　선행사　　　　　　　　　　　　　　　　분사구문(~와 비교해서)
those [who listened to less rhythmic music].

[문제편 p.014]

10-12 쌍둥이 자매와의 연습으로 슛 감각을 향상시킨 Chanel

[본문 해석]

(A)
단지 연습 경기이기는 했지만 농구공은 마치 Chanel의 것인 듯했다. 그녀는 자기 쌍둥이 자매인 Vasha에게 공을 패스하지 않기로 결심했다. 대신 (a) 그녀는 멈춰서서 점프해 공을 골대 쪽으로 던졌지만, 그것은 백보드를 맞고 튕겨 나갔다. 「Chanel은 팀원들이 실망하는 것을 볼 수 있었다.」 상대 팀이 공을 가져가서 이내 득점했고 경기는 끝났다.
　　　　　　└ : 12번 ①의 근거 일치

(D)
연습 경기가 끝났을 때, Chanel은 눈이 눈물로 따끔거리는 것을 느꼈다. "괜찮아," Vasha가 위로하는 목소리로 말했다. Chanel은 그녀에게 고마웠지만, Vasha 덕분에 기분이 더 나아지지는 않았다. Vasha는 그녀의 쌍둥이가 나아지도록 돕고 싶었다. 그녀는 자기 쌍둥이에게 (e) 자신과 함께 연습하자고 권유했다. 「방과 후에 그들은 농구공을 가지고 농구 슛을 연습하기 시작했다.」
　　　　　　　　　　　　　　└ : 12번 ⑤의 근거 일치

(C)
처음에 Chanel은 Vasha와 연습하는 것이 좋지 않았는데, Vasha가 슛을 할 때마다 슛이 들어갔기 때문이었다. 하지만 Chanel은 자기 차례마다 슛을 넣지 못했다. (c) 그녀는 슛을 넣지 못해 좌절했다. "포기하지 마!" 슛이 실패할 때마다 Vasha가 외쳤다. 「12번의 연이은 실패 후에 13번째 슛이 들어갔고, 그녀가 "마침내 내가 해냈어!"라고 외쳤다.」 그녀의 쌍둥이는 말했다. "(d) 네가 해낼 줄 알았어! 자, 계속 연습하자!"
　　　　　　　└ : 12번 ④의 근거 불일치

(B)
「다음날 Chanel은 라이벌 학교와의 챔피언십 경기에 출전했다.」 팽팽한 경기였
　　　　　　　　　　　　　　　　└ : 12번 ②의 근거 일치
고, 경기가 10초 남은 상황에서 Chanel이 Vasha에게 공을 패스받았을 때 점수는 동점이었다. (b) 그녀는 공중으로 뛰어올라 공을 던졌다. 「그것은 곧바로 골대 안으로 들어갔다! Chanel의 마지막 슛으로 인해 그녀의 팀은 우승팀이 되었다.」 Vasha와 모든 다른 팀원들은 그녀에게 환호를 보냈다.
　　　　　　　　　　　　　　└ : 12번 ③의 근거 일치

- bounce off 튕겨져 나오다
- intense ⓐ 격렬한
- leap ⓥ 뛰어오르다
- give up 포기하다
- scream ⓥ 비명을 지르다
- comfort ⓥ 위로하다

- disappointed ⓐ 실망한
- tie ⓥ 동점을 이루다
- cheer for ~을 응원하다
- in a row 연속으로
- sting ⓥ 따끔거리다, 쓰라리다
- appreciate ⓥ 고마워하다

구문 풀이

(C) 4행 She got frustrated at not making a shot.
　　　　　　　　　　　전치사┘　　동명사(부정 표현)

10 글의 순서 파악 정답률 75% | 정답 ⑤

주어진 글 (A)에 이어질 내용을 순서에 맞게 배열한 것으로 가장 적절한 것은?

① (B) - (D) - (C)　　　　② (C) - (B) - (D)
③ (C) - (D) - (B)　　　　④ (D) - (B) - (C)
✔ (D) - (C) - (B)

Why? 왜 정답일까?

연습 게임에서 Chanel이 결정적인 슛을 실패해 팀에 패배를 안겼다는 내용의 (A) 뒤에는, 경기 후 쌍둥이 자매 Vasha가 함께 연습하자고 제안했다는 내용의 (D), Vasha와 계속 연습하며 Chanel이 다시 슛을 성공하게 되었다는 내용의 (C), 슛 감각을 완전히 찾은 Chanel이 본 게임에서는 멋지게 결정 골을 넣었다는 내용의 (B)가 차례로 연결되어야 한다. 따라서 글의 순서로 가장 적절한 것은 ⑤ '(D) - (C) - (B)'이다.

11 지칭 추론 정답률 64% | 정답 ⑤

밑줄 친 (a) ~ (e) 중에서 가리키는 대상이 나머지 넷과 다른 것은?

① (a)　　② (b)　　③ (c)　　④ (d)　　✔ (e)

Why? 왜 정답일까?

(a), (b), (c), (d)는 Chanel, (e)는 Vasha를 가리키므로, (a) ~ (e) 중에서 가리키는 대상이 다른 하나는 ⑤ '(e)'이다.

12 세부 내용 파악
정답률 84% | 정답 ④

윗글의 Chanel에 관한 내용으로 적절하지 않은 것은?

① 연습 경기 중에 팀원들의 실망한 모습을 보았다.
② 라이벌 학교와의 챔피언십 경기에 출전했다.
③ 팀을 우승시키는 마지막 숏을 성공했다.
☑ 숏 연습에서 연이은 실패 후에 12번째 숏이 들어갔다.
⑤ 방과 후에 농구 숏을 연습하기 시작했다.

Why? 왜 정답일까?

(C) 'After twelve misses in a row, her thirteenth shot went in ~'에서 Chanel은 숏을 12번 실패한 후 13번째 숏을 성공시켰음을 알 수 있다. 따라서 내용과 일치하지 않는 것은 ④ '숏 연습에서 연이은 실패 후에 12번째 숏이 들어갔다.'이다.

Why? 왜 오답일까?

① (A) 'Chanel could see that her teammates were disappointed.'의 내용과 일치한다.
② (B) 'Chanel played in the championship game against a rival school.'의 내용과 일치한다.
③ (B) 'Chanel's last shot had made her team the champions.'의 내용과 일치한다.
⑤ (D) 'After school, they ~ started practicing their basketball shots.'의 내용과 일치한다.

DAY 03 20분 미니 모의고사

01 ①	02 ⑤	03 ⑤	04 ④	05 ⑤
06 ③	07 ①	08 ①	09 ③	10 ②
11 ④	12 ⑤			

01 웹툰 제작 관련 강의 홍보
정답률 93% | 정답 ①

다음 글의 목적으로 가장 적절한 것은?

☑ 웹툰 제작 온라인 강좌를 홍보하려고
② 웹툰 작가 채용 정보를 제공하려고
③ 신작 웹툰 공개 일정을 공지하려고
④ 웹툰 창작 대회에 출품을 권유하려고
⑤ 기초적인 웹툰 제작 방법을 설명하려고

[본문 해석]

저는 Charlie Reeves이고 Toon Skills Company의 경영자입니다. 여러분이 새로운 웹툰 제작 기술과 기법에 관심이 있으시다면, 이 게시물은 여러분을 위한 것입니다. 올해, 저희는 특별 온라인 강좌를 시작했는데, 여기에는 웹툰 제작에 관한 다양한 콘텐츠가 담겨 있습니다. 각 강좌는 여러분의 그리기와 스토리텔링 기술을 향상하는 데 도움을 주는 10차시로 설계되어 있습니다. 게다가, 이 강좌들은 초급에서 고급까지 어떤 수준에든 적합하게 구성되어 있습니다. 비용은 한 강좌당 45달러이며, 강좌는 6개월 동안 원하는 만큼 여러 번 보실 수 있습니다. 재능이 있고 노련한 강사들이 담당하는 저희 강좌는 여러분에게 창의력의 새로운 세계를 열어줄 것입니다. 이제 https://webtoonskills.com에서 여러분의 웹툰 세계를 창조하기 시작할 때입니다.

Why? 왜 정답일까?

올해 런칭한 웹툰 제작 온라인 강좌를 홍보하는 글이므로(This year, we've launched special online courses, which contain a variety of contents about webtoon production.), 글의 목적으로 가장 적절한 것은 ① '웹툰 제작 온라인 강좌를 홍보하려고'이다.

- technique ⓝ 기술
- consist of ~로 구성되다
- be designed to ~하도록 설계되다
- cost ⓥ ~의 비용이 들게 하다
- contain ⓥ 포함하다
- improve ⓥ 향상하다
- suit ⓥ 적합하다
- experienced ⓐ 숙련된

구문 풀이

13행 It's time to start creating your webtoon world at https://
= It's time you should start = It's time you started(가정법 과거)
webtoonskills.com.

02 일과 상황을 수용하고 받아들이기
정답률 73% | 정답 ⑤

다음 글에서 필자가 주장하는 바로 가장 적절한 것은?

① 창의력을 기르려면 익숙한 환경에서 벗어나야 한다.
② 상대방의 무리한 요구는 최대한 분명하게 거절해야 한다.
③ 주어진 과업을 정확하게 파악한 후에 일을 시작해야 한다.
④ 효율적으로 일을 처리하기 위해 좋아하는 일부터 해야 한다.
☑ 원치 않는 일을 해야만 할 때 수용적인 태도를 갖춰야 한다.

[본문 해석]

사람들은 원하지 않는 일을 더 해야 할수록, 자신과 다른 사람에게 불편한 환경을 만들 가능성이 더 커진다. 만약 여러분이 하는 일을 싫어하지만 그럼에도 불구하고 해야 한다면, 여러분은 그 일을 싫어하는 것과 그 일을 끝내야 한다는 사실을 받아들이는 것 중 하나를 선택할 수 있다. 어느 쪽이든, 여러분은 그 일을 할 것이다. 증오의 영역에서 그 일을 한다면, 여러분 자신과 주변 사람들을 향한 증오를 키우게 된다. (하지만) 수용의 영역에서 그 일을 한다면 자신을 향한 연민을 갖게 되며 그 과업을 달성할 더 적합한 방법을 찾을 기회를 갖게 된다. 과업이 완료되어야 한다는 사실을 받아들이기로 한다면, 여러분의 상황이 삶이 준 선물임을 인식하는 것으로부터 시작하라. 이는 여러분이 그것을 수용의 교훈으로 여기게 도울 것이다.

Why? 왜 정답일까?

일이 싫더라도 끝내야 한다는 것을 받아들이기로 했다면, 그것을 삶이 준 선물로 받아들이고 수용의 교훈으로 삼으라(If you decide to accept the fact that your task has to be done, start from recognising that your situation is a gift from life; ~ see it as a lesson in acceptance.)는 내용의 글이다. 따라서 필자가 주장하는 바로 가장 적절한 것은 ⑤ '원치 않는 일을 해야만 할 때 수용적인 태도를 갖춰야 한다.'이다.

- unwanted ⓐ 원치 않는
- environment ⓝ 환경
- develop ⓥ 키우다, 발전시키다
- compassion ⓝ 연민, 동정
- accomplish ⓥ 달성하다, 이루다
- unpleasant ⓐ 불쾌한
- nonetheless [ad] 그럼에도 불구하고
- acceptance ⓝ 수용
- allow for ~을 허용하다, 고려하다
- task ⓝ 과제

구문 풀이

1행 The more people have to do unwanted things the more
「the+비교급 ~, the+비교급 … : ~할수록 더 …하다」
chances are that they create unpleasant environment for themselves
접속사
and others.

★★★ 1등급 대비 고난도 3점 문제

03 사회적 삶의 연극적 속성 정답률 38% | 정답 ⑤

밑줄 친 constantly wearing masks가 다음 글에서 의미하는 바로 가장 적절한 것은? [3점]

① protecting our faces from harmful external forces
위험한 외부적 힘으로부터 우리 얼굴을 보호하고 있는
② performing on stage to show off our acting skills
우리의 연기력을 뽐내기 위해 무대에 공연하고 있는
③ feeling confident by beating others in competition
경쟁에서 남을 이겨서 자신감을 느끼고 있는
④ doing completely the opposite of what others expect
다른 사람들이 기대하는 것과 완전히 반대로 행동하고 있는
⑤ adjusting our behavior based on the social context given
주어진 사회적 상황에 기초하여 우리의 행동을 적용시키는

[본문 해석]

수 세기에 걸쳐 다양한 작가와 사상가들은 외부의 관점에서 인간들을 바라보며 사회적 삶의 연극적 속성과 마주해왔다. 이것을 표현하는 가장 유명한 명언은 셰익스피어에게서 비롯되는데, "모든 세상은 연극 무대이고, 모든 인간은 단지 배우일 뿐이다. 그들은 퇴장하고 입장한다. 그리고 일생 동안 한 인간은 다양한 역할을 연기한다." 만약 연극과 배우들이 전통적으로 가면의 이미지로 표현된다면, 셰익스피어와 같은 작가들은 우리 모두는 끊임없이 가면을 쓰고 있다는 것을 암시하고 있는 것이다. 어떤 사람들은 다른 사람보다 더 나은 배우이다. 연극 Othello 속 Iago와 같은 악역들은 그들의 적대적 의도를 친근한 미소 뒤에 숨길 수 있다. 다른 사람들은 더 큰 자신감과 허세를 가지고 연기를 할 수 있고, 그들은 주로 리더가 된다. 훌륭한 연기력을 가지고 있는 사람들은 우리의 복잡한 사회적 환경을 더 잘 헤쳐 나갈 수 있고 앞서갈 수 있다.

Why? 왜 정답일까?

삶을 연극 무대에 비유하고 있는 글로, 인간은 배우와 같아서 살면서 다양한 역할을 맡게 된다("All the world's a stage, / And all the men and women merely players; / ~ one man in his time plays many parts.")는 셰익스피어의 인용구가 주제를 잘 제시하고 있다. 특히 밑줄 뒤의 두 문장에서 적의를 친근한 미소 뒤에 숨긴 채 행동하거나, 자신감과 허세를 잘 가장하여 리더가 되는 경우를 언급하고 있다. 이는 사람들이 상황에 따라 자신이 필요한 대로 처세하기 위해 일정한 역할이나 특성을 꾸며낼 수 있음을 뜻하는 것이다. 따라서 밑줄 친 부분이 의미하는 바로 가장 적절한 것은 ⑤ '주어진 사회적 상황에 기초하여 우리의 행동을 적용시키는'이다.

- perspective ⓝ 관점
- merely [ad] 단지
- constantly [ad] 끊임없이
- navigate ⓥ (길을 가며) 방향을 찾다
- show off 뽐내다
- theatrical ⓐ 연극적인
- represent ⓥ 표현하다, 나타내다, 대표하다
- confidence ⓝ 자신감
- harmful ⓐ 해로운, 위험한

구문 풀이

1행 Over the centuries various writers and thinkers, looking at
기간 부사구   주어   분사구문
humans from an outside perspective, have been struck by the
현재완료 수동태
theatrical quality of social life.

▶ 많이 틀린 이유는?
이 글은 삶이 연극과 같다는 내용을 제시하고 있으며, 밑줄 친 부분의 masks는 우리가 사회적 상황에서 연기를 하듯 어떤 모습을 꾸며내어 대처하거나 특정한 역할을 담당한다는 것을 비유한 표현이다. ②는 이 masks를 삶에서의 연기가 아닌 무대에서의 연기와 연관짓고 있어 답으로 적절하지 않다.

▶ 문제 해결 방법은?
글에 인용구가 나오면 주제와 직결된다. 여기서도 삶이 연기와 다를 바 없다는 셰익스피어의 인용구를 토대로 '연기, 연극'이 비유적인 표현임을 이해해야 한다.

---

04 캐나다의 무급 돌봄 제공 비율 정답률 86% | 정답 ④

다음 도표의 내용과 일치하지 않는 것은?

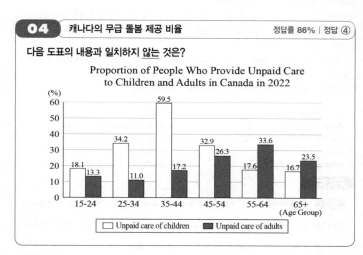

Proportion of People Who Provide Unpaid Care
to Children and Adults in Canada in 2022

[본문 해석]

위 그래프는 2022년 캐나다의 연령 집단별 아동과 성인에게 무급 돌봄을 제공한 사람의 비율을 보여 준다. ① 특히 35 ~ 44세 집단은 아동에게 무급 돌봄을 제공하는 사람의 비율이 가장 높았는데, 이는 59.5퍼센트에 달했다. ② 하지만 성인에게 무급 돌봄을 제공하는 사람의 가장 높은 비율은 55 ~ 64세 집단에서 발견되었다. ③ 25 ~ 34세 집단에 비해, 15 ~ 24세 집단은 아동에게 무급 돌봄을 제공하는 사람의 비율이 더 낮았고, 성인에게 무급 돌봄을 제공하는 사람의 비율이 더 높았다. ④ 45 ~ 54세 집단에서 성인에게 무급 돌봄을 제공하는 사람의 비율은 35 ~ 44세 집단의 비율보다 두 배 넘게 높았다. ⑤ 55 ~ 64세 집단과 65세 이상 집단은 아동에게 무급 돌봄을 제공하는 사람의 비율이 1퍼센트 포인트 미만의 차이로 비슷한 비율을 보였다.

Why? 왜 정답일까?

도표에 따르면 45 ~ 54세 집단에서 성인에게 무급 돌봄을 제공하는 사람의 비율은 26.3%이고, 35 ~ 44세 집단의 비율은 17.2%이므로 두 배 넘게 차이나지 않는다는 것을 알 수 있다. 따라서 도표와 일치하지 않는 것은 ④이다.

- unpaid ⓐ 무급의
- reach ⓥ 도달하다
- care ⓝ 돌봄, 치료

구문 풀이

3행 Notably, the 35-44 group had the highest percentage of
최상급
individuals providing unpaid care to children, reaching 59.5%.
현재분사

---

05 경제 성장의 영향에 대처하기 정답률 48% | 정답 ⑤

다음 글의 밑줄 친 부분 중, 어법상 틀린 것은? [3점]

[본문 해석]

World Bank와 같은 기관들은 '선진' 국가와 '개발도상' 국가를 구별하기 위해 부를 이용하지만, 그들은 또한 발전이 경제 성장 그 이상이라는 데 동의한다. '발전'은 경제 성장에 의해 야기되거나 경제 성장을 수반하는 사회적이고 환경적인 변화도 포함할 수 있으며, 그 변화의 일부는 긍정적이기에 (일부는) 부정적일지도 모른다. 경제 성장이 인간과 지구에 어떻게 영향을 미치고 있는지에 대한 문제가 다뤄질 필요가 있다는 인식이 커졌고, 계속해서 커지고 있다. 국가들은 경제 활동이나 프로젝트의 폐해를 피해가 나타난 이후보다, 그것이 계획되는 때인 초기에 줄이려고 노력하는 것이 비용이 덜 들고 훨씬 적은 고통을 야기한

다는 것을 서서히 깨닫고 있다. 이렇게 하는 것은 쉽지 않고 항상 불완전하다. 그러나 그러한 노력의 필요성에 대한 인식은 새로운 제품과 서비스를 만드는 데만 집중했던 이전의 널리 퍼진 태도보다 더 큰 이해와 도덕적 관심을 나타낸다.

Why? 왜 정답일까?

than 앞에 일반동사 indicates가 나오므로, than 뒤의 대동사는 do 동사 형태여야 한다. 이때 문맥상 시제가 과거이므로 was를 did로 고쳐야 한다. 따라서 어법상 틀린 것은 ⑤이다.

Why? 왜 오답일까?

① use가 포함된 3형식의 완전한 구조 뒤에 '~하기 위해'라는 목적의 의미로 주절을 보충하는 to부정사가 바르게 쓰였다.
② 콤마 앞으로 접속사 없이 문장이 연결되므로, some of 뒤에 관계대명사가 필요하다. 따라서 앞에 나온 복수 명사 changes를 대신하면서 두 문장을 연결하는 접속사 역할을 하는 which가 알맞게 쓰였다.
③ 주어인 the question이 단수 명사이므로, 동사 또한 단수형인 needs로 바르게 쓰였다.
④ 비교급 less를 강조하는 부사로 much가 바르게 쓰였다.

- institution ⑪ 기관
- differentiate ⑰ 구별하다
- environmental ⓐ 환경적인
- awareness ⑪ 인식
- suffering ⑪ 고통
- wealth ⑪ 부
- economic growth 경제 성장
- accompany ⑰ 동반하다
- address ⑰ 다루다, 처리하다
- imperfect ⓐ 불완전한

구문 풀이

4행 "Development" can also include the social and environmental
─────────── 선행사
changes [that are caused by or accompany economic growth], some
─── 주격 관·대
of which are positive and thus may be negative.
= the changes

---

06 친족을 묘사하는 체계가 비교적 단순한 영어 정답률 60% | 정답 ③

(A), (B), (C)의 각 네모 안에서 어법에 맞는 표현으로 가장 적절한 것은?

	(A)	(B)	(C)
①	described	which	have
②	described	in which	has
✓③	described	in which	have
④	describing	which	has
⑤	describing	in which	has

[본문 해석]

영어 사용자들은 가족 관계를 묘사하는 가장 단순한 체계 중 하나를 지닌다. 많은 아프리카 언어 사용자들은 남성과 여성 친척 양쪽 모두를 묘사하는 데 "cousin"과 같은 한 단어를 사용하는 것, 또는 묘사되는 사람이 말하는 사람의 아버지와 혈연관계인지 아니면 어머니와 혈연관계인지 구별하지 않는 것을 불합리하다고 여길 것이다. brother-in-law를 아내의 남자 형제인지 여자 형제의 남편인지 구별할 수 없다는 것은 많은 문화에 존재하는 인간관계의 구조 속에서 혼란스럽게 보일 것이다. 마찬가지로, "uncle"이라는 한 단어가 아버지의 형제와 어머니의 형제에게 적용되는 상황을 어떻게 이해할 수 있겠는가? 하와이 언어는 동일한 용어를 사용하여 아버지와 아버지의 남자 형제를 지칭한다. Jinghpaw 언어로 사고하는 Northern Burma의 사람들은 친족을 묘사하기 위한 18개의 기본 용어가 있다. 이 용어 중 어떤 것도 영어로 바로 번역될 수 없다.

Why? 왜 정답일까?

(A) the person이 '묘사하는' 주체가 아니고 '묘사되는' 대상이므로 과거분사인 described를 쓰는 것이 적절하다.
(B) 앞에 장소 명사로 취급되는 a situation이 나오고 뒤에 완전한 절이 나오므로 in which를 쓰는 것이 적절하다.
(C) 주어가 People of Northern Burma이고 뒤에 나온 who절은 수식을 위한 삽입절이다. 그러므로 복수 주어에 맞추어 have를 쓰는 것이 적절하다. 정답은 ③이다.

- absurd ⓐ 불합리한
- brother-in-law 시아주버니, 처남, 자형 등
- structure ⑪ 구조
- refer to ~을 지칭하다, 언급하다
- translate ⑰ 번역하다
- distinguish ⑰ 구별하다
- confusing ⓐ 혼란스러운, 혼란을 주는
- apply to ~에 적용되다
- kin ⑪ 친족

구문 풀이

7행 To be unable to distinguish a brother-in-law as the brother
─── 주어(~것)
of one's wife or the husband of one's sister would seem confusing
─── 동사 ─── 주격 보어(형용사)
within the structure of personal relationships [existing in many
└─ 전치사(~내에) ─── 현재분사
cultures].

---

07 사냥의 역사를 지니고 있는 음악 정답률 57% | 정답 ①

다음 빈칸에 들어갈 말로 가장 적절한 것을 고르시오.

✓① hunt - 사냥
② law - 법
③ charity - 자선 (행위)
④ remedy - 치료법
⑤ dance - 춤

[본문 해석]

심지어 모든 음악 단체 중 가장 훌륭한 단체인 교향악단도 자신의 DNA 안에 사냥의 유산을 지니고 있다. 교향악단에 있는 다양한 악기들은 다음의 원시적인 기원으로 거슬러 올라갈 수 있는데, 그것들의 초기 형태는 동물(뿔, 가죽, 내장, 뼈) 또는 동물을 진압하기 위해 사용된 무기(막대, 활)로 만들어졌다. 음악 그 자체에서, 세계의 주요한 교향악단의 핵심 레퍼토리로 남아 있는 기념비적인 교향곡들의 강력한 공격성과 경외감을 자아내는 당당함에서 이러한 역사를 듣는다면 우리가 틀린 것인가? 베토벤, 브람스, 말러, 브루크너, 베를리오즈, 차이코프스키, 쇼스타코비치 및 다른 위대한 작곡가들의 음악을 들으며, 나는 소리를 지배의 원천이자 상징으로, 공격적인 힘에 대한 의지의 표현으로 사용하면서 동물을 쫓기 시작하는 사람들 무리의 이미지를 쉽게 떠올릴 수 있다.

Why? 왜 정답일까?

두 번째 문장에서 초기 악기는 동물의 신체 부위로 만들어지거나 동물을 진압하기 위한 무기(either from the animal ~ or the weapons employed in bringing the animal under control)에서 기원했다고 설명한다. 마지막 문장에서는 유명한 음악가의 음악을 들으면 과거 조상들이 소리로 공격의 의지를 표명하면서 동물들을 사냥하던 모습을 상상할 수 있다고 언급한다. 따라서 빈칸에 들어갈 말로 가장 적절한 것은 ① '사냥'이다.

- respectable ⓐ 훌륭한, 존경할 만한
- trace back to ~으로 거슬러 올라가다
- hide ⑪ (동물의) 가죽
- awe-inspiring ⓐ 경외감을 불러일으키는
- monumental ⓐ 기념비적인, 엄청난
- predatory ⓐ 포식하는, 생물을 잡아먹는
- institution ⑪ 기관, 제도
- primitive ⓐ 원시적인
- aggression ⑪ 공격성
- assertiveness ⑪ 적극성, 자기 주장
- summon up (생각 등을) 불러일으키다

구문 풀이

11행 Listening to Beethoven, Brahms, Mahler, Bruckner, Berlioz,
└─ 분사구문(~하면서)
Tchaikovsky, Shostakovich, and other great composers, I can easily
─── 동사구
summon up images of bands of men starting to chase animals,
─── 목적어 ── 꾸밈 받는 명사 └ 현재분사
using sound as a source and symbol of dominance, an expression
└─ 분사구문(~하면서) ─ 전치사(~로서)
of the will to predatory power.

★★★ 1등급 대비 고난도 2점 문제

08 다른 사람의 도움이 자존감에 해가 되는 순간 정답률 44% | 정답 ①

다음 빈칸에 들어갈 말로 가장 적절한 것을 고르시오.

✓① make you feel bad about yourself
당신이 스스로를 안 좋게 느끼도록 만들
② improve your ability to deal with challenges
어려움에 대처하는 능력을 높여줄
③ be seen as a way of asking for another favor
또 다른 부탁을 하는 방법으로 여겨질
④ trick you into thinking that you were successful
스스로 성공했다고 착각하게 할
⑤ discourage the person trying to model your behavior
당신의 행동을 본보기로 삼으려는 사람을 낙담시킬

[본문 해석]

도움이 효과적이지 않을 수 있는 몇몇 이유들이 있다. 한 가지 가능한 이유는 도움을 받는 것이 자존감에 타격이 될 수 있다는 것이다. Lehigh 대학의 Christopher Burke와 Jessica Goren에 의한 최근 한 연구는 이 가능성을 조사했다. 자존감 위협 모델 이론에 따르면, 도움은 협력적이고 애정 있는 것으로

여겨질 수도 있고, 혹은 만약 그 도움이 무능함을 암시하는 것으로 해석된다면 위협적으로 보여질 수 있다. Burke와 Goren에 따르면 도움이 자기 연관적이거나 자기 정의적인 영역 — 다시 말해, 자신의 성공과 성취가 특히 중요한 영역 — 안에 있는 경우, 그것은 특히 위협으로 보여질 가능성이 있다. 자기 연관적인 일로 도움을 받는 것은 당신이 스스로를 안 좋게 느끼도록 만들 수 있고, 이것은 도움의 잠재적인 긍정적 영향에 해를 줄 수 있다. 예를 들어, 만약 당신의 자아 개념이 훌륭한 요리 실력에 일부 기초한다면, 친구가 당신이 손님들을 위해 식사를 준비하는 것을 도울 때 이는 당신의 자아에 타격이 될 수 있는데 이는 당신이 생각했던 만큼 유능한 요리사가 아니라는 뜻이기 때문이다.

Why? 왜 정답일까?

도움이 효과적이지 않은 순간 중 하나는 도움이 자존감에 타격을 줄 때(One possible reason is that receiving help could be a blow to self-esteem.)임을 설명하는 글이므로, 빈칸에 들어갈 말로 가장 적절한 것은 ① '당신이 스스로를 안 좋게 느끼도록 만들'이다.

- blow ⓝ 타격, 충격
- threat ⓝ 위협
- self-relevant 자아 관련의
- self-concept ⓝ 자아 개념
- trick A into B A를 속여 B하게 하다
- self-esteem ⓝ 자아 존중감
- incompetence ⓝ 무능
- undermine ⓥ 손상시키다
- rest on ~에 놓여 있다
- discourage ⓥ 낙담시키다

구문 풀이

17행 ~ it may be a blow to your ego when a friend helps you prepare a meal for guests because it suggests that you're not the master chef [(you thought) you were].
선행사 ┘ 삽입절
[ ]: 형용사절
(were의 보어가 없는 불완전한 절)

★★ 문제 해결 꿀~팁 ★★

▶ 많이 틀린 이유는?
'~ support is especially likely to be seen as threatening ~' 문장에서 과업의 자기 관련성이 높은(self-relevant or self-defining) 경우 타인의 도움이 오히려 위험으로 여겨질 수 있다고 한다. ②의 경우, 이런 과업에서 타인의 도움을 받으면 위기 대처 능력이 '향상된다'는 의미이므로 주제와 정반대된다. ④는 자기 관련성이 높은 과업에서 타인의 도움을 받을 때 '우리가 성공했다는 착각에 빠질 수 있다'는 의미인데, 성공에 대한 착각은 글에서 언급되지 않았다.
▶ 문제 해결 방법은?
마지막 문장의 a blow to your ego를 ①에서 feel bad about yourself로 바꾸었다.

---

09 머리카락의 영적 중요성 정답률 66% | 정답 ③

다음 글에서 전체 흐름과 관계 없는 문장은?

[본문 해석]
과거 17세기 정도에 머리카락은 아프리카에서 특별한 영적 중요성을 가졌다. 많은 아프리카의 문화들은 신체에서 머리를 지배, 소통, 그리고 정체성의 중심이라고 여겼다. ① 머리카락은 개인을 인격화하는 힘의 원천으로 여겨졌고 영적인 목적을 위해서나 심지어 주문을 걸기 위해서 사용될 수 있었다. ② 머리카락은 신체의 가장 높은 지점에 있기 때문에, 그 자체로 신성한 영혼들과 소통할 수 있는 수단이었고 행운을 가져오거나 악으로부터 지켜준다고 생각되는 방식으로 다루어졌다. ③ 사람들은 서로의 머리카락을 스타일링해 주면서 사귀는 기회를 가졌고 머리카락에 대한 공유된 전통이 대대로 전해졌다. ④ 작가 Ayana Byrd와 Lori Tharps에 따르면, "신과 영혼들로부터의 의사소통이 머리카락을 통과하여 영혼에 다다른다고 여겨졌다." ⑤ 예를 들어 Cameroon에서는 치료 주술사들이 치료 물약을 보호하고 그 효과성을 높이기 위해 머리카락을 자신의 물약을 담은 용기에 붙였다.

Why? 왜 정답일까?

아프리카 문화권에서 머리카락은 영적 의미를 가진 대상으로 이해되었다는 내용의 글로, ①, ②, ④, ⑤는 모두 주제를 뒷받침한다. 하지만 ③은 사람들이 머리 스타일을 만져주며 서로 사귀었고 머리카락에 관한 공유된 전통이 대대로 전해졌다는 무관한 내용을 다룬다. 따라서 전체 흐름과 관계없는 문장은 ③이다.

- spiritual ⓐ 영적인
- identity ⓝ 정체성
- cast a spell 주문을 걸다
- significance ⓝ 중요성
- personify ⓥ 인격화하다
- divine ⓐ 성스러운, 신성한

- socialize ⓥ (사람을) 사귀다. 어울리다
- enhance ⓥ 강화하다, 향상시키다
- pass down 전해주다

구문 풀이

4행 Hair was regarded as a source of power [that personified
「A + be regarded as + B : A가 B로 간주되다」 주격 관계대명사 / 동사1
the individual and could be used for spiritual purposes or
동사2 부사구1
even to cast a spell].
부사구2(목적)

★★★ 1등급 대비 고난도 2점 문제

10 잊힐 권리 정답률 30% | 정답 ②

주어진 글 다음에 이어질 글의 순서로 가장 적절한 것을 고르시오.

① (A) − (C) − (B)
② (B) − (A) − (C) ✓
③ (B) − (C) − (A)
④ (C) − (A) − (B)
⑤ (C) − (B) − (A)

[본문 해석]
잊힐 권리는 사생활 권리와 구별되지만 연관성이 있는 권리이다. 사생활 권리는 무엇보다도 전통적으로 보호되거나 공개되지 않아야 할 개인적인 것으로 여겨지는 정보에 대한 권리이다.

(B) 반면에 잊힐 권리는 공공의 영역에 있었던 정보에 적용될 수 있다. 잊힐 권리는 개인이 특정 시점의 정보에 의해 영원히 규정되지 않을 권리를 폭넓게 포함한다.

(A) 그러한 권리의 한 가지 이유는 개인이 자기 삶을 영위하고 삶의 특정한 사건이나 기간에 의해 한정되지 않도록 해 주는 것이다. 예를 들어, 영국과 프랑스와 같은 일부 국가에서는 과거의 범죄 유죄 판결조차도 결국 '다 소모되고' 한 사람의 삶에 계속 영향을 미치지 않아야 한다고 오랫동안 인식되어 왔다.

(C) 잊힐 권리를 지지하는 이유에도 불구하고, 잊힐 권리는 다른 권리와 때때로 충돌할 수 있다. 예를 들어, 공식적인 예외가 안보와 공중 보건의 이유로 인해 때때로 생겨난다.

Why? 왜 정답일까?

잊힐 권리의 개념과 필요성을 설명하는 글이다. 주어진 글에서 '사생활 권리'를 잊힐 권리와 대비되는 개념으로 언급한 후, in contrast로 시작하는 (B)는 잊힐 권리로 다시 돌아와 예시와 함께 의미를 설명한다. (A)에서는 잊힐 권리가 왜 필요한지 이유를 설명하고, (C)에서는 그런 이유에도 불구하고 가끔 예외 상황은 생길 수 있음을 덧붙인다. 따라서 글의 순서로 가장 적절한 것은 ② '(B) − (A) − (C)'이다.

- right to be forgotten 잊힐 권리
- reveal ⓥ 드러내다, 폭로하다
- criminal ⓐ 형사상의, 범죄의
- spent ⓐ 소모된, 영향력이 없어진
- formal ⓐ 공식적인
- right to privacy 사생활 권리
- define ⓥ 규정하다, 한정짓다
- conviction ⓝ 유죄 판결
- domain ⓝ 영역
- public health 공중 보건

구문 풀이

2행 The right to privacy is, (among other things), the right for
동사 ( ): 삽입구 주격 보어
information traditionally regarded as protected or personal not to
~라고 여겨지는
be revealed.

★★ 문제 해결 꿀~팁 ★★

▶ 많이 틀린 이유는?
주어진 글과 (B)를 연결하고 난 다음이 문제이다. (B)의 마지막은 '잊힐 권리'의 범위(includes ~)를 언급하며 끝나는데, (A)는 이 권리가 필요한 이유를, (C)는 이 권리가 다른 권리와 충돌을 일으킨다는 내용을 각각 다룬다. 즉 (C)에서 글의 흐름이 전환되고 있으므로 (B) − (C)를 바로 연결하는 ③은 답으로 적절치 않다.
▶ 문제 해결 방법은?
(A)의 motivation이 바로 '이유'를 말하는 표현이다. (B)에서 잊힐 권리의 개념과 범위를 소개한 뒤, 이런 권리를 지지하는 '한 가지 이유'를 말하는 (A)가 먼저 나오고, '그런 이유에도 불구하고' 권리 충돌이 발생한다는 내용의 (C)가 마지막에 나와야 적절하다.

DAY 03

[문제편 p.021]

11-12 분석에 의한 마비 현상

[본문 해석]

「분석에 의한 마비는 특정 문제를 지나치게 생각하고 분석하지만 여전히 결정을 내리지 못하는 상태이다.」(「 」: 11번의 근거) 여우와 고양이의 한 유명한 고대 우화는 이 분석에 의한 마비 상황을 가장 간단한 방법으로 설명한다. 이야기에서, 여우와 고양이는 그들이 사냥꾼으로부터 탈출할 수 있는 얼마나 많은 방법이 있는지 논의한다. 고양이는 재빨리 나무에 오른다. 반면에 여우는 그가 알고 있는 모든 탈출 방법을 분석하기 시작한다. 하지만 어떤 것이 가장 좋을지 결정하지 못한 채, 그는 행동하지 (a) 못하고 개들에게 잡힌다. 이 이야기는 분석 마비 현상을 완벽하게 설명하는데, 이용 가능한 대안들에 대한 지나친 생각 때문에 행동하거나 결정하지 (b) 못하는 것이다. 사람들은 비록 문제의 해결책을 찾으려는 좋은 의도로 시작하지만, 그들은 종종 잘못된 결정을 초래할지 모를 다양한 요인에 대해 무한히 분석하는 것을 경험한다. 그들은 이용 가능한 정보에 만족하지 못하고 그들의 결정을 완벽하게 하기 위해 여전히 (c) 더 많은 데이터가 필요하다고 생각한다. 「대부분 이러한 분석에 의한 마비 상황은 누군가가 처참한 잠재적 결과를 초래할 수 있는 잘못된 결정을 할까 봐 두려워할 때 (d) 발생하고, 그들의 경력이나 조직의 생산성에 영향을 미칠 수 있다.」(「 」: 12번의 근거) 그래서 그것이 사람들이 일반적으로 막대한 이해관계가 수반되는 결정을 내릴 때 (e) 자신이 있는(→ 지나치게 조심하는) 이유이다.

- end up ~ing 결국 ~하게 되다
- illustrate ⓥ (예를 들어 분명하게) 보여주다
- inability ⓝ ~할 수 없음, 무능력
- intention ⓝ 의도
- catastrophic ⓐ 처참한, 재앙 같은
- productivity ⓝ 생산성
- fable ⓝ 우화
- phenomenon ⓝ 현상
- alternative ⓝ 대안 ⓐ 대체의
- indefinitely ad 무한히
- consequence ⓝ 결과, 영향
- keep A from B A가 B하지 못하게 하다

구문 풀이

9행 But (being) unable to decide which one would be the best, he fails to act and gets caught by the dogs.
(being): 생략(분사구문) 형용사 보어 / which one: 의문형용사(어떤) / fails to act: 동사구1(~하지 못하다) / gets caught: 동사구2

11 제목 파악
정답률 71% | 정답 ④

윗글의 제목으로 가장 적절한 것은?

① Best Ways to Keep You from Overthinking
당신이 너무 많은 생각을 하지 않게 할 최선의 방법
② Overthinking or Overdoing: Which Is Worse?
과한 생각 또는 과한 행동: 어느 것이 더 나쁠까?
③ Costs and Benefits of Having Various Alternatives
다양한 대안을 갖고 있는 것의 비용과 이점
✔④ Overthinking: A Barrier to Effective Decision-making
과한 생각: 효과적인 의사결정의 장애물
⑤ Trapped in Moral Dilemma: Harmful for Your Survival
도덕적 딜레마에 갇히는 것: 생존에 해롭다

Why? 왜 정답일까?

첫 문장에서 핵심 소재인 '분석에 의한 마비 현상'을 정의 내린 후 예시를 통해 개념을 쉽게 설명해주는 글이다. '**Paralysis by analysis is a state of overthinking and analyzing a particular problem, but you still end up not making a decision.**'에서 분석에 의한 마비 상황이란 어떤 문제에 대해 생각이 너무 많아서 쉽게 결정을 내리지 못하는 상태라고 언급하는 것으로 볼 때, 글의 제목으로 가장 적절한 것은 ④ '과한 생각: 효과적인 의사결정의 장애물'이다.

12 어휘 추론
정답률 55% | 정답 ⑤

밑줄 친 (a)~(e) 중에서 문맥상 낱말의 쓰임이 적절하지 않은 것은? [3점]

① (a) ② (b) ③ (c) ④ (d) ✔⑤ (e)

Why? 왜 정답일까?

'**Most often this situation of paralysis by analysis arises when somebody is afraid of making an erroneous decision that can lead to potential catastrophic consequences:** ~'에서 분석에 의한 마비 현상은 잘못된 결정으로 처참한 결과가 발생할까봐 우려되는 상황에서 발생한다고 언급한다. 이를 근거로 보면, **(e)**가 포함된 문장은 사람들이 막대한 이해관계가 수반되는 결정을 해야 할 때 '망설이는' 이유가 바로 분석에 의한 마비 현상 때문이라는 의미여야 하므로, **(e)**의 **confident**를 **overcautious**로 고쳐야 한다. 따라서 문맥상 낱말의 쓰임이 적절하지 않은 것은 ⑤ '**(e)**'이다.

DAY 04 20분 미니 모의고사

01 ④	02 ③	03 ②	04 ⑤	05 ④
06 ①	07 ①	08 ③	09 ④	10 ④
11 ③	12 ③			

01 낙관적인 상상의 부작용
정답률 47% | 정답 ④

다음 글의 요지로 가장 적절한 것은?

① 과도한 목표 지향적 태도는 삶의 만족감을 떨어뜨린다.
② 긍정적 자세로 역경을 극복할 때 잠재 능력이 발휘된다.
③ 편안함을 느끼는 상황에서 자기 개선에 대한 동기가 생긴다.
✔④ 낙관적인 상상은 소망을 실현하는 데 필요한 동력을 약화시킨다.
⑤ 막연한 목표보다는 명확하고 구체적인 목표가 실현 가능성이 크다.

[본문 해석]

낙관적인 상상이 우리가 긴장을 푸는 데 도움이 되어서 그것이 생물학적 검사로 나타날 정도라는 것은 주목할 만하다. 만약 여러분이 긴장을 풀고 싶다면 심호흡하거나 마사지를 받거나 산책을 할 수도 있지만, 단순히 눈을 감고 여러분이 누릴지도 모를 미래의 결과에 대해 상상해 볼 수도 있다. 하지만 여러분의 목표가 소망을 실현하는 것인 경우라면 어떨까? 여러분이 *가장 피해야 할* 상태는 긴장이 풀려 있는 것이다. 여러분은 소파에서 일어나 (지금 쪄 있는) 살을 빼거나, (원하는) 직업을 찾거나 (붙고 싶은) 시험공부를 할 수 있을 만큼 충분히 활력을 얻어야 하고, 피할 수 없는 장애물이나 문제가 발생할 때도 계속 전념할 수 있도록 충분히 동기 부여되어야 한다. '꿈꾸라. 소망하라. 실현하라.'라는 원칙은 사실이 아니며, 우리는 이제 그 이유를 안다. 꿈꾸고 있을 때, 여러분은 그걸 하는 데 필요한 에너지를 약화시킨다. 여러분은 완전한 행복, 고요, 그리고 비활동의 일시적인 상태에 빠지게 된다.

Why? 왜 정답일까?

'**But what about ~**' 문장 이후로 주제가 제시되는데, 낙관적 상상이 긴장을 푸는 데는 도움이 되지만 목표 실현에는 도움이 안 된다(~ **in dreaming it, you undercut the energy you need to do it.**)는 것이다. 따라서 글의 요지로 가장 적절한 것은 ④ '낙관적인 상상은 소망을 실현하는 데 필요한 동력을 약화시킨다.'이다.

- remarkable ⓐ 두드러지는
- unwind ⓥ 긴장을 풀다, (감긴 것을) 풀다
- objective ⓝ 목표
- inevitable ⓐ 피할 수 없는, 필연적인
- arise ⓥ 발생하다
- undercut ⓥ 약화하다
- inactivity ⓝ 무활동
- physiological ⓐ 생리학적인
- outcome ⓝ 결과
- be motivated to ~하도록 동기 부여받다
- obstacle ⓝ 장애물
- hold true 사실이다
- temporary ⓐ 일시적인

구문 풀이

1행 It's remarkable {that positive fantasies help us relax to such an extent that it shows up in physiological tests}. ({ }: 진주어)
help: 동사 / us: 목적어 / relax: 목·보(원형부정사) / such an extent that: ~할 정도로

02 환경에 대한 인간 지배의 시작
정답률 61% | 정답 ③

다음 글의 제목으로 가장 적절한 것은?

① Strategies for Industrial Innovations
산업 혁신을 위한 전략
② Urbanization: A Road to a Better Life
도시화: 더 나은 삶으로 가는 길
✔③ Industrial Development Hurt the Environment
산업 발달이 환경을 해쳤다
④ Technology: A Key to Sustainable Development
기술: 지속 가능한 발전의 열쇠
⑤ The Driving Force of Capitalism Was Not Greed
자본주의의 원동력은 탐욕이 아니었다

[본문 해석]

환경에 대한 인간 지배의 실현은 1700년대 후반 산업 혁명과 함께 시작되었다. 제조업의 발달은 사회와 경제를 변화시키면서 환경에 중대한 영향을 미쳤다. 증기 기관의 발달이 기계화를 통한 상품의 대량 생산으로 이어지면서 미국 사회는 여러 산업의 자본주의적 목표에 따라 구축되었다. 수제 상품과 농업에 기

반을 둔 경제를 가진 시골의 농업 사회는 산업화된 제조업 경제를 기반으로 한 대규모 공장이 있는 도시에서의 삶을 위해 버려졌다. 직물, 철, 철강 생산의 혁신은 사기업의 이윤을 증대하였다. 동시에, 그런 산업들은 환경에 권력을 행사하였고 공공 토지와 수로에 유해한 부산물을 내버리기 시작했다.

Why? 왜 정답일까?

첫 문장에서 환경에 대한 인간의 지배가 산업화와 함께 시작되었다(The realization of human domination over the environment began in the late 1700s with the industrial revolution.)고 언급한 뒤, 산업 발달과 함께 착취되고 오염되기 시작한 환경에 관해 서술하고 있다. 따라서 글의 제목으로 가장 적절한 것은 ③ '산업 발달이 환경을 해쳤다'이다.

- realization ⓝ 실현
- industrial revolution 산업 혁명
- significant ⓐ 중대한
- mechanize ⓥ 기계화하다
- abandon ⓥ 버리다
- authority ⓝ 권위
- by-product ⓝ 부산물
- driving force 추진력, 원동력
- domination ⓝ 지배
- transform ⓥ 변모시키다
- capitalistic ⓐ 자본주의적인
- mass ⓝ 대량, 많음
- exert ⓥ (힘, 영향 등을) 행사하다, 가하다
- hazardous ⓐ 유해한
- sustainable ⓐ 지속 가능한
- greed ⓝ 탐욕

구문 풀이

1행 The realization of human domination over the environment [주어] began in the late 1700s with the industrial revolution. [동사(과거)] [시간 부사구]

---

03 Charles H. Townes의 생애 정답률 91% | 정답 ②

Charles H. Townes에 관한 다음 글의 내용과 일치하지 않는 것은?
① 어린 시절에 농장에서 성장하였다.
✓② 박사 학위를 받기 전에 Bell Labs에서 일했다.
③ 1958년에 레이저의 개념을 제안하였다.
④ 1964년에 노벨 물리학상을 수상하였다.
⑤ 달 착륙 프로젝트에 관여하였다.

[본문 해석]

가장 영향력 있는 미국의 물리학자 중 한 사람인 Charles H. Townes는 South Carolina에서 태어났다. 「어린 시절에 그는 하늘에 있는 별들을 연구하면서 농장에서 성장했다.」「1939년에 그는 California Institute of Technology에서 박사 학위를 받았고 그 후 뉴욕시에 있는 Bell Labs에 일자리를 얻었다.」 제2차 세계 대전 후에 그는 Columbia 대학교에서 물리학 부교수가 되었다. 「1958년에 Townes와 그의 공동 연구자는 레이저의 개념을 제안했다.」 레이저 기술은 산업과 연구에서 빠르게 인정받았다. 「1964년에 그는 노벨 물리학상을 받았다.」「그는 또한 달 착륙 프로젝트인 아폴로 계획에 관여했다.」 인터넷과 모든 디지털 미디어는 레이저 없이는 상상할 수 없을 것이라는 점에서 그의 공헌은 대단히 귀중하다.

Why? 왜 정답일까?

'He earned his doctoral degree from the California Institute of Technology in 1939, and then he took a job at Bell Labs in New York City.'에 따르면, Charles H. Townes는 박사 학위를 취득하고 나서 Bell Labs에서 근무했으므로, 내용과 일치하지 않는 것은 ② '박사 학위를 받기 전에 Bell Labs에서 일했다.'이다.

Why? 왜 오답일까?

① 'In his childhood, he grew up on a farm, studying the stars in the sky.'의 내용과 일치한다.
③ 'In 1958, Townes and his co-researcher proposed the concept of the laser.'의 내용과 일치한다.
④ 'He received the Nobel Prize in Physics in 1964.'의 내용과 일치한다.
⑤ 'He was also involved in Project Apollo, the moon landing project.'의 내용과 일치한다.

- physicist ⓝ 물리학자
- doctoral degree 박사 학위
- lab (laboratory) ⓝ 연구소, 실험실
- co-researcher ⓝ 공동 연구자
- acceptance ⓝ 인정
- earn ⓥ 얻다, 벌다
- take a job 취직하다
- associate professor 부교수
- propose ⓥ 제안하다
- industry ⓝ 업계

- be involved in ~에 관여하다
- priceless ⓐ 대단히 귀중한
- contribution ⓝ 공헌, 기여
- unimaginable ⓐ 상상할 수 없는

구문 풀이

13행 His contribution is priceless because the Internet and all digital [가정법 과거 주절] media would be unimaginable without the laser.
= if it were not for

---

04 심해 유기체들의 특성 정답률 64% | 정답 ⑤

다음 글의 밑줄 친 부분 중, 어법상 틀린 것은? [3점]

[본문 해석]

심해에 사는 유기체들은 몸에 물을 저장하여 고압에 적응해 왔고, 일부는 거의 물로만 구성되어 있다. 대부분의 심해 유기체들은 부레가 없다. 그들은 주변 환경에 체온을 맞추는 냉혈 유기체들로, 이는 그들이 낮은 신진대사를 유지하고 있는 동안 차가운 물에서 생존하게 한다. 구할 수 있는 드문 먹이를 찾는 것이 많은 에너지를 소비하기 때문에, 많은 종들은 신진대사를 아주 많이 낮추어 오랜 기간 먹이 없이 생존이 가능하다. 심해의 많은 포식성 물고기는 거대한 입과 날카로운 이빨을 가지고 있고, 이는 물고기들이 먹이를 붙잡고 제압하게 한다. 해양의 잔광 구역에서 먹이를 잡는 일부 포식자들은 뛰어난 시력을 가지고 있는 반면, 다른 포식자들은 먹이나 짝을 끌어들이기 위해 빛을 만들어 낼 수 있다.

Why? 왜 정답일까?

주어가 복수 명사인 Some predators이므로, 동사 또한 단수형인 has가 아닌 have로 써 주어야 적절하다. 주어와 동사 사이의 'hunting ~'은 주어를 꾸민다. 따라서 어법상 틀린 것은 ⑤이다.

Why? 왜 오답일까?

① 앞에 완전한 주절이 나온 뒤 의미상 주어 some 뒤로 분사구문이 이어지는 것이다. 따라서 현재분사 consisting은 알맞게 쓰였다.
② allow는 목적격 보어 자리에 to부정사를 쓰는 동사이므로, allowing them 뒤로 to survive가 알맞게 쓰였다.
③ 뒤에 주어가 없는 관계절이 나와 the sparse food를 꾸미고 있으므로, 주격 관계대명사 that은 알맞게 쓰였다.
④ 앞에 나온 불가산명사 prey를 가리키기 위해 단수 대명사 it을 쓴 것은 적절하다.

- entirely ⓐⓓ 전적으로
- sparse ⓐ 드문, (밀도가) 희박한
- predatory ⓐ 포식성의
- enormous ⓐ 거대한
- residual ⓐ 잔여의
- metabolism ⓝ 신진대사
- expend ⓥ 소비하다
- be equipped with ~을 갖추다
- overpower ⓥ 제압하다, 압도하다

구문 풀이

7행 Many species lower their metabolism so much that they are [so ~ that : 너무 ~해서 …하다] able to survive without food for long periods of time, as finding the [접속사(이유)] [주어(동명사구)] sparse food [that is available] expends a lot of energy.
[ ] : the sparse food 수식 → 동사(단수)

---

05 용어를 통한 문제 인식 정답률 53% | 정답 ④

다음 글의 밑줄 친 부분 중, 문맥상 낱말의 쓰임이 적절하지 않은 것은? [3점]

[본문 해석]

사진이 생생한 색으로 되어 있지 않았던 시기로 돌아가 보자. 그 기간 동안, 사람들은 오늘날 우리가 부르듯이 사진을 '흑백 사진'이 아닌 '사진'이라고 불렀다. 색의 가능성은 존재하지 않았고, 따라서 '흑백'이라는 형용사를 삽입하는 것은 ① 불필요했다. 하지만, 우리가 컬러 사진의 존재 전에 '흑백'이라는 어구를 정말로 포함시켰다고 가정해 보자. 그 현실을 ② 강조함으로써, 우리는 현재의 한계를 의식하게 되고, 따라서 새로운 가능성과 잠재적 기회에 마음을 연다. 제1차 세계대전은 우리가 제2차 세계대전에 깊이 휘말린 ③ 후에야 비로소 그 이름이 붙여졌다. 1940년대의 끔찍한 시기 이전에, 제1차 세계대전은 단순히 '대전쟁', 또는 더 심하게는 '모든 전쟁을 끝내는 전쟁'이라고 불렸다. 만약 우리가 1918년으로 돌아가 그것을 '제1차 세계대전' 이라고 불렀더라면 어땠을까? 그러한 명칭은 두 번째 세계적 충돌의 가능성을 정부와 개인에게 ④ 예측

할 수 없는(→ 더 큰) 현실로 만들었을지도 모른다. 우리가 문제를 명시적으로
⑤ 확인했을 때, 우리는 그것을 의식하게 된다.

Why? 왜 정답일까?

글 전반부에서 흑백 사진이 표준이어서 사람들이 흑백 사진을 그냥 '사진'이라고 부르던
시절에 만일 '흑백 사진'이라는 용어를 썼다면 '컬러 사진'이라는 새로운 기회에 대한
인식이 깨어났을지도 모른다고 설명한다. 이어서 제1차 세계대전이 비슷한 예로 언급되
는데, 만일 제2차 세계대전이 일어날 줄 모르는 상황 속에서 이미 '제1차 세계대전'이라
는 용어를 썼다면 사람들이 '제2차' 세계대전의 가능성을 '더' 현실적으로 인지했을 것이
라는 내용이 서술되고 있다. 이러한 흐름으로 보아, ④의 unpredictable을 greater
로 고쳐야 한다. 따라서 문맥상 낱말의 쓰임이 적절하지 않은 것은 ④이다.

● unnecessary ⓐ 불필요한 　● insert ⓥ 삽입하다
● existence ⓝ 존재 　● highlight ⓥ 강조하다
● limitation ⓝ 한계 　● embattle ⓥ 전쟁 준비를 갖추다
● conflict ⓝ 충돌, 갈등 　● unpredictable ⓐ 예측 불가능한
● explicitly ⓐ 명시적으로 　● identify ⓥ 확인하다, 알아보다

구문 풀이

11행 World War I was given that name only after we were deeply
　　　　　주어　　　4형식 수동태　　목적어　　접속사(~하고 나서야 비로소)
embattled in World War II.

---

06 규제에서 꽃피는 기업의 혁신 　정답률 58% | 정답 ①

다음 빈칸에 들어갈 말로 가장 적절한 것을 고르시오.

✓ innovation – 혁신 　② resistance – 저항
③ fairness – 공정함 　④ neglect – 방치
⑤ unity – 통합

[본문 해석]

비즈니스 전략과 환경을 연구하는 과정에서, Michael Porter는 기업이 규제로
부터 이익을 얻는 것처럼 보인다는 독특한 패턴을 발견했다. 그는 또한 더 엄
격한 규제가 느슨한 규제보다 더 많은 혁신을 유발하고 있다는 것을 발견했다.
네덜란드의 꽃 산업은 하나의 예시다. 수년 동안, 네덜란드의 세계적으로 유명
한 튤립과 다른 꽃들을 생산하는 회사들은 또한 비료와 농약으로 그 나라의 물
과 토양을 오염시키고 있었다. 1991년, 네덜란드 정부는 2000년까지 농약 사
용을 절반으로 줄이도록 고안된 정책을 채택했는데, 이것은 그들이 궁극적으
로 달성한 목표였다. 점점 더 엄격한 규제에 직면하면서, 온실 재배자들은 더
적은 양의 농약으로 상품의 품질을 유지하려면 새로운 방법을 개발해야만 한
다는 것을 깨달았다. 이에 그들은 폐쇄 루프 방식으로 물을 순환시키고 암모
배양판에서 꽃을 키우는 재배 방식으로 전환했다. 새로운 시스템은 환경에 배
출되는 오염을 감소시켰을 뿐만 아니라, 회사들이 재배 조건을 더 잘 통제할
수 있게 해 이익을 증가시켰다.

Why? 왜 정답일까?

네덜란드의 꽃 산업을 예로 들어, 국가적인 엄격한 규제가 생산 주체들로 하여금 새로운
방법과 혁신을 시도하도록 격려한다(Businesses seemed to be profiting from
regulation.)는 것을 보여주는 글이다. 따라서 빈칸에 들어갈 말로 가장 적절한 것은
① '혁신'이다.

● peculiar ⓐ 특이한 　● prompt ⓥ 유발하다
● illustration ⓝ (잘 보여주는) 예 　● world-renowned ⓐ 세계적으로 유명한
● contaminate ⓥ 오염시키다 　● fertilizer ⓝ 비료
● pesticide ⓝ 살충제 　● cultivation ⓝ 경작, 재배
● substrate ⓝ 배양판 　● resistance ⓝ 저항
● neglect ⓝ 방치, 태만, 소홀

구문 풀이

12행 Facing increasingly strict regulation, greenhouse growers
　　　　분사구문(= Faced with)
realized (that) they had to develop new methods if they were going
　　　　생략(명사절 접속사)
to maintain product quality with fewer pesticides.

★★★ 1등급 대비 고난도 3점 문제

07 찰나의 인식에 의해 형성되는 직감 　정답률 46% | 정답 ①

다음 빈칸에 들어갈 말로 가장 적절한 것을 고르시오. [3점]

✓ result of our cognitive processing system
　우리의 인지 처리 체계의 결과
② instance of discarding negative memories
　부정적 기억을 버리는 것의 예시
③ mechanism of overcoming our internal conflicts
　우리의 내적 갈등을 극복하는 기제
④ visual representation of our emotional vulnerability
　우리의 정서적 취약성의 시각적 표현
⑤ concrete signal of miscommunication within the brain
　뇌 속의 의사소통 오류에 대한 구체적 신호

[본문 해석]

우리는 우리의 직감이 단지 내면의 느낌, 즉 비밀스러운 내적 목소리라고 생각
할지도 모르지만, 사실 그것은 얼굴 표정 또는 시각적 불일치와 같이 너무 빨
리 지나가서 보통 우리가 그것을 알아차렸음을 의식하지도 못하는, 우리 주변
의 가시적인 무언가에 대한 인식에 의해 형성된다. 오늘날 심리학자들은 이러
한 순간을 '시각적 연결시키기 게임'으로 생각한다. 그렇다면 스트레스를 받거
나, 서두르고 있거나 피곤한 사람이 이 시각적 연결시키기에 의존할 가능성이
더 높다. 그들이 눈앞의 상황을 볼 때 정신의 지식 저장고 안에 보관된 과거 경
험의 바다와 그것을 재빨리 연결해 보고, 그다음 연결에 기초하여 앞에 있는
정보에 의미를 부여한다. 그리고 나서 뇌가 창자로 신호를 보내는데 이것은 수
백 개의 신경세포를 가지고 있다. 따라서 우리가 뱃속에서 받는 본능적인 느낌
과 우리가 느끼는 긴장감은 우리의 인지 처리 체계의 결과이다.

Why? 왜 정답일까?

첫 문장에서 우리의 직감은 단지 내면의 느낌에 불과한 것이 아니라 아주 찰나에 이루어
지는, 주변 정보에 대한 처리에 기반하여 형성된다(~ shaped by a perception ~
so fleeting that often we're not even aware we're notice it.)고 한다. 이를
가리켜 '시각적 연결시키기 게임'이라고 정리한 후 예시가 이어지고, 빈칸은 예시의 결론
부분에 있으므로 첫 문장의 주제와 동일한 내용일 것이다. 따라서 빈칸에 들어갈 말로 가
장 적절한 것은 ① '우리의 인지 처리 체계의 결과'이다.

● instinct ⓝ 본능, 직감 　● interior ⓐ 내부의
● inconsistency ⓝ 불일치, 모순 　● fleeting ⓐ 순식간의, 잠깐 동안의
● assign A to B A를 B에 부여하다 　● nerve cell 신경세포
● discard ⓥ 버리다 　● miscommunication ⓝ 의사소통의 오류
● vulnerability ⓝ 취약성, 연약함 　● concrete ⓐ 구체적인

구문 풀이

1행 We might think that our gut instinct is just an inner feeling —
　　　　　　　　　　　　　　　　　　　　　　　　　　　　　→ 동격 ←
a secret interior voice — but in fact it is shaped by a perception of
something visible around us, such as a facial expression or a visual
　　　　　-thing + 형용사　　　　　　　　　　　　　　　　　선행사
inconsistency [(which is) so fleeting that often we're not even aware
　　　　　　　　　　　생략　　　「so ~ that … : 너무 ~해서 …하다」
we've noticed it].

★★ 문제 해결 꿀~팁 ★★

▶ 많이 틀린 이유는?
글에 따르면 직감은 그저 느낌이 아니라, 우리도 모르는 새에 스쳐간 정보를 재빨리
분석한 결과이다. 이 일련의 과정은 '시각적 연결시키기 게임'과 비슷하다고 하는데,
이는 정보 분석의 과정을 비유하는 설명일 뿐 직감 자체가 시각적 표현이라는 의미는
아니다. 따라서 ④는 빈칸에 적합하지 않다.

▶ 문제 해결 방법은?
빈칸이 마지막 문장에 있으면 앞에 제시된 요지를 반복하거나 예시를 일반화하는 말
을 답으로 골라야 한다. 이 문제에서도 예시 앞의 주제인 첫 문장이 가장 큰 힌트이다.

★★★ 1등급 대비 고난도 3점 문제

08 일부 아프리카 부족의 음악의 즉흥성 　정답률 33% | 정답 ③

글의 흐름으로 보아, 주어진 문장이 들어가기에 가장 적절한 곳을 고르시오. [3점]

[본문 해석]

서양에서 개인 작곡가는 음악이 연주되기 오래 전에 음악을 작곡한다. 우리가
듣는 패턴들과 멜로디들은 사전에 계획되고 의도된다. ① 그러나 일부 아프리
카 부족의 음악은 연주자들의 협연의 결과로 즉석에서 생겨난다. ② 모든 연주
자가 어느 한 박자에서 쉴 때의 휴지(休止)이든, 모든 연주자가 함께 연주할 때
의 강박(强拍)이든 간에 들리는 패턴은 계획된 것이 아니라 우연히 얻은 것이
다. ③ 전반적인 휴지가 4박자와 13박자에 나타날 때, 그것은 각각의 음악가가

"4박자와 13박자에 나는 쉴 거야."라고 생각하고 있기 때문이 아니다. 오히려, 이것은 모든 연주자의 패턴이 동시에 쉬는 것으로 한데 모아질 때 무작위로 일어난다. ④ 그 음악가들도 아마 4박자와 13박자에 휴지를 듣고서 청중만큼 놀란다. ⑤ 확실히 그 놀라움은 부족의 음악가들이 음악을 연주할 때 경험하는 기쁨 중 하나이다.

Why? 왜 정답일까?

일부 아프리카 부족의 음악 연주에서 관찰되는 우연성과 즉흥성을 설명한 글이다. ③ 앞에서 모든 연주자가 연주 도중 함께 쉬든 혹은 함께 특정 박자를 세게 치든 모든 것은 계획에 따른 것이 아니라 우연히 이루어진다고 서술한다. 주어진 문장은 이에 대한 예로 4박과 13박에서 휴지가 일어났을 때를 언급하며 이것이 모든 연주자가 생각하고 있던 것이 아니라고 설명한다. ③ 뒤의 문장은 주어진 문장에 Rather로 연결되며 '그렇다기보다는' 각 연주자의 연주 패턴이 동시에 쉬는 것으로 우연히 한데 모일 때 전체 휴지가 무작위로 발생하는 것임을 설명한다. 따라서 주어진 문장이 들어가기에 가장 적절한 곳은 ③이다.

- **composer** ⓝ 작곡가
- **on the spur of the moment** 즉석에서
- **randomly** ⓐⓓ 무작위로
- **tribal** ⓐ 부족의
- **accent** ⓥ 강조하다
- **simultaneous** ⓐ 동시의

구문 풀이

8행 The patterns heard, (whether they are the silences when all
　　　　주어　　과거분사　「whether＋A＋or＋B : A이든 B이든」
players rest on a beat or the accented beats when all play together),
are not planned but serendipitous.　　　　( ) : 부사절
동사 「not＋A＋but＋B : A가 아니라 B인」

★★ 문제 해결 꿀~팁 ★★

▶ 많이 틀린 이유는?
④ 앞에서 모두가 4박과 13박에서 멈추는 현상이 '계획되지 않고 무작위로' 일어난다고 말한 데 이어, ④ 뒤에서는 그래서 아마 음악가들도 청중만큼 '놀랄' 수도 있다고 설명하고 있다. 즉 놀람의 이유가 무작위로 일어난 휴지(休止) 때문이므로 ④ 앞뒤는 논리적으로 자연스럽게 연결된다.

▶ 문제 해결 방법은?
앞에 not A가 나오면 but B를 떠올려야 한다. 여기서도 주어진 문장에 not(it is not because ~)이 나오므로 뒤에 but B가 이어져야 하는데, ③ 뒤의 문장이 but을 대신할 수 있는 Rather(오히려, 대신에)로 시작하며 자연스럽게 이어진다.

★★★ 1등급 대비 고난도 2점 문제

09 뇌에 가해지는 인지적 부담에 따른 충동 억제 정도　정답률 31% | 정답 ④

다음 글의 내용을 한 문장으로 요약하고자 한다. 빈칸 (A), (B)에 들어갈 말로 가장 적절한 것은?

	(A)		(B)
①	limited 제한된	……	powerful 강력한
②	limited 제한된	……	divided 분리된
③	varied 달라지는	……	passive 수동적인
✔④	increased 증가된	……	dominant 우세해지게
⑤	increased 증가된	……	weakened 약화된

[본문 해석]

Iowa 대학교에서, 학생들에게 그들이 암기해야 하는 숫자를 잠시 보여 주었다. 그러고 나서 그들에게 과일 샐러드나 초콜릿 케이크 중 하나를 선택하게 했다. 학생들이 외운 숫자가 일곱 자리일 때, 그들 중 63%가 케이크를 선택했다. 그러나 그들이 기억하도록 요청받은 숫자가 두 자리밖에 되지 않았을 때, 59%가 과일 샐러드를 선택했다. 우리의 숙고하는 뇌는 과일 샐러드가 우리의 건강에 더 좋다는 것을 알지만, 우리의 반사적인 뇌는 그 부드럽고 살이 찌는 초콜릿 케이크를 원한다. 만약 숙고하는 뇌가 일곱 자리 숫자를 기억하려고 애쓰는 일과 같은 다른 어떤 것을 해결하느라 바쁘다면, 충동이 쉽게 이길 수 있다. 반면에, 우리가 다른 것에 관해 너무 열심히 생각하고 있지 않다면(두 자리 숫자를 외우는 것처럼 사소하게 주의를 산만하게 하는 일만 있을 때), 숙고하는 (뇌의) 계통은 반사적인 쪽의 감정적인 충동을 억제할 수 있다.

➡ 위 실험에 따르면, 뇌에 가해지는 (A) 증가된 지적 부담은 뇌의 반사적인 부분이 (B) 우세해지게 한다.

Why? 왜 정답일까?

실험 결과를 제시하는 'If the reflective brain is busy figuring something else out ― like trying to remember a seven-digit number ― then impulse can easily win.' 이후로 뇌에 부담된 인지 과업이 많다면 충동에 대한 억제가 덜 일어나지만, 인지 과업이 적은 경우에는 억제가 잘 이루어진다고 언급하고 있다. 이에 근거할 때, 요약문은 뇌에 부담된 인지적 부담이 '늘어나면' 반사, 즉 충동을 따르려는 경향이 '우세해진다'는 내용이어야 하므로, 요약문의 빈칸에 들어갈 말로 가장 적절한 것은 ④ '(A) increased(증가된), (B) dominant(우세해지게)'이다.

- **briefly** ⓐⓓ 잠시, 짧게
- **fatten** ⓥ 살찌게 하다
- **impulse** ⓝ 충동
- **deny** ⓥ 부인하다
- **limited** ⓐ 제한된, 한정된
- **dominant** ⓐ 지배적인
- **digit** ⓝ 숫자
- **be busy ~ing** ~하느라 바쁘다
- **distraction** ⓝ 주의를 산만하게 하는 것
- **intellective** ⓐ 인지적인, 지적인
- **passive** ⓐ 수동적인

구문 풀이

2행 Then they were offered the choice of either a fruit salad or a
　　　　　4형식 수동태(~을 제공받다)　목적어　「either＋A＋or＋B : A와 B 중 하나」
chocolate cake.

★★ 문제 해결 꿀~팁 ★★

▶ 많이 틀린 이유는?
마지막 두 문장에서 뇌에 인지적 부담이 많이 가해지면 충동에 지기 쉽지만, 뇌에 인지적 부담이 적게 가해지면 충동을 억제하기가 쉽다고 했다. ①의 경우, 인지적 부담이 '제한되면' 뇌의 반사적인 부분, 즉 충동에 의해 좌우되는 부분이 '우세해진다'는 의미이므로 주제와 반대되는 선택지이다. 마찬가지로 ⑤ 또한 인지적 부담이 '커지면' 충동에 의해 좌우되는 부분이 '약해진다'는 의미이므로 주제와 반대된다.

▶ 문제 해결 방법은?
마지막 두 문장의 내용을 '인지적 부담↑ 충동↑, 인지적 부담↓ 충동↓'과 같이 간단히 도식화해보면 요약문에 들어갈 단어를 쉽게 찾을 수 있다.

10-12 온 세상을 녹색으로 칠하려 했던 남자

[본문 해석]

(A)
「심한 눈 통증으로 괴로워하는 아주 부유한 남자가 있었다. 그는 많은 의사와 상담했고, 이들 중 여러 명에게 치료받았다.」그는 멈추지 않고 수많은 의료 전문가들과 상담했으며, 많은 약물을 복용했고 주사를 수백 번 맞았다. 하지만 통증은 지속되었고, 전보다 심해졌다. 결국 (a) 그는 자신 같은 질환의 환자들을 치료하는 것으로 유명한 한 수도사에 대해 듣게 되었다. 며칠 후, 그 수도사는 고통받는 그 남자에게 불려갔다.
「 」: 12번 ①의 근거 일치

(D)
수도사는 그 부자의 문제를 이해했고 일정 시간 동안 (e) 그가 녹색에만 집중하고 눈으로 다른 색을 봐서는 안 된다고 말했다. 「부자는 그것이 이상한 처방이라고 생각했지만, 절박해서 그것을 시도하기로 하였다.」「그는 페인트공들을 불러 모았고 녹색 페인트를 많이 구매하여 수도사가 제안한 대로 그가 볼 가능성이 있는 모든 물체를 녹색으로 칠하라고 지시했다.」
「 」: 12번 ④의 근거 일치
「 」: 12번 ⑤의 근거 일치

(B)
며칠 후 (b) 그 남자 주변의 모든 것은 녹색이 되었다. 부자는 주변의 어떤 것도 다른 색이 되지 않도록 확실히 하였다. 「며칠 후 수도사가 그를 찾아왔을 때, 그는 붉은 옷을 입고 있었기 때문에 부자의 하인들은 녹색 페인트통을 들고 달려와서 그의 몸 전체에 부었다.」(c) 그는 하인들에게 왜 그들이 그렇게 했는지 물었다.
「 」: 12번 ②의 근거 일치

(C)
그들은 대답했다, "우리는 주인님이 다른 어떤 색도 보게 할 수 없어요." 이것을 듣고 수도사는 웃으며 말했다. 「"만약에 당신들이 단돈 몇 달러밖에 하지 않는 녹색 안경 하나만 구매했다면, 이러한 벽, 나무, 항아리, 그리고 다른 모든 것을 지킬 수 있었을 것이고 또한 (d) 그의 재산의 많은 부분을 아낄 수 있었을 것입니다.」당신들은 온 세상을 녹색으로 칠할 수는 없어요."
「 」: 12번 ③의 근거 불일치

- **wealthy** ⓐ 부유한
- **medical expert** 의료 전문가
- **severe** ⓐ 심각한
- **medicate** ⓥ 약을 투여하다

● undergo ⓥ 겪다, 경험하다 ● persist ⓥ 지속되다
● call for 데리러 가다, 부르다 ● desperate ⓐ 절박한

구문 풀이

[C] 2행 Hearing this, the monk laughed and said "If only you had
「if (only) + 주어 + had p.p. ~
purchased a pair of green glasses for just a few dollars, you could
주어 + 조동사 과거형 +
have saved these walls, trees, pots, and everything else ~"
have p.p.: 가정법 과거완료

[D] 6행 He ~ ordered that every object [he was likely to see]
동사(명령) 접속사 주어
(should) be painted green just as the monk had suggested.
동사구

---

10 글의 순서 파악 정답률 83% | 정답 ④

주어진 글 (A)에 이어질 내용을 순서에 맞게 배열한 것으로 가장 적절한 것은?

① (B) – (D) – (C) ② (C) – (B) – (D)
③ (C) – (D) – (B) ✔④ (D) – (B) – (C)
⑤ (D) – (C) – (B)

Why? 왜 정답일까?

한 부자가 눈 통증이 너무 심해 여러 의사를 전전하다 수도사를 불러들였다는 내용의 (A) 뒤에는, 초록색만 봐야 한다는 수도사의 처방에 따라 부자가 하인들을 시켜 모든 사물을 녹색으로 칠하게 했다는 내용의 (D)가 이어진다. 한편, (B)에서는 며칠 후 수도사가 붉은 옷을 입고 부자의 집을 방문하자 하인들이 수도사의 몸에 초록색 페인트를 부었다는 내용이 전개되고, (C)에서는 그 이유를 들은 수도사가 그저 초록색 안경 하나만 샀으면 됐을 것이라고 알려주었다는 내용이 이어진다. 따라서 글의 순서로 가장 적절한 것은 ④ '(D) – (B) – (C)'이다.

---

11 지칭 추론 정답률 70% | 정답 ③

밑줄 친 (a) ~ (e) 중에서 가리키는 대상이 나머지 넷과 다른 것은?

① (a) ② (b) ✔③ (c) ④ (d) ⑤ (e)

Why? 왜 정답일까?

(a), (b), (d), (e)는 the wealthy man, (c)는 the monk를 가리키므로, (a) ~ (e) 중에서 가리키는 대상이 다른 하나는 ③ '(c)'이다.

---

12 세부 내용 파악 정답률 78% | 정답 ③

윗글에 관한 내용으로 적절하지 않은 것은?

① 부자는 눈 통증으로 여러 명의 의사에게 치료받았다.
② 수도사는 붉은 옷을 입고 부자를 다시 찾아갔다.
✔③ 하인들은 녹색 안경을 구입했다.
④ 부자는 수도사의 처방이 이상하다고 생각했다.
⑤ 부자는 주변을 모두 녹색으로 칠하게 했다.

Why? 왜 정답일까?

(C) 'If only you had purchased a pair of green glasses for just a few dollars, you could have saved ~'에서 수도사는 만일 부자가 주변을 온통 초록색으로 칠하는 대신 그저 녹색 안경 하나만 샀다면 많은 자원을 아꼈을 것이라고 말해주고 있다. 즉, 녹색 안경을 산 것은 실제 일어난 일이 아니므로, 내용과 일치하지 않는 것은 ③ '하인들은 녹색 안경을 구입했다.'이다.

Why? 왜 오답일까?

① (A) 'There was a very wealthy man who was bothered by severe eye pain. He consulted many doctors and was treated by several of them.'의 내용과 일치한다.
② (B) '~ because he was wearing red clothes.'의 내용과 일치한다.
④ (D) 'The wealthy man thought it was a strange prescription, ~'의 내용과 일치한다.
⑤ (D) '~ ordered that every object he was likely to see be painted green just as the monk had suggested.'의 내용과 일치한다.

DAY 05 ◂ 20분 미니 모의고사

01 ②	02 ④	03 ⑤	04 ③	05 ④
06 ④	07 ③	08 ⑤	09 ④	10 ⑤
11 ②	12 ③			

01 과학 교사 워크숍 특강 의뢰 정답률 94% | 정답 ②

다음 글의 목적으로 가장 적절한 것은?

① 과학 교육 정책 협의회 참여를 독려하려고
✔② 과학 교사 워크숍의 특강을 부탁하려고
③ 과학 교사 채용 계획을 공지하려고
④ 과학 교육 프로그램 개발을 요청하려고
⑤ 과학 교육 워크숍 일정의 변경을 안내하려고

[본문 해석]

Green 씨께,

저의 이름은 Donna Williams이며, Rogan 고등학교의 과학 교사입니다. 저는 우리 학교의 과학 교사들을 위한 특별 워크숍을 계획하고 있습니다. 저희는 온라인 과학 수업을 가르치는 방법을 배우는 데 관심을 가지고 있습니다. 저는 과학 수업에 인터넷 플랫폼을 사용하는 데 대한 귀하의 아이디어에 감명을 받았습니다. 귀하가 온라인 교육의 전문가이기에, 저는 다음 달에 계획된 워크숍에서 귀하가 특별 강연을 해주시기를 부탁드리고자 합니다. 저희 교사들이 성공적인 온라인 과학 수업을 해내는 데 강의가 도움이 되리라고 확신하며 귀하의 통찰력으로부터 저희가 배울 수 있기를 희망합니다. 귀하의 답변을 고대하고 있겠습니다.

Donna Williams 드림

Why? 왜 정답일까?

두 번째 문장에서 필자는 과학 교사를 위한 특별 워크숍을 계획 중이라고 언급한 뒤, '~ I would like to ask you to deliver a special lecture at the workshop scheduled for next month.'에서 특강을 부탁하고 싶다고 말한다. 따라서 글의 목적으로 가장 적절한 것은 ② '과학 교사 워크숍의 특강을 부탁하려고'이다.

● be impressed with ~에 감명받다 ● expert ⓝ 전문가
● deliver a lecture 강의를 하다 ● scheduled ⓐ 계획된, 예정된
● manage ⓥ 운영하다, 관리하다 ● insight ⓝ 통찰력
● look forward to ~을 고대하다

구문 풀이

10행 I am sure (that) the lecture will help our teachers manage
생략 5형식 동사 목적어 목적격 보어
successful online science classes, and I hope (that) we can learn
생략
from your insights.

---

02 조직원에 대한 평가의 명확성 정답률 42% | 정답 ④

다음 글에서 필자가 주장하는 바로 가장 적절한 것은?

① 조직이 구성원에게 제공하는 보상은 즉각적이어야 한다.
② 조직의 발전을 위해 구성원은 동료의 능력을 신뢰해야 한다.
③ 조직 내 구성원의 능력에 맞는 명확한 목표를 설정해야 한다.
✔④ 조직의 신뢰 형성을 위해 구성원에 대한 평가 요소가 명확해야 한다.
⑤ 구성원의 의견 수용을 위해 신뢰에 기반한 조직 문화가 구축되어야 한다.

[본문 해석]

조직에서의 명확성은 모두가 계속 조화롭게 일하게 하고, 신뢰와 투명성 같은 핵심적인 리더십 요소에 활력을 준다. 조직에서 누가 또는 무엇이 평가되고 있든 간에 그들이 무엇을 평가받는지는 분명해야 하고, 사람들은 그것을 알고 있어야 한다. 만약 여러분 조직에 있는 개개인들이 무엇에 대해 평가되고 있는지를 알지 못한 채로 평가받는다면, 이것은 불신을 초래하고 여러분의 조직이 명확성으로부터 멀어지게 할 수 있다. 여러분의 조직이 생산적이고 응집력이 높고 성공적이게 하려면 신뢰가 필수적이다. 조직에 대한 신뢰를 갖지 못하는

것은 어떤 평가 결과에든 부정적인 영향을 끼칠 것이다. 그것은 또한 조직의 성장을 상당히 방해할 것이다. 정확한 평가를 수행하려면 신뢰는 필수적이며, 이는 명확성으로부터 온다. 결국 평가는 여러분이 더 분명하게 볼 수 있도록 도와주는데, 이는 이후 여러분의 조직이 최적의 성공에 도달할 힘을 준다.

Why? 왜 정답일까?

'To conduct accurate assessments, trust is a must—which comes through clarity.'에서 정확한 평가를 하려면 신뢰가 갖춰져야 하고, 신뢰는 명확성에서 나온다는 핵심 내용을 제시한다. 따라서 필자가 주장하는 바로 가장 적절한 것은 ④ '조직의 신뢰 형성을 위해 구성원에 대한 평가 요소가 명확해야 한다.'이다.

- clarity ⓝ 명확성
- in one accord 합심하여, 이구동성으로
- transparency ⓝ 투명성
- be aware of ~을 알다
- mistrust ⓝ 불신
- cohesive ⓐ 응집력 있는
- failure to ~하지 못하는 것
- significantly ⓐⓓ 현저히, 상당히
- growth ⓝ 성장
- in turn 결국
- optimal ⓐ 최적의
- organization ⓝ 조직
- component ⓝ 구성 요소
- assess ⓥ 평가하다
- individual ⓝ 개인
- productive ⓐ 생산적인
- essential ⓐ 필수적인
- negative ⓐ 부정적인
- hinder ⓥ 막다, 방해하다
- accurate ⓐ 정확한
- empower ⓥ 권한을 부여하다

구문 풀이

3행 No matter who or what is being assessed in your organization,
누가 혹은 무엇이 ~하든 간에(= whoever or whatever)
what they are being assessed on must be clear and the people
주어1(명사절)　　　　　　동사1　　　　주어2
must be aware of it.
동사2

03 인간이 바다의 침입종 확산에 미친 영향　　정답률 52% | 정답 ⑤

다음 글의 주제로 가장 적절한 것은?

① benefits of recreational ocean fishing
취미로 하는 바다 낚시의 이점
② ways to maintain marine biodiversity
해양 생물 다양성을 유지하는 방법
③ potential value of the ocean for ecotourism
생태 관광에 있어 해양의 잠재적 가치
④ contribution of ocean farming to food supply
바다 양식의 식량 공급에 대한 기여
✔⑤ human influence on the spread of invasive species
침입종의 확산에 대한 인간의 영향

[본문 해석]

굴, 습지 풀, 그리고 물고기를 포함한 많은 해양 종들은 그것들이 미칠 수 있는 영향에 대한 정보가 거의 없는 상태에서 의도적으로 식량이나 침식 방제를 위해 도입되었다. 어패류는 양식을 위해 전 세계에 의도적으로 도입되어 음식과 일자리를 제공하지만, 탈출해서 토착종, 생태계 기능, 또는 생계에 위협이 될 수 있다. 대서양 연어는 Washington State와 British Columbia의 해양 그물 어장에서 길러진다. 매년 많은 연어가 탈출해, 그들은 Washington State, British Columbia, Alaska의 해수와 담수에서 모두 발견된다. 취미로 하는 낚시 또한 침입종을 전파시킬 수 있다. Maine의 미끼용 벌레들은 전국적으로 인기가 있다. 그것들은 보통 많은 다른 유기체들을 포함하는 해초에 싸여 있다. 만약 해초가 버려지면, 해초나 해초 위에 있는 유기체들은 새로운 영역에서 군락을 이룰 수 있다. 낚시용 장화, 여가용 보트와 트레일러는 유기체를 한 장소에서 집어 올려 다른 곳으로 옮길 수 있다.

Why? 왜 정답일까?

첫 두 문장에서 많은 해양종이 사전 정보 없이 식량이나 침식 방제를 위해 인간에 의해 의도적으로 도입되어 이득도 주지만 생태계에 대한 악영향도 준다(Fish and shellfish have been intentionally introduced all over the world ~, but they can ~ become a threat to native species, ecosystem function, or livelihoods.)고 언급하고 있다. 따라서 글의 주제로 가장 적절한 것은 ⑤ '침입종의 확산에 대한 인간의 영향'이다.

- oyster ⓝ (바다) 굴
- deliberately ⓐⓓ 의도적으로
- intentionally ⓐⓓ 의도적으로
- livelihood ⓝ 생계 (수단)
- rear ⓥ 기르다, 재배하다
- freshwater ⓝ 담수, 민물
- invasive ⓐ 침입의
- marsh ⓝ 습지
- erosion ⓝ 침식
- threat ⓝ 위협
- salmon ⓝ 연어
- saltwater ⓝ 해수, 바닷물
- spread ⓥ 퍼뜨리다
- discard ⓥ 버리다

구문 풀이

1행 Many marine species (including oysters, marsh grasses,
주어
and fish) were deliberately introduced for food or for erosion control,
동사구　　　　　　　　　　부사구1　　　　　부사구2
with little knowledge of the impacts [they could have].
선행사

04 독일의 연령별 독서 빈도 비율　　정답률 73% | 정답 ③

다음 도표의 내용과 일치하지 <u>않는</u> 것은?

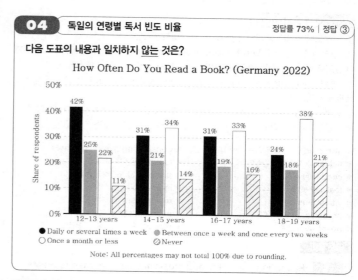

How Often Do You Read a Book? (Germany 2022)

(Y축: Share of respondents, 0% ~ 50%)

- 12-13 years: 42%, 25%, 22%, 11%
- 14-15 years: 31%, 21%, 34%, 14%
- 16-17 years: 31%, 19%, 33%, 16%
- 18-19 years: 24%, 18%, 38%, 21%

● Daily or several times a week　● Between once a week and once every two weeks
○ Once a month or less　◪ Never

Note: All percentages may not total 100% due to rounding.

[본문 해석]

위 그래프는 2022년 독일의 어린이와 젊은 성인이 책을 얼마나 자주 읽었는지를 연령 집단에 따라 보여 준다. ① 12 ~ 13세 연령 집단을 제외한 각각의 연령 집단에서 월 1회 또는 그 미만으로 책을 읽었다고 말한 이들은 가장 높은 비율을 차지했다. ② 12 ~ 13세 연령 집단에서 42%가 매일 또는 일주일에 여러 번 책을 읽었다고 말했고, 이는 그 집단 내에서 가장 높은 비율이었다. ③ <u>14 ~ 15세 연령 집단에서 매일 또는 일주일에 여러 번 책을 읽은 십 대의 비율은 같은 연령 집단 내에서 전혀 책을 읽지 않은 이들 비율의 3배였다.</u> ④ 16 ~ 17세 연령 집단에서 1주에 한 번에서 2주에 한 번 책을 읽은 이들의 비율은 20% 미만이었다. ⑤ 18 ~ 19세 연령 집단의 5분의 1 이상이 아무 책도 읽지 않았다고 답했다.

Why? 왜 정답일까?

도표에 따르면 14 ~ 15세 연령 집단에서 책을 매일 혹은 일주일에 여러 번 읽은 이들은 31%, 책을 전혀 읽지 않은 이들은 14%이다. 따라서 도표와 일치하지 않는 것은 이를 3배 차이로 잘못 설명한 ③이다.

- German ⓐ 독일의
- age group 연령 집단
- proportion ⓝ 비율
- share ⓝ 몫, 점유율
- respond ⓥ 대답하다
- according to ~에 따라
- account for ~을 차지하다
- daily ⓐⓓ 매일
- one fifth 5분의 1

구문 풀이

13행 More than one fifth of the age group of 18 to 19 years
분수 표현(분자 : 기수 / 분모 : 서수)
responded that they never read any book.
접속사(~것)

05 사람들이 녹음된 음악에 끌리는 이유　　정답률 55% | 정답 ④

다음 글의 밑줄 친 부분 중, 어법상 틀린 것은? [3점]

[본문 해석]

개인용 음악 플레이어가 흔하고 사람들이 헤드폰으로 음악을 많이 듣는 것을 특히 고려할 때, 요즘 우리 중 그렇게나 많은 사람이 녹음된 음악에 끌리는 이유가 있다. 녹음 엔지니어와 음악가는 우리 청각 환경의 중요한 특징들을 분간하도록 진화한 신경회로를 이용함으로써 우리의 뇌를 자극하는 특수 효과를 만들어 내는 것을 배웠다. 이러한 특수 효과들은 원리상 3-D 아트, 모션 픽처, 또는 착시와 비슷하지만, 그것들 중에 어느 것도 우리의 뇌가 그것들을 인식하기 위한 특수한 방법을 진화시킬 만큼 충분히 오랫동안 주변에 존재하지는 않았다. 오히려 3-D 아트, 모션 픽처, 그리고 착시는 다른 것들을 성취하기 위해

DAY 05

자리 잡고 있는 인식 체계를 이용한다. 그것들(특수 효과들)이 이러한 신경회로를 새로운 방식으로 사용하기 때문에, 우리는 그것들이 특히 흥미롭다고 여긴다. 동일한 것이 현대의 녹음된 음악이 만들어지는 방법에도 적용된다.

Why? 왜 정답일까?

find의 목적어인 them은 앞 문장에 나오는 3-D art, motion pictures, and visual illusions를 받는데, 이들은 '흥미롭게 하는' 주체이다. 따라서 interested를 interesting으로 고쳐야 한다. 어법상 틀린 것은 ④이다.

Why? 왜 오답일까?

① '~하도록'의 의미를 나타내는 to부정사가 바르게 쓰였다.
② 앞에 나오는 명사 3-D art, motion pictures, or visual illusions를 대신하면서 앞뒤로 절을 연결하는 계속적 용법의 관계대명사 which가 바르게 쓰였다.
③ 선행사 systems가 복수 명사이므로 관계절의 동사 자리에 are라는 복수 동사가 바르게 쓰였다.
⑤ 방법의 way, 이유의 reason이 선행사일 때 that은 흔히 관계부사를 대체한다. 여기서도 관계부사 역할의 that이 바르게 쓰였고, 이어서 완전한 구조가 뒤따랐다.

- **attracted to** ~에 끌리는, 매혹되는
- **tickle** ⓥ 자극하다, 간질이다
- **circuit** ⓝ 회로
- **feature** ⓝ 특징
- **visual illusion** 착시
- **perceive** ⓥ 인식하다
- **novel** ⓐ 새로운
- **considering** [prep] ~을 고려할 때
- **exploit** ⓥ 이용하다
- **discern** ⓥ 분간하다, 식별하다
- **in principle** 원리적으로
- **mechanism** ⓝ 기제
- **accomplish** ⓥ 성취하다
- **true of** ~에 해당되는, 적용되는

구문 풀이

4행 Recording engineers and musicians have learned to create special effects [that tickle our brains by exploiting neural circuits {that evolved to discern important features of our auditory environment}].
(선행사 / 관계절 동사(복수) / ~함으로써 / 선행사 / 부사적 용법(~하도록))

---

06 카페인을 분해하는 속도   정답률 63% | 정답 ④

다음 글의 밑줄 친 부분 중, 문맥상 낱말의 쓰임이 적절하지 않은 것은?

[본문 해석]

카페인의 '충격'은 확실히 점차 사라진다. 카페인은 여러분 간 속의 효소에 의해 신체로부터 ① 제거되는데, 이 효소는 시간이 지남에 따라 그것을 점진적으로 분해한다. 대체로 유전적 특징 때문에, 어떤 사람들은 카페인을 분해하는 더 효율적인 형태의 효소를 갖고 있는데, 이는 간이 그것을 혈류로부터 더 빠르게 제거하도록 ② 허용한다. 이 몇 안 되는 사람들은 저녁과 함께 에스프레소를 마시고도 아무 문제 없이 한밤중에 깊이 잠들 수 있다. 그러나 다른 사람들은 더 느리게 작용하는 형태의 효소를 가지고 있다. 이들의 신체는 같은 양의 카페인을 제거하는 데 훨씬 ③ 더 오래 걸린다. 결과적으로, 그들은 카페인의 효과에 매우 ④ 둔감하다(→ 민감하다). 아침에 마시는 차 또는 커피 한 잔은 그날 대부분 동안 지속될 것이고, 심지어 이른 오후라도 혹시 또 한 잔을 마신다면 이들은 저녁에 잠들기가 어렵다는 것을 깨닫는다. 또한, 노화는 카페인 제거 속도를 ⑤ 변화시킨다. 즉, 우리가 나이 들수록 우리 뇌와 신체가 카페인을 제거하는 데 더 오래 걸리고, 따라서 우리는 노후에 카페인의 수면을 방해하는 효과에 더 민감해진다.

Why? 왜 정답일까?

'Others, however, ~' 이후로 카페인 분해 속도가 느린 사람들을 언급한다. 이들은 카페인을 몸 밖으로 배출하는 시간이 '더 오래' 걸리기 때문에, 한 잔만 먹어도 효과가 오래 가서 카페인의 영향에 '더 취약하다'는 설명이 적합하다. 즉 ④에는 insensitive 대신 sensitive가 적합하므로, 문맥상 낱말의 쓰임이 적절하지 않은 것은 ④이다.

- **jolt** ⓝ 충격
- **enzyme** ⓝ 효소
- **gradually** [ad] 점점
- **genetics** ⓝ 유전적 특징
- **bloodstream** ⓝ 혈류
- **fast asleep** 깊이 잠든
- **insensitive** ⓐ 둔감한
- **clearance** ⓝ 없애기, 정리
- **disrupt** ⓥ 지장을 주다
- **wear off** 차츰 사라지다, 없어지다
- **liver** ⓝ 간
- **degrade** ⓥ 분해하다, 저하시키다
- **efficient** ⓐ 효율적인
- **rare** ⓐ 몇 안 되는, 드문
- **eliminate** ⓥ 제거하다
- **alter** ⓥ 변화시키다
- **sensitive** ⓐ 민감한

구문 풀이

13행 One cup of tea or coffee in the morning will last much of the day, and should they have a second cup, even early in the afternoon, (가정법 미래(=if they should have ~)) they will find it difficult to fall asleep in the evening. (동사 / 목적격 보어 / 진목적어(~것) / 가목적어)

---

07 농지 분산의 이점   정답률 57% | 정답 ③

다음 빈칸에 들어갈 말로 가장 적절한 것을 고르시오. [3점]

① land leveling – 땅 평평하게 고르기
② weed trimming – 잡초 손질
✓③ field scattering – 농지 흩어놓기
④ organic farming – 유기농법
⑤ soil fertilization – 토지 비옥하게 만들기

[본문 해석]

여러 해에 걸쳐서 평균을 내는, 최고로 가능한 시간 평균적인 농작물 생산량을 만드는 것은 농부의 목표가 아니다. 당신의 시간 평균적인 생산량이 (농사 결과가) 좋았던 9년과 농사에 실패한 1년을 합친 결과로 엄청나게 높더라도, 당신은 훌륭한 시간 평균적인 생산량에 있어서 스스로를 축하하려고 돌아보기도 전에 농사에 실패한 바로 그 한 해에 굶어 죽을 것이다. 대신에, 농부의 목표는 시간 평균적인 생산량이 가장 높지 않을지라도, 굶어 죽지 않을 수준 이상의 생산량을 매년 확실히 만들어내는 것이다. 그것이 바로 농지 흩어놓기가 합리적인 이유이다. 만일 당신이 그냥 하나의 큰 농지를 가지고 있다면, 그것이 평균적으로 아무리 좋다고 할지라도, 당신은 유일한 농지가 낮은 생산량을 내는 그 가끔 오는 불가피한 때가 오면 굶주리게 될 것이다. 그러나 만일 당신이 서로 상관없는 다른 농지들을 가지고 있다면, 어느 해에 당신의 다른 농지들이 빈약하게 생산하고 있을 때조차도 당신의 농지 중 일부는 잘 생산할 것이다.

Why? 왜 정답일까?

빈칸 뒤에서 큰 농지를 하나 가지고 있을 때와 여러 개의 분산된 농지를 갖고 있을 때를 대조하며, 전자의 경우 그 농지 수확이 낮으면 꼼짝없이 위기를 맞지만 후자의 경우 어느 한 땅이 안 좋아도 다른 땅이 벌충해줄 수 있어 좋다(But if you have many different fields, varying independently of each other, then in any given year some of your fields will produce well ~)고 설명하고 있다. 따라서 빈칸에 들어갈 말로 가장 적절한 것은 ③ '농지 흩어놓기'이다.

- **peasant** ⓝ 농부, 소작농
- **marvelously** [ad] 놀랍도록
- **occasional** ⓐ 이따금의
- **leveling** (땅) 고름, 평평하게 함
- **fertilization** ⓝ (땅) 비옥하게 하기
- **yield** ⓝ 수확량, 산출량
- **starve to death** 굶어 죽다
- **inevitable** ⓐ 불가피한
- **independently of** ~와 상관없이
- **scatter** ⓥ 흩어놓다

구문 풀이

3행 If your time-averaged yield is marvelously high as a result of (접속사(조건) / 현재시제 / ~의 결과로) the combination of nine great years and one year of crop failure, you will still starve to death in that one year of crop failure before you can (미래시제) look back to congratulate yourself on your great time-averaged yield. (부사적 용법(목적))

★★★ 1등급 대비 고난도 3점 문제

08 유전자 발현에 영향을 주는 음식   정답률 37% | 정답 ⑤

다음 빈칸에 들어갈 말로 가장 적절한 것을 고르시오. [3점]

① identical twins have the same genetic makeup
일란성 쌍둥이는 똑같은 유전자 구성을 지니고 있다
② our preference for food is influenced by genes
우리의 음식 선호는 유전자에 영향을 받는다
③ balanced diet is essential for our mental health
균형잡힌 식사가 우리의 정신 건강에 필수적이다
④ genetic engineering can cure some fatal diseases
유전공학은 몇몇 치명적인 질병을 고칠 수 있다
✓⑤ foods can immediately influence the genetic blueprint
식품이 유전자 청사진에 직접 영향을 줄 수 있다

[본문 해석]

성장하고 있는 유전학 분야는 많은 과학자가 여러 해 동안 의구심을 가져왔던 것, 즉 식품이 유전자 청사진에 직접 영향을 줄 수 있다는 것을 우리에게 보여

주고 있다. 이 정보는 유전자가 우리의 통제 하에 있는 것이지 우리가 복종해야 하는 것이 아니라는 것을 더 잘 이해하도록 도와준다. 일란성 쌍둥이를 생각해보자. 두 사람은 모두 똑같은 유전자를 부여받는다. 중년에, 쌍둥이 중 한 명은 암에 걸리고, 다른 한 명은 암 없이 건강하게 오래 산다. 특정 유전자가 쌍둥이 중 한 명에게 암에 걸리도록 명령했지만, 나머지 한 명에서는 똑같은 유전자가 그 질병을 발생시키지 않았다. 한 가지 가능성은 쌍둥이 중 건강한 사람이 암 유전자, 즉 나머지 한 명이 병에 걸리도록 명령했던 바로 그 유전자를 차단하는 식사를 했다는 것이다. 여러 해 동안 과학자들은 화학적 독소(예를 들어 담배)와 같은 다른 환경적 요인들이 유전자에 작용하여 암의 원인이 될 수 있다는 것을 인정해 왔다. 음식이 유전자 발현에 특정한 영향을 미친다는 생각은 비교적 새로운 것이다.

Why? 왜 정답일까?

유전자가 완전히 서로 같지만 둘 중 한 사람만 암에 걸린 일란성 쌍둥이를 생각해 볼 때, 음식이 유전자 발현에 특정한 영향을 끼친다는 사실(The notion that food has a specific influence on gene expression ~)을 알 수 있음을 소개한 글이다. 따라서 빈칸에 들어갈 말로 가장 적절한 것은 ⑤ '식품이 유전자 청사진에 직접 영향을 줄 수 있다'이다.

- genetics ⓝ 유전학
- under control 통제 하에 있는, 통제되는
- identical twin 일란성 쌍둥이
- initiate ⓥ 시작되게 하다
- contribute to ~의 원인이 되다
- makeup ⓝ 구성
- immediately ⓐⓓ 직접적으로, 즉각
- suspect ⓥ 의심하다
- obey ⓥ 복종하다
- instruct ⓥ 명령하다, 지시하다
- environmental ⓐ 환경적인
- relatively ⓐⓓ 비교적
- preference ⓝ 선호
- blueprint ⓝ 청사진, 설계도

구문 풀이

10행 One possibility is that the healthy twin had a diet [that turned off the cancer gene] — the same gene [that instructed the other person to get sick].

★★ 문제 해결 꿀~팁 ★★

▶ 많이 틀린 이유는?
우리가 먹는 음식이 유전자 발현에 영향을 미칠 수 있다는 내용으로 ④에서 언급하는 genetic engineering(유전공학)이나 fatal diseases(치명적인 질병)에 대한 언급은 없다. 또한 ②는 유전자가 음식 선호에 영향을 준다는 내용으로 이 글의 내용과 반대되는 내용이다.

▶ 문제 해결 방법은?
글의 주제가 처음과 마지막에서 두 번 언급되고 있고 이를 예를 들어 설명한 내용이 가운데에 배치된 글이다. 빈칸이 주제를 나타내고 있으므로 예시를 잘 파악하고 주제가 다시 언급되는 부분에 주목하여 읽는다.

09 런던 택시 운전사들의 두뇌 특징 정답률 58% | 정답 ④

다음 글에서 전체 흐름과 관계 <u>없는</u> 문장은?

[본문 해석]

런던에서 택시 운전면허를 받기 전에, 사람은 'The Knowledge'라는 위협적인 이름의 매우 어려운 시험을 통과해야 한다. ① 이 시험은 Greater London 지역의 2만 개 이상 거리의 구획을 암기하는 것을 포함하는데, 이는 엄청난 양의 기억 자원을 포함하는 기술이다. ② 사실, 택시 운전사 훈련에 등록한 사람 중 50% 미만이 시험을 통과하는데, 심지어 그것을 2~3년을 공부한 후에도 그러하다! ③ 그리고 밝혀진 바에 따르면, 런던 택시 운전사들의 두뇌는 초인적인 기억 노력을 반영하는 방식 면에서 택시 운전을 하지 않는 사람들과 다르다. ④ 즉, 그들은 운전 면허청에서 발급된 정식 운전면허증을 최소 1년 동안 소지해야 한다. ⑤ 사실, 공간 기억과 가장 자주 연관된 뇌 부위, 즉 해마라 불리는 해마 모양을 한 뇌 영역의 꼬리 부분은 이들 택시 운전사들에게서 평균보다 더 크다.

Why? 왜 정답일까?

런던의 택시 운전 면허 시험은 대단히 방대한 기억 자원을 요하고, 이에 따라 공간 기억을 다루는 해마 부위가 택시 운전사들의 뇌에서 평균보다 더 크다. 하지만 ④는 운전사들의 면허 소지 기간에 관한 내용이므로 흐름상 어색하다. 따라서 전체 흐름과 관계 없는 문장은 ④이다.

[문제편 p.032]

- license ⓥ 면허를 주다 ⓝ 면허
- intimidating ⓐ 위협적인
- cabbie(cabby) ⓝ 택시 기사
- hippocampus ⓝ (대뇌의) 해마
- cab ⓝ 택시
- feat ⓝ 능력, 기술
- herculean ⓐ 초인적인

구문 풀이

14행 In fact, the part of the brain [that has been most frequently associated with spatial memory], the tail of the sea horse-shaped brain region called the hippocampus, is *bigger* than average in these taxi drivers.

★★★ 1등급 대비 고난도 3점 문제

10 편향의 영향력을 제한하기 위한 노력 정답률 39% | 정답 ⑤

주어진 글 다음에 이어질 글의 순서로 가장 적절한 것을 고르시오. [3점]

① (A) – (C) – (B)
② (B) – (A) – (C)
③ (B) – (C) – (A)
④ (C) – (A) – (B)
⑤ (C) – (B) – (A) ✓

[본문 해석]

우리는 우리의 편향을 완전히 없앨 수 없다는 것을 알고 있기 때문에, 우리는 편향이 우리의 결정과 판단의 객관성과 합리성에 끼칠 수 있는 해로운 영향들을 제한하도록 노력할 필요가 있다.

(C) 우리가 언제 우리의 인지적 편향 중 하나가 활성화되는지를 인지하고, 그 편향을 극복하기 위한 의식적 결정을 내리는 것이 중요하다. 우리는 편향이 우리의 의사 결정 과정과 삶에 끼치는 영향력을 인지할 필요가 있다.

(B) 그때 우리는 편향과 싸우기 위해 적절한 반(反) 편향 전략을 선택할 수 있다. 우리가 전략을 실행해 본 이후에, 우리는 그것이 우리가 희망했던 방식대로 작동했는지를 보기 위해 한 번 더 확인해야 한다.

(A) 만약 그러했다면, 우리는 넘어가서 객관적이고 정보에 근거한 결정을 내릴 수 있다. 만약 그러지 않았다면, 우리는 우리가 이성적 판단을 내릴 준비가 될 때까지 똑같은 전략을 다시 시도하거나 새로운 것을 실행한다.

Why? 왜 정답일까?

편향의 영향력을 제한하기 위해 노력할 필요가 있다는 내용의 주어진 글 뒤에는, 우리가 편향이 언제 작용하는지를 이해하고 이를 극복하기 위한 의식적인 결정을 내릴 수 있어야 한다는 설명으로 주어진 글의 내용을 뒷받침하는 (C)가 먼저 연결된다. 이어서 (B)는 (C)의 후반부 내용을 받아 '편향이 삶에 미치는 영향력을 우리가 인지할 때' 바로 반 편향 전략 사용으로 나아갈 수 있다는 내용을 제시한다. 마지막으로 (A)는 (B)의 후반부 내용을 받아 전략이 우리가 기대한 대로 작용했는지 그렇지 못했는지에 따라 이어지는 결과를 소개하고 있다. 따라서 글의 순서로 가장 적절한 것은 ⑤ '(C) – (B) – (A)'이다.

- eliminate ⓥ 없애다, 제거하다
- harmful ⓐ 해로운
- rationality ⓝ 합리성
- implement ⓥ 실행하다
- combat ⓥ 싸우다
- overcome ⓥ 극복하다
- bias ⓝ 편향, 편견
- objectivity ⓝ 객관성
- informed ⓐ 정보에 근거한
- appropriate ⓐ 적절한
- cognitive ⓐ 인지적인

구문 풀이

10행 After we have implemented a strategy, we should check in again to see if it worked in the way [we had hoped].

★★ 문제 해결 꿀~팁 ★★

▶ 많이 틀린 이유는?
(C)에 이어 (A)와 (B) 중 어느 단락이 이어질지 파악하는 것이 풀이의 관건이다. (C) 뒤에 (A)가 바로 이어질 경우, '편견이 우리의 의사 결정에 영향을 미친다면 우리가 객관적이고 정보에 근거한 판단을 내릴 수 있다'는 의미가 완성되어 맥락에 부합하지 않는다.

▶ 문제 해결 방법은?
(B) 후반부의 'if it worked in the way we had hoped'를 (A)에서 'if it did ~'와 'if it didn't ~'로 나누어 설명하고 있음을 파악하면 쉽게 답을 고를 수 있다.

DAY 05

[Day 05] 미니 모의고사 **021**

11-12 과정상 오류로 인한 연구의 타당성 저해

[본문 해석]

우리는 주어진 연구의 결과가 타당성을 가질 것이라고 당연하게 여길 수 없다. 한 연구자가 일탈 행동을 연구하는 상황을 생각해보자. 특히, 그녀는 대학생들이 시험에서 부정행위를 하는 정도를 조사하고 있다. 시험을 감독하는 사람들이 (규모가) 더 작은 반에서보다 큰 반에서 학생들을 감독하는 것이 더 (a) 어렵다고 추론하여 그녀는 더 높은 비율의 부정행위가 작은 반보다 큰 반의 시험에서 발생할 것이라고 가정한다. 『이러한 가설을 검증하기 위해 그녀는 큰 반과 작은 반 둘 다에서 부정행위에 대한 자료를 수집하고 그 자료를 분석한다. 그녀의 결과는 더 큰 반에서 학생당 (b) 더 많은 부정행위가 발생한다는 것을 보여준다.』 그러므로 그 자료는 명백히 그 연구자의 연구 가설을 (c) 거부한다 (→ 지지한다). 『그러나 며칠 후에 한 동료가 그녀의 연구에서 모든 작은 반에서는 단답형과 서술형 시험을 사용한 반면, 모든 큰 반에서는 선다형 시험을 사용했다는 것을 지적한다. 그 연구자는 즉각 외부 변인(시험 형식)이 독립 변인(수업 크기)을 간섭하고 있고 그녀의 자료에서 한 (d) 원인으로 작용하고 있을지도 모른다는 것을 깨닫는다. 그녀의 연구 가설에 대한 명백한 지지는 가공물에 불과할 수도 있다. 아마도 진짜 결과는 더 많은 부정행위가 수업 (e) 크기와는 관계없이 서술형 시험에서보다 선다형 시험에서 발생했다는 점일 것이다.』

「 」: 12번의 근거
「 」: 11번의 근거

- take for granted ~을 당연히 여기다
- investigator ⓝ 연구자
- extent ⓝ 정도
- hypothesize ⓥ 가정하다, 가설을 세우다
- apparently 〔ad〕 명백히, 분명히
- extraneous ⓐ 외부의, 관련 없는
- interfere with ~에 간섭하다
- subjective ⓐ 주관적인
- experimental ⓐ 실험의
- discourage A from B A가 B하지 못하게 하다
- finding ⓝ 결과
- deviant ⓐ 벗어난
- cheating ⓝ 부정행위
- analyze ⓥ 분석하다
- multiple-choice 선다형의
- variable ⓝ 변인, 변수
- regardless of ~에 관계없이
- objective ⓐ 객관적인
- limitation ⓝ 한계

구문 풀이

6행 Reasoning that it is more difficult for people [monitoring an
분사구문   가주어   의미상 주어
exam] to keep students under surveillance in large classes than in
진주어
smaller ones, / she hypothesizes that a higher rate of cheating
                주어   동사   접속사   주어
will occur on exams in large classes than in small (classes).
자동사   생략

★★★ 1등급 대비 고난도 2점 문제

11 제목 파악 정답률 36% | 정답 ②

윗글의 제목으로 가장 적절한 것은?

① Investigator's Attitude: Subjective vs. Objective
   연구자의 태도: 주관적 vs. 객관적
✓ Research Error from Wrong Experimental Design
   잘못된 실험 설계로 인한 연구 오류
③ Test Your Hypothesis to Obtain Academic Support
   학술적 지지를 얻기 위해 가설을 검증해 보라
④ Limitations of Multiple-choice Exams in Large Classes
   규모가 큰 반에서 치르는 선다형 시험의 한계
⑤ Is There Any Way to Discourage Students from Cheating?
   학생들이 컨닝을 하지 못하게 할 방법이 있는가?

Why? 왜 정답일까?

첫 문장에서 연구의 타당성은 결과가 타당하다고 해서 당연히 전제될 수 없다고 진술한 뒤, 이를 뒷받침하기 위해 실험 결과에 영향을 줄 수 있는 변인을 다 통제하지 못한 채 실험을 진행하고는 가설이 타당하다고 잘못 결론을 내리는 연구자의 예를 든 글이다. 특히 'A few days later, however, ~'에서 연구자가 동료의 지적을 받고 실험 결과에 본래 의도했던 수업 크기라는 독립 변인뿐 아니라 시험 형태라는 다른 변인이 개입되었을 수도 있다는 점을 깨닫는다는 내용이 언급되고, 이를 근거로 마지막 두 문장은 기존의 실험 결과가 단지 '가공된' 결과임에 불과할 수도 있다는 결론을 제시하고 있다. 따라서 글의 제목으로 가장 적절한 것은 ② '잘못된 실험 설계로 인한 연구 오류'이다.

★★ 문제 해결 꿀~팁 ★★

▶ 많이 틀린 이유는?
규모가 큰 반과 작은 반에서 시험 유형을 통제하지 않은 채 부정행위를 유발하는 요인

을 밝혀내려 했던 실험을 소개한 글이다. 본문이 '선다형 시험의 한계'를 지적하는 글은 아니므로 최다 오답인 ④는 정답에서 제외된다.

▶ 문제 해결 방법은?
본문은 연구의 타당성을 장담할 수 없는 이유는 연구 과정이나 실험 설계에 오류가 있을 수 있기 때문이라는 내용으로 요약될 수 있으므로, 가장 적절한 선택지는 Wrong Experimental Design을 포함한 ②이다.

12 어휘 추론 정답률 51% | 정답 ③

밑줄 친 (a) ~ (e) 중에서 문맥상 낱말의 쓰임이 적절하지 않은 것은?

① (a)   ② (b)   ✓ (c)   ④ (d)   ⑤ (e)

Why? 왜 정답일까?

'To test this hypothesis, she collects data on cheating in both large classes and small ones and then analyzes the data. Her results show that more cheating per student occurs in the larger classes.'을 보면 큰 수업에서 부정행위가 더 많이 일어날 것으로 추측한 연구자가 데이터를 모아 분석한 결과 자신의 가설이 맞다는 것을 확인한 경우를 언급하고 있다. 이를 근거로 볼 때, (c)의 **reject**를 **support**로 고쳐야 한다. 따라서 문맥상 낱말의 쓰임이 적절하지 않은 것은 ③ '(c)'이다.

DAY 06 20분 미니 모의고사

01 ①	02 ①	03 ③	04 ④	05 ④
06 ③	07 ④	08 ⑤	09 ②	10 ③
11 ②	12 ②			

---

01 새 직장 첫 출근날
정답률 94% | 정답 ①

다음 글에 드러난 David의 심경 변화로 가장 적절한 것은?

☑ nervous → relieved
　초조한　　안도한
② lonely → hopeful
　쓸쓸한　　희망찬
③ pleased → confused
　기쁜　　　당황한
④ indifferent → delighted
　무관심한　　즐거운
⑤ bored → thrilled
　지루한　　짜릿한

[본문 해석]

David는 밴쿠버에서 새로운 일을 시작하게 되었고, 자신이 탈 버스를 기다리고 있었다. 그는 계속 자기 시계와 버스가 올 방향을 번갈아 보았다. 그는 "내가 탈 버스가 아직 안 오네. 첫날 지각할 수는 없어."라고 생각했다. David는 마음을 놓을 수가 없었다. 그가 다시 고개를 들었을 때, 그는 바로 직장으로 가는 다른 버스가 오고 있는 것을 보았다. 그 버스는 그의 앞에 서서 문을 열었다. 그는 버스에 오르며, "후유! 다행히도 지각하지 않도록 이 버스가 딱 맞춰 왔네."라고 생각했다. 그는 버스의 빈 좌석에 등을 기대며 깊은 한숨을 내쉬었고, 마침내 긴장을 풀 수 있었다.

Why? 왜 정답일까?

기다리던 버스가 오지 않아 초조해하던(David couldn't feel at ease.) David가 다른 버스를 잡아 타고 안도했다는(~ finally able to relax.) 내용이다. 따라서 David의 심경 변화로 가장 적절한 것은 ① '초조한 → 안도한'이다.

- **back and forth** 앞뒤로, 이리저리
- **luckily** [ad] 다행히
- **lean back** 뒤로 기대다
- **take a deep breath** 심호흡하다
- **confused** ⓐ 혼란스러운
- **bored** ⓐ 지루한
- **feel at ease** 마음을 놓다, 안도하다
- **just in time** 딱 맞춰서
- **unoccupied** ⓐ 비어 있는
- **relieved** ⓐ 안도한
- **delighted** ⓐ 기쁜
- **thrilled** ⓐ 짜릿한

구문 풀이

10행 He leaned back on an unoccupied seat in the bus and took
　　　　　　　　　　　　　　　　　　　　동사1
a deep breath, (being) finally able to relax.
　　　　　　　분사구문(생략)

---

02 도시 재생에서 가장 중요한 요소
정답률 83% | 정답 ①

다음 글의 요지로 가장 적절한 것은?

☑ 도시 재생을 위한 공공정책은 건설보다 사람에 중점을 두어야 한다.
② 대중 교통 이용이 편리하도록 도시 교통 체계를 구축해야 한다.
③ 사회기반시설 확충을 통해 지역 경제를 활성화해야 한다.
④ 에너지를 절감할 수 있는 친환경 건물을 설계해야 한다.
⑤ 문화유산 보존을 우선하는 도시 계획을 수립해야 한다.

[본문 해석]

문제가 있는 도시의 너무 많은 공무원들은 새로운 경기장 또는 경전철 시스템, 컨벤션 센터, 주택 프로젝트와 같은 대규모 건설 프로젝트를 통해 그들의 도시를 이전의 영광으로 되돌릴 수 있다고 잘못 상상하고 있다. 거의 예외 없이 어떤 공공 정책도 도시 변화의 흐름을 늦출 수는 없다. 우리는 Rust Belt에 사는 가난한 사람들의 요구를 무시해서는 안 되고 공공 정책이 가난한 지역을 돕는 것이 아닌 가난한 *사람*들을 돕도록 해야 한다. 반짝이는 새로운 부동산은 쇠퇴하는 도시를 꾸밀 수는 있지만, 이것은 기저에 있는 문제를 해결하지는 못한다. 쇠퇴하는 도시의 특징은 이들이 경제력에 비해서 *너무 많은* 주택과 기반시설을 가지고 있다는 것이다. 그 모든 건축물의 공급과 너무 적은 수요로 인해 더 많은 공급을 만들어 내기 위해 공공 자금을 사용하는 것은 의미가 없다. 건물 중심의 도시 재생의 어리석음은 우리에게 도시는 구조물이 아니라 사람이라는 것을 상기시킨다.

Why? 왜 정답일까?

'~ public policy should help poor *people*, not poor *places*.'와 'The folly of building-centric urban renewal reminds us that cities aren't structures; cities are people.'에서 도시 재생을 위한 공공 정책은 장소나 건설이 아닌 사람에 집중해야 한다는 논지를 일관되게 제시하는 것으로 볼 때, 글의 요지로 가장 적절한 것은 ① '도시 재생을 위한 공공정책은 건설보다 사람에 중점을 두어야 한다.'이다.

- **official** ⓝ 공무원
- **massive** ⓐ 거대한
- **light rail** 경(輕)철도
- **exception** ⓝ 예외
- **ignore** ⓥ 무시하다
- **underlying** ⓐ 기저에 있는, 근본적인
- **infrastructure** ⓝ 기반 시설
- **renewal** ⓝ 재생, 부활
- **lead back to** ~로 되돌리다
- **construction** ⓝ 건설
- **housing** ⓝ 주택 (공급)
- **tidal** ⓐ (바다) 조수의
- **decline** ⓥ 쇠퇴하다
- **hallmark** ⓝ 특징
- **folly** ⓝ 어리석음, 판단력 부족

구문 풀이

1행 Too many officials in troubled cities wrongly imagine that
　　　　　　　　주어　　　　　　　　　　　　　　　　동사　접속사(~것)
they can lead their city back to its former glories with some massive
construction project — (a new stadium or light rail system, a convention
center, or a housing project).
( ): 동격(= some massive construction project)

---

03 뉴스 정보가 제시되는 방식
정답률 60% | 정답 ③

다음 글의 제목으로 가장 적절한 것은?

① Inverted Pyramid: Logically Impossible Structure
　역 피라미드: 논리적으로 불가능한 구조
② Curiosity Is What Makes Readers Keep Reading
　호기심은 독자가 읽기를 계속하게 만드는 것이다
☑ Where to Put Key Points in News Writing
　뉴스 작성 시 요점을 어디에 둘 것인가
④ The More Information, the Less Attention
　정보가 더 많을수록 관심이 더 적어진다
⑤ Readers, Tell the Facts from the Fakes!
　독자들이여, 사실과 거짓을 구별하라!

[본문 해석]

뉴스 리포터들은 가장 중요한 정보로 이야기를 시작하도록 배운다. 리드라고 불리는 첫 번째 문장은 이야기의 가장 본질적인 요소들을 담는다. 좋은 리드는 많은 정보를 전달할 수 있다. 리드 후에, 정보는 중요도가 감소하는 순서로 제시된다. 언론인들은 이것을 '역 피라미드' 구조라고 부르는데, 가장 중요한 정보(피라미드의 가장 넓은 부분)가 맨 위에 있는 것이다. 역 피라미드는 독자들에게 아주 좋다. 독자의 주의 지속 시간이 어떻든 간에 — 독자가 리드만 읽든 전체 이야기를 읽든 — 역 피라미드는 독자가 얻는 정보를 극대화한다. 다른 방법을 생각해 보라. 만약 뉴스 이야기들이 마지막에 극적인 결말이 있는 미스터리처럼 쓰여진다면, 이야기 중반부에서 중단한 독자들은 요점을 놓칠 것이다. 누가 대통령 선거 혹은 슈퍼볼(매년 미국 프로 미식축구의 우승팀을 결정하는 경기)에서 이겼는지 알아내기 위해 이야기의 마지막 문장까지 기다린다고 상상해 보라.

Why? 왜 정답일까?

첫 두 문장에 따르면 뉴스에서 가장 중요한 정보는 리드라고 불리는 첫 번째 문장에 제시된다(News reporters are taught to start their stories with the most important information. The first sentence, called the lead, contains the most essential elements of the story.)고 한다. 이어서 중요도가 덜할수록 정보가 나중에 제시된다는 설명이 뒤따르고 있다. 따라서 글의 제목으로 가장 적절한 것은 ③ '뉴스 작성 시 요점을 어디에 둘 것인가'이다.

- **essential** ⓐ 필수적인, 본질적인
- **attention span** 주의 지속 시간
- **payoff** ⓝ (뜻밖의) 결말
- **presidential** ⓐ 대통령 (선거)의
- **tell A from B** A와 B를 구별하다
- **convey** ⓥ 전달하다
- **alternative** ⓝ 대안
- **break off** (갑자기) 중단하다
- **logically** [ad] 논리적으로

구문 풀이

9행 No matter what the reader's attention span — whether she
　　　= whatever(무엇이 ~이든 간에)　　　　　　　　부사절 접속사(~이든 아니든)
reads only the lead or the entire story — the inverted pyramid
　　　　　　　　　　　　　　　　　　　　　　　　　주어
maximizes the information [she gets].
　　동사　　　목적어(선행사)

DAY 06

04 제왕나비의 특징
정답률 91% | 정답 ④

monarch butterfly에 관한 다음 글의 내용과 일치하지 <u>않는</u> 것은?
① 날개의 바깥 가장자리에 흰 점이 있다.
② 뒷날개는 앞날개보다 색이 더 밝다.
③ 알은 약 3일에서 5일 후에 부화한다.
☑ 북부 주의 추운 겨울 기온에 잘 버틴다.
⑤ 4천 킬로미터 넘게 날 수 있다.

[본문 해석]

제왕나비는 날개에 밝은색의 예쁜 얼룩무늬가 있다. 『날개 바깥쪽 가장자리에 흰 점들이 있다.』 『뒷날개는 둥글고, 앞날개보다 더 밝은색을 띤다.』 몸통은 검은 바탕에 흰 점이 있다. 『어미 나비는 밀크위드 잎 밑면에 오직 한 개의 알만 낳고, 그것은 약 3일에서 5일 후에 부화한다.』 제왕나비는 3월부터 10월까지 미국 전역에서 따뜻한 햇살을 받으며 날아다니는 것을 좋아한다. 『제왕나비는 북부 주의 추운 겨울 기온에 살아남을 수 없다.』 그래서, 그것은 매우 현명하게 북부 주에서 남부로 이주하여 동면한다. 『제왕나비는 더 따뜻한 지방으로 4천 킬로미터 넘게 날 수 있는 유일한 곤충이다.』
①의 근거 일치 / ②의 근거 일치 / ③의 근거 일치 / ④의 근거 불일치 / ⑤의 근거 일치

Why? 왜 정답일까?

'The monarch cannot survive the cold winter temperatures of the northern states.'에서 제왕나비는(미국) 북부 주의 겨울 온도에서 생존할 수 없다고 하므로, 내용과 일치하지 않는 것은 ④ '북부 주의 추운 겨울 기온에 잘 버틴다.'이다.

Why? 왜 오답일까?

① 'The wings have white spots on the outer margins.'의 내용과 일치한다.
② 'The hind wings are ~ lighter in color than the front wings.'의 내용과 일치한다.
③ '~ which hatches about three to five days later.'의 내용과 일치한다.
⑤ 'The monarch is the only insect that can fly more than four thousand kilometers to a warmer climate.'의 내용과 일치한다.

- **monarch** ⓝ 제왕, 군주
- **spot** ⓝ 점
- **rounded** ⓐ 둥근
- **underside** ⓝ 아랫면, 밑면
- **migrate** ⓥ 이주하다
- **splash** ⓥ 알록달록하게 장식하다
- **margin** ⓝ 가장자리
- **lay** ⓥ (알을) 낳다
- **hatch** ⓥ 부화하다

구문 풀이

5행 The mother butterfly lays only one egg on the underside of milkweed leaves, which hatches about three to five days later.
선행사 / 주격 관·대 동사(단수)

★★★ 1등급 대비 고난도 3점 문제

05 자기 보고 데이터의 한계
정답률 40% | 정답 ④

다음 글의 밑줄 친 부분 중, 어법상 틀린 것은? [3점]

[본문 해석]

연구 심리학자들은 종종 *자기 보고 데이터*로 작업하는데, 이는 자신들의 행동에 대한 참가자들의 구두 설명으로 구성되어 있다. 변인을 측정하기 위해 설문지, 면접 또는 성격 특성 목록이 사용될 때마다 여기 해당한다. 자기 보고 방법은 꽤 유용할 수 있다. 그것들은 사람들이 자신을 풀타임으로 관찰할 수 있는 유일한 기회를 갖는다는 사실을 이용한다. 그러나, 자기 보고는 몇 가지 종류의 왜곡으로 오염될 수 있다. 이러한 왜곡 중 가장 문제가 되는 하나는 사회적 바람직성 편향인데, 이것은 자신에 관한 질문에 사회적으로 승인된 답을 제공하는 경향이다. 이러한 편향에 영향을 받은 피실험자들은 특히 민감한 문제에 대해 질문받을 때 호의적인 인상을 만들기 위해 더 노력한다. 예를 들어, 많은 설문 조사 응답자들은 사실은 안 했다고 밝히는 것이 가능할 때도 선거에서 투표했다거나 자선 단체에 기부했다고 보고할 것이다.

Why? 왜 정답일까?

문맥상 실험 대상자(subjects)가 질문을 '받는' 상황이므로 ask 대신 are asked를 써야 한다. 타동사 뒤에 목적어도 없다는 점에서 수동태가 필요하다는 힌트를 추가로 얻을 수 있다. 따라서 어법상 틀린 것은 ④이다.

Why? 왜 오답일까?

① '~할 때마다'라는 의미의 복합관계부사 whenever이다.
② to observe의 목적어 themselves는 to observe의 의미상 주어인 people과 동일한 대상이다. 이렇게 같은 행위에 걸리는 주어와 목적어가 같으면 목적어 자리에 재귀대명사를 쓴다.
③ 과거분사 approved를 꾸미는 부사 socially이다.
⑤ voted와 병렬 연결되는 과거시제 동사 gave이다.

- **verbal** ⓐ 구두의
- **questionnaire** ⓝ 설문지
- **plague** ⓥ 괴롭히다, 감염시키다
- **subject** ⓝ 실험 대상자
- **sensitive** ⓐ 민감한
- **account** ⓝ 설명
- **variable** ⓝ 변수, 변인
- **distortion** ⓝ 왜곡
- **bias** ⓝ 편향
- **vote** ⓥ 투표하다

구문 풀이

5행 They take advantage of the fact [that people have a unique opportunity to observe themselves full-time]. [ ]: 동격절(= the fact)

★★ 문제 해결 꿀~팁 ★★

▶ 많이 틀린 이유는?
⑤의 병렬구조는 전체적인 문맥을 살펴봐야 하기 때문에 까다로웠을 수 있다. 최근의 출제 트렌드 상 병렬구조는 형태만 기계적으로 맞추기보다 의미를 고려해야 하는 유형으로 나오기 때문에 주의가 필요하다.
▶ 문제 해결 방법은?
④의 '능동태 vs. 수동태'는 최다 출제 포인트 중 하나이다. '태'란 주어-동사의 관계를 나타내므로, 동사에 밑줄이 있으면 주어와의 관계를 1순위로 살피도록 한다.

06 갑작스러운 성공 또는 부의 위험성
정답률 47% | 정답 ③

다음 글의 밑줄 친 부분 중, 문맥상 낱말의 쓰임이 적절하지 <u>않은</u> 것은? [3점]

[본문 해석]

갑작스러운 성공이나 상금은 아주 위험할 수 있다. 신경학적으로 흥분과 에너지의 강력한 분출을 유발하는 화학물질들이 뇌에서 분비되고, 이 경험을 ① 반복하고자 하는 욕구로 이어진다. 그것이 어떤 종류의 중독 또는 광적 행동의 출발점일 수 있다. 또한, 이익이 빨리 얻어질 때, 우리는 진정한 성공이 정말 지속되기 위해서는 노력을 통해야 한다는 기본적인 지혜를 보지 못하고 ② 놓치는 경향이 있다. 우리는 그처럼 ③ 어렵게 얻은(→ 갑작스러운) 이익에 있어 운이 하는 역할을 고려하지 않는다. 우리는 그만큼의 돈이나 관심을 얻는 것으로부터의 그 황홀감을 되찾기 위해 계속해서 시도한다. 우리는 우월감을 느낀다. 우리는 특히 우리에게 경고를 하려고 하는 누구에게든 ④ 저항하게 된다 — 그들은 이해하지 못한다고 우리는 스스로에게 말한다. 이것은 지속될 수 없기 때문에 우리는 필연적이고도 몹시 고통스러운 ⑤ 추락을 경험하고, 이는 그 사이클의 우울기로 이어진다. 도박꾼들이 가장 이러기 쉽지만, 이것은 거품 경제일 때의 사업가들과 대중으로부터 갑작스러운 관심을 얻은 사람들에게도 똑같이 적용된다.

Why? 왜 정답일까?

③ 앞의 문장에서 우리는 갑작스럽게 성공을 거머쥐다 보면 진정한 성공을 지속시키기 위해 노력이 필요하다는 기본적인 지혜를 놓칠 수 있다고 언급한다. 이 뒤에는 우리가 '갑자기 쉽게 얻은' 성공에 운이 개입하였음을 고려하지 않는다는 내용이 연결되어야 하므로, ③의 hard-earned는 sudden으로 고쳐야 한다. 따라서 문맥상 낱말의 쓰임이 적절하지 않은 것은 ③이다.

- **neurologically** ⓐd 신경학적으로
- **addiction** ⓝ 중독
- **last** ⓥ 지속되다
- **hard-earned** 어렵게 얻은
- **superiority** ⓝ 우월함
- **sustain** ⓥ 지속시키다, 지탱하다
- **depression** ⓝ 우울, 낮게 패인 곳
- **burst** ⓝ 분출
- **manic** ⓐ 광적인
- **take into account** ~을 고려하다
- **recapture** ⓥ 되찾다
- **resistant** ⓐ 저항하는
- **inevitable** ⓐ 필연적인, 불가피한
- **prone to** ~하기 쉬운

구문 풀이

12행 We become especially resistant to anyone who tries to warn us — they don't understand, we tell ourselves.
2형식 동사 / 형용사 보어 / =whoever / 직접 목적어 / 주어 동사 / 간접 목적어

★★★ 1등급 대비 고난도 2점 문제

07 | 자유 놀이의 기능 | 정답률 29% | 정답 ④

다음 빈칸에 들어갈 말로 가장 적절한 것을 고르시오.

① noisy – 시끄럽지
② sociable – 사교적이지
③ complicated – 복잡하지
✓④ helpless – 무력하지
⑤ selective – 선택적이지

[본문 해석]

자유 놀이는 아이들에게 자신이 <u>무력하지</u> 않다는 것을 가르치는 자연적 수단이다. <u>어른과 떨어져 놀면서, 아이들은 통제력을 정말로 가지고 그것을 발휘하는 것을 연습할 수 있다.</u> 자유 놀이를 통해, 아이들은 스스로 결정을 내리고, 자신들만의 문제를 해결하고, 규칙을 만들고 지키며, 복종적이거나 반항적인 아랫사람보다는 동등한 사람 자격으로 다른 사람과 어울리는 것을 배운다. 활동적인 야외 놀이를 통해, 아이들은 의도적으로 자기 자신에게 적절한 수준의 두려움을 주고, 그렇게 하여 자기 신체뿐만 아니라 두려움 또한 통제하는 법을 배운다. 사회적인 놀이를 통해 아이들은 어떻게 다른 사람과 협상하고, 다른 사람을 기쁘게 하며, 갈등으로부터 생길 수 있는 분노를 다스리고 극복할 수 있는지를 배운다. 이러한 교훈 중 어느 것도 언어적 수단을 통해서는 배울 수 없다. 그것들은 오로지 경험을 통해서만 배울 수 있는데, 그것은 자유 놀이가 제공하는 것이다.

Why? 왜 정답일까?

두 번째 문장에서 자유 놀이를 통해 아이들은 통제력을 갖고 발휘하는 연습(~ do have control and can practice asserting it.)을 해볼 수 있다는 핵심 내용이 나온다. 이어서 글 전체에 걸쳐 아이들은 놀이 속에서 스스로 결정하고 문제를 해결하며, 타인과 동등한 인격체로 어울리고 협상하는 법을 익히는 한편, 자신의 감정을 통제하는 법도 익혀나간다는 보충 설명이 제시된다. 이때 빈칸 바로 앞에는 not이 있으므로, 빈칸에는 '통제력이 없는' 상태에 관한 말이 들어가야 'not+빈칸'이 주제를 나타낼 수 있다. 따라서 빈칸에 들어갈 말로 가장 적절한 것은 ④ '무력하지'이다.

- assert ⓥ (권리 등을) 행사하다, 주장하다
- rebellious ⓐ 반항적인
- deliberately ⓐ 의도적으로
- moderate ⓐ 적당한
- negotiate ⓥ 협상하다
- arise from ~에서 발생하다
- verbal ⓐ 언어적인
- helpless ⓐ 무력한
- obedient ⓐ 복종하는
- subordinate ⓝ 하급자, 부하
- dose ⓥ (약을) 투여하다, 먹이다
- thereby ⓐ 그렇게 함으로써
- overcome ⓥ 극복하다
- conflict ⓝ 갈등
- sociable ⓐ 사교적인
- selective ⓐ 선택적인

구문 풀이

11행 In social play children learn how to negotiate with others,
　　　　　　　　　　　　　　　　　　　　 명사구1
how to please others, and how to manage and overcome the anger
명사구2　　　　　　　　　　 명사구3(~하는 방법)
[that can arise from conflicts].
[ ] : anger 수식

★★ 문제 해결 꿀~팁 ★★

▶ 많이 틀린 이유는?
글에 get along with others, social play 등의 표현이 나와 ②가 답으로 적절해 보일 수 있다. 하지만 아이들의 놀이의 의미를 설명하는 두 번째 문장을 보면, 놀이를 통해 아이들은 스스로 '통제력'을 지니고 있음을 알고, 그것을 행사하는 방법을 익히게 된다고 한다. 이는 아이들이 '무력한 존재가 아니라' 놀이 속 경험을 통해 행동이나 감정의 조절, 사회적 규칙 등을 배워갈 수 있는 힘을 지닌 존재라는 뜻이다.

▶ 문제 해결 방법은?
빈칸 앞에 not이 있으므로, 'not+빈칸'이 함께 주제를 나타내려면 빈칸에는 주제와 반대되는 말이 들어가야 한다. 즉 do have control과 의미상 반대되는 표현이 빈칸에 적합하다.

★★★ 1등급 대비 고난도 3점 문제

08 | 소리의 밝기 | 정답률 41% | 정답 ⑤

글의 흐름으로 보아, 주어진 문장이 들어가기에 가장 적절한 곳을 고르시오. [3점]

[본문 해석]

소리의 밝기는 더 높은 주파수에서의 많은 에너지를 의미하며, 이는 소리로부

터 쉽게 계산될 수 있다. 바이올린은 플루트에 비해 더 많은 상음(上音)을 가지고 있고 더 밝게 들린다. ① 오보에가 클래식 기타보다 더 밝고, 크래시 심벌이 더블 베이스보다 더 밝다. ② 이것은 명백하고 실제로 사람들은 밝음을 좋아한다. ③ 한 가지 이유는 그것이 소리를 주관적으로 더 크게 들리도록 만든다는 것이며, 이는 현대 전자 음악과 19세기 클래식 음악에서 소리의 세기 전쟁의 일환이다. ④ 모든 음향 기사들은 만약 방금 이 곡을 녹음한 음악가에게 곡을 틀어 주고 약간의 더 높은 주파수를 더하면, 그 음악가는 곧바로 그 곡을 훨씬 더 좋아하게 되리라는 것을 안다. ⑤ 하지만 이것은 일시적인 효과이고, 장기적으로 사람들은 그러한 소리가 너무 밝다는 것을 알게 된다. 따라서 그러한 곡을 너무 밝게 틀어 주지 않는 것이 현명한데 왜냐하면, 그 음악가에게 더 적은 밝기가 결국 음악에 더 도움이 된다는 것을 납득시키는 데 보통 시간이 꽤 걸리기 때문이다.

Why? 왜 정답일까?

소리는 밝을수록 더 크게 느껴진다는 설명 뒤로, ⑤ 앞의 문장은 만일 음악을 녹음해서 조금 더 높은 주파수를 첨가해 틀어주면 음악가가 그 소리를 더 좋아하게 될 것이라는 예를 든다. 하지만 ⑤ 뒤의 문장은 곡을 너무 밝게 틀어주지 않는 것이 현명하다는 내용이므로, 밝은 소리가 선호될 것이라는 ⑤ 앞의 내용과 상충한다. 따라서 But으로 시작하며 밝아진 소리에 대한 선호가 일시적임을 지적하는 주어진 문장이 들어가기에 가장 적절한 곳은 ⑤이다.

- short-lived ⓐ 단기적인
- overtone ⓝ 상음(上音)
- loudness ⓝ 소리의 세기
- track ⓝ (테이프로 녹음한) 곡
- record ⓥ 녹음하다
- convince ⓥ 납득시키다
- frequency ⓝ 주파수
- subjectively ⓐ 주관적으로
- sound engineer ⓝ 음향기사
- musician ⓝ 음악가
- immediately ⓐ 즉시, 곧바로
- serve ⓥ 도움이 되다

구문 풀이

16행 So it is wise not to play back such a track with too much
　　　　　가주어　　　　　　　　　　　진주어
brightness, as it normally takes quite some time to convince the
「it takes + 시간 + to부정사 : ~이 …하는 데 ~의 시간이 걸리다」
musician that less brightness serves his music better in the end.

★★ 문제 해결 꿀~팁 ★★

▶ 많이 틀린 이유는?
③에 주어진 문장을 넣으면 '밝은 소리는 주관적으로 크게 들린다 → 그런데 이 효과는 일시적이다 → 그 이유는 소리가 크게 들리기 때문이다'라는 흐름이 얼핏 자연스러워 보인다. 하지만 ③을 답으로 고르면, ⑤ 앞뒤의 흐름 단절이 해소되지 않은 상태로 남기 때문에 전체적인 논리 전개가 부자연스럽다.

▶ 문제 해결 방법은?
⑤ 뒤의 문장에 So가 있고, So 뒤로 곡을 너무 밝게 틀어주면 안 된다는 결론이 나오므로, ⑤ 앞에는 '밝게 틀어주는 것의 한계'를 언급하는 말이 나와야 한다. 본문에서 이 한계는 ⑤ 앞 문장이 아닌, 주어진 문장에서 언급된다(find such sounds too bright).

09 | 그린워싱의 교묘한 수법 | 정답률 59% | 정답 ②

다음 글의 내용을 한 문장으로 요약하고자 한다. 빈칸 (A), (B)에 들어갈 말로 가장 적절한 것은? [3점]

	(A)		(B)
①	permanently 영구적으로	……	manipulated 조종당한
✓②	temporarily 일시적으로		misinformed 잘못된 정보를 받은
③	momentarily 잠시		advocated 옹호된
④	ultimately 궁극적으로	……	underestimated 과소평가된
⑤	consistently 지속적으로	……	analyzed 분석된

[본문 해석]

그린워싱은 소비자가 재화나 서비스를 실제보다 더 친환경적이라고 생각하도록 현혹시키는 것을 포함한다. 그린워싱은 법에 의해 요구되는 환경적 주장을 하는 것, 그래서 무의미한 것(예를 들어 '염화불화탄소 없음')에서부터 과대 광고(환경적 주장을 과장하는 것), 사기에까지 이르는 것을 포함한다. 연구자들에 따르면, 제품에 관한 주장은 종종 지나치게 모호하거나 현혹적이다. 몇몇 제품들에는 실제로 식물과 동물을 포함해서 모든 것에 화학물질이 들어있음에

DAY 06

도 '화학물질 없음'이라고 표기되어 있다. 현혹적이고 확인할 수 없는 주장이 가장 많이 포함된 제품들은 세탁 세제, 가정용 세제, 그리고 페인트였다. 환경 옹호자들이 동의하기로, 소비자들이 구매하는 제품의 환경적 영향력에 대하여 확실히 정보를 적절하게 제공받게 하려면 여전히 갈 길이 멀다. 그린워싱의 가장 흔한 이유는 환경적으로 의식 있는 소비자들을 유인하기 위해서이다. 많은 소비자들은 구매를 끝내기 전까지 거짓 주장을 발견하지 못한다. 그러므로 그린워싱은 단기적으로는 판매량을 증가시킬 수도 있다. 하지만, 이 전략은 자신들이 기만당하고 있다는 것을 소비자들이 알게 될 때 심각하게 역효과를 낼 수 있다.

➡ 그린워싱이 환경적인 의식이 있는 소비자들을 속여 (A) 일시적으로 회사에 이익을 가져다줄 수 있지만, 소비자들이 (B) 잘못된 정보를 받은 것을 알게 됐을 때 회사는 심각한 문제에 직면할 것이다.

Why? 왜 정답일까?

마지막 네 문장에 핵심 내용이 제시된다. 그린워싱은 흔히 환경에 신경을 쓰는 소비자들을 유인하기 위해 이용되고, 실제로 단기적으로는 회사에 이득을 가져다주지만, 결과적으로 소비자들이 속았다는 것을 깨달으면 심각한 역효과를 초래할 수 있다(~ greenwashing may increase sales in the short term. However, this strategy can seriously backfire when consumers find out they are being deceived.)는 것이다. 따라서 요약문의 빈칸 (A), (B)에 들어갈 말로 가장 적절한 것은 ② '(A) temporarily (일시적으로), (B) misinformed(잘못된 정보를 받은)'이다.

- **greenwashing** ⓝ 그린워싱, 위장 환경주의
- **environmentally friendly** 환경 친화적인
- **make a claim** 주장하다
- **puffery** ⓝ 과대 선전
- **label** ⓥ 이름을 붙이다, 명명하다
- **unverifiable** ⓐ 증명할 수 없는
- **advocate** ⓝ 옹호자, 지지자
- **adequately** ⓐⓓ 적절하게
- **impact** ⓝ 영향, 충격
- **in the short term** 단기적으로
- **deceive** ⓥ 속이다
- **manipulate** ⓥ 조종하다
- **momentarily** ⓐⓓ 잠시
- **mislead** ⓥ 현혹하다, 오도하다
- **range from A to B** A부터 B에 이르다
- **irrelevant** ⓐ 부적절한, 관련이 없는
- **vague** ⓐ 애매모호한
- **chemical** ⓝ 화학물질 ⓐ 화학의
- **detergent** ⓝ 세제
- **ensure** ⓥ 확실히 하다, 보장하다
- **informed** ⓐ 정보를 제공받은
- **attract** ⓥ 유인하다, 끌다
- **backfire** ⓥ 역효과를 낳다
- **permanently** ⓐⓓ 영구적으로
- **temporarily** ⓐⓓ 일시적으로
- **underestimate** ⓥ 과소평가하다

구문 풀이

1행 Greenwashing involves misleading a consumer into thinking
　　　　　　　　　　　　　목적어(동명사)
a good or service is more environmentally friendly than it really is.
　　　　　　　　　　　　　　　　　　　　　　대동사(= is environmentally friendly)

10-12　내면의 용기로 풍요로움을 쌓아온 Jack

[본문 해석]

(A)
1960년대에 Jack이 20대 초반의 청년이었을 때, 그는 자기가 기대받았던 대로 아버지의 보험 회사에서 일하려고 했다. 『그의 두 형은 쉽게 적응했고 자기 일을 즐기는 것처럼 보였다.』그러나 Jack은 보험 업계에 싫증이 났다. "그것은 지루함 그 이상으로 나빴다."라고 그는 말했다. "나는 내면이 죽어가는 것 같았다." Jack은 미용에 매력을 느꼈고, 활기찬 분위기의 미용실을 갖는 것을 꿈꿨다. 그는 (a) 자신이 미용의 창의적이고 사회적인 면을 즐길 것이고, 성공할 것이라고 믿었다.

(C)
『26세에 Jack은 아버지에게 가서 회사를 떠나 미용사가 되겠다는 의사를 밝혔다.』Jack이 예상했던 대로, 그의 아버지는 화를 내며 Jack이 이기적이고 배은망덕하며 남자답지 못하다고 비난했다. 아버지의 분노 앞에서, Jack은 혼란과 두려움을 느꼈다. 그의 결심은 약해졌다. 그러나 그때 어떤 힘이 (d) 그의 가슴을 채웠고 그는 자기 결정에 확고해졌다. 『자신의 길을 가면서, Jack은 번창하는 미용실 세 군데를 운영했을 뿐만 아니라, 또한 고객들이 힘든 시기에 직면했을 때 그들의 말을 들어주고 격려해주어 그들이 내면의 아름다움을 경험하도록 도왔다.』

(D)
『자기 일에 대한 그의 사랑으로 인해 그는 요양원에서 시간과 재능을 기부하게 되었고, 이는 결과적으로 그가 호스피스 자원봉사가 되고, 마침내 자기 지역

사회에서 호스피스 프로그램을 위한 기금 모금 운동을 시작하는 결과로 이어졌다.』그리고 이 모든 것은 그의 삶에서 또 다른 용기 있는 움직임을 위한 견고한 디딤돌을 놓았다. Jack과 그의 아내 Michele이 건강한 아이들 둘을 낳고 나서 고아가 된 아이를 가정에 데려오기로 결정했을 때, (e) 그의 아버지는 그들과 의절하겠다고 위협했다.

(B)
Jack은 아버지가 입양을 두려워하고 있으며, 특히 이 경우에는 아이가 그들 가족과 다른 인종적 배경 출신이었기 때문임을 이해했다. 『Jack과 Michele은 거부의 위험을 무릅쓰고 입양을 진행했다.』몇 년이 걸렸지만, 결국 Jack의 아버지는 어린 손녀를 사랑했고 (b) 자기 아들의 독립적인 선택을 받아들였다. Jack은 비록 자주 두려움을 느꼈고 여전히 그렇지만, 항상 자신에게 용기가 있다는 것을 깨달았다. 사실, 용기는 (c) 그가 삶에 풍요로움을 쌓아온 발판이었다.

- **insurance** ⓝ 보험
- **rejection** ⓝ 거부
- **scaffolding** ⓝ 발판
- **rage** ⓥ 분노하다
- **selfish** ⓐ 이기적인
- **unmanly** ⓐ 남자답지 못한
- **fury** ⓝ 분노
- **flourishing** ⓐ 무성한, 번영하는
- **hospice** ⓝ 호스피스(말기 환자용 병원)
- **orphaned** ⓐ 고아인
- **adoption** ⓝ 입양
- **courage** ⓝ 용기
- **anticipate** ⓥ 예상하다
- **accuse A of B** A를 B에 대해 비난하다
- **ungrateful** ⓐ 배은망덕한
- **in the face of** ~에도 불구하고
- **resolve** ⓝ 결심 ⓥ 결심하다
- **in turn** 결과적으로
- **fundraising** ⓝ 모금
- **disown** ⓥ 의절하다

구문 풀이

(B) 9행 In fact, courage was the scaffolding around which he had
　　　　　　　　　　　　　　　　　　　　　　　　　　= where
built richness into his life.

(D) 6행 When, (after having two healthy children of their own),
　　　　　　　　接속사　　= after they had
Jack and his wife, Michele, decided to bring an orphaned child into
　　　주어　　　　　　　　동사
their family, his father threatened to disown them.
　　　　　　　주어　　　동사구(~하겠다고 협박하다)

10　글의 순서 파악　　정답률 74% | 정답 ③

주어진 글 (A)에 이어질 내용을 순서에 맞게 배열한 것으로 가장 적절한 것은?
① (B) - (D) - (C)　　　　② (C) - (B) - (D)
✓③ (C) - (D) - (B)　　　　④ (D) - (B) - (C)
⑤ (D) - (C) - (B)

Why? 왜 정답일까?

Jack이 아버지의 보험 회사에서 일하다가 미용에 관심을 갖게 되었다는 (A) 뒤로, Jack이 비난을 무릅쓰고 회사를 나와 미용실을 성공적으로 운영하기 시작했다는 (C), Jack이 각종 봉사를 이어가다가 아이 입양 문제로 다시금 아버지와 대립했다는 (D), 입양을 감행한 Jack이 결국 손녀와 잘 지내기 시작한 아버지를 보며 자기 안의 용기를 깨달았다는 (B)가 차례로 연결되어야 자연스럽다. 따라서 글의 순서로 가장 적절한 것은 ③ '(C) - (D) - (B)'이다.

11　지칭 추론　　정답률 70% | 정답 ②

밑줄 친 (a) ~ (e) 중에서 가리키는 대상이 나머지 넷과 다른 것은?
① (a)　✓② (b)　③ (c)　④ (d)　⑤ (e)

Why? 왜 정답일까?

(a), (c), (d), (e)는 Jack을, (b)는 his father를 가리키므로, (a) ~ (e) 중에서 가리키는 대상이 다른 하나는 ② '(b)'이다.

12　세부 내용 파악　　정답률 77% | 정답 ②

윗글의 Jack에 관한 내용으로 적절하지 않은 것은?
① 두 형은 자신들의 일을 즐기는 것으로 보였다.
✓② 아버지의 반대로 입양을 포기했다.
③ 아버지에게 회사를 떠나겠다는 의사를 밝혔다.
④ 세 개의 번창하는 미용실을 운영했다.

⑤ 지역사회에서 모금 운동을 시작했다.

Why? 왜 정답일까?

(B) 'Jack and Michele risked rejection and went ahead with the adoption.' 에서 아버지의 반대를 감수하고 Jack은 아내와 함께 아이를 입양했다고 하므로, 내용과 일치하지 않는 것은 ② '아버지의 반대로 입양을 포기했다.'이다.

Why? 왜 오답일까?

① (A) 'His two older brothers fit in easily and seemed to enjoy their work.'의 내용과 일치한다.

③ (C) 'When he was twenty-six, Jack approached his father and expressed his intentions of leaving the business to become a hairstylist.' 의 내용과 일치한다.

④ (C) 'In following his path, Jack not only ran three flourishing hair shops ~'의 내용과 일치한다.

⑤ (D) '~ eventually to starting fundraising efforts for the hospice program in his community.'의 내용과 일치한다.

DAY 07 | 20분 미니 모의고사

01 ③	02 ③	03 ①	04 ②	05 ③
06 ②	07 ①	08 ①	09 ③	10 ③
11 ②	12 ③			

01 기차표 날짜 변경 요청
정답률 86% | 정답 ③

다음 글의 목적으로 가장 적절한 것은?

① 특가로 제공되는 기차표를 구매하려고
② 축구 경기 입장권의 환불을 요구하려고
☑ 다른 날짜로 기차표 변경을 요청하려고
④ 기차표 예약이 가능한 날짜를 알아보려고
⑤ 축구 경기 날짜가 연기되었는지를 확인하려고

[본문 해석]

전화로 설명드렸듯이, 이번 주 토요일이 National Soccer Championship에서 Riverside Warriors가 Greenville Trojans와 시합할 날과 같은 날이어서 그날 Springfield에 사시는 저희 부모님을 뵈러 혼자 두 아이를 데리고 기차 여행을 하고 싶지 않습니다. 그래서 제 기차표를 다음 주말(4월 23일)로 바꿔 주시면 정말 감사하겠습니다. 특가로 제공되는 원래 기차표는 교환할 수 없다는 것을 잘 알지만, 기차표를 예매할 당시에는 축구 경기에 관해 알지 못했으니 이렇게 해 주시면 정말 감사하겠습니다. 미리 감사드립니다.

Why? 왜 정답일까?

'I would really appreciate it, therefore, if you could change my tickets to the following weekend (April 23).'에서 기차표 날짜를 변경해줬으면 좋겠다는 내용이 나오는 것으로 보아, 글의 목적으로 가장 적절한 것은 ③ '다른 날짜로 기차표 변경을 요청하려고'이다.

- **by oneself** 혼자
- **fully** ad 충분히
- **non-exchangeable** ⓐ 교환 불가한
- **book** ⓥ 예약하다
- **appreciate** ⓥ 감사하다, (제대로) 이해하다
- **special-offer** 특가로 제공되는
- **match** ⓝ 경기
- **grateful** ⓐ 고마워하는

구문 풀이

1행 As I explained on the telephone, I don't want to take my two
접속사(~듯이)
children by myself on a train trip to visit my parents in Springfield
혼자서 ······· 부사적용법(~하기 위해)
this Saturday since it is the same day [(that) the Riverside Warriors
접속사(~ 때문에) ······· 선행사(시간) ······· 생략
will play the Greenville Trojans in the National Soccer Championship].

02 소셜 미디어 활용 시 조직의 목표를 고려할 필요성
정답률 77% | 정답 ③

다음 글에서 필자가 주장하는 바로 가장 적절한 것은?

① 기업 이미지에 부합하는 소셜 미디어를 직접 개발하여 운영해야 한다.
② 기업은 사회적 가치와 요구를 반영하여 사업 목표를 수립해야 한다.
☑ 기업은 소셜 미디어를 활용할 때 사업 목표를 토대로 해야 한다.
④ 소셜 미디어로 제품을 홍보할 때는 구체적인 정보를 제공해야 한다.
⑤ 소비자의 의견을 수렴하기 위해 소셜 미디어를 적극 활용해야 한다.

[본문 해석]

조직이 소셜 미디어로 실험하는 것을 처음 고려할 때 범하는 가장 일반적인 실수 중 하나는 너무 지나치게 소셜 미디어 도구와 플랫폼에 중점을 두고 조직 자체의 사업 목표에는 충분히 중점을 두지 않는 것이다. 기업을 위한 소셜 웹에서의 성공의 실제는 소셜 미디어 프로그램을 고안하는 것이 최신 소셜 미디어 도구와 채널에 대한 통찰력이 아니라 조직 자체의 목적과 목표에 대한 철저한 이해와 더불어 시작된다는 것이다. 소셜 미디어 프로그램은 그저 '다른 모든 이가 하고 있기' 때문에 인기 소셜 네트워크상에서 '존재'를 관리해야 할 막연한 필요를 이행하는 것이 아니다. '소셜 미디어에 있다는 것' 자체로는 아무 쓸모도 없다. 조금이라도 어떤 쓸모가 있으려면, 소셜 미디어상의 존재는 조직과 조직의 고객을 위해 문제를 해결하거나 어떤 종류의 개선이라는 결과(될 수

있으면 측정 가능한 결과)를 가져와야 한다. 어떤 일이든, 목적이 성공을 이끌어낸다. 소셜 미디어의 세계도 다르지 않다.

Why? 왜 정답일까?

'The reality of success in the social web for businesses ~'에서 기업이 소셜 웹에서 성공하는 데 실제적으로 중요한 요인은 조직 자체의 목표를 이해하는 것이라고 언급하는 것으로 볼 때, 필자가 주장하는 바로 가장 적절한 것은 ③ '기업은 소셜 미디어를 활용할 때 사업 목표를 토대로 해야 한다.'이다. 참고로 마지막 두 문장에서 논지가 반복되고 있다.

- **objective** ⓝ 목표
- **latest** ⓐ 최신(식)의, 최근의
- **merely** ⓐ 그저, 단지
- **vague** ⓐ 막연한
- **serve a purpose** 쓸모가 있다
- **measurable** ⓐ 측정 가능한
- **reality** ⓝ 현실, 사실, 실체
- **thorough** ⓐ 철저한
- **fulfillment** ⓝ 이행, 달성
- **in and of itself** 그 자체로는
- **preferably** ⓐ 될 수 있으면, 가급적

구문 풀이

5행 The reality of success in the social web for businesses is 주어 / 접속사(~것) / 동사(단수) that creating a social media program begins not {with insight into 주어(동명사구) / 동사(단수) / 'not+{A}+ the latest social media tools and channels} but {with a thorough but+{B}: {A}가 아니라 {B}인 understanding of the organization's own goals and objectives}.

★★★ 1등급 대비 고난도 2점 문제

03 명문화되지 않은 규칙의 완고함   정답률 48% | 정답 ①

밑줄 친 the silent killers가 다음 글에서 의미하는 바로 가장 적절한 것은?

① hidden rules that govern our actions unconsciously
  우리의 행동을 무의식적으로 통제하는 숨겨진 규칙
② noises that restrict one's level of concentration
  사람들의 집중력을 제한하는 소음
③ surroundings that lead to the death of a cat
  고양이의 죽음을 초래하는 환경
④ internal forces that slowly lower our self-esteem
  우리의 자존감을 서서히 낮추는 내부적인 힘
⑤ experiences that discourage us from following rules
  우리가 규칙을 준수하지 않게 만드는 경험

[본문 해석]

작가 Elizabeth Gilbert는 명상할 때 신도들을 이끌었던 위대한 성자의 우화에 대해 이야기한다. 신도들이 선의 순간에 막 빠질 때, 야옹 하고 울고 모든 사람들을 귀찮게 하며 사원을 돌아다니는 고양이에 의해 방해를 받곤 했다. 성자는 간단한 해결책을 생각해 냈다. 그는 명상 시간 동안 고양이를 기둥에 묶기 시작했다. 이 해결책, 즉 먼저 고양이를 기둥에 묶고, 그다음에 명상하는 것은 빠르게 하나의 의식으로 발전했다. 고양이가 결국 자연사했을 때, 종교적 위기가 뒤따랐다. 신도들이 어떻게 해야 하는 것인가? 어떻게 고양이를 기둥에 묶지 않고 그들이 명상을 할 수 있을 것인가? 이 이야기는 내가 보이지 않는 규칙이라고 부르는 것을 보여 준다. 이것들은 불필요하게 규칙으로 굳어진 습관과 행동들이다. 비록 쓰여진 규칙들은 변화에 저항할 수 있지만, 보이지 않는 규칙들은 더 완고하다. 그것들은 침묵의 살인자이다.

Why? 왜 정답일까?

명상에 앞서 명상을 방해하는 고양이를 매번 기둥에 묶어두는 일부터 하는 것이 규칙처럼 자리잡자, 막상 고양이가 죽었을 때 사람들이 어찌할 바를 몰랐다는 일화가 제시되고 있다. 즉 이는 '불필요한' 규칙 또는 습관에 불과하지만 명문화되어 있지 않아 도리어 사람들의 의식 속에 더 완고하게 자리잡게 되었다는 것(These are habits and behaviors that have unnecessarily rigidified into rules. Although written rules can be resistant to change, invisible ones are more stubborn.)이 글의 논지이다. 밑줄 친 부분에서 이러한 규칙이 '침묵의 살인자'와 같다고 언급한 것은 이 규칙이 우리의 행동을 얼마나 강하게 통제하고 있는지를 비유적으로 나타낸 것이다. 따라서 밑줄 친 부분이 의미하는 바로 가장 적절한 것은 ① '우리의 행동을 무의식적으로 통제하는 숨겨진 규칙'이다.

- **fable** ⓝ 우화
- **disrupt** ⓥ 방해하다, 지장을 주다
- **ritual** ⓝ 의식
- **crisis** ⓝ 위기
- **invisible** ⓐ 보이지 않는
- **resistant** ⓐ (~에) 저항하는, 내성이 있는
- **restrict** ⓥ 제한하다
- **meditation** ⓝ 명상
- **come up with** ~을 떠올리다
- **religious** ⓐ 종교적인
- **illustrate** ⓥ (예를 들어 분명히) 보여주다
- **unnecessarily** ⓐ 불필요하게
- **stubborn** ⓐ 완고한

구문 풀이

2행 Just as the followers were dropping into their zen moment, 접속사(바로 ~할 때) they would be disrupted by a cat [that would walk through the temple 조동사(과거의 습관) / 수동태 / 선행사 meowing and bothering everyone]. 분사구문1 / 분사구문2

★★ 문제 해결 꿀~팁 ★★

▶ 많이 틀린 이유는?
글로 쓰이지 않은 규칙은 우리 일상에 완고하게 자리잡았을 때 대단한 영향력을 행사한다는 내용의 글이다. 명상을 방해하는 고양이에 관한 이야기는 예시일 뿐이므로 '침묵의 살인자'라는 표현 자체가 고양이를 죽게 하는 환경과 관련되어 있다는 의미의 ③은 답으로 부적절하다.

▶ 문제 해결 방법은?
밑줄 친 부분의 silent는 규칙이 우리 일상을 '우리도 모르게' 통제하고 있다는 의미를, killer는 그 통제가 매우 완고하고 강력하다는 의미를 나타낸다. ①의 hidden, govern, unconsciously를 주의 깊게 보도록 한다.

04 아이의 행동 제한을 설정할 때 고려할 사항   정답률 74% | 정답 ②

다음 글의 주제로 가장 적절한 것은?

① ways of giving reward and punishment fairly
  보상과 처벌을 공정하게 주는 방법
② considerations when placing limits on children's behavior
  아이들의 행동에 제한을 설정할 때의 고려사항들
③ increasing necessity of parents' participation in discipline
  훈육에 있어 부모 참여의 필요성 증가
④ impact of caregivers' personality on children's development
  아동 발달에 양육자의 성격이 미치는 영향
⑤ reasons for encouraging children to do socially right things
  아이들에게 사회적으로 옳은 일을 하도록 격려해야 하는 이유

[본문 해석]

행동이 통제되지 않는 아이는 행동에 대한 분명한 제한이 설정되고 시행될 때 개선된다. 그러나 부모들은 어디에 제한을 두고 어떻게 그것이 시행될지에 대해 반드시 합의를 해야 한다. 제한과 그 제한을 깨뜨리는 것의 결과는 반드시 아이에게 분명하게 제시되어야 한다. 제한의 시행은 일관성 있고 단호해야 한다. 너무 많은 제한은 배우기 어렵고 자율성의 정상적 발달을 저해할지도 모른다. 제한은 아이의 나이, 기질, 발달 수준의 측면에서 합당해야 한다. 효과적이려면 부모 모두가 (그리고 가정의 다른 어른들도) 제한을 시행해야 한다. 그렇지 않으면, 아이들은 효과적으로 부모를 따로 떼어서 좀 더 멋대로 하게 하는 부모에게 제한을 시험해 보려 한다. 모든 상황에서 효과적이기 위해서는 처벌은 간결하고 행동과 직접적으로 관련 있어야 한다.

Why? 왜 정답일까?

첫 두 문장인 'A child whose behavior is out of control improves when clear limits on their behavior are set and enforced. However, parents must agree on where a limit will be set and how it will be enforced.'에서 아이의 행동을 개선하기 위한 제한은 어디에 설정되고 어떻게 시행될지에 대한 부모 간의 합의를 바탕으로 만들어져야 한다는 핵심 내용을 제시하고 있다. 따라서 글의 주제로 가장 적절한 것은 ② '아이들의 행동에 제한을 설정할 때의 고려사항들'이다.

- **enforce** ⓥ 시행하다
- **present** ⓥ 제시하다
- **spoil** ⓥ 망치다
- **temperament** ⓝ 기질
- **split** ⓥ 갈라놓다, 분리시키다
- **fairly** ⓐ 공정하게, 꽤
- **consequence** ⓝ 결과
- **consistent** ⓐ 일관성 있는
- **autonomy** ⓝ 자율성
- **effectively** ⓐ 효과적으로
- **punishment** ⓝ 처벌
- **discipline** ⓝ 훈육, 규율

구문 풀이

1행 A child [whose behavior is out of control] improves when 주어 / 소유격 관계대명사 / 접속사(~할 때) 자동사 clear limits on their behavior are set and enforced. 주어 / 동사구(수동태)

05 사회적 관계의 필수적 기반 역할을 하는 도덕성   정답률 53% | 정답 ③

다음 글의 밑줄 친 부분 중, 어법상 틀린 것은? [3점]

[본문 해석]

모든 사회적 상호 작용은 관련된 당사자들이 그들의 행동을 조정할 수 있는 어떤 공통의 기반을 요구한다. 인간과 그 외의 영장류들이 사는 상호 의존적인 집단에서, 개인들은 사회적 관계를 확립하고 유지하기 위해 훨씬 더 큰 공통의 기반을 가져야 한다. 이러한 공통의 기반은 도덕성이다. 이는 도덕성이 사회적 관계의 행위에서 옳고 그름을 판단하기 위한 공유된 일련의 기준으로 자주 정의되는 이유이다. 도덕성은 어떻게 개념화되더라도 (신뢰성, 협력, 정의 혹은 배려든 간에) 항상 사회적 관계에서 사람을 대하는 것에 관한 것이다. 이것이 아마 공유된 도덕 관념이 사회적 관계에 필수적이라는 광범위한 관점에 걸쳐 놀라운 일치가 있는 이유이다. 진화 생물학자와 사회학자와 철학자 모두 인간이 의존하는 집단 내에서의 상호 의존적 관계가 공유된 도덕성 없이는 가능하지 않다는 사회 심리학자의 의견에 동의하는 듯하다.

Why? 왜 정답일까?

No matter how(어떻게 ~하더라도)와 whether(~이든 아니든)가 이끄는 부사절에 이어 주어 morality가 나오므로, 주어와 호응하는 동사가 뒤따라야 한다. 따라서 준동사 to be를 동사 is로 고쳐야 한다. 어법상 틀린 것은 ③이다.

Why? 왜 오답일까?

① 선행사 the interdependent groups 뒤로 1형식의 완전한 관계절이 연결되는 것으로 보아 '전치사＋관계대명사' 형태의 in which를 쓴 것은 적절하다. 이는 여기서 where와 같다.
② 전치사 for 뒤로 동명사 judging을 쓴 것은 적절하다.
④ agreement의 내용을 보충 설명하는 완전한 동격절을 연결하기 위해 접속사 that을 쓴 것은 적절하다.
⑤ 주어인 the interdependent relationships가 복수 명사이므로 복수 동사 are가 적절하게 쓰였다.

- coordinate ⓥ 조정하다
- primate ⓝ 영장류
- morality ⓝ 도덕성
- trustworthiness ⓝ 신뢰성
- evolutionary ⓐ 진화의
- interdependent ⓐ 상호 의존적인
- establish ⓥ 확립하다
- conceptualize ⓥ 개념화하다
- perspective ⓝ 관점

구문 풀이

9행 No matter how it is conceptualized — whether as
　　　= however(어떻게 ~하더라도)　　　　　~이든 아니든
trustworthiness, cooperation, justice, or caring — morality is always
　　　　　　　　　　　　　　　　　　　　　　　　　주어　　　　동사
about the treatment of people in social relationships.

06　객관적인 카메라 　　　　정답률 40% | 정답 ②

다음 글의 밑줄 친 부분 중, 문맥상 낱말의 쓰임이 적절하지 않은 것은? [3점]

[본문 해석]

객관적인 관점은 John Ford의 '카메라의 철학'에 의해 설명된다. Ford는 카메라를 창문이라고 생각했고 관객은 창문 안쪽 사람과 사건을 바라보면서 창문 ① 밖에 있다고 생각했다. 우리는 사건들이 멀리서 일어나고 있는 것처럼 그것들을 바라보도록 요청받고, 참여하도록 요청받지 않는다. 객관적인 관점은 이런 창문 효과를 ② 피하기(→ 만들기) 위해 정적인 카메라를 가능한 한 많이 이용하고, 카메라에 관심을 끄는 것 없이 배우와 사건에 집중한다. 객관적인 카메라는 카메라와 대상 간의 감정적인 거리를 보여 주는데, 카메라는 이야기의 등장인물과 사건을 가능한 한 ③ 있는 그대로 그저 기록하고 있는 것으로 보인다. 대부분의 경우, 감독은 자연스럽고 일반적인 종류의 카메라 위치와 카메라 각도를 사용한다. 객관적인 카메라는 사건에 관해 논평하거나 ④ 해석하지 않고 그것이 전개되게 하면서 그저 그것을 기록한다. 우리는 냉담한 관찰자의 관점에서 사건을 본다. 만약 카메라가 움직인다면 그것은 눈에 띄지 않게, 가능한 한 카메라 자체에 관심을 불러일으키는 일이 ⑤ 거의 없이 그렇게 한다.

Why? 왜 정답일까?

'~ it concentrates on the actors and the action without drawing attention to the camera.'와 'We see the action from the viewpoint of an impersonal observer.'에서 객관적인 카메라는 우리가 카메라 자체에 관심을 두지 않은 채 관찰자의 시점에서 사건을 바라보도록 도와준다고 한다. 이를 근거로 볼 때, 객관적 카메라는 첫 두 문장에서 언급한 카메라의 '창문 효과'를 피하지 않고 적절히 이용하여 관객이 인물과 사건으로부터 거리를 두게 해 준다는 것을 알 수 있다. 따라서 ②의 avoid를 produce로 고쳐야 한다. 문맥상 낱말의 쓰임이 적절하지 않은 것은 ②이다.

- objective ⓐ 객관적인
- philosophy ⓝ 철학
- static ⓐ 정적인
- draw attention to ~에 관심을 끌다
- comment on ~에 대해 논평하다
- unfold ⓥ 펼쳐지다, 펴다
- unnoticeably ⓐⓓ 눈에 띄지 않게
- illustrate ⓥ 자세히 설명하다
- at a distance 멀리 떨어져서
- concentrate on ~에 집중하다
- straightforwardly ⓐⓓ 있는 그대로
- interpret ⓥ 해석하다
- impersonal ⓐ 냉담한

구문 풀이

　　　　　　　「as if + 주어 + 과거 동사 : 마치 (현재 ~하지 않는데) ~한 것처럼」
4행 We are asked to watch the actions as if they were taking
　　　　　　「be asked + to부정사 : ~하도록 요청받다」
place at a distance, and we are not asked to participate.

07　자기 소유의 물건의 가치를 과대평가하는 경향 　정답률 71% | 정답 ①

다음 빈칸에 들어갈 말로 가장 적절한 것을 고르시오.

✓ ① overvalue - 과대평가할
② exchange - 교환할
③ disregard - 무시할
④ conceal - 숨길
⑤ share - 공유할

[본문 해석]

일단 우리가 어떤 것을 소유하면, 우리는 그것을 과대평가할 가능성이 훨씬 더 높다. Duke 대학에서 실시된 한 연구에서, 극도로 성가신 추첨(참여하기 위해 하루 이상 줄을 서서 기다려야 하는 것)에서 농구 티켓을 얻은 학생들은 평균적으로 2,400달러 아래로는 자신의 티켓을 팔지 않을 것이라고 말했다. 그러나 기다렸지만 티켓을 얻지 못한 학생들은 단지 평균적으로 티켓당 170달러를 지불할 것이라고 말했다. 일단 학생이 티켓을 소유하면 그 또는 그녀는 실제로 그러한 것보다 그것이 시장에서 훨씬 더 많은 가치가 있다고 여겼다. 또 다른 사례에서 2008년의 주택시장 붕괴 동안에 부동산 웹 사이트가 주택 소유자들이 느끼기에 그 붕괴가 자신들의 주택의 가격에 어떻게 영향을 미쳤는지를 알아보기 위해 설문조사를 실시했다. 인근의 압류를 인식하고 있는 응답자 중 92%가 이것이 자신의 지역에 있는 주택의 가격을 손상시켰다고 단언했다. 하지만 그들 소유의 주택 가격에 대해 질문을 받았을 때, 62%는 그것이 상승했다고 믿었다.

Why? 왜 정답일까?

첫 문장인 주제문을 완성하는 빈칸 문제로, 빈칸 이후의 두 예시를 적절히 일반화하여 빈칸에 들어갈 말을 추론해야 한다. 예시의 결론 문장에서 각각 티켓을 소유한 학생은 실제보다 티켓의 가치를 높게 보았고, 자기 소유의 주택가에 대해 질문을 받은 사람들은 가격이 상승했다고 믿었다는 내용이 나온다. 이를 일반화하면, 사람들은 자신이 소유하게 된 것의 가치를 실제보다 크게 추산하는 경향이 있다는 결론을 도출할 수 있다. 따라서 빈칸에 들어갈 말로 가장 적절한 것은 ① '과대평가할'이다.

- extremely ⓐⓓ 극도로
- wait in line 줄을 서서 기다리다
- real estate 부동산
- overvalue ⓥ 과대평가하다
- lottery ⓝ 추첨, 도박, 복권
- crash ⓝ 붕괴, 도산
- assert ⓥ 단언하다, 확고히 하다
- disregard ⓥ 무시하다

구문 풀이

2행 In a study conducted at Duke University, / students [who won
　　　　　　　　　　　　　과거분사　　　　　　　　　주어(선행사) 주격 관계대명사
basketball tickets in an extremely onerous lottery] / (one [that they
　　　　　　　　　　　　　　　　　　　　　　　= a lottery 목적격 관계대명사
had to wait in line to enter for more than a day]) / said (that) they
　　　　　　　　　　부사적 용법(~하기 위해)　　　　　　동사 생략(접속사)
wouldn't sell their tickets for less than, on average, $2,400.

★★★ 1등급 대비 고난도 3점 문제

08　어느 정도의 정부 개입이 필요한 자유 시장 경제 　정답률 33% | 정답 ①

다음 빈칸에 들어갈 말로 가장 적절한 것을 고르시오. [3점]

✓ ① markets are rarely left entirely free
시장이 완전히 자유로운 상태로 맡겨지는 경우는 드물다
② governments are reluctant to intervene
정부는 개입하기를 꺼린다
③ supply and demand are not always balanced
수요와 공급은 항상 균형이 맞는 것은 아니다
④ economic inequality continues to get worse
경제적 불평등은 계속해서 심해지고 있다
⑤ competition does not guarantee the maximum profit
경쟁은 최대 이익을 보장해주지 못한다

DAY 07

[본문 해석]

오늘날 세계 대부분에서 자본주의와 자유 시장은 경제적 자원을 분배하고 경제적 생산을 장려하기 위한 최고의 시스템을 구성하는 것으로 받아들여지고 있다. 국가들은 사회주의나 공산주의와 같은 다른 시스템들을 시도했지만, 많은 경우 그들은 자유 시장으로 완전히 전환하거나 자유 시장의 측면들을 받아들였다. 자유 시장 시스템의 광범위한 수용에도 불구하고, 시장이 완전히 자유로운 상태로 맡겨지는 경우는 드물다. 정부의 개입은 법과 규정의 제정과 집행에서부터 미국의 담보 기관과 같은 실체를 통한 직접적인 경제 참여에 이르기까지 다양한 형태를 취한다. 그러나 아마도 가장 중요한 형태의 정부 개입은 중앙은행과 국가 재무기관이 경기 주기의 흥망성쇠를 통제하고 영향을 미치려는 시도로 나타날 것이다.

Why? 왜 정답일까?

빈칸 앞에서 오늘날 세계 대부분의 국가가 자유 시장 경제를 받아들였다고 이야기하는데, 빈칸 뒤에서는 자유 시장 경제 체제 안에서도 이루어질 수밖에 없는 정부 개입(Government involvement)에 관해 설명하고 있다. 따라서 빈칸에 들어갈 말로 가장 적절한 것은 ① '시장이 완전히 자유로운 상태로 맡겨지는 경우는 드물다'이다.

- capitalism ⓝ 자본주의
- constitute ⓥ 구성하다
- resource ⓝ 자원
- communism ⓝ 공산주의
- acceptance ⓝ 수용
- enforcement ⓝ 시행, 집행
- mortgage ⓝ (담보) 대출
- central bank 중앙은행
- ups and downs 흥망성쇠
- reluctant ⓐ 꺼리는, 마지못해 하는
- supply and demand 수요와 공급
- free market 자유 시장
- allocate ⓥ 배분하다, 할당하다
- socialism ⓝ 사회주의
- wholesale ⓐⓓ 완전히, 모조리
- involvement ⓝ 개입
- regulation ⓝ 규정, 규제
- perhaps ⓐⓓ 아마도
- treasury ⓝ 재무부, 금고
- entirely ⓐⓓ 완전히
- intervene ⓥ 개입하다

구문 풀이

7행 Despite the widespread acceptance of the freemarket
전치사(~에도 불구하고)
system, markets are rarely left entirely free.
5형식 수동태   보어(형용사구)

★★ 문제 해결 꿀~팁 ★★

▶ 많이 틀린 이유는?
②는 '정부가 개입을 꺼린다'는 의미인데, 빈칸 뒤를 보면 실제 자본주의 체계에서 일어나는 다양한 정부 개입의 형태를 언급하고 있다. 이는 정부가 시장 개입을 자제한다기보다 오히려 단행한다는 뜻이다.
▶ 문제 해결 방법은?
글 중간에 나온 빈칸에 대한 힌트는 빈칸 뒤에 있음을 명심하자. 여기서도 빈칸 뒤를 보면, 정부 개입은 실제로 다양한 형태로 발생하고, 그중에서도 가장 중요한 개입은 중앙 은행이나 국가 재무기관의 조치로 나타난다는 내용이 제시된다. 이를 토대로 볼 때, '정부 개입이 이뤄진다 = 시장을 가만히 내버려두는 경우는 잘 없다'는 내용이 빈칸에 들어가야 한다.

---

09 인간의 과정의 특성 고려하기   정답률 54% | 정답 ③

다음 글에서 전체 흐름과 관계 없는 문장은?

[본문 해석]

인간의 과정은 그 결과에 있어서 이성적인 과정과 다르다. 이상적인 수행 척도를 고려할 때, 만일 하나의 과정이 현재의 정보를 바탕으로 맞는 일을 항상 수행한다면 그 과정은 *이성적*이다. 요컨대 이성적인 과정은 책에 나와 있는 규칙대로 진행하고, 책은 실제로 옳다고 간주한다. ① 인간의 과정은 본능, 직관 그리고 책을 반드시 반영하지는 않는 다른 변인들을 포함하며, 심지어 기존의 데이터를 고려하지 않을 수도 있다. ② 예를 들어, 자동차를 운전하는 이성적인 방식은 항상 법규를 따르는 것이다. ③ 마찬가지로, 보행자 횡단 신호는 나라에 따라 다르고, 길을 건너는 사람의 모양이 서로 다르다. ④ 그러나 차량 흐름은 이성적이지 않아서, 만일 여러분이 법규를 정확히 따른다면 다른 운전자는 법규를 정확히 따르지 않기 때문에 여러분은 결국 어딘가에 갇혀 꼼짝 못하는 결과를 맞게 될 것이다. ⑤ 따라서 자율 주행 자동차는 성공을 거두려면 이성적이기보다는 인간적으로 행동해야 한다.

Why? 왜 정답일까?

인간의 과정은 반드시 합리적으로 움직이지는 않는다는 일반적 내용 뒤로, 인간의 과정

이 꼭 책에 나오는 것 같지는 않다고 주제를 한 번 더 풀어 설명하는 ①, 예를 제시하는 ②와 ④, 이를 토대로 자율 주행 차가 나아갈 방향을 결론 짓는 ⑤가 자연스럽게 연결된다. 하지만 ③은 교통 법규의 세부적 내용이 나라마다 다르다는 의미여서 앞뒤 내용과 연결되지 않는다. 따라서 전체 흐름과 관계 없는 문장은 ③이다.

- ideal ⓐ 이상적인
- intuition ⓝ 직관
- existing ⓐ 기존의
- pedestrian ⓝ 보행자
- end up 결국 ~하다
- self-driving car 자율 주행 자동차
- instinct ⓝ 본능
- variable ⓝ 변수
- likewise ⓐⓓ 마찬가지로
- precisely ⓐⓓ 정확하게
- stuck ⓐ (어딘가에) 갇힌

구문 풀이

15행 To be successful, a self-driving car must therefore act humanly, rather than rationally.
「A + rather than + B : B라기보다는 A인(A, B는 병렬)」

★★★ 1등급 대비 고난도 3점 문제

10 행동에 관한 경제학적 관점   정답률 31% | 정답 ③

주어진 글 다음에 이어질 글의 순서로 가장 적절한 것을 고르시오. [3점]
① (A) – (C) – (B)
② (B) – (A) – (C)
✓ (B) – (C) – (A)
④ (C) – (A) – (B)
⑤ (C) – (B) – (A)

[본문 해석]

한 사람의 선호도 구조를 알아내는 것, 즉 한 상품을 소비하여 얻는 만족도가 또 다른 상품을 소비하여 얻는 만족도보다 더 큰지를 이해하는 데 성공한 경제학자에게 있어, 행동을 기저에 있는 호불호의 변화 측면에서 설명하는 것은 대체로 아주 문제가 많다.

(B) 예를 들어 베이비 붐과 그 이후의 출생률 급락이 변동 없는 선호도를 배경으로 한 상대적 비용의 변화보다는, 아기에 대한 대중의 내재적 선호가 증가했다가 이후 떨어진 것에서 비롯되었다고 주장하는 것은 사회과학자를 불안정한 입지에 둔다.

(C) 경제학에서 출생률에 대한 그러한 주장은 사망률의 상승과 하락이 죽음에 대한 내재적 욕구 변화의 증가에서 비롯된다고 말하는 것과 같다. 경제학자에게는 기호의 변화보다는 소득과 물가의 변화가 출생률에 영향을 미친다.

(A) 예를 들어 소득이 증가할 때 사람들은 자녀에 대한 내재적 욕구가 그대로 유지되더라도 더 많은 자녀(또는 여러분이 나중에 알게 되겠지만, 아이로부터 오는 더 큰 만족감)를 원한다.

Why? 왜 정답일까?

경제학적으로 볼 때 선호 변화로 행동을 설명하는 것은 문제가 있다는 주어진 글에 이어, (B)는 베이비 붐 시대의 인구 증가와 그 이후 세대의 인구 감소를 설명할 때를 예로 든다. (C)는 (B)에서 소개되었듯이 아기에 대한 대중의 선호 변화라는 관점에서 인구 증감을 설명하는 '그러한 주장'이 경제학적으로 타당하지 않다는 내용을 제시한다. 마지막으로 (A)는 (C)의 마지막 부분에서 언급되었듯이, 선호도보다는 '소득'의 변화가 출산율에 영향을 미칠 수 있음을 구체적 사례로 설명한다. 따라서 글의 순서로 가장 적절한 것은 ③ '(B) – (C) – (A)'이다.

- underlying ⓐ 기저에 있는
- problematic ⓐ 문제가 있는
- inherent ⓐ 내재된
- baby bust 출생률 급감
- stable ⓐ 안정된
- be equivalent to ~와 같다
- mortality ⓝ 사망률
- like and dislikes 호불호
- income ⓝ 소득, 수입
- inherent ⓐ 내재된
- baby boom 베이비 붐
- taste ⓝ 취향
- unsound ⓐ 불안정한, 불건전한
- rise and fall 증감, 흥망성쇠
- be attributed to ~에서 비롯되다, 기인하다

구문 풀이

1행 To an economist [who succeeds in figuring out a person's
주격 관계대명사
preference structure] — understanding {whether the satisfaction
동명사 주어1   { } : 명사절(~인지 아닌지)
gained from consuming one good} is greater than that of another —
동사1
explaining behavior in terms of changes in underlying likes and dislikes
동명사 주어2
is usually highly problematic.
동사2

★★ 문제 해결 꿀~팁 ★★

▶ 많이 틀린 이유는?
④는 정답과 마찬가지로 (C) – (A)를 잘 연결했지만 (B)를 맨 뒤에 배치했는데, 이는 적절한 선택이 아니다. 주어진 글에서 '출생률에 관한 주장'을 다루지 않았는데, (C)에서는 '그러한 주장'을 언급하기 때문이다. 이 주장을 언급한 단락은 (B)이다. 따라서 (B)가 먼저 배치된 후 '그러한 주장'에 관해 평가하는 (C)를 배치하는 것이 옳다.

▶ 문제 해결 방법은?
어떤 두 단락이 인접한다면, 앞 단락의 마지막 부분에서 언급된 내용이 뒷 단락의 처음 부분에서 다시 언급된다. 가령 (C)의 첫 문장에서 '출생률에 관한 그러한 주장'을 언급하려면 앞에 '베이비 붐, 출산율'과 관련된 '주장'을 제시하는 (B)가 나와야 하는 식이다.

11-12 이메일을 더 친환경적으로 사용하기 위해 노력할 필요성

[본문 해석]

요즘 같은 시대에 이메일이 없는 우리의 삶을 상상하기 어렵다. 그러나 얼마나 자주 우리는 이러한 가상 메시지의 환경적 영향을 고려하는가? 얼핏 보면 디지털 메시지가 자원을 (a) 절약하는 것처럼 보인다. 전통적인 편지와는 달리, 종이나 우표가 필요하지 않다. 즉, 어떤 것도 포장되거나 운송될 필요가 없다. 우리 중 많은 사람은 이메일을 사용하는 것이 컴퓨터 전원을 켜는 데 사용되는 전기 정도만 필요로 한다고 추정하는 경향이 있다. 특히 데이터 전송과 저장에 관해, 네트워크 실행에 수반되는 보이지 않는 에너지 사용을 (b) 간과하기 쉽다.

세계의 모든 받은편지함에 있는 모든 이메일은 서버에 저장된다. 엄청난 양의 데이터는 엄청난 양의 서버 팜을 필요로 하는데, 이것은 정보를 저장하고 전송하는 수백만 대의 컴퓨터가 있는 거대한 센터이다. 이러한 서버는 하루 24시간 (c) 최소한의(→ 엄청나게 많은) 양의 에너지를 소비하며 냉각을 위해 수많은 리터의 물 또는 에어컨 시스템이 필요하다. 『더 많은 메시지를 보내고, 받고, 저장할수록 (d) 더 많은 서버가 필요한데, 이는 더 많은 에너지 소비와 더 많은 탄소 배출을 의미한다.』 『분명히, 환경 의식이 있는 방식으로 전자 메시지를 보내고 받는 것은 결코 기후 변화를 멈추기에 충분하지 않다. 그러나 몇몇 주의 깊고 신중한 변화로 (e) 불필요한 CO₂ 배출은 쉽게 회피될 수 있다.』
『 』:12번의 근거
『 』:11번의 근거

- impact ⓝ 영향
- at first glance 언뜻 보기에는
- package ⓥ 포장하다
- overlook ⓥ 간과하다
- particularly ⓐⓓ 특히
- incredible ⓐ 믿어지지 않을 정도인
- gigantic ⓐ 거대한
- consume ⓥ 소비하다, 소모하다
- countless ⓐ 무수히 많은
- carbon ⓝ 탄소
- environmentally conscious 환경 의식이 있는
- mindful ⓐ 의식하는, 유념하는
- virtual ⓐ 가상의
- resource ⓝ 자원, 재원(財源)
- transport ⓥ 운송하다, 수송하다
- invisible ⓐ 눈에 보이지 않는
- when it comes to ~에 관해서
- quantity ⓝ 양
- transmit ⓥ 전송하다
- minimum ⓐ 최소한의, 최저의
- air conditioning 에어컨
- emission ⓝ (빛·열·가스 등의) 배출
- unnecessary ⓐ 불필요한

구문 풀이

14행 The incredible quantity of data requires huge server farms — (gigantic centres with millions of computers [which store and transmit information]).
선행사 : millions of computers
주격 관·대 : which
( ) : 동격(= server farms)

---

11 제목 파악
정답률 75% | 정답 ②

윗글의 제목으로 가장 적절한 것은?

① Recycling Makes Your Life Even Better
  재활용은 여러분의 삶을 훨씬 더 좋게 만든다
✔ Eco-friendly Use of Email Saves the Earth
  이메일의 친환경적 사용이 지구를 지킨다
③ Traditional Letters: The Bridge Between Us
  전통적 편지: 우리를 연결해주는 다리
④ Email Servers: Records of Past and Present
  이메일 서버: 과거와 현재의 기록
⑤ Technicians Looking for Alternative Energy
  대체 에너지를 찾고 있는 기술자들

Why? 왜 정답일까?

통념과는 달리 이메일을 사용하는 데에는 많은 에너지와 자원이 들어가므로, 보다 환경

을 생각하는 방식으로 이메일을 이용하기 위해 노력해야 한다는 내용의 글이다. 특히 마지막 두 문장에서, 환경 의식이 있는 방식으로 이메일을 사용하고자 노력한다고 해서 바로 기후 변화가 멈춰지는 것은 아니지만, 적어도 불필요한 탄소 배출을 줄일 수는 있게 될 것이라고 언급하며 변화를 촉구하고 있다. 따라서 글의 제목으로 가장 적절한 것은 ② '이메일의 친환경적 사용이 지구를 지킨다'이다.

12 어휘 추론
정답률 74% | 정답 ③

밑줄 친 (a) ~ (e) 중에서 문맥상 낱말의 쓰임이 적절하지 않은 것은?

① (a) ② (b) ✔ (c) ④ (d) ⑤ (e)

Why? 왜 정답일까?

이메일을 더 많이 보낼수록 서버가 더 많이 필요하고, 에너지 소비량과 탄소 배출량이 증가한다(**The more messages we send, receive and store, the more servers are needed — which means more energy consumed, and more carbon emissions.**)는 내용으로 보아, (c)가 포함된 문장 또한 이메일 서버 팜의 '많은' 에너지 소비에 관해 언급해야 한다. 따라서 (c)의 minimum을 massive로 고쳐야 한다.

DAY 07

DAY 08 › 20분 미니 모의고사

01 ①	02 ②	03 ⑤	04 ④	05 ⑤
06 ③	07 ②	08 ⑤	09 ①	10 ④
11 ②	12 ③			

---

01 파트너 대신 발표를 무사히 마치고 안도한 필자   정답률 84% | 정답 ①

다음 글에 드러난 'I'의 심경 변화로 가장 적절한 것은?

✓① panicked → relieved
　당황한　　안도한
② sorrowful → indifferent
　슬픈　　　　무관심한
③ sympathetic → content
　연민 어린　　만족한
④ jealous → delighted
　질투하는　　기쁜
⑤ confused → humiliated
　혼란스러운　굴욕스러운

[본문 해석]

그날, Dan과 나는 발표를 하기로 돼 있었다. 수업이 시작된 직후에 내 전화가 진동했다. "나 제때 도착할 수 없어. 도로에서 교통사고가 났어!"라고 Dan이 보낸 문자 메시지였다. 나는 거의 쓰러질 뻔했다. '어떻게 하지?' Dan은 우리 차례 전에 나타나지 않았고 곧 나는 반 전체 학생 앞에 서 있었다. 나는 겨우 내 부분을 다 끝냈고 어떻게 할지 생각하면서 정신이 몇 초간 명해졌다. '정신 차려!' 나는 재빨리 정신을 가다듬고 내가 할 수 있는 한 최선을 다해 Dan의 발표 부분을 해 나갔다. 잠시 후, 나는 혼자서 전체 발표를 끝냈다. 그제서야 긴장감이 사라졌다. 나는 우리 교수님의 웃음 띤 얼굴을 볼 수 있었다.

Why? 왜 정답일까?

발표를 함께 하기로 한 친구가 제때 도착하지 못해 기절할 정도로 아찔해했던(I almost fainted. 'What should I do?') 필자가 무사히 발표를 마치고 긴장이 풀렸다(Only then did the tension vanish.)는 내용의 글이다. 따라서 'I'의 심경 변화로 가장 적절한 것은 ① '당황한 → 안도한'이다.

- buzz ⓥ (윙윙) 울리다
- go blank (마음 따위가) 텅 비다
- come to one's senses 정신을 차리다
- vanish ⓥ 사라지다
- panicked ⓐ 당황한, 공포에 질린
- content ⓐ 만족한
- faint ⓥ 기절하다
- hold oneself together 정신을 차리다
- tension ⓝ 긴장
- beaming ⓐ 미소 띤, 기쁨에 넘치는
- sympathetic ⓐ 연민 어린
- humiliated ⓐ 굴욕을 느끼는, 수치스러운

구문 풀이

12행 Only then did the tension vanish.
「준부정어 + 조동사 + 주어 + 동사원형 : 도치 구문」

---

02 부모 본인의 평정심 유지하기   정답률 77% | 정답 ②

다음 글의 요지로 가장 적절한 것은?

① 자녀의 행동 변화를 위해 부모의 즉각적인 반응이 필요하다.
✓② 부모의 내적 성장을 통한 평정심 유지가 양육에 중요하다.
③ 부모는 자녀가 감정을 다스릴 수 있게 도와주어야 한다.
④ 부모와 자녀는 건설적인 의견을 나눌 수 있어야 한다.
⑤ 바람직한 양육은 자녀에게 모범을 보이는 것이다.

[본문 해석]

대부분의 부모들은 자녀가 그저 '잘 행동하면' 부모로서 침착함을 유지할 수 있다고 생각한다. 진실은 우리가 감정과 행동을 관리하는 것이 부모로서 평안함을 느끼도록 해준다는 것이다. 궁극적으로 우리는 우리의 자녀나 그들이 마주할 장애물을 통제할 수는 없지만, 항상 우리 자신의 행동을 통제할 수 있다. 양육은 우리 자녀가 무엇을 하는지에 대한 것이 아니라 우리가 어떻게 반응하는지에 대한 것이다. 사실, 우리가 양육이라고 부르는 것의 대부분은 부모와 자녀 사이가 아니라 부모 안에서 발생한다. 폭풍이 일어나려고 할 때, 부모의 반응은 그것을 잠재우거나, 아니면 최대치의 해일을 유발할 것이다. 그 모든 아이 같은 행동—그리고 그 이면의 폭풍 같은 감정—에 건설적으로 반응할 수 있을 만큼 침착함을 유지하는 것은 우리에게도 성장을 요구한다. 만약 우리 버튼이 눌리는 그런 순간을 그저 반응하는 목적이 아니라 성찰하는 데 이용할 수 있다면, 우리는 우리가 언제 평정심을 잃는지 알아차릴 수 있고 다시 제자리로

돌아갈 수 있다. 이러한 내면의 성장이 세상에서 가장 힘든 일이지만, 그것은 당신이 하루하루 더욱 평안한 부모가 될 수 있도록 해주는 것이다.

Why? 왜 정답일까?

부모가 평정심을 유지하려면 자녀의 행동이나 반응보다는, 자기 자신의 감정과 행동을 관리하는 데 노력을 들일 필요가 있으며(The truth is that managing our own emotions and actions is what allows us to feel peaceful as parents.), 이러한 내적 성장이 더 좋은 부모가 되도록 이끌어준다(This inner growth is ~ what enables you to become a more peaceful parent, one day at a time.)는 내용의 글이다. 따라서 글의 요지로 가장 적절한 것은 ② '부모의 내적 성장을 통한 평정심 유지가 양육에 중요하다.'이다.

- obstacle ⓝ 장애물
- brew ⓥ (불쾌한 일이 일어나려고) 태동하다
- childish ⓐ 유치한
- steer ⓥ 조종하다
- parenting ⓝ 양육
- constructively ⓐd 건설적으로
- equilibrium ⓝ 평정, 균형
- back on track 정상 궤도로 돌아온

구문 풀이

11행 Staying calm enough to respond constructively to all that
　동명사구 주어
childish behavior — (and the stormy emotions behind it) — requires
　　　　　　　　　　　삽입구　　　　　　　　　　　　　　동사(단수)
that we (should) grow, too.
　　　　생략

---

03 과잉 관광의 개념   정답률 65% | 정답 ⑤

다음 글의 제목으로 가장 적절한 것은? [3점]

① The Solutions to Overtourism: From Complex to Simple
　과잉 관광의 해결책: 복잡한 것에서 단순한 것으로
② What Makes Popular Destinations Attractive to Visitors?
　무엇이 인기 있는 목적지를 방문객에게 매력적으로 만드는가?
③ Are Tourist Attractions Winners or Losers of Overtourism?
　관광 명소는 과잉 관광의 승자인가 아니면 패자인가?
④ The Severity of Overtourism: Much Worse than Imagined
　과잉 관광의 심각성: 상상했던 것보다 훨씬 더 나쁜
✓⑤ Overtourism: Not Simply a Matter of People and Places
　과잉 관광: 단순히 사람과 장소의 문제가 아니다

[본문 해석]

과잉 관광의 개념은 관광학과 사회 과학 전반에서 흔히 볼 수 있는 사람과 장소에 관한 특정한 가정에 기초한다. 둘(사람과 장소) 다 명확하게 정의되고 경계가 정해졌다고 간주된다. 사람들은 주인이나 손님의 역할을 하는 경계가 확실한 사회적 행위자로 구성된다. 장소도 마찬가지로 명확한 경계가 있는 안정적인 용기로 취급된다. 그러므로 장소는 관광객으로 가득 찰 수 있고, 따라서 과잉 관광으로 고통받을 수 있다. 하지만 어느 한 장소가 사람으로 가득 차 있다는 것은 무엇을 의미하는가? 사실, 제한된 수용력을 가지고 있고 실제로 더 많은 방문객을 수용할 공간이 없는 특정 명소의 사례들이 있다. 특히 에펠탑과 같은 일부 인공 건축물의 경우이다. 그러나 장소가 목적지로 홍보되고 과잉 관광의 피해지로 묘사되는 도시, 지역 또는 심지어 국가 전체와 같은 장소에서는 상황이 더 복잡해진다. 과도하거나 균형이 안 맞는 것은 매우 상대적이며 자연적 (질적) 저하와 경제적 유출(정치 및 지방 권력 역학은 말할 것도 없이)과 같은, 물리적 수용력 이외의 다른 측면과 더 관련이 있을 수도 있다.

Why? 왜 정답일까?

과잉 관광을 사람과 장소의 개념만으로 바라볼 수 없고 다른 측면과 관련이 더 있을 수도 있다(What is excessive or out of proportion is highly relative and might be more related to other aspects than physical capacity, ~)는 글의 결론으로 볼 때, 글의 제목으로 가장 적절한 것은 ⑤ '과잉 관광: 단순히 사람과 장소의 문제가 아니다'이다.

- rest on ~에 기초하다
- define ⓥ 규정하다
- frame ⓥ 틀에 맞춰 만들다
- host ⓝ 주최자, 주인
- container ⓝ 용기, 그릇
- suffer from ~로 고통받다, 시달리다
- capacity ⓝ 수용력
- not least 특히
- construction ⓝ 건물, 구성
- victim ⓝ 피해자
- out of proportion 균형이 안 맞는
- degradation ⓝ (질적) 저하
- not to mention ~은 말할 것도 없이
- assumption ⓝ 가정
- demarcate ⓥ 경계를 정하다
- bounded ⓐ 경계가 확실한
- stable ⓐ 안정적인
- hence ⓐd 따라서
- attraction ⓝ (관광) 명소
- room for ~을 위한 공간, 여지
- man-made ⓐ 인공의
- destination ⓝ 목적지
- excessive ⓐ 과도한
- relative ⓐ 상대적인
- leakage ⓝ 유출
- severity ⓝ 심각성

구문 풀이

14행 However, with places (such as cities, regions or even whole
〔with + 명사 +
countries) being promoted as destinations and described as victims
분사1 +   분사2 : 부대상황 분사구문〕
of overtourism, things become more complex.

---

04 휴대용 사진 프린터 설명서 　　　　정답률 90% | 정답 ④

EZ Portable Photo Printer 사용에 관한 다음 안내문의 내용과 일치하는 것은?
① LED 표시기의 흰색은 충전 중임을 나타낸다.
② 전원 버튼을 한 번 누르면 전원이 꺼진다.
③ 배터리가 완전히 충전되는 데 2시간 이상 걸린다.
✔ 무선 연결을 위해 앱을 다운로드해야 한다.
⑤ 인화지를 로고가 위로 향하도록 넣어야 한다.

[본문 해석]

EZ 휴대용 사진 프린터 사용자 설명서

LED 표시기에 대한 유의 사항
• 『흰색: 전원 켜짐』━━『 』:①의 근거 불일치
• 빨간색: 배터리 충전 중

작동 방법
• 프린터를 켜려면 전원 버튼을 누르세요.
• 『프린터를 끄려면 전원 버튼을 두 번 누르세요.』━『 』:②의 근거 불일치
• 배터리를 충전하려면, 케이블을 USB 포트에 연결하세요. 『완전 충전은 60 ~ 90분이 소요됩니다.』━『 』:③의 근거 불일치
• 『프린터에 무선으로 연결하려면, 모바일 기기에 'EZ Printer App'을 다운받으세요.』━『 』:④의 근거 일치

인화지 장착 방법
• 프린터의 상단 덮개를 들어 올리세요.
• 『인화지를 로고가 아래로 향하도록 넣으세요.』━『 』:⑤의 근거 불일치

Why? 왜 정답일까?

'To connect to the printer wirelessly, download the 'EZ Printer App' on your mobile device.'에서 프린터를 무선 연결하려면 앱을 다운로드해야 한다고 하므로, 안내문의 내용과 일치하는 것은 ④ '무선 연결을 위해 앱을 다운로드해야 한다.'이다.

Why? 왜 오답일까?

① 'White: Power on'에서 LED 표시기의 흰색은 전원이 켜져 있다는 의미라고 하였다. 충전 중을 표시하는 색은 빨간색이다.
② 'Press the power button twice to turn the printer off.'에서 전원을 끄려면 버튼을 두 번 누르라고 하였다.
③ 'It takes 60 – 90 minutes for a full charge.'에서 완전 충전까지는 60분에서 90분이 걸린다고 하였다.
⑤ 'Insert the photo paper with any logos facing downward.'에서 인화지는 로고가 아래로 향하도록 넣어야 한다고 하였다.

● **portable** ⓐ 휴대 가능한
● **wirelessly** ⒜ 무선으로
● **indicator** ⓝ 표시(기), 장치, 지표
● **load** ⓥ 장착하다, 싣다

★★★ 1등급 대비 고난도 2점 문제

05 협력과 문제 해결을 뒷받침하는 포용성 　　정답률 30% | 정답 ⑤

다음 글의 밑줄 친 부분 중, 어법상 틀린 것은?

[본문 해석]

오늘날 조직, 지도자, 그리고 가족의 요구에 관해 곰곰이 생각할 때 우리는 독특한 특성 중 하나가 포용성이라는 것을 깨닫는다. 왜 그런가? 포용성은 모든 사람이 자신의 관계에서 궁극적으로 원하는 것인 협력을 뒷받침하기 때문이다. 그러나 대다수의 지도자, 조직, 그리고 가정은 보통 가장 연장자, 가장 교육을 많이 받은 사람, 그리고/또는 가장 부유한 사람인 한 사람이 모든 결정을 내리고, 토론이나 다른 사람의 관여가 거의 없이 그들의 결정이 지배하고 결과적으로 배타성을 초래하는 낡은 패러다임의 언어를 여전히 사용하고 있다. 오늘날 이 사람은 어떤 조직의 관리자, 최고 경영자, 또는 다른 상급 지도자일 수

있다. 다른 사람들이 자신의 생각을 제시할 필요가 없는데 왜냐하면 그것은 부적절한 것으로 여겨지기 때문이다. 그러나 연구에 따르면 문제 해결에 있어서 배타성은, 심지어 천재와 함께하는 것이더라도, 포용성만큼 효과적이지 않은데, 포용성이 있는 경우에는 모든 사람의 생각을 듣게 되고 해결책은 협력을 통해 발전된다.

Why? 왜 정답일까?

'everyone's ideas are heard and a solution is developed ~'는 완전한 수동태 문장이므로, 불완전한 절을 수반하는 관계대명사 which 뒤에 나올 수 없다. 따라서 which를 관계부사로 바꾸어야 하는데, 여기서는 선행사 inclusivity를 공간처럼 취급하여 which 대신 where를 써야 한다. 어법상 틀린 것은 ⑤이다.

Why? 왜 오답일까?

① 'one of the + 복수 명사'가 that절의 주어이므로 뒤따르는 동사가 단수형인 is로 바르게 쓰였다.
② 앞에 선행사가 없고, 뒤따르는 'everyone ultimately wants'는 동사의 목적어가 빠진 불완전한 문장이다. 따라서 선행사가 없는 맥락에서 선행사의 역할을 대신하며 불완전한 관계절을 수반하는 what이 바르게 쓰였다.
③ 현재분사 resulting이 전치사 in과 짝을 이루어 '(결과적으로) ~을 초래하는'이라는 의미를 나타내며 뒤에 목적어 exclusivity를 수반한 구조로 바르게 쓰였다.
④ 5형식 동사 consider는 주로 명사 또는 형용사 보어를 수반하는데, 특히 형용사 보어가 쓰인 'consider + 명 + 형'을 수동태로 바꾸면 '명 + be considered + 형'이 된다. 따라서 are considered라는 수동태 뒤에 형용사 inadequate가 바르게 쓰였다.

● **reflect on** ~에 대해 곰곰이 생각하다
● **characteristic** ⓝ 특성
● **support** ⓥ 뒷받침하다
● **collaboration** ⓝ 협력
● **typically** ⒜ 보통, 대개
● **wealthy** ⓐ 부유한
● **exclusivity** ⓝ 배타성
● **genius** ⓝ 천재
● **organization** ⓝ 조직
● **inclusivity** ⓝ 포용성
● **ultimately** ⒜ 궁극적으로
● **majority** ⓝ 대다수
● **educated** ⓐ 교육을 받은, 교양 있는
● **rule** ⓥ 지배하다, 통치하다
● **inadequate** ⓐ 부적절한

구문 풀이

15행 Yet research shows that exclusivity in problem solving, even
　　　　　　　　　　接속사(~것)　　　　주어
with a genius, is not as effective as inclusivity, where everyone's ideas
　　　　　　　동사　　　　　　　　　　　선행사　　관계부사　　주어1
are heard and a solution is developed through collaboration.
동사1　　　　　　주어2　　　　　동사2

★★ 문제 해결 꿀~팁 ★★

▶ 많이 틀린 이유는?
④ '형용사 vs. 부사'는 자주 출제되는 문법 포인트이지만, 이 문제에서는 5형식 동사 consider의 수동태를 결합시켜 난이도를 높였다. consider는 능동태로 쓸 때 뒤에 목적어와 목적격 보어를 수반하지만, 목적어를 주어로 삼아 수동태인 be considered 형태로 쓰이면 뒤에 보어만을 수반한다. 이 보어 자리에는 명사 또는 형용사가 들어갈 수 있고, inadequate는 형용사이므로, ④는 어법상 바르게 쓰였다. 해석하면 '부적절하게 여겨진다'이기 때문에 부사처럼 느껴지지만, 보어 자리이기 때문에 부사인 inadequately를 써서는 안 된다는 점에 주의해야 한다.
▶ 문제 해결 방법은?
정답인 ⑤ '관계대명사 vs. 관계부사'는 가장 많이 출제되는 문법 포인트 중 하나로, 앞보다는 뒤를 보아 어법상 적절한지를 판단해야 한다. 뒤에 주어, 목적어, 보어 중 하나가 빠진 불완전한 문장이 나오면 관계대명사를, 수동태나 자동사 등이 쓰인 완전한 문장이 나오면 관계부사를 써야 한다.

---

06 신체의 움직임과 감정 간의 관계 　　정답률 66% | 정답 ③

(A), (B), (C)의 각 네모 안에서 문맥에 맞는 낱말로 가장 적절한 것은?

	(A)	(B)	(C)
①	active 활동인	excess 초과	deconstruct 해체하다
②	active 활동적인	lack 부족	intensify 강화하다
✔③	active 활동적인	lack 부족	deconstruct 해체하기
④	inactive 비활동적인	lack 부족	intensify 강화하다
⑤	inactive 비활동적인	excess 초과	intensify 강화하다

DAY 08

[본문 해석]
많은 사람은 신체 움직임이 때때로 부정적인 감정들을 떨쳐버릴 수 있음을 발견한다. 만약 우리가 부정적인 기분이라면, 일상생활에서 (A) 활동적인 상태이고 싶어 하기를 멈추는 것이 매우 쉬울 수 있다. 이것이 또한 우울증을 겪는 많은 사람이 계속 잠을 자고, 외출을 하거나 운동을 하려는 동기가 없는 것으로 발견되는 이유이다. 불행히도, 이러한 운동의 (B) 부족이 실제로 많은 부정적인 감정을 악화시킬 수 있다. 운동과 움직임은 우리가 부정적인 에너지를 제거하기 시작하는 훌륭한 방법이다. 많은 사람은 화날 때 운동을 하거나 청소를 하고 싶은 상태가 된다는 점을 깨닫는다. 이것은 사실상 여러분이 하는 매우 건강하고 긍정적인 일이며, 그것(부정적인 감정)들이 더 이상 여러분의 삶에 영향을 미치지 않고 관계를 해치지 않도록 여러분이 부정적인 감정들을 (C) 해체하기 시작하는 훌륭한 방법이다.

Why? 왜 정답일까?

(A) 'This is why many people who suffer from depression are also found sleeping in and having no motivation to go outside or exercise.'에서 우울증을 경험하는 사람들은 신체를 움직이려는 동기가 부족하다고 말한다. 따라서 부정적인 감정을 겪을 때 '활동적인' 상태이기를 멈추려 한다는 뜻으로서 (A)에는 active가 들어가야 적절하다.
(B) 글에 따르면 몸을 움직이는 것은 부정적인 감정을 떨쳐내는 좋은 수단이므로, 몸을 움직이지 '않는' 사람은 그러한 감정들을 해소하지 못하여 도리어 감정이 악화될 것임을 유추할 수 있다. 따라서 (B)에는 lack이 들어가야 적절하다.
(C) 'Exercise and movement is a great way for us to start getting rid of negative energies.'에서 운동과 움직임은 부정적인 감정을 '제거하는' 좋은 방법이라고 말하므로, (C)에 적절한 말은 deconstruct이다. 따라서 각 네모 안에서 문맥에 맞는 낱말로 가장 적절한 것은 ③ '(A) active(활동적인) – (B) lack(부족) – (C) deconstruct(해체하기)'이다.

- **dispel** ⓥ 떨쳐버리다, 없애다
- **depression** ⓝ 우울(증)
- **deconstruct** ⓥ 해체하다
- **negative** ⓐ 부정적인
- **compound** ⓥ 악화시키다
- **no longer** 더 이상 ~ 않다

구문 풀이

4행 This is why many people [who suffer from depression] 〔주어〕
are also found sleeping in and having no motivation to go outside 〔동사(~한 상태로 발견되다)〕 →현재분사1 현재분사2
or exercise.

★★★ 1등급 대비 고난도 3점 문제

07 섣부른 결정으로 인한 실패를 피하는 방법   정답률 26% | 정답 ②

다음 빈칸에 들어갈 말로 가장 적절한 것을 고르시오. [3점]
① justifying layoffs – 해고를 정당화하는
✓ exercising patience – 인내심을 발휘하는
③ increasing employment – 고용을 늘리는
④ sticking to his opinions – 자기 의견을 고수하는
⑤ training unskilled members – 미숙한 구성원들을 훈련시키는

[본문 해석]
리더들이 종종 빨리 결정들을 내려야 하는 큰 압박에 직면하지만, 섣부른 결정들은 결정 실패의 주된 원인이다. 이것은 주로 리더들이 근원적인 문제들을 탐색하는 데 시간을 보내기보다는 결정의 피상적인 문제에 반응하기 때문이다. Bob Carlson은 다양한 문제들에 직면했을 때 인내심을 발휘하는 리더의 좋은 예이다. 2001년 초의 경기 침체기에, Reell Precision Manufacturing은 총수입의 30퍼센트 하락에 직면했다. 몇몇의 고위 지도자 팀의 구성원들은 해고에 찬성했고 몇몇은 임금 삭감에 찬성했다. 경제적 압박의 긴장 상태를 완화하기 위해서 결정을 밀어붙이거나 투표를 요청하는 것이 쉬웠을 테지만, 공동 최고 경영자로서, Bob Carlson은 그 팀이 함께 노력하고 모든 문제들을 검토하도록 도왔다. 그 팀은 마침내 자신들이 최선의 능력으로 두 가지 가능한 결정 모두의 영향을 철저하게 검토했다는 것을 아는 상태로 임금 삭감에 동의했다.

Why? 왜 정답일까?

빈칸 뒤에 제시된 예에 따르면 경기 침체기를 맞아 해고 또는 임금 삭감이라는 두 가지 안 중 하나를 선택해야 하는 상황에서, 회사의 공동 경영자였던 Bob Carlson은 팀원들 모두가 함께 노력하고 모든 문제를 검토하도록 도와주었다(~ as co-CEO, Bob Carlson helped the team work together and examine all of the issues.)

고 한다. 이는 리더가 섣불리 결정하지 않고 팀원들의 논의와 검토 과정을 '인내심 있게 기다리는' 행위로 볼 수 있으므로, 빈칸에 들어갈 말로 가장 적절한 것은 ② '인내심을 발휘하는'이다.

- **enormous** ⓐ 거대한
- **primarily** [ad] 주로
- **underlying** ⓐ 근본적인
- **manufacturing** ⓝ 제조업
- **layoff** ⓝ 해고
- **call for** ~을 요구하다[청하다]
- **ease** ⓥ (고통·불편 등을) 덜어주다
- **examine** ⓥ 검토하다
- **justify** ⓥ 정당화하다
- **premature** ⓐ 너무 이른, 시기상조의
- **superficial** ⓐ 피상적인
- **in the face of** ~에 직면하여
- **favor** ⓥ 찬성하다, 선호하다
- **reduction** ⓝ 삭감, 감소
- **in order to** (목적) 위하여
- **tension** ⓝ 긴장 상태, 긴장
- **thoroughly** [ad] 철저하게
- **stick to** ~을 고수하다

구문 풀이

16행 The team finally agreed on salary reductions, knowing 〔분사구문〕
that, (to the best of their ability), they had thoroughly examined 〔접속사(~것)〕 ( ): 삽입구 주어 동사(과거완료)
the implications of both possible decisions.

★★ 문제 해결 꿀~팁 ★★

▶ 많이 틀린 이유는?
리더들이 섣부른 결정을 내리는 이유를 진단하고 이를 해결할 방법을 제시하는 글이다. '해고'는 예시의 일부로 언급될 뿐 글의 핵심 소재가 아니므로 ①은 답으로 부적절하다. ④는 리더가 '자기 의견만 고수한다'라는 의미인데, 이는 글의 주제와 정반대된다.

▶ 문제 해결 방법은?
글에 'patience(인내심)'이라는 단어가 직접 등장하지는 않지만, 예시에서 리더가 팀원들로 하여금 모든 해결책을 꼼꼼히 검토해볼 수 있도록 도와주었다는 내용을 통해, 섣불리 혼자 결정하지 않고 '시간을 들여 기다리는 것'이 필요하다는 결론을 내릴 수 있다.

★★★ 1등급 대비 고난도 3점 문제

08 임무가 종료된 인공 위성의 처리 문제   정답률 41% | 정답 ⑤

글의 흐름으로 보아, 주어진 문장이 들어가기에 가장 적절한 곳을 고르시오. [3점]

[본문 해석]
국제연합은 모든 기업들이 인공위성의 임무 종료 후 25년 이내에 위성을 궤도에서 제거해 줄 것을 요청하고 있다. 하지만 인공위성이 작동하지 않을 수 있기(그리고 종종 정말로 작동하지 않기) 때문에 이것은 시행하기에 까다롭다. ① 이 문제를 해결하기 위해 전세계의 몇몇 회사들이 새로운 해결책을 내놓았다. ② 이것은 수명이 다한 인공위성을 궤도에서 제거하고, 대기권으로 다시 끌어들이는 것을 포함하는데, 여기서 그것은 다 타 버리게 될 것이다. ③ 우리가 이렇게 할(인공위성을 대기권으로 끌고 들어올) 수 있는 방법은 위성이 궤도에서 떨어져 나오도록 대기 항력을 증가시키면서 위성을 작살을 이용해서 잡거나, 거대한 그물로 잡거나, 자석을 이용하여 잡거나, 레이저를 발사하여 가열하는 것을 포함한다. ④ 하지만, 이러한 방법은 오직 지구 궤도를 도는 큰 위성들에게만 유용하다. ⑤ 우리가 페인트 조각이나 금속 같은 작은 잔해물을 치울 수 있는 방법은 정말로 없다. 우리는 그것들이 자연적으로 지구의 대기로 다시 들어오기를 기다려야 할 뿐이다.

Why? 왜 정답일까?

⑤ 앞의 문장에서 임무가 종료된 인공위성을 대기권으로 끌어들여 태우는 방법은 지구 궤도를 도는 큰 위성들에게만 유용하다고 언급한다. 주어진 문장은 우리가 '작은' 잔해물을 처리할 방법이 없다고 언급하며 ⑤ 앞의 문장 내용을 보충 설명한다. ⑤ 뒤의 문장은 주어진 문장에서 언급된 smaller pieces of debris를 them으로 받으며, 작은 잔해물은 알아서 대기로 들어오기를 바랄 수밖에 없다고 언급한다. 따라서 주어진 문장이 들어가기에 가장 적절한 곳은 ⑤이다.

- **debris** ⓝ 잔해
- **orbit** ⓝ 궤도
- **tricky** ⓐ 까다로운
- **tackle** ⓥ 다루다, 해결하다
- **novel** ⓐ 새로운, 신기한
- **atmosphere** ⓝ (지구의) 대기
- **magnet** ⓝ 자석, 자철
- **fall out of** ~을 빠져나오다, 떨어져 나오다
- **satellite** ⓝ 인공위성
- **mission** ⓝ 임무
- **enforce** ⓥ 시행하다
- **come up with** ~을 떠올리다
- **drag** ⓝ 항력, 끌림
- **burn up** 타 버리다
- **heat up** 데우다, 열을 가하다
- **method** ⓝ 방법

구문 풀이

14행 Upon seeing the incorrect answers of others, participants
「upon + 동명사 : ~하자마자」   주어
were also drawn toward the wrong answers themselves.
동사(수동태)   재귀대명사(주어 강조)

구문 풀이

11행 Ways [we could do this] include using a harpoon to grab a
주어(복수)   동사 목적어1
satellite, catching it in a huge net, using magnets to grab it, or even
목적어2   목적어3
firing lasers to heat up the satellite, increasing its atmospheric drag
목적어4   분사구문(~하면서)
so that it falls out of orbit.
접속사(~하도록, ~하기 위해)

★★ 문제 해결 꿀~팁 ★★

▶ 많이 틀린 이유는?
수명이 다한 인공위성의 사후 처리에 관한 글로, 대명사 힌트를 잘 활용하면 오답을 쉽게 소거할 수 있다. ③ 앞에서 인공위성을 다시 대기로 끌어들여 없애는 방법을 언급한 데 이어, ③ 뒤이자 ④ 앞의 문장에서는 이를 do this로 가리킨다. 또한 이 문장의 'using ~, catching ~, using ~, or even firing ~'을 ④ 뒤에서 these methods로 가리킨다. 즉 ③, ④ 앞뒤에서 대명사 사용이 모두 적절하기 때문에 주어진 문장은 이 두 곳에 들어갈 수 없다.

▶ 문제 해결 방법은?
정답을 골라내는 데에도 대명사 힌트가 큰 역할을 한다. ⑤ 앞의 문장에서는 대기로 끌어당기는 갖가지 방법이 큰 인공위성(large satellites)에만 적용될 수 있다고 하는데, ⑤ 뒤의 문장은 '이 방법을 사용하지 못하고 그저 자연스럽게 지구로 다시 오기를 기다려야 하는' 대상을 them으로 가리키고 있다. 즉 them이 large satellites와 일치하지 않으므로, 주어진 문장이 ⑤에 들어가야 함을 알 수 있다.

10-12 Henrietta의 마음 따뜻한 일화

[본문 해석]

(A)

Henrietta는 가장 위대한 '노래의 여왕' 중 한 명이다. (a) 그녀가 독일이 배출한 가장 위대한 가수라는 남들의 부러움을 살 위치에 도달하기 전 그녀는 혹독한 시련을 겪어야 했다. 『경력 초기에 그녀는 라이벌이었던 Amelia의 친구들에 의해 비엔나 무대에서 야유를 받고 쫓겨났다.』 그러나 이 좌절에도 불구하고, Henrietta는 모든 유럽이 그녀의 발아래에 있을 때까지 견뎠다.
└「」: 12번 ①의 근거 일치

(D)

수년 후, Henrietta의 명성이 절정에 달했을 때, 그녀는 어느 날 베를린의 거리를 차를 타고 지나가고 있었다. 『곧 그녀는 눈먼 여성을 데리고 가는 여자 아이와 마주쳤다.』 그녀는 여성의 무력함에 마음이 움직였고, 충동적으로 아이를 (e) 자기 쪽으로 오라고 손짓하며, "이리 와, 애야. 네가 손을 잡고 데리고 가는 사람은 누구니?"라고 말했다.
└「」: 12번 ⑤의 근거 일치

(B)

대답은 이랬다. "저분은 제 어머니, Amelia Steininger예요. 그녀는 훌륭한 가수였지만 목소리를 잃었고, 그 일로 너무 많이 울어서 (b) 그녀는 이제 더 이상 앞을 볼 수 없게 됐어요." Henrietta는 그들의 주소를 묻고 나서 아이에게 "어머니께 오래된 지인이 오늘 오후에 방문할 것이라고 말하렴."이라고 말했다. 『그녀는 그들의 거처를 찾아내서 모녀를 돌보았다.』 『그녀의 요청에 따라 숙련된 의사가 Amelia의 시력을 회복시키려 했지만 허사였다.』
└「」: 12번 ②의 근거 일치   └「」: 12번 ③의 근거 불일치

(C)

그러나 Henrietta가 (c) 자기 예전 경쟁자에게 베푼 친절은 여기서 그치지 않았다. 『그다음 주에 그녀는 그 불쌍한 여성을 위한 자선 콘서트를 열었고,』 (사람들은) Henrietta가 그 자리에서 (d) 그녀가 전에 한 번도 불러본 적 없는 방식으로 불렀다고 했다. 그리고 많은 청중의 박수와 함께 지상 사람들의 선행에 기뻐하는 천국에 있는 천사들의 박수가 섞여 있었다는 것을 누가 의심할 수 있겠는가?
└「」: 12번 ④의 근거 일치

구문 풀이

(C) 2행 The next week she gave a benefit concert for the poor
woman, and it was said that on that occasion Henrietta sang as she
= Henrietta was said to sing on that occasion ~
had never sung before.

---

10 글의 순서 파악   정답률 71% | 정답 ④

주어진 글 (A)에 이어질 내용을 순서에 맞게 배열한 것으로 가장 적절한 것은?

① (B) − (D) − (C)   ② (C) − (B) − (D)
③ (C) − (D) − (B)   ✓ (D) − (B) − (C)
⑤ (D) − (C) − (B)

Why? 왜 정답일까?

Henrietta가 '노래의 여왕'이 되기 전 경쟁자 Amelia의 친구들 때문에 좌절을 겪었다는 내용의 (A) 뒤로, (D)에서는 '수년이 지나 그녀가 명성을 얻은 후' 길을 가다가 어느

---

09 기억의 왜곡을 유발하는 외부적 요인   정답률 53% | 정답 ①

다음 글의 내용을 한 문장으로 요약하고자 한다. 빈칸 (A), (B)에 들어갈 말로 가장 적절한 것은?

	(A)	(B)
✓	stable 안정된	falsified 왜곡된
②	fragile 허술한	modified 수정된
③	stable 안정된	intensified 강화된
④	fragile 허술한	solidified 공고해진
⑤	concrete 수동적인	maintained 유지하는

[본문 해석]

2011년 Micah Edelson과 그의 동료들이 기억 조작의 외부 요인들에 대한 흥미로운 실험을 했다. 그들의 실험에서 참가자들은 2분짜리 다큐멘터리 영상을 보고 나서 그 영상에 대한 일련의 질문을 받았다. 그 영상을 본 직후 참가자들은 응답에서 거의 실수를 하지 않았고 세부 사항들을 정확하게 기억해 낼 수 있었다. 4일 후에 그들은 여전히 세부 사항들을 기억할 수 있었고 영상에 관한 어떤 잘못된 정보가 제시되었을 때에도 자신의 기억이 흔들리게 두지 않았다. 그러나 참가자들이 그 영상에 관한 다른 참가자들이 한 거짓 응답을 봤을 때 이것이 바뀌었다. 다른 사람들의 올바르지 않은 응답을 보자마자 참가자들 자신 또한 잘못된 응답 쪽으로 이끌려 갔다. 심지어 그들이 다른 응답들은 조작되었으며 그 다큐멘터리와 아무 상관이 없다는 것을 알아낸 뒤에도, 이는 너무 늦어버린 후였다. 참가자들은 더 이상 진실과 허구를 구분할 수 없었다. 그들은 이미 자신의 기억을 집단에 맞게끔 수정했다.

➡ 실험에 따르면 참가자들이 거짓된 정보 자체를 제공받았을 때 그들의 기억은 (A) 안정된 상태로 남아있었으나 다른 참가자들의 거짓 응답에 노출되었을 때 그들의 기억이 (B) 왜곡되었다.

Why? 왜 정답일까?

'This changed, however, when participants were shown fake responses about the film made by other participants.' 이후로, 사람들은 본래 혼자서는 정확히 기억하고 있던 것도 다른 사람들이 제공했다는 '잘못된' 정보에 노출되면 혼동하기 시작한다는 내용이 이어지고 있다. 이는 마지막 문장에서 말하듯이 사람들이 집단 기억에 맞추어 자신의 기억을 수정하는 경향이 있기(They had already modified their memories to fit the group.) 때문임을 알 수 있다. 따라서 요약문의 빈칸에 들어갈 말로 가장 적절한 것은 ① 'A) stable(안정된), (B) falsified(왜곡된)'이다.

DAY 08

모녀를 마주쳤다고 한다. 이어서 **(B)**에서는 그 모녀가 Amelia 모녀였다는 내용과 함께 Henrietta가 이들을 챙겼다는 내용이, **(C)**에서는 Henrietta가 추가로 베푼 선행에 관한 내용이 전개된다. 따라서 글의 순서로 가장 적절한 것은 ④ '**(D)** – **(B)** – **(C)**'이다.

11 지칭 추론 정답률 60% | 정답 ②

밑줄 친 (a) ~ (e) 중에서 가리키는 대상이 나머지 넷과 <u>다른</u> 것은?
① (a) ✓② (b) ③ (c) ④ (d) ⑤ (e)

Why? 왜 정답일까?

(a), (c), (d), (e)는 Henrietta, (b)는 Amelia를 가리키므로, (a) ~ (e) 중에서 가리키는 대상이 다른 하나는 ② '(b)'이다.

12 세부 내용 파악 정답률 77% | 정답 ③

윗글에 관한 내용으로 적절하지 않은 것은?
① Amelia와 Henrietta는 라이벌 관계였다.
② Henrietta는 모녀의 거처를 찾아내서 그들을 돌보았다.
✓③ 숙련된 의사가 Amelia의 시력을 회복시켰다.
④ 불쌍한 여성을 위해 Henrietta는 자선 콘서트를 열었다.
⑤ Henrietta는 눈먼 여성을 데리고 가는 여자 아이와 마주쳤다.

Why? 왜 정답일까?

(B) '~ a skilled doctor tried to restore Amelia's sight, but it was in vain.'에 따르면 숙련된 의사가 Amelia의 시력을 회복시키고자 했지만 허사로 돌아갔다고 하므로, 내용과 일치하지 않는 것은 ③ '숙련된 의사가 Amelia의 시력을 회복시켰다.'이다.

Why? 왜 오답일까?

① (A) '~ she was hissed off a Vienna stage by the friends of her rival, Amelia.'의 내용과 일치한다.
② (B) 'She searched out their place and undertook the care of both mother and daughter.'의 내용과 일치한다.
④ (C) 'The next week she gave a benefit concert for the poor woman, ~'의 내용과 일치한다.
⑤ (D) 'Soon she came across a little girl leading a blind woman.'의 내용과 일치한다.

DAY 09 20분 미니 모의고사

01 ①	02 ②	03 ①	04 ②	05 ④
06 ③	07 ④	08 ④	09 ④	10 ③
11 ⑤	12 ⑤			

01 강당 수리 예정 안내 정답률 84% | 정답 ①

다음 글의 목적으로 가장 적절한 것은?
✓① 수리로 인한 강당 폐쇄를 안내하려고
② 캠퍼스 투어 프로그램 일정을 조정하려고
③ 강당 사용을 위한 신청 방법을 공지하려고
④ 강당 신축을 위한 기금 모금 행사를 홍보하려고
⑤ 집짓기 행사에 참여할 자원 봉사자를 모집하려고

[본문 해석]

Douglas school의 학부모님과 학생 여러분에게,

여러분들도 아시다시피, 우리 학교는 150년도 더 전에 지어졌습니다. 우리는 학교의 역사가 자랑스럽지만, 학교의 시설들이 현대 교육을 위해 정확히 맞지는 않습니다. 학교 재단에 아낌없이 기부해 주신 덕분에, 우리는 구식이 되어버린 캠퍼스의 그러한 요소들에 대한 보수를 시작할 수 있을 것입니다. 우리는 이 보수작업으로 우리 학생들에게 가능한 최고의 교육을 제공하는 데 도움이 되기를 바랍니다. 강당이 수리로 인해 폐쇄되는 첫 번째 건물이 될 것이라는 점을 이 편지로 알려드립니다. 학생들은 수리가 진행되는 동안 약 한 달 동안 강당을 이용할 수 없게 됩니다. 이 짧은 불편함이 향후 몇 년 동안 지역사회 전체의 혜택을 어떻게 장려할 것인지 이해해 주시기를 바랍니다.

교감 Kyla Andrews 드림

Why? 왜 정답일까?

글 후반부에서 캠퍼스 내 보수작업이 강당에서 처음 진행됨에 따라 앞으로 한 달간 강당을 이용할 수 없게 된다고 하므로(I'm writing to inform you that the auditorium will be the first building closed for repairs.), 글의 목적으로 가장 적절한 것은 ① '수리로 인한 강당 폐쇄를 안내하려고'이다.

- **facility** ⓝ 시설
- **donation** ⓝ 기부, 기증
- **renovate** ⓥ 수리하다, 보수하다
- **auditorium** ⓝ 강당
- **repair** ⓝ 수리, 보수
- **inconvenience** ⓝ 불편, 폐
- **generous** ⓐ 관대한, 너그러운
- **foundation** ⓝ 재단
- **outdated** ⓐ 구식인, 시대에 뒤처진
- **inform** (~에게 …을) 알리다
- **brief** ⓐ 짧은, 잠시 동안의

구문 풀이

> **9행** I'm writing to inform you that the auditorium will be the first
> 　　　　　　　　부사적 용법(목적)　　　접속사(~것)
> building closed for repairs.
> 　　　과거분사구

02 성공하게 도와준 사람들에게 감사하는 마음 갖기 정답률 91% | 정답 ②

다음 글에서 필자가 주장하는 바로 가장 적절한 것은?
① 원만한 인간관계를 위하여 사고의 유연성을 길러야 한다.
✓② 성공에 도움을 준 사람들에게 감사하는 마음을 가져야 한다.
③ 자신의 분야에서 성공하기 위해서는 경험의 폭을 넓혀야 한다.
④ 원하는 직업을 갖기 위해서는 다른 사람의 조언을 경청해야 한다.
⑤ 타인의 시선을 의식하지 않고 부단히 새로운 일에 도전해야 한다.

[본문 해석]

개인의 성취와 인정을 향한 질주 속에서, 성공한 대다수의 사람들은 자신의 작은 시작을 잊는다. 그들은 종종 성공으로 가는 과정에서 자신을 도와준 사람들을 잊는다. 당신이 어디서 왔는지 잊어버리고, 상황이 힘들고 진척이 없을 때 곁에 있어 준 사람들을 소홀히 한다면, 당신의 성공은 가치가 없다. 누구도 다른 사람의 도움 없이는 성공할 수 없다. 도움을 주는 부모님, 친구, 조언자, 코치들이 있다. 당신은 당신을 도와준 사람들 모두에게 감사할 필요가 있다. 감사

는 당신과 다른 사람들을 연결해 주는 접착제이다. 그것은 당신을 위해 과거에 있었고 마지막에도 있을 것 같은 사람들과 당신을 계속해서 연결해 주는 다리이다. 관계, 그리고 당신이 다른 사람들을 대하는 방식이 당신의 진정한 성공을 결정한다.

Why? 왜 정답일까?

'You need to be grateful to all of those who helped you.'에서 성공에 도움을 주었던 사람들에게 고마워하는 마음을 지니라고 하므로, 필자가 주장하는 바로 가장 적절한 것은 ② '성공에 도움을 준 사람들에게 감사하는 마음을 가져야 한다.'이다.

- **achievement** ⓝ 성취
- **make it** 성공하다
- **neglect** ⓥ 소홀히 하다
- **gratitude** ⓝ 감사
- **recognition** ⓝ 인정, 표창
- **humble** ⓐ 작은, 변변찮은, 겸손한
- **valueless** ⓐ 가치 없는
- **determine** ⓥ 결정하다

구문 풀이

1행 In the rush towards individual achievement and recognition, the majority of those [who make it] forget their humble beginnings.
주어(부분 of 전체) / 동사(복수)

03 일기 쓰기의 발달과 자아 성찰   정답률 61% | 정답 ①

밑줄 친 make oneself public to oneself가 다음 글에서 의미하는 바로 가장 적절한 것은? [3점]

✓① use writing as a means of reflecting on oneself
글을 자신을 되돌아보는 수단으로 사용하곤
② build one's identity by reading others' diaries
타인의 일기를 읽으며 자신의 정체성을 확립하곤
③ exchange feedback in the process of writing
글 쓰는 과정에서 의견을 교환하곤
④ create an alternate ego to present to others
다른 사람에게 보여주기 위한 대체적 자아를 창조하곤
⑤ develop topics for writing about selfhood
자아에 관한 글을 쓰기 위한 주제를 개발하곤

[본문 해석]

18세기와 19세기에 발달한 상태가 된 개인 일기는 근대적 주체성을 구축하는 데 중심물이 되었는데, 그것의 중심에는 세계와 자아에 대한 이해에 이성과 비판의 적용이 있었고, 이는 새로운 종류의 지식을 창조할 수 있게 해주었다. 일기는 그것을 통해 계몽되고 자유로운 주체가 구성될 수 있는 중심 매체였다. 그것은 개인이 자신의 행방, 감정, 생각에 대해 매일 쓸 수 있는 공간을 제공했다. 시간이 지나고, (일기를) 다시 읽어보면서, 이질적인 항목, 사건 및 우연이 자신에 관한 통찰력과 이야기로 만들어질 수 있었으며, 주체성의 형성이 가능해졌다. '말로 만들어지고 또한 탐구되는 자아'라는 개념이 나타나는 것은 바로 그런 맥락에서다. 일기는 개인적이고 사적인 것이었다. 사람들은 자신을 위해 쓰곤 했는데, Habermas의 명확한 표현을 빌리면, 자기 자신을 스스로에게 공개적으로 만들곤 했다. 자아를 사적 영역에서 공개함으로써, 자아는 또한 자기 점검과 자기 비판의 대상이 되었다.

Why? 왜 정답일까?

일기 쓰기가 근대적 주체성을 구축하는 데 핵심이 되었다는 내용의 글이다. 특히 마지막 문장에서, 일기를 통해 자아를 사적 영역에 공개해 놓자 자아에 대한 자기 점검과 비판이 가능해졌다고 말한다. 이는 곧 일기 쓰기가 자신을 '되돌아보는' 도구가 되었다는 의미로 이해할 수 있으므로, 밑줄 친 부분의 의미로 가장 적절한 것은 ① '글을 자신을 되돌아보는 수단으로 사용하곤(use writing as a means of reflecting on oneself)'이다.

- **come of age** 충분히 발달한 상태에 이르다
- **centerpiece** ⓝ 가장 핵심적인 것
- **at the heart of** ~의 중심에 있는
- **reason** ⓝ 이성, 이유
- **whereabout** ⓝ 행방, 소재
- **entry** ⓝ (사전, 장부, 일기 등의) 항목
- **render** ⓥ 만들다
- **explore** ⓥ 탐구하다
- **private** ⓐ 사적인
- **formulation** ⓝ (특정 방식으로의) 표현
- **sphere** ⓝ 영역
- **as a means of** ~의 수단으로
- **personal** ⓐ 사적인, 개인적인
- **subjectivity** ⓝ 주체성, 주관성
- **application** ⓝ 적용
- **enlightened** ⓐ 계몽된, 깨우친
- **disparate** ⓐ 이질적인
- **happenstance** ⓝ 우연
- **allow for** ~을 허용하다, 고려하다, 참작하다
- **emerge** ⓥ 생겨나다, 발생하다, 떠오르다
- **for oneself** 자신을 위해, 스스로
- **public** ⓐ 공개된, 공적인
- **inspection** ⓝ 점검, 조사
- **alternate** ⓐ 교체의, 번갈아 나오는

구문 풀이

6행 Diaries were central media through which enlightened and free subjects could be constructed.
「전치사 + 관계대명사」 / 완전한 문장

04 전쟁에서 노래와 춤을 이용하는 것의 이점   정답률 52% | 정답 ②

다음 글의 주제로 가장 적절한 것은?

① cultural differences in honoring war victims
전쟁 희생자를 기념하는 데 있어 문화적 차이
✓② benefits of utilizing sound and motion in warfare
전쟁에서 소리와 움직임을 이용하는 것의 이점
③ functions of music in preventing or resolving conflicts
갈등을 방지하거나 해결하는 데 있어서의 음악의 기능
④ strategies of analyzing an enemy's vulnerable points in war
전쟁에서 적의 취약점을 분석하는 전략
⑤ effects of religious dances on lowering anxiety on the battlefield
종교적인 춤이 전쟁터에서 불안을 낮추는 데 끼치는 영향

[본문 해석]

북미 원주민들은 공격을 개시하기 위한 준비로 종종 노래를 불렀고 춤을 췄다. 이러한 준비의 노래에서 비롯된 감정적이고 신경 화학적인 흥분 상태가 공격을 수행하는 힘을 제공해주었다. 무의식적이고 억제되지 않는 행동으로 시작됐을지도 모르는 것, 즉 격분하여 노래를 부르고 북을 치며 희생자를 공격하는 것은 승리자들이 자신들이 공격 중인 사람들에게 자신들의 행동이 미치는 영향을 직접 목격하면서 전략이 되었을 수도 있다. 비록 전쟁의 춤이 적에게 곧 있을 공격을 경고해 주는 위험을 감수하는 것임에도 불구하고, 공격자들에게 주는 정서적 자극과 동시에 움직이게 하는 이점이 기습의 상실을 보상해 줄 수 있다. 노래하고, 춤추고, 행진했던 사람들은 그러한 장관을 목격한 적들을 겁먹게 했을 뿐만 아니라 전쟁터에서 강한 우세를 누렸을지도 모른다. 19세기와 20세기의 독일인들은 스코틀랜드인들을 가장 무서워했는데, (이들의) 백파이프와 북은 순전한 시끄러움과 시각적인 장관으로 (적을) 교란시켰다.

Why? 왜 정답일까?

전쟁에서 노래와 춤을 이용하는 쪽이 우세를 누렸다(Humans who sang, danced, and marched may have enjoyed a strong advantage on the battlefield as well as intimidated enemies who witnessed such a spectacle.)는 점을 언급하며 그 이유를 추측하는 글이므로, 글의 주제로 가장 적절한 것은 ② '전쟁에서 소리와 움직임을 이용하는 것의 이점'이다.

- **launch** ⓥ 개시하다, 시작하다
- **synchronize** ⓥ 동시에 움직이게 하다
- **intimidate** ⓥ 위협하다
- **sheer** ⓐ 순전한, 큰
- **religious** ⓐ 종교적인
- **arousal** ⓝ 자극, 흥분
- **compensate for** ~을 보충하다, 보상하다
- **disturb** ⓥ 교란시키다
- **vulnerable** ⓐ 취약한
- **anxiety** ⓝ 불안, 걱정

구문 풀이

4행 What may have begun as an unconscious, uncontrolled act —
명사절 주어
(rushing their victims with singing and beating drums in a frenzy) —
( ): 삽입구
could have become a strategy as the victors saw firsthand the
동사구(과거에 대한 추측: ~했을 수도 있다)
effect [their actions had on those they were attacking.]

05 사회적 비교의 결과   정답률 56% | 정답 ④

다음 글의 밑줄 친 부분 중, 어법상 틀린 것은? [3점]

[본문 해석]

타인과 견주어 우리 자신을 평가해서는 안 된다는 많은 경고에도 불구하고, 우리 대부분은 여전히 그렇게 하고 있다. 우리는 의미를 추구하는 존재일 뿐만 아니라 사회적인 존재라서, 우리 자신을 평가하고, 지위를 개선하며, 자존감을 높이기 위해 끊임없이 사람들끼리 비교한다. 그러나 사회적 비교의 문제는 그것이 흔히 역효과를 낸다는 것이다. 우리보다 더 잘하고 있는 사람과 우리 자신을 비교할 때, 우리는 흔히 그만큼 잘하지 못하는 것에 대해서 무능하다고 느낀다. 이것은 때로는 심리학자들이 악성 질투라고 부르는 것, 즉 누군가가 불행을 만나기를 바라는 욕망("그녀가 지금 가진 것을 가지고 있지 않으면 좋을 텐데.")으로 이어진다. 마찬가지로, 우리보다 더 못하고 있는 사람과 자신을 비교하는 것은 경멸, 즉 다른 사람이 우리의 호의를 받을 가치가 없다는 느낌("그녀는 내가 주목할 가치가 없어.")으로 이어질 위험이 있다. 그렇지 않고, 우리 자신을 타인과 비교하는 것은 또한 양성 질투, 즉 다른 사람이 불행해지기를 바라지 않고 그들의 성취를 재생산하려는 열망("그녀가 가진 것을 나도 가지면 좋을 텐데.")으로 이어질 수 있으며, 이는 몇몇 상황에서 우리가 최근의 실패에도 불구하고 노력을 더 하도록 우리에게 영감을 주고 동기를 부여한다고 알려져 왔다.

[문제편 p.054]

Why? 왜 정답일까?

동명사구 주어인 'comparing ourselves with someone ~'는 단수 동사와 함께 쓰므로, risk를 risks로 고쳐야 한다. 따라서 어법상 틀린 것은 ④이다.

Why? 왜 오답일까?

① creatures를 받는 복수의 부정대명사 ones가 바르게 쓰였다.
② 2형식 동사 feel 뒤에서 주격 보어 역할을 하기 위해 형용사 inadequate가 바르게 쓰였다.
③ the desire는 to부정사구의 꾸밈을 받는 명사이므로, 형용사적 용법의 to meet이 바르게 쓰였다.
⑤ 선행사 the longing을 받으면서 뒤에 주어가 없는 관계절을 이끌기 위해 which가 바르게 쓰였다. 이 which는 콤마 뒤에서 선행사를 보충 설명하는 계속적 용법으로 쓰였다.

- **abundant** ⓐ 많은, 풍부한
- **measure A against B** B에 견주어 A를 평가하다, 측정하다
- **enhance** ⓥ 높이다, 향상시키다
- **self-esteem** ⓝ 자존감
- **inadequate** ⓐ 부족한, 무능한
- **malignant** ⓐ 악의 있는
- **risk** ⓥ (~의 위험을) 감수하다
- **undeserving** ⓐ (~을 가질) 자격이 없는
- **beneficence** ⓝ 선행, 자선
- **benign** ⓐ 양성의, 상냥한
- **circumstance** ⓝ 상황
- **in spite of** ~에도 불구하고

구문 풀이

1행 Despite abundant warnings {that we shouldn't measure
　　　전치사　　　명사구　　　{ }: 동격절(= warnings)
ourselves against others}, most of us still do.
　　　　　　　　　　　　　　　= measure ~ others

★★★ 1등급 대비 고난도 2점 문제

06 Adam Smith의 전문화 개념　　　정답률 45% | 정답 ③

다음 글의 밑줄 친 부분 중, 문맥상 낱말의 쓰임이 적절하지 **않은** 것은?

[본문 해석]

Adam Smith는 전문화, 즉 우리 각자가 하나의 특정한 기술에 집중하는 것이 모든 사람의 복지의 전반적인 향상으로 이어진다고 지적했다. 그 개념은 간단하고 강력하다. 예컨대 식량 재배, 의류 생산, 혹은 주택 건설과 같은 단 하나의 분야에만 전문화함으로써, 각각의 노동자는 특정한 활동에 ① 숙달하게 된다. 하지만 전문화는 전문가가 그 이후 자신의 생산물을 다른 활동 라인 전문가들의 생산물과 ② 거래할 수 있을 때만 성립한다. 만약 그 ③ 부족한(→ 넘치는) 식량을 의류, 주거지 등등으로 교환할 시장 판매처가 없다면 한 가구가 필요로 하는 양보다 더 많이 식량을 생산하는 것은 의미가 없을 것이다. 동시에, 시장에서 식량을 구매할 능력이 없다면, 전문 주택 건축가나 전문 의류 제작자가 되는 것은 불가능할 텐데, 스스로의 생존을 위해 농사를 지어야 할 ④ 필요성이 있기 때문이다. 따라서 Smith는 시장의 규모는 전문화의 정도에 따라 결정되는 반면에, 노동의 분업은 시장의 규모에 의해 ⑤ 제한된다는 것을 알았다.

Why? 왜 정답일까?

②가 포함된 문장에서 전문화는 시장 거래가 가능할 때만 의의가 있다고 하는데, 이러한 거래는 한 가정에서 필요한 양 '이상의', 즉 '남는' 생산물을 대상으로 할 것이기에, ③의 scarce를 excess로 고쳐야 한다. 따라서 문맥상 낱말의 쓰임이 적절하지 않은 것은 ③이다.

- **specialization** ⓝ 전문화
- **specific** ⓐ 특정한
- **improvement** ⓝ 향상, 개선
- **raise** ⓥ 기르다, 키우다
- **make sense** 말이 되다, 의의가 있다
- **subsequently** ⓐⓓ 차후에
- **trade** ⓥ 교역하다, 거래하다
- **and so forth** 기타 등등
- **division of labor** 분업

구문 풀이

13행 At the same time, without the ability to buy food on the
　　　　　　　　　　　　= if it were not for(~이 없다면)
market, it would not be possible to be a specialist home builder or
　　　　　　가정법 과거 주절
clothing maker, ~

★★ 문제 해결 꿀~팁 ★★

▶ 많이 틀린 이유는?
전문화의 이점을 언급하는 글로, 특히 글 중간의 however 뒤에서는 이 전문화가 시장의 존재를 전제로 한다는 내용을 다루고 있다. 시장이 있어야 많이 생산된 식량을

교환할 수도 있고, 식량이 아닌 '다른' 재화를 생산해 식량과 바꿀 수도 있게 되므로 결국 시장의 규모가 분업이나 전문화의 정도까지도 '결정한다'는 것이다. ⑤는 시장의 규모에 따라 분업, 즉 전문화의 정도에 영향이 간다는 의미로 limited를 적절히 썼다.

▶ 문제 해결 방법은?
③이 포함된 문장은 문맥상 시장이 있어서 '남는' 음식을 처분할 수 없다면 음식을 더 많이 생산할 필요가 없을 것이라는 의미이다.

07 과학과 예술 분야에서 창의성의 보편성　　　정답률 40% | 정답 ④

다음 빈칸에 들어갈 말로 가장 적절한 것을 고르시오. [3점]

① formality – 형식성
② objectivity – 객관성
③ complexity – 복잡성
✔ universality – 보편성
⑤ uncertainty – 불확실성

[본문 해석]

상당한 수의 과학자들과 예술가들이 창의성의 보편성에 대해 주목해 왔다. 1980년에 열린 제16차 노벨 회의에서 과학자들, 음악가들 그리고 철학자들은 Freeman Dyson의 말을 인용하여 "여러분이 창조와 행위에 관해 이야기하고 있는 한 과학과 예술 사이의 유사성은 매우 높습니다. 창조는 분명 매우 유사합니다. 행위의 솜씨에서 나오는 미적 쾌감은 과학에서도 매우 큽니다."라는 것에 모두 동의했다. 몇 년 후, 또 다른 여러 학문 분야에 걸친 회의에서 물리학자인 Murray Gell-Mann은 "모두가 아이디어가 어디에서 오는지에 대해 동의합니다. 우리는 화가 여러 명, 시인 한 명, 작가 두서넛 명 그리고 물리학자들을 포함하여 약 10년 전 이곳에서 세미나를 했습니다. 모두는 그것이 어떻게 진행되는지에 대해 동의합니다. 이 사람들 모두는 자신들이 예술적인 일을 하고 있든 과학적인 일을 하고 있든 문제를 해결하려고 노력하고 있습니다."라는 것을 알아냈다.

Why? 왜 정답일까?

과학과 예술이라는 서로 다른 분야에서도 창조의 행위는 서로 유사하며(~ the analogies between science and art are very good as long as you are talking about the creation and the performance. The creation is certainly very analogous.), 과학자들과 예술가들 모두 아이디어가 어디서 나오고 창조가 어떻게 진행되는가에 대해 의견을 같이한다는 내용의 글이다. 따라서 주제를 요약해 나타내는 빈칸에 들어갈 말로 가장 적절한 것은 ④ '보편성'이다.

- **a good many** 상당한 수의
- **quote** ⓥ 인용하다
- **analogy** ⓝ 유사성, 유추
- **aesthetic** ⓐ 미적인
- **craftsmanship** ⓝ (훌륭한) 솜씨
- **multidisciplinary** ⓐ 여러 학문 분야에 걸친

구문 풀이

2행 At the Sixteenth Nobel Conference, (which was) held in 1980, /
　　　　　　　　　　　　　　　선행사　　　생략
scientists, musicians, and philosophers all agreed, to quote Freeman
　　　　　주어　　　　　　　　　　동사
Dyson, {that "the analogies between science and art are very good /
　　　　　　　　주어　　　　　　　　　　　　　　　동사
as long as you are talking about the creation and the performance}.
~하는 한　　　　　　　　　　　　　　　　　　　　{ }: 목적어

★★★ 1등급 대비 고난도 3점 문제

08 문화적 산물이 사람들에게 미치는 영향　　　정답률 40% | 정답 ④

다음 빈칸에 들어갈 말로 가장 적절한 것을 고르시오. [3점]

① can provide many valuable views
　여러 가치 있는 시각을 제공해줄 수 있다
② reflects the idea of the sociologists
　사회학자들의 생각을 반영한다
③ forms prejudices to certain characters
　특정 캐릭터에 대한 편견을 형성한다
✔ will have the same effect on everyone
　모든 사람에게 똑같은 영향을 줄 것이라
⑤ might resolve social conflicts among people
　사람들 사이의 사회적 갈등을 해결해줄지 모른다

[본문 해석]

사회학자들은 사람들이 그들 자신의 관점이나 가치를 그들이 직면하는 문화로 가져온다는 것을 입증해 왔는데, 책, TV 프로그램, 영화, 음악은 모두에게 영향을 줄지도 모르지만 다양한 사람들에게 다양한 방식으로 영향을 준다. 한 연구에서, Neil Vidmar와 Milton Rokeach는 인종에 관한 다양한 관점을 가진 시

청자들에게 시트콤 *All in the Family*의 에피소드들을 보여주었다. 이 쇼는 보다 진보적인 가족 구성원들과 자주 싸움에 휘말리는 편협한 고집쟁이 Archie Bunker라는 인물에 초점을 맞춘다. Vidmar와 Rokeach는 Archie Bunker의 관점을 공유하지 않는 시청자들이 Archie의 어처구니없는 인종 차별주의를 비웃는 방식에 있어 그 쇼가 아주 재미있다고 생각했다는 것을 발견했는데, 실은 이것이 제작자의 의도였다. 그러나 반면에, 스스로가 고집쟁이인 시청자들은 Archie Bunker가 그 쇼의 영웅이라고 생각했고, 제작자가 Bunker의 어리석은 가족들을 비웃으려 한다고 생각했다! 이것은 왜 특정 문화적 산물이 <u>모든 사람</u>에게 똑같은 영향을 줄 것이라고 가정하는 것이 잘못인지를 보여준다.

Why? 왜 정답일까?

첫 문장인 '~ books, TV programs, movies, and music may affect everyone, but they affect different people in different ways.'에서 책, TV 프로, 영화, 음악 등은 모두에게 영향을 주기는 하지만 그 영향의 대상과 양상은 다양하다는 주제를 제시하고 있다. 이를 근거로 할 때, 어느 시각이 '잘못된' 것인지를 지적하는 빈칸에는 주제와는 반대로 모두에게 같은 영향이 갈 것으로 생각한다는 내용이 들어가야 하므로, 답으로 가장 적절한 것은 ④ '모든 사람에게 똑같은 영향을 줄 것이라'이다.

- encounter ⓥ 직면하다, 마주치다
- progressive ⓐ 진보적인
- racism ⓝ 인종 차별주의
- assume ⓥ 가정하다
- have an effect on ~에게 영향을 주다
- intolerant ⓐ 편협한
- absurd ⓐ 어처구니없는, 불합리한
- demonstrate ⓥ 분명히 보여주다
- prejudice ⓝ 편견
- resolve ⓥ 해결하다

구문 풀이

17행 This demonstrates why it's a mistake to assume that a (의문부사 ↳가주어 진주어 접속사(~것)) certain cultural product will have the same effect on everyone.

★★ 문제 해결 꿀~팁 ★★

▶ 많이 틀린 이유는?
첫 문장에 따르면 각종 문화적 산물이 사람마다 미치는 영향이 다른데, 이는 사람들이 문화적 산물을 접할 때 각기 자기만의 견해와 가치관을 투영하기 때문이다. 이를 근거로 할 때, 문화적 산물이 사람들에게 가치로운 견해를 '주는' 입장이라고 서술한 ①은 글의 내용과 맞지 않다. ③ 또한 문화적 산물을 특정 캐릭터들에 대한 편견을 형성시키는 주체로 보고 있어 답으로 부적절하다.

▶ 문제 해결 방법은?
첫 문장에서 주제를 제시한 후 이를 뒷받침하는 연구의 내용을 후술한 글이다. 따라서 연구의 결론을 나타내는 빈칸 문장은 첫 문장과 동일한 내용일 것임을 예측할 수 있다.

09 인간의 사고력에 대한 믿음
정답률 49% | 정답 ④

다음 글에서 전체 흐름과 관계 <u>없는</u> 문장은?

[본문 해석]
서구권 문화에는 인간이 본질적으로 이성적이며, 사실과 허구를 능숙하게 가려내고, 최종적으로 세상에 대한 영원한 진리에 도달한다는 널리 스며 있는 관념이 있다. ① 이러한 사고방식은 인간은 논리의 규칙을 따르고, 가능성을 정확히 계산하며, 모든 이용 가능한 정보에 의해 완벽히 정보를 갖춘 판단을 세상에 대해 내린다고 주장한다. ② 반대로 효과적이고 정보를 잘 갖춘 판단을 내리지 못하는 것은 흔히 인간 사고의 실패 탓으로 여겨지는데, 예를 들어 심리적 장애나 인지적 편견에서 비롯된다고 여겨진다. ③ 이러한 상황에서 우리가 성공할 것인가 실패할 것인가는 개개인이 이성적이고 지적인지 아닌지의 문제인 것으로 판명된다. ④ 이성적인 판단을 내리는 우리의 능력은 우리의 개인적 심리보다 우리의 사회적 상호작용과 더욱 관련이 있다. ⑤ 그러므로 우리가 더 참된 신념과 더 나은 판단과 같은 더 나은 결과를 성취하기를 원한다면, 우리는 개개인의 사고를 향상하는 것에 집중할 필요가 있다.

Why? 왜 정답일까?

서구권에서 인간은 이성적 존재로 여겨지기에 판단의 실패는 개인의 능력 부족 탓으로 여겨지며, 문제 해결의 실마리 또한 개인의 능력 향상에 있다고 간주된다는 내용의 글이다. 하지만 ④는 인간의 이성적 사고 능력이 개인의 심리보다는 사회적 상호작용과 더 관련이 있다는 내용이므로 흐름에서 벗어난다. 따라서 전체 흐름과 관계 없는 문장은 ④이다.

- sort A from B A와 B를 가려내다
- timeless ⓐ 영원한
- probability ⓝ 확률, 가능성
- be attributed to ~의 탓이다
- ultimately ⓐⓓ 궁극적으로
- calculate ⓥ 계산하다
- accurately ⓐⓓ 정확하게
- have to do with ~와 관련이 있다

구문 풀이

1행 There is a pervasive idea in Western culture {that humans (동사 주어) are essentially rational, skillfully sorting fact from fiction, and, ultimately, arriving at timeless truths about the world}. { } : 주어 동격

★★★ 1등급 대비 고난도 3점 문제

10 언어 프레이밍의 중요성
정답률 46% | 정답 ③

글의 흐름으로 보아, 주어진 문장이 들어가기에 가장 적절한 곳을 고르시오. [3점]

[본문 해석]
프레이밍은 많은 영역에서 중요하다. ① 신용 카드가 1970년대에 인기 있는 지불 방식이 되기 시작했을 때, 몇몇 소매상들은 현금 고객과 신용 카드 고객에게 다른 가격을 청구하기를 원했다. ② 이것을 막기 위해서, 신용 카드 회사들은 소매상들이 현금 고객과 신용 카드 고객에게 다른 가격을 청구하는 것을 막는 규정을 채택했다. ③ 하지만, 그러한 규정들을 금지하기 위한 법안이 의회에 제출되었을 때, 신용 카드 압력단체는 언어로 주의를 돌렸다. 그 단체가 선호하는 것은 만약 회사가 다른 가격을 현금 고객과 신용 카드 고객에게 청구한다면, 현금 가격을 보통 가격으로 만들고 신용 카드 고객에게 추가금을 청구하는 방안보다는, 신용 카드 가격이 '정상'(디폴트) 가격, 현금 가격이 할인으로 여겨져야 한다는 것이었다. ④ 신용 카드 회사들은 심리학자들이 '프레이밍'이라고 부르게 된 것에 대한 훌륭한 직관적 이해를 하고 있었다. ⑤ 이러한 발상은 선택이 어느 정도는 문제들이 언급되는 방식에 달려있다는 것이다.

Why? 왜 정답일까?

어떤 문제가 어떤 표현으로 언급되는지, 즉 문제가 '프레이밍'되는 방식이 중요하다는 내용을 다룬 글이다. ③ 앞의 두 문장에서 신용 카드가 널리 사용되면서 소매상들이 현금 지불 시의 가격과 카드 지불 시의 가격을 달리하고 싶어 하자 카드 회사에서 이를 막는 규정을 채택했다는 내용을 말하는데, 주어진 문장에서는 이때 카드 회사의 주의가 '언어'로 향했다는 점을 환기시킨다. ③ 뒤의 문장에서는 카드 회사에서 카드 지불 시의 가격을 '정상' 가격, 현금 가격을 '할인' 가격으로 명명함으로써 문제의 인식을 달리하려고 시도했다는 내용을 이어서 말한다. 따라서 주어진 문장이 들어가기에 가장 적절한 곳은 ③이다.

- bill ⓝ (국회에 제출된) 법안
- domain ⓝ 영역, 분야
- merchant ⓝ 상인, 무역상
- default ⓝ 디폴트, (기본으로) 내정된 값
- outlaw ⓥ 금지하다, 불법화하다
- retail ⓝ 소매 ⓐ 소매의
- charge A to B A를 B에 부과하다
- surcharge ⓝ 추가 요금

구문 풀이

10행 Its preference was that (if a company charged different prices (접속사 ( ) : 부사절) to cash and credit customers), the credit price should be considered (주어 조동사 수동태) the "normal" (default) price and the cash price (should be considered) (주격 보어1 주어2 생략) a discount — rather than the alternative of making the cash price (주격 보어2 전치사 ↳ 동명사1 목적어) the usual price and charging a surcharge to credit card customers. (목적격 보어 동명사2)

★★ 문제 해결 꿀~팁 ★★

▶ 많이 틀린 이유는?
문제를 기술하는 언어 표현이 중요하다는 주제를 신용 카드 회사의 예로 제시하는 글로서, 주어진 문장은 예시 부분에 있다. 주어진 문장은 However로 시작하며 '언어'에 대한 관심을 환기하므로, 이미 가격의 '표현' 문제를 언급하고 있는 'Its preference was that ~'보다 앞에 나와야 한다.

▶ 문제 해결 방법은?
③ 뒤의 대명사 Its에 주목한다. ③ 앞의 문장에서 '카드 회사'는 credit card companies와 같이 복수형으로 제시되므로 ③ 뒤에서 이를 단수대명사 Its로 받을 수는 없다. 따라서 이 Its는 주어진 문장의 the card lobby를 받는다고 보아야 한다.

11-12 평범하지 않은 것이 더 잘 기억나는 이유

[본문 해석]
「평범하지 않은 사건들이나 경험들은 당신의 뇌가 기억된 사건들의 창고에서 그것들에 접근하려고 할 때 더 잘 기억되는 경향이 있는데, 그것들과 경쟁하는

DAY 09

것이 없기 때문이다.」 다시 말해, 2주 전 목요일에 아침 식사로 무엇을 먹었는 지 기억하기가 (a) 어려울 수 있는 이유는 아마도 그 목요일이나 그 특정 아침 식사에 대해 특별한 게 없었기 때문이다. 그 결과, 당신의 모든 아침 식사 기억 은 일종의 일반적인 아침 식사에 대한 인상으로 (b) 합쳐진다. 여러분의 기억 력은 유사한 사건들을 병합하는데, 그것은 그렇게 하는 것이 더 효율적일 뿐만 아니라, 이것이 우리가 어떤 것들을 배우는 방법의 기본이기 때문이다. 우리의 뇌는 경험을 함께 묶는 추상적인 규칙들을 추출한다.

이것은 (c) 일상적인 것들에 특히 해당된다. 만약 당신의 아침 식사가 항상 같다 면—예를 들어, 우유를 곁들인 시리얼, 오렌지 주스 한 잔, 커피 한 잔—당신 의 뇌가 특정한 한 아침 식사에서 그 세부 사항을 추출하기는 쉽지 않다. 그래 서 아이러니하게도, 일상화된 행동의 경우, 당신은 그 행동의 일반적인 내용 (가령 당신이 먹었던 것, 당신은 항상 같은 것을 먹기 때문에)은 「기억할 수 있 지만, 그 한 가지 예의 (d) 세부 사항들(쓰레기 트럭이 지나가는 소리나 창문을 지나치는 새소리 같이)은 매우 특이하지 않다면 상기하기가 매우 어려울 수 있 다.」 반면에, 만약 당신이 일상을 깨뜨리는 특이한 일을 했다면—어쩌면 아침 식사로 남은 피자를 먹고 와이셔츠에 토마토 소스를 쏟았을 수도 있다—당신 은 그것을 기억하기 (e) 덜(→더) 쉽다.

`「」:11번의 근거` (옆 표시)
`「」:12번의 근거` (옆 표시)

- out of (the) ordinary 평범하지 않은
- merge ⓥ 병합하다
- routinize ⓥ 일상화하다, 습관화하다
- distinctive ⓐ 독특한
- spill ⓥ 쏟다
- generic ⓐ 일반적인
- extract ⓥ 추출하다
- garbage ⓝ 쓰레기
- leftover ⓐ 남긴 ⓝ 남은 음식

구문 풀이

1행 Events or experiences [that are out of ordinary] tend to be
(주어) (동사구)
remembered better because there is nothing competing with them
(현재분사구)
when your brain tries to access them from its storehouse of
(= events or experiences)
remembered events.

11 제목 파악 | 정답률 46% | 정답 ⑤

윗글의 제목으로 가장 적절한 것은?

① Repetition Makes Your Memory Sharp!
반복은 여러분의 기억이 예리해지게 한다!
② How Does Your Memory Get Distorted?
기억은 어떻게 왜곡되는가?
③ What to Consider in Routinizing Your Work
작업을 일상화할 때 고려해야 할 것
④ Merging Experiences: Key to Remembering Details
기억의 통합: 세부 사항을 기억하는 데 있어 핵심
✓⑤ The More Unique Events, the More Vivid Recollection
사건이 더 특이할수록, 기억은 더 생생해진다

Why? 왜 정답일까?

특이한 사건이 보통 사건보다 기억이 잘 나는(Events or experiences that are out of ordinary tend to be remembered better ~) 이유에 관한 글이므로, 글의 제목 으로 가장 적절한 것은 ⑤ '사건이 더 특이할수록, 기억은 더 생생해진다'이다.

12 어휘 추론 | 정답률 69% | 정답 ⑤

밑줄 친 (a) ~ (e) 중에서 문맥상 낱말의 쓰임이 적절하지 않은 것은?

① (a)   ② (b)   ③ (c)   ④ (d)   ✓⑤ (e)

Why? 왜 정답일까?

(e)가 포함된 문장 바로 앞에서, 어떤 사건의 세부 사항은 '특이하지 않은 이상' 일반적인 기억 속에 통합되어 버려 구체적으로 상기되기 어렵다고 한다(particulars to that one instance can be very difficult to call up (such as the sound of a garbage truck going by or a bird that passed by your window) *unless* they were especially distinctive). 이러한 흐름으로 보아, (e)의 less를 more로 고쳐야 흐름에 적합하다. 따라서 낱말의 쓰임이 문맥상 적절하지 않은 것은 ⑤ '(e)'이다.

DAY 10 20분 미니 모의고사

01 ③	02 ⑤	03 ②	04 ⑤	05 ⑤
06 ②	07 ②	08 ③	09 ①	10 ④
11 ⑤	12 ③			

01 동료의 격려로 힘을 되찾은 Jamie | 정답률 88% | 정답 ③

다음 글에 드러난 Jamie의 심경 변화로 가장 적절한 것은?

① indifferent → regretful
무관심한 후회하는
② pleased → bored
기쁜 지루한
✓③ frustrated → encouraged
좌절한 고무된
④ nervous → fearful
초조한 무서워하는
⑤ calm → excited
차분한 신이 난

[본문 해석]

Jamie는 자신의 모든 에너지를 달리기 경주의 마지막 한 바퀴에 쏟아부으며 결승 선을 통과했다. 실망스럽게도, 그녀는 개인 최고 기록을 깨는 데 또 실패했다. Jamie는 기어코 자기 기록을 깨기 위해 몇 달 동안 자신을 몰아붙였지만, 그것 은 모두 수포로 돌아갔다. 그녀가 실패에 관해 어떤 기분을 느끼는지 알아차린 팀 동료인 Ken은 그녀에게 다가와 말했다. "Jamie, 비록 오늘 네가 개인 최고 기록을 세우지 못했지만 너의 경기력은 극적으로 향상됐어. 네 달리기 기량이 아주 많이 발전했어! 다음 경주에서 너는 분명히 개인 최고 기록을 깰 거야!" 그의 말을 들은 후, 그녀는 자신감을 느꼈다. 이제 목표를 계속 밀고 나갈 의욕 을 갖게 된 Jamie는 미소를 지으며 대답했다. "네 말이 맞아! 다음 경주에서 나 는 틀림없이 최고 기록을 깰 거야!"

Why? 왜 정답일까?

기록 경신에 실패해서 실망했던(To her disappointment ~) Jamie가 팀원의 응원 을 받고 자신감(felt confident)과 의욕(motivated)을 되찾았다는 내용이다. 따라서 Jamie의 심경 변화로 가장 적절한 것은 ③ '좌절한 → 고무된(frustrated → encouraged)'이다.

- put energy into ~에 에너지를 쏟다
- fail to ~하지 못하다
- break a record 기록을 깨다
- approach ⓥ 다가오다, 접근하다
- dramatically ⓐⓓ 극적으로
- definitely ⓐⓓ 확실히
- be motivated to ~할 의욕을 갖다
- frustrated ⓐ 좌절한
- cross the finish line 결승선을 통과하다
- beat a record 기록을 깨다
- for nothing 헛되이
- performance ⓝ 경기, 수행, 성과, 공연
- progress ⓥ 나아지다, 발전하다
- confident ⓐ 자신 있는
- regretful ⓐ 후회하는
- fearful ⓐ 무서워하는

구문 풀이

4행 Jamie had pushed herself for months to finally break her
(과거완료(was보다 과거)) (목적(finally는 to부정사 수식))
record, but it was all for nothing.

02 변화를 받아들이고 성장하는 것의 중요성 | 정답률 60% | 정답 ⑤

다음 글의 요지로 가장 적절한 것은?

① 다양한 업종의 경력이 있으면 구직 활동에 유리하다.
② 직원의 다양한 능력을 활용하면 업계를 주도할 수 있다.
③ 기술이 발전함에 따라 단순 반복 업무가 사라지고 있다.
④ 자신의 약점을 인정하면 동료들로부터 도움을 얻기 쉽다.
✓⑤ 변화를 받아들이지 못하면 업계에서의 적합성을 잃게 된다.

[본문 해석]

성장과 발전에 실패한 브랜드는 그 적합성을 잃는다. 한때 여러분의 회사에서 승진 가도에 있었는데 더 이상 회사에 있지 않거나, 더 나쁜 예로는 경력의 정 체기에 든 것으로 보이는 지인을 생각해 보라. 그 사람이 야심에 찬 행동을 하 지 않았다고 가정하면, 대개 이 사람은 자기 업계에서 적합성을 유지하고 발전 을 포용하지 못한 것의 희생자이다. 개인용 컴퓨터 사용 기술이 이 기술을 접한 첫 물결의 경영 지도자에게 미친 영향을 생각해 보라. 기술을 포용한 이들은 그것을 그들의 작업 스타일에 흡수시켜서 탁월해질 수 있었다. 여러 번 (기술에) 저항한 이들은 경력을 발전시키기 위한 기회를 거의 찾을 수 없었고, 많은 경우

이들은 결국 적합성을 유지하고 기술을 새롭게 하는 데 실패하여 이른 은퇴를 통해 해고되었다.

Why? 왜 정답일까?

첫 문장에서 성장과 발전에 실패한 브랜드는 그 적합성을 잃게 된다고 한다. 두 번째 문장부터는 이를 직장 상황에 적용하여, 변화에 적응해 자신의 가치를 높이지 못한 직원들은 일찍이 도태되는 결과를 맞는다고 설명하고 있다. 따라서 글의 요지로 가장 적절한 것은 ⑤ '변화를 받아들이지 못하면 업계에서의 적합성을 잃게 된다.'이다.

- relevance ⓝ 적합성, 적절성
- assume ⓥ 가정하다
- victim ⓝ 희생자
- industry ⓝ 업계, 산업
- integrate ⓥ 통합하다
- let go ~을 해고하다
- hit a plateau 정체기에 들다
- ambitious ⓐ 야망 있는
- embrace ⓥ 포용하다
- executive ⓐ 경영의, 간부의
- resistant ⓐ 저항하는, 내성 있는
- retirement ⓝ 은퇴

구문 풀이

1행 Brands [that fail to grow and develop] lose their relevance.
주어 [ ]: 주어 수식 동사(복수)

---

03 자유 시장의 순기능   정답률 57% | 정답 ②

다음 글의 제목으로 가장 적절한 것은?
① Trade War: A Reflection of Human's Innate Violence
무역 전쟁: 인간의 타고난 폭력의 반영
✓② Free Market: Winning Together over Losing Together
자유 시장: 함께 지기보다 함께 이기기
③ New Economic Framework Stabilizes the Free Market
새로운 경제 체제는 자유 시장을 안정시킨다
④ Violence Is the Invisible Hand That Disrupts Capitalism!
폭력은 자본주의를 교란하는 보이지 않는 손이다!
⑤ How Are Governments Involved in Controlling the Market?
정부는 시장 통제에 어떻게 관여하는가?

[본문 해석]

자유 시장은 마르크스주의가 결코 할 수 없었던 방식으로 사람들을 자유롭게 해 왔다. 게다가 하버드 대학 경제 역사학자인 A. O. Hirschman이 대표적 연구인 *The Passions and the Interests*에서 보여주었듯이, 시장은 계몽주의 사상가들인 Adam Smith, David Hume 그리고 Montesquieu에 의해 인류의 가장 큰 전통적 약점들 중 하나인 폭력에 대한 강력한 해결책으로 여겨졌다. Montesquieu가 말했던 바로, 두 국가는 만나서 두 가지 중 하나를 할 수 있는데, 즉 전쟁을 벌이거나 거래를 할 수 있다. 만약 그들이 전쟁을 벌인다면, 둘 다 장기적으로 손해를 볼 가능성이 있다. 만약 그들이 거래를 한다면, 둘 다 이득을 얻을 것이다. 물론 그것이 유럽 연합의 설립 이면에 있는 논리였다. 즉 연합의 국가들, 특히 프랑스와 독일의 운명을 한데 묶었는데, 그렇게 함으로써 그들은 20세기 전반에 너무나도 파괴적인 대가를 치르며 벌였던 전쟁을 다시는 벌이지 않는다는 저항할 수 없는 이해관계를 가졌을 것이다.

Why? 왜 정답일까?

'~ the market was seen ~ as a powerful solution to ~ violence.'에서 자유 시장은 국가 간 폭력에 대한 강력한 해결책으로 여겨졌다는 핵심 내용을 제시한다. 이어서 예시에 따르면 어떤 두 국가가 만났을 때 전쟁 또는 거래라는 선택지가 주어지는데, 전쟁은 둘 다에 실이 되는 한편 거래는 둘 다에 득이 되기에 유럽 연합 등의 기구가 출현하여 자유 시장을 촉진하고 전쟁을 억제하는 기능을 수행하게 되었다고 한다. 따라서 글의 제목으로 가장 적절한 것은 자유 시장의 순기능을 적절히 요약한 ② '자유 시장: 함께 지기보다 함께 이기기'이다.

- classic ⓐ 전형적인, 고전적인
- wage war 전쟁을 벌이다
- overwhelming ⓐ 저항할 수 없는, 압도적인
- reflection ⓝ 반영, 성찰
- Enlightenment ⓝ (18세기) 계몽주의
- establishment ⓝ 설립
- devastating ⓐ 참담한
- disrupt ⓥ 교란시키다

구문 풀이

11행 That, of course, was the logic behind the establishment of
주어 보어
the European Union: {to lock together the destinies of its nations,
{ }: 보어 동격
(especially France and Germany), in such a way [that they would
( ): 삽입구 선행사
have an overwhelming interest not to wage war again as they had
접속사(~듯이)
done to such devastating cost in the first half of the twentieth
century]}.

---

04 Carl-Gustaf Rossby의 생애   정답률 90% | 정답 ⑤

Carl-Gustaf Rossby에 관한 다음 글의 내용과 일치하지 않는 것은?
① Stockholm에서 성장하면서 전통적인 교육을 받았다.
② University of Stockholm에서 수리 물리학 학위를 받았다.
③ 1925년에 장학금을 받았다.
④ polar front theory를 지지했다.
✓⑤ University of Stockholm에 마련된 직책을 거절했다.

[본문 해석]

Carl-Gustaf Rossby는 Bergen 대학에서 노르웨이 기상학자인 Vilhelm Bjerknes와 함께 일했던 저명한 스칸디나비아 연구자들 중 한 명이었다. 『Stockholm에서 성장하면서, Rossby는 전통적인 교육을 받았다.』①의 근거 일치 『그는 1918년에 University of Stockholm에서 수리 물리학 학위를 받았지만,』②의 근거 일치 Bjerknes의 강의를 듣고 나서 아마도 Stockholm에 대한 지루함 때문에 Bergen에 새로 설립된 지구 물리학 연구소로 옮겼다. 『1925년에 Rossby는 스웨덴-미국 재단으로부터 장학금을 받아 미국으로 갔고, 그곳에서 미국 기상국에 입사했다.』③의 근거 일치 일기 예보에 대한 그의 실질적인 경험을 일부 바탕으로 하여, 『Rossby는 고온 기단과 저온 기단 사이의 경계에서 발생하는 사이클론 순환을 설명하는 'polar front theory'의 지지자가 되었다.』④의 근거 일치 『1947년에 Rossby는 University of Stockholm에 자신을 위해 마련된 기상 연구소장 직책을 받아들였고, 그곳에서 10년 후 생을 마감할 때까지 재직했다.』⑤의 근거 불일치

Why? 왜 정답일까?

'In 1947, Rossby accepted the chair of the Institute of Meteorology, which had been set up for him at the University of Stockholm, ~'에 따르면 Carl-Gustaf Rossby는 University of Stockholm에 마련된 기상 연구소장 직책을 수락했고, 여기서 사망할 때까지 재직했다고 한다. 따라서 내용과 일치하지 않는 것은 ⑤ 'University of Stockholm에 마련된 직책을 거절했다.'이다.

Why? 왜 오답일까?

① 'While growing up in Stockholm, Rossby received a traditional education.'의 내용과 일치한다.
② 'He earned a degree in mathematical physics at the University of Stockholm in 1918, ~'의 내용과 일치한다.
③ 'In 1925, Rossby received a scholarship ~'의 내용과 일치한다.
④ '~ Rossby had become a supporter of the "polar front theory," ~'의 내용과 일치한다.

- notable ⓐ 저명한
- earn a degree 학위를 받다
- practical ⓐ 실질적인, 현실적인
- cyclonic ⓐ 사이클론의, 격렬한
- meteorologist ⓝ 기상학자
- receive a scholarship 장학금을 받다
- weather forecasting 기상 예보
- circulation ⓝ 순환

구문 풀이

12행 Based in part on his practical experience in weather
분사구문
forecasting, Rossby had become a supporter of the "polar front theory,"
주어 선행사
which explains the cyclonic circulation [that develops at the boundary
계속적 용법
between warm and cold air masses].

★★★ 1등급 대비 고난도 3점 문제

05 긍정적 강화에 대한 실험   정답률 34% | 정답 ⑤

다음 글의 밑줄 친 부분 중, 어법상 틀린 것은? [3점]

[본문 해석]

Harvard에서 연구원으로 일하는 동안, B. F. Skinner는 후에 'Skinner box'로 알려지게 된 발명품을 사용하여, 쥐를 대상으로 일련의 실험을 수행했다. 이 상자들 중 하나에 쥐 한 마리를 넣었는데, 이 상자에는 내부에 끼워져 있는 특별한 막대가 있었다. 쥐는 이 막대를 누를 때마다 음식을 받았다. 막대를 누르는 비율이 자동으로 기록되었다. 처음에 쥐는 우연히, 또는 단순히 호기심으로 막대를 눌렀을 것이고, 그리고 그 결과로 약간의 음식을 받았을 것이다. 시간이 지나면서, 쥐는 막대가 눌러질 때마다 음식이 나타난다는 것을 학습했고, 먹이를 받기 위해 일부러 그것을 누르기 시작했다. 막대 누르는 행동에 대해

음식이라는 '긍정적인 강화'가 주어진 쥐들에게서 나온 결과를 그렇지 않았거나(강화가 없었거나) 음식을 다른 비율로 받은 쥐들과 비교해보니, 쥐의 행동의 결과로 음식이 나타났을 때, 이것이 쥐의 향후 행동에 영향을 미쳤다는 것이 분명해졌다.

Why? 왜 정답일까?

마지막 문장에서 주절이 'it became clear ~'이고 Comparing이 접속사 없이 분사구문으로 쓰인 것으로 볼 때, 문장에 또 다른 동사가 나올 수 없다. 즉 gives는 동사가 아닌 준동사로 바뀌어야 하는데, 여기서는 앞에 나오는 명사 rats를 꾸밀 수 있도록 gives를 과거분사인 given으로 바꾸는 것이 적절하다. 따라서 어법상 틀린 것은 ⑤이다. rats가 '주는' 주체가 아니라 '받는' 대상이기 때문에 giving이 아닌 given을 쓴다는 점에 주의한다.

Why? 왜 오답일까?

① 사물 선행사 one of these boxes를 보충 설명하기 위해 주어가 없는 불완전한 문장을 연결하는 which가 바르게 쓰였다.
② 수동태 동사 was recorded를 꾸미기 위해 부사 automatically가 적절하게 쓰였다.
③ 등위접속사 and 앞뒤로 동사구 might press와 병렬을 이루는 또 다른 동사가 필요하므로 receive가 바르게 쓰였다.
④ 단수 명사 the bar를 받는 단수 대명사 it이 바르게 쓰였다.

- **carry out** ~을 수행하다
- **automatically** [ad] 자동적으로
- **accidentally** [ad] 우연히
- **purposefully** [ad] 일부러, 목적을 갖고
- **reinforcement** ⑪ 강화
- **present A with B** A에게 B를 주다
- **initially** [ad] 처음에
- **as a consequence** 그 결과

구문 풀이

12행 Comparing results from rats [(that were) given the "positive
「compare + A + 선행사   생략
reinforcement" of food for their bar-pressing behavior] with those
                                        with + B : A와 B를 비교하다」
[that were not, or were presented with food at different rates], it
                                                가주어
became clear {that when food appeared as a consequence of the
rat's actions, this influenced its future behavior}. { }: 진주어

★★ 문제 해결 꿀~팁 ★★

▶ 많이 틀린 이유는?
③은 and 앞뒤의 병렬구조를 묻는 선택지이다. 'or simply out of curiosity', 'as a consequence' 등 불필요한 부사구를 지워보면 'might press ~'와 'receive ~'가 병렬구조임을 알 수 있다.
▶ 문제 해결 방법은?
정답인 ⑤가 포함된 문장은 분사구문, 관계절, 가주어-진주어 구문 등이 함께 쓰여 그 구조가 복잡하다. 수식어구를 전부 괄호로 묶으면, 주절인 'it became clear ~' 앞의 분사구문은 Comparing A (~) with B (~)의 구조를 띠고, ⑤는 이중 A의 일부인 rats를 꾸미는 수식어구 자리임을 파악할 수 있다.

★★★ 1등급 대비 고난도 2점 문제

06 오래된 이야기를 더 잘 믿는 사람들 정답률 38% | 정답 ②

다음 글의 밑줄 친 부분 중, 문맥상 낱말의 쓰임이 적절하지 않은 것은?

[본문 해석]

등골이 오싹한 유령 이야기는 정말 무섭다면 들려주기에 재밌고, 만약 당신이 그 이야기가 사실이라고 주장하면 훨씬 더 그렇다. 사람들은 그런 이야기를 전달하는 것으로부터 ① 스릴을 느낀다. 같은 것이 기적 이야기에도 적용된다. 만약 기적에 대한 소문이 어떤 책에 쓰인다면, 특히 그 책이 아주 오래되었을 경우 그 소문은 ② 믿기(→ 의문을 제기하기) 힘들어진다. 만약 소문이 충분히 ③ 오래된 것이라면, 그것은 대신 '전통'으로 불리기 시작하고, 그러면 사람들은 그것을 한결 더 믿는다. 이것은 다소 이상한데, 그 이유는 그들이 (근거 없이) 주장된 사건 그 자체에 시간상 가까운 최근의 소문보다 오래된 소문이 ④ 왜곡될 시간이 더 많다는 점을 깨달을 것이라고 당신이 생각할 수 있기 때문이다. Elvis Presley와 Michael Jackson은 전통이 생겨나기에는 너무 ⑤ 최근에 살아서 "Elvis가 화성에서 목격되었다"와 같은 이야기를 믿는 사람은 많지 않다.

Why? 왜 정답일까?

'If a rumor is old enough, ~' 이후로 오래된 소문일수록 '전통'처럼 취급되어 사람

들이 더 잘 믿는다는 내용이 언급되고 있다. 이에 근거할 때, 아주 오래된 책에 적힌 이야기는 사람들의 믿음을 더 많이 사게 되어 이 이야기에 대한 '의문을 제기하기가' 어려워질 것을 유추할 수 있다. 따라서 ②의 **believe**는 **challenge**로 고쳐야 한다. 문맥상 낱말의 쓰임이 적절하지 않은 것은 ②이다.

- **spine-tingling** 등골이 오싹한, 스릴 넘치는
- **ancient** ⓐ 아주 오래된, 고대의
- **alleged** ⓐ (증거 없이) 주장된, ~이라고들 말하는
- **pass on** ~을 전해주다
- **distort** ⓥ 왜곡하다

구문 풀이

9행 This is rather odd because you might think (that) they would
        접속사(~ 때문에)   생략(접속사)
realize that older rumors have had more time to get distorted than
    접속사(~것)   현재완료
younger rumors [that are close in time to the alleged events
    선행사   주격 관계대명사
themselves].
재귀대명사(events 강조)

★★ 문제 해결 꿀~팁 ★★

▶ 많이 틀린 이유는?
④가 포함된 문장은 오래된 루머가 왜 신뢰를 얻는지에 대한 의문을 제기하고 있다. 즉 더 오래된 루머는 생겨난 지 오래라 그만큼 '왜곡될' 기회도 더 많았을 텐데 왜 더 믿을 만하다고 여겨지는지 궁금해한다는 의미를 나타내기 위해 ④의 **distorted**가 바르게 쓰였다. 또한 ⑤가 포함된 문장의 so 뒤에서 사람들이 Elvis에 관한 루머를 잘 믿지 않는다고 언급하는데, 이는 글의 논리에 따르면 그가 비교적 '최근에' 살았던 사람이기 때문일 것임을 유추할 수 있다. 따라서 **recently**도 맞게 쓰였다.
▶ 문제 해결 방법은?
'소문이 오래될수록 더 잘 믿어진다'는 주제문과 'especially if the book ~'를 힌트로 삼도록 한다.

★★★ 1등급 대비 고난도 3점 문제

07 우정이 싹트게 하는 요인 정답률 34% | 정답 ②

다음 빈칸에 들어갈 말로 가장 적절한 것을 고르시오. [3점]
① shared value - 공유된 가치
② physical space - 물리적 공간 ✓
③ conscious effort - 의식적 노력
④ similar character - 비슷한 성격
⑤ psychological support - 심리적 지지

[본문 해석]

심리학자 Leon Festinger, Stanley Schachter, 그리고 사회학자 Kurt Back은 우정이 어떻게 형성되는지 궁금해 하기 시작했다. 왜 몇몇 타인들은 지속적인 우정을 쌓는 반면, 다른 이들은 기본적인 상투적인 말을 넘어서는 데 어려움을 겪을까? 몇몇 전문가들은 우정 형성이 유아기로 거슬러 올라갈 수 있다고 설명했는데, 그 시기에 아이들은 훗날 삶에서 그들을 결합시키거나 분리시킬 수도 있는 가치, 신념, 그리고 태도를 습득했다. 그러나 Festinger, Schachter, 그리고 Back은 다른 이론을 추구하였다. 그 연구자들은 물리적 공간이 우정 형성의 핵심이라고, 즉 "우정은 집을 오가거나 동네 주변을 걸어 다니면서 이루어지는 짧고 수동적인 접촉에 근거하여 발달하는 것 같다."라고 믿었다. 그들의 관점에서는 유사한 태도를 지닌 사람들이 친구가 된다기보다는 그날 동안 서로를 지나쳐 가는 사람들이 친구가 되는 경향이 있고 그래서 시간이 지남에 따라 유사한 태도를 받아들이게 되었다.

Why? 왜 정답일까?

빈칸 뒤의 인용구 'friendships are likely to develop on the basis of brief and passive contacts made going to and from home or walking about the neighborhood.'에서 우정은 집을 오가거나 동네 주변을 걸어 다니며 우연히 만나거나 접촉한 사람들 사이에서 발달하는 듯하다는 연구자들의 믿음을 제시하고 있으므로, 빈칸에 들어갈 말로 가장 적절한 것은 ② '물리적 공간'이다.

- **psychologist** ⑪ 심리학자
- **wonder** ⓥ 궁금하다, 궁금해 하다
- **struggle** ⓥ 투쟁하다, 노력하다
- **infancy** ⑪ 유아기
- **attitude** ⑪ 태도
- **separate** ⓥ 분리시키다
- **passive** ⓐ 수동적인
- **similar** ⓐ 유사한
- **sociologist** ⑪ 사회학자
- **lasting** ⓐ 지속적인
- **be traced to** ~로 거슬러 올라가다
- **acquire** ⓥ 습득하다
- **bind** ⓥ 묶다, 결속하다
- **pursue** ⓥ 추구하다
- **on the basis of** ~을 기반으로

구문 풀이

13행 In their view, it wasn't so much {that people with similar
「not so much + A + but + B : A라기보다 B인」　　주어
attitudes became friends}, but rather {that people [who passed each
동사　　　　　　　　　　　　　　　　　　주어
other during the day] tended to become friends and so came to adopt
동사1　　　　　　　　　　　　　　　동사2
similar attitudes over time}.

★★ 문제 해결 꿀~팁 ★★

▶ 많이 틀린 이유는?
빈칸이 글 중간에 나오므로 뒤에 주로 힌트가 있다. 최다 오답인 ④는 서로 스쳐가는 사람들이 친구가 되고 나중에야 비슷한 태도를 받아들이는 것이라는 내용의 마지막 문장을 근거로 할 때 답으로 부적절하다.

▶ 문제 해결 방법은?
'~ on the basis of brief and passive contacts made going to and from home or walking about the neighborhood.'와 'people who passed each other during the day'가 서로 같은 내용임에 유의한다. 즉 주변에서 오며 가며 자주 보고 스치는 사람끼리 친구가 된다는 것이 글의 주제이다.

08 조수간만의 차 　　정답률 35% | 정답 ③

글의 흐름으로 보아, 주어진 문장이 들어가기에 가장 적절한 곳을 고르시오. [3점]

[본문 해석]
우리 행성의 여러 부분에 대한 달 중력의 차이는 효과적으로 '잡아 늘리는 힘'을 만든다. ① 그것은 우리 행성이 달이 보이는 쪽으로 약간 늘어나고, 그것에 직각을 이루는 선을 따라 약간 눌리게 만든다. ② 달의 중력으로 발생하는 조수의 팽창은 땅과 물을 포함한 우리 행성 전체에 안팎으로 영향을 미친다. ③ 하지만 암석의 단단함은 땅이 물보다는 훨씬 적은 양만큼 조수와 함께 오르락내리락한다는 것을 의미하며, 이 이유로 우리는 오로지 바다의 조수만을 알아차리게 된다. 또한, 그 팽창은 왜 일반적으로 매일 바다에서 두 번의 만조(그리고 두 번의 간조)가 발생하는지 설명한다. ④ 지구가 고무줄처럼 늘어나기 때문에, 바다는 달을 향하는 쪽에서도, 달에서 멀어지는 쪽에서도 팽창해 나간다. ⑤ 지구가 자전함에 따라 우리는 매일 이 두 개의 조수 팽창부를 통과하게 되어서, 우리가 각각 두 개의 팽창부에 있을 때 만조를 겪고 그 사이 중간 지점에 있을 때 간조를 겪는다.

Why? 왜 정답일까?
조수간만의 차가 발생하는 이유를 설명하는 글이다. 달의 중력은 지구의 영역마다 다르게 작용하기 때문에 지구는 달을 보는 쪽을 따라 늘어나고, 이와 직각을 이루는 지점에서는 줄어든다는 배경 설명이 ③ 앞까지 이어진다. 이때 주어진 문장은 암석으로 이뤄진 지구의 땅은 팽창과 수축이 덜 드러나는 반면, 바다의 물은 보다 크게 차이를 보인다고 설명한다. **also**로 시작하는 ③ 뒤의 문장부터는 조수간만의 차가 일어나는 횟수에 관해 언급하며 앞과 내용상 달라진다. 따라서 주어진 문장이 들어가기에 가장 적절한 곳은 ③이다.

- **rigidity** ⓝ 단단함
- **slightly** ⓐⓓ 약간
- **inside and out** 안팎으로
- **carry through** 헤쳐나가다, 달성하다
- **tide** ⓝ 조수, 밀물과 썰물
- **perpendicular** ⓐ 직각을 이루는
- **bulge** ⓥ 팽창하다 ⓝ 튀어나온 것
- **midpoint** ⓝ 중간 지점

구문 풀이
1행 However, the rigidity of rock means that land rises and falls
with the tides by a much smaller amount than water, which is why
선행사(문장)　　　　　　　　　　　　　　　　계속적 용법
we notice only the ocean tides.

09 행동이 결정이나 생각에 무의식적으로 미치는 영향 　정답률 57% | 정답 ①

다음 글의 내용을 한 문장으로 요약하고자 한다. 빈칸 (A), (B)에 들어갈 말로 가장 적절한 것은?

	(A)	(B)		(A)	(B)
✔	favorably 호의적으로	behavior 행동	②	favorably 호의적으로	instinct 본능
③	unfavorably 호의적이지 않게	feeling 감정	④	unfavorably 호의적이지 않게	gesture 몸짓
⑤	irrationally 불합리하게	prejudice 편견			

[본문 해석]
사람들은 특정한 생각을 할 때 매우 예측 가능하게 행동한다. 그들은 동의할 때 고개를 끄덕인다. 여기까지는 놀랍지 않지만, '고유 수용 심리학'이라고 알려진 한 연구 분야에 따르면, 그 과정은 거꾸로도 작용한다. 사람들을 특정한 방식으로 행동하게 하면, 당신은 그들이 특정한 생각을 갖게 하는 것이다. 이 관념은 처음에는 논란의 여지가 있었지만, 다행히도 설득력 있는 실험으로 뒷받침되었다. 한 연구에서, 참가자들은 큰 컴퓨터 화면을 가로질러 움직이는 다양한 제품들에 시선을 고정하고, 그 제품들이 자신한테 매력적인지 아닌지를 나타내도록 요청받았다. 일부 제품은 수직으로 움직였고(참가자들이 보는 동안 고개를 끄덕이게 하면서), 다른 제품은 수평으로 움직였다(좌우로 머리를 움직이게 하면서). 참가자들은 '예'와 '아니오'라는 머리 움직임이 결정에 핵심적인 역할을 했다는 사실을 인지하지 못한 채 수직으로 움직이는 제품을 선호했다.

➡ 한 연구에서, 참가자들은 고개를 위아래로 움직일 때 컴퓨터 화면에 나오는 제품들에 (A) 호의적으로 반응했는데, 이는 이들의 결정이 (B) 행동에 의해서 무의식적으로 영향을 받는다는 것을 보여주었다.

Why? 왜 정답일까?
사람들이 특정한 행동을 하면 특정한 생각을 품게 될 수 있다(Get people to behave in a certain way and you cause them to have certain thoughts.)는 내용이다. 이에 대한 근거로 사람들로 하여금 고개를 끄덕이거나 가로저으며 제품 만족도를 평가하게 했을 때 고개를 끄덕였던 제품에 대한 선호가 실제로 더 높게 나타났다(Participants preferred vertically moving products without being aware that their "yes" and "no" head movements had played a key role in their decisions.)는 실험이 언급되고 있다. 따라서 요약문의 빈칸 (A), (B)에 들어갈 말로 가장 적절한 것은 ① '(A) favorably(호의적으로), (B) behavior(행동)'이다.

- **controversial** ⓐ 논쟁의 여지가 있는
- **vertically** ⓐⓓ 수직으로, 세로로
- **unconsciously** ⓐⓓ 무의식적으로
- **fixate on** ~에 고정시키다
- **horizontally** ⓐⓓ 수평으로, 가로로
- **prejudice** ⓝ 편견

구문 풀이
5행 →명령문(~하라) Get people to behave in a certain way and you cause them
목적어　목적격 보어　　　　　　　　　　　접속사(그러면)
to have certain thoughts.

10-12 소년이 홀로 차분할 수 있었던 이유

[본문 해석]
(A)
한 사업가가 비행기에 탑승했다. 『자리에 도착한 후, 그는 여행 동반자들, 즉 창가에 앉아 있는 중년 여성과 통로 쪽 좌석에 앉아 있는 어린 소년과 인사를 나눴다. 가방을 머리 위 짐칸에 넣은 후, 그는 그들 사이에 앉았다.』 비행기가 이륙한 후, 그는 어린 소년과 대화를 시작했다. 그는 (a) 그의 아들과 나이가 비슷해 보였고 색칠 공부 책을 칠하느라 바빴다.
　　　　　　　　　　　　　　　　　　　『』: 12번 ①의 근거 일치

(D)
그는 소년에게 그의 나이, 취미, 좋아하는 동물과 같은 몇 가지 일상적인 질문을 했다. 그는 그런 어린 소년이 혼자 여행하는 것이 이상하다고 생각해서 그가 괜찮은지 확인하기 위해 (e) 그를 지켜보기로 했다. 비행 시작 1시간여 만에 비행기가 갑자기 난기류를 타기 시작했다. 『조종사는 악천후를 만났기 때문에 안전벨트를 매고 침착하라고 모든 사람들에게 말했다.』 ─『』: 12번 ⑤의 근거 일치

(B)
　　　　　　　　　　　　　　　　　　　　　─『』: 12번 ②의 근거 일치
『비행기가 여러 차례 오르락내리락하자 사람들은 긴장해 자리에 똑바로 앉았다.』 그 남자도 긴장해서 (b) 자기 좌석을 최대한 꽉 잡고 있었다. 그러는 동안에도, 어린 소년은 조용히 (c) 그의 옆에 앉아 있었다. 『그의 색칠 공부 책과 크레용은 앞 좌석 주머니에 가지런히 치워져 있었고,』 그의 손은 차분히 다리 위에 놓여 있었다. 놀랍게도, 그는 전혀 걱정하지 않는 것처럼 보였다.
　　　　　　　　　　　　　　　　　─『』: 12번 ③의 근거 불일치

(C)
그러다가 갑자기 난기류가 끝났다. 조종사는 험난한 비행에 대해 사과하고 곧 착륙할 것이라고 알렸다. 비행기가 하강하기 시작했을 때, 그 남자는 어린 소년에게 말했다. "너는 어린 아이에 불과하지만, (d) 나는 평생 (너보다) 더 용감한 사람을 만난 적이 없어! 어른들 모두가 두려워하는데 어떻게 그렇게 침착하게 있었는지 말해 주겠니?" 그의 눈을 바라보며 소년은 말했다. "『저희 아빠가 이 비행기 조종사인데, 아빠가 저를 집으로 데려가고 있어요.』" ─『』: 12번 ④의 근거 일치

- **board** ⓥ 탑승하다
- **middle-aged** ⓐ 중년의
- **take off** 이륙하다
- **neatly** 〔ad〕 가지런히, 깔끔하게
- **bumpy ride** 험난한 주행, 곤란, 우여곡절
- **keep an eye on** ~을 주시하다
- **greet** ⓥ 인사하다
- **overhead bin** 짐 넣는 곳
- **grab** ⓥ 쥐다, 잡다
- **rest on** ~ 위에 놓여 있다
- **descent** ⓝ 하강
- **rough weather** 악천후

구문 풀이

[A] 1행 Arriving at his seat, he greeted his travel companions:
분사구문(~하자)   →동격←
a middle-aged woman sitting at the window, and a little boy sitting
in the aisle seat.

[B] 2행 The man was also nervous and grabbing his seat as tightly
as he could.
「as + 원급 + as ~ can[could] : 최대한 ~하게」

[D] 3행 He found it strange {that such a young boy would be traveling
5형식 동사 ᒼ 목적격 보어 { } : 진목적어(명사절)
alone}, ~

---

10 글의 순서 파악   정답률 78% | 정답 ④

주어진 글 (A)에 이어질 내용을 순서에 맞게 배열한 것으로 가장 적절한 것은?

① (B) – (D) – (C)
② (C) – (B) – (D)
③ (C) – (D) – (B)
☑ (D) – (B) – (C)
⑤ (D) – (C) – (B)

Why? 왜 정답일까?

비행기에 탄 사업가가 옆자리의 한 소년을 만났다는 내용의 **(A)** 뒤로, 두 사람이 탄 비행기가 난기류를 만났다는 내용의 **(D)**, 모두가 두려워하는 와중에 소년이 혼자 걱정하지 않는 듯 보였다는 내용의 **(B)**, 남자가 소년에게 그 이유를 묻자 소년이 아버지가 조종사라고 답했다는 내용의 **(C)**가 차례로 이어져야 한다. 따라서 글의 순서로 가장 적절한 것은 ④ '**(D) – (B) – (C)**'이다.

---

11 지칭 추론   정답률 76% | 정답 ⑤

밑줄 친 (a) ~ (e) 중에서 가리키는 대상이 나머지 넷과 <u>다른</u> 것은?

① (a)   ② (b)   ③ (c)   ④ (d)   ☑ (e)

Why? 왜 정답일까?

(a), (b), (c), (d)는 the businessman, (e)는 the young boy를 가리키므로, (a) ~ (e) 중에서 가리키는 대상이 다른 하나는 ⑤ '(e)'이다.

---

12 세부 내용 파악   정답률 82% | 정답 ③

윗글에 관한 내용으로 적절하지 <u>않은</u> 것은?

① 사업가는 중년 여성과 소년 사이에 앉았다.
② 비행기가 오르락내리락하자 사람들은 긴장했다.
☑ 소년은 색칠 공부 책과 크레용을 가방에 넣었다.
④ 소년은 자신의 아버지가 조종사라고 말했다.
⑤ 조종사는 사람들에게 안전벨트를 매고 침착하라고 말했다.

Why? 왜 정답일까?

(B) 'His coloring book and crayons were put away neatly in the seat pocket in front of him. ~'에서 소년은 색칠 공부 책과 크레용을 앞 좌석 주머니에 치워놓고 차분하게 있었다고 하므로, 내용과 일치하지 않는 것은 ③ '소년은 색칠 공부 책과 크레용을 가방에 넣었다.'이다.

Why? 왜 오답일까?

① **(A)** 'After putting his bag in the overhead bin, he took his place between them.'의 내용과 일치한다.
② **(B)** 'As the plane rose and fell several times, people got nervous and sat up in their seats.'의 내용과 일치한다.
④ **(C)** '~ he said, "My father is the pilot, ~'의 내용과 일치한다.
⑤ **(D)** 'The pilot told everyone to fasten their seat belts and remain calm, ~'의 내용과 일치한다.

DAY 11   20분 미니 모의고사

01 ②	02 ④	03 ③	04 ⑤	05 ③
06 ④	07 ⑤	08 ④	09 ③	10 ①
11 ①	12 ⑤			

---

01 협력의 기술을 지도하기   정답률 91% | 정답 ②

다음 글에서 필자가 주장하는 바로 가장 적절한 것은?

① 학생의 참여가 활발한 수업 방법을 개발해야 한다.
☑ 학생에게 성공적인 협동을 위한 기술을 가르쳐야 한다.
③ 학생의 의견을 존중하는 학교 분위기를 조성해야 한다.
④ 학생의 전인적 발달을 위해 체육활동을 강화해야 한다.
⑤ 정보를 올바르게 선별하도록 미디어 교육을 실시해야 한다.

[본문 해석]

선생님의 지도 없이는 학생들은 협력의 가치를 인정하는 개인적 발달의 여정에 나서지 않을 것이다. 하고 싶은 대로 내버려 두면, 그들은 본능적으로 서로 점점 더 경쟁적이 될 것이다. 그들은 스포츠 경기장에서와 마찬가지로 교실 환경 내의 점수, 성적표, 피드백을 비교할 것이다. 우리는 학생들에게 승자와 패자에 대해 가르칠 필요가 없다. 운동장과 미디어가 그들을 위해 그렇게 하는 것이다. 하지만, 우리는 그들에게 삶에 승리보다 더 많은 것이 있다는 것과 성공적인 협력을 위해 필요한 기술에 대해 정말로 가르쳐 줄 필요가 있다. 성공적으로 함께 일하는 그룹은 고도의 대인 의식뿐만 아니라 다양한 사회적 기술을 가진 개인들을 필요로 한다. 일부 학생들은 본래 이러한 기술에 대한 타고난 이해를 가지고 있지만, 그들은 항상 소수이다. 당신의 교실에 또래들 사이의 협력을 불러일으키기 위해서, 당신은 의식적이고 주의 깊게 이러한 기술들을 가르쳐야 하고, 학창시절 내내 계속해서 그것들을 육성해야 한다.

Why? 왜 정답일까?

'However, we do need to teach them that there is more to life than winning and about the skills they need for successful cooperation.'에서 선생님은 학생들에게 성공적인 협력을 위해 필요한 기술을 지도해야 한다고 하므로, 필자가 주장하는 바로 가장 적절한 것은 ② '학생에게 성공적인 협동을 위한 기술을 가르쳐야 한다.'이다.

- **embark on** ~에 착수하다
- **arena** ⓝ 경기장, 무대
- **interpersonal** ⓐ 대인 관계에 관련된
- **nurture** ⓥ 육성하다
- **instinctively** 〔ad〕 본능적으로
- **a multitude of** 다수의, 아주 많은
- **inherently** 〔ad〕 본래, 선천적으로
- **continuously** 〔ad〕 계속해서

구문 풀이

3행 Left to their own devices, they will instinctively become
수동분사구문(= If they are left ~)   주어   동사구
increasingly competitive with each other.
주격 보어(형용사구)

---

02 새로운 시작과 연관된 날짜와 목표 추진의 동기   정답률 80% | 정답 ④

다음 글의 요지로 가장 적절한 것은?

① 새로운 시작을 하기 전에 장기적인 계획을 세우는 것이 바람직하다.
② 자신이 해야 할 일을 일정표에 표시하는 것이 목표 달성에 효과적이다.
③ 문제 행동을 개선하기 위해 원인이 되는 요소를 파악할 필요가 있다.
☑ 날짜가 시작이라는 의미와 관련지어질 때 목표 추구에 강한 동기가 부여된다.
⑤ 상세한 일정표를 작성하는 것은 여러 목표를 동시에 달성하는 데 도움이 된다.

[본문 해석]

한 연구에서 연구자들이 어떤 날짜가 새로운 시작(예컨대 '봄의 첫날')과 관련이 있다고 제시했을 때, 학생들은 연구자들이 그 날짜를 평범한 날(예컨대 '3월의 세 번째 목요일')로 제시했을 때에 비해 그날을 목표 추구를 시작할 더 매력적인 시기로 간주했다. 새로운 운동 습관을 시작하는 것이든, 혹은 소셜 미디

어에 시간을 덜 쓰는 것이든, 연구자들이 제시하는 날짜가 새로운 시작과 관련될 때 더 많은 학생들이 바로 그때 변화를 시작하려고 했다. 그리고 다른 팀에 의한 더 최근의 연구는 목표를 추구하는 사람들에게 수정된 주간 일정표를 보여줘서 비슷한 이점을 얻었다는 것을 알아냈다. 달력이 오늘을 (월요일이든 일요일이든) 한 주의 첫날로 표현했을 때, 사람들은 자기 목표에 대한 즉각적인 진전을 이루는 데 더 의욕적인 기분을 느낀다고 보고했다.

Why? 왜 정답일까?

두 연구를 예로 들어 날짜가 달이든 주이든 시작과 관련되어 있을 때 목표 추구에 더 강한 동기가 부여된다는 결론을 이끌어내는 글이다. 따라서 글의 요지로 가장 적절한 것은 ④ '날짜가 시작이라는 의미와 관련지어질 때 목표 추구에 강한 동기가 부여된다.'이다.

- **kick-start** ⓥ 시동을 걸다
- **present A as B** A를 B라고 제시하다
- **depict** ⓥ 묘사하다, 설명하다
- **pursuit** ⓝ 추구
- **unremarkable** ⓐ 특별할 것 없는, 평범한
- **progress** ⓝ 진전

구문 풀이

1행 ~ when researchers suggested that a date was associated 〔접속사(~것)〕
with a new beginning (such as "the first day of spring"), students
viewed it as a more attractive time to kick-start goal pursuit
「view+A+as+B : A를 B라고 여기다」 「비교급+than : ~보다 더 …한」
than when researchers presented it as an unremarkable day (such
as "the third Thursday in March"). 〔= the date〕

---

03 인간의 기계화를 유도하는 상황   정답률 53% | 정답 ③

다음 글의 주제로 가장 적절한 것은? [3점]

① difficulties of overcoming human weaknesses to avoid failure
실패를 피하기 위해 인간의 약점을 극복하는 것의 어려움
② benefits of allowing machines and humans to work together
기계와 인간이 함께 일하게 하는 것의 이점
✓③ issues of allocating unfit tasks to humans in automated systems
자동화 시스템에서 인간에게 부적합한 과제를 주는 것의 문제
④ reasons why humans continue to pursue machine automation
인간이 기계 자동화를 계속 추구하는 이유
⑤ influences of human actions on a machine's performance
인간의 행동이 기계의 성능에 미치는 영향

[본문 해석]

사람과 기계를 협업 시스템으로 생각하지 않고 자동화될 수 있는 작업은 무엇이든 기계에 할당하고 그 나머지를 사람들에게 맡길 때 어려움이 발생한다. 이것은 결국 사람들에게 기계와 똑같이, 즉 인간의 능력과는 다른 방식으로 행동할 것을 요구하게 된다. 우리는 사람들이 기계를 감시하기를 기대하는데, 이는 오랫동안 경계를 게을리하지 않는 것을 의미하며, 그것은 우리가 잘하지 못하는 것이다. 우리는 사람들에게 기계에 의해 요구되는 극도의 정밀함과 정확성을 가지고 반복적인 작업을 할 것을 요구하는데, 이 또한 우리가 잘하지 못하는 것이다. 우리가 이런 식으로 어떤 과제의 기계적 구성요소와 인간적 구성요소를 나눌 때, 우리는 인간의 강점과 능력을 이용하지 못하고, 그 대신 유전적으로, 생물학적으로 부적합한 영역에 의존하게 되는 것이다. 하지만, 사람들이 실패할 때, 그들은 비난을 받는다.

Why? 왜 정답일까?

첫 두 문장에서 인간과 기계를 상보적인 협업 관계로 취급하지 않고 자동화할 수 있는 것은 모두 기계로 돌린 후 인간에게 남은 것을 맡길 때 인간은 기계화될 것을 요구받는 문제에 직면한다(~. This ends up requiring people to behave in machine-like fashion, in ways that differ from human capabilities.)고 언급하고 있다. 따라서 글의 주제로 가장 적절한 것은 ③ '자동화 시스템에서 인간에게 부적합한 과제를 주는 것의 문제'이다.

- **arise** ⓥ 발생하다
- **assign** ⓥ 할당하다
- **keep alert** 경계를 게을리 하지 않다
- **component** ⓝ 구성요소
- **genetically** ⓐⓓ 유전적으로
- **collaborative** ⓐ 협업의
- **end up ~ing** 결국 ~하게 되다
- **precision** ⓝ 정밀함
- **take advantage of** ~을 이용하다
- **unsuited** ⓐ 부적합한

구문 풀이

1행 Difficulties arise when we do not think of people and
〔주어〕〔동사〕〔접속사〕〔동사1 「think of+A+as+B : A를 B로 간주하다」〕
machines as collaborative systems, but assign whatever tasks can
〔동사2〕〔복합관계형용사(~하는 어떤 …이든지)〕
be automated to the machines and leave the rest to people.
〔동사3〕

---

04 비교 우위에 따라 일을 분담할 필요성   정답률 56% | 정답 ⑤

다음 글의 밑줄 친 부분 중, 어법상 틀린 것은?

[본문 해석]

모든 것을 당신 스스로 생산하려고 노력하는 것은 당신이 고비용 공급자가 되는 많은 것들을 생산하기 위해 당신의 시간과 자원을 사용하고 있다는 것을 의미한다. 이것은 더 낮은 생산량과 수입으로 해석될 수 있다. 예를 들면, 비록 대부분의 의사가 자료 기록과 진료 예약 잡기에 능숙할지라도, 이러한 서비스를 수행할 누군가를 고용하는 것은 일반적으로 그들에게 이익이 된다. 기록을 하기 위해 의사가 사용하는 시간은 그들이 환자를 진료하면서 보낼 수 있었을 시간이다. 그들이 환자와 보내게 되는 시간은 많은 가치를 가지기 때문에 의사들에게 자료 기록을 하는 기회비용은 높을 것이다. 따라서 의사는 자료를 기록하고 관리하기 위해 누군가 다른 사람을 고용하는 것이 이득이라는 것을 거의 항상 알게 될 것이다. 더군다나 의사가 진료 제공을 전문으로 하고, 자료 기록에 비교 우위를 가지고 있는 사람을 고용하면, 그렇게 하지 않을 때 얻을 수 있는 것보다 그 비용은 더 낮아질 것이고 공동의 결과물이 더 커질 것이다.

Why? 왜 정답일까?

등위 접속사 and 앞에 주어 the doctor에 연결되는 3인칭 단수 동사 specializes가 나오므로, hiring은 specializes와 병렬을 이루도록 hires로 고쳐야 한다. 따라서 어법상 틀린 것은 ⑤이다.

Why? 왜 오답일까?

① 관계절인 'you are a high-cost provider'가 완전하므로 '전치사+관계대명사' 형태인 for which는 적절하다.
② 진주어인 'to hire someone ~'와 대응될 말로서 가주어 it의 쓰임은 적절하다.
③ 앞에 나오는 명사 the time이 '쓰이는' 대상이므로 수동의 의미를 나타내는 과거분사 spent의 쓰임은 적절하다.
④ 5형식 동사 find 뒤로 가목적어 it과 목적격 보어가 이어지는 구조이므로 형용사 advantageous의 쓰임은 적절하다.

- **high-cost** 고비용의, 비용이 많이 드는
- **production** ⓝ 생산
- **generally** ⓐⓓ 일반적으로
- **advantageous** ⓐ 이로운, 유리한
- **provision** ⓝ 공급, 제공
- **comparative advantage** 비교 우위
- **achievable** ⓐ 달성 가능한
- **translate into** ~로 번역되다
- **arrange** ⓥ 준비하다, 마련하다
- **opportunity cost** 기회비용
- **specialize in** ~을 전문으로 하다
- **physician** ⓝ 의사
- **joint** ⓐ 공동의

구문 풀이

14행 Moreover, when the doctor specializes in the provision of
〔시간 접속사〕〔동사1〕
physician services and hires someone [who has a comparative
〔동사2〕〔선행사〕
advantage in record keeping], costs will be lower and joint output
〔주어1〕〔동사1〕〔주어2〕
(will be) larger than would otherwise be achievable.
〔생략(동사2)〕〔가정법 과거 의미 내포(~하지 않는다면 …할 것보다)〕

★★★ 1등급 대비 고난도 3점 문제

05 인간의 판단과 통계 자료의 결합   정답률 43% | 정답 ③

다음 글의 밑줄 친 부분 중, 문맥상 낱말의 쓰임이 적절하지 않은 것은? [3점]

[본문 해석]

Robert Blattberg와 Steven Hoch는 변화하는 환경에서 일관성이 항상 장점인지가 분명하지 않다는 것과, 인간이 판단하는 것의 이점 중 하나는 변화를 감지하는 능력이라는 데 주목했다. 따라서 변화하는 환경에서는 인간의 판단과 통계 모델들을 결합하는 것이 ① 유리할 수 있다. Blattberg와 Hoch는 슈퍼마켓 관리자들에게 특정한 제품에 대한 수요를 예측하게 한 다음, 이 판단을 ② 지난 데이터에 근거한 통계 모델의 예측과 평균을 내어 종합적인 예측을 생성해서 이러한 가능성을 조사했다. (그들의) 논리는 통계 모델들은 변동이 없는 조건을 ③ 부정하기(→ 가정하기) 때문에 경쟁자들에 의해 취해진 행동이나 신제품의 도입과 같은 새로운 사건이 수요에 미치는 영향을 설명할 수 없다는 것이었다. 하지만 인간은 이러한 새로운 요인들을 판단에 ④ 통합할 수 있다. 종합된 것, 즉 인간의 판단과 통계 모델의 평균이 통계 모델이나 관리자들이 각자 처리하는 것보다 더 ⑤ 정확하다는 것이 증명되었다.

Why? 왜 정답일까?

상황이 일관적이지 않고 변화하는 중일 때는 통계 자료에 더해 인간의 판단력을 결합해야 더 정확한 결정을 내릴 수 있다는 내용이다. ④가 포함된 문장에서 역접어(however)와 함께, 인간은 변화하는 상황을 고려해 판단을 내릴 수 있다고 한다. 이러한 문맥으로 보아, ③이 포함된 however 앞 문장은 '인간과는 달리' 통계 자료는 일관된 상황만을 '전제로 한다'는 의미여야 하므로, ③의 deny는 assume으로 바뀌어야 적절하다. 따라서 문맥상 낱말의 쓰임이 적절하지 않은 것은 ③이다.

- consistency ⓝ 일관성
- detect ⓥ 감지하다
- forecast ⓥ 예측하다
- deny ⓥ 부인하다
- take action 행동을 취하다, 조치를 취하다
- virtue ⓝ 미덕
- statistical ⓐ 통계적인
- composite ⓐ 종합적인 ⓝ 종합적 것
- novel ⓐ 새로운, 신기한
- accurate ⓐ 정확한

구문 풀이

2행 ~ it is not clear [that consistency is always a virtue] and
　　　　　　　　　　가주어
[that one of the advantages of human judgment is the ability to detect
　　주어(one of the + 복수 명사)　　　　　　　　　　동사(단수)
change]. [ ] : 진주어

★★ 문제 해결 꿀~팁 ★★

▶ 많이 틀린 이유는?
첫 문장에서 인간 판단력의 이점은 '변화를 감지하는(detect change)' 능력이라고 했는데, 이 말을 ④가 포함된 문장에서는 '새로운 요인을 포함한다(incorporate these novel factors)'는 말로 바꾸었다. 따라서 ④는 문맥상 어색하지 않다.
▶ 문제 해결 방법은?
and 앞뒤는 서로 같은 내용이 연결되어야 하는데, ③의 deny는 같은 문장의 and 뒤에 나오는 'cannot account for ~ novel events'와 정반대된다. 따라서 ③이 어색한 것을 바로 파악할 수 있다.

★★★ 1등급 대비 고난도 3점 문제

06 온라인에 저장된 정보의 양면적인 특성　정답률 37% | 정답 ④

다음 빈칸에 들어갈 말로 가장 적절한 것을 고르시오. [3점]
① scarcity – 희소성
② creativity – 창의력
③ acceleration – 가속화
✓ permanency – 영속성
⑤ mysteriousness – 신비성

[본문 해석]
온라인 환경은 거기에서 일어나는 일이 무엇이든지 간에 얼마나 쉽게 저장할 수 있는지, 즉 내가 그것의 *기록 가능성*과 *저장 가능성*이라고 부르는 것에 있어서 아주 다양하다. 비록 소셜 미디어의 디자인, 활동, 멤버십이 시간이 지남에 따라 바뀔지도 모르겠지만, 사람들이 게시했던 내용은 보통 훼손되지 않고 남아 있다. 이메일, 동영상, 음성, 텍스트 메시지는 저장될 수 있다. 완벽한 보존이 가능할 때, 시간은 멈춰 있다. 당신은 원할 때마다 그러한 과거의 사건들을 다시 돌아보기 위해 되돌아 갈 수 있다. 또 다른 상황에서, 우리가 받았다고 기억하는 듯한 이메일이 우리의 받은 편지함에서 불가사의하게 사라질 때처럼, 어떤 것이 어떤 식으로든 존재했었는지에 대한 실재 검증에 심지어 이의를 제기하면서, 영속성은 우리 손가락 사이로 빠져나간다. 손가락으로 우연하게 살짝 톡 친 것이 그렇게 하지 않았으면 영원히 존재했을 문서를 무(無)의 상태로 보내 버릴 수 있다.

Why? 왜 정답일까?

In other situations 앞뒤로 온라인에 저장된 정보에 관한 서로 다른 내용이 대조된다. 이 앞에서는 정보가 온라인에서 비교적 한결같은 상태로 보존될 수 있다는 내용을 다루지만, 뒤에서는 손가락으로 우연히 살짝 잘못 건드리기만 해도 문서가 무의 상태로 돌아가 버릴 수도 있다는(The slightest accidental tap of the finger can send an otherwise everlasting document into nothingness.)는 내용을 다루고 있다. 빈칸은 In other situations 뒤에 있으므로, 빈칸을 포함한 문장은 정보의 '영속성'이 순식간에 우리 손을 빠져나갈 수도 있다는 의미를 나타내야 한다. 따라서 빈칸에 들어갈 말로 가장 적절한 것은 ④ '영속성'이다.

- recordability ⓝ 기록 가능성
- intact ⓐ 손상되지 않은, 온전한
- suspend ⓥ (공식적으로) 멈추다, 유예하다
- inbox ⓝ 받은 편지함, 수신함
- preservability ⓝ 저장 가능성, 보존 가능성
- preservation ⓝ 보존
- reexamine ⓥ 다시 검토하다
- accidental ⓐ 우연한, 돌발적인

- otherwise ⓐ그렇지 않으면
- nothingness ⓝ 무, 공허, 존재하지 않음
- everlasting ⓐ 영원한, 변치 않는

구문 풀이

1행 Online environments vary widely in {how easily you can
　　　　　　　　　자동사(다르다)　　　의문부사　{ } : 서로 동격
save whatever happens there}, {what I call its *recordability* and
　　　복합관계대명사(무엇이 ~하든 간에)　　관계대명사
preservability}.

★★ 문제 해결 꿀~팁 ★★

▶ 많이 틀린 이유는?
온라인에 저장된 정보의 특성을 설명하는 추상적인 글이다. ①의 '희소성'은 본문의 다른 부분에서 언급된 바 없으며, ⑤는 빈칸 뒤의 'mysteriously'를 품사만 바꾼 것이다.
▶ 문제 해결 방법은?
In other situations를 기점으로 글의 흐름이 반전되며, 빈칸은 이 뒤에 있으므로 답의 근거 또한 후반부에서 찾는 것이 정석이다. 하지만 빈칸 뒤의 'slips between our fingers'가 '~이 빠져나간다'라는 뜻으로서 부정적인 의미를 내포하므로, 빈칸에는 In other situations 뒤가 아닌 앞을 요약하는 표현이 들어가야 적절하다.

07 생물학적 작용의 한계에서 비롯되는 인식의 한계　정답률 49% | 정답 ⑤

다음 빈칸에 들어갈 말로 가장 적절한 것을 고르시오.
① hindered by other wavelengths – 다른 파장에 의해 방해받는다
② derived from our imagination – 우리의 상상에서 나온다
③ perceived through all senses – 모든 감각을 통해 인식된다
④ filtered by our stereotypes – 우리의 고정관념에 의해 걸러진다
✓ limited by our biology – 우리의 생물학적 작용에 의해 제한된다

[본문 해석]
색은 파장에 대한 해석으로, 내부에서만 존재하는 것이다. 그리고 이것은 더 생소해지는데, 우리가 말하고 있는 파장은 빨간색에서 보라색까지 이어지는 파장의 스펙트럼인 '가시광선'이라고 부르는 것만을 포함하기 때문이다. 그러나 가시광선은 전자기 스펙트럼의 극히 일부만을 구성해서 그중 10조 분의 1도 되지 않는다. 전파, 마이크로파, X선, 감마선, 휴대폰 통화, 와이파이 등 나머지 모든 스펙트럼이 지금 우리를 통해 흐르고 있으며, 우리는 이 모든 것을 완전히 알지 못한다. 이것은 우리가 스펙트럼의 다른 부분으로부터 이러한 신호를 포착할 수 있는 어떤 특별한 생물학적 수용체도 가지고 있지 않기 때문이다. 우리가 볼 수 있는 현실의 단면은 우리의 생물학적 작용에 의해 제한된다.

Why? 왜 정답일까?

우리 주변에는 온갖 종류의 스펙트럼이 흐르고 있지만 우리는 생물학적 수용체의 한계상 극히 일부만 인식할 수 있다(~ we don't have any specialized biological receptors to pick up on these signals from other parts of the spectrum.)는 설명으로 보아, 빈칸에 들어갈 말로 가장 적절한 것은 ⑤ '우리의 생물학적 작용에 의해 제한된다'이다.

- interpretation ⓝ 해석
- internally ⓐ 내부적으로
- constitute ⓥ 구성하다
- rest ⓝ 나머지
- conversation ⓝ 대화
- specialized ⓐ 전문화된, 분화된
- hinder ⓥ 방해하다
- perceive ⓥ 인식하다
- wavelength ⓝ 파장, 주파수
- visible light 가시광선
- fraction ⓝ 부분, 파편
- radio waves 무선 전파
- unaware ⓐ 알지 못하는
- pick up on ~을 알아차리다
- derive ⓥ ~에서 나오다
- stereotype ⓝ 고정관념

구문 풀이

2행 And it gets stranger, because the wavelengths we're talking
about involve only {what we call "visible light"}, a spectrum of
　　　　　　　　　　{ } : 선행사　　　　　　　선행사 동격
wavelengths [that runs from red to violet].
　　　　　　주격 관·대

08 마케팅에서 입장을 취하는 것의 중요성　정답률 60% | 정답 ④

다음 글에서 전체 흐름과 관계 <u>없는</u> 문장은?

[본문 해석]

입장을 취하는 것은 당신의 사람, 부족, 청중인 그 개개인들에게 당신이 횃불이 되기 때문에 중요하다. ① 당신이 당신의 견해를 깃발처럼 들 때, 사람들은 당신을 어디서 찾아야 할지를 안다. 그것은 집합 지점이 된다. ② 당신의 관점을 보여주는 것은 당신이 그저 물건과 서비스만 파는 것이 아님을 장래 (및 현재) 고객들이 깨닫게 한다. ③ 최고의 마케팅은 결코 제품이나 서비스를 판매하는 것에 대한 것이 아니라 입장을 취하는 데 관한 것으로, 청중들은 그저 당신의 행동에 동의하기 때문에 그들이 당신이 마케팅하고 있는 것을 반드시 원하게 될 만큼 충분히 믿어야 하는 이유를 그들에게 보여주는 것이다. ④ 만약 당신이 기존의 고객을 유지하고 싶다면, 당신은 고객이 상품 개발 과정에 참여하면서 팀의 또 다른 구성원이 된 기분을 느낄 수 있게 할 방법을 만들어낼 필요가 있다. ⑤ 상품은 기능하지 않으면 바꾸거나 고칠 수 있지만, 집합 지점은 당신의 행위 이면에 있는 가치 및 의미와 같은 선상에 있다.

Why? 왜 정답일까?

마케팅에서 특정 입장을 취하는 것이 중요하다는 내용으로, 첫 문장과 문장 ③이 핵심 내용을 잘 제시한다. 반면 ④는 고객을 상품 개발 과정에 참여시켜 기존 고객을 유지할 방법에 관해 논하므로 글의 흐름에서 벗어난다. 따라서 전체 흐름과 관계 없는 문장은 ④이다.

- take a stand 입장을 취하다
- viewpoint ⓝ 견해, 시각
- believe in ~을 믿다
- agree with ~에 동의하다
- existing ⓐ 기존의
- align with ~와 나란히 있다
- tribe ⓝ 부족
- prospective ⓐ 장래의
- at any cost 반드시, 기필코
- retain ⓥ 보유하다, 유지하다
- product development 상품 개발

구문 풀이

5행 Displaying your perspective lets prospective (and current)
　　　　　　　　　　　　　사역동사　　　　　　목적어
customers know that you don't just sell your products or services.
원형부정사

★★★ 1등급 대비 고난도 2점 문제

09 발췌본의 유용함과 한계　　　정답률 29% | 정답 ③

주어진 글 다음에 이어질 글의 순서로 가장 적절한 것을 고르시오.

① (A) – (C) – (B)　　　　② (B) – (A) – (C)
③ (B) – (C) – (A)　　　　④ (C) – (A) – (B)
⑤ (C) – (B) – (A)

[본문 해석]

일부 문학 작품의 길이가 압도적이라는 데는 의심의 여지가 없다. 수업 시간에 작품을 몇 시간, 몇 주 동안 읽거나 번역하는 것은 너무나 지루한 경험일 수 있어서 많은 학생이 다시는 외국어 서적을 절대 펴고 싶어 하지 않는다.

(B) 발췌본은 한 가지 해결책을 제공한다. 장점들은 분명하다. 즉, 다양한 작품에서 가져온 일련의 단락을 읽는 것은 교실에서 더 많은 다양성을 만들어 내서, 교사는 단조로움을 피할 가능성이 더 큰 한편으로, 여전히 최소한이라도 어떤 작가의 특별한 묘미를 학습자에게 맛보게 한다.

(C) 반면에, '짧은 토막글'만 접한 학생은 책의 전반적인 구성을 아는 만족감을 결코 가질 수 없을 것이며, 결국 그 만족감은 모국어로 된 어떤 글을 읽을 때 우리 대부분이 찾고자 하는 것이다.

(A) 게다가 짧은 발췌로는 충분히 설명될 수 없는 문학적인 특징이 몇 가지 있는데, 예를 들면 줄거리나 등장인물의 전개와 더불어 이것이 내포하는 독자의 점진적 몰입, 또는 대조적인 관점의 병치를 통한 복잡한 주제 전개 등이 있다.

Why? 왜 정답일까?

긴 문학 작품을 다루는 경우를 언급하는 주어진 글 뒤로, 발췌본을 활용하는 것이 해결책이 될 수 있다는 내용의 (B), On the other hand로 흐름을 반전시키며 발췌본에 한계가 있음을 설명하는 (C), Moreover와 함께 한계점을 추가로 열거하는 (A)가 차례로 연결된다. 따라서 글의 순서로 가장 적절한 것은 ③ '(B) – (C) – (A)'이다.

- doubt ⓝ 의심, 의혹
- overwhelming ⓐ 압도적인
- week after week 여러 주 동안
- adequately [ad] 충분히
- excerpt ⓝ 발췌
- literary ⓐ 문학의
- translate ⓥ 번역하다
- moreover [ad] 게다가, 더욱이
- illustrate ⓥ 설명하다, 예증하다
- plot ⓝ 줄거리

- for instance 예를 들어
- involvement ⓝ 몰입, 몰두
- unfolding ⓝ 전개, 펼침
- contrasting ⓐ 대조되는, 상충하는
- passage ⓝ 단락
- flavour ⓝ 묘미, 맛
- satisfaction ⓝ 만족감
- gradual ⓐ 점진적인
- imply ⓥ 내포하다
- juxtaposition ⓝ 병치
- extract ⓝ 발췌(본) ⓥ 발췌하다, 뽑아내다
- monotony ⓝ 단조로움
- chunk ⓝ 토막, 덩어리
- pattern ⓝ 구성, 양식

구문 풀이

2행 Reading or translating a work in class, hour after hour, week
　　　　주어(동명사구)
after week, can be such a boring experience that many students
　　　　　동사　　「such ~ that … : 너무 ~해서 …하다」
never want to open a foreign language book again.

★★ 문제 해결 꿀~팁 ★★

▶ 많이 틀린 이유는?
발췌본의 한계를 연이어 설명하는 (C) – (A)의 연결고리를 파악했다면, (B)의 순서를 잡는 것이 관건이다. 주어진 글에서 '발췌본'에 관한 언급이 아예 나오지 않는데, 바로 On the other hand로 시작하는 (C)가 연결되어 발췌본의 한계를 지적하면 글의 흐름이 어색하다. 따라서 (C) 앞에 (B)가 나와 '발췌본'이라는 소재를 등장시켜야 흐름이 매끄러워진다.

▶ 문제 해결 방법은?
주어진 글이 아닌 (B)에서 중심 소재가 등장하므로, 일단 (B)가 전제되어야 나머지 단락을 연결할 수 있다는 점을 파악하도록 한다.

10 선택 구조의 변화로 시작된 식습관의 변화　　정답률 64% | 정답 ①

다음 글의 내용을 한 문장으로 요약하고자 한다. 빈칸 (A), (B)에 들어갈 말로 가장 적절한 것은?

	(A)		(B)		(A)		(B)
✓	placement 배치	……	lowered 줄인다	②	placement 배치	……	boosted 증가시킨다
③	price 가격	……	lowered 줄인다	④	price 가격	……	boosted 증가시킨다
⑤	flavor 맛	……	maintained 유지시킨다				

[본문 해석]

Boston의 1차 진료 의사인 Anne Thorndike는 아주 좋은 생각을 했다. 그녀는 의지력이나 동기를 바꾸지 않고 가벼운 방식으로 수천 명의 병원 직원들과 방문객들의 식습관을 개선할 수 있다고 믿었다. 사실, 그녀는 그들에게 말해줄 계획을 세우지 않았다. Thorndike는 병원 구내식당의 '선택 구조'를 바꾸기 위해서 연구를 설계했다. 그녀는 공간 안에 음료가 놓여 있는 방식을 바꾸는 것으로 시작했다. 원래, 구내식당 내의 금전등록기 옆에 있는 냉장고들은 탄산음료로만 채워져 있었다. 그녀는 각각의 냉장고에 선택 사항으로 물을 추가했다. 게다가, 그녀는 공간 전체에 있는 음식을 두는 장소 옆에 물병이 담긴 바구니들을 놓았다. 탄산음료는 여전히 기본 냉장고에 있었지만, 물은 이제 음료를 둔 모든 곳에서 이용 가능하게 되었다. 다음 3개월 동안, 병원의 탄산음료 판매 숫자는 11.4퍼센트만큼 떨어졌다. 반면에, 물병의 판매는 25.8퍼센트만큼 증가했다.

→ Thorndike에 의해 수행된 연구는 병원 구내식당에 음료를 (A) 배치하는 것이 사람들이 하는 선택에 영향을 주어, 탄산음료의 소비를 (B) 줄인다는 것을 보여주었다.

Why? 왜 정답일까?

개인의 의지력 또는 동기를 자극하지 않고 단지 개인이 선택할 수 있는 구조만 바꾸어도 개인의 식습관 변화가 일어날 수 있다는 내용의 글이다. 글의 마지막 세 문장에 따르면, 구내식당에 음료 비치 코너에 물을 추가하여 어디서든 물을 이용할 수 있게 하자, 탄산음료가 선택 사항에서 빠지지 않았음에도 불구하고 물 소비가 증가하고 탄산음료 소비가 떨어졌다고 한다. 이를 근거로 볼 때, 요약문은 구내식당의 음료 '배치'가 사람들의 선택에 영향을 미칠 수 있으며, 이를 잘 활용하면 사람들의 탄산음료 소비를 '줄일' 수 있다는 의미를 나타내야 한다. 따라서 요약문의 빈칸 (A), (B)에 들어갈 말로 가장 적절한 것은 ① '(A) placement(배치) – (B) lowered(줄인다)'이다.

- primary ⓐ (순서·단계상으로) 최초의
- improve ⓥ 향상시키다
- motivation ⓝ 동기
- design ⓥ 설계하다
- physician ⓝ (내과) 의사
- willpower ⓝ 의지력
- slight ⓐ 약간의, 조금의, 경미한
- study ⓝ 연구

- alter ⓥ 바꾸다
- arrange ⓥ 배열하다
- refrigerator ⓝ 냉장고
- cash register 금전 등록기
- additionally ⓐⓓ 추가적으로, 게다가
- meanwhile ⓐⓓ 한편, 반면에
- lowered ⓐ 낮아진
- flavor ⓝ 맛

- architecture ⓝ 구성, 건축
- originally ⓐⓓ 본래, 원래
- locate ⓥ 위치하고 있다
- be filled with ~로 채워지다
- available ⓐ 구할[이용할] 수 있는
- perform ⓥ (일·과제·의무 등을) 행하다
- boosted ⓥ 증가하다
- maintain ⓥ 유지하다

구문 풀이

9행 Originally, the refrigerators located next to the cash registers
　　　　주어　　　　　　　　　　　　　과거분사
in the cafeteria were filled with only soda.
　　　　　　　　동사구(~로 채워지다)

11-12　사회성으로 인한 인간의 뇌 발달

[본문 해석]

『진화생물학자들은 사회성이 우리의 복잡한 뇌의 진화를 이끌었다고 믿는다.』 ← :11번의 근거
화석 증거는 13만 년 전이라는 먼 옛날에 *호모사피엔스*가 거래하러, 음식을 공유하러, 그리고 의심의 여지없이 잡담을 하러 150마일 이상을 이동하는 것이 (a) 이상한 일이 아니었다는 것을 보여준다. 네안데르탈인과는 다르게 그들의 사회 집단은 그들 자신의 가족을 훨씬 넘어서서 뻗어 있었다. 누가 누구와 관련이 있는지 그리고 그들이 어디에 사는지 모든 그런 (b) 연결을 기억하는 것은 상당한 처리 능력을 요구했다.

그것은 또한 길 찾기 요령을 요구했다. 구석기 시대 황야의 수십 혹은 수백 제곱마일을 가로지르는 사회 관계망을 (c) 유지하려고 한다고 상상해 보라. 여러분은 친구들이 어디에 있는지 알아내기 위해 그들에게 문자 메시지를 보낼 수도 없다. 여러분은 나가서 그들을 방문하거나, 마지막으로 그들을 어디에서 보았는지 기억해 내거나 혹은 그들이 어디로 갔을지 상상해야만 했다. 이것을 하기 위해, 여러분은 길 찾기 능력, 공간 인식, 방향 감각, 풍경의 지도를 머릿속에 저장하는 능력, 그리고 여기저기를 이동할 동기를 필요로 했다. 『캐나다 인류학자인 Ariane Burke는 우리의 조상이 자신의 이웃과 연락하고 지내려고 하는 동안 이러한 모든 특징들을 (d) 발달시켰다고 믿는다. 마침내 우리의 두뇌가 길 찾기를 위한 준비를 하게 된 것이다.』 ← :12번의 근거 한편, 네안데르탈인은 그만큼 멀리 이동하지 않았고 다양한 공간 능력을 전혀 발전시키지 못했다. 수준 높은 사냥꾼이었고 추위에 잘 적응했으며 어둠 속에서도 볼 수 있었음에도 불구하고, 그들은 멸종하게 되었다. 선사 시대의 불모지에서는 그 어떤 것도 친구 집단보다 (e) 쓸모없는(→ 도움이 되는) 것은 없었다.

- sociability ⓝ 사교성, 사회성
- considerable ⓐ 상당한
- spatial ⓐ 공간의
- anthropologist ⓝ 인류학자
- keep in touch with ~와 연락하다
- sophisticated ⓐ 수준 높은, 정교한
- prehistoric ⓐ 선사 시대의

- extend ⓥ 뻗다, 확장하다
- wilderness ⓝ 황무지
- landscape ⓝ 풍경
- attribute ⓝ 특성
- primed for ~의 준비가 된
- extinct ⓐ 멸종된
- badland ⓝ 악지, 불모지

구문 풀이

2행 Fossil evidence shows that as far back as 130,000 years ago,
　　　　　　　　　　　　　　접속사(~것)
it was not unusual for Homo sapiens to travel more than a hundred
가주어　　　　　　　　　의미상 주어　　　진주어 to부정사구
and fifty miles to trade, share food and, no doubt, gossip.
　　　　　　　부정사구1　　부정사구2　　　　　　　　　　부정사구3(~하기 위해)

11　제목 파악　　　정답률 58% | 정답 ①

윗글의 제목으로 가장 적절한 것은?

☑ ① Social Networks: An Evolutionary Advantage
　　사회적 연결망: 진화적 이점
② Our Brain Forced Us to Stay Close to Our Family!
　　우리 뇌는 우리가 가족의 근처에 있도록 강요했다!
③ How We Split from Our Way and Kept Going on My Way
　　우리는 어떻게 우리의 길에서 벗어나 나의 길을 가는가
④ Why Do Some People Have Difficulty in Social Relationships?
　　왜 어떤 사람들은 사회적 관계에 어려움을 겪는가?
⑤ Being Connected to Each Other Leads to Communicative Skills
　　서로 연결되는 것이 의사소통 능력으로 이어진다

Why?　왜 정답일까?

첫 문장인 '~ sociability drove the evolution of our complex brains.'에서 인간의 사회성은 인간의 뇌 발달을 이끌어낸 요소라는 주제를 제시하므로, 글의 제목으로 가장 적절한 것은 ① '사회적 연결망: 진화적 이점'이다.

12　어휘 추론　　　정답률 61% | 정답 ⑤

밑줄 친 (a) ~ (e) 중에서 문맥상 낱말의 쓰임이 적절하지 않은 것은? [3점]

① (a)　② (b)　③ (c)　④ (d)　☑ ⑤ (e)

Why?　왜 정답일까?

'~ our ancestors developed all these attributes while trying to keep in touch with their neighbours. Eventually, our brains became primed for wayfinding.'에서 인간은 이웃과 계속 연락하고 지내려고 노력하는 동안 길 찾기에 필요한 능력을 갖추게 되었다고 언급한다. 즉 '친구 집단'이 우리의 뇌 발달에 도움이 되었다는 것이다. 이를 근거로 할 때, (e)의 useless는 반의어인 useful로 고쳐야 한다. 문맥상 낱말의 쓰임이 적절하지 않은 것은 ⑤ '(e)'이다.

DAY 12 — 20분 미니 모의고사

01 ③	02 ⑤	03 ②	04 ⑤	05 ⑤
06 ④	07 ①	08 ⑤	09 ①	10 ②
11 ③	12 ⑤			

---

01 상품권 기부 요청   정답률 92% | 정답 ③

다음 글의 목적으로 가장 적절한 것은?

① 행사 홍보물 게시가 가능한지를 문의하려고
② 학교 퀴즈 행사에 사용할 물품 제작을 의뢰하려고
☑ 우승 상품으로 사용할 상품권을 기부해 줄 것을 요청하려고
④ 학교 행사로 예상되는 소음 발생에 대해 양해를 구하려고
⑤ 퀴즈 행사 개최를 위한 장소 사용 허가를 받으려고

[본문 해석]

지역 상점 주인분들께

제 이름은 Carol Williams이고 Yellowstone 고등학교의 학생회장입니다. 저희는 3월 30일에 연례 퀴즈의 밤을 개최할 것이고, 우승팀에게 상품을 제공할 계획입니다. 그러나 이 행사는 유용한 상품과 서비스를 제공해 주는 지역 상점의 후원 없이는 불가능할 것입니다. 저희가 상품으로 사용할 상품권을 흔쾌히 기부해 주실 수 있으신가요? 어떤 액수의 상품권 기부든 감사히 여길 것입니다. 귀하의 관대함에 대한 대가로 저희 답안지에 귀하의 사업 광고를 싣겠습니다. 시간 내셔서 이 편지를 읽고 저희 요청을 고려해주셔서 감사합니다. 만약 기부를 원하시거나 더 많은 정보가 필요하시면 제게 전화나 이메일을 주십시오. 귀하로부터 곧 소식 듣기를 기대하겠습니다.

Carol Williams 드림

Why? 왜 정답일까?

편지 중반에 퀴즈의 밤 행사의 우승 상품으로 사용할 상품권을 기부해줄 수 없는지(Would you be willing to donate a gift certificate that we can use as a prize?) 묻는 말이 나오므로, 글의 목적으로 가장 적절한 것은 ③ '우승 상품으로 사용할 상품권을 기부해 줄 것을 요청하려고'이다.

- student council 학생회
- support ⓝ 후원, 지지
- be willing to 기꺼이 ~하다
- grateful for ~에 감사하는
- generosity ⓝ 관대함
- host ⓥ 주최하다
- valuable ⓐ 가치 있는
- gift certificate 상품권
- in exchange for ~에 대한 대가로

구문 풀이

8행 Would you be willing to donate a gift certificate [that we can use as a prize]?
「be willing to + 동사원형: 기꺼이 ~하다」
[ ]: 목적격 관계대명사절

---

02 침묵 효과가 발생하는 이유   정답률 69% | 정답 ⑤

밑줄 친 the innocent messenger who falls before a firing line이 다음 글에서 의미하는 바로 가장 적절한 것은? [3점]

① the employee being criticized for being silent
침묵해서 비난당하는 직원
② the peacemaker who pursues non-violent solutions
비폭력적 해결책을 추구하는 중재자
③ the negotiator who looks for a mutual understanding
상호 이해를 탐색하는 협상가
④ the subordinate who wants to get attention from the boss
상사에게 관심을 얻으려는 부하직원
☑ the person who gets the blame for reporting unpleasant news
불쾌한 소식을 전했다고 비난받는 사람

[본문 해석]

나쁜 소식부터 처리하고 넘어가려고 하는 것보다 아마도 더 나쁜 것은 그것을 부드럽게 말하거나 전혀 다루지 않으려고 하는 것이다. 1970년대 초반에 심리학자인 Sidney Rosen과 Abraham Tesser가 만든 용어인 이 '침묵 효과'는 사람들이 다른 사람들의 부정적인 감정의 표적이 되는 것을 피하고 싶기 때문에 발생한다. 우리 모두는 변화를 이끌 기회를 가지고 있으나, 그것은 종종 우리의 상사에게 나쁜 소식을 전달하기 위한 용기를 필요로 한다. 우리는 사선 앞에서 쓰러지는 무고한 전령이 되고 싶어 하지는 않는다. 우리의 생존 본능이 발동하면, 이것은 어떤 상황의 진상이 희석될 때까지 우리의 용기를 무효화시킬 수 있다. "침묵 효과와 그로 인해 발생하는 (언어) 필터링은 가파른 위계 관계에서 파괴적인 결과를 가져올 수 있다"라고 조직 심리학자 Robert Sutton은 말한다. "나쁜 소식으로 시작한 것이 단계를 올라갈수록 점점 좋아진다. 그 이유는 각 단계의 상사가 자기 부하직원으로부터 그 소식을 듣고 나서 다음 단계로 올려 보내기 전에 그것을 다소 덜 나쁘게 들리도록 만들기 때문이다."

Why? 왜 정답일까?

사람들은 타인의 부정적 감정에 희생되고 싶어 하지 않으며(people want to avoid becoming the target of others' negative emotions), 생존하겠다는 본능 때문에 나쁜 소식을 전해야만 하는 상황에서 용기가 수그러든다(our survival instincts ~ can override our courage until the truth of a situation gets watered down.)는 내용으로 보아, 우리가 되고 싶지 않은 모습을 묘사하는 밑줄 친 부분의 의미로 가장 적절한 것은 ⑤ '불쾌한 소식을 전했다고 비난받는 사람'이다.

- out of the way 처리된, 끝난
- superior ⓝ 상사, 윗사람
- kick in 효과가 나타나다
- water down (물로) 희석하다
- hierarchy ⓝ 위계질서
- mutual ⓐ 서로의, 상호의
- mum ⓝ 침묵 ⓐ 잠자코 있는
- firing line (화기가 발사되는) 사선, 방화선
- override ⓥ 중단시키다
- devastating ⓐ 파괴적인
- subordinate ⓝ 부하직원

구문 풀이

1행 Perhaps worse than attempting to get the bad news out of
「보어(비교급 형용사)+
the way is attempting to soften it or simply not address it at all.
동사 + 주어 : 도치 구문」

★★★ 1등급 대비 고난도 2점 문제

03 시간에 기반을 두는 촉각   정답률 45% | 정답 ②

다음 글의 제목으로 가장 적절한 것은?

① Touch and Movement: Two Major Elements of Humanity
촉각과 움직임: 인간의 두 가지 주요 요소
☑ Time Does Matter: A Hidden Essence of Touch
시간이 진정 중요하다: 촉각의 숨겨진 본질
③ How to Use the Five Senses in a Timely Manner
오감을 적시에 사용하는 방법
④ The Role of Touch in Forming the Concept of Time
시간 개념 형성에서 촉각의 역할
⑤ The Surprising Function of Touch as a Booster of Knowledge
지식의 촉진제로서 촉각의 놀라운 기능

[본문 해석]

사람들은 보통 촉각을 시간의 현상으로 생각하지 않지만, 그것은 공간적인 만큼 전적으로 시간에 기반을 두고 있다. 직접 알아보려면 실험을 해볼 수 있다. 친구에게 손바닥이 위로 향하게 한 채 손을 동그랗게 모아 쥐고 눈을 감으라고 요청해 보라. 그의 손바닥에 작고 평범한 물건을 올려놓고 — 반지, 지우개, 무엇이든 괜찮다 — 손의 어떤 부분도 움직이지 말고 그것이 무엇인지 알아보라고 요청해 보라. 그는 무게와 아마 전체적인 크기 외에 아무것도 모를 것이다. 그런 다음 그에게 눈을 감은 채로 그 물건 위로 손가락을 움직여보라고 말하라. 그는 거의 틀림없이 그것이 무엇인지 즉시 알아낼 것이다. 손가락이 움직이게 함으로써 촉각이라는 감각적 지각에 시간을 더했다. 망막의 중심에 있는 중심와(窩)와 손가락 끝 사이에 직접적인 유사함이 있는데, 둘 다 몹시 예민하다는 것이다. 어둠 속에서 셔츠 단추를 잠그거나 현관문을 여는 것과 같이 촉각을 복합하게 사용하는 능력은 지속적이고도 시간에 따라 달라지는 촉각의 패턴에 의존한다.

Why? 왜 정답일까?

첫 문장인 'People don't usually think of touch as a temporal phenomenon, but it is every bit as time-based as it is spatial.'에서 사람들의 생각과는 달리 촉각은 시간에 기반을 둔 감각이라는 주제를 제시한 후, 이를 뒷받침하는 예를 들고 있다. 따라서 글의 제목으로 가장 적절한 것은 ② '시간이 진정 중요하다: 촉각의 숨겨진 본질'이다.

- temporal ⓐ 시간의
- spatial ⓐ 공간적인
- experiment ⓝ 실험
- palm ⓝ 손바닥
- identify ⓥ 알아내다
- every bit 전적으로
- carry out ~을 수행하다
- cup ⓥ 손을 컵 모양으로 모아 쥐다
- ordinary ⓐ 평범한, 일상적인
- clue ⓝ 단서, 실마리

[문제편 p.071]

- **overall** ⓐ 종합[전반]적인, 전체의
- **sensory** ⓐ 감각적인
- **acuity** ⓝ 예민함
- **humanity** ⓝ 인류, 인간성
- **timely** ⓐ 시기적절한, 때맞춘
- **at once** 동시에, 즉시
- **perception** ⓝ 지각, 인지
- **time-varying** 시간에 따라 달라지는
- **matter** ⓥ 중요하다, 문제되다
- **booster** ⓝ 촉진제

구문 풀이

13행 There's a direct analogy between the fovea at the center of
(선행사1)
your retina and your fingertips, both of which have high acuity.
(선행사2) (계속적 용법) (동사(복수))

★★ 문제 해결 꿀~팁 ★★

▶ 많이 틀린 이유는?
첫 문장에서 언급했듯 이 글은 촉각이 시간에 기반을 둔 감각임을 설명하고 있지만, 촉각이 시간 개념 형성에 있어 수행하는 '역할'에 관해서는 언급하고 있지 않다. 따라서 Role을 언급하는 ④는 Touch, Time이라는 키워드가 모두 포함되어 있더라도 정답이 아니다.

▶ 문제 해결 방법은?
두 번째 문장부터 예가 열거되는 것으로 보아 첫 문장이 주제문이고, 마지막 문장에서 주제와 같은 내용의 결론을 다시 언급하고 있다. 따라서 중간보다는 처음과 끝에 무게를 두어 독해하고 답을 추론토록 한다.

---

04 평화 마라톤 축제
정답률 94% | 정답 ⑤

Peace Marathon Festival에 관한 다음 안내문의 내용과 일치하지 <u>않는</u> 것은?

① 출발 시각은 오전 10시이다.
② 5 킬로미터 코스는 참가에 나이 제한이 없다.
③ 참가자는 선착순 1,000명으로 제한된다.
④ 모든 참가자들에게 기념품과 메달이 주어진다.
☑ 물은 결승선에서만 제공된다.

[본문 해석]

Peace Marathon Festival(평화 마라톤 축제)

평화 마라톤 축제는 세계 평화를 장려하고 도움이 필요한 사람들을 위한 온정을 나누기 위해 개최됩니다. 달리기를 즐기는 데 동참하고 더 나은 세상을 만들어 주세요.

일시 & 장소
• 2023년 9월 3일, 일요일 『(출발 시각: 오전 10시)』— 「」: ①의 근거 일치
• 시민 스타디움

참가비 & 자격
• 풀 & 하프: $30 (20세 이상)
• 『10km & 5km: $15 (나이 제한 없음)』— 「」: ②의 근거 일치

등록
• 『참가자는 1,000명으로 제한됩니다. (선착순입니다.)』— 「」: ③의 근거 일치
• ipmarathon.com에서 온라인으로만 가능

참고
• 『모든 참가자들에게 기념품과 메달이 주어집니다.』— 「」: ④의 근거 일치
• 탈의실은 무료로 이용 가능합니다.
• 『물은 2.5km마다, 그리고 결승선에서 제공됩니다.』— 「」: ⑤의 근거 불일치

Why? 왜 정답일까?

'Water will be provided every 2.5 km and at the finish line.'에서 물은 결승선뿐 아니라 2.5km 단위로 제공된다는 것을 알 수 있다. 따라서 안내문의 내용과 일치하지 않는 것은 ⑤ '물은 결승선에서만 제공된다.'이다.

Why? 왜 오답일까?

① 'Start time: 10 a.m.)'의 내용과 일치한다.
② '10 km & 5 km: $15 (No age limit)'의 내용과 일치한다.
③ 'The number of participants is limited to 1,000. (First come, first served.)'의 내용과 일치한다.
④ 'Souvenirs and medals will be given to all participants.'의 내용과 일치한다.

- **compassion** ⓝ 연민, 동정
- **qualification** ⓝ 자격 (사항)

---

05 기준점 편향
정답률 37% | 정답 ⑤

다음 글의 밑줄 친 부분 중, 어법상 틀린 것은? [3점]

[본문 해석]

기준점 편향은 초기 정보의 상대적인 질이나 적절성과 상관없이, 여러분이 어떠한 상황에서 나중에 도착하는 정보에 비해 일찍 도착하는 정보에 더 비중을 두는 경향이 있을 때 저지르는 인지 오류를 말한다. 여러분이 어떠한 상황을 보기 시작할 때 처음으로 제시되는 어떤 정보든 '기준점'을 형성할 수 있고, 생각의 방향을 이 기준점에서 벗어나도록 바꾸는 것은 논리적으로 그래야 하는 것보다도 상당히 더 어려워진다. 응급 진료에서 기준점 편향의 고전적인 예는 '부상자 분류 편향'인데, 이는 여러분이 환자에 대해 어떠한 첫인상을 갖거나 받든 그것이 그 환자를 보는 다음의 모든 의료 종사자들에게 영향을 미치는 경향이 있다는 것이다. 예를 들어 이따금 가슴까지 아래로 퍼지는 쑤시는 턱 통증으로 응급 치료를 받으러 온 두 명의 환자들을 상상해 보라. 환자를 예진하는 의료 종사자들이 어떻게 차트에 분류하는가의 차이, 예를 들어 '턱 통증' 대 '가슴 통증' 중 무엇으로 분류하는지는 그 환자들이 어떻게 치료받는가에 있어 중대한 차이를 초래할 수도 있는 기준점을 만든다.

Why? 왜 정답일까?

복수 명사 주어 Differences 뒤로 동사가 필요하므로 creating을 create로 고쳐야 한다. 따라서 어법상 틀린 것은 ⑤이다.

Why? 왜 오답일까?

① '~에 비해'라는 뜻의 분사구문 관용표현인 compared to[with]가 어법상 알맞다.
② 가주어 it에 대응되는 진주어 to alter가 어법상 알맞다.
③ 뒤에 주어인 명사절 'whatever the first impression you develop, or are given, ~', 동사 'tends to ~'로 구성된 완전한 문장이 나오므로 관계부사 where가 어법상 알맞다. triage bias는 공간 선행사로 취급되었다.
④ 선행사 aching jaw pain이 불가산 명사이므로, 이를 꾸미는 주격 관계대명사절의 동사 또한 단수형으로 써야 한다. 따라서 extends가 어법상 알맞다.

- **anchor** ⓝ 기준점
- **give weight to** ~을 중요시하다
- **relevance** ⓝ 적절성
- **bias** ⓝ 편향
- **subsequent** ⓐ 다음의, 이후의
- **occasionally** ⓐⓓ 때때로
- **cognitive** ⓐ 인지적인
- **regardless of** ~와 관계없이
- **significantly** ⓐⓓ 상당히
- **triage bias** 부상자 분류
- **present** ⓥ (환자가) 진찰을 받으러 가다

구문 풀이

5행 {Whatever data is presented to you first when you start to
(복합관계형용사(어떤 ~이든지))
look at a situation} can form an "anchor" and it becomes significantly
({ }: 주어1) (동사1) (주어2(가주어)) (동사2)
more challenging to alter your mental course away from this anchor
(보어) (진주어)
than it logically should be.

★★ 문제 해결 꿀~팁 ★★

▶ 많이 틀린 이유는?
③은 관계부사의 쓰임을 묻고 있다. where가 나오면 흔히 which와 비교해야 하는데, 뒤에 완전한 문장이 나오면 관계부사 where를, 뒤에 불완전한 문장이 나오면 관계대명사 which를 쓴다.
이 문제에서 where 뒤의 구조를 분석하면 'whatever ~ about a patient'가 '~하는 어떤 것이든'이라는 의미의 명사절 주어이고, tends to influence가 동사구, 'all subsequent providers ~'가 목적어이다. 따라서 which가 아닌 where를 쓴 것이 알맞다.

▶ 문제 해결 방법은?
복합관계사 whatever가 주어, 목적어, 보어 역할을 하는 명사절을 이끈다는 사실을 기억해 둔다. 또한, 어법 문제에서 수식어구를 동반한 긴 주어가 나오면 동사가 어디에 있는지 체크하고, 동사의 수 일치 또한 확인하도록 한다.

---

06 Voltaire의 사상과 작품 행보
정답률 34% | 정답 ④

다음 글의 밑줄 친 부분 중, 문맥상 낱말의 쓰임이 적절하지 <u>않은</u> 것은? [3점]

[본문 해석]

언론의 자유와 종교적 관용의 옹호자인 Voltaire는 논란이 많았던 인물이었다. 예를 들어 그는 "나는 여러분이 하는 말을 싫어하지만 그것을 말할 여러분의 권리를 사력을 다해 옹호할 것이다,"라고 말했다고 여겨지는데, 그것은 여러분이 경멸하는 의견조차도 들을 자격이 있다는 생각에 대한 강력한 ① 변론이었다. 하지만 18세기 유럽에서는 가톨릭 교회가 무엇이 출판될 수 있는지를 엄격히 ② 통제하였다. Voltaire의 많은 희곡과 책이 검열을 받았고 공개적으로 불태워졌으며, 그는 세력이 있는 귀족을 ③ 모욕했기 때문에 파리의 Bastille 감옥에 수감되기까지 하였다. 하지만 이 중 어떤 것도 그가 그의 주변 사람들의 편견과 가식에 도전하는 것을 막지 못했다. 그의 철학 단편 소설인 *Candide*에서, 그는 당대의 다른 사상가들이 표명했던 인류와 우주에 대한 종교적인 낙관론을 완전히 ④ 지지했고(→ 훼손했고), 이를 매우 재미있는 방식으로 하여 그 책은 즉시 베스트셀러가 되었다. 현명하게도, Voltaire는 속표지에서 자신의 이름을 ⑤ 지웠는데, 만약 그렇지 않았다면 그 책의 출판은 종교적 신념을 조롱한 이유로 다시 그를 감옥에 갇히게 했을지도 모른다.

Why? 왜 정답일까?

마지막 문장에서 Voltaire가 쓴 책은 종교적 신념을 조롱하는 내용을 담고 있었음을 알 수 있으므로, ④가 포함된 문장에서 종교적 낙관론을 '지지했다'는 뜻을 나타내는 **supported**는 이 낙관론을 '훼손했다'는 의미의 **undermined**로 고쳐야 한다. 따라서 문맥상 적절하지 않은 낱말은 ④이다.

- religious ⓐ 종교적인
- controversial ⓐ 논란이 많은
- right ⓝ 권리
- censor ⓥ 검열하다
- insult ⓥ 모욕하다
- philosophical ⓐ 철학적인
- humanity ⓝ 인류, 인간성
- publication ⓝ 출판
- toleration ⓝ 관용
- declare ⓥ 선언하다
- defense ⓝ 변론
- imprison ⓥ 감금하다
- pretension ⓝ 가식, 허세
- optimism ⓝ 낙관론
- leave off (명단 등에서) ~을 빼다, 제외하다
- make fun of ~을 조롱하다

구문 풀이

2행 He is, for instance, supposed to have declared, {"I hate
　　　　　　　　　　　　　　完了 부정사(과거)　　　동사1
what you say, but will defend to the death your right to say it,"}
　　　　　　　　　동사2　　　　　　　　　　목적어　　형용사적 용법
a powerful defense of the idea [that even views (that you despise)
　　　　　{　}와 동격　　　　　동격 접속사　　주어　↑목적격 관계대명사
deserve to be heard].
~할 자격이 있다

★★ 문제 해결 꿀~팁 ★★

▶ 많이 틀린 이유는?
최다 오답인 ⑤에서 'leave + 목적어 + off'는 '~을 빼다, 제외하다'라는 뜻이다. 뒤에서 '그렇게 하지 않았다면' Voltaire가 종교적 신념을 모독한 죄로 다시 감옥에 갔을 것이라 언급하는 것으로 볼 때, Voltaire가 자신이 쓴 책에서 이름을 '지웠고' 따라서 그가 그 책을 썼다는 것을 사람들이 몰랐기에 재수감될 위기를 면했다는 설명은 자연스럽다.

▶ 문제 해결 방법은?
어휘는 빈칸이 여러 개 있는 문제로 이해하고 선택지마다 정확한 근거를 지문에서 찾도록 한다. ④의 경우 마지막 문장에서 '종교적 신념을 조롱한' 책을 썼다고 언급하므로 종교적 낙관주의를 '지지했다'는 설명이 부적절함을 알 수 있다.

---

07 천천히 변하는 뇌
정답률 69% | 정답 ①

다음 빈칸에 들어갈 말로 가장 적절한 것을 고르시오. [3점]

✓ stability - 안정감
② maturity - 성숙함
③ curiosity - 호기심
④ variability - 가변성
⑤ productivity - 생산성

[본문 해석]

뇌의 진정한 본질은 무엇인가? 뇌는 천천히 변화하는 기계이며, 그것은 좋은 것이다. 만약 여러분의 뇌가 하룻밤 사이에 완전히 변할 수 있다면 여러분은 불안정해질 것이다. 여러분의 평소 행동 양식이 잠에서 깨서, 커피와 베이글을 먹으며 신문을 읽고, 개를 산책시키고, 뉴스를 보는 것이라고 해 보자. 이것은 여러분의 습관적인 일상이다. 그런데 어느 날 밤, 여러분이 새벽 3시에 전화를 받고 속옷 차림으로 여러분의 이웃을 확인해 보기 위해 뛰쳐나가야만 한다. 만약 여러분의 뇌가 이 새로운 일상을 자기 것으로 만들어 여러분이 매일 새벽

3시에 속옷 차림으로 계속해서 밖으로 뛰쳐나가야 한다면 어떻겠는가? 누구도 그러길 원치 않을 것이므로 우리의 뇌가 그것보다 더 많은 반복이 필요하다는 것은 좋은 것이다! 천천히 변하는 우리 뇌가 우리에게 제공해 주는 안정감을 받아들이고 고마워하자.

Why? 왜 정답일까?

첫 문장에서 뇌의 본질은 무엇인가 라는 질문을 던진 뒤 이에 대한 답으로서 '뇌는 천천히 변한다'는 내용이 제시되고 있다. 특히 'If your brain could completely change overnight, you would be unstable.'에서는 만일 뇌가 지금과는 달리 하루아침에 빠르게 변할 수 있었더라면 불안정했을 것이라는 말을 통해 천천히 변하는 뇌가 인간에게 '안정감'을 줄 수 있다는 내용을 나타내고 있다. 따라서 빈칸에 들어갈 말로 가장 적절한 것은 ① '안정감'이다.

- nature ⓝ 본질, 천성
- completely ⓐⅾ 완전히
- norm ⓝ 행동 양식, 표준, 규범
- routine ⓝ (판에 박힌) 일상
- repetition ⓝ 반복
- slow-changing 천천히 변하는
- overnight ⓐⅾ 하룻밤 사이에, 간밤에
- habitual ⓐ 습관적인
- latch on to ~을 붙들다, ~에 들러붙다
- thankful ⓐ 고마워하는

구문 풀이

2행 If your brain could completely change overnight, / you would
「if + 주어 + 과거 동사 +　　　　　　　　　　주어 + 조동사 과거 + 동사원형 : 가정법 과거」
be unstable.

---

08 객관적 증거에 의한 믿음의 검증
정답률 41% | 정답 ⑤

글의 흐름으로 보아, 주어진 문장이 들어가기에 가장 적절한 곳을 고르시오. [3점]

[본문 해석]

전부는 아니지만 대부분의 믿음은 검증 시험을 받을 수 있다. 이것은 믿음이 옳거나 그른지를 확인하기 위해 시험될 수 있다는 것을 의미한다. ① 믿음은 그 사람의 외부에 있는 객관적인 기준을 통해 진실임이 입증되거나 거짓임이 입증될 수 있다. ② 지구가 평평하고 구가 아니라고 믿는 사람들이 있다. ③ 우리는 지구가 실제로 구라는 객관적인 증거를 가지고 있기 때문에, 지구가 평평하다는 믿음은 거짓임이 증명될 수 있다. ④ 또한, 내일 비가 올 것이라는 믿음은 내일까지 기다려 비가 오는지 안 오는지 봄으로써 진실인지 확인될 수 있다. ⑤ 하지만, (9999년이 되면 지구가 자전하는 것을 멈출 것이라는 믿음이나 1억 광년 떨어진 행성에 생명체가 있다는 것 같은) 어떤 종류의 믿음은 우리가 일생 동안 외부 증거를 얻을 수 없기 때문에 진실인지 확인될 수 없다. 또한, (신의 존재와 본질과 같은) 형이상학적 믿음은 모든 사람이 진리 기준으로 기꺼이 사용할 증거를 만드는 데 있어서 상당한 난제가 된다.

Why? 왜 정답일까?

⑤ 앞에서 지구가 둥글다는 믿음과 내일 비가 올 것이라는 믿음을 예로 들어, 믿음을 외부의 객관적 기준으로 검증할 수 있는 경우를 언급하고 있다. 이와는 반대로 주어진 문장은 지구가 미래 어느 시점에는 자전을 멈출 것이라는 믿음, 또는 외계 생명체가 있다는 믿음 등은 이를 뒷받침하는 외부적 증거를 얻을 수 없기 때문에 검증이 이루어지기 어렵다는 내용을 제시하고 있다. 이어서 ⑤ 뒤의 문장은 주어진 문장과 **Also**로 연결되며, 신의 존재 등에 관한 형이상학적 믿음 또한 객관적 증거로 뒷받침되기 어려울 수 있다는 점을 추가로 제시한다. 따라서 주어진 문장이 들어가기에 가장 적절한 곳은 ⑤이다.

- external ⓐ 외부의, 외적인
- verify ⓥ 검증하다, 확인하다
- criterion ⓝ 기준 (*pl.* criteria)
- meta-physical ⓐ 형이상학의
- nature ⓝ 본질
- generate ⓥ 만들어 내다
- axis ⓝ 축
- objective ⓐ 객관적인
- sphere ⓝ 구
- existence ⓝ 존재, 실재
- considerable ⓐ 상당한
- willing ⓐ 기꺼이 ~하려는

구문 풀이

13행 Also, the belief {that it will rain tomorrow} can be tested for
　　　　　　　　　　{　}:동격절(= the belief)　　　조동사 수동태
truth by waiting until tomorrow and seeing whether it rains or not.
　　　　　전치사 동명사1　　　　　　　동명사2 명사절 접속사(~인지 아닌지)

---

09 인간이 서로 돕고 사는 이유
정답률 61% | 정답 ①

다음 글의 내용을 한 문장으로 요약하고자 한다. 빈칸 (A), (B)에 들어갈 말로 가장 적절한 것은?

[문제편 p.073]

[문제편 p.075]

(A)	(B)
✔① advantages 이익	repay 되갚다
② patience 인내	evaluate 평가하다
③ wisdom 지혜	forget 잊다
④ advantages 이익	accept 받아들이다
⑤ patience 인내	appreciate 감사하다

[본문 해석]

우리는 왜 돕는가? 널리 받아들여지는 한 가지 관점은 자기 이익이 인간의 모든 상호 작용의 기초가 되고, 우리의 지속적인 목표는 보상을 극대화하고 비용을 최소화하는 것이라는 것이다. 회계사들은 그것을 *비용-수익 분석*이라고 부른다. 철학자들은 그것을 *공리주의*라고 부른다. 사회 심리학자들은 그것을 사회적 교환 이론이라고 부른다. 만약 당신이 헌혈할지를 생각한다면, 당신은 그렇게 하는 것의 이익들(죄책감 감소, 사회적 인정, 그리고 좋은 감정) 대비 비용들(시간, 불편함, 그리고 걱정)을 따져 볼지도 모른다. 만약 그 보상들이 비용들을 초과한다면 당신은 도울 것이다. 다른 사람들은 우리가 어떻게 행동해야 하는지를 규정하는 규범들을 통해서, 우리가 그렇게 하도록 사회화되어 왔기 때문에 돕는다고 믿는다. 사회화를 통해서 우리는 상호성 규범, 즉 우리는 우리를 도와주었던 사람들에게 해가 아닌 도움을 돌려주어야 한다는 기대를 배운다. 유사한 지위의 타인들과의 관계에서, 상호성 규범은 우리로 하여금 대략 우리가 받은 만큼 (호의, 선물들, 혹은 사회적 초대를) 주도록 강요한다.

➡ 사람들은 돕는 것이 그들에게 (A) 이익을 주기 때문만이 아니라, 타인이 그들에게 한 것을 (B) 되갚아야 한다고 사회적으로 학습되기 때문에 돕는다.

Why? 왜 정답일까?

인간이 서로 돕고 사는 이유에 관해 설명한 글로, 'One widely held view is that self-interest underlies all human interactions, that our constant goal is to maximize rewards and minimize costs.'에서는 인간이 자기 이익을 추구하는 존재이기 때문에 비용을 초과하는 이득이 있을 때 남을 돕는다고 설명한다. 이어서 'Others believe that ~ we learn the reciprocity norm: ~'에서는 우리가 상호성의 규범, 즉 자신에게 도움을 제공했던 사람에게 보답을 해야 한다는 점을 학습하기 때문에 도움을 베풀게 되는 것임을 추가적으로 설명한다. 따라서 요약문의 빈칸에 들어갈 말로 가장 적절한 것은 ① '(A) advantages(이익), (B) repay(되갚다)'이다.

- underlie ⓥ ~의 기초를 이루다
- analysis ⓝ 분석
- utilitarianism ⓝ 공리주의
- approval ⓝ 인정, 승인
- prescribe ⓥ 규정하다, 처방하다
- compel ⓥ 강요하다
- accountant ⓝ 회계사
- philosopher ⓝ 철학자
- weigh ⓥ (결정을 내리기 전에) 따져 보다
- discomfort ⓝ 불편함
- reciprocity ⓝ 상호성

구문 풀이

14행 Through socialization, we learn the reciprocity norm: the expectation that we should return help, not harm, to those [who have helped us].
동격 / 동격 접속사 / 주어 / 동사 / 목적어(B+(but) not+A : A가 아니라 B인) / 선행사

10-12 잘 웃는 John의 특별한 재능

[본문 해석]

(A)

John은 민감한 소년이었다. 심지어 그의 머리카락도 간지럼을 탔다. 산들바람이 그의 머리카락에 닿으면 그는 웃음을 터뜨리곤 했다. 그리고 간지럼으로 인한 웃음이 시작되면, 아무도 그를 멈추게 할 수 없었다. John의 웃음은 전염성이 매우 강해서 John이 간지럼을 타기 시작하면 모두 결국 끝없이 웃게 되었다. 『간지럼을 잘 타는 것을 억제하기 위해 수없이 많은 다양한 모자를 써 보기도 했고, 초강력 헤어스프레이를 사용해 보기도 하며, 머리를 밀기도 하는 등 온갖 노력을 했다.』 하지만 어떤 것도 효과가 없었다. 어느 날 그는 거리에서 어떤 광대를 만났다. 그 광대는 매우 늙어서 걸음도 겨우 걸었지만 John이 울고 있는 것을 보았을 때 (a) 그를 격려하러 갔다.
└─『』:12번 ①의 근거 일치

(C)

John을 웃게 하는 데 오래 걸리지 않았고, 그들은 이야기를 나누기 시작했다.

John은 (c) 그에게 간지럼을 타는 자신의 문제에 관해 말했다. 『그리고 나서 그는 광대에게 그렇게 늙어서도 어떻게 광대 일을 계속할 수 있는지 물었다.』 "나를 대신할 사람은 없고, 내게는 해야 할 매우 중요한 일이 있단다."라고 그 광대는 말했다. 『그리고 나서 그는 John을 여러 병원과 보호 시설, 학교로 데려갔다.』
└─『』:12번 ③의 근거 일치
└─『』:12번 ④의 근거 일치

(B)

가는 곳마다 아프거나 고아가 된 아이들, 매우 심각한 문제를 가진 아이들로 가득했다. 하지만 그들은 그 광대를 보자마자, 그들의 표정은 완전히 바뀌고 미소로 밝아졌다. 그날은 훨씬 더 특별했는데, 『모든 쇼에서 John의 전염성 있는 웃음이 결국 아이들을 많이 웃게 만들곤 했기 때문이다.』 그 늙은 광대는 (b) 그에게 윙크하며 말했다. "이제 이 일이 얼마나 중요한 일인지 알겠니? 그래서 내 나이에도 나는 은퇴할 수가 없단다."
└─『』:12번 ②의 근거 일치

(D)

그리고 그는 "아무나 그 일을 할 수 있는 게 아니란다. 웃음에 특별한 재능이 있는 사람이어야 한단다."라고 덧붙여 말했다. 이 말을 했을 때 바람이 다시 John의 간지럼과 (d) 그의 웃음을 터지게 했다. 『얼마 후, John은 그 늙은 광대의 뒤를 잇기로 했다.』 그날 이후로 특별한 재능 덕분에 남다르다는 사실은 실제로 (e) John을 행복하게 만들었다.
└─『』:12번 ⑤의 근거 불일치

- sensitive ⓐ 민감한
- contagious ⓐ 전염되는
- shave ⓥ 면도하다, 깎다
- light up with ~로 빛나다
- carry on 계속해서 ~하다
- set off 유발하다, 일으키다
- burst out laughing 웃음을 터뜨리다
- end up in 결국 ~로 끝나다
- orphaned ⓐ 고아가 된
- retire ⓥ 은퇴하다
- replace ⓥ 대체하다

구문 풀이

(A) 4행 John's laughter was so contagious that when John started feeling ticklish, everyone ended up in endless laughter.
「so ~ that … : 너무 ~해서 …하다」

(B) 4행 That day was even more special, because in every show John's contagious laughter would end up making the kids laugh a lot.
「end up+동명사 : 결국 ~하게 되다」 원형부사구

(D) 2행 This said, the wind again set off John's ticklishness and his laughter.
분사구문(수동) / 의미상 주어 / 주어 / 동사

(D) 5행 From that day onward, the fact {that John was different} actually made him happy, thanks to his special gift.
주어 / { } : 동격절 / 동사 / 목적어 / 목적격 보어

10 글의 순서 파악   정답률 77% | 정답 ②

주어진 글 (A)에 이어질 내용을 순서에 맞게 배열한 것으로 가장 적절한 것은?

① (B) - (D) - (C)   ✔② (C) - (B) - (D)
③ (C) - (D) - (B)   ④ (D) - (B) - (C)
⑤ (D) - (C) - (B)

Why? 왜 정답일까?

간지럼을 잘 타고 잘 웃는 John이 어느 날 광대를 만났다는 내용의 (A) 뒤에는, John이 광대에게 자신의 문제를 상담하며 광대 일에 관해 물었다는 내용의 (C)가 연결된다. 이어서 (B)에서는 광대가 John을 데리고 웃음이 필요한 사람들에게로 향했다고 하고, (D)에서는 광대와 함께 다니며 자신의 장점을 깨달은 John이 광대의 뒤를 잇기로 결심했다고 한다. 따라서 글의 순서로 가장 적절한 것은 ② '(C) - (B) - (D)'이다.

11 지칭 추론   정답률 71% | 정답 ③

밑줄 친 (a)~(e) 중에서 가리키는 대상이 나머지 넷과 다른 것은?

① (a)   ② (b)   ✔③ (c)   ④ (d)   ⑤ (e)

Why? 왜 정답일까?

(a), (b), (d), (e)는 John, (c)는 (A)의 The clown을 가리키므로, (a)~(e) 중에서 가리키는 대상이 다른 하나는 ③ '(c)'이다.

12 세부 내용 파악
정답률 85% | 정답 ⑤

윗글의 John에 관한 내용으로 적절하지 않은 것은?

① 간지럼을 타지 않으려고 온갖 시도를 했다.
② 전염성 있는 웃음으로 아이들을 많이 웃게 했다.
③ 광대에게 그렇게 늙어서도 어떻게 계속 일할 수 있는지 물었다.
④ 광대와 함께 여러 병원과 보호 시설, 학교에 갔다.
☑ 광대의 뒤를 잇지 않기로 했다.

Why? 왜 정답일까?

(D) 'After a while, John decided to replace the old clown.'에서 늙은 광대와 하루를 보내고 난 얼마 후 John은 광대의 뒤를 잇기로 결심했다고 하므로, 내용과 일치하지 않는 것은 ⑤ '광대의 뒤를 잇지 않기로 했다.'이다.

Why? 왜 오답일까?

① (A) 'He tried everything to control his ticklishness: ~'의 내용과 일치한다.
② (B) '~ John's contagious laughter would end up making the kids laugh a lot.'의 내용과 일치한다.
③ (C) 'Then he asked the clown how such an old man could carry on being a clown.'의 내용과 일치한다.
④ (C) 'And then he took John to many hospitals, shelters, and schools.'의 내용과 일치한다.

[문제편 p.075]

DAY 13 · 20분 미니 모의고사

01 ①	02 ③	03 ①	04 ④	05 ⑤
06 ②	07 ②	08 ④	09 ③	10 ②
11 ②	12 ⑤			

DAY 13

---

01 기다리던 인턴십 합격 편지를 받은 Ester
정답률 84% | 정답 ①

다음 글에 드러난 Ester의 심경 변화로 가장 적절한 것은?

☑ anticipating → excited
　기대하는　　　신난
② confident → ashamed
　자신 있는　　부끄러운
③ curious → embarrassed
　호기심 어린　당황한
④ surprised → confused
　놀란　　　　혼란스러운
⑤ indifferent → grateful
　무관심한　　고마운

[본문 해석]

밖에서 호버 엔진의 윙윙거리는 소리가 들리자마자 Ester는 일어섰다. "편지다." 소리치며 그녀는 계단을 세 칸씩 뛰어내려가 문을 확 열었다. 비가 쏟아지고 있었지만 그녀는 빗속으로 뛰어나갔다. 그녀는 우체통을 마주하고 있었다. 안에는 뜯지 않은 편지 한 통이 들어 있었다. 그녀는 이것이 그녀가 간절히 기다리고 있던 게 틀림없다고 확신했다. 망설임 없이 그녀는 봉투를 뜯어서 열었다. 그녀는 종이를 꺼내 펼쳤다. 편지에는 '우리 회사에 지원해 주셔서 감사합니다. 우리는 당신을 인턴십 프로그램에 초대하고 싶습니다. 우리는 당신을 곧 뵙기를 기대합니다.'라고 쓰여 있었다. 그녀는 펄쩍펄쩍 뛰며 다시 편지를 내려다보았다. 그녀는 이 소식을 가족들에게 빨리 전하고 싶었다.

Why? 왜 정답일까?

어떤 편지를 기다리고 있던(She was sure this must be what she was eagerly waiting for.) Ester가 인턴십 합격 통지를 받고 몹시 기뻐했다(She couldn't wait to tell this news to her family.)는 내용이다. 따라서 Ester의 심경 변화로 가장 적절한 것은 ① '기대하는 → 신난'이다.

- hum ⓝ 웅웅거리는 소리
- swing open 활짝 열다
- face ⓥ 마주보다, 직면하다
- unopened ⓐ 개봉되지 않은
- pull out 꺼내다
- apply to ~에 지원하다
- look down at ~을 내려다보다
- anticipating ⓐ 기대하는
- stairs ⓝ 계단
- pour ⓥ (비가) 퍼붓다
- mailbox ⓝ 우편함
- eagerly [ad] 간절히
- unfold ⓥ 펼치다
- look forward to ~을 기대하다
- can't wait to ~하기를 몹시 기대하다
- embarrassed ⓐ 당황한

구문 풀이

6행 She was sure this must be {what she was eagerly waiting for}.
　　　　　　　　　　　　~임에 틀림없다　　　{ }: must be의 보어(명사절)

---

02 풍부한 다문화 경험을 자녀에게 제공하기
정답률 95% | 정답 ③

다음 글에서 필자가 주장하는 바로 가장 적절한 것은?

① 자녀가 전통문화를 자랑스럽게 여기게 해야 한다.
② 자녀가 주어진 문제를 깊이 있게 탐구하도록 이끌어야 한다.
☑ 자녀가 다른 문화를 가능한 한 자주 접할 수 있게 해야 한다.
④ 창의성 발달을 위해 자녀의 실수에 대해 너그러워야 한다.
⑤ 경험한 것을 돌이켜 볼 시간을 자녀에게 주어야 한다.

[본문 해석]

우리는 더 글로벌한 사회로 나아가고 있지만, 다양한 민족 집단들은 전통적으로 상당히 다르게 일을 하고 있어, 새로운 관점이 개방적인 아이를 만드는 데 가치가 있다. 광범위한 다문화 경험은 아이를 더 창의적으로 (얼마나 많은 생각을 떠올릴 수 있는지와 연상 능력으로 측정됨) 만들고 아이가 자신의 생각을 확장하기 위해 다른 문화로부터 색다른 생각을 포착할 수 있게 한다. 부모로서 가능한 한 자주 자녀가 다른 문화를 접하게 해야 한다. 할 수 있다면 자녀와 다른 나라로 여행하고, 가능하면 거기서 살라. 둘 다 가능하지 않은 경우에는 지역 축제 탐방하기와 다른 문화에 대한 도서관 책 빌리기, 집에서 다른 문화의 음식 요리하기와 같이 국내에서 할 수 있는 일이 많다.

Why? 왜 정답일까?

'As a parent, you should expose your children to other cultures as often as possible.'에서 자녀에게 다른 문화를 가급적 많이 접할 수 있게 해 주어야 한다고 하므로, 필자의 주장으로 가장 적절한 것은 ③ '자녀가 다른 문화를 가능한 한 자주 접할 수 있게 해야 한다.'이다.

- ethnic @ 민족의
- perspective ⓝ 관점, 시각
- open-minded @ (사고가) 개방적인
- multicultural @ 다문화적인
- association ⓝ 연상, 연관
- capture ⓥ 포착하다, 붙잡다
- expand ⓥ 확장하다
- at home 국내에서

- traditionally ⓐⓓ 전통적으로
- valuable @ 가치가 있는
- extensive @ 광범위한
- come up with ~을 떠올리다
- allow ⓥ 허락하다, 가능하게 하다
- unconventional @ 색다른
- expose ⓥ 접하게 하다
- explore ⓥ 탐방하다, 탐험하다

구문 풀이

4행 Extensive multicultural experience makes kids more
　　　　　　　　　　　　　　　　　　　　동사1 목적어1 목적격 보어1(형용사)
creative (measured {by how many ideas they can come up with} and
　　　　　　　　　　　　　　　　　　　　　{ }: 전치사구 병렬
{by association skills}) and allows them to capture unconventional
　　　　　　　　　　　　　동사2 목적어2   목적격 보어2
ideas from other cultures to expand on their own ideas.
　　　　　　　　　　　　　　　부사적 용법(~하기 위해)

---

03 아이에 따라 양육 방식을 맞춤 설계하기　　　정답률 86% | 정답 ①

다음 글의 요지로 가장 적절한 것은?
☑ ① 자녀의 특성에 맞는 개별화된 양육이 필요하다.
② 식물을 키우는 것이 자녀의 창의성 발달에 도움이 된다.
③ 정서적 교감은 자녀의 바람직한 인격 형성에 필수적이다.
④ 자녀에게 타인을 존중하는 태도를 가르치는 것이 중요하다.
⑤ 전문가에 의해 검증된 양육 방식을 따르는 것이 바람직하다.

[본문 해석]

대중적인 양육법을 단순히 채택하는 것의 문제는 그것이 방정식의 가장 중요한 변수, 즉 자녀의 독특함을 무시한다는 것이다. 그래서, 한 가지 양육 방식이 모든 아이들에게 효과가 있을 것이라고 주장하기보다는, 정원사 안내서의 일부를 참고할 수도 있다. 정원사가 의문이나 거부감 없이 식물의 요구 사항을 받아들이고 각각의 식물이 자라고 번성하는 데 필요한 적절한 조건을 제공하는 것처럼, 우리 부모도 역시 아이들 각각의 타고난 욕구에 맞는 양육을 맞춤 설계할 필요가 있다. 그것이 어려워 보일지 모르지만, 가능하다. 일단 우리가 우리 아이들이 진정 어떤 아이인지를 알게 되면, 우리가 양육하도록 축복 받은 각각의 아이에게 보다 긍정적이고 수용적이도록 양육 방식에 변화를 줄 방법을 알아내기 시작할 수 있다.

Why? 왜 정답일까?

'~ so, too, do we parents need to custom-design our parenting to fit the natural needs of each individual child.'에서 부모는 아이들 각각의 필요에 맞는 양육 방식을 맞춤 설계할 필요성이 있다고 하므로, 글의 요지로 가장 적절한 것은 ① '자녀의 특성에 맞는 개별화된 양육이 필요하다.'이다.

- adopt ⓥ 채택하다
- parenting ⓝ 양육
- variable ⓝ 변수 @ 가변적인
- gardner ⓝ 정원사, 원예사
- handbook ⓝ 안내서
- requirement ⓝ 필요조건
- flourish ⓥ 번성하다
- blessed @ 축복 받은

- method ⓝ 방법
- ignore ⓥ 무시하다
- uniqueness ⓝ 독특함, 고유함
- insist ⓥ 주장하다
- resistance ⓝ 저항
- provide ⓥ 제공하다
- possible @ 가능한

구문 풀이

6행 Just as the gardener accepts, (without question or resistance),
　　　　　접속사(~와 마찬가지로)　　　( ): 삽입구
the plant's requirements and provides the right conditions [each plant
　　　　　목적어1　　　　　　동사2　　　　목적어2(선행사)
needs to grow and flourish], so, too, do we parents need to custom-
　　　　　　　　　　　　　　　'so + 조동사 + 주어 + 동사원형': 긍정 동의(~도 그렇다)
design our parenting to fit the natural needs of each individual child.

---

04 미국인 연령대별 선호 거주지 비율　　　정답률 93% | 정답 ④

다음 도표의 내용과 일치하지 <u>않는</u> 것은?

Americans' Preferred Type of Place to Live
(surveyed in 2020)

Note: Percentages may not sum to 100% due to rounding.

[본문 해석]

위의 그래프는 2020년 조사를 기반으로 연령대별로 미국인이 선호하는 거주지 유형의 비율을 보여준다. ① 각기 세 가지 연령대에서 읍내/시골 지역은 가장 선호되는 거주지 유형이었다. ② 18 ~ 34세 그룹에서는 대도시/소도시를 선호하는 비율이 대도시/소도시 근교를 선호하는 비율보다 더 높았다. ③ 35 ~ 54세 연령층에서는 대도시/소도시 근교를 선호하는 비율이 대도시/소도시를 선호하는 비율을 앞질렀다. ④ 55세 이상 연령층에서는 세 가지 선호하는 거주지 유형 중에서 대도시/소도시를 선택한 비율이 가장 낮았다. ⑤ 세 가지 선호하는 거주지 유형의 각각의 비율은 세 연령대에 걸쳐 20%보다 더 높았다.

Why? 왜 정답일까?

도표에 따르면, 55세 이상 연령층에서 가장 적게 선택된 항목은 '대도시/소도시'(26%)가 아닌, '대도시/소도시 근교'(22%)이다. 따라서 도표와 일치하지 않는 것은 ④이다.

- place to live 살 곳, 거주지
- age group 연령 집단
- percentage ⓝ 백분율, 비율
- rounding ⓝ 반올림

- survey ⓥ 설문 조사하다 ⓝ 설문 조사
- suburb ⓝ 근교, 교외
- sum to 더해서 ~가 되다
- exceed ⓥ 능가하다

---

05 확실성에 대한 선호로 생존해가는 인간　　　정답률 58% | 정답 ⑤

다음 글의 밑줄 친 부분 중, 어법상 틀린 것은? [3점]

[본문 해석]

인간은 확실성을 좋아한다. 이 선호는 검치호와 독이 있는 딸기류 열매 곁에서 살아남아야 했던 우리의 고대 선조들로부터 유래한다. 우리의 뇌는 우리가 위협에 주의하고 그것에서 벗어나 이후 살아남을 수 있게 진화했다. 사실, 우리는 무언가에 대해 더 확신할수록 옳은 선택을 할 가능성이 더 크다는 것을 학습했다. 이 딸기류 열매는 지난번과 모양이 같은가? 같은 크기인가? 그게 그렇다는 것을 확실히 안다면, 내 뇌는 내가 그것을 먹도록 지시할 텐데, 그것이 안전하다는 것을 내가 알기 때문이다. 그리고 만약 내게 확신이 없다면, 내 뇌는 나를 보호하고자 위험 신호를 보낼 것이다. 그 모든 수천 년 전의 확실성에 대한 의존은 현재까지 우리의 생존을 책임졌고, 그 위험을 알리는 시스템은 계속하여 우리를 지키고 있다. 이것은 우리의 뇌가 새롭거나 모호하거나 예측할 수 없는 매일의 사건과 경험을 불확실한 것으로 명명함으로써 이루어진다. 그런 후 우리의 뇌는 그 불확실한 요소로부터 우리를 안전하게 지키기 위해 감각, 사고, 그리고 행동 계획을 만들어 내고, 우리는 살아서 또 다른 날을 보게 된다.

Why? 왜 정답일까?

주어 Our brains 뒤로 동사가 필요하므로 generating을 generate로 고쳐야 한다. 뒤에 따로 술어가 나오지 않는 것으로 보아 ⑤가 곧 술어 자리이기 때문이다. 따라서 어법상 틀린 것은 ⑤이다.

Why? 왜 오답일까?

① our ancient ancestors가 사람 선행사이므로 이를 수식하는 주격 관계대명사 who를 썼다.
② keep away의 주어는 Our brains인데 목적어는 threats이므로, '자기 자신'을 가리키는 재귀대명사 themselves가 아닌 인칭대명사 them을 썼다.
③ 'the + 비교급 ~, the + 비교급 …(~할수록 더 …하다)' 구문이다. 비교급의 품사가

형용사일지 부사일지 알려면 비교급 뒤를 보면 되는데, 여기서는 we were와 같이 2형식 문장이 나온다. 즉 ③이 were의 보어 자리이므로 형용사인 certain이 적절하게 쓰였다. ④ it is (the same shape and size)의 의미이므로 be동사가 알맞게 쓰였다.

- **certainty** ⓝ 확실성
- **saber-toothed tiger** 검치호
- **threat** ⓝ 위협
- **send out** 내보내다
- **dependence** ⓝ 의존
- **unpredictable** ⓐ 예측 불가한
- **stem from** ~에서 기원하다
- **attend to** ~에 주의를 기울이다
- **uncertain** ⓐ 확신이 없는
- **alert** ⓐ 경고, 경계 태세 ⓐ 경계하는, 기민한
- **vague** ⓐ 희미한
- **generate** ⓥ 만들어내다

구문 풀이

8행 〔접속사(조건)〕 If I know for certain it is, my brain will direct me to eat it 〔현재시제〕 ... 〔미래시제〕 because I know it's safe.

06 이야기와 신뢰
정답률 63% | 정답 ②

(A), (B), (C)의 각 네모 안에서 문맥에 맞는 낱말로 가장 적절한 것은? [3점]

(A)	(B)	(C)
① exists 존재한다	deceptive 기만적인	Respecting 존중하는 것
✓② exists 존재한다	sacrificial 희생적인	Respecting 존중하는 것
③ exists 존재한다	sacrificial 희생적인	Wasting 낭비하는 것
④ vanishes 사라진다	sacrificial 희생적인	Respecting 존중하는 것
⑤ vanishes 사라진다	deceptive 기만적인	Wasting 낭비하는 것

[본문 해석]

이야기는 오직 이야기하는 사람만큼만 믿을 만하다. 이야기가 효과적이려면 신뢰가 확립되어야 한다. 그렇다, 신뢰다. 누군가가 여러분의 말을 듣기 위해 멈출 때마다, 무언의 신뢰라는 요소가 (A) 존재한다. 여러분의 이야기를 듣는 사람은 여러분이 가치 있는 어떤 것, 즉 그의 시간을 낭비하지 않을 어떤 것을 그에게 말할 것이라고 무의식적으로 신뢰한다. 그가 여러분에게 주는 몇 분간의 관심은 (B) 희생적이다. 그는 다른 어딘가에 자신의 시간을 보내는 걸 선택할 수 있었지만 대화에서 여러분의 말을 존중하기 위해 멈추었다. 여기가 이야기가 들어오는 곳이다. 이야기는 요점을 분명하게 설명하고, 종종 주제들을 쉽게 연결하기 때문에 신뢰가 *빨리* 확립될 수 있으며, 이러한 이야기의 시간적 요소를 인지하는 것이 신뢰에 필수적이다. 여러분의 이야기를 듣는 사람의 시간을 (C) 존중하는 것이 여러분의 문장 맨 앞의 대문자(시작점)이다. *만약* 신뢰가 얻어지고 당연하게 여겨지지 않는다면 그것은 대화를 들을 만한 가치가 있는 문장으로 이끈다.

Why? 왜 정답일까?

(A) 뒤에서 청자는 화자가 가치 있는 어떤 것을 이야기하리라고 무의식적으로 '신뢰한다'고 언급하는 것으로 보아, (A)에는 신뢰가 '있다'는 의미를 완성하는 exists가 들어가야 적절하다.
(B) 뒤에서 대화 상대방은 다른 일을 할 수도 있는 시간에 우리 이야기를 듣기로 선택했다는 이야기가 나오는데, 이는 상대가 우리를 위해 '희생하고' 있다는 사실을 상기시키는 진술이다. 따라서 (B)에는 sacrificial이 들어가야 적절하다.
(C) 앞에서 대화의 시간적 요소를 '인지하라'고 언급하므로, (C)에는 이를 달리 표현한 Respecting이 들어가야 적절하다. 따라서 각 네모 안에서 문맥에 맞는 낱말로 가장 적절한 것은 ② '(A) exists(존재한다) − (B) sacrificial(희생적인) − (C) Respecting(존중하는 것)'이다.

- **establish** ⓥ 확립하다
- **vanish** ⓥ 사라지다
- **worthwhile** ⓐ 가치 있는
- **sacrificial** ⓐ 희생적인
- **illustrate** ⓥ 분명하게 보였다
- **essential** ⓐ 필수적인, 본질적인
- **unspoken** ⓐ 무언의, 이야기되지 않은
- **unconsciously** ⓐ 무의식적으로
- **deceptive** ⓐ 기만적인
- **part** ⓝ (배역의) 말, 대사
- **bridge** ⓥ 연결하다

구문 풀이

14행 〔동명사구 주어〕 Respecting your listener's time is the capital letter 〔동사(단수)〕 at the beginning of your sentence — it leads the conversation into 〔~의 시작점에〕 〔「lead + A + into + B : A를 B로 이끌다」〕 a sentence worth listening to if trust is earned and not taken for 〔「worth + 동명사 : ~할 가치가 있는」〕 granted.

---

07 예측 불가능한 자극이 있을 때 일어나는 학습
정답률 57% | 정답 ②

다음 빈칸에 들어갈 말로 가장 적절한 것을 고르시오.
① audible – 잘 들리는지
② predictable – 예측 가능한지 ✓
③ objective – 객관적인지
④ countable – 셀 수 있는지
⑤ recorded – 녹음된 것인지

[본문 해석]

어떤 학습도 오류 신호 없이는 가능하지 않다. 유기체는 사건이 기대에 어긋날 때에만 학습한다. 다시 말해 놀람은 학습의 근본적인 동력 중 하나이다. 일련의 똑같은 음인 AAAAA를 듣는 것을 상상해 보라. 각각의 음은 여러분의 뇌의 청각 영역에서 반응을 끌어내지만, 음이 반복되면서 그 반응은 점진적으로 감소한다. 이것은 '적응'이라 불리며, 뇌가 다음 사건을 예상하는 법을 배울 것임을 알려주는 현혹될 정도로 단순해 보이는 현상이다. 문득, 그 음이 AAAAA#으로 바뀐다. 당신의 일차 청각 피질은 즉시 강한 놀람의 반응을 보이는데, 즉 적응이 점차 사라질 뿐만 아니라 예상치 못한 소리에 대한 반응으로 추가적인 뉴런이 힘차게 활성화되기 시작한다. 그리고 적응을 유발하는 것은 단순한 반복이 아니며, 중요한 것은 그 음이 예측 가능한지이다. 예를 들어 만약 당신이 ABABA와 같이 일련의 교차하는 음을 듣는다면, 당신의 뇌는 이 교차에 익숙해지고, 당신의 청각 영역 내 활동은 다시 감소한다. 그러나 이번에는 놀람의 반응을 일으키는 것은 바로 ABABB와 같은 예상치 못한 반복이다.

Why? 왜 정답일까?

첫 세 문장에서 학습이 가능한 것은 오류 신호, 즉 '예측을 벗어나는 놀람'이 있을 때라고 한다(Organisms only learn when events violate their expectations. In other words, surprise is one of the fundamental drivers of learning.). 이어서 우리 뇌는 자극에 '적응하는' 능력을 지니고 있기에 반복되는 패턴에 주의를 덜 기울이고, 예측에 벗어나는 변칙이 주어질 때 '놀라면서' 비로소 학습하려 한다는 설명이 제시된다. 따라서 빈칸에 들어갈 말로 가장 적절한 것은 ② '예측 가능한지'이다.

- **violate** ⓥ 위반하다
- **identical** ⓐ 동일한
- **draw out** ~을 끌어내다
- **progressively** ⓐ 점진적으로
- **phenomenon** ⓝ 현상
- **primary** ⓐ 1차의, 주요한, 기본적인
- **vigorously** ⓐ 힘차게
- **audible** ⓐ 잘 들리는, 들을 수 있는
- **fundamental** ⓐ 근본적인
- **note** ⓝ 음
- **auditory** ⓐ 청각의
- **deceptively** ⓐ 현혹될 정도로
- **anticipate** ⓥ 기대하다, 예상하다
- **cortex** ⓝ (대뇌의) 피질
- **alternate** ⓥ 번갈아 나오다, 교대로 나오다
- **predictable** ⓐ 예측 가능한

구문 풀이

11행 Your primary auditory cortex immediately shows a strong surprise reaction: not only does the adaptation fade away, but 〔「부정어구 + 조동사 + 주어 + 동사원형 : 도치 구문」〕 additional neurons begin to vigorously fire in response to the unexpected sound.

★★★ 1등급 대비 고난도 3점 문제

08 혁신에 대한 동기 부여
정답률 37% | 정답 ④

다음 빈칸에 들어갈 말로 가장 적절한 것을 고르시오. [3점]
① the unknown is more helpful than the negative
미지의 것이 부정적인 것보다 더 도움이 되기
② it highlights the progress they've already made
그들이 이미 이룬 진전을 강조하기
③ it is not irrational but is consumer-based practice
불합리하지 않지만 소비자 중심의 관행이기
✓④ it reframes a gain-framed activity in terms of losses
손실의 관점에서 수익 (창출로) 구조화된 활동을 재구조화하기
⑤ they discuss how well it fits their profit-sharing plans
그것이 그들의 수익 공유 계획에 얼마나 적합한지 그들이 논의하기

[본문 해석]

거대 제약회사 Merck에서 CEO인 Kenneth Frazier는 그의 간부들이 혁신과 변화를 이끄는 데 보다 적극적인 역할을 취하도록 동기를 부여하기로 결심하였다. 그는 그들이 급진적인 무엇인가를 하도록 요청하였는데, Merck를 폐업시킬 아이디어들을 만들어내라는 것이었다. 다음 두 시간 동안 회사 간부들은 Merck의 주요 경쟁사 가운데 하나인 체하면서 그룹으로 작업을 하였다. 그들이 그들의 회사를 짓밟을 만한 약과 그들이 놓쳤던 주요 시장에 대한 아이디어를 발전시키는 동안 에너지가 치솟았다. 그러고 나서, 그들의 과제는 그들의 역할을 반대로 하여 이러한 위험을 어떻게 방어할 수 있는지를 알아내는 것이었다. 이러한 "회사 무너뜨리기" 활동은 손실의 관점에서 수익 (창출로) 구조

DAY 13

화된 활동을 재구조화하기 때문에 강력하다. 혁신 기회에 대해 심사숙고할 때, 리더들은 위험을 무릅쓰지 않는 경향이 있었다. 그들이 그들의 경쟁자들이 그들을 어떻게 폐업시킬 수 있을지를 고려했을 때, 그들은 혁신하지 않는 것이 위험한 것이라는 것을 깨달았다. 혁신의 다급함이 명확해졌다.

Why? 왜 정답일까?

간부들에게 혁신의 동기를 부여하기 위해 경쟁사의 입장에서 회사를 망하게 할 아이디어를 먼저 떠올려 보게 했던 Merck 사의 이야기를 다룬 글이다. 'Then, their challenge was to reverse their roles and figure out how to defend against these threats.'에서 뒤이어 간부들은 다시 입장을 바꾸어 회사가 그런 아이디어들로 망하지 않기 위해서는 어떻게 해야 하는가를 알아내야 했다는 이야기가 나오는데, 이는 곧 회사가 손실을 보거나 큰 위기에 처하는 상황을 먼저 생각해본 뒤 그에 맞추어서 혁신의 기회를 재고할 기회를 갖게 된 것으로 이해할 수 있다. 따라서 빈칸에 들어갈 말로 가장 적절한 것은 ④ '손실의 관점에서 수익 (창출로) 구조화된 활동을 재구조화하기'이다.

- **pharmaceutical** ⓐ 제약의, 약학의
- **executive** ⓝ 임원, 간부
- **radical** ⓐ 급진적인
- **put out of business** ~을 문 닫게 하다
- **competitor** ⓝ 경쟁자, 경쟁 상대
- **reverse** ⓥ 뒤집다
- **threat** ⓝ 위협
- **urgency** ⓝ 다급함
- **unknown** ⓐ 미지의
- **reframe** ⓥ 다시 구성하다
- **motivate** ⓥ 동기를 부여하다
- **innovation** ⓝ 혁신
- **generate** ⓥ 만들어내다, 창출하다
- **pretend** ⓥ ~인 척하다
- **soar** ⓥ 치솟다, 급등하다
- **defend** ⓥ 방어하다, 막다
- **be inclined to** ~하는 경향이 있다
- **apparent** ⓐ 명백한
- **irrational** ⓐ 비이성적인

구문 풀이

7행 Energy soared / as they developed ideas for drugs [that would crush theirs] and key markets [they had missed].
주어 / 자동사 / ~하면서, ~함에 따라 / 전치사 / 목적어1 / 목적어2

★★ 문제 해결 꿀~팁 ★★

▶ 많이 틀린 이유는?
오답률이 선택지 별로 고르게 포진한 것으로 볼 때, 매력적인 오답이 두드러지지는 않았지만 정답 선택지의 표현이 어려워 틀린 수험생이 많았다는 점을 유추할 수 있다.
▶ 문제 해결 방법은?
경쟁사 입장에서 회사에 손실을 끼칠 방법을 먼저 생각하게 한 후 이를 방어할 아이디어를 다시 찾게 함으로써 혁신의 필요성을 일깨웠다는 것이 글의 주제이다. ④의 a gain-framed activity가 '혁신'을, 'reframes ~ in terms of losses'가 실험의 과정을 묘사한다.

★★★ 1등급 대비 고난도 2점 문제

09 | 과거 유럽의 통치 권력 | 정답률 35% | 정답 ③

다음 글에서 전체 흐름과 관계 <u>없는</u> 문장은?

[본문 해석]
유럽 초기 민주주의의 아이러니는 바로 유럽의 통치자들이 매우 오랫동안 현저하게 약했기 때문에 그것이 번성하고 번영했다는 것이다.① 로마의 멸망 후 천 년 넘게, 유럽의 통치자들은 백성들이 생산하고 있었던 것을 평가해 이를 바탕으로 상당한 세금을 부과할 능력이 부족했다. ② 유럽의 연약함을 설명하는 가장 눈에 띄는 방법은 그들이 거둔 세입이 얼마나 적은지를 보여주는 것이다. ③ 이러한 이유로, 유럽의 세금 징수원은 막대한 액수의 세입을 거둘 수 있었고, 그리하여 사회가 어떻게 기능해야 하는지에 큰 영향을 미쳤다. ④ 유럽인들은 결국 강력한 세입 징수 시스템을 개발했지만, 그렇게 하는 데 엄청나게 오랜 시간이 걸렸다. ⑤ 중세 시대와 초기 근대의 일부 동안, 중국의 황제들과 이슬람 문명의 칼리프들은 작은 도시 국가를 제외한 그 어느 유럽 통치자들보다 경제적 생산물 중 훨씬 많은 양을 뜯어낼 수 있었다.

Why? 왜 정답일까?

유럽의 적은 세금 수입을 보면 유럽의 통치 권력이 강하지 않았다는 것을 알 수 있다는 내용인데, ③은 유럽의 징수원이 막대한 세금을 거둬들일 수 있었다는 모순되는 내용이다. 따라서 전체 흐름과 관계 없는 문장은 ③이다.

- **democracy** ⓝ 민주주의
- **prosper** ⓥ 번영하다
- **assess** ⓥ 평가하다
- **thrive** ⓥ 번성하다
- **remarkably** ⓐⓓ 현저하게
- **levy** ⓥ 부과하다

- **substantial** ⓐ 상당한
- **illustrate** ⓥ 분명히 보여주다
- **huge** ⓐ 거대한, 막대한
- **medieval** ⓐ 중세의
- **emperor** ⓝ 황제
- **extract** ⓥ 뜯어내다, 얻어내다
- **striking** ⓐ 눈에 띄는
- **revenue** ⓝ 세입, 수입
- **awfully** ⓐⓓ 몹시, 지독히
- **era** ⓝ 시대
- **caliph** ⓝ 칼리프(과거 이슬람 국가의 통치자)
- **with the exception of** ~을 제외하고

구문 풀이

11행 Europeans would eventually develop strong systems of revenue collection, but it took them an awfully long time to do so.
= it took an awfully long time for them to do so(의미상 주어 활용)

★★ 문제 해결 꿀~팁 ★★

▶ 많이 틀린 이유는?
유럽의 통치 권력이 약했다는 것을 적은 세금 수입으로 알 수 있다는 내용인데, ④에서 갑자기 '세금 징수 체계'를 언급하므로 흐름상 부자연스러워 보일 수 있다. 하지만 이 문장의 진짜 의미는 유럽에서 (세금을 더 잘 거두기 위해) 세입 체계를 만들기는 했지만 그렇게 하는 데도 시간이 오래 걸렸을 정도로 '통치 권력이 약했다'는 것이다.
▶ 문제 해결 방법은?
모든 문장에서 '세금 징수'가 언급되고 있으므로, 소재가 어긋나는 문장은 없다. 이럴 때는 주제와 반대되는 문장이 없는지 살펴보면 된다.

★★★ 1등급 대비 고난도 3점 문제

10 | 농경 이후 사회의 인구 | 정답률 37% | 정답 ②

주어진 글 다음에 이어질 글의 순서로 가장 적절한 것을 고르시오. [3점]
① (A) − (C) − (B)
② (B) − (A) − (C)
③ (B) − (C) − (A)
④ (C) − (A) − (B)
⑤ (C) − (B) − (A)

[본문 해석]
농경 이후에 존재했던 사람들이 더 행복했든, 더 건강했든, 아니면 둘 다 아니었든 간에 관계없이, 더 많은 수의 사람들이 있었다는 것은 부인할 수 없다. 농경은 더 많은 사람을 부양하는 동시에, 그들을 지탱해 주는 농작물을 기를 더 많은 사람을 필요로 한다.

(B) 물론, 추정치는 다양하지만, 증거에 따르면 농경이 확립된 후 전 세계적으로 인구가 1 ~ 5백만 명에서 수억 명으로 증가했다.

(A) 그리고 더 많은 인구는 더 큰 가족을 위해 더 큰 상자의 시리얼을 사는 것 같이 단지 모든 것의 규모를 확장하는 것을 의미하지는 않는다. 그것은 사람들의 생활 방식에 질적인 변화를 가져온다.

(C) 예를 들어 더 많은 사람은 더 많은 종류의 질병을 의미하는데, 특히 그 사람들이 한 곳에 정착해 있을 때 그렇다. 그러한 사람들의 집단은 또한 음식을 장기간 보관할 수 있고, 이것은 가진 자와 가지지 못한 자가 있는 사회를 만들어 낸다.

Why? 왜 정답일까?

농경 이후 사회의 인구는 이전보다 더 많아졌다는 내용을 제시하는 주어진 글 뒤에는, 농경 이후의 인구 증가를 수치로 보여주는 (B), 농경이 사람들의 생활 방식에 질적인 변화를 가져왔다는 내용의 (A), 질적 변화에 대한 예를 드는 (C)가 차례로 이어져야 한다. 따라서 글의 순서로 가장 적절한 것은 ② '(B) − (A) − (C)'이다.

- **regardless of** ~에 관계없이
- **undeniable** ⓐ 부인할 수 없는
- **require** ⓥ 필요로 하다, 요구하다
- **sustain** ⓥ 지탱하다, 부양하다
- **increase** ⓥ 증가하다
- **estimate** ⓝ 추정치 ⓥ 추정하다
- **evidence** ⓝ 증거
- **established** ⓐ 확립된
- **agriculture** ⓝ 농경
- **support** ⓥ 부양하다, 지지하다
- **crop** ⓝ 농작물
- **population** ⓝ 인구
- **qualitative** ⓐ 질적인
- **vary** ⓥ 다양하다, 다르다
- **point to** ~을 보여주다, 시사하다
- **store** ⓥ 저장하다

구문 풀이

10행 Estimates vary, of course, but evidence points to an increase
주어1 / 동사1(자동사) / 주어2 / 동사2(~을 시사하다)
in the human population from 1-5 million people worldwide to a few
「from + A + to + B : A에서 B까지」
hundred million / once agriculture had become established.
일단 ~한 후에 / 과거완료

maintenance of the machines, which resulted in lower production and thus a loss of profits.'에서 기계의 과도한 사용으로 인한 부정적 결과가 잘 나타나므로, 이를 반영한 글의 제목으로 가장 적절한 것은 ② '과도한 사용을 막기 위해 기계에게 휴식을 주라'이다.

12 어휘 추론

정답률 41% | 정답 ⑤

밑줄 친 (a) ~ (e) 중에서 문맥상 낱말의 쓰임이 적절하지 **않은** 것은?

① (a) ② (b) ③ (c) ④ (d) ☑ (e)

Why? 왜 정답일까?

'The new manager had to put significant time and effort into repair and maintenance of the machines, which resulted in lower production and thus a loss of profits.'에서 내내 돌아가던 기계가 부품이 많이 닳고 상하는 바람에 기존의 관리자 이후에 부임해 온 사람은 기계를 유지 보수하는 데 많은 시간과 비용을 써야만 했다고 설명하고 있다. 이를 근거로 볼 때, 마지막 문장은 제때 유지 보수에 관심을 기울이지 않았던 것이 장기적으로는 '부정적인' 결과를 초래했다는 결론으로 끝나야 하므로, (e)의 positive는 negative로 고쳐야 한다. 따라서 문맥상 낱말의 쓰임이 적절하지 않은 것은 ⑤ '(e)'이다.

▶ 많이 틀린 이유는?
(B)는 농경 이후 세계 인구가 1 ~ 5백만에서 수억까지 증가했다는 내용으로 끝나는데 (C)는 사람들이 많아지면 질병도 많아진다는 내용으로 이어지고 있어 두 단락 사이에 논리적 연관성이 없다. 따라서 (B) 뒤로 '사람들이 많아지면 삶에서 단순히 양적인 변화뿐 아니라 질적인 변화도 야기된다'는 내용을 제시하는 (A)가 먼저 나온 후 '질적인 변화'를 부가 설명하는 (C)가 연결되어야 한다.
▶ 문제 해결 방법은?
For example 등 연결어는 순서 문제 풀이에 큰 힌트를 제공한다. 여기서도 (C)의 For example 뒤로 소개되는 예시가 (A)와 (B) 중 어느 단락과 연결되는지를 중점적으로 파악해보면 정답을 찾을 수 있다.

11-12 적절한 휴지기와 유지 보수의 중요성

[본문 해석]
한 조직이 질 좋은 제품을 더 낮은 가격으로 생산할 수 있는 새로운 기계를 수입했다. 한 관리자는 상대적으로 짧은 시간에 많은 양을 책임지고 있었다. 그는 새로운 기계를 (a) 꽉 채워 사용하는 것으로 시작했다. 그는 그것을 최대 성능으로 24시간 7일 내내 작동시켰다. 그는 비가동 시간, 회복을 위한 휴지기, 또는 기계의 일반적인 유지 보수에는 최소의 주의를 기울였다. 그 기계가 새것이었으므로 그것은 계속해서 결과물을 만들어 냈고, 그리하여 그 조직의 수익성은 (b) 치솟았으며 그 관리자는 성과를 인정받았다. 이제 얼마의 시간이 흘러, 이 관리자는 승진하였고 다른 지점으로 옮겼다. 새로운 관리자가 제조 지점 운영을 담당하기 위해 그의 자리를 채우러 왔다. 그러나 이 관리자는 과도한 사용과 유지 보수를 위한 비가동 시간의 부재로 인해 기계의 많은 부품들이 상당히 (c) 닳았고 대체되거나 수리될 필요가 있다는 것을 깨달았다. 『새 관리자는 상당한 시간과 노력을 그 기계의 수리와 유지 보수에 들여야만 했고, 그것은 생산 감소와 그에 따른 이익의 손실을 초래했다.』 이전의 관리자는 비록 단기간에 좋은 결과를 얻었을지라도 생산 목표만을 신경 썼고 기계를 (d) 무시했다. 그러나 궁극적으로 회복과 유지 보수에 주의를 기울이지 않은 것은 장기간의 (e) 긍정적인(→ 부정적인) 결과들을 초래했다.

『 』: 11, 12번의 근거

- **import** ⓥ 수입하다
- **utilization** ⓝ 사용
- **maintenance** ⓝ 유지 보수
- **appreciate** ⓥ (진가를) 인정하다
- **significantly** ad 상당히
- **ultimately** ad 궁극적으로
- **maximize** ⓥ 최대화하다
- **quantity** ⓝ 양
- **downtime** ⓝ (기계 등의) 비가동 시간
- **profitability** ⓝ 수익성
- **promote** ⓥ 승진하다
- **worn** ⓐ 닳은, 해진
- **consequence** ⓝ 결과

구문 풀이

15행 But this manager realized that with heavy utilization and
접속사(~것)
without any downtime for maintenance, a lot of the parts of the
주어(복수)
machinery were significantly worn and needed to be replaced or
동사구1   동사구2
repaired.

11 제목 파악

정답률 45% | 정답 ②

윗글의 제목으로 가장 적절한 것은?
① Why Are Quality Products Important?
  왜 양질의 제품이 중요한가?
☑ Give Machines a Break to Avoid Overuse
  과도한 사용을 막기 위해 기계에게 휴식을 주라
③ Providing Incentives to Maximize Workers' Abilities
  근로자의 능력을 최대화하기 위해 인센티브를 제공하는 것
④ Tip for Managers: The Right Man in the Right Place
  관리자들을 위한 조언: 적재적소(적당한 사람을 적합한 곳에)
⑤ Wars for High Productivity in a World of Competition
  경쟁의 세계에서 높은 생산성을 위한 전쟁

Why? 왜 정답일까?

생산성이 좋은 기계를 쉴 틈 없이 최대 능력치로 가동했다가 결국에는 많은 부품이 빨리 닳게 되어 유지 보수 비용과 생산성 면에서 손해가 야기되었다는 내용을 다룬 글이다. 특히 'The new manager had to put significant time and effort into repair and

DAY 14 · 20분 미니 모의고사

01 ①	02 ⑤	03 ②	04 ③	05 ⑤
06 ④	07 ①	08 ③	09 ②	10 ⑤
11 ④	12 ⑤			

---

01 자녀의 결석 사유 등록 요청하기   정답률 72% | 정답 ①

다음 글의 목적으로 가장 적절한 것은?

☑ 자녀의 결석 사유를 등록해 줄 것을 요청하려고
② 학교 홈페이지의 일시적 운영 중단을 공지하려고
③ 자녀가 지각하지 않도록 부모의 지도를 당부하려고
④ 방과 후 프로그램에 대한 부모의 관심을 독려하려고
⑤ 인정 결석은 최대 7일까지 허용된다는 것을 안내하려고

[본문 해석]

친애하는 부모님께

학생의 잠재력을 극대화하는 데는 학교에 규칙적으로 출석하는 것이 필수적입니다. 최근에, 우리는 전 학년에 걸쳐 승인되지 않은 결석 수에 대해 우려하고 있습니다. 저는 부모로서 귀하의 역할이 학교 결석을 승인하는 것임을 더 명확히 하고 싶습니다. 학부모들은 결석 기간과 관계 없이 첫날로부터 7일 이내에 결석에 대한 설명을 학교에 제공해야 합니다. 7일의 기간 내에 설명이 주어지지 않을 경우, 학교는 결석을 정당하지 않은 것으로 학생부에 기록할 것입니다. 반드시 학부모 포털 사이트에 들어가서 자녀가 결석할 때마다 사유를 등록해 주십시오. 자녀가 불이익에 처하지 않도록 모든 결석을 승인해 주십시오. 협조해 주셔서 대단히 감사합니다.

교감 Natalie Brown 드림

Why? 왜 정답일까?

부모에게 자녀의 결석 사유를 꼭 등록해 달라고 요청하는 글이므로(Please ~ register the reason ~), 글의 목적으로 가장 적절한 것은 ① '자녀의 결석 사유를 등록해 줄 것을 요청하려고'이다.

- **attendance** ⓝ 출석, 참석
- **absence** ⓝ 결석
- **within** prep ~ 이내에
- **student's record** 학생부
- **unapproved** ⓐ 승인되지 않은
- **clarify** ⓥ 밝히다
- **unjustified** ⓐ 정당하지 않은
- **disadvantage** ⓝ 불리(한 점)

구문 풀이

9행 Where an explanation has not been received within the
부사절 접속사(~할 경우에) / 현재완료 수동태
7-day time frame, the school will record the absence as unjustified
미래시제
on the student's record.

---

02 데이터베이스와 즉흥성   정답률 70% | 정답 ⑤

밑줄 친 playing intellectual air guitar가 다음 글에서 의미하는 바로 가장 적절한 것은? [3점]

① acquiring necessary experience to enhance their creativity
자신들의 창의력을 향상하기 위해 필요한 경험을 습득하고 있는
② exhibiting artistic talent coupled with solid knowledge of music
탄탄한 음악 지식과 결합된 예술적 재능을 드러내고 있는
③ posing as experts by demonstrating their in-depth knowledge
자신들의 심층 지식을 보여줌으로써 전문가인 체하고 있는
④ performing musical pieces to attract a highly educated audience
고학력 청중을 끌어들이기 위해 음악 작품을 공연하고 있는
☑ displaying seemingly creative ability not rooted in firm knowledge
확실한 지식에 기반을 두지 않은, 겉보기에만 창의적인 능력을 보여주는

[본문 해석]

데이터베이스에 근거한 직감만을 혹은 즉흥적인 직감만을 다루는 어떤 학습 환경이든 우리 능력의 절반은 무시한다. 그것은 반드시 실패한다. 그것은 내게 재즈 기타리스트가 생각나게 한다. 음악 이론에 대해 많이 알고 있지만, 라이브 콘서트에서 즉흥 연주하는 법을 모른다면, 그들은 성공하지 못할 것이다. 일부 학교와 직장에서는 안정적이고, 기계적으로 암기한 데이터베이스를 강조한다. 그들은 수백만 년 동안 우리에게 주입되어 온 즉흥적인 직감을 무시한

다. (그 결과) 창의력이 고전한다. 다른 학교와 직장에서는 애초에 지식의 축적을 정착시키지 않고 창의적인 데이터베이스의 사용을 강조한다. 그들은 풍부하게 구조화된 데이터베이스를 암기하고 저장하는 것을 포함하는, 어떤 주제에 대한 깊은 이해를 얻고자 하는 우리의 욕구를 무시한다. (결과적으로) 여러분은 훌륭한 즉흥 연주자이지만 깊이 있는 지식은 없는 사람들을 얻게 된다. 여러분은 여러분이 일하는 곳에서 이런 누군가를 알지도 모른다. 그들은 재즈 뮤지션처럼 보이고 즉흥 연주를 하는 모습을 지니고 있을지 모르지만, 결국 그들은 아무것도 모른다. 그들은 지적으로 기타 연주 흉내를 내고 있는 것이다.

Why? 왜 정답일까?

첫 두 문장에서 데이터베이스와 즉흥성 중 하나만을 강조하는 학습 환경은 결국 우리의 창의력을 악화시킨다는 핵심 내용을 제시한 후, 재즈 기타리스트의 비유가 이어지고 있다. 이 기타 리스트들이 아무리 많은 이론 지식을 갖추고 있어도 즉흥 연주를 하지 못한다면 성공할 수 없는 것처럼, 우리가 데이터베이스와 더불어 진정으로 창의적인 직감을 활용할 수 없다면 성공할 수 없을 것이라는 내용이 언급되고 있다. 이에 근거할 때, 마지막 문장에서 데이터베이스만을 강조하는 사람들이 '기타를 연주하는 흉내만 내고 있을 뿐'이라고 지적한 것은 이들이 겉으로 보기에만 창의적일 뿐, 실제로 창의적이거나 어떤 주제에 대한 깊은 이해를 갖추고 있지는 않다고 지적한 것과 같다. 따라서 밑줄 친 부분이 의미하는 바로 가장 적절한 것은 ⑤ '확실한 지식에 기반을 두지 않은, 겉보기에만 창의적인 능력을 보여주는'이다.

- **ignore** ⓥ 무시하다
- **emphasize** ⓥ 강조하다
- **obtain** ⓥ 얻다
- **enhance** ⓥ 높이다
- **seemingly** ad 겉보기에는
- **jam** ⓥ 즉흥 연주를 하다
- **stable** ⓐ 안정적인
- **acquire** ⓥ 습득하다
- **exhibit** ⓥ 드러내다

구문 풀이

1행 Any learning environment [that deals with only the database
주어 / 주격 관계대명사
instincts or only the improvisatory instincts] ignores one half of our
단수 동사
ability.

---

03 자전거 타기의 의미 변화   정답률 50% | 정답 ②

다음 글의 제목으로 가장 적절한 것은?

① Cycling Contributes to a City's Atmosphere and Identity
자전거 타기는 도시 분위기와 정체성에 이바지한다
☑ The Rise of Cycling: A New Status Symbol of City Dwellers
자전거 타기의 증가: 도시 거주자들에게 있어 지위의 새로운 상징물
③ Cycling Is Wealth-Building but Worsens Social Inequality
자전거 타기는 부를 축적하지만 사회적 불평등을 악화시킨다
④ How to Encourage and Sustain the Bicycle Craze in Urban Areas
도시 지역의 자전거 열풍을 촉진하고 유지시킬 방법
⑤ Expanding Bike Lane Networks Can Lead to More Inclusive Cities
자전거 도로망 확장이 더 폭넓은 도시를 만든다

[본문 해석]

최근 '라이프스타일로서의 자전거' 열풍은 유럽, 미국, 호주, 그리고 아시아의 몇몇 도시 지역에서 적극적으로 자전거를 타는 사람들 수의 증가와 자전거 타기 클럽 회원의 성장으로 나타났다. 그것은 또한 자전거의 상징적인 재해석과 동반되었다. 자전거가 수년 간 가난과 연관지어진 이후로, 비싼 여가용 자전거나 여가용에서 영감을 얻은 통근용 자전거가 도시 환경에서 갑자기 열망의 상품이 되었다. 오늘날 자전거 타기는 그것의 표현적 가치, 그것이 정체성 형성에서 수행하는 역할, 그리고 그것이 타인에게 깊은 인상을 주고 사회적 지위를 나타내는 데 있어서의 효과성 때문에 수행되기도 하는 활동이 되었다. 어느 정도는 자전거 타기가 부유한 사람들의 상징적 표시로 바뀌었다. 분명히, 가치를 지닌 소비 행위는 결코 자전거 타기에 한정되지 않는다. 그러나 정체성 형성과 과시적 소비와의 연관성은 자전거 타기에 있어 특히 분명해졌다.

Why? 왜 정답일까?

자전거의 의미가 과거와 달라졌음을 설명하는 글이다. 과거에는 자전거가 가난과 주로 연관되었지만, 오늘날에는 비싼 여가용 자전거 등이 개발되면서 자전거가 도시 사람들의 정체성 형성과 과시적 소비와 관련성을 띠게 되었다(cycling has become an activity which is also performed for its demonstrative value, its role in identity construction and its effectiveness in impressing others and signaling social status)는 내용이다. 따라서 글의 제목으로 가장 적절한 것은 ② '자전거 타기의 증가: 도시 거주자들에게 있어 지위의 새로운 상징물'이다.

- **accompany** ⓥ 동반하다, 수반하다
- **poverty** ⓝ 가난
- **reinterpretation** ⓝ 재해석
- **inspire** ⓥ 영감을 주다

- demonstrative ⓐ 표현적인
- effectiveness ⓝ 유효성
- well-off ⓐ 부유한
- by no means 결코 ~않다
- manifest ⓥ 나타나는, 분명한
- inequality ⓝ 불평등
- construction ⓝ 구축, 건설
- social status 사회적 지위
- value-laden ⓐ 가치 판단적인
- conspicuous ⓐ 눈에 잘 띄는
- dweller ⓝ 거주자

구문 풀이

1행 The recent "cycling as a lifestyle" craze has expressed itself
재귀대명사(= The recent ~ craze)
in an increase in the number of active cyclists ~

---

04   Camille Flammarion의 생애   정답률 90% | 정답 ③

Camille Flammarion에 관한 다음 글의 내용과 일치하지 않는 것은?

① 어린 나이에 천문학에 흥미가 생겼다.
② 1858년에 Le Verrier의 조수가 되었다.
☑ 19세에 쓴 책에서 외계 생명체의 존재를 부인했다.
④ 자신의 자금으로 Juvisy에 천문대를 세웠다.
⑤ French Astronomical Society를 설립했다.

[본문 해석]

Camille Flammarion은 프랑스 Montigny-le-Roi에서 태어났다. 『그는 어린 나이에 천문학에 흥미가 생겼고, 불과 16세에 그는 세상의 기원에 관한 책을 썼다.』 그 원고는 그 당시 출판되지 않았지만, Paris Observatory의 소장이었던 Urbain Le Verrier의 관심을 끌게 되었다. 『그는 1858년에 Le Verrier의 조수가 되었고 계산원으로 일했다.』 『19세에 그는 *The Plurality of Inhabited Worlds*라는 또 다른 책을 썼는데, 이 책에서 그는 외계에 생명체가 존재한다고 열정적으로 주장했다.』 그의 가장 성공적인 저서인 *Popular Astronomy*는 1880년에 출판되었고, 결국 130,000부가 판매되었다. 『그는 자신의 자금으로 Juvisy에 천문대를 세웠고, 매년 5월에서 11월까지 거기서 지냈다.』 『1887년에 그는 French Astronomical Society를 설립했고 거기서 월간 간행물의 편집자로 일했다.』

Why? 왜 정답일까?

'At nineteen, he wrote another book called *The Plurality of Inhabited Worlds*, in which he passionately claimed that life exists outside the planet Earth.'에서 Camille Flammarion은 외계 생명체의 존재 가능성을 열정적으로 주장했다고 하므로, 내용과 일치하지 않는 것은 ③ '19세에 쓴 책에서 외계 생명체의 존재를 부인했다.'이다.

Why? 왜 오답일까?

① 'He became interested in astronomy at an early age, ~'의 내용과 일치한다.
② 'He became an assistant to Le Verrier in 1858 and worked as a calculator.'의 내용과 일치한다.
④ 'With his own funds, he built an observatory at Juvisy ~'의 내용과 일치한다.
⑤ 'In 1887, he founded the French Astronomical Society ~'의 내용과 일치한다.

- astronomy ⓝ 천문학
- publish ⓥ 출판하다, 게재하다
- calculator ⓝ 계산원, 계산기
- inhabit ⓥ 거주하다
- serve as ~로 일하다, ~의 역할을 하다
- manuscript ⓝ 원고
- observatory ⓝ 천문대
- plurality ⓝ 다원성, 많은 수
- passionately ⓐⓓ 열정적으로
- publication ⓝ 간행물, 발행

구문 풀이

8행 At nineteen, he wrote another book called *The Plurality of*
선행사
Inhabited Worlds, in which he passionately claimed {that life exists
전치사 + 관계대명사   명사절(claimed의 목적어)
outside the planet Earth}.

★★★ 1등급 대비 고난도 2점 문제

05   공동체에 더 많은 공로를 돌릴 필요성   정답률 37% | 정답 ⑤

다음 글의 밑줄 친 부분 중, 어법상 틀린 것은?

[본문 해석]

모든 농부들은 밭을 준비하는 것이 어려운 부분임을 안다. 씨앗을 심고 그것들이 자라는 것을 보는 것은 쉽다. 과학과 산업의 경우, 공동체가 밭을 준비하지만, 사회는 우연히 성공적인 씨앗을 심은 개인에게 모든 공로를 돌리는 경향이 있다. 씨를 심는 것은 반드시 엄청난 지능을 필요로 하지는 않지만, 씨앗이 번성하게 해 주는 환경을 만드는 것은 필요로 한다. 우리는 과학, 정치, 사업 그리고 일상에서 공동체에 좀 더 많은 공로를 인정해 줄 필요가 있다. Martin Luther King Jr.는 위대한 사람이었다. 아마도 그의 가장 큰 강점은 모든 역경에 맞서 사회의 인종에 대한 인식과 법의 공정성에서의 혁명적인 변화들을 성취하기 위해서 사람들이 함께 일하도록 고무시키는 능력이었다. 그러나 그가 성취한 것을 진정으로 이해하려면 이 사람 너머를 보는 것이 요구된다. 그를 모든 위대한 것들의 표명으로 여기는 대신에 우리는 미국이 위대해질 수 있음을 보여주게 하는 데 있어 그의 역할을 인정해야 한다.

Why? 왜 정답일까?

앞에 선행사가 없고 뒤에 'he accomplished'라는 목적어가 없는 절이 뒤따르는 것으로 보아 that 대신 선행사를 포함하는 관계대명사 what을 써야 한다. 따라서 어법상 틀린 것은 ⑤이다.

Why? 왜 오답일까?

① getting의 목적어인 the field가 '준비된 상태로 만들어지는' 대상이므로 과거분사 목적격 보어인 prepared가 적절하게 쓰였다.
② 앞에 나온 복수 명사 seeds를 받기 위해 복수 대명사 them이 바르게 쓰였다.
③ 주어가 동명사인 creating이고 앞에 일반동사 require가 나오므로 단수 대동사 does가 바르게 쓰였다.
④ his ability를 꾸미는 말로 to inspire가 바르게 쓰였다. attempt, ability, chance, opportunity, effort 등은 to부정사의 꾸밈을 받는 명사임을 기억해 둔다.

- industry ⓝ 산업
- overwhelming ⓐ 엄청난, 압도적인
- against all odds 모든 역경을 딛고
- perception ⓝ 인식
- fairness ⓝ 공정함
- accomplish ⓥ 성취하다, 달성하다
- give credit to ~에게 공로를 주다, ~을 믿다
- prosper ⓥ 번성하다
- revolutionary ⓐ 혁명적인
- race ⓝ 인종
- accomplish ⓥ 성취하다, 달성하다
- appreciate ⓥ (진가를) 인정하다

구문 풀이

「inspire + 목적어 + to부정사 : ~이 …하도록 고무시키다」
11행 Perhaps his greatest strength was his ability to inspire people
주어   동사   보어
to work together to achieve, (against all odds), revolutionary changes
목적어(~하기 위해)   ( ):삽입구   to achieve의 목적어
in society's perception of race and in the fairness of the law.

★★ 문제 해결 꿀~팁 ★★

▶ 많이 틀린 이유는?
③의 대동사는 앞에 나오는 동사와 대동사의 주어를 보아 결정한다. 세미콜론(;) 앞에 require라는 일반동사가 나오고, 주어가 단수 취급되는 동명사구 'creating ~'이므로 do/does/did 중 does가 바르게 쓰였다.

▶ 문제 해결 방법은?
정답인 ⑤의 'that vs. what'은 어법 문항에서 가장 많이 출제되는 포인트이므로 경우를 나누어 잘 기억해 둔다. 앞에 선행사가 있으면 관계대명사 that, 앞에 선행사가 없고 뒤에 완전한 문장이 나오면 접속사 that, 앞에 선행사가 없고 뒤에도 불완전한 문장이 나오면 관계대명사 what을 쓴다.

---

06   합리적인 선택에 혼란을 주는 선택 항목 과잉   정답률 57% | 정답 ④

다음 글의 밑줄 친 부분 중, 문맥상 낱말의 쓰임이 적절하지 않은 것은?

[본문 해석]

오늘날 시장에서 선택 항목의 과잉은 더 많은 선택의 자유를 준다. 그러나 행복의 관점에서 치러야 할 대가가 있을 것이다. 심리학자 David Myers와 Robert Lane의 연구에 따르면 모든 이런 선택은 자주 사람들을 ① 우울하게 만든다. 연구자들은 일부 쇼핑객들에게는 24개의 잼을 맛보게 했고 다른 사람들에게는 단 6개만 맛보게 했다. ② 더 적은 선택 항목을 가진 사람들이 맛볼 때 더 행복해했다. 훨씬 더 놀랍게도, 더 넓은 범위의 선택 사항을 가진 사람들 중 오직 당시 3%만이 잼을 구매한 반면, 더 적은 선택 사항을 가진 사람들 중에서는 그 당시 31%가 잼을 구매했다. 아이러니한 점은 사람들이 거의 항상 ③ 더 많은 선택 항목을 원한다고 말한다는 것이다. 그러나 더 많은 선택 항목을 가질수록

그들은 더 ④ 안도한다(→ 마비된다). 사리에 밝은 레스토랑 사장들은 더 적은 선택 항목을 제공한다. 이는 고객들이 더 편안함을 느끼게 하고, 그들이 쉽게 고르고 선택에 더 만족하도록 ⑤ 촉진한다.

Why? 왜 정답일까?

'The overabundance of options in today's marketplace gives you more freedom of choice. However, there may be a price to pay in terms of happiness.'에서 선택 항목이 많은 것은 자유를 주는 반면 행복의 측면에서는 대가를 치르게 한다고 말하므로, ④의 경우처럼 더 많은 선택 항목을 가진 사람들은 '안도'와는 반대로 'paralyzed(마비된, 불안한)'한 기분을 느끼게 될 것이다. 따라서 문맥상 적절하지 않은 어휘는 ④이다.

- overabundance ⓝ 과잉
- depressed ⓐ 우울한
- surprisingly [ad] 놀랍게도
- relieved ⓐ 안도한
- prompt ⓥ 촉진하다
- in terms of ~의 관점에서
- researcher ⓝ 연구자
- purchase ⓥ 구매하다
- savvy ⓐ 사리에 밝은
- satisfied ⓐ 만족한

구문 풀이

12행 The ironic thing about this is [that people nearly always

　　　　　　　주어　　　　　동사 접속사(~것)
say they want more choices].
└─(접속사 that 생략)

13행 Yet, the more options they have, the more relieved they
　　　　「the + 비교급 ~　　　　the + 비교급 … : ~할수록 더 …하다」
become.

★★★ 1등급 대비 고난도 2점 문제

07 철학적 대화에서 이루어지는 무지의 인식　　정답률 36% | 정답 ①

다음 빈칸에 들어갈 말로 가장 적절한 것을 고르시오.

☑ recognition of ignorance – 무지의 인식
② emphasis on self-assurance – 자기 확신에 대한 강조
③ conformity to established values – 확립된 가치관에 대한 순응
④ achievements of ancient thinkers – 고대 사상가들의 업적
⑤ comprehension of natural phenomena – 자연 현상에 대한 이해

[본문 해석]

철학적 활동은 무지의 인식에 기초를 둔다. 지식에 대한 철학자의 갈망은 그 답이 결코 발견되지 않는다 하더라도 질문에 대한 더 나은 답을 찾으려는 시도를 통해 나타나게 된다. 동시에, 철학자는 또한 지나치게 확신하는 것이 다른 가능성들과 더 나은 가능성들의 발견을 방해할 수 있다는 것을 알고 있다. 철학적 대화에서 참여자들은 자신이 알지 못하거나 이해하지 못하는 것이 있다는 것을 인식한다. 그 대화의 목표는 아무도 전부터 알지 못했거나 이해하지 못했다는 생각에 도달하는 것이다. 철학이 존재하지 않는 전통적 학교에서, 학생들은 흔히 사실적 질문에 대해 공부하고, 교육과정에 실린 특정한 내용을 배우며, 철학적인 문제를 해결하도록 요구받지 않는다. 하지만 우리는 누구도 알지 못하는 것에 대한 인식이 지식을 습득하는 좋은 방법이 될 수 있다는 것을 안다. 지식과 이해는 사색과 토론을 통해 발달한다. 생각을 말로 표현하는 것은 생각을 더 분명하게 만든다. 따라서 학생들은 틀린 것을 말하거나 처음에 그들이 옳다는 것을 확신하지 못하는 상태로 이야기하는 것을 두려워해서는 안 된다.

Why? 왜 정답일까?

'In a philosophical dialogue, the participants are aware that there are things they do not know or understand.'에서 철학적 대화를 하다 보면 사람들은 자신이 모르고 있거나 이해하지 못하고 있는 것이 있음을 알게 된다고 언급한 후, 'However, we know that awareness of what one does not know can be a good way to acquire knowledge.'에서는 이러한 무지에 대한 인식이 우리가 지식을 습득하는 좋은 방법이 될 수 있다고 설명한다. 따라서 빈칸에 들어갈 말로 가장 적절한 것은 ① '무지의 인식'이다.

- philosophical ⓐ 철학적인
- discovery ⓝ 발견
- specific ⓐ 특정한
- acquire ⓥ 습득하다
- ignorance ⓝ 무지
- self-assurance ⓝ 자기 확신
- phenomenon ⓝ 현상
- hinder ⓥ 방해하다
- factual ⓐ 사실적인
- awareness ⓝ 인식
- put into words 말로 옮기다
- emphasis ⓝ 강조
- conformity ⓝ 순응

구문 풀이

10행 In traditional schools, where philosophy is not present,
　　　　　　　　　　선행사　　　　　관계부사
students often work with factual questions, they learn specific
　주어1　　　　동사1　　　　　　　　　　　　　　　　주어2 동사2
content listed in the curriculum, and they are not required to solve
　　　　　　　　　　　　　　　　　　　주어3　　　　　동사3
philosophical problems.

★★ 문제 해결 꿀~팁 ★★

▶ 많이 틀린 이유는?
'In a philosophical dialogue, ~'와 'The goal of the dialogue ~'에서 철학적 대화를 통해 인간은 스스로 알지 못하거나 모르고 있다는 사실을 인지하게 된다고 했다. 따라서 철학적 대화나 활동을 통해 인간이 자기 확신에 이른다는 내용인, self-assurance를 포함한 ②는 답으로 적절하지 않다.

▶ 문제 해결 방법은?
주제를 제시하는 However가 포함된 문장의 'awareness of what one does not know'를 재진술한 표현이 바로 ①의 'recognition of ignorance'임을 파악하면 쉽게 답을 고를 수 있다.

★★★ 1등급 대비 고난도 3점 문제

08 생각과 행동의 전파　　정답률 50% | 정답 ③

글의 흐름으로 보아, 주어진 문장이 들어가기에 가장 적절한 곳을 고르시오. [3점]

[본문 해석]

20세기 후반 연구자들은 뉴스, 소문, 혁신이 얼마나 빨리 그리고 얼마나 멀리 이동하는지를 측정하고자 했다. ① 더 최근의 연구는 생각, 즉 감정 상태와 상황까지도 사회 관계망을 통해 전파될 수 있다는 것을 보여주었다. ② 이러한 종류의 전염의 증거는 분명한데, '학구적인 룸메이트와 함께 하는 학생들은 더욱 학구적이 되고, 폭식하는 사람 옆에 앉아 식사하는 사람은 더 많은 음식을 먹는다.' ③ 그러나 Christakis와 Fowler에 따르면 우리는 우리의 친구의 친구의 친구를 훨씬 넘어서서(다시 말해 고작 세 단계의 분절을 건너서는) 생각과 행동을 전파할 수 없다. 이것은 생각이나 행동의 전파와 수용이 편지나 어떤 고용 기회가 있다는 말을 전달하는 것보다 더 강한 연결을 요구하기 때문이다. ④ 단지 사람을 아는 것은 그들이 더 공부하거나 과식하도록 영향을 미칠 수 있는 것과는 같지 않다. ⑤ 모방은 그것이 무의식적일 때조차도 실로 가장 순수한 형태의 아첨이다.

Why? 왜 정답일까?

③ 앞에서 뉴스, 소문, 혁신뿐 아니라 감정 상태와 상황 또한 흔히 사람들 간에 전염처럼 번질 수 있다고 언급한 데 이어, 주어진 문장은 친구의 친구의 친구, 즉 세 단계를 걸쳐 아는 사람들을 넘어서면 그 전파력이 잘 발휘되지 않는다는 상반된 내용을 제시한다. ③ 뒤의 문장은 주어진 문장 내용을 This로 받으며, 생각이나 행동의 전파 또는 수용이 편지나 정보를 단순히 전달하는 경우보다 더 강한 유대나 연결을 요구하기 때문이라는 이유를 제시한다. 따라서 주어진 문장이 들어가기에 가장 적절한 곳은 ③이다.

- transmit ⓥ 전달하다
- innovation ⓝ 혁신
- studious ⓐ 학구적인
- relaying ⓝ (정보나 뉴스 등의) 전달
- unconscious ⓐ 무의식적인
- separation ⓝ 단절, 분리
- contagion ⓝ 전염
- reception ⓝ 수용
- merely [ad] 단지, 그저

구문 풀이

7행 More recent research has shown that ideas — (even emotional
　　　　　　　　　　　　　　　접속사(~것)└┘ 주어　　　( ): 삽입구
states and conditions) — can be transmitted through a social network.
　　　　　　　　　　　　　　　　조동사 수동태

★★ 문제 해결 꿀~팁 ★★

▶ 많이 틀린 이유는?
④ 앞에서 생각이나 행동을 전파할 때는 단순히 소식이나 정보를 전달할 때보다 더 강한 연결이 필요하다고 설명한다. 이어서 ④ 뒤의 문장에서는 단지 사람을 안다고 해서 그 사람의 행동에 영향을 미칠 수 있다고 볼 수는 없다고 언급한다. 즉 ④ 앞뒤로 생각이나 행동에 영향을 미치려면 '알고 있는 것 이상'의 강한 연결고리가 필요하다는 내용이 일관성 있게 제시되므로, 주어진 문장은 ④에 들어갈 수 없다.

▶ 문제 해결 방법은?
③ 앞뒤로 '생각·행동이 사회 관계망을 통해 전파되는 경우 **vs.** 그 전파가 어려운 경우'가 대비되고 있음을 파악하도록 한다.

---

09 과학자와 운동선수의 차이점
정답률 53% | 정답 ②

다음 글의 내용을 한 문장으로 요약하고자 한다. 빈칸 (A), (B)에 들어갈 말로 가장 적절한 것은?

(A)		(B)		(A)		(B)
① confident 자신 있는	·····	keep 유지해야		✓② skeptical 회의적인	·····	eliminate 없애야
③ arrogant 거만한	·····	express 표현해야		④ critical 비판적인	·····	keep 유지해야
⑤ stubborn 고집 센	·····	eliminate 제거하다				

[본문 해석]

퍼포먼스 심리학의 큰 아이러니는 개개의 운동선수들이 능력이 되는 한 이길 것이라고 믿도록 가르친다는 것이다. 어느 누구도 의심하지 않는다. 어느 누구도 내면의 회의에 빠지지 않는다. 그것이 스포츠 심리학의 논리이다. 하지만 오직 한 사람만이 이길 수 있다. 그것이 스포츠의 논리이다. 과학자와 운동선수의 차이점을 주목하라. 의심은 과학자의 일상적인 업무이다. 진보는 이론을 반박하는 증거에 집중하고 그에 따라 이론을 개선하여 이루어진다. 회의론은 과학적 진보의 추진 연료이다. 하지만 운동선수에게 의심은 독이다. 진보는 증거를 무시함으로써 만들어지고, 그것은 의심과 불확실성에 영향을 받지 않는 사고방식을 만드는 것이다. 다시 말하지만, 이성적인 시각에서 보면 이는 미친 짓이나 다름없다. 왜 운동선수는 자신이 질 거라는 모든 가능성이 있다는 것을 알면서도 이길 것이라고 확신해야 하는가? 선수는 이기려면 증거가 아니라 마음이 유용하게 해낼 수 있는 것이 무엇이든 그것에 자기 신념을 할당해야 하기 때문이다.

➡ 과학적 진보를 이루기 위해 (A) 회의적인 태도가 요구되는 과학자들과는 달리, 스포츠 심리학은 운동선수들이 성공하려면 이길 수 있는지에 대한 불확실한 감정을 (B) 없애야 한다고 한다.

Why? 왜 정답일까?

과학자들과 운동선수 간에 차이가 있다(the difference between a scientist and an athlete)는 내용 뒤로, 과학자는 의심을 추진력으로 삼는 반면에 운동선수는 의심 대신 확신을 지녀야 한다(Skepticism is the rocket fuel of scientific advance. But doubt, to an athlete, is poison.)는 설명이 이어진다. 따라서 요약문의 빈칸 (A), (B)에 들어갈 말로 가장 적절한 것은 ② 'A) skeptical(회의적인), (B) eliminate (없애야)'이다.

- **irony** ⓝ 아이러니, 반어
- **skepticism** ⓝ 회의론
- **athlete** ⓝ 운동선수
- **evidence** ⓝ 증거
- **improve** ⓥ 개선하다
- **scientific** ⓐ 과학적인
- **mindset** ⓝ 사고방식
- **rational** ⓐ 이성적인
- **nothing less than** 다름 아닌
- **proportion** ⓥ 적절한 비율로 조화시키다
- **skeptical** ⓐ 회의적인
- **arrogant** ⓐ 거만한

- **indulge** ⓥ (~에) 빠지다, 탐닉하다
- **logic** ⓝ 논리
- **stock in trade** 상투적 요소, 장사 도구
- **refute** ⓥ 반박하다
- **accordingly** ⓐⓓ 그에 따라
- **progress** ⓝ 진보
- **immune** ⓐ ~의 영향을 받지 않는
- **perspective** ⓝ 관점, 시각
- **convince** ⓥ 확신시키다
- **get away with** ~을 잘 해내다
- **eliminate** ⓥ 없애다, 제거하다
- **stubborn** ⓐ 고집 센, 완고한

구문 풀이

1행 The great irony of performance psychology is {that it teaches
　　　　　　주어　　　　　　　　　　　　　　　동사(단수)　　　동사
each sportsman to believe, (as far as he is able), that he will win}.
목적어　　　목적격 보어　　　( ): 삽입절　　　{ }: 주격 보어(명사절)

10-12 Wylder의 첫 훈련

[본문 해석]

(A)

초가을의 더운 날이었다. Wylder는 첫 훈련을 하러 학교 운동장으로 향하고 있었다. 「그는 성공적인 실력 테스트 후 다른 학생 다섯 명과 함께 팀에 막 합

류했다.」 운동장에 다가가면서, (a) 그는 선수들이 양말을 당겨 올리고 정강이 보호대를 착용하면서 준비하는 것을 보았다. 그러나 그들은 함께가 아니었다. 새 선수들은 차고 옆 그늘에 앉아 있던 반면 다른 선수들은 오른편 골대 옆의 양지에 서 있었다. 그런 다음 McGraw 코치가 도착해서 선수들을 보았다.

(D)

McGraw 코치도 새로운 아이들과 다른 아이들이 따로 떨어져서 무리를 짓고 있는 패턴을 보았다. 그는 '이건 바꿔야겠군.'이라고 생각했다. 그는 승리하는 팀을 원했다. 그렇게 하려면, 그는 관계를 형성해야 했다. 「그는 걸어가면서 "너희들 여기 중앙에 와서 앉았으면 좋겠다."라며 선수들을 불렀다.」 McGraw 는 "너!"라고 소리치며 Wylder를 가리켰다. "여기 필드 쪽에 필드 쪽에 와서 앉아라. 그리고 Jonny! 너 저기 앉아라!" 그는 (앉을 위치들을) 가리키기 시작했고, 그들이 반드시 서로 섞이도록 했다. Wylder는 코치가 무엇을 하려는지 알아차렸고, 그래서 (e) 그는 운동장 안으로 뛰어 들어갔다.

(C)

「재배열이 마음에 들 때까지 McGraw는 각 선수를 불러내면서 계속 가리켰다.」 그는 "자, 이렇게 되어갈 거다. 우리는 서로 신뢰하고 함께 경기하는 방식을 배워야 해. 이게 팀이 경기하는 방식이다. 이게 내가 경기장 안과 밖에서 너희 들에게 바라는 거야. 함께하는 것 말이다."라고 말했다. 선수들은 서로 쳐다 보았다. 「거의 곧바로, McGraw는 그들의 자세와 얼굴 변화를 알아차렸다.」 (d) 그는 그들 중 몇몇이 미소 짓기 시작한 것을 보았다.

(B)

'와,' Wylder는 생각했다. 「잔디 위 새로운 자리에서, 그는 다리를 쭉 폈다.」 그는 듣고 있는 (코치의) 말이 마음에 들었다. (b) 그는 새로운 공동체 정신의 감각, 더 깊은 연대감을 느꼈다. 코치가 이것에 관해 말하는 것을 듣고, 그가 그 도전 에 정면으로 맞서는 것을 보는 것은 고무적이었다. 이제 그의 연설이 끝났다. 선수들은 몸을 풀려고 일어서서 운동장을 걸어 다니기 시작했다. 코치를 지나쳐 걸어가면서, 존경의 마음을 담아 (e) 그의 눈을 내리깐 채로, Wylder는 McGraw 에게 낮은 목소리로 말했다. "잘하셨습니다. 코치님. 좋았습니다."

- **tryout** ⓝ 실력 테스트, 적격 시험
- **strap on** (시계, 배낭 등을) 차다
- **pole** ⓝ 기둥
- **stretch out** ~을 펴다
- **head-on** ⓐⓓ 정면으로 ⓐ 정면으로 맞서는
- **rearrangement** ⓝ 재배치
- **hop** ⓥ (깡충깡충) 뛰다
- **pull up** 끌어올리다
- **shin** ⓝ 정강이
- **location** ⓝ 위치, 장소
- **encouraging** ⓐ 고무적인
- **warm up** 몸을 풀다
- **separately** ⓐⓓ 따로

구문 풀이

(A) 4행 Approaching the field, he saw players getting ready, pulling
분사구문(~하면서)　　　　　　지각동사　　목적격 보어1　　목적격 보어2
up their socks and strapping on shin guards.
목적격 보어3

---

10 글의 순서 파악
정답률 59% | 정답 ⑤

주어진 글 (A)에 이어질 내용을 순서에 맞게 배열한 것으로 가장 적절한 것은?

① (B) - (D) - (C)　　　　② (C) - (B) - (D)
③ (C) - (D) - (B)　　　　④ (D) - (B) - (C)
✓⑤ (D) - (C) - (B)

Why? 왜 정답일까?

Wylder의 첫 훈련 날 운동장에 선수들이 서로 갈라져 있었다는 (A) 뒤로, 코치인 McGraw가 선수들을 서로 섞으려고 자리를 지정해주기 시작했다는 (D), 재배치 이후 선수들의 표정이 달라졌다는 (C), Wylder가 McGraw 코치의 뜻에 공감하며 그에게 존경을 표현했다는 (B)가 차례로 이어지는 것이 자연스럽다. 따라서 글의 순서로 가장 적절한 것은 ⑤ 'D) - (C) - (B)'이다.

---

11 지칭 추론
정답률 69% | 정답 ④

밑줄 친 (a) ~ (e) 중에서 가리키는 대상이 나머지 넷과 다른 것은?

① (a)　　② (b)　　③ (c)　　✓④ (d)　　⑤ (e)

Why? 왜 정답일까?

(a), (b), (c), (e)는 Wylder, (d)는 Coach McGraw를 가리키므로, (a) ~ (e) 중에서 가리키는 대상이 다른 하나는 ④ '(d)'이다.

---

12 세부 내용 파악   정답률 75% | 정답 ⑤

윗글에 관한 내용으로 적절하지 <u>않은</u> 것은?

① Wylder는 다섯 명의 다른 학생과 팀에 합류했다.
② Wylder는 잔디 위의 새로운 자리에서 다리를 쭉 폈다.
③ McGraw는 재배열이 마음에 들 때까지 선수들을 불러냈다.
④ McGraw는 선수들의 자세와 얼굴의 변화를 알아차렸다.
☑ McGraw는 선수들에게 운동장 밖으로 나가라고 말했다.

Why? 왜 정답일까?

(D) '"I want you guys to come over here in the middle and sit," ~'에 따르면 코치인 McGraw는 선수들을 운동 중간에 와서 앉으라고 불렀다. 따라서 내용과 일치하지 않는 것은 ⑤ 'McGraw는 선수들에게 운동장 밖으로 나가라고 말했다.'이다.

Why? 왜 오답일까?

① (A) 'He had just joined the team with five other students after a successful tryout.'의 내용과 일치한다.
② (B) 'From his new location on the grass, he stretched out his legs.'의 내용과 일치한다.
③ (C) '~ calling each player out, until he was satisfied with the rearrangement.'의 내용과 일치한다.
④ (C) 'Almost immediately, McGraw noticed a change in their postures and faces.'의 내용과 일치한다.

DAY 15   20분 미니 모의고사

01 ②	02 ②	03 ③	04 ③	05 ④
06 ③	07 ①	08 ②	09 ④	10 ③
11 ⑤	12 ④			

---

01 카페 개업을 앞둔 Isabel   정답률 78% | 정답 ②

다음 글에 드러난 Isabel의 심경 변화로 가장 적절한 것은?

① calm → surprised
   평온한   놀란
☑ doubtful → confident
   의심하는   자신 있는
③ envious → delighted
   부러워하는   기쁜
④ grateful → frightened
   고마워하는   겁에 질린
⑤ indifferent → uneasy
   무관심한   불안한

[본문 해석]

개업식날, Isabel은 초조한 기대감을 품고 카페에 매우 일찍 도착한다. 그녀는 카페를 둘러보지만, 뭔가 빠졌다는 느낌을 떨쳐 낼 수 없다. 컵과 숟가락, 접시를 차려 놓으며 Isabel의 의심은 커진다. 그녀는 카페를 완벽하게 만들기 위해 뭘 더 할 수 있을지를 상상하려고 애쓰며 주변을 둘러보지만, 아무것도 머릿속에 떠오르지 않는다. 그때, 갑작스러운 영감의 폭발과 함께, Isabel은 붓을 쥐고 꽃과 나무를 더해 텅 빈 벽을 풍경화로 변화시킨다. 그림을 그리면서, 그녀의 불안도 서서히 사라지기 시작한다. 아름답게 완성된 그녀의 작품을 보며, 그녀는 카페가 성공할 거라고 확신한다. '자, 성공이 확실히 보장되지는 않았지만, 나는 분명 이르게 될 거야.'라고 혼자 생각한다.

Why? 왜 정답일까?

카페 개업을 앞두고 뭔가 빠진 느낌에 의심(doubts)을 품었던 Isabel이 벽면에 그림을 그려넣고는 카페가 잘 될거라는 확신을 느꼈다(she is certain that the cafe will be a success)는 내용이다. 따라서 Isabel의 심경 변화로 가장 적절한 것은 ② '의심하는 → 자신 있는'이다.

- anticipation ⓝ 기대
- set out 차려내다, 착수하다, 시작하다
- sudden ⓐ 갑작스러운
- inspiration ⓝ 영감
- transform ⓥ 변모시키다
- fade ⓥ 옅어지다
- certain ⓐ 확신하는
- envious ⓐ 부러워하는
- frightened ⓐ 겁에 질린
- shake off 떨쳐내다
- doubt ⓝ 의심
- burst ⓝ 폭발
- grab ⓥ 집어들다
- landscape ⓝ 풍경(화)
- handiwork ⓝ (솜씨를 발휘한) 작품, 피조물
- guarantee ⓥ 보장하다, 보증하다
- grateful ⓐ 고마워하는
- uneasy ⓐ 불안한

구문 풀이

5행 She looks around the cafe, but she can't shake off the feeling [that something is missing].
[ ] : 동격(= the feeling)

---

02 외부자의 눈으로 조직을 비판하기   정답률 74% | 정답 ②

다음 글에서 필자가 주장하는 바로 가장 적절한 것은?

① 조직 내의 의사소통이 원활한지 수시로 살피라.
☑ 외부자의 관점으로 자기 조직을 비판적으로 바라보라.
③ 관심사의 공유를 통해 직장 동료와의 관계를 개선하라.
④ 과거의 성공에 도취되어 자기 계발을 소홀히 하지 말라.
⑤ 동료의 실수를 비판하기보다는 먼저 이해하려고 노력하라.

[본문 해석]

여러분의 상황이 어떠하든, 여러분이 내부자이건 외부자이건, 여러분은 어제의 정답에 이의를 제기하는 목소리가 될 필요가 있다. 외부자를 조직에 가치 있게 만드는 특성들에 관해 생각해 보라. 그들은 내부자가 너무 가까이 있어서 정말 알아차릴 수 없는 문제들을 볼 수 있는 관점을 가진 사람들이다. 그들은 자신의 일자리나 자신의 경력을 걸지 않고 이런 문제들을 지적하고 그것들을 비판할 수 있는 자유를 가진 사람들이다. 외부자의 사고방식을 채택하는 것의 일부는 이렇게 분리된, 덜 감정적인 관점으로 여러분의 조직을 스스로 둘러보도록 강제하는 것이다. 여러분이 자신의 동료를 모르고 그들과 공유된 경험으

로 결속되어 있다고 느끼지 않는다면 여러분은 그들에 관해 어떻게 생각하겠는가? 여러분이 자신의 생각을 경영진에게 말할 직업 안정성이나 자신감을 갖고 있지 않을지도 모르지만 여러분은 자신의 조직에 관해 이런 '외부자의' 평가를 독자적으로 할 수 있고 경력을 발전시키기 위해 여러분이 판단한 것을 이용할 수 있다.

Why? 왜 정답일까?

첫 문장에서 상황과 입지가 어떠하든 조직 내에서 기존의 답에 의문을 제기하는 사람이 될 필요가 있다고 언급한 후, 마지막 문장에서 외부자로서의 시각을 갖추고 조직을 비판적으로 바라보며 경력을 발전시킬 것을 조언하고 있다. 따라서 필자가 주장하는 바로 가장 적절한 것은 ② '외부자의 관점으로 자기 조직을 비판적으로 바라보라.'이다.

- challenge ⓥ 이의를 제기하다, 반박하다
- perspective ⓝ 관점, 시각
- risk ⓥ ~을 걸다, 위태롭게 하다
- disassociated ⓐ 고립된, 결속되지 않은
- confidence ⓝ 자신감
- characteristic ⓝ 특성, 특징
- criticize ⓥ 비판하다
- mentality ⓝ 사고방식
- security ⓝ 안정성
- assessment ⓝ 평가

구문 풀이

1행 No matter what your situation (is), whether you are an insider
＝whatever(무엇이 ~이든 간에)　　　「whether + A + or + B : A이든 B이든」
or an outsider, you need to become the voice [that challenges
　　　　　　　　　　　　　　　　　　　선행사　　주격 관계대명사
yesterday's answers].

---

03 수작업 활동이 정신 건강에 미치는 긍정적 영향 정답률 83% | 정답 ③

다음 글의 요지로 가장 적절한 것은?
① 긍정적인 감정은 타인에게 쉽게 전이된다.
② 감정 조절은 대인 관계 능력의 핵심 요소이다.
✓ 수작업 활동은 정신 건강에 도움을 줄 수 있다.
④ 과도한 신체활동은 호르몬 분비의 불균형을 초래한다.
⑤ 취미 활동을 통해 여러 분야의 사람들을 만날 수 있다.

[본문 해석]

심리학 교수인 Kelly Lambert 박사의 연구는 그녀가 '노력 주도 보상 회로'라고 부르는 것을 잘 작동되는 상태로 유지하는 것이, 당신이 당신 주변의 환경에서나 당신의 정서 생활에서의 도전들을 더 효과적이고 효율적으로 처리하는 데 도움이 된다고 설명한다. 목도리를 뜨거나 처음부터 직접 요리하거나 정원을 손질하는 것과 같이 여러분이 보고 만질 수 있는 결과를 만들어내는 수작업 활동을 하는 것은 보상 회로가 최적으로 작동하도록 활성화시킨다. 그녀는 문서로 기록된 미국인들의 우울증 증가는 목적이 있는 신체 활동의 감소와 직접적으로 관련이 있을 수도 있다고 주장한다. 우리가 손으로 일을 할 때, 신경 화학 물질인 도파민과 세로토닌의 분비를 증가시키는데, 둘 다 긍정적인 감정을 발생시키는 것을 담당한다. 그녀는 또한 우리의 손으로 작업하는 것은 우리에게 환경에 대한 더 큰 통제감과 우리 주변 세계와의 더 많은 연결을 준다고 설명한다. 이 모든 것이 스트레스와 불안의 감소에 기여하고 우울증 발생에 대한 회복력을 키워준다.

Why? 왜 정답일까?

마지막 세 문장에서 손으로 하는 활동은 긍정적인 감정을 발생시키는 화학 물질의 분비를 촉진하고, 환경에 대한 통제감과 주변 세계에 대한 연결감을 주어서 불안을 감소시키고 우울증 발생을 막는 데 도움을 준다고 설명하고 있다. 따라서 글의 요지로 가장 적절한 것은 이러한 수작업 활동의 효과를 일반화해 서술한 ③ '수작업 활동은 정신 건강에 도움을 줄 수 있다.'이다.

- hands-on 손으로 하는, 직접 해보는
- tend ⓥ 돌보다, 보살피다
- depression ⓝ 우울(증), 침체
- neurochemical ⓝ 신경 화학 물질
- resilience ⓝ 회복력, 탄력성
- from scratch 처음부터
- optimally ⓐⓓ 최적으로
- correlate ⓥ 연관성이 있다
- anxiety ⓝ 불안
- onset ⓝ (특히 불쾌한 일의) 시작

구문 풀이

6행 Doing hands-on activities [that produce results {you can
　　　동명사구 주어　　　　　　선행사　　주격 관·대 동사(복수)　　목적어
see and touch}] — such as knitting a scarf, cooking from scratch, or
　　　　　　　　　　　　　　　　　　동명사1　　　　　동명사2
tending a garden — fuels the reward circuit so that it functions
동명사3　　　　　　　동사(단수)　　　　　　접속사(~하도록)
optimally.

---

04 수중 야간 행사 정답률 96% | 정답 ③

Goldbeach SeaWorld Sleepovers에 관한 다음 안내문의 내용과 일치하는 것은?
① 7세 이하의 어린이가 참가할 수 있다.
② 평일에 진행된다.
✓ 참가비에 아침 식사가 포함된다.
④ 모든 활동은 야외에서 진행된다.
⑤ 사진 촬영은 언제든지 할 수 있다.

[본문 해석]

Goldbeach SeaWorld 하룻밤 행사

여러분의 자녀는 해양 동물들을 좋아하나요? Goldbeach SeaWorld에서의 하룻밤 행사는 분명히 자녀들에게 신나는 하룻밤 동안의 경험이 될 것입니다. 환상적인 수중 하룻밤 행사를 함께하세요.

참가자:
- 「8세 ~ 12세의 아동」—「」: ①의 근거 불일치
- 아동은 보호자를 동반하여야 합니다.

일시: 「2022년 5월 매주 토요일 오후 5시 ~ 일요일 오전 10시」—「」: ②의 근거 불일치

활동: 가이드 투어, 수중 쇼, 인어와 사진 찍는 시간

참가비:
- 「1인당 $50 (저녁 식사 및 아침 식사 포함)」—「」: ③의 근거 일치

참고 사항
- 침낭 및 기타 개인용품은 제공되지 않습니다.
- 「모든 활동은 실내에서 이루어집니다.」—「」: ④의 근거 불일치
- 「오후 10시부터 오전 7시까지는 사진 촬영이 허용되지 않습니다.」—「」: ⑤의 근거 불일치

더 많은 정보를 원하시면 우리 웹 사이트 www.goldbeach-seaworld.com을 방문하시면 됩니다.

Why? 왜 정답일까?

'(dinner and breakfast included)'에서 참가비에 저녁 및 아침 식사가 포함된다고 하므로, 안내문의 내용과 일치하는 것은 ③ '참가비에 아침 식사가 포함된다.'이다.

Why? 왜 오답일까?

① 'Children ages 8 to 12'에서 8 ~ 12세 사이의 어린이가 참가할 수 있다고 하였다.
② 'Saturdays 5 p.m. to Sundays 10 a.m. in May, 2022'에서 행사는 주말에 진행된다고 하였다.
④ 'All activities take place indoors.'에서 모든 활동은 실내에서 이루어진다고 하였다.
⑤ 'Taking photos is not allowed from 10 p.m. to 7 a.m.'에서 사진 촬영은 오후 10시부터 오전 7시까지 허용되지 않는다고 하였다.

- sleepover ⓝ 밤샘 파티, 함께 자며 놀기
- surely ⓐⓓ 분명히, 틀림없이
- accompany ⓥ 동반하다, 동행하다
- session ⓝ 시간[기간]
- marine ⓐ 해양의, 바다의
- overnight ⓐ 하룻밤 사이의
- guardian ⓝ 보호자
- mermaid ⓝ 인어

---

05 선매 행위의 개념과 종류 정답률 67% | 정답 ④

다음 글의 밑줄 친 부분 중, 어법상 틀린 것은? [3점]

[본문 해석]

선매 행위는 경쟁자가 어떤 특정한 활동을 시작하는 것을 막고자 어떤 전략이 만들어진다는 것을 의미한다. 어떤 경우 선제적 조치는 단순히 경쟁자들이 똑같이 하지 못하게 할 수 있는 어떤 의도의 공표일 수도 있다. 선매 행위 개념은 때로 타이밍이 매우 중요하다는 것을 암시하는데, 즉 어떤 시점의 결정이나 조치는 다른 시점에 행하는 것보다 훨씬 더 득이 될 수 있다. 선매 행위에는 새로운 진입자가 시장에 진출하기 이전과 진출 도중에 광고의 가중치를 높이는 것이 포함될 수 있다. 그 취지는 신규 진입자의 광고가 잠재적 구매자들에게 인상을 남기는 것을 더 어렵게 만드는 것이다. 제품 확산은 또 다른 잠재적인 선매 행위 전략이다. 그 개념은 수용되지 않는 시장 수요 방식이 거의 없도록 다양한 제품 변형을 출시하는 것이다. 거의 틀림없이, 만약 시장이 제품 변형으로 이미 채워져 있다면 경쟁자들은 아직 점유되지 않은 시장 수요 주머니를 찾기가 더 어렵다.

Why? 왜 정답일까?

주격 관계대명사절의 동사는 선행사와 수 일치되는데, **market demand**가 불가산명사임에도 불구하고 **that** 뒤에 복수 동사 **are**가 나왔다. 이는 어법상 옳지 않으므로, **are**를 **is**로 고쳐야 한다. 따라서 어법상 틀린 것은 ④이다.

Why? 왜 오답일까?

① **some intent**를 꾸미면서 뒤에 주어가 없는 불완전한 구조를 연결하고자 주격 관계대명사 **that**을 썼다.
② 비교의 **than** 뒤에 '~하는 것'이라는 의미의 동명사 **doing**을 썼다.
③ 일반적인 시간 선행사 **the time**이 생략된 자리에 관계부사 **when**이 알맞게 쓰였다.
⑤ '**pockets of market demand**'가 '손이 안 닿은' 대상이므로 과거분사 **untapped**가 알맞게 쓰였다.

- **pre-emption** ⓝ 선매 행위
- **weight** ⓥ 가중치를 두다 ⓝ 가중치, 무게
- **proliferation** ⓝ 확산
- **arguably** ⓐ𝑑 거의 틀림없이
- **rewarding** ⓐ 보람된
- **entrant** ⓝ 갓 들어온 사람, 진입자, 출전자
- **accommodate** ⓥ 수용하다
- **untapped** ⓐ 아직 손대지 않은

구문 풀이

3행 In some case a pre-emptive move may simply be an announcement of some intent [that might discourage rivals from
선행사　　　　　　　「discourage + A + from + B :
doing the same].　[ ] : 주격 관계대명사절　　A가 B하지 못하게 막다」

---

06 부유국의 보호 무역 조치   정답률 41% | 정답 ③

다음 글의 밑줄 친 부분 중, 문맥상 낱말의 쓰임이 적절하지 않은 것은? [3점]

[본문 해석]

지난 수십 년 동안, 가난한 나라들의 부채를 줄이려는 몇 가지 합의가 있었지만, (무역 장벽 등) 다른 경제적 과제는 ① 남아 있다. 할당제, 보조금, 수출 제한과 같은 비관세 무역 조치가 점점 더 널리 퍼지고 있으며, 무역과 무관한 정책적 이유로 제정될 수 있다. 그러나 그것들은 부유한 국가들이 부과한 비관세 조치의 요건을 준수할 자원이 부족한 국가들의 수출에 ② 차별적인 영향을 끼친다. 예를 들어, ③ 가난한(→ 부유한) 국가들이 자국 농부들에게 주는 막대한 보조금은 전 세계 나머지 국가들의 농부들이 그들과 경쟁하기 매우 힘들게 만든다. 또 다른 예는 국내 보건 또는 안전 규제인데, 이것은 구체적으로 수입을 타겟으로 하진 않지만, 수입자 시장에 맞추려는 외국 제조업체에 상당한 비용을 ④ 부과할 수 있다. 개발도상국 시장의 산업은 이러한 추가 비용을 부담하는 데 더 많은 ⑤ 어려움을 겪을 수 있다.

Why? 왜 정답일까?

가난한 국가들의 국가 부채를 줄이려는 노력이 많이 있었지만 이를 가로막는 부유국의 경제 조치가 여전히 있다는 내용이다. 그런데 ③은 '가난한' 국가가 자국 농부들을 타국 농부들과의 경쟁으로부터 보호하려 한다는 의미이므로 흐름상 어색하다. 따라서 문맥상 낱말의 쓰임이 적절하지 않은 것은 ③이고, 이를 **wealthy**로 고쳐야 한다.

- **trade barrier** 무역 장벽
- **quota** ⓝ 할당(제)
- **restriction** ⓝ 제한, 규제
- **enact** ⓥ 제정하다
- **comply with** ~을 준수하다
- **domestic** ⓐ 국내의, 가정의
- **conform to** ~에 맞추다, 순응하다
- **nontariff** ⓐ 비관세의
- **subsidy** ⓝ 보조금
- **prevalent** ⓐ 만연한, 널리 퍼진
- **discriminatory** ⓐ 차별적인
- **impose** ⓥ 부과하다
- **significant** ⓐ 상당한

구문 풀이

10행 For example, the huge subsidies [that wealthy nations give
가목적어　　　　　　　　주어　　　　목적격 관·대
to their farmers] make it very difficult for farmers (in the rest of the
　　　　　　　동사　목적격 보어　　　　　　의미상 주어
world) to compete with them.
　진목적어

---

07 행동의 연쇄 반응   정답률 61% | 정답 ①

다음 빈칸에 들어갈 말로 가장 적절한 것을 고르시오.

① isolation – 고립
② comfort – 위안
③ observation – 관찰
④ fairness – 공정함
⑤ harmony – 조화

[본문 해석]

한 구매가 또 다른 구매로 이어지는 경향에는 이름이 있는데, 바로 Diderot 효과이다. Diderot 효과는 새로운 소유물을 얻는 것이 종종 추가적인 구매들로 이어지는 소비의 소용돌이를 만든다고 말한다. 당신은 이러한 경향을 어디서든지 발견할 수 있다. 당신은 드레스를 사고 어울리는 새 신발과 귀걸이를 사야 한다. 당신은 아이를 위해 장난감을 사고 곧 그것과 어울리는 모든 액세서리들을 구매하는 자신을 발견한다. 이것은 구매의 연쇄 반응이다. 많은 인간의 행동들은 이 순환을 따른다. 당신은 종종 당신이 방금 끝낸 것에 근거하여 다음에 무엇을 할지 결정한다. 화장실에 가는 것은 손을 씻고 말리는 것으로 이어지고, 이로 인해 당신은 더러운 수건을 세탁실에 넣을 필요가 있다는 생각이 들고, 그래서 당신은 쇼핑 목록에 세탁 세제를 더하고, 기타 등등을 한다. 고립되어 일어나는 행동은 없다. 각 행동은 다음 행동을 유발하는 신호가 된다.

Why? 왜 정답일까?

마지막 문장인 'Each action becomes a cue that triggers the next behavior.'에서 한 행동은 다음 행동을 유발하는 신호가 된다고 언급하는 것으로 보아, 빈칸이 포함된 문장은 그 어떤 행동도 '따로' 일어나지 않는다는 의미를 나타내야 한다. 따라서 빈칸에 들어갈 말로 가장 적절한 것은 ① '고립'이다.

- **state** ⓥ 진술하다
- **possession** ⓝ 소유물
- **consumption** ⓝ 소비
- **spot** ⓥ 발견하다
- **go with** ~와 어울리다
- **remind** ⓥ 상기시키다
- **detergent** ⓝ 세제
- **isolation** ⓝ 고립
- **obtain** ⓥ 얻다, 입수하다
- **spiral** ⓝ 소용돌이
- **additional** ⓐ 추가의
- **pattern** ⓝ (정형화된) 양식, 패턴, 경향
- **chain reaction** 연쇄 반응
- **laundry** ⓝ 세탁실
- **trigger** ⓥ 유발하다
- **fairness** ⓝ 공정함, 공평함

구문 풀이

1행 The tendency for one purchase to lead to another one has
　　　　　주어　　　　　　의미상 주어　　　형용사적 용법　　　동사(단수)
a name: the Diderot Effect.
동격(= a name)

★★★ 1등급 대비 고난도 3점 문제

08 인간의 인지 작용   정답률 33% | 정답 ②

다음 빈칸에 들어갈 말로 가장 적절한 것을 고르시오. [3점]

① tend to favor learners with great social skills
　사교성이 뛰어난 학습자를 선호하는 경향이 있다
② are marked by a steady elimination of information
　정보의 지속적인 제거로 특징지어진다
③ require an external aid to support our memory capacity
　우리 기억력을 보조하고자 외부의 도움을 필요로 한다
④ are determined by the accuracy of incoming information
　유입되는 정보의 정확성에 의해 결정된다
⑤ are facilitated by embracing chaotic situations as they are
　혼돈의 상황을 있는 그대로 받아들이는 것으로부터 촉진된다

[본문 해석]

인간 사고의 많은 부분은 정보를 걸러내고 나머지는 처리하기 쉬운 상태로 분류하도록 설계된다. 특히 문화와 사회에서 이용할 수 있는 엄청난 양의 정보를 고려할 때, 우리 감각에서 오는 데이터의 유입은 압도적인 혼란을 낳을 수 있다. 모든 감각적 인상과 가능한 정보 중에서, 우리의 개인적인 필요와 가장 관련된 적은 양을 찾아서 그것을 사용 가능한 지식체로 구성하는 게 중요하다. 예상들은 이 작업의 일부를 수행하여 예상되는 것과 무관한 정보를 걸러내는 데 도움이 되고, 명확한 모순에 우리의 주의를 집중시킨다. 학습과 기억의 과정은 정보의 지속적인 제거로 특징지어진다. 사람들은 그들 주변 세계의 일부분만을 인지한다. 그런 다음, 그들이 알아차린 것의 일부만 처리되어 기억에 저장된다. 그리고 기억에 넘겨진 것의 일부만 생각해 낼 수 있다.

Why? 왜 정답일까?

빈칸 뒤에서 우리는 세계의 일부만 인지하고, 인지한 것 중 일부만 저장하고, 저장된 것의 일부만 회상할 수 있다고 한다. 말인즉 정보를 점점 줄여가는 것이 우리의 인지 과정이라는 것이므로, 빈칸에 들어갈 말로 가장 적절한 것은 ② '정보의 지속적인 제거로 특징지어진다'이다.

- **screen out** 차단하다
- **inflow** ⓝ 유입
- **chaos** ⓝ 혼돈
- **vital** ⓐ 매우 중요한
- **accomplish** ⓥ 해내다, 성취하다
- **manageable** ⓐ 처리하기 쉬운
- **overwhelming** ⓐ 압도적인
- **enormous** ⓐ 막대한
- **stock** ⓝ 저장, 축적 ⓥ 저장하다, 보관하다
- **irrelevant** ⓐ 무관한

- **contradiction** ⓝ 모순
- **commit A to memory** A를 기억하다
- **accuracy** ⓝ 정확성
- **fraction** ⓝ 부분
- **retrieve** ⓥ 생각해 내다
- **facilitate** ⓥ 촉진하다

구문 풀이

6행 Out of all the sensory impressions and possible information,
～ 중에서
it is vital to find a small amount [that is most relevant to our individual
가주어   진주어1   선행사   주격 관·대
needs] and to organize that into a usable stock of knowledge.
진주어2   대명사(= the small amount)

★★ 문제 해결 꿀~팁 ★★

▶ 많이 틀린 이유는?
외부에서 들어오는 데이터나 정보를 차단하고 줄여야 한다는 내용 때문에 '기억력을 외부에서 보조해줘야 한다'는 의미의 ③을 고르게 될 수도 있다. 하지만 '외부의 보조'에 관해서는 전혀 언급되지 않았다.

▶ 문제 해결 방법은?
빈칸 뒤가 인간의 인지적 과정을 잘 요약하고 있다. 주변 정보를 선별적으로 받아들이고, 받아들인 정보 중 일부만을 저장하고, 저장된 정보 중 일부만을 기억하게 된다는 것은 결국 '계속 정보를 지워간다'는 의미와 같다. 본문의 **screen out**이 ②의 **elimination**과 연결된다.

---

09 디지털 기기의 작동 원리에 대한 이해
정답률 55% | 정답 ④

다음 글에서 전체 흐름과 관계 없는 문장은?

[본문 해석]
오늘날의 '디지털 원주민'들은 디지털 기술에 몰입한 채로 성장했고, 자기가 가진 기기의 힘을 충분히 활용할 수 있는 기술적 소질을 가지고 있다. ① 하지만 그들이 어떤 앱을 사용해야 하는지 혹은 어떤 웹 사이트를 방문해야 하는지 알고 있을지라도, 터치스크린 뒤에 숨겨진 작동 방식을 반드시 이해한다는 것은 아니다. ② 사람들이 기계의 역학과 용도를 이해하려면 기술 활용 능력이 필요하다. ③ 100년 전 공장 근로자들이 엔진의 기본 구조를 이해할 필요가 있었던 것과 마찬가지로, 우리는 우리의 기기 뒤에 숨겨진 기본 원리를 이해할 필요가 있다. ④ 기기의 수명은 하드웨어의 구조뿐만 아니라 기기를 작동하는 소프트웨어의 우수성에 달려 있다. ⑤ 이것은 우리가 소프트웨어와 하드웨어를 최대한 유용하게 사용하여, 성취하고 만들어 낼 수 있는 우리의 능력을 극대화한다.

Why? 왜 정답일까?
디지털 기기의 작동 원리를 이해할 필요가 있다는 내용의 글로, ④의 경우 디지털 기기의 수명을 결정짓는 요소에 관해 이야기하므로 흐름상 무관하다. 따라서 전체 흐름과 관계 없는 문장은 ④이다.

- **immersed in** ～에 몰입한
- **utilize** ⓥ 이용하다, 활용하다
- **elemental** ⓐ 기본적인
- **operate** ⓥ 작동하다, 조작하다
- **maximize** ⓥ 극대화하다
- **aptitude** ⓝ 소질, 적성
- **literacy** ⓝ (글을) 읽고 쓰는 능력, 문해력
- **lifespan** ⓝ 수명
- **empower** ⓥ 권한을 주다

구문 풀이

6행 People need technological literacy if they are to understand
be to 용법(의도 : ～하려면)
machines' mechanics and uses.

---

10 연꽃 식물의 잎 정화 원리를 이용한 페인트 개발
정답률 71% | 정답 ③

주어진 글 다음에 이어질 글의 순서로 가장 적절한 것을 고르시오.

① (A) − (C) − (B)
② (B) − (A) − (C)
✓③ (B) − (C) − (A)
④ (C) − (A) − (B)
⑤ (C) − (B) − (A)

[본문 해석]
연꽃 식물(흰 수련)은 호수와 연못의 더럽고 진흙투성이인 바닥에서 성장하지만, 그러함에도 불구하고 그것의 잎은 항상 깨끗하다.

(B) 그것은 먼지 같은 가장 작은 입자가 그 식물에 떨어질 때마다, 즉시 잎을

흔들어서 먼지 입자들을 어떠한 특정 장소로 향하도록 하기 때문이다. 잎에 떨어지는 빗방울들이 그 동일한 장소로 보내져 먼지를 씻어낸다.

(C) 연꽃의 이러한 특성은 연구자들이 새로운 주택용 페인트를 고안하도록 이끌었다. 연구자들은 연꽃잎이 하는 것과 대체로 똑같이 비가 올 때 깨끗하게 씻기는 페인트를 어떻게 개발할지에 대한 연구를 시작했다.

(A) 이 연구의 결과로 한 독일 회사가 주택용 페인트를 생산했다. 유럽과 아시아의 시장에서 이 제품은 심지어 세제나 모래 분사 세척 없이 5년 동안 깨끗한 상태로 유지된다고 보증했다.

Why? 왜 정답일까?
연꽃 식물이 더러운 환경에서 자람에도 잎은 늘 깨끗하다고 설명한 주어진 글 뒤에는, 주어진 글의 내용을 That으로 받아 그 이유를 설명하는 (B)가 먼저 이어져야 한다. (B)에서는 먼지 같은 입자가 떨어질 때마다 연꽃이 잎을 즉시 흔들어서 입자들을 다른 곳으로 보낸다는 점을 언급하는데, (C)는 이를 This property of the lotus로 가리키며, 이 특성을 접목하여 탄생한 것이 새로운 주택용 페인트임을 설명한다. (A)에서는 (C)의 후반부에 이어 페인트 개발에 관한 연구와 그 결과를 언급하고 있다. 따라서 글의 순서로 가장 적절한 것은 ③ '(B) − (C) − (A)'이다.

- **lotus** ⓝ 연꽃, 수련
- **guarantee** ⓝ 보증 ⓥ 보장하다
- **sandblasting** ⓝ 모래 분사
- **property** ⓝ 특성
- **investigation** ⓝ 연구, 조사
- **detergent** ⓝ 세제
- **particle** ⓝ 입자

구문 풀이

15행 Researchers began working on how to develop paints [that
주격 관계대명사
「how +to부정사 : 어떻게 ～할지」 선행사
wash clean in the rain], in much the same way as lotus leaves do.
～와 대체로 똑같이   = wash clean

11-12 토론에서의 집단 양극화 현상

[본문 해석]
상식에 따르면 다른 의견을 내는 사람들과의 토론은 그 집단 내의 모든 사람들에게 좀 더 온건한 태도를 만들어 낼 것이라고 한다. 놀랍게도, 이것이 항상 사실은 아니다. 집단 양극화에서, 일정 기간의 토론은 집단 구성원들이 이미 선호하는 경향이 있던 방향으로 더 극단적인 입장을 취하도록 압박한다. 「집단 양극화는 태도의 방향을 (a) 뒤집는 것이 아니라, 오히려 처음에 가졌던 태도를 강화한다.」「두 가지 압력들이 집단 토론 후에 개인들이 더 극단적인 입장을 취하도록 압박하는 것으로 보인다.」첫째, 순응과 소속 욕구는 집단 양극화에 기여한다. 만약 어떤 집단의 다수가 특정한 방향으로 기울어 있다면, 그 다수에게 (b) 동의하고, 어쩌면 심지어 그 주장에서 한 걸음 더 나아가는 것보다 더 나은 소속 방법이 무엇이겠는가? 또한 생각이 비슷한 사람들은 서로 뭉치는 경향이 있는데, 이는 기존 의견에 대한 (c) 강화를 제공하고, 그러한 의견에 대한 사람들의 확신을 높이고, 그러한 의견에 대한 새로운 근거 및 상반되는 관점에 대한 반론의 발견을 야기하며, 상충되는 생각에의 노출을 줄일 수 있다. 둘째, 주제에 대한 토론에의 노출은 태도를 (d) 바꿀(→ 유지할) 새로운 이유를 도입한다. 만약 당신이 이미 총기 규제에 반대하고 있으며 당신의 입장을 지지하는 추가적인 주장을 듣는다면, 당신은 결국 원래보다 더 (e) 반대하게 될지도 모른다.

- **common sense** 상식
- **be not the case** 사실이 아니다
- **polarization** ⓝ 양극화
- **like-minded** ⓐ 생각이 비슷한
- **counterargument** ⓝ 반론
- **gun control** 총기 규제
- **companion** ⓝ 동반자
- **moderate** ⓐ 온건한, 중간의
- **inclined to** ～하는 경향이 있는
- **lean** ⓥ 기울다, 기대다
- **reinforcement** ⓝ 강화
- **opposing** ⓐ 상반되는, 대립되는
- **end up** 결국 ～이 되다
- **foster** ⓥ 기르다, 육성하다

구문 풀이

17행 There is also a tendency for like-minded people to affiliate
주어(선행사)   의미상 주어   형용사적 용법
with one another, which can provide reinforcement for existing
계속적 용법   동사1
opinions, increase people's confidence in those opinions, lead to
동사2   동사3
the discovery (of new reasons for those opinions and counterarguments
to opposing views), and reduce exposure to conflicting ideas.
동사4

DAY 15

★★★ 1등급 대비 고난도 2점 문제

11 제목 파악   정답률 41% | 정답 ⑤

윗글의 제목으로 가장 적절한 것은?

① Have More Companions and Perform Better!
동반자를 더 많이 두어 성과를 높여라!

② Group Competition: Not Necessarily Harmful
집단 경쟁: 반드시 해롭지는 않다

③ Exposure to New Ideas Weakens Group Identity
새로운 아이디어에 대한 노출은 집단 정체성을 약화시킨다

④ Sharing Ideas: The Surest Way to Foster Creativity
아이디어 공유: 창의력을 키우는 가장 확실한 방법

✔ ⑤ Black Gets Darker, White Gets Brighter in Group Discussion
집단 토론에서 검은색은 더 검어지고, 흰색은 더 희어진다

Why? 왜 정답일까?

토론 중 집단 양극화 현상으로 원래 갖고 있던 견해가 강화된다(Group polarization ~ accentuates the attitudes held at the beginning.)는 내용을 설명한 글이므로, 글의 제목으로 가장 적절한 것은 ⑤ '집단 토론에서 검은색은 더 검어지고, 흰색은 더 희어진다'이다.

★★ 문제 해결 꿀~팁 ★★

▶ 많이 틀린 이유는?

이 글의 주제는 다른 의견을 가진 사람들끼리 토론한 뒤 서로 견해가 중화되지 않고 도리어 강화될 수 있다는 것이다. 그러나 최다 오답인 ③은 새로운 아이디어를 접하는 것이 집단 정체성을 '약하게 만든다'는 의미로, 주제를 거꾸로 진술하고 있다.

▶ 문제 해결 방법은?

제목 문제에 비유적 표현이 나오면 한 번 더 주의 깊게 살펴야 한다. 'Black Gets Darker, White Gets Brighter'는 '검은 것이 더 검어지고, 흰 것이 더 희어진다'는 의미인데, 이는 토론을 통해 각자의 견해가 중립적이 되기는커녕 서로 더 극단으로 향하는 상황을 올바르게 묘사한다.

★★★ 1등급 대비 고난도 3점 문제

12 어휘 추론   정답률 36% | 정답 ④

밑줄 친 (a) ~ (e) 중에서 문맥상 낱말의 쓰임이 적절하지 않은 것은? [3점]

① (a)   ② (b)   ③ (c)   ✔ ④ (d)   ⑤ (e)

Why? 왜 정답일까?

'Two pressures appear to push individuals to take more extreme positions following a group discussion.' 이후로 집단 양극화로 개인이 원래 갖고 있던 견해를 강화해 나가게 되는 이유를 제시한다. (d)가 포함된 문장은 사람들이 견해를 '바꾸지' 않고 '고수하는' 두 번째 이유에 관한 설명이므로, changing을 holding으로 고쳐야 한다. 따라서 문맥상 낱말의 쓰임이 적절하지 않은 것은 ④ '(d)'이다.

★★ 문제 해결 꿀~팁 ★★

▶ 많이 틀린 이유는?

최다 오답인 ③은 서로 생각이 비슷한 사람끼리 뭉치면 나타나는 결과를 설명하며, 비슷한 사람끼리 있으면 원래 가졌던 견해를 '강화'하게 된다는 의미로 reinforcement를 적절히 썼다. 한편, ⑤를 고른 학생들도 많은데, 원래 총기 난사에 '반대하던' 상황에서 추가적인 반대 근거를 들면 '더 반대하게' 될 수 있다는 의미로 opposed를 쓴 것은 적절하다.

▶ 문제 해결 방법은?

④와 ⑤는 사실상 함께 판단해야 하는 선택지이다. ④가 포함된 문장에 대해 예를 드는 문장이 마지막 문장, 즉 ⑤가 포함된 문장이기 때문이다. 마지막 문장의 핵심 내용은 원래 반대하던 사람이 추가로 반대할 이유를 접하면 '더 심하게' 반대하게 된다는 것이다. 이는 기존의 견해를 '바꾸는' 상황이 아니라 '유지하는' 상황에 해당한다.

DAY 16 — 20분 미니 모의고사

01 ⑤	02 ①	03 ①	04 ⑤	05 ③
06 ①	07 ②	08 ④	09 ①	10 ⑤
11 ④	12 ④			

01 버스 무정차 시정 요청   정답률 90% | 정답 ⑤

다음 글의 목적으로 가장 적절한 것은?

① 버스 운전기사 채용 계획을 문의하려고
② 버스 정류장의 위치 변경을 요청하려고
③ 도로 공사로 인한 소음에 대해 항의하려고
④ 출퇴근 시간의 버스 배차 간격 단축을 제안하려고
✔ ⑤ 버스 정류장 무정차 통과에 대한 시정을 요구하려고

[본문 해석]

담당자 귀하

35번 버스에서 자주 발생하는 문제에 대해 귀하의 주의를 환기하고 싶습니다. Fenny Road를 따라 중간쯤 버스 정류장이 있고, 그곳에 35번 버스가 정차하게 되어 있습니다. 그러나 귀사의 버스 기사들 중 일부는 이 버스 정류장을 인식하지 못하거나 무슨 이유인지 그것을 무시하기로 해서 버스가 꽉 차지 않았는데도 지나쳐가는 것으로 보입니다. 기사들에게 이 버스 정류장이 존재하고, 그곳에 정차할 준비를 해야 한다는 것을 상기시켜 주시면 고맙겠습니다. 곧 이 서비스가 개선되기를 기대합니다.

John Williams 드림

Why? 왜 정답일까?

버스가 종종 정차하지 않고 지나는 정류장에 대해 기사들의 주의를 환기시켜 달라고 요구하는 글이다(I would be grateful if you could remind your drivers that this bus stop exists and that they should be prepared to stop at it.). 따라서 글의 목적으로 가장 적절한 것은 ⑤ '버스 정류장 무정차 통과에 대한 시정을 요구하려고'이다.

- to whom it may concern 담당자 귀하
- frequently [ad] 자주
- be supposed to ~하기로 되어 있다
- unaware @ 모르는
- draw Ⓥ 끌다
- attention ⑩ 주의
- appear Ⓥ ~처럼 보이다
- grateful @ 고마워하는

구문 풀이

3행 There is a bus stop about halfway along Fenny Road,
약, 대략
at which the No. 35 buses are supposed to stop.
계속적 용법(= where)   ~하기로 되어 있다

★★★ 1등급 대비 고난도 3점 문제

02 버렸던 방식을 되짚으며 창작을 하는 예술가들   정답률 35% | 정답 ①

밑줄 친 got "colder"가 다음 글에서 의미하는 바로 가장 적절한 것은? [3점]

✔ ① moved away from the desired outcome
바라던 결과에서 멀어졌다

② lost his reputation due to public criticism
대중의 비판으로 인해 명성을 잃었다

③ became unwilling to follow new art trends
새로운 예술 사조를 따르기를 꺼렸다

④ appreciated others' artwork with less enthusiasm
남들의 예술작품을 덜 열정적으로 감상했다

⑤ imitated masters' styles rather than creating his own
자신의 스타일을 만들기보다 거장들의 스타일을 모방했다

[본문 해석]

만약 창작자들이 그들이 언제 걸작을 만들어가고 있는지를 안다면, 그들의 작품은 오직 앞으로만 나아갈 것이다. 그들은 금광을 발견했을 때 아이디어를 만들어내는 노력을 멈출 것이다. 하지만 사실 그들은 (창작 과정을) 되짚어가서 이전에 부적당하다고 폐기했던 버전으로 되돌아간다. 베토벤의 가장 유명한 작품인 제5번 교향곡에서 그는 제1악장의 결말 부분이 너무 짧다고 느껴져 폐기했고, 결국 나중에야 그것에 복귀했다. 베토벤이 비범한 작품과 평범한 작품

을 구분할 수 있었다면 그는 자기 작곡을 바로 성공으로 받아들였을 것이다. 피카소가 파시즘에 저항하여 유명한 *Guernica*를 그릴 때, 그는 79점의 다른 스케치들을 그렸다. 이 그림의 많은 이미지들은 이후의 변형물이 아니라, 그의 초기 스케치에 바탕을 두었다. 만약 피카소가 작품을 만들면서 자신의 작품을 판단할 수 있었다면, 그는 일관되게 '더 뜨거워지고' 나중에 그린 스케치를 사용했을 것이다. 하지만 실제로는 그가 '더 차가워진' 것은 그만큼 흔한 일이었다.

Why? 왜 정답일까?

첫 두 문장에서 예술가들은 창작 도중에는 어떤 것이 걸작인지 바로 파악할 수 없기에 작품을 만들어가는 과정을 때때로 되짚어가며 버렸던 것을 다시 가져와 작품을 완성한다고 설명한 후, 베토벤과 피카소의 예를 들고 있다. 특히 피카소의 예에서, 피카소가 만일 작품을 그리던 도중에 어느 스케치가 괜찮은지를 알아볼 수 있었다면 피카소는 초기 스케치를 되살릴 필요 없이 꾸준히 '더 뜨거워졌을' 것이라고 언급하고 있다. 여기서 '뜨거워지다'는 피카소가 걸작에 일관되게 가까워지는 과정을 비유한 표현으로 볼 수 있다. 이에 근거할 때, 피카소가 실제로는 '더 차가워졌다'는 말은 피카소가 걸작에 꾸준히 가까워지지 못하고 초기 스케치에 미치지 못하는 중간 스케치들을 생산해내는 과정을 묘사한 말로 볼 수 있다. 따라서 밑줄 친 부분이 의미하는 바로 가장 적절한 것은 ① '바라던 결과에서 멀어졌다'이다.

- **fashion** ⓥ (특히 손으로) 만들다, 빚다
- **strike gold** 노다지를 캐다
- **discard A as B** A를 B로 간주해서 폐기하다
- **scrap** ⓥ 폐기하다, 버리다
- **composition** ⓝ 작곡, 구성
- **variation** ⓝ 변형, 변주
- **generation** ⓝ 발생, 유발, 생성
- **backtrack** ⓥ (왔던 길을) 되짚어가다
- **inadequate** ⓐ 부당한, 불충분한
- **distinguish A from B** A와 B를 구별하다
- **in protest of** ~에 저항하는
- **consistently** ⓐⓓ 일관되게

구문 풀이

9행 Had Beethoven been able to distinguish an extraordinary
「had + 주어 + p.p. : 가정법 과거완료 종속절(if 생략 후 도치)」
from an ordinary work, he would have accepted his composition
「주어 + 조동사 과거형 + have p.p. : 가정법 과거완료 주절」
immediately as a hit.

★★ 문제 해결 꿀~팁 ★★

▶ 많이 틀린 이유는?
예술가들의 창작 과정이 항상 앞으로만 향하지는 않는다는 내용의 글로, '예술 사조'나 '거장의 스타일을 모방하는' 행위 등은 언급되지 않기 때문에 ③, ⑤는 모두 오답이다.

▶ 문제 해결 방법은?
앞에 나온 get "warmer"의 의미를 잘 이해해야 한다. 이는 피카소가 *Guernica*를 작업하는 도중 어느 스케치가 더 나은지를 바로 판단할 수 있었다면 제작 과정에서 계속 더 발전된 쪽으로 나아가는 요소들만 선택했을 것이기 때문에 그가 추구하는 좋은 작품에 '꾸준히 더 가까워졌을' 것이라는 의미를 나타내는 표현이다. 밑줄 친 got "colder"는 이와 반대되는 의미로 이해해야 한다.

---

03 메시지를 표현하는 빌딩 정답률 72% | 정답 ①

다음 글의 제목으로 가장 적절한 것은?

✔ ① Buildings Do Talk in Their Own Ways!
빌딩은 자기 식대로 분명 말한다!
② Design of Buildings Starts from Nature
건물 설계는 자연에서 시작된다
③ Language of Buildings: Too Vague to Grasp
건물의 언어: 너무 모호해서 이해할 수 없다
④ Which Is More Important, Safety or Beauty?
안전과 아름다움, 무엇이 더 중요한가?
⑤ How Do Architects Attach Emotions to Buildings?
건축가들은 건물에 어떻게 감정을 부여하는가?

[본문 해석]

빌딩은 무생물이지만, 표현을 제대로 하지 못하는 사물은 아니다. 아무리 단순한 집이라도 항상 진술을 하는데, 그것은 말보다 벽돌과 돌, 나무와 유리로 표현되지만 꽤 크고 명확하다. 잡초와 버려진 자동차로 둘러싸인 녹슨 트레일러나 높은 벽을 가진 아주 새로운 소형 저택을 볼 때, 우리는 즉시 메시지를 받는다. 이 두 경우 모두, 비록 다른 억양이지만, "여기에 들어오지 말라"는 것이다. 물론 우리와 소통하는 것은 집뿐만이 아니다. 교회, 박물관, 학교, 병원, 식당, 사무실 등 모든 종류의 건물들이 우리에게 소리 없이 말한다. 때때로 그 진술은 의도적이다. 가게나 레스토랑은 주로 저소득층 또는 고소득층 고객을 맞이하기 위해서 설계될 수 있다. 건물들은 우리가 그들의 메시지를 의식적으로 명심하지는 않더라도 우리에게 무엇을 생각하고 어떻게 행동해야 하는지를 알려준다.

Why? 왜 정답일까?

첫 문장과 마지막 문장을 통해, 건물은 아무 표현을 하지 하는 무생물이 아니므로 우리에게 메시지를 전달한다(Buildings tell us what to think and how to act, ~)는 주제를 파악할 수 있다. 따라서 글의 주제로 가장 적절한 것은 ① '빌딩은 자기 식대로 분명 말한다!'이다.

- **inanimate** ⓐ 무생물의
- **brick** ⓝ 벽돌
- **abandon** ⓥ 버리다
- **statement** ⓝ 진술
- **low-income** ⓐ 저소득의
- **consciously** ⓐⓓ 의식적으로
- **make a statement** 말하다, 진술하다
- **weed** ⓝ 잡초
- **instantly** ⓐⓓ 즉시
- **deliberate** ⓐ 의도적인, 고의의
- **register** ⓥ 알아채다, 기억하다
- **grasp** ⓥ 이해하다

구문 풀이

2행 Even the simplest house always makes a statement,
one (expressed in brick and stone, in wood and glass, rather than in
부정대명사(= a statement)
words — but no less loud and obvious). ( ) : 과거분사구(one 수식)

---

04 Niklas Luhmann의 생애 정답률 96% | 정답 ⑤

Niklas Luhmann에 관한 다음 글의 내용과 일치하지 않는 것은?

① 제2차 세계 대전 이후에 법을 공부했다.
② State of Lower Saxony에서 교육 개혁을 담당했다.
③ Harvard University에 있을 때 Talcott Parsons의 영향을 받았다.
④ 다양한 주제에 관해 연구했다.
✔ ⑤ 그의 책은 번역하기가 쉽다고 알려져 있다.

[본문 해석]

20세기의 유명한 사회학자 Niklas Luhmann은 1927년 독일 Lüeburg에서 태어났다. 『제2차 세계 대전 후, 그는 University of Freiburg에서 1949년까지 법학을 공부했다.』 『경력 초기에 그는 State of Lower Saxony에서 일했는데, 그곳에서 그는 교육 개혁을 담당했다.』 『1960년에서 1961년에 Luhmann은 Harvard University에서 사회학을 공부할 기회가 있었는데, 그곳에서 그는 가장 유명한 사회 체계 이론가 중 한 명이었던 Talcott Parsons의 영향을 받았다.』 나중에 Luhmann은 본인의 사회 체계 이론을 개발했다. 1968년에 그는 University of Bielefeld에서 사회학 교수가 되었다. 『그는 대중 매체와 법을 포함한 다양한 주제를 연구했다.』 『비록 그의 책들은 번역하기 어렵다고 알려져 있지만 실제로 다른 언어들로 널리 번역되었다.』

(『』: ①의 근거 일치 / ②의 근거 일치 / ③의 근거 일치 / ④의 근거 일치 / ⑤의 근거 불일치)

Why? 왜 정답일까?

마지막 문장(Although his books are known to be difficult to translate ~)에서 Luhmann의 책은 번역하기 어렵다고 알려져 있다고 하므로, 내용과 일치하지 않는 것은 ⑤ '그의 책은 번역하기가 쉽다고 알려져 있다.'이다.

Why? 왜 오답일까?

① 'After World War II, he studied law ~'의 내용과 일치한다.
② '~ he worked for the State of Lower Saxony, where he was in charge of educational reform.'의 내용과 일치한다.
③ 'Luhmann had the chance to study sociology at Harvard University, where he was influenced by Talcott Parsons, ~'의 내용과 일치한다.
④ 'He researched a variety of subjects, ~'의 내용과 일치한다.

- **renowned** ⓐ 유명한
- **in charge of** ~을 담당하는, 책임지는
- **reform** ⓝ 개혁
- **theorist** ⓝ 이론가
- **research** ⓥ 연구하다 ⓝ 연구
- **mass media** 대중 매체
- **translate** ⓥ 번역하다
- **sociologist** ⓝ 사회학자
- **educational** ⓐ 교육적인
- **influence** ⓥ 영향을 주다 ⓝ 영향
- **professor** ⓝ 교수
- **subject** ⓝ 주제, 피실험자
- **be known to** ~한 것으로 알려지다
- **widely** ⓐⓓ 널리

구문 풀이

6행 Luhmann had the chance to study sociology at
형용사적 용법
Harvard University, where he was influenced by Talcott Parsons,
장소 선행사   관계부사   사람
one of the most famous social system theorists.
동격(앞의 사람 설명)

DAY 16

★★★ 1등급 대비 고난도 3점 문제

05 곤충의 몸 구성
정답률 46% | 정답 ③

다음 글의 밑줄 친 부분 중, 어법상 틀린 것은? [3점]

[본문 해석]

야외에서 곤충의 성공적인 생존의 비결 중 하나는 그들의 작은 몸이 탈수되지 않도록 돕는 단단한 밀랍 같은 층인 외피에 있다. 그들은 공기로부터 산소를 흡수하기 위해 몸의 마디에 있는 좁은 호흡구들을 사용하는데, 이들은 공기를 수동적으로 흡입하고 필요할 때 열리고 닫힐 수 있다. 혈관에 담긴 피 대신 그들은 자유롭게 흐르는 혈림프를 갖고 있는데, 이는 그들의 몸이 단단하게 유지되도록 돕고 움직임을 거들고 영양분과 노폐물이 몸의 적절한 부위로 이동하는 것을 도와준다. 신경 체계가 모듈식으로 되어 있는데, 어떤 의미에서는 몸의 각 마디가 그 자체의 개별적이고 자율적인 뇌를 갖고 있으며, 몇몇 다른 몸의 체계가 유사한 모듈화를 보여 준다. 이것들은 곤충의 몸이 우리의 것과는 완전히 다르게 구조화되어 있고 기능하는 많은 방식들 중 몇 가지일 뿐이다.

Why? 왜 정답일까?

분사의 꾸밈을 받는 명사 blood가 혈관 속에 '포함되는' 대상이므로, 현재분사 containing 대신 과거분사 contained를 사용해야 한다. 어법상 틀린 것은 ③이다.

Why? 왜 오답일까?

① 'one of the + 복수 명사'가 주어이므로 단수 동사인 lies가 바르게 쓰였다.
② 관계절의 동사인 take in을 꾸미기 위해 부사인 passively가 바르게 쓰였다.
④ 단수 취급하는 'each of the + 복수 명사'의 소유격을 나타내기 위해 단수 대명사 its가 바르게 쓰였다.
⑤ 관계절에 are structured라는 수동태 동사와 자동사 function을 포함한 완전한 구조가 나온다. 따라서 관계부사와 마찬가지로 뒤에 완전한 절을 수반하는 '전치사 + 관계대명사' 형태의 in which가 바르게 쓰였다.

- **open air** 야외, 옥외
- **covering** ⓝ 외피, 피복
- **segment** ⓝ (동물의) 몸의 마디
- **as needed** 필요에 따라
- **rigid** ⓐ 단단한, 엄격한
- **appropriate** ⓐ 적절한
- **in a sense** 어떤 의미에서
- **outer** ⓐ 외부의, 바깥 표면의
- **dehydrate** ⓥ 탈수 상태가 되다, 건조시키다
- **passively** ⓐⓓ 수동적으로
- **vessel** ⓝ 혈관
- **nutrient** ⓝ 영양분
- **nervous** ⓐ 신경의
- **autonomous** ⓐ 자율적인

구문 풀이

1행 One of the keys to insects' successful survival in the open
「one of the + 복수 명사 : ~ 중 하나」　　「help + 원형부정사 : ~하는 것을 돕다」
air lies in their outer covering — a hard waxy layer [that helps prevent
동사(단수)　　　　　　　　　　　　　　동격(=their ~ covering)　주격 관·대
their tiny bodies from dehydrating].

★★ 문제 해결 꿀~팁 ★★

▶ 많이 틀린 이유는?
② '형용사 vs. 부사', ④ '대명사의 수 일치', ⑤ '전치사 + 관계대명사' 등 빈출 포인트로 구성된 어법 문제이다. 특히 ⑤의 경우 뒤에 나오는 문장 구조를 잘 파악해야 한다. '전치사 + 관계대명사'는 관계부사와 기능상 같아서 뒤에 완전한 절이 연결되어야 한다.

▶ 문제 해결 방법은?
③ '현재분사 vs. 과거분사'는 분사가 꾸미거나 보충 설명하는 명사가 분사의 행위 주체인지 아니면 행위 대상인지를 구별해야 한다. 여기서는 분사의 수식을 받는 blood가 혈관에 무언가를 '포함시키는' 주체가 아니라 혈관에 '담기는' 대상이므로 과거분사를 써야 한다.

06 공예와 순수 예술
정답률 51% | 정답 ①

(A), (B), (C)의 각 네모 안에서 문맥에 맞는 낱말로 가장 적절한 것은? [3점]

(A)	(B)	(C)
✓ creative 창의적인	satisfying 충족시키는	gone 사라진
② creative 창의적인	ignoring 무시하는	gone 사라진
③ creative 창의적인	satisfying 충족시키는	born 실린
④ practical 실용적인	ignoring 무시하는	born 실린
⑤ practical 실용적인	satisfying 충족시키는	gone 사라진

[본문 해석]

우리의 문화는 순수 예술 — 즐거움 외에는 어떤 기능도 가지고 있지 않은 창조적 생산물 — 쪽으로 편향되어 있다. 공예품은 덜 가치가 있는데 그것들은 일상의 기능을 제공하기 때문에 순수하게 (A) 창의적이지 않다. 하지만 이러한 구분은 문화적으로 그리고 역사적으로 상대적이다. 대부분의 현대 고급 예술은 일종의 공예로 시작했다. 우리가 오늘날 "고전 음악"이라고 부르는 것의 작곡과 연주는 가톨릭 미사에서 요구되는 기능 또는 왕실 후원자의 특정한 오락적 요구를 (B) 충족시키는 공예 음악의 형태로 시작했다. 예를 들면, 실내악은 실제로 방들 — 부유한 가정의 작고 사적인 방들 — 에서 종종 배경음악으로 연주되도록 설계되었다. 바흐에서 쇼팽에 이르는 유명한 작곡가들에 의해서 작곡된 춤곡들은 원래는 정말로 춤을 동반했다. 하지만 오늘날, 그것들이 작곡된 맥락과 기능들이 (C) 사라진 채로, 우리는 이러한 작품들을 순수 예술로 듣는다.

Why? 왜 정답일까?

(A) '~ because they serve an everyday function, ~'에서 공예품은 일상의 기능을 제공한다고 하므로 순수하게 창의의 의미만을 지니고 있지 않다는 뜻에서 (A)에는 creative가 들어가는 것이 적절하다. 앞에 not이 있으므로 creative를 그대로 넣음에 주의한다.

(B) 공예는 기능을 제공한다는 앞의 내용을 근거로 볼 때, 공예 음악 또한 특정한 기능이나 필요를 '충족했다'는 뜻에서 (B)에는 satisfying이 들어가는 것이 적절하다.

(C) 과거의 춤곡은 본디 춤의 배경음악을 제공한다는 기능적인 목적을 수행했지만 시간이 지나며 그러한 기능이 '사라졌기에' 순수 예술로 남게 되었다(~ we listen to these works as fine art.)는 내용을 설명하는 맥락이므로, (C)에는 gone이 들어가는 것이 적절하다. 따라서 문맥에 맞는 낱말로 가장 적절한 것은 ① '(A) creative(창의적인) – (B) satisfying(충족시키는) – (C) gone(사라진)'이다.

- **bias** ⓥ 편향시키다
- **purely** ⓐⓓ 순수하게
- **division** ⓝ 구분, 분리
- **contemporary** ⓐ 현대의, 동시대의
- **specific** ⓐ 특정한
- **intimate** ⓐ 사적인, 개인적인; 친밀한
- **background** ⓐ 배경의
- **accompany** ⓥ 동반하다, 수반하다
- **other than** ~ 외에
- **practical** ⓐ 실용적인
- **relative** ⓐ 상대적인
- **composition** ⓝ 작곡, 구성
- **royal** ⓐ 국왕의, 왕실의
- **wealthy** ⓐ 부유한
- **compose** ⓥ 구성하다
- **context** ⓝ 맥락

구문 풀이

7행 The composition and performance of {what we now call
주어　　　　　　　　　　　　　　　　관계대명사　5형식 동사
"classical music"} began as a form of craft music [satisfying required
목적격 보어(명사)　자동사　　　　　　　　　　현재분사　　목적어1
functions in the Catholic mass, or the specific entertainment needs
목적어2
of royal patrons].

★★★ 1등급 대비 고난도 3점 문제

07 아이의 혼자 있을 수 있는 능력의 발달
정답률 26% | 정답 ②

다음 빈칸에 들어갈 말로 가장 적절한 것을 고르시오. [3점]

① Hardship – 고난　　　　　✓ Attachment – 애착
③ Creativity – 창의력　　　　④ Compliment – 칭찬
⑤ Responsibility – 책임감

[본문 해석]

아이들은 관심을 가져주는 타인이 있을 때 혼자 있을 수 있는 능력을 발달시킨다. 여러분이 어린 아이를 자연에서 조용히 산책시킬 때 다가오는 고요를 생각해 보아라. 그 아이는, 그에게 이러한 경험을 처음으로 하게 한 누군가와 '함께' 있다는 것에 도움을 받아, 자연 속에서 혼자 있는 것이 어떤 것인지에 대해 점점 알아 간다고 느끼게 된다. 점차적으로, 그 아이는 혼자 산책한다. 또는 두 살짜리 딸아이를 목욕시키는 엄마가, 딸이 엄마가 함께 있고 자신에게 시간을 내어줄 수 있다는 것을 내내 아는 상태로 이야기를 만들고 생각을 하며 혼자 있는 법을 배우면서 목욕 장난감을 가지고 공상에 잠길 수 있게 하는 것을 생각해 보아라. 점차적으로, 혼자서 하는 목욕은 그 아이가 상상을 하며 편안해 하는 시간이 된다. 애착은 혼자 있는 것을 가능하게 한다.

Why? 왜 정답일까?

첫 문장인 'Children develop the capacity for solitude in the presence of an attentive other.'에서 아이들은 관심을 주는 타인이 있을 때 혼자 있을 수 있게 된다는 핵심 내용이 제시되므로, 빈칸에 들어갈 말로 가장 적절한 것은 ② '애착'이다.

- **solitude** ⓝ 혼자 있음, 고독
- **attentive** ⓐ 관심을 가져주는
- **gradually** ⓐⓓ 점차적으로
- **presence** ⓝ 존재
- **increasingly** ⓐⓓ 점점
- **available** ⓐ (사람이) 시간이 있는

구문 풀이

7행 Or imagine a mother giving her two-year-old daughter a bath,
명령문 「imagine + 목적어 + 현재분사 : ~이 …하는 것을 상상하다」
allowing the girl's reverie with her bath toys as she makes up stories
분사구문1(a mother 설명)   ~하면서   동사1
and learns to be alone with her thoughts, all the while knowing (that)
동사2   분사구문2(the girl 설명) ↵ 접속사(생략)
her mother is present and available to her.

★★ 문제 해결 꿀~팁 ★★

▶ **많이 틀린 이유는?**
글 중간의 예시에 주목하면 ③ '창의력'이 답처럼 보일 수 있다. 하지만 주제문인 첫 문장에서 관심 있는 타인의 존재를 중요하게 언급하는 것으로 볼 때 이는 답으로 부적절하다.

▶ **문제 해결 방법은?**
빈칸 문제에서 빈칸은 글의 주제와 관련되어 있다. 따라서 이 글처럼 '주제 - 예시' 구조로 이루어진 글에서는 주제문인 첫 문장을 근거로 답을 찾아야 한다. 또한, 예시에서도 'being "with" someone'이라는 키워드를 제시하고 있다.

08 과학 실험의 조작과 통제   정답률 49% | 정답 ④

글의 흐름으로 보아, 주어진 문장이 들어가기에 가장 적절한 곳을 고르시오.

[본문 해석]

실험 방법의 근본적인 본질은 조작과 통제이다. 과학자들은 관심 변인을 조작하고, 차이가 있는지 확인한다. 동시에, 다른 모든 변인의 잠재적 영향을 통제하려고 시도한다. 사건의 근본적인 원인을 식별하는 데 있어 통제된 실험의 중요성은 아무리 강조해도 지나치지 않다. ① 현실의 통제되지 않은 세계에서, 변인들은 종종 상관관계가 있다. ② 예를 들어, 비타민 보충제를 섭취하는 사람들은 비타민을 섭취하지 않는 사람들과는 다른 식습관과 운동 습관을 지닐 수 있다. ③ 그 결과, 만약 우리가 비타민의 건강에 미치는 효과를 연구하고 싶다면, 우리는 단지 현실 세계만 관찰할 수 없는데, 왜냐하면 이러한 요소(비타민, 식단, 운동) 중 어느 것이든 건강에 영향을 미칠 수 있기 때문이다. ④ 오히려, 우리는 현실 세계에서 실제로 일어나지 않는 상황을 만들어야 한다. 그것이 바로 과학 실험이 하는 일이다. ⑤ 그것들은 그 밖의 다른 모든 것을 일정하게 유지하면서, 한 번에 하나의 특정 변인을 조작해 세상에서 자연적으로 발생하는 관계를 분리하려고 애쓴다.

Why? 왜 정답일까?

과학 실험의 조작과 통제를 설명하는 글이다. ④ 앞에서 현실 세계만 관찰해서는 여러 변인의 상호작용으로 인해 연구가 잘 이뤄지지 않는다고 하고, 주어진 문장에서는 '그래서 오히려' 현실에 없는 상황을 만들어야 한다고 설명하고 있다. ④ 뒤는 바로 '그 일'이 과학 실험에서 일어나는 일이라는 내용으로 주어진 문장과 자연스럽게 연결된다. 따라서 주어진 문장이 들어가기에 가장 적절한 곳은 ④이다.

- **fundamental** ⓐ 근본적인
- **underlying** ⓐ 근본적인, 기저에 있는
- **constant** ⓐ 일정한
- **manipulation** ⓝ 조작
- **correlate** ⓥ 상호 관련시키다

구문 풀이

1행 Rather, we have to create a situation [that doesn't actually
                                      선행사   주격 관·대   동사(단수)
occur in the real world].

09 좌우보다 위아래나 앞뒤를 구별하기 쉬운 이유   정답률 53% | 정답 ①

다음 글의 내용을 한 문장으로 요약하고자 한다. 빈칸 (A), (B)에 들어갈 말로 가장 적절한 것은?

	(A)	(B)		(A)	(B)
✔	spatial 공간적	······ significant 유의미한	②	spatial 공간적	······ scarce 드문
③	auditory 청각적	······ different 서로 다른	④	cultural 문화적	······ accessible 이해하기 쉬운
⑤	cultural 문화적	······ desirable 바람직한			

[본문 해석]

오른쪽과 왼쪽의 방향을 구분하라고 요구받으면 어린아이는 당황할 수 있다. 하지만 그 아이는 위아래나 앞뒤의 방향을 알아내는 데에는 전혀 어려움이 없을 것이다. 과학자들이 주장하기로 이것이 발생하는 이유는 비록 우리가 세 가지 차원을 경험하지만 두 가지만이 우리의 진화에 강력한 영향을 미쳤기 때문이다. 바로 중력으로 정의되는 수직적 차원과, 이동하는 종의 경우 감각 먹이 섭취 기제의 배치로 정의되는 앞뒤 차원이다. 이것들은 수직 대 수평, 원거리 대 근거리에 대한 우리의 지각과 (독수리처럼) 위 또는 (뱀처럼) 아래로부터의 위험 탐색에 영향을 미친다. 그러나 좌우 축은 자연에서는 그만큼 중요하지 않다. 곰은 왼쪽에서든 오른쪽에서든 똑같이 위험하지만, 거꾸로 뒤집혀 있다면 그렇지 않다. 사실, 우리가 식물이나 동물, 자동차, 도로 표지판 같이 인간이 만든 물체가 포함된 장면을 관찰할 때, 만약 그 인공적인 물체들을 관찰한다면 좌우가 뒤바뀐 것을 겨우 구별할 수 있을 뿐이다.

➡ 수직적 차원과 앞뒤 차원은 우리의 (A) 공간적 지각의 진화에 영향을 미쳤기 때문에 쉽게 인식되지만, 자연에서 (B) 유의미하지 않은 좌우 축은 우리에게 즉각 이해되지 않는다.

Why? 왜 정답일까?

수직적 차원과 앞뒤 차원은 인간의 공간 지각에 많은 영향을 미쳤지만(~ the vertical dimension ~ and, ~ the front/back dimension ~. These influence our perception. ~) 좌우 축은 그 영향이 덜했다(~ the left-right axis is not as relevant in nature.)는 내용이다. 따라서 요약문의 빈칸 (A), (B)에 들어갈 말로 가장 적절한 것은 ① '(A) spatial(공간적), (B) significant(유의미한)'이다.

- **puzzled** ⓐ 혼란스러워하는
- **dimension** ⓝ 차원
- **gravity** ⓝ 중력
- **horizontal** ⓐ 수평적인
- **artificial** ⓐ 인공적인
- **scarce** ⓐ 드문
- **accessible** ⓐ 이해하기 쉬운, 접근 가능한
- **distinguish** ⓥ 구별하다
- **vertical** ⓐ 수직적인
- **perception** ⓝ 지각, 인식
- **axis** ⓝ 축
- **significant** ⓐ 유의미한, 중요한
- **auditory** ⓐ 청각적인
- **desirable** ⓐ 바람직한

구문 풀이

3행 But that same child may have no difficulty in determining
「have no difficulty in + 동명사 : ~하는 데 어려움이 없다」
the directions of up and down or back and front.

10-12 노숙자 여자의 따뜻한 마음에 감동한 Jennifer

[본문 해석]

(A)

Jennifer는 집으로 가던 중이었다. 『그녀는 커피를 사기 위해 주유소에 들르기로 결정했다.』 ─ 「」: 12번 ①의 근거 일치 커피값을 지불한 후에 그녀는 자신의 차로 돌아왔는데, 차의 시동을 걸기 전에 그녀는 건물 앞 바깥에서 서 있는 한 여자에게 주목했다. (a) 그녀는 여자의 겉모습을 보고 노숙자임을 알 수 있었다. 그녀의 옷은 닳았고 그녀는 거죽과 뼈만 남아 있었다. 이 사람은 먹을 것을 사기 위한 충분한 돈을 가지고 있지 않았음이 틀림없어. Jennifer는 그녀에게 동정심을 느끼며 혼자 생각했다.

(D)

갑자기 개 한 마리가 건물 앞으로 걸어갔다. 개를 사랑하는 사람인 Jennifer는 그 개가 저먼 셰퍼드라는 것을 알아챘다. 『그녀는 또한 그 개가 어미라는 것을 알 수 있었는데, 왜냐하면 누구든 그 개가 강아지들에게 젖을 먹여 왔음을 알아챌 수 있었기 때문이었다.』 ─ 「」: 12번 ⑤의 근거 일치 그 개는 먹을 것을 너무나 필요로 하고 있었고 (e) 그녀는 개에게 너무나 안쓰러움을 느꼈다. 그녀는 만약 그 개가 곧 먹지 않는다면, 그 개와 강아지들이 살아남을 수 없을지도 모른다는 것을 알았다.

(C)

Jennifer는 자신의 차에 앉아서 개를 쳐다보았다. 『그녀는 사람들이 개에게 관심을 보이지 않고 지나가는 것을 알아챘다.』 ─ 「」: 12번 ③의 근거 일치 그러나 그럼에도 (c) 그녀는 어떤 것도 하지 않았다. 하지만 누군가는 했다. Jennifer가 생각하기에 자신이 먹을 것을 살 돈이 전혀 없었던 노숙자 여자가 가게에 들어갔다. 그리고 그녀가 한 일로 Jennifer는 눈물을 흘렸다. 『그녀는 가게에 들어가서 개의 먹이 한 캔을 샀고 그 개에게 먹였다.』 ─ 「」: 12번 ④의 근거 불일치 (d) 그녀는 또한 그 일을 하면서 매우 행복해 보였다.

(B)

그 장면을 본 것이 Jennifer의 삶을 완전히 바꾸었다. 『실은 그날은 어머니날이었다.』 ─ 「」: 12번 ②의 근거 일치 (b) 그녀에게 이타적인 베풂과 사랑이 무엇인지를 보여 주는 데 한 명의

노숙자 여자가 필요했다. 그날 이후로 Jennifer는 곤경에 처한 사람들, 특히 아이들을 키우기 위해 애쓰는 엄마들을 돕고 있다. 노숙자 여자가 Jennifer를 더 나은 사람으로 만들었다.

- **appearance** ⓝ 겉모습
- **entirely** [ad] 완전히
- **bring tears to one's eyes** ~의 눈물을 짓게 하다
- **in need of** ~이 필요한
- **pity** ⓝ 유감, 연민
- **selfless** ⓐ 이타적인

구문 풀이

(A) 8행 *She must have not had enough money to get something to eat.*
「must have p.p. : ~했음에 틀림없다」

(C) 4행 The homeless woman, {who (Jennifer thought) did not have
　　　　　주어(선행사)　　　주격 관·대　　（ ）: 삽입절
money to buy herself anything to eat}, went into the store.
　　　{ }: 주어 보충　　　　　　동사

(D) 2행 Being a dog lover, Jennifer noticed that the dog was a
분사구문(=As she was ~)　　　　　　　접속사(~것)
German Shepherd.

10　글의 순서 파악　　정답률 66% | 정답 ⑤

주어진 글 (A)에 이어질 내용을 순서에 맞게 배열한 것으로 가장 적절한 것은?
① (B) – (D) – (C)　　　② (C) – (B) – (D)
③ (C) – (D) – (B)　　　④ (D) – (B) – (C)
☑(D) – (C) – (B)

Why? 왜 정답일까?

커피를 사러 주유소에 들렀던 Jennifer가 남루한 차림의 노숙자 여자를 우연히 보았다는 내용의 **(A)** 뒤로, 이어서 Jennifer가 굶주린 어미 개를 보았다는 내용의 **(D)**, 모두가 외면하고 있던 개에게 노숙자 여자가 먹을 것을 사 먹이는 것을 보고 Jennifer가 감동을 받았다는 내용의 **(C)**, 이후로 Jennifer가 어려운 사람들을 돕기 시작했다는 내용의 **(B)**가 차례로 연결된다. 따라서 글의 순서로 가장 적절한 것은 ⑤ '(D) – (C) – (B)'이다.

11　지칭 추론　　정답률 66% | 정답 ④

밑줄 친 (a) ~ (e) 중에서 가리키는 대상이 나머지 넷과 다른 것은?
① (a)　　② (b)　　③ (c)　　☑(d)　　⑤ (e)

Why? 왜 정답일까?

(a), (b), (c), (e)는 Jennifer, (d)는 the homeless woman을 가리키므로, (a) ~ (e) 중에서 가리키는 대상이 다른 하나는 ④ '(d)'이다.

12　세부 내용 파악　　정답률 68% | 정답 ④

윗글에 관한 내용으로 적절하지 않은 것은?
① Jennifer는 커피를 사기 위해 주유소에 들렀다.
② 사건이 일어난 날은 어머니날이었다.
③ 지나가던 사람들은 개에게 관심을 보이지 않았다.
☑Jennifer는 가게에 들어가서 개의 먹이를 샀다.
⑤ Jennifer는 개가 어미 개라는 것을 알았다.

Why? 왜 정답일까?

(C) 'She had gone into the store, bought a can of dog food, and fed that dog.'에서 상점으로 들어가 개 먹이를 사서 나온 사람은 Jennifer가 아닌 노숙자 여자이다. 따라서 내용과 일치하지 않는 것은 ④ 'Jennifer는 가게에 들어가서 개의 먹이를 샀다.'이다.

Why? 왜 오답일까?

① (A) 'She decided to stop at a gas station to get coffee.'의 내용과 일치한다.
② (B) '~ that day was Mother's Day.'의 내용과 일치한다.
③ (C) 'She noticed that people were walking by without paying attention to the dog.'의 내용과 일치한다.
⑤ (D) 'She could also tell that the dog was a mother, ~'의 내용과 일치한다.

---

01 ②	02 ⑤	03 ②	04 ③	05 ②
06 ③	07 ⑤	08 ⑤	09 ③	10 ⑤
11 ③	12 ②			

01　신기술의 영향 골고루 평가하기　　정답률 85% | 정답 ②

다음 글에서 필자가 주장하는 바로 가장 적절한 것은?
① 기술 혁신을 저해하는 과도한 법률적 규제를 완화해야 한다.
☑기술의 도입으로 인한 잠재적인 영향들을 충분히 고려해야 한다.
③ 혁신적 농업 기술을 적용할 때는 환경적인 측면을 검토해야 한다.
④ 기술 진보가 가져온 일자리 위협에 대한 대비책을 마련해야 한다.
⑤ 기술 발전을 위해서는 혁신적 사고와 창의성이 뒷받침되어야 한다.

[본문 해석]

신기술의 도입은 지속 가능한 발전에 긍정적인 영향과 부정적인 영향을 둘 다 분명히 미친다. 기술 자원을 잘 관리하려면 그것들을 충분히 고려해야 한다. 원자력과 농업과 같은 분야의 기술 발전은 환경적 이익뿐만 아니라 환경이나 인간의 건강에 대한 위험이 어떻게 기술 발전에 수반될 수 있는지에 대한 예를 제공한다. 새로운 기술은 또한 심오한 사회적 영향을 끼친다. 산업혁명 이후 기술의 발전은 직장에서 요구되는 기술의 본질을 변화시켜 고용 패턴에 영향을 미치며 특정 유형의 일자리를 창출하고 다른 유형의 일자리는 소멸시켰다. 신기술은 모든 잠재적 영향, 즉 긍정적이고 부정적인 영향에 관해 다 평가되어야 한다.

Why? 왜 정답일까?

신기술의 잠재적 영향을 좋은 것이든 나쁜 것이든 완전히 평가해야 한다(**New technologies need to be assessed for their full potential impacts, both positive and negative.**)는 내용이므로, 필자가 주장하는 바로 가장 적절한 것은 ② '기술의 도입으로 인한 잠재적인 영향들을 충분히 고려해야 한다.'이다.

- **introduction** ⓝ 소개, 도입
- **negative** ⓐ 부정적인
- **sustainable development** (환경적으로) 지속 가능한 개발
- **take into account** ~을 고려하다
- **nuclear** ⓐ 핵의
- **benefit** ⓝ 이점
- **profound** ⓐ 심오한, 깊은
- **positive** ⓐ 긍정적인
- **impact** ⓝ 영향
- **sector** ⓝ 부문
- **agriculture** ⓝ 농업
- **risk** ⓝ 위험 ⓥ 위험을 감수하다
- **assess** ⓥ 평가하다

구문 풀이

6행 Technological developments in sectors such as nuclear energy
　　　　　　　주어　　　　　　　　　　　~와 같은
and agriculture provide examples of {how not only environmental
　　　　　　　동사(복수)　　　　　　　　「not only + A + but also + B : A뿐 아니라 B도」
benefits but also risks to the environment or human health can
accompany technological advances}.　{ }: of의 목적어(간접의문문)

02　습관에 관한 타인의 조언　　정답률 82% | 정답 ⑤

다음 글의 요지로 가장 적절한 것은?
① 한번 잘못 들인 습관은 바로잡기가 어렵다.
② 꾸준한 반복을 통해 올바른 습관을 들일 수 있다.
③ 친구나 가족의 조언은 항상 귀담아들을 필요가 있다.
④ 사소하더라도 좋은 습관을 들이면 인생이 바뀔 수 있다.
☑타인에게 유익했던 습관이 자신에게는 효과가 없을 수 있다.

[본문 해석]

친구나 가족의 조언은 모든 것 중에서 가장 좋은 뜻으로 하는 말이지만, 새로운 습관에 자신을 맞추는 최선의 방법은 아니다. 핫 요가가 여러분 친구의 삶을 바꿔 놓았을지 모르지만, 그것이 여러분에게 맞는 운동임을 의미할까? 우리 모두에게는 새벽 4시 30분에 일어나는 새로운 습관이 자신의 삶을 바꿨고 우리도 그렇게 해야 한다고 확언하는 친구들이 있다. 나는 엄청 일찍 일어나는 것이 사람들의 삶을 때로는 좋은 방식으로, 때로는 그렇지 않게 바꾼다는 것을 의심하지 않는다. 그러나 주의하라. 이 습관이 특히 잠을 더 적게 자는 것을 의

미한다면, 그것이 실제로 여러분의 삶을 더 낫게 만들지 알 수 없다. 그러니, 친구에게 효과가 있었던 것을 시도해 볼 수 있지만, 친구의 해결책이 여러분을 똑같은 방식으로 바꾸지 않는다고 해서 자책하지 말라. 이 모든 접근법은 추측과 우연을 포함한다. 그리고 그것은 여러분 삶의 변화를 위해 노력하는 좋은 방법은 아니다.

Why? 왜 정답일까?

첫 문장과 마지막 세 문장을 통해, 생활 습관에 관한 친구와 가족의 조언이 우리에게 꼭 맞지는 않을 수도 있으므로 시도해본 뒤 효과가 없다고 해서 자책하지 말라(~ don't beat yourself up if your friend's answer doesn't change you in the same way.)는 내용이 주제임을 알 수 있다. 따라서 글의 요지로 가장 적절한 것은 ⑤ '타인에게 유익했던 습관이 자신에게는 효과가 없을 수 있다.'이다.

- **well-meaning** ⓐ 선의로 하는
- **practice** ⓝ 연습
- **doubt** ⓥ 의심하다
- **especially** ⓐⓓ 특히
- **approach** ⓝ 접근법
- **strive for** ~을 위해 노력하다
- **habit** ⓝ 버릇, 습관
- **swear** ⓥ 장담하다, 맹세하다
- **cautious** ⓐ 조심하는, 신중한
- **beat oneself up** 자책하다
- **involve** ⓥ 포함하다, 수반하다

구문 풀이

5행 We all have friends [who *swear* {(that) their new habit of getting up at 4:30 a.m. changed their lives} and {that we have to do it}].
선행사 / 주격 관·대 / 동사 / 생략 / { } : 목적어

---

03 예측 불가능성을 향하는 인간의 성향
정답률 63% | 정답 ②

다음 글의 주제로 가장 적절한 것은?

① considerations in learning foreign languages
   외국어 학습에서의 고려 사항
✓② people's inclination towards unpredictability
   예측 불가능성을 향하는 인간의 성향
③ hidden devices to make a movie plot unexpected
   영화 줄거리를 예측 불가하게 만들기 위한 숨겨진 장치들
④ positive effects of routine on human brain function
   일상이 인간의 뇌 기능에 미치는 긍정적 영향
⑤ danger of predicting the future based on the present
   현재에 근거해 미래를 예측하는 것의 위험성

[본문 해석]

영화 *Groundhog Day*에서, Bill Murray가 연기한 기상캐스터는 하루를 반복해서 다시 살아야 한다. 끝이 없어 보이는 이 고리에 직면하여, 그는 결국 같은 날을 같은 방식으로 두 번 사는 것에 저항한다. 그는 프랑스어를 배우고, 위대한 피아노 연주자가 되고, 이웃들과 친구가 되고, 가난한 사람들을 도와준다. 우리는 왜 그를 응원하는가? 왜냐하면 반복되는 것이 매력적일지라도, 우리는 완벽한 예측 가능성을 원하지 않기 때문이다. 놀라움은 우리를 끌어들인다. 그것은 우리를 자동 조종 장치에서 벗어나게 한다. 그것은 우리가 경험을 계속 인식하게 한다. 실제로, 보상과 관련된 신경 전달 물질 체계는 놀라움의 수준과 관련이 있다. 규칙적이고, 예측 가능한 때에 전달되는 보상은 임의적으로 예측 불가능한 때에 전달되는 동일한 보상보다 뇌에서 훨씬 적은 활동을 산출한다. 놀라움은 만족감을 준다.

Why? 왜 정답일까?

글 중간의 질문에 답을 제시하는 문장에서 주제가 드러나는데, 우리는 완전한 예측 가능성을 원하지 않는다(Because we don't want perfect predictability, ~)는 것이다. 이어서 'Surprise engages us.'와 'Surprise gratifies.'에서 놀라움, 즉 예측 불가 요소는 우리를 끌어들이는 속성이 있으며, 우리에게 만족감을 준다고 한다. 따라서 글의 주제로 가장 적절한 것은 ② '예측 불가능성을 향하는 인간의 성향'이다.

- **confront** ⓥ 직면하다
- **rebel against** ~에 저항하다
- **cheer on** ~을 응원하다
- **appealing** ⓐ 매력적인
- **neurotransmitter** ⓝ 신경 전달 물질
- **yield** ⓥ 산출하다
- **inclination** ⓝ 성향, 경향
- **routine** ⓝ 일상
- **seemingly** ⓐⓓ 겉보기에
- **befriend** ⓥ ~와 친구가 되다
- **predictability** ⓝ 예측 가능성
- **engage** ⓥ 사로잡다
- **predictable** ⓐ 예측할 수 있는
- **gratify** ⓥ 기쁘게 하다, 충족시키다
- **plot** ⓝ 줄거리
- **function** ⓝ 기능

구문 풀이

3행 Confronted with this seemingly endless loop, he eventually
수동분사구문(= As he is confronted ~)
rebels against living through the same day the same way twice.

---

04 OECD 회원국들의 부문별 원유 수요
정답률 87% | 정답 ③

다음 도표의 내용과 일치하지 않는 것은?

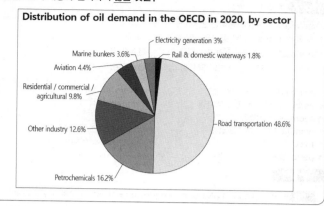

Distribution of oil demand in the OECD in 2020, by sector
- Electricity generation 3%
- Rail & domestic waterways 1.8%
- Marine bunkers 3.6%
- Aviation 4.4%
- Residential / commercial / agricultural 9.8%
- Other industry 12.6%
- Petrochemicals 16.2%
- Road transportation 48.6%

[본문 해석]

위 그래프는 2020년 OECD에서의 원유 수요에 따른 부문별 분포를 보여준다. ① 48.6%를 차지한 도로 교통 부문은 OECD 회원국들에서 가장 큰 원유 수요 부문이었다. ② 석유화학 부문의 원유 수요 비율은 도로 교통 부문의 원유 수요 비율의 3분의 1이었다. ③ 기타 산업 부문과 석유화학 부문 사이의 원유 수요 차이는 항공 부문과 전기 생성 부문 사이의 원유 수요 차이보다 작았다. ④ 주거, 상업, 그리고 농업 부문의 원유 수요는 OECD의 총 원유 수요의 9.8%를 차지했는데, 이는 전체 부문 중 네 번째로 컸다. ⑤ 해상 벙커 부문의 원유 수요 비율은 철도와 국내 수로 부문의 원유 수요 비율의 두 배였다.

Why? 왜 정답일까?

도표에 따르면 기타 산업과 석유화학 부문은 3.6%만큼, 항공 부문과 전기 생성 부문은 1.4%만큼 차이가 난다. 즉 기타 산업 부문과 석유화학 부문 사이의 차이가 더 크므로, 도표의 내용과 일치하지 않는 것은 ③이다.

- **distribution** ⓝ 분배, 분포
- **take up** ~을 차지하다
- **aviation** ⓝ 항공
- **domestic** ⓐ 국내의, 가정의
- **sector** ⓝ 부문, 분야
- **petrochemical** ⓐ 석유화학의
- **residential** ⓐ 거주의, 주거의

구문 풀이

7행 The difference (in oil demand) (between the Other industry sector and the Petrochemicals sector) was smaller than the difference (in oil demand) (between the Aviation sector and the Electricity generation sector).
주어 / 동사(단수) / 「비교급+than : ~보다 더 …한」

---

05 생산자와 소비자에게 영향을 주는 판매 유효 기간
정답률 50% | 정답 ②

다음 글의 밑줄 친 부분 중, 어법상 틀린 것은?

[본문 해석]

우리가 판매 유효 기한에 따라 움직인다는 것은 의심할 여지가 거의 없다. 일단 어떤 품목이 그 기한을 지나면 폐기물 흐름으로 들어가고, 이는 물품의 탄소 발자국을 더욱더 증가시킨다. 그러한 품목들이 이미 수백 마일을 이동해 선반에 도달했고, 일단 버려지면 그것들은 새로운 탄소 마일 여정을 시작한다는 것을 기억하라. 그러나 우리 모두는 판매 유효 기한에 대해 알아서 판단을 내린다. 가령, 제2차 세계 대전 중에 자란 사람들은 그런 경고가 조장한다고 생각하는 끔찍한 낭비를 흔히 경멸한다. 식품 제조업자는 뭔가 만들거나 재배할 때, 제품이 선반에 도달할 무렵에는 그것이 이미 매우 오랫동안, 그리고 아마 상당한 거리를 이동해 왔다는 관점을 지닌다. 그래서 제조업자는 제품이 이를테면 90일 이내에는 무리 없이 소비될 수 있고, 90일에서 이동에 필요한 여러 날을 빼면 판매 유효 기한이 나온다고 판단한다. 그러나 그것이 유독해지는지는 개인이 각자 결정할 수 있는 것이다. 상하기 쉬운 제품을 대량으로 사지 않는 것이 이치에 맞아 보이겠지만, 상하지 않는 품목들의 경우에는 비용 효율이 높아질 수도 있다.

Why? 왜 정답일까?

Remember의 목적절에서 접속사 that은 생략되고 주어 those items와 동사 have already travelled가 나왔으므로, ②는 주절을 보충 설명하는 부사구 자리이다. 즉

DAY 17

동사 reach 대신 to부정사 to reach의 형태로 써야 적합하다. 따라서 어법상 틀린 것은 ②이다.

Why? 왜 오답일까?

① 콤마 뒤로 주절을 보충하는 분사구문이다.
③ 주어가 those이므로 동사의 복수형을 적절히 썼다.
④ a view를 설명하는 동격 명사절을 이끄는 접속사이다.
⑤ '~인지 아닌지'라는 의미의 명사절 접속사 whether이다.

- sell-by date 판매 유효 기한
- carbon footprint 탄소 발자국
- scornful ⓐ 경멸하는
- manufacturer ⓝ 제조업체
- toxic ⓐ 유독한
- perishable ⓐ 상하기 쉬운
- stream ⓝ 흐름
- bring up 양육하다
- terrible ⓐ 끔찍한
- consume ⓥ 소비하다
- make sense 이치에 맞다

구문 풀이

6행 But we all make our own judgement about sell-by dates;
those (brought up during the Second World War) are often scornful
주어 / 과거분사 / →생략(목적격 관·대) / 동사(복수)
of the terrible waste [(that) (they believe) such caution encourages].
선행사 / 삽입절

★★★ 1등급 대비 고난도 2점 문제

06 유기농 방식의 한계와 가치 / 정답률 38% | 정답 ③

다음 글의 밑줄 친 부분 중, 문맥상 낱말의 쓰임이 적절하지 <u>않은</u> 것은?

[본문 해석]

천연 제품들만 투입물로 사용되는 방식으로 정의되는 '유기농' 방식은 생물권에 해를 덜 끼친다고 시사되어 왔다. 그러나 '유기농' 경작 방식의 대규모 채택은 많은 주요 작물의 산출량을 ① 감소시키고 생산비를 증가시킬 것이다. 무기질 질소 공급은 많은 비(非)콩과 작물 종의 생산성을 중상 수준으로 유지하는데 ② 필수적인데, 그것은 질소성 물질의 유기적 공급이 무기질 질소 비료보다 흔히 제한적이거나 더 비싸기 때문이다. 게다가, '친환경 거름' 작물로 거름이나 콩과 식물을 광범위하게 사용하는 것에는 ③ 이점(→ 제약)이 있다. 많은 경우, 화학 물질이 사용될 수 없으면 잡초 방제가 매우 어렵거나 많은 손이 필요할 수 있는데, 사회가 부유해짐에 따라 이 작업을 기꺼이 하려는 사람이 ④ 더 적을 것이다. 그러나 윤작의 합리적인 사용과 경작과 가축 경영의 특정한 조합과 같은 '유기농' 경작에서 사용되는 몇몇 방식들은 농촌 생태계의 지속 가능성에 중요하게 ⑤ 기여할 수 있다.

Why? 왜 정답일까?

In addition 앞에서 질소성 물질을 유기농식으로 공급하는 것은 무기 비료를 쓰는 것보다 제한적이거나 비용이 더 많이 든다고 했다. 이는 유기농법의 이점보다는 한계에 가까운 내용이고, ③이 포함된 문장은 앞에 이어 또 다른 '제약'을 언급하는 것이므로 benefits 대신 constraints를 써야 자연스럽다. 따라서 문맥상 낱말의 쓰임이 적절하지 않은 것은 ③이다. 참고로 'In many cases, ~' 문장은 유기농 방법을 쓰면 잡초 방제가 어렵다는 내용으로 ③의 '제약'을 보충 설명한다.

- be defined as ~라고 정의되다
- biosphere ⓝ 생물권
- inorganic ⓐ 무기물의
- extensive ⓐ 광범위한
- sensible ⓐ 합리적인
- sustainability ⓝ 지속 가능성
- damaging ⓐ 해로운
- adoption ⓝ 채택, 이용
- productivity ⓝ 생산성
- wealthy ⓐ 부유한
- crop rotation 윤작, (작물) 돌려심기
- rural ⓐ 농촌의, 시골의

구문 풀이

1행 It has been suggested {that "organic" methods, (defined as
가주어 / 주어 / ( ): 삽입(분사구문)
those in which only natural products can be used as inputs), would be
동사
less damaging to the biosphere}. { }: 진주어

★★ 문제 해결 꿀~팁 ★★

▶ 많이 틀린 이유는?
밑줄 앞뒤 단서를 잘 이용해야 한다. 'In many cases, weed control can be very difficult or require much hand labor ~'에서, 잡초 방제는 화학 약품 없이는 손일을 많이 요구해서 어려운 작업이라고 했다. 이를 근거로 볼 때, 최다 오답

인 ④ 자리에는 사람들이 '점점 덜' 이런 일을 하고 싶어 할 것이라는 의미의 fewer가 바르게 쓰였다.

▶ 문제 해결 방법은?
In addition이 큰 힌트이다. in addition은 앞 내용과 흐름 반전 없이 같은 맥락으로 연결되면서 추가적인 내용을 보탤 때 쓰는 연결어이다. 여기서 In addition 앞을 보면, 무기 비료가 아닌 유기농 방법을 사용해 질소를 공급하려면 비용도 더 많이 들고, 제한도 더 많다고 했다. 따라서 In addition 뒤에도 유기농 방법에 따르는 '제약'을 언급해야 자연스럽게 연결됨을 알 수 있다.

07 생각을 일상 언어로 풀어보기 / 정답률 47% | 정답 ⑤

다음 빈칸에 들어갈 말로 가장 적절한 것을 고르시오. [3점]

① finish writing quickly – 글쓰기를 빨리 끝낼
② reduce sentence errors – 문장의 오류를 줄일
③ appeal to various readers – 다양한 독자의 흥미를 끌
④ come up with creative ideas – 창의적인 생각을 떠올릴
✓⑤ clarify your ideas to yourself – 자신의 생각을 스스로에게 명료하게 할

[본문 해석]

학문적인 언어를 일상 언어로 바꿔 보는 것은 여러분이 작가로서 <u>자신의 생각을 스스로에게 명료하게 할</u> 수 있는 필수적인 도구가 될 수 있다. 왜냐하면, 글쓰기 이론가들이 흔히 지적하듯이, 글쓰기는 일반적으로 머릿속에 완전하게 만들어진 한 가지 생각으로 시작하여, 그 생각을 본래 그대로의 상태로 페이지 위에 단순히 옮겨 쓰는 과정이 아니기 때문이다. 도리어 글쓰기는 글쓰기 과정을 사용하여 우리의 생각이 무엇인지를 알아내는 발견의 수단인 경우가 더 흔하다. 이래서 글을 쓰는 사람들은 결국 페이지 위에 적히는 내용이 처음에 시작할 때 그렇게 되리라고 생각했던 것과 상당히 다르다는 것을 발견하고는 자주 놀란다. 우리가 여기서 하고자 하는 말은 일상 언어가 이런 발견 과정에 흔히 매우 중요하다는 것이다. 여러분의 생각을 더 평범하고 더 간단한 말로 바꿔 보는 것은 여러분이 처음에 그럴 것이라고 상상했던 것이 아니라 실제 여러분의 생각이 무엇인지 알아내도록 도와줄 수 있을 것이다.

Why? 왜 정답일까?

'Translating your ideas into more common, simpler terms can help you figure out what your ideas really are, as opposed to what you initially imagined they were.'에서 머릿속 생각을 쉬운 말로 풀어보면 그 생각의 내용이 실제로 어떤지 깨닫는 데 도움이 될 것이라고 하므로, 빈칸에 들어갈 말로 가장 적절한 것은 ⑤ '자신의 생각을 <u>스스로에게 명료하게 할</u>'이다.

- translate A into B A를 B로 번역하다
- theorist ⓝ 이론가
- unchanged ⓐ 변하지 않은
- end up with 결국 ~하게 되다
- as opposed to ~이 아니라
- come up with ~을 떠올리다
- essential ⓐ 필수적인
- generally ⓐd 일반적으로
- discovery ⓝ 발견
- crucial ⓐ 중요한
- initially ⓐd 처음에
- clarify ⓥ 명확하게 하다

구문 풀이

3행 For, as writing theorists often note, writing is generally not
a process [in which we start with a fully formed idea in our heads
선행사 / 「전치사+관·대」 / 선행사 / 전명구
{that we then simply transcribe in an unchanged state onto the
목적격 관·대
page}]. { }: a fully formed idea 수식

★★★ 1등급 대비 고난도 3점 문제

08 시장 사고방식에 의한 관습의 변질 / 정답률 20% | 정답 ⑤

다음 빈칸에 들어갈 말로 가장 적절한 것을 고르시오. [3점]

① people can put aside their interests for the common good
사람들이 공익을 위해 그들의 이익을 제쳐둘 수 있는지
② changing an existing agreement can cause a sense of guilt
기존의 합의를 바꾸는 것은 죄책감을 유발할 수 있는지
③ imposing a fine can compensate for broken social contracts
벌금 부과가 사회 계약 위반을 보상할 수 있는지
④ social bonds can be insufficient to change people's behavior
사회적 유대감이 사람들의 행동을 바꾸기에 불충분할 수 있는지
✓⑤ a market mindset can transform and undermine an institution
시장 사고방식이 관습을 변질시키고 훼손시킬 수 있는지

[본문 해석]

어떻게 시장 사고방식이 관습을 변질시키고 훼손시킬 수 있는지에 대한 한 생생한 예가 Dan Ariely의 저서 *Predictably Irrational*에서 주어진다. 그는 아이를 데리러 늦게 도착한 부모들에게 벌금을 부과하기로 결정했던 이스라엘의 한 어린이집에 관한 이야기를 들려주는데, 이는 벌금이 그들의 그런 행동을 막을 수 있기를 바라서였다. 실제로는 정반대의 일이 일어났다. 벌금 부과 전에 부모들은 늦게 도착한 것에 대해 죄책감을 느꼈고, 죄책감은 늦는 사람이 얼마 없도록 하는 데 효과적이었다. 일단 벌금이 도입되자 부모들의 마음속에서 전체 시나리오가 사회 계약에서 시장 계약으로 바뀌었던 것으로 보인다. 근본적으로 그들은 방과 후에 아이를 돌봐주는 데 대해 어린이집에 비용을 지불하고 있었다. 일부 부모들은 그것이 값어치를 한다고 생각했고 늦은 도착의 비율이 증가했다. 중요하게는, 어린이집이 벌금을 포기하고 이전 방식으로 돌아갔을 때, 늦은 도착은 벌금 기간 중 달했던 그 높은 수준으로 유지되었다.

Why? 왜 정답일까?

예시에 따르면 어린이집이 아이를 늦게 데리러 온 부모들에 벌금을 물리기 시작하자 부모들이 점차 어린이집에 지불하는 '비용'을 의식하게 되면서 오히려 더 많이 늦게 왔다고 한다. 이어서 마지막 문장에서는 이후 결국 어린이집이 벌금을 없앴음에도 이 늦는 비율이 줄어들지 않았다고 한다. 즉 이 예시는 사회 계약으로 인식되던 관계가 '시장 계약'으로 변화했을 때 기존의 관습이 어떻게 무너지는지를 보여준다고 정리할 수 있다. 따라서 빈칸에 들어갈 말로 가장 적절한 것은 ⑤ '시장 사고방식이 관습을 변질시키고 훼손시킬 수 있는지'이다.

- **vivid** ⓐ 생생한
- **discourage A from B** A를 B하지 못하게 하다
- **opposite** ⓐ 반대의
- **guilty** ⓐ 죄책감이 드는
- **contract** ⓝ 계약
- **worth** ⓐ ~의 가치가 있는
- **put aside** ~을 무시하다, 제쳐두다
- **insufficient** ⓐ 불충분한
- **institution** ⓝ 제도, 관습
- **irrational** ⓐ 불합리한
- **imposition** ⓝ 부과
- **introduce** ⓥ 도입하다
- **look after** ~을 맡다[돌보다/간사하다]
- **abandon** ⓥ (하다가) 포기하다
- **compensate for** ~을 보상하다
- **undermine** ⓥ 훼손하다, 약화시키다

구문 풀이

14행 Some parents thought `it worth the price`, and the rate of late arrivals increased.
(목적어 / 5형식 동사 / 목적격 보어(worth + 명사 : ~할 가치가 있는))

★★ 문제 해결 꿀~팁 ★★

▶ 많이 틀린 이유는?

글에 따르면 부모들과 어린이집은 본래 '사회 계약' 관계에 있었지만, 어린이집이 지각하는 부모들에게 벌금을 물리기 시작하며 '돈'이 매개가 되는 '시장 계약'으로 관계가 변화했다고 한다. 오답 중 ③은 벌금이 사회 계약을 복구시키는 수단이 될 수 있다는 의미이므로 답으로 적절하지 않다. 또한, 이 글이 사회적 유대 관계가 행동을 바꾼다는 내용도 아니므로 ④도 답으로 부적절하다.

▶ 문제 해결 방법은?

⑤의 an institution은 본문의 a social contract과 문맥적 의미가 같다. 즉 부모들에게 벌금을 물리기 이전에 '부모가 어린이집에 제때 와 아이를 데려가기로 하는' 암묵적 합의가 있었던 상황을 요약하는 말이다.

---

09 사회적 증거

정답률 69% | 정답 ③

다음 글에서 전체 흐름과 관계 없는 문장은?

[본문 해석]

소셜 미디어에서 생겨난 흥미로운 현상은 *사회적 증거*라는 개념이다. 사람은 다른 사람들이 이미 새로운 가치나 아이디어를 받아들였다는 것을 알 때 그렇게 하기가 더 쉽다. ① 만약 그들이 새로운 아이디어를 받아들이고 있다고 보는 그 사람이 우연히도 친구라면, 그때 사회적 증거는 사람들이 자신의 친한 친구들의 판단에 두는 신뢰에 의존할 뿐만 아니라 또래 압력을 발휘함으로써 훨씬 더 큰 힘을 갖게 된다. ② 예를 들어, 어떤 문제에 대한 영상은 그 자체로 논란이 될 수 있지만 그것이 수천 개의 좋아요를 얻으면 더 신뢰할 수 있다. ③ 친구에게 좋아함의 감정을 표현할 때 표정과 같은 비언어적 신호를 이용해 그것들을 표현할 수 있다. ④ 만약에 한 친구가 당신에게 영상을 추천한다면, 많은 경우 영상이 제시하는 아이디어의 신뢰도는 당신이 영상을 추천하는 친구에게 부여하는 신뢰도와 정비례하여 상승할 것이다. ⑤ 이것이 소셜 미디어의 힘이고 영상이나 '게시물'이 '입소문이 날' 수 있는 이유의 일부이다.

Why? 왜 정답일까?

소셜 미디어의 발전과 함께 등장한 사회적 증거 개념을 설명한 글로, ①, ②, ④, ⑤는 주제에 부합한다. 하지만 ③은 비언어적 신호를 통해 친구에게 호의를 표시하는 경우에 관해 언급하고 있어 흐름에서 벗어난다. 따라서 전체 흐름과 관계 없는 문장은 ③이다.

- **phenomenon** ⓝ 현상
- **controversial** ⓐ 논란의 여지가 있는
- **nonverbal** ⓐ 비언어적인
- **rely on** ~에 의존하다
- **credible** ⓐ 신뢰할 만한
- **in proportion to** ~에 비례하여

구문 풀이

4행 If the person [(whom) they see accepting the new idea]
(접속사 / 주어 / 생략 / 주어 지각동사 목적격 보어)
happens to be a friend, then social proof has even more power by
(동사(단수) / 전치사)
exerting peer pressure as well as relying on the trust [that people
(동명사1 / 동명사2 / 선행사 / 목적격 관계대명사)
put in the judgments of their close friends].

★★★ 1등급 대비 고난도 3점 문제

10 온라인 공간의 특성

정답률 44% | 정답 ⑤

주어진 글 다음에 이어질 글의 순서로 가장 적절한 것을 고르시오. [3점]

① (A) – (C) – (B)
② (B) – (A) – (C)
③ (B) – (C) – (A)
④ (C) – (A) – (B)
✓⑤ (C) – (B) – (A)

[본문 해석]

온라인 세상은 완전히 사람에 의해 만들어지고 설계된 인공의 세계이다. 그 근본적인 시스템의 디자인은 우리가 어떻게 보이고 우리가 다른 사람들에게서 무엇을 보는지를 형성한다.

(C) 그것은 대화의 구조와, 누가 어떤 정보에 접근할 수 있는지를 결정한다. 물리적인 도시의 건축가들은 사람들이 가게 될 길과 그들이 보게 될 광경을 결정한다. 그들은 경외감을 불러일으키는 대성당들과 명랑함을 북돋는 학교들을 지어 사람들의 기분에 영향을 미친다.

(B) 그러나, 건축가들이 그러한 건물들의 거주자들이 어떻게 자신들을 나타내는지 또는 서로를 어떻게 바라보는지를 통제하지는 않는 반면, 가상공간의 설계자들은 그렇게 하며, 그들은 사용자들의 사회적 경험에 훨씬 더 큰 영향을 준다.

(A) 그들은 우리가 서로의 얼굴을 볼지 아니면 대신 이름만으로 서로를 알지를 결정한다. 그들은 구독자의 규모와 구성을 드러낼 수 있거나, 실제로는 수백 만 명이 읽고 있을지라도 한 사람이 오직 소수에게만 친밀하게 글을 쓰고 있다는 인상을 줄 수 있다.

Why? 왜 정답일까?

주어진 글에서 온라인 세상은 기본적으로 인간이 만들고 설계한 인공적 세계임을 말한 데 이어, (C)에서는 실제 물리적인 세계를 대조의 대상으로 언급한다. (B)에서는 however로 흐름을 뒤집으며 사이버 공간에 다시 주목하고, (A)는 문두의 대명사 They를 통해 (B)의 'the designers of virtual spaces'를 가리키며 (B)와 동일한 이야기 흐름을 이어 간다. 따라서 글의 순서로 가장 적절한 것은 ⑤ '(C) – (B) – (A)'이다.

- **artificial** ⓐ 인공적인, 인위적인
- **determine** ⓥ 결정하다
- **impression** ⓝ 인상
- **influence** ⓝ 영향(력)
- **have access to** ~에 접근하다
- **cathedral** ⓝ 대성당
- **underlying** ⓐ 근본적인, 기저에 있는
- **makeup** ⓝ 구성, 구조
- **intimately** ⓐ𝖽 친밀하게
- **structure** ⓝ 구조
- **architect** ⓝ 건축가
- **playfulness** ⓝ 명랑함, 우스꽝스러움, 재미

구문 풀이

6행 They can reveal the size and makeup of an audience, / or
(동사1)
provide the impression {that one is writing intimately to only a few, /
(동사2 / 접속사 / 몇 안 되는 (사람들))
even if millions are in fact reading}.
(비록 ~일지라도 / { } : 동격 명사절)

★★ 문제 해결 꿀~팁 ★★

▶ 많이 틀린 이유는?

(A), (B)의 순서를 제대로 잡는 것이 올바른 문제 풀이의 관건이다. (C)에서 가상 공

간을 설계하는 사람과 대비되는 개념으로 물리적인 공간의 건축가를 언급하므로, 이들을 연이어 언급하는 (B)가 먼저 나오고, 이어서 다시 가상 공간 설계자들을 언급하며 주제를 정리하는 (A)가 마지막에 나오는 것이 적절하다.

▶ 문제 해결 방법은?
(A)의 They, (B)의 however 등 지시사와 접속부사에 주목하도록 한다. They 앞에는 반드시 복수의 명사가 지시 대상으로 나오게 되며, However 앞에는 반드시 뒤와 상반되는 내용이 미리 제시되어야 한다.

11-12 정보를 얻지 못할 때 세부 사항을 꾸며내 우리를 '속이는' 뇌

[본문 해석]

신경 심리학자 Michael Gazzaniga는 우리 뇌가 우리를 속이는 일관성 있는 (하지만 꼭 사실은 아닌) 이야기를 만들어 내는 데 (a) 탁월함을 보여 주는 연구를 수행했다. 이 연구에서는 분리 뇌 환자들에게 왼쪽 눈에만 보이도록 이미지를 보여 주고 왼손으로 관련 있는 카드를 선택하도록 요청했다. 왼쪽 눈의 시력과 왼쪽 몸의 움직임은 우뇌에 의해 제어된다. 『분리 뇌 환자에게 있어 우뇌와 좌뇌 사이의 연결은 끊어져 있는데, 이는 한쪽 뇌에서 다른 쪽 뇌로 정보가 건너갈 수 없다는 것을 의미한다.』 따라서 이 실험에서 우뇌가 모든 작업을 수행하고 있었고, 좌뇌는 무슨 일이 일어나고 있는지 (b) 알고(→ 모르고) 있었다.
└ : 12번의 근거
그 뒤 Gazzaniga는 참가자들에게 그들이 고른 그 카드를 왜 선택했는지 물었다. 언어는 좌뇌에서 처리되고 생성되기 때문에 좌뇌가 응답하도록 요구된다. 그러나 그 실험의 설계 때문에 오직 우뇌만이 왜 그 참가자가 그 카드를 선택했는지 알고 있었다. 결과적으로 Gazzaniga는 참가자들이 질문에 답할 것을 요청받았을 때 (c) 침묵할 것이라고 예상했다. 하지만 그 대신, 모든 피실험자는 응답을 꾸며 냈다. 좌뇌는 우뇌에 의해 행해진 행동에 대한 (d) 설명을 제공하라는 요청을 받고 있었다. 좌뇌는 답을 알지 못했다. 그러나 그것이 좌뇌가 답을 꾸며 내는 것을 막지는 못했다. 하지만 그 대답은 사실 근거를 가지고 있지 않았다. 자, 만약 이 연구가 분리 뇌 환자에만 제한됐다면, 그것은 흥미롭지만 우리와 매우 (e) 관련 있는 일은 아닐 것이다. 밝혀지기로, 분리 뇌 환자들이 이유를 꾸며 내는 유일한 사람은 아니다. 우리 모두 그렇게 한다. 『우리 모두는 자신에 대한 일관성 있는 이야기를 필요로 하고, 그 이야기에서 정보가 빠져 있을 때, 우리의 뇌는 그저 세부 사항을 채워넣는다.』 └ : 11번의 근거

- **neuropsychologist** ⓝ 신경 심리학자
- **deceive** ⓥ 속이다
- **hemisphere** ⓝ 반구, (뇌의 한쪽) 뇌
- **generate** ⓥ 만들어내다, 생성하다
- **fabricate** ⓥ 꾸며내다, 날조하다
- **behavior** ⓝ 행동
- **basis** ⓝ 근거, 기반
- **deceptive** ⓐ 속이는, 교묘한
- **activate** ⓥ 활성화하다
- **coherent** ⓐ 일관성 있는
- **split** ⓐ 분리된, 쪼개진
- **process** ⓥ 처리하다
- **respond** ⓥ 반응하다, 응수하다
- **rationalization** ⓝ 합리적 설명, 합리화
- **keep A from B** A가 B하지 못하게 하다
- **relevant** ⓐ 관련 있는, 적절한
- **insight** ⓝ 통찰력
- **dominance** ⓝ 우세

구문 풀이

15행 Gazzaniga then asked participants [why they chose the card that they did].
　　　　　　　　　　　　　　4형식 동사　　　간접목적어
[ ] : 직접목적어(간접의문문)
대동사(= chose)

11 제목 파악　　　　　　　정답률 41% | 정답 ③

윗글의 제목으로 가장 적절한 것은?

① Which Side of the Brain Do We Tend to Use More?
우리는 어느 쪽 뇌를 더 사용하는 경향이 있을까?
② How Our Brain's Hemispheres Interact in Storytelling
이야기를 할 때 우리 뇌의 두 반구가 상호작용하는 방식
✔ The Deceptive Brain: Insights from a Split-Brain Patient Study
속이는 뇌: 분리 뇌 환자 연구에서 나온 통찰
④ To Be Creative, Activate Both Hemispheres of Your Brain!
창의적이 되려면, 여러분 뇌 양쪽을 모두 활성화하라!
⑤ The Dominance of the Left Brain in Image Processing
이미지 처리에 있어 좌뇌의 우세

Why? 왜 정답일까?

분리 뇌 환자들의 연구 사례를 통해, 우리 뇌는 정보가 없을 때 세부 사항을 '그저 채워넣기' 위해 꼭 사실은 아닐 수도 있는 정보를 만들어 낸다(**We all need a coherent story**

---

about ourselves, and when information in that story is missing, our brains simply fill in the details.)는 결론을 이끌어내는 글이다. 따라서 글의 제목으로 가장 적절한 것은 ③ '속이는 뇌: 분리 뇌 환자 연구에서 나온 통찰'이다.

12 어휘 추론　　　　　　　정답률 39% | 정답 ②

밑줄 친 (a) ~ (e) 중에서 문맥상 낱말의 쓰임이 적절하지 않은 것은? [3점]

① (a)　　✔ (b)　　③ (c)　　④ (d)　　⑤ (e)

Why? 왜 정답일까?

분리 뇌 환자들의 상태를 설명하는 'In a split-brain patient, the connection between the right and left hemispheres has been broken, meaning no information can cross from one hemisphere to the other.'에서, 이런 환자들의 두 뇌 사이에는 연결이 끊어져 있어 어느 한쪽 뇌에서 받아들인 정보가 다른 쪽 뇌에 전달되지 않는다고 설명한다. 이를 근거로 볼 때, 우뇌가 하는 일을 좌뇌는 '모른다'는 의미가 되도록 (b)의 aware를 unaware로 고쳐야 한다. 따라서 문맥상 낱말의 쓰임이 적절하지 않은 것은 ② '(b)'이다.

DAY 18 20분 미니 모의고사

01 ⑤	02 ⑤	03 ⑤	04 ④	05 ②
06 ⑤	07 ①	08 ①	09 ①	10 ④
11 ④	12 ⑤			

01 책 읽어 주기 자원봉사 참여 요청
정답률 93% | 정답 ⑤

다음 글의 목적으로 가장 적절한 것은?

① 도서관의 운영 시간 연장을 제안하려고
② 봉사 활동 시간이 변경된 것을 안내하려고
③ 독서 토론 수업에 참여할 아동을 모집하려고
④ 봉사 활동에 참여하지 못하게 된 것을 사과하려고
☑ 책 읽어 주기 자원봉사에 참여해 줄 것을 요청하려고

[본문 해석]

Stevens씨께,

제 이름은 Peter Watson이고, 저는 Springton 도서관의 관리자입니다. 우리 도서관의 스토리텔링 프로그램에 많은 분들이 참석해주셔서 프로그램을 주 6일로 확대하는 것을 계획 중입니다. 이것은 아이들에게 책을 읽어 줄 자원봉사자를 더 많이 모집해야 한다는 것을 의미합니다. 사람들은 우리 자원봉사자 중 한 명이 올 수 없었을 때 당신이 대신 채워준 일주일에 대해서 아직도 이야기합니다. 당신은 정말 그 이야기들에 생동감을 불어넣었죠! 그래서, 매주 금요일 오전 10시부터 11시까지 한 시간 동안 미취학 아동들에게 책을 읽어 줄 의향이 있으십니까? 당신이 이 기회를 받아들여서 더 많은 아이들이 당신의 목소리를 듣게 되길 바랍니다. 당신의 긍정적인 답변을 기다리겠습니다.

Peter Watson 드림

Why? 왜 정답일까?

미취학 아동들에게 책을 읽어주는 자원봉사에 참여할 의향이 있는지(So, would you be willing to read to the preschoolers for an hour, from 10 to 11 a.m. every Friday?) 묻는 내용의 글이므로, 글의 목적으로 가장 적절한 것은 ⑤ '책 읽어 주기 자원봉사에 참여해 줄 것을 요청하려고'이다.

- **well-attended** ⓐ 많은 사람들이 참석하는
- **recruit** ⓥ 모집하다
- **bring to life** (이야기를) 생동감 있게 하다
- **opportunity** ⓝ 기회
- **expand** ⓥ 확대하다
- **fill in** ~을 대신하다, 채워넣다
- **preschooler** ⓝ 미취학 아동
- **positive** ⓐ 긍정적인

구문 풀이

3행 Our storytelling program has been so well-attended that we
「so ~ that … : 너무 ~해서 …하다」
are planning to expand the program to 6 days each week.

02 인간의 도덕적 발달 과정에 대한 이해
정답률 63% | 정답 ⑤

다음 글의 주제로 가장 적절한 것은?

① evolution of human morality from a cultural perspective
문화적 관점으로부터의 인간 도덕성의 진화
② difficulties in studying the evolutionary process of genes
유전자의 진화 과정 연구에서의 어려움
③ increasing necessity of educating children as moral agents
도덕적 행위자로서 아이를 교육해야 할 필요성의 증가
④ nature versus nurture controversies in developmental biology
발달 생물학에서의 천성 대 양육 논쟁
☑ complicated gene-environment interplay in moral development
도덕적 발달에 있어서 유전-환경의 복잡한 상호 작용

[본문 해석]

인간은 유능한 도덕적 행위자로서 세상에 들어오지 않는다. 또한 모든 이가 그 상태로 세상을 떠나지도 않는다. 하지만 그 사이의 어딘가에서, 대부분의 사람들은 그들에게 도덕적 행위자 공동체의 구성원 자격을 주는 얼마간의 예의를 습득한다. 유전자, 발달, 그리고 학습은 모두 예의 바른 인간이 되는 과정에 기여한다. 하지만 천성과 양육 사이의 상호 작용은 매우 복잡하며, 발달 생물학자들은 그저 그것이 얼마나 복잡한지를 간신히 이해하기 시작하고 있을 뿐이다. 세포, 유기체, 사회 집단, 그리고 문화에 의해 제공되는 맥락이 없으면,

DNA는 비활성이다. 사람들은 도덕적이도록 '유전적으로 프로그램이 짜여 있다'고 말하는 누구든 유전자가 작동하는 방식에 대한 지나치게 단순화된 견해를 가지고 있다. 유전자와 환경은 아이들의 도덕적 발달 과정, 또는 다른 어떤 발달 과정이, 천성 대 양육이라는 견지에서 논의될 수 있다고 생각하는 것을 무의미하게 만드는 방식으로 상호 작용한다. 발달 생물학자들은 이제 그것이 진정 둘 다, 즉 양육을 통한 천성이라는 것을 안다. 인간 종의 도덕적 진화와 발달에 대한 완전한 과학적 설명은 까마득히 멀다.

Why? 왜 정답일까?

'The interaction between nature and nurture is, however, highly complex. ~'에서 도덕적 발달 과정에 있어 천성과 양육의 상호 작용은 대단히 복잡하다고 언급한 데 이어, 마지막 세 문장에서 인간의 도덕적 발달 과정은 천성과 양육을 대립적으로 보는 시각으로 이해할 수 없고 오히려 양육을 통한 천성의 발현으로 이해할 수 있다고 설명하고 있다. 따라서 글의 주제로 가장 적절한 것은 ⑤ '도덕적 발달에 있어서 유전-환경의 복잡한 상호 작용'이다.

- **competent** ⓐ 유능한
- **contribute** ⓥ 한 원인이 되다
- **grasp** ⓥ 움켜잡다
- **interplay** ⓝ 상호 작용
- **qualify** ⓥ 자격을 주다
- **decent** ⓐ 예의 바른
- **nonsensical** ⓐ 무의미한

구문 풀이

14행 Genes and environment interact in ways [that make it
주어 / 동사 / 5형식 동사 / 가목적어
nonsensical to think {that the process of moral development in
목적격 보어 / 진목적어 / 접속사1 / 주어1
children, or any other developmental process, can be discussed
주어2 / 조동사 수동태
in terms of nature versus nurture}].
~의 관점에서

03 언어의 변화
정답률 53% | 정답 ⑤

다음 글의 제목으로 가장 적절한 것은?

① Original Meanings of Words Fade with Time
단어의 원래 의미는 시간이 가며 퇴색된다
② Dictionary: A Gradual Continuation of the Past
사전: 과거의 점진적 지속
③ Literature: The Driving Force Behind New Words
문학: 새로운 단어 이면의 원동력
④ How Can We Bridge the Ever-Widening Language Gap?
계속해서 넓어지는 언어 격차를 어떻게 줄일 수 있을까?
☑ Language Evolution Makes Even Shakespeare Semi-literate!
언어 변화는 심지어 셰익스피어도 글을 반만 이해하게 한다!

[본문 해석]

새로운 상황, 생각, 감정에 반응하여 새로운 단어들과 표현들이 계속해서 생겨난다. Oxford 영어 사전은 그 언어에 등장한 새로운 단어들과 표현들의 추가분을 출판한다. 어떤 사람들은 이런 일을 한탄하고 그것을 올바른 영어에서 벗어났다고 본다. 그러나 영어의 철자와 구두법을 공식화하려는 시도는 18세기에 이르러서야 이루어졌다. 21세기에 우리가 사용하는 언어는 셰익스피어에게는 사실상 이해되기 어려울 것이며, 우리에게도 그의 말하기 방식이 그럴 것이다. Alvin Toffler는 셰익스피어가 현재 영어에서 일반적으로 사용되는 450,000개의 단어 중 약 250,000개만을 이해할 것이라고 추정했다. 다시 말해서, 가령 만약 셰익스피어가 오늘날 런던에 나타난다면, 그는 평균적으로 우리의 어휘에 있는 9개의 단어당 5개만 이해할 것이다.

Why? 왜 정답일까?

언어는 계속해서 변하고, 그에 따라 심지어 언어 사용의 대가라고 여겨지는 셰익스피어조차 오늘날의 언어를 절반 정도밖에 이해하지 못할 것이라는(The language we speak in the twenty-first century would be virtually unintelligible to Shakespeare, and so would his way of speaking to us. / ~ if Shakespeare were to materialize in London today he would understand, on average, only five out of every nine words in our vocabulary.) 비유가 제시되고 있다. 따라서 글의 제목으로 가장 적절한 것은 이 비유를 그대로 차용한 ⑤ '언어 변화는 심지어 셰익스피어도 글을 반만 이해하게 한다!'이다.

- **continually** ⓐ 지속적으로
- **publish** ⓥ 출판하다
- **deplore** ⓥ 한탄하다
- **drift** ⓝ 표류, 부유
- **formalize** ⓥ 공식화하다
- **virtually** ⓐ 거의, 사실상
- **in response to** ~에 반응하여
- **supplement** ⓝ 보충
- **see A as B** A를 B라고 여기다
- **attempt** ⓝ 시도, 노력
- **punctuation** ⓝ 구두법
- **unintelligible to** ~가 이해할 수 없는

DAY 18

- **estimate** ⓥ 추정하다
- **so to speak** 가령, 말하자면
- **vocabulary** ⓝ 어휘
- **literature** ⓝ 문학
- **bridge** ⓥ 격차를 줄이다, 다리를 놓다
- **in use** 사용 중인
- **materialize** ⓥ (갑자기) 나타나다
- **fade** ⓥ 바래다, 옅어지다
- **driving force** 원동력
- **ever-widening** ⓐ 점점 커지는

구문 풀이

6행 But *it was* only in the eighteenth century *that* any attempt
「*it was* ~ *that* …: …한 것은 바로 ~였다(강조 구문)」
was made to formalize spelling and punctuation of English at all.
부사적 용법(목적)

---

04 John Bowlby의 생애   정답률 91% | 정답 ④

John Bowlby에 관한 다음 글의 내용과 일치하지 <u>않는</u> 것은?

① 아버지는 왕의 의료진의 일원이었다.
② 어머니와 많은 시간을 보내지 못했다.
③ 기숙 학교로 보내진 것이 성장에 있어 충격적인 일이었다.
✓ Trinity 대학에 심리학을 공부하기 위해 입학했다.
⑤ 세계 보건 기구에서 정신 건강 자문 위원으로 일했다.

[본문 해석]
영국 발달 심리학자이자 정신과 의사인 John Bowlby는 1907년에 상위 중산 계급 가정에서 태어났다. 「왕의 의료진의 일원이었던 그의 아버지는 자주 집을 비웠다.」 「Bowlby는 주로 유모에게 보살핌을 받았고 어머니와 많은 시간을 보내지 못했는데, 이는 당시 그의 계급에서 관례적이었다.」 「Bowlby는 7살에 기숙 학교로 보내졌다. 그는 나중에 이것을 자신의 성장에 있어 충격적인 일이었다고 회상했다.」 그러나 이 경험은 Bowlby에게 큰 영향을 미쳤던 것으로 판명되었고 그의 연구는 아동의 발달에 중점을 두었다. 「아버지의 제안에 따라, Bowlby는 Cambridge의 Trinity 대학에 의학을 공부하기 위해 입학했으나 3년째 되던 해에 관심 분야를 심리학으로 바꿨다.」 「1950년대에 Bowlby는 잠시 세계 보건 기구에서 정신 건강 자문 위원으로 활동했다.」 그의 애착 이론은 어린 시절의 사회적 발달을 이해하는 데 있어 주요한 접근법으로 평가되어 오고 있다.

Why? 왜 정답일까?
'Following his father's suggestion, Bowlby enrolled at Trinity College, Cambridge to study medicine, but by his third year, he changed his focus to psychology.'에 따르면 Bowlby는 의학을 공부하러 Trinity 대학에 입학했지만 3년째 되던 해에 심리학으로 관심을 틀었다고 한다. 따라서 내용과 일치하지 않는 것은 ④ 'Trinity 대학에 심리학을 공부하기 위해 입학했다.'이다.

Why? 왜 오답일까?
① 'His father, who was a member of the King's medical staff, ~'의 내용과 일치한다.
② 'Bowlby ~ did not spend much time with his mother, ~'의 내용과 일치한다.
③ 'Bowlby was sent to a boarding school at the age of seven. He later recalled this as being traumatic to his development.'의 내용과 일치한다.
⑤ '~ Bowlby briefly worked as a mental health consultant for the World Health Organization.'의 내용과 일치한다.

- **psychiatrist** ⓝ 정신과 의사
- **nanny** ⓝ 유모
- **boarding school** 기숙 학교
- **enroll at** ~에 등록하다
- **dominant** ⓐ 지배적인
- **primarily** ⓐⓓ 주로
- **customary** ⓐ 관습적인
- **have an impact on** ~에 영향을 미치다
- **attachment** ⓝ (유아와 부모의) 애착

★★★ 1등급 대비 고난도 3점 문제

05 인간의 도구 사용   정답률 32% | 정답 ②

다음 글의 밑줄 친 부분 중, 어법상 틀린 것은? [3점]

[본문 해석]
인간은 점점 확장되는 도구 세트를 이용하기 시작했다는 점에서 유일무이할 뿐만 아니라 외부 에너지원을 이용하는 복잡한 형태를 만들어 낸 지구상 유일한 종이다. 이것은 근본적인 새로운 발전이었는데 거대한 역사상 전례가 없었

다. 이러한 능력은 인간이 불을 통제하기 시작했던 150만 년 전에서 50만 년 전 사이에 처음으로 생겨났을지도 모른다. 기류 및 수류에 저장된 에너지의 일부가 적어도 5만 년 전부터 운항에, 그리고 훨씬 후에는 최초의 기계에 동력을 제공하는 데에도 사용되었다. 1만 년 전 즈음에, 인간은 식물을 경작하고 동물을 길들여서 이런 중요한 물질 및 에너지 흐름을 통제하는 법을 배웠다. 곧 인간은 동물의 근력을 이용하는 법도 배우게 되었다. 약 250년 전에는, 화석 연료가 많은 다양한 종류의 기계에 동력을 공급하는 데 대규모로 사용되기 시작하였고, 그렇게 함으로써 오늘날 우리에게 익숙한 사실상 무한한 양의 인공적인 복잡성을 만들어내었다.

Why? 왜 정답일까?
②의 which는 관계대명사이므로 뒤에 'there were no precedents in big history'와 같이 완전한 절을 수반할 수 없다. 따라서 '~에 대한 선례'라는 의미를 나타낼 때 쓰는 전치사 for를 이용하여 which를 '전치사+관계대명사' 형태의 for which로 고쳐야 한다. 어법상 틀린 것은 ②이다.

Why? 왜 오답일까?
① Not only가 문두에 나온 도치구문에서 동사 are의 보어가 필요하므로 형용사 unique의 쓰임은 어법상 맞다.
③ '부분+of+전체'가 주어일 경우 동사의 수는 전체 명사에 일치시키는데, 여기서는 전체에 해당하는 the energy가 불가산 명사이므로 동사를 단수형인 was로 쓴 것은 어법상 맞다.
④ learned의 목적어인 to cultivate와 병렬구조를 이루는 to tame에서 to는 생략 가능하므로 tame을 쓴 것은 어법상 맞다.
⑤ 앞에 완전한 주절이 나오고 주절의 의미를 보충하는 분사구문이 이어지는 맥락에서 뒤에 목적어인 'the ~ artificial complexity'가 있으므로 현재분사 creating을 쓴 것은 어법상 맞다.

- **ever-widening** 점점 확장되는
- **complexity** ⓝ 복잡성
- **fundamental** ⓐ 근본적인
- **emerge** ⓥ 생겨나다, 출현하다
- **power** ⓥ 동력을 제공하다
- **tame** ⓥ 길들이다
- **artificial** ⓐ 인공적인
- **construct** ⓥ 만들다, 구성하다
- **external** ⓐ 외부의
- **precedent** ⓝ 선례
- **navigation** ⓝ 운항, 항해
- **cultivate** ⓥ 경작하다
- **unlimited** ⓐ 무제한의

구문 풀이

1행 Not only are humans unique in the sense that they began to
「부정어구+동사+주어: 도치 구문」   ~라는 점에서
use an ever-widening tool set, (but) we are also the only species on
선행사
this planet [that has constructed forms of complexity {that use external
주격 관계대명사   선행사   관계절 동사(복수)
energy sources}].

★★ 문제 해결 꿀~팁 ★★

▶ 많이 틀린 이유는?
최다 오답인 ③은 수 일치라는 빈출 개념을 묻고 있다. 앞에 나오는 'air and water flows'를 주어로 혼동하면 was를 were로 고쳐야 한다고 생각할 수 있지만 이는 주어를 꾸미는 과거분사구의 일부이다. 진짜 주어가 'some of the energy'이고 '부분+of+전체' 구조에서는 전체 명사에 수를 일치시킨다는 개념을 알고 있다면 was가 적절함을 파악할 수 있다.

▶ 문제 해결 방법은?
②에서처럼 관계대명사에 밑줄이 있을 때에는 뒤에 나오는 절이 불완전한지 여부를 가장 먼저 검토해야 한다. 여기서는 'there were no precedents ~'가 완전한 1형식 구조이므로 which가 관계부사 또는 '전치사+관계대명사' 형태로 바뀌어야 함을 알 수 있다.

---

06 화가들의 제한적인 색상 선택   정답률 50% | 정답 ⑤

다음 글의 밑줄 친 부분 중, 문맥상 낱말의 쓰임이 적절하지 <u>않은</u> 것은? [3점]

[본문 해석]
이론상으로 화가들은 무한한 범위의 색을 마음대로 사용할 수 있는데, 합성 화학에서 유채색의 ① 폭발적 증가를 이룬 현대에 특히 그렇다. 그러나 화가들이 모든 색을 동시에 사용하는 것은 아닌데, 사실 많은 화가들은 눈에 띄게 ② 제한적으로 색을 선택하여 사용해 왔다. Mondrian은 자신의 검정색 선이 그려진 격자무늬를 채우기 위해 대개 빨강, 노랑, 그리고 파랑의 3원색으로 스스로를

제한했고, Kasimir Malevich는 비슷하게 스스로 부과한 제한에 따라 작업했다. Yves Klein에게는 한 가지 색이면 ③ 충분했고, Franz Klein의 예술(작품)은 보통 흰색 바탕 위에 검정색이었다. 여기에는 ④ 새로울 것이 없었는데, 그리스와 로마 사람들은 단지 빨간색, 노란색, 검정색 그리고 흰색만을 사용하는 경향이 있었다. 왜 그랬을까? 일반화할 수는 없지만, 고대와 현대에서 모두 (범위가) ⑤ 확대된(→ 제한된) 팔레트가[색이] 명확성과 이해 가능성에 도움을 주고 중요한 구성 요소인 모양과 형태에 주의를 집중할 수 있도록 도움을 주었던 것 같다.

Why? 왜 정답일까?

다양한 색을 이용할 수 있게 된 현대에 이르러서도 많은 화가들은 고대 시절 화가들이 그랬듯이 제한된 색을 쓰곤 하는데(And yet painters don't use all the colours at once, and indeed many have used a remarkably restrictive selection.) 이것이 모양과 형태에 보다 주의를 기울이게 도와줄 것임을 설명한 글이다. 즉 색이 '제한적으로' 선택되는 이유를 언급하는 것이 글의 핵심이므로, ⑤의 expanded를 limited 로 고쳐야 한다. 따라서 낱말의 쓰임이 적절하지 않은 것은 ⑤이다.

- in principle 원칙적으로, 이론상으로
- at one's disposal ~의 마음대로 이용할 수 있는
- explosion ⓝ 폭발적 증가, 폭발
- remarkably ⓐⓓ 눈에 띄게, 두드러지게
- primary ⓝ 원색 ⓐ 주요한, 기본적인
- typically ⓐⓓ 보통, 대개, 전형적으로
- antiquity ⓝ 고대, 아주 오래됨
- expand ⓥ 확장시키다
- clarity ⓝ 명확성
- component ⓝ 구성 요소
- infinite ⓐ 무한한
- synthetic ⓐ 합성한
- restrictive ⓐ 제한적인
- self-imposed 스스로 부과한
- generalize ⓥ 일반화하다
- modernity ⓝ 현대, 현대적임
- aid ⓥ (일이 수월해지도록) 돕다
- comprehensibility ⓝ 이해 가능성

구문 풀이

13행 It's impossible to generalize, but both in antiquity and modernity it seems likely {that the limited palette aided clarity and comprehensibility, and helped to focus attention on the components [that mattered]: shape and form}.
= the components

★★★ 1등급 대비 고난도 3점 문제

07 생존 편향의 개념과 사례   정답률 40% | 정답 ①

다음 빈칸에 들어갈 말로 가장 적절한 것을 고르시오. [3점]

✓ ① the areas that were not hit – (총알을) 맞지 않은 부분
② high technologies to make airplanes – 비행기를 만드는 고도의 기술
③ military plans for bombing the targets – 목표물을 폭격하기 위한 군사 계획
④ the data that analyzed broken parts – 부서진 부품을 분석한 데이터
⑤ the commanders of the army – 군대의 지휘관들

[본문 해석]

'생존 편향'은 흔한 논리적 오류이다. 우리는 생존자들의 성공담을 듣는 경향이 있는데, 왜냐하면 이야기를 해 줄 다른 이들은 주변에 없기 때문이다. 역사상 극적인 예는 2차 세계대전 동안 폭격기를 더 안전하게 만들 방법을 정하기 위해 미국 공군에 의해 고용된 통계학자 Abraham Wald의 경우이다. 살아 돌아온 비행기는 날개, 본체, 그리고 꼬리 부분을 따라 총알 자국이 있는 경향이 있었고, 그 부분들이 가장 총알을 자주 맞는 것처럼 보였기 때문에 지휘관들은 이 부분들을 강화하기를 원했다. 그러나 Wald는 중요한 것은 이 총알 구멍들이 비행기를 파괴한 것이 아니며, 보호가 더 필요한 쪽은 (총알을) 맞지 않은 부분이라는 것을 알게 되었다. 그 부분들은 만약 비행기가 총알을 맞았다면 다시 그것(비행기)을 볼 수 없게 했을 부분들이었다. 그 논리에 기초한 그의 계산은 오늘날에도 여전히 사용되며, 그것은 많은 조종사들의 목숨을 구했다.

Why? 왜 정답일까?

2차 세계대전에서 폭격기를 만들 당시, 미국 공군에서는 총알을 자주 맞는 부분을 강화하기를 원했지만, 통계학자인 Abraham Wald는 혹시라도 총알을 맞았다면 큰 타격을 입었을(~ if a plane was struck by a bullet, it would never be seen again.) '다른' 부분들에 초점을 두기를 주장했고, 이것이 오늘날까지도 많은 조종사들의 목숨을 살리는 결과로 이어졌다는 내용을 다룬 글이다. 따라서 빈칸에 들어갈 말로 가장 적절한 것은 ① '(총알을) 맞지 않은 부분'이다.

- survivorship ⓝ 생존
- logical ⓐ 논리적인
- be prone to ~하기 쉽다
- determine ⓥ 결정하다
- reinforce ⓥ 강화하다, 보강하다
- calculation ⓝ 계산
- military ⓐ 군사적인, 무력의
- bias ⓝ 편견, 편향
- fallacy ⓝ 오류
- statistician ⓝ 통계학자
- commander ⓝ 지휘관, 사령관
- protection ⓝ 보호
- in use 사용 중인, 쓰이고 있는

구문 풀이

3행 A dramatic example from history is the case of statistician Abraham Wald [who, (during World War Ⅱ), was hired by the U.S. Air Force / to determine how to make their bomber planes safer].
선행사 / 주격 관계대명사 / 동사 / ~하기 위해 / 『의문사 + to부정사(~하는 방법)』

★★ 문제 해결 꿀~팁 ★★

▶ 많이 틀린 이유는?
앞에서 제시된 '생존 편향'이라는 개념과 예시의 연결이 쉽지 않아 읽기 어려운 지문이다. 이런 경우에는 예시 자체에 집중하여 답을 찾는다. 빈칸 바로 뒤의 문장에서, '총알을 맞았다면 비행기를 볼 수 없게 되었을 만큼 타격을 입었을 다른 부분'이란 것은 결국 '여태까지는 총알을 비껴갔(기에 비행기가 살아남을 수 있었)던' 부분을 뜻한다. 최다 오답인 ④는 '(이미 총알을 맞아) 부서진 부분', 즉 Wald가 아닌 사령관들이 주목했던 부분으로서 핵심과는 반대되는 내용이다.

▶ 문제 해결 방법은?
근거 문장에 내포된 가정법에 주의를 기울여 답을 찾도록 한다.

★★★ 1등급 대비 고난도 3점 문제

08 인간의 비언어적 의사소통   정답률 31% | 정답 ①

글의 흐름으로 보아, 주어진 문장이 들어가기에 가장 적절한 곳을 고르시오. [3점]

[본문 해석]

수십만 년 동안 우리의 수렵－채집인 조상들은 비언어적 신호들을 통해서 서로 끊임없이 의사소통해야만 생존할 수 있었다. 언어의 발명 이전에 오랜 시간에 걸쳐 발달되어, 그렇게 인간의 얼굴은 매우 표현적이고 몸짓은 매우 정교해지게 되었다. ① 우리는 우리의 감정을 전달하고자 하는 끊임없는 욕망을 지니고 있지만 동시에 적절한 사회적 기능을 위해 그것들을 감추고자 하는 욕구를 지니고 있다. 이 반대 세력들이 우리 내면에서 다투면서, 우리는 우리가 전달하는 것을 완전히 통제할 수 없다. ② 우리의 진짜 감정은 몸짓, 목소리의 톤, 얼굴 표정, 그리고 자세의 형태로 끊임없이 새어 나온다. ③ 그러나 우리는 사람들의 비언어적 신호에 주의를 기울이도록 훈련받지 않는다. ④ 순전한 습관으로 우리는 사람들이 하는 말에 집착하며 동시에 또한 우리가 다음번에 말할 것을 생각한다. ⑤ 이것이 의미하는 것은 우리 모두가 소유한 잠재적인 사회적 기술들 중 오직 작은 부분만을 우리가 사용하고 있다는 것이다.

Why? 왜 정답일까?

인간의 비언어적 의사소통에 관해 설명한 글로, ① 뒤의 지시어에 주목한다. ① 뒤의 문장에서 these counterforces를 언급하는데 앞에는 '상충되는 힘'으로 나타낼 만한 것이 없다. 이때 주어진 문장은 인간이 감정을 나타내고 싶어 하지만 동시에 감정을 감추고 싶어 한다는 내용이므로, 이 'desire to communicate ~'와 'need to conceal ~'을 ① 뒤의 문장에서 these counterforces로 가리키고 있음을 알 수 있다. 따라서 주어진 문장이 들어가기에 가장 적절한 곳은 ①이다.

- continual ⓐ 끊임없는
- communicate ⓥ 전달하다
- functioning ⓝ 기능
- expressive ⓐ (감정을) 나타내는
- battle ⓥ 다투다
- leak out 새어 나오다
- posture ⓝ 자세
- potential ⓐ 잠재적인
- desire ⓝ 욕망, 욕구
- proper ⓐ 적절한
- nonverbal ⓐ 비언어적인
- elaborate ⓐ 정교한
- continually ⓐⓓ 끊임없이
- in the form of ~의 형태로
- fixate on ~에 집착하다, ~을 고수하다
- possess ⓥ 소유하다

구문 풀이

7행 Developed over so much time, before the invention of language, that is how the human face became so expressive, and gestures (became) so elaborate.
수동분사구문 / 그렇게 ~하게 되다 / 주어1 / 동사1 / 주어2 / 동사2(중복되어 생략)

★★ 문제 해결 꿀~팁 ★★

▶ 많이 틀린 이유는?

'With these counterforces ~' 이후로 네 문장에 걸쳐 우리가 우리의 의사소통 내용을 완벽히 통제하지 못하기에 비언어적 단서의 형태로 자꾸 진정한 감정을 내비치게 되지만, 우리는 비언어적 단서에 주목하도록 훈련받지 않아서 주로 언어적 단서에 집착한다는 내용이 논리적 공백 없이 기술되어 있다. 따라서 ②, ③, ④는 모두 오답이다.

▶ 문제 해결 방법은?

① 뒤의 these counterforces가 가리키는 바에 주목한다. 만일 주어진 문장이 ①에 들어가지 않으면, these counterforces로 받을 만한 명사는 human face와 gestures 뿐인데, '얼굴과 몸짓'을 '상충하는 힘'으로 일반화하기에는 근거가 부족하다.

---

09 도움을 주려는 동기에 대한 연구
정답률 45% | 정답 ①

다음 글의 내용을 한 문장으로 요약하고자 한다. 빈칸 (A), (B)에 들어갈 말로 가장 적절한 것은?

	(A)		(B)
✓①	sustained 지속될	⋯⋯	decline 감소
②	sustained 지속될	⋯⋯	maximization 극대화
③	indirect 간접적일	⋯⋯	variation 변화
④	discouraged 좌절될	⋯⋯	reduction 감소
⑤	discouraged 좌절될	⋯⋯	increase 증가

[본문 해석]

2006년에 연구자들은 미국을 향한 9.11 테러 공격 이후에 도움을 주려는 동기에 대한 연구를 수행했다. 이 연구에서, 그들은 타인에게 초점을 맞춘 동기(다른 사람의 곤란을 줄이기 위해 베푸는 것) 때문에 돈, 혈액, 물품, 또는 다른 형태의 도움을 주었던 사람들이 원래 동기가 자신의 고통을 줄이는 것이었던 사람들에 비해 일 년 후에도 여전히 지원을 제공할 가능성이 거의 네 배 더 높다는 것을 발견했다. 이 결과는 감정적 자극의 차이에서 비롯된 것 같다. 9.11의 사건들은 미국 전역의 사람들에게 감정적으로 영향을 미쳤다. 자기 고통을 줄이기 위해 베푼 사람들은 초기의 베품을 통해 그 감정적 고통을 해소하면서 감정적 자극을 줄였다. 하지만, 다른 사람들의 고통을 줄이기 위해 베푼 사람들은 공격 이후 오랫동안 계속 고생하는 피해자들에게 계속해서 공감했다.

➡ 한 연구는 베푸는 행위가 타인에 초점을 맞춘 동기보다는 자기 중심적 동기에 의해 유도될 때 (A) 지속될 가능성이 더 낮았는데, 아마도 감정적 자극의 (B) 감소 때문이라는 것을 발견했다.

Why? 왜 정답일까?

베푸는 행위가 자기 중심적 동기에 바탕을 둘 때에는 도움의 행위가 덜 지속되는 경향이 있었는데, 아마도 감정적 자극이 줄어들면서 그런 것 같다(Those who gave to reduce their own distress reduced their emotional arousal with their initial gift, discharging that emotional distress.)는 연구 내용을 소개하는 글이다. 따라서 요약문의 빈칸 (A), (B)에 들어갈 말로 가장 적절한 것은 ① '(A) sustained (지속될), (B) decline(감소)'이다.

- **motivation** ⓝ 동기
- **against** [prep] ~에 반대하여
- **discomfort** ⓝ 불편
- **stem from** ~에서 기인하다
- **arousal** ⓝ 자극
- **throughout** [prep] ~을 통틀어
- **discharge** ⓥ 해소하다, 내보내다
- **sustain** ⓥ 지속되다
- **discourage** ⓥ 낙담시키다, 좌절시키다
- **terrorist attack** 테러 사건
- **assistance** ⓝ 도움, 원조
- **distress** ⓝ (정신적) 고통
- **emotional** ⓐ 감정적인
- **affect** ⓥ 영향을 미치다
- **initial** ⓐ 처음의
- **struggle** ⓥ 고생하다
- **indirect** ⓐ 간접적인

구문 풀이

19행 A study found that the act of giving was less likely to be
　　　　　　　　　접속사(~것)　　　　　　　　~할 가능성이 적다
sustained when (it was) driven by self-centered motives rather than
　　　　　　　　(생략)
by other-focused motives, possibly because of the decline in emotional
　　　　　　　　　　　　　　　　　　전치사(~ 때문에)
arousal.

10-12 발레에 재능을 갖고 태어난 Melanie

[본문 해석]

(A)

옛날에 Melanie라는 소녀가 살았다. 그녀는 발레 댄서가 되고 싶었다. 「어느 날, Melanie의 엄마는 Melanie가 발레리나의 흠 없는 스텝과 열정을 갖고 춤추는 것을 보았다.」 "놀랍지 않아요? Melanie는 정규 교육을 받지 않고도 춤을 너무 잘 춰요!"라고 그녀의 엄마가 말했다. "아이가 기술을 연마하는 것을 돕기 위해 (a) 아이가 전문적인 수업을 받도록 해야겠어요.

(D)

「다음날, Melanie는 지역 댄스 학원에 엄마와 동행했다.」 댄스 교사인 Mr. Edler를 만나자마자 엄마는 Melanie를 학원에 받아달라고 요청했다. 교사는 Melanie에게 오디션을 보라고 했다. (e) 그녀는 기뻐하며 그에게 자신이 가장 좋아하는 댄스 스텝을 보여 주었다. 「하지만, 그는 그녀의 춤에 관심이 없었다.」 그는 댄스실에서 다른 일들로 바빴다. "이제 가셔도 됩니다! 이 소녀는 평범합니다. 댄서가 되길 꿈꾸며 시간을 낭비하게 하지 마세요."라고 그가 말했다. Melanie와 엄마는 이 말을 듣고 충격을 받았다.

(B)

실망하여 그들은 집으로 돌아왔고, Melanie의 뺨에 눈물이 흘러내렸다. 자신감과 자아가 상처받은 채, Melanie는 결코 다시는 춤을 추지 않았다. (b) 그녀는 학업을 마치고 학교 교사가 되었다. 어느 날, 그녀가 근무하는 학교의 발레 강사가 늦게 (학교에) 오는 중이었고, Melanie는 학생들이 학교를 배회하지 않도록 지켜봐 달라는 요청을 받았다. 발레실 안으로 들어가자, Melanie는 자신을 통제할 수 없었다. 「그녀는 소녀들에게 몇 가지 스텝을 가르쳤고 얼마 동안 계속해서 춤을 추었다.」 시간과 그녀를 둘러싼 사람들도 인식하지도 못한 채, (c) 그녀는 자신만의 작은 춤의 세계에 빠져 있었다.

(C)

바로 그때, 발레 강사가 교실로 들어와 Melanie의 훌륭한 기술을 보고 놀랐다. "대단한 공연이에요!"라고 강사는 눈을 반짝이며 말했다. Melanie는 자신 앞에 서 있는 강사를 보고 당황했다. "죄송해요, 강사님!"이라고 그녀는 말했다. "뭐가요?"라고 강사가 물었다. "당신은 진정한 발레리나예요!" 강사는 Melanie에게 발레 교습소로 (d) 자신과 함께 가자고 요청했고, 이후 Melanie는 결코 무용을 그만두지 않았다. 「오늘날, 그녀는 세계적으로 유명한 발레 무용수이다.」

- **flawless** ⓐ 흠 없는
- **formal** ⓐ 공식적인, 형식적인
- **cheek** ⓝ 볼, 뺨
- **ego** ⓝ 자아, 에고
- **run late** 늦다
- **control oneself** 자제하다, 통제하다
- **sparkle** ⓝ 반짝거림
- **accompany** ⓥ 동반하다, 데리고 가다
- **request** ⓥ 요청하다
- **average** ⓐ 평균의
- **aspire** ⓥ 열망하다, 바라다
- **enthusiasm** ⓝ 열정
- **polish** ⓥ 연마하다, 다듬다
- **confidence** ⓝ 자신감
- **instructor** ⓝ 강사
- **roam** ⓥ 이리저리 돌아다니다, 배회하다
- **unaware** ⓐ 알지 못하는
- **embarrassed** ⓐ 당황한
- **world-renowned** ⓐ 세계적으로 유명한
- **admit** ⓥ (입학 등을) 받아주다
- **waste** ⓥ 낭비하다

구문 풀이

(A) 2행 One day, Melanie's mother saw her dancing with the flawless
　　　　　　　　　　　　　　지각동사　목적어　　→목적격 보어(현재분사)
steps and enthusiasm of a ballerina.

(B) 5행 One day, the ballet instructor at her school was running late,
and Melanie was asked to keep an eye on the class so that they
　　　　　　　「be asked + to부정사 : ~하도록 요청받다」　　접속사(~하도록)
wouldn't roam around the school.

(C) 4행 Melanie was embarrassed to see the instructor in front of her.
　　　　　　　　　　　　감정 형용사　　부사적 용법(감정의 원인)

(D) 2행 Upon meeting the dance teacher, Mr. Edler, her mother
　　　　　　　~하자마자　　　　　　　　　　　동격
requested to admit Melanie to his institute.
　　동사　　　　목적어

---

10 글의 순서 파악
정답률 85% | 정답 ④

주어진 글 (A)에 이어질 내용을 순서에 맞게 배열한 것으로 가장 적절한 것은?

① (B) - (D) - (C)　　　　　② (C) - (B) - (D)

③ (C) − (D) − (B)   ✔ (D) − (B) − (C)
⑤ (D) − (C) − (B)

Why? 왜 정답일까?

배운 적이 없어도 춤을 잘 추었던 Melanie를 보고 엄마가 감탄했다는 내용의 **(A)** 뒤에는, 다음날 Melanie와 엄마가 학원에 찾아가서 춤을 선보였지만 평균에 불과하다는 말을 듣고 낙심했다는 내용의 **(D)**가 먼저 이어진다. 이어서 **(B)**에서는 이후 커서 교사가 된 Melanie가 어느 날 우연히 늦게 온 발레 강사를 대신해 아이들에게 스텝을 가르쳐주다가 혼자만의 춤에 빠져들었다는 내용이 전개된다. 마지막으로 **(C)**에서는 Melanie의 실력에 감탄한 발레 강사가 Melanie에게 발레 수업을 권했고, 마침내 Melanie가 유명한 발레리나가 되었다는 결말이 제시된다. 따라서 글의 순서로 가장 적절한 것은 ④ '**(D)** − **(B)** − **(C)**'이다.

---

11   지칭 추론   정답률 70% | 정답 ④

밑줄 친 (a) ~ (e) 중에서 가리키는 대상이 나머지 넷과 다른 것은?

① (a)   ② (b)   ③ (c)   ✔ (d)   ⑤ (e)

Why? 왜 정답일까?

(a), (b), (c), (e)는 Melanie, (d)는 the ballet instructor at her school을 가리키므로, (a) ~ (e) 중에서 가리키는 대상이 다른 하나는 ④ '(d)'이다.

---

12   세부 내용 파악   정답률 80% | 정답 ⑤

윗글에 관한 내용으로 적절하지 않은 것은?

① 엄마는 Melanie가 발레리나의 열정을 가지고 춤추는 것을 보았다.
② Melanie는 학생들에게 스텝을 가르쳤다.
③ Melanie는 세계적으로 유명한 발레 댄서이다.
④ Melanie는 지역 댄스 학원에 엄마와 동행했다.
✔ Mr. Edler는 Melanie의 춤에 관심을 보였다.

Why? 왜 정답일까?

(D) 'However, he wasn't interested in her dance.'에서 Melanie가 찾아갔던 댄스 학원의 Mr. Edler는 Melanie의 춤에 관심을 보이지 않았다고 하므로, 내용과 일치하지 않는 것은 ⑤ 'Mr. Edler는 Melanie의 춤에 관심을 보였다.'이다.

Why? 왜 오답일까?

① (A) 'One day, Melanie's mother saw her dancing with ~ enthusiasm of a ballerina.'의 내용과 일치한다.
② (B) 'She taught the students some steps ~'의 내용과 일치한다.
③ (C) 'Today, she is a world-renowned ballet dancer.'의 내용과 일치한다.
④ (D) 'The following day, Melanie accompanied her mother to a local dance institute.'의 내용과 일치한다.

DAY 19   20분 미니 모의고사

01 ②	02 ⑤	03 ⑤	04 ⑤	05 ④
06 ⑤	07 ②	08 ⑤	09 ④	10 ④
11 ④	12 ②			

01   자녀를 비판적으로 비교하는 말 하지 않기   정답률 79% | 정답 ②

다음 글에서 필자가 주장하는 바로 가장 적절한 것은?

① 아이를 칭찬할 때는 일관성 있게 하라.
✔ 자녀를 서로 비교하는 발언을 자제하라.
③ 아이의 발전을 위하여 경쟁을 활용하라.
④ 아이에게 실패를 두려워하지 말라고 가르쳐라.
⑤ 자녀가 구체적인 목표를 설정하도록 조언하라.

[본문 해석]

형제간의 경쟁은 특히 의지가 강한 아이들 사이에서 자연스러운 것이다. 부모로서, 위험들 중 하나는 아이들을 서로 호의적이지 않게 비교하는 것인데, 왜냐하면 그들은 항상 경쟁 우위를 찾기 때문이다. 문제는 아이가 얼마나 빨리 달릴 수 있느냐가 아니라, 누가 먼저 결승선을 통과하느냐이다. 아이는 자신이 얼마나 키가 큰지 신경 쓰지 않으며, 누가 가장 큰지에 매우 관심이 있다. 아이들은 스케이트보드 타는 능력에서부터 누가 가장 많은 친구를 가지고 있는지에 이르기까지 모든 것에 대해 자신을 동료들과 비교해서 체계적으로 평가한다. 그들은 자기 가족 내에서 공개적으로 이야기되는 어떠한 실패에든 특히 민감하다. 따라서, 가정의 소소한 평화를 원하는 부모들은 일상적으로 한 아이를 다른 아이보다 편애하는 비교의 발언에 대해 경계해야 한다. 이 원칙을 위반하는 것은 그들 사이에 훨씬 더 큰 경쟁을 만드는 것이다.

Why? 왜 정답일까?

'Accordingly, parents who want a little peace at home should guard against comparative comments that routinely favor one child over another.'에서 가정의 평화를 유지하고 싶은 부모라면 자녀끼리 비교하는 발언을 하지 말아야 한다고 언급하는 것으로 볼 때, 필자가 주장하는 바로 가장 적절한 것은 ② '자녀를 서로 비교하는 발언을 자제하라.'이다.

- rivalry ⓝ 경쟁
- compare ⓥ (A와 B를) 비교하다
- competitive advantage 경쟁 우위
- systematically ⓐⓓ 체계적으로
- sensitive ⓐ 민감한, 예민한
- openly ⓐⓓ 공개적으로
- guard against 경계하다, 조심하다
- routinely ⓐⓓ 일상적으로
- strong-willed ⓐ 의지가 강한
- unfavorably ⓐⓓ 비판적으로
- vitally ⓐⓓ 극도로, 지극히
- measure ⓥ 측정하다, 재다
- failure ⓝ 실패
- accordingly ⓐⓓ 따라서
- comparative ⓐ 비교의
- violate ⓥ 위반하다

구문 풀이

2행 As parents, one of the dangers **is** comparing children unfavorably with each other, since they are always looking for a competitive advantage.
전치사(~로서) / 주어 / 동사(단수) / 주격 보어(동명사) / 접속사(~이기 때문에)

---

02   맹점에 관해 조언해줄 수 있는 사람을 곁에 두기   정답률 71% | 정답 ⑤

다음 글의 요지로 가장 적절한 것은?

① 모르는 부분을 인정하고 질문하는 것이 중요하다.
② 폭넓은 인간관계는 성공에 결정적인 영향을 미친다.
③ 자기발전은 실수를 기회로 만드는 능력에서 비롯된다.
④ 주변에 관심을 가지고 타인을 도와주는 것이 바람직하다.
✔ 자신의 맹점을 인지하도록 도와줄 수 있는 사람이 필요하다.

[본문 해석]

개인의 맹점은 다른 사람들에게는 보이지만 당신에게는 보이지 않는 부분이다. 맹점이 지닌 발달상의 어려움은 당신이 무엇을 모르는지 모른다는 것이다. 옆 차선의 트럭을 볼 수 없는 당신 차의 사이드미러 속 부분과 같이, 개인의 맹점

DAY 19

은 당신이 그것의 존재를 완전히 인지하지 못하기 때문에 쉽게 간과될 수 있다. 그것들은 마찬가지로 똑같이 위험할 수 있다. 당신이 보지 못하는 그 트럭? 그것은 정말 존재한다! 당신의 맹점도 그러하다. 당신이 그것을 볼 수 없다고 해서 그것이 당신을 칠 수 없음을 의미하는 것은 아니다. 여기서 당신이 다른 사람의 도움을 구해야 한다. 당신은 기꺼이 그 거울을 들고, 그 트럭을 볼 수 있을 정도로 충분히 당신을 잘 알 뿐만 아니라 또한 트럭이 존재한다는 것을 당신에게 알려 줄 만큼 충분히 당신을 아끼는 이런 특별한 동료들을 만들어야 한다.

Why? 왜 정답일까?

마지막 두 문장인 'This is where you need to enlist the help of others. You have to develop a crew of special people, people who are willing to hold up that mirror, who not only know you well enough to see that truck, but who also care enough about you to let you know that it's there.'에서 개인의 맹점은 타인에게는 보이지만 자신에게는 보이지 않는 부분이므로 자신에게 맹점에 관해 조언을 해줄 수 있는 특별한 동료를 곁에 두어야 한다는 조언을 제시하고 있다. 따라서 글의 요지로 가장 적절한 것은 ⑤ '자신의 맹점을 인지하도록 도와줄 수 있는 사람이 필요하다.'이다.

- blind spot 맹점
- overlook ⓥ 간과하다
- equally [ad] 똑같이
- enlist ⓥ (협조나 도움을) 구하다, 요청하다
- developmental ⓐ 발달상의
- unaware ⓐ 인지하지 못하는
- run over (차 등이) ~을 치다

구문 풀이

12행 You have to develop a crew of special people, people [who are willing to hold up that mirror], [who not only know you well enough (동격)(기꺼이 ~하다)(not only+A+) to see that truck, but who also care enough about you to let you know (but also+B : A뿐만 아니라 B도)(형/부+enough+to부정사 : ~할 만큼 충분히 ···한/하게) that it's there].

---

03 집에서 요리하는 일이 줄어들면서 생긴 변화 정답률 63% | 정답 ⑤

다음 글의 주제로 가장 적절한 것은?

① current trends in commercial cooking equipment
상업용 조리 장치의 최근 동향
② environmental impacts of shifts in dietary patterns
식생활 패턴의 변화가 환경에 미치는 영향
③ cost-effective ways to cook healthy meals at home
집에서 건강한 음식을 요리하는 가성비 좋은 방법
④ reasons behind the decline of the food service industry
외식업 쇠퇴의 이면에 있는 이유
⑤ benefits of reduced domestic cooking duties through outsourcing
(기업에의) 외부 위탁을 통한, 집에서 요리하는 일이 감소한 것의 이득

[본문 해석]

생물 인류학자인 Richard Wrangham이 말하는 것만큼 요리가 인간의 정체성, 생물학 및 문화에 중요하다면, 우리 시대의 요리 감소가 현대 생활에 심각한 결과로 이어진다는 것은 당연하고, 실제로 그랬다. 그게 다 나쁜 걸까? 전혀 그렇지 않다. 요리의 많은 부분을 기업에 위탁한 것은 전통적으로 그들의 전적인 책임이라 여겨진 가족을 먹이는 일을 여성들에게서 덜어주었고, 그들이 집 밖에서 일하고 직업을 갖기 더 쉽게 했다. 그것은 그토록 큰 성 역할 및 가정 역학의 큰 변화가 촉발한 많은 가정 내 갈등을 막아냈다. 그것은 더 많은 근무 일과 일정이 지나치게 바쁜 아이들을 포함한 집안의 다른 곤란을 덜어주었고, 이제 우리가 시간을 아껴 다른 일에 시간을 들이게 했다. 그것은 또한 우리의 식단을 상당히 다양하게 해주었고, 요리 기술이 없고 돈이 거의 없는 사람들까지도 완전히 색다른 요리를 즐길 수 있게 해 주었다. 필요한 것은 전자레인지 뿐이다.

Why? 왜 정답일까?

요리를 기업들에 맡기면서 여성들이 밖에서 일하기 더 쉬워지고 가정 내 곤란이나 갈등은 줄어들었으며 식단은 다양해졌다는 내용이다. 따라서 글의 주제로 가장 적절한 것은 ⑤ '(기업에의) 외부 위탁을 통한, 집에서 요리하는 일이 감소한 것의 이득'이다.

- anthropologist ⓝ 인류학자
- decline ⓝ 감소, 쇠퇴 ⓥ 줄어들다
- outsource (외부에) 위탁하다
- exclusive ⓐ 전적인, 배타적인
- domestic ⓐ 가정의
- be bound to ~하게 마련이다
- pursuit ⓝ 활동, 취미
- dietary ⓐ 식단의
- stand to reason 당연하다, 이치에 맞다
- consequence ⓝ 결과, 영향
- corporation ⓝ 회사, 기업
- head off ~을 막다, 차단하다
- gender role 성 역할
- spark ⓥ 촉발하다
- substantially [ad] 상당히
- cost-effective ⓐ 가성비 좋은

구문 풀이

1행 If cooking is as central to human identity, biology, and culture (as + 원급 +) as the biological anthropologist Richard Wrangham suggests, it (as : ~만큼 ···한)(가주어) stands to reason {that the decline of cooking in our time would have ({ } : 진주어) serious consequences for modern life}, and so it has. (대동사(=has had serious consequences))

---

04 국가별 소매 판매 온라인 점유율 정답률 93% | 정답 ⑤

다음 도표의 내용과 일치하지 않는 것은?

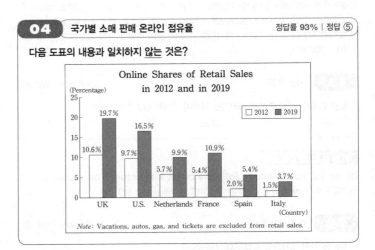

Online Shares of Retail Sales
in 2012 and in 2019

(Percentage)
□ 2012 ■ 2019

UK 10.6% / 19.7%
U.S. 9.7% / 16.5%
Netherlands 5.7% / 9.9%
France 5.4% / 10.9%
Spain 2.0% / 5.4%
Italy 1.5% / 3.7%
(Country)

Note: Vacations, autos, gas, and tickets are excluded from retail sales.

[본문 해석]

위 도표는 2012년과 2019년에 6개국의 소매 판매의 온라인 점유율을 보여준다. 소매 판매의 온라인 점유율은 주어진 나라에서 온라인으로 이루어진 소매 판매의 비율을 말한다. ① 각국에서 2019년의 소매 판매의 온라인 점유율은 2012년보다 더 컸다. ② 여섯 나라 중에서 영국은 2019년에 19.7%로 소매 판매의 온라인 점유율이 가장 컸다. ③ 2019년에 미국은 16.5%로 소매 판매의 온라인 점유율이 두 번째로 컸다. ④ 2012년에 네덜란드의 소매 판매의 온라인 점유율은 프랑스보다 더 컸던 반면, 2019년에는 그 반대였다. ⑤ 스페인과 이탈리아의 경우에, 각국에서 소매 판매의 온라인 점유율이 2012년과 2019년에 모두 5.0%에 미치지 못했다.

Why? 왜 정답일까?

도표에 따르면 2019년 스페인에서 소매 판매의 온라인 점유율은 5.0%를 넘겼다 (5.4%). 따라서 도표와 일치하지 않는 것은 ⑤이다.

- share ⓝ 점유율
- own ⓥ 소유하다
- case ⓝ (특정한 상황의) 경우, 사례
- retail sales ⓝ 소매 판매
- reverse ⓝ 반대, 역

---

05 자기 행동의 영향력을 금방 인식하는 유아 정답률 54% | 정답 ④

다음 글의 밑줄 친 부분 중, 어법상 틀린 것은? [3점]

[본문 해석]

유아들은 자신의 행동과 그에 따른 외부 변화 사이에서의 관계를 알아차림으로써, 그들이 인지된 변화의 주체라는 인식, 즉 자아 효능감을 발전시킨다. 유아들은 자신의 행동이 물리적 환경에 미치는 영향을 알아차릴 수 있지만, 유아들이 가장 쉽게 자기 행동의 결과를 인지하는 상황은 바로 초기 사회적 상호작용이다. 사람들은 유아들이 확실히 그들 쪽으로 향하게 할 지각적 특성을 가지고 있다. 사람들은 얼굴 표정이 시각적으로 구별되고 달라진다. 사람들은 소리를 만들고, 촉각을 제공하고, 흥미로운 냄새를 가지고 있다. 또한, 사람들은 유아들이 매력적이라고 느끼는 방식으로 얼굴 표정을 과장하고 목소리를 조절하며 유아들과 관계를 맺는다. 그러나 다른 무엇보다 중요한 것은, 이러한 익살스러운 행동이 유아들의 발성, 얼굴 표정, 몸짓에 호응해준다는 것인데, 사람들은 유아들의 행동에 맞춰 자기 행동의 속도와 수준을 다양하게 한다. 결과적으로 초기 사회적 상호 작용은 유아들이 자기 행동의 영향을 쉽게 알아차릴 수 있는 맥락을 제공한다.

Why? 왜 정답일까?

④가 포함된 주격 관계대명사 that절의 선행사는 ways인데, 이는 '매혹시키는' 주체이므로 fascinated 대신 fascinating을 써야 한다. 따라서 어법상 틀린 것은 ④이다.

Why? 왜 오답일까?

① a sense를 보충 설명하는 동격 명사절의 접속사 that이 바르게 쓰였다. that 뒤에 완전한 2형식 구조가 나왔음을 참고한다.
② 동사 perceive를 꾸미기 위해 부사 readily가 바르게 쓰였다.
③ 선행사 perceptual characteristics가 복수 명사이므로, 주격 관계대명사 that 뒤의 동사 또한 복수 동사여야 한다. 따라서 assure가 바르게 쓰였다.
⑤ 관계부사 where가 장소의 선행사 a context를 어법상 적절하게 꾸미고 있다.

- notice ⓥ 알아차리다
- external ⓐ 외부적인
- agent ⓝ 주체, 행위자
- perceptual ⓐ 지각과 관련된
- virtually [ad] 실제로
- engage with ~와 관계를 맺다
- fascinated ⓐ 매혹된
- responsive to ~에 잘 호응하는
- resultant ⓐ 그로 인한
- self-efficacy ⓝ 자기 효능감
- readily [ad] 쉽게, 순조롭게
- characteristic ⓝ 특성
- assure ⓥ 확실히 하다
- exaggerate ⓥ 과장하다
- most importantly 가장 중요한 것은
- consequentially [ad] 결과적으로

구문 풀이

11행 In addition, people engage with infants by exaggerating their facial expressions and inflecting their voices in ways [that infants find fascinating].

---

06 고대 이집트인과 메소포타미아인들의 자연관   정답률 49% | 정답 ⑤

(A), (B), (C)의 각 네모 안에서 문맥에 맞는 낱말로 가장 적절한 것은?

	(A)	(B)	(C)
①	assistant 조력자	distinguishable 구별할 수 있는	neglect 무시하다
②	assistant 조력자	indistinguishable 구별할 수 없는	recognize 인식하다
③	opponent 적	distinguishable 구별할 수 있는	recognize 인식하다
④	opponent 적	indistinguishable 구별할 수 없는	neglect 무시하다
⑤✓	opponent 적	indistinguishable 구별할 수 없는	recognize 인식하다

[본문 해석]

고대 이집트와 메소포타미아 사람들은 서구 사회의 철학적 선조였다. 그들의 세계관 속에서 자연은 삶의 투쟁 속에 있는 (A) 적은 아니었다. 오히려, 인간과 자연은 같은 처지로서 같은 이야기 속에 있는 동반자였다. 인간은 자신과 다른 사람들을 생각하듯이 자연 세계를 생각했다. 자연 세계는 인간들처럼 생각, 욕구 그리고 감정을 가지고 있었다. 그러므로 인간과 자연의 영역은 (B) 구분이 불분명했으며 인지적으로 달리 이해될 필요는 없었다. 자연 현상들은 인간 경험과 똑같은 방식으로 상상되었다. 이러한 근동 지역의 고대인들은 인과 관계를 진정 (C) 인식하고는 있었지만, 그것에 대해서 숙고할 때에는 '무엇'의 관점보다는 '누구'의 관점에서 접근했다. 나일강이 불어났을 때, 그것은 그 강이 원했기 때문이지 비가 왔기 때문은 아니었다.

Why? 왜 정답일까?

(A) 'Rather, man and nature were in the same boat, companions in the same story.'에서 고대 이집트인과 메소포타미아인들은 자연을 인간과 같은 입장에 있는 동반자로 보았다고 하는데, 네모 앞에 not이 있으므로 (A)에는 자연과 인간이 '적이 아니었다'는 의미를 완성하는 opponent가 적절하다.

(B) 'The natural world had thoughts, desires, and emotions, just like humans.'에서 자연은 인간과 마찬가지로 생각, 욕구, 감정을 지닌 존재로 이해되었다고 하므로, (B)에는 자연과 인간이 서로 구분되어 취급되지 않았다는 의미의 indistinguishable이 적절하다.

(C) but 앞뒤로 고대 사람들이 인과관계에 대해 '인식하기는 했지만' 인과관계의 관점보다는 행위자의 관점에서 자연 현상을 이해했다는 내용이 대비를 이루므로, (C)에는 recognize가 적절하다. 따라서 (A), (B), (C)의 각 네모 안에서 문맥에 맞는 낱말로 가장 적절한 것은 ⑤ '(A) opponent(적) – (B) indistinguishable(구별할 수 없는) – (C) recognize(인식하다)'이다.

- philosophical ⓐ 철학의
- concept ⓝ 개념, 생각
- in the same boat 처지가 같은
- emotion ⓝ 감정
- distinguishable ⓐ 구별할 수 있는
- cognitively [ad] 인지적으로
- forebear ⓝ 선조, 조상
- opponent ⓝ 적, 경쟁자
- companion ⓝ 동반자
- realm ⓝ 영역
- indistinguishable ⓐ 구별할 수 없는
- neglect ⓥ 무시하다

- recognize ⓥ 인식하다
- cause and effect 원인과 결과
- rather than ~라기 보다
- relation ⓝ 관계
- speculate ⓥ 숙고하다, 추측하다

구문 풀이

13행 These ancients of the Near East did recognize the relation of cause and effect, but (when speculating about it) they came from a "who" (perspective) rather than a "what" perspective.
「A + rather than + B : B라기보다 A」

---

07 상대적 비교에 따라 결정되는 음식 양   정답률 54% | 정답 ②

다음 빈칸에 들어갈 말로 가장 적절한 것을 고르시오.
① Originality - 독창성
②✓ Relativity - 상대성
③ Visualization - 시각화
④ Imitation - 모방
⑤ Forgetfulness - 건망증

[본문 해석]

상대성은 여러 면에서 그리고 삶의 많은 다른 영역에 걸쳐 정신을 위한 일반적인 메커니즘으로 작용한다. 예를 들어, *Mindless Eating*의 저자 Brian Wansink는 이것이 우리의 허리 둘레에도 영향을 미칠 수 있다는 것을 보여주었다. 우리는 단순히 우리가 실제로 먹는 음식 양의 함수로서가 아니라 대안과의 비교를 통해서 우리가 먹을 양을 결정한다. 우리가 메뉴에 있는 8온스, 10온스, 12온스의 버거 세 개 중 하나를 선택해야 한다고 하자. 우리는 10온스 버거를 고르고 식사가 끝날 때쯤이면 완벽하게 만족할 수 있을 것이다. 하지만 만약 대신에 우리의 선택권이 10온스, 12온스, 14온스라면, 우리는 다시 중간의 것을 선택할 것이고, 비록 우리가 더 많이 먹었더라도, 식사가 끝날 때 매일 영양분을 섭취하거나 포만감을 느끼기 위해 필요하지 않았던 12온스의 햄버거에 똑같이 행복감과 만족감을 다시 느낄 수 있을 것이다.

Why? 왜 정답일까?

예시 앞의 'We decide how much to eat not simply as a function of how much food we actually consume, but by a comparison to its alternatives.'에서 우리는 대안 간의 비교를 통해 얼마나 먹을지를 결정하게 된다고 하므로, 빈칸에 들어갈 말로 가장 적절한 것은 '비교'를 다른 말로 재진술한 ② '상대성'이다.

- mechanism ⓝ 방법, 메커니즘
- function ⓝ (수학) 함수
- comparison ⓝ 비교
- satisfied ⓐ 만족하는
- nourishment ⓝ 영양분
- relativity ⓝ 상대성
- waistline ⓝ 허리둘레
- consume ⓥ 먹다, 마시다
- alternative ⓝ 대안
- equally [ad] 똑같이, 동일하게
- originality ⓝ 독창성
- forgetfulness ⓝ 건망증, 잘 잊어버림

구문 풀이

5행 We decide how much to eat not simply as a function (of how much food we actually consume), but by a comparison (to its alternatives).
「not simply[only] + A + but (also) + B : A뿐 아니라 B도」

★★★ 1등급 대비 고난도 3점 문제

08 확실성을 추구하는 인간   정답률 43% | 정답 ⑤

다음 빈칸에 들어갈 말로 가장 적절한 것을 고르시오. [3점]
① weigh the pros and cons of our actions
  우리 행동의 장단점을 따져 본다
② develop the patience to bear ambiguity
  모호함을 참을 수 있는 인내심을 기른다
③ enjoy adventure rather than settle down
  안주하기보다 모험을 즐긴다
④ gain insight from solving complex problems
  복잡한 문제를 해결하여 통찰력을 얻는다
⑤✓ lose our ability to interact with the unknown
  미지의 것과 상호 작용하는 우리의 능력을 잃어버린다

[본문 해석]

현대 세계에서 우리는 불확실한 곳에서 확실성을 찾는다. 우리는 혼란 속에서 질서를, 애매모호함에서 정답을, 복잡함에서 확신을 찾는다. 베스트셀러 작가인 Yuval Noah Harari가 말하기를, "우리는 세상을 이해하려고 하는 것보다 세상을 통제하려고 하는 것에 훨씬 더 많은 시간과 노력을 쏟는다." 우리는 쉽게 따라할 수 있는 공식을 찾는다. 시간이 지나면서 우리는 미지의 것과 상호 작

DAY 19

용하는 우리의 능력을 잃어버린다. 우리의 접근법은 내게 밤에 가로등 아래에서 자신의 열쇠를 찾는 술 취한 남자에 대한 전형적인 이야기를 떠올리게 한다. 그는 자신이 열쇠를 어두운 길 어딘가에서 잃어버렸다는 것을 알지만 가로등 밑에서 그것을 찾는데, 왜냐하면 그곳에 빛이 있기 때문이다. 확실성에 대한 우리의 열망은 우리가 가로등 아래에서 열쇠를 찾음으로써 겉으로 보기에 안전한 해결책을 추구하도록 이끈다. 어둠 속으로 위험한 걸음을 내딛는 대신, 우리는 우리의 현재 상태가 아무리 열등할지 몰라도 그 안에 머문다.

Why? 왜 정답일까?

마지막 두 문장에서 우리는 확실성을 추구하기 때문에 겉보기에 안전해 보이는 선택지를 취하려 하며, 미지의 어둠 속을 탐색하는 대신 부족하고 열등한 현재 상태일지라도 그대로 유지하려는 경향이 있다(Our yearning for certainty leads us to pursue seemingly safe solutions ~. Instead of taking the risky walk into the dark, we stay within our current state, however inferior it may be.)고 언급한다. 따라서 빈칸에 들어갈 말로 가장 적절한 것은 새롭고 불확실한 것을 점점 덜 알아보려 한다는 의미의 ⑤ '미지의 것과 상호 작용하는 우리의 능력을 잃어버린다'이다.

- certainty ⑩ 확실성
- ambiguity ⑩ 애매모호함
- complexity ⑩ 복잡성
- formula ⑩ 공식, 제조법
- pursue ⑩ 추구하다
- inferior ⑩ 열등한
- patience ⑩ 인내심
- insight ⑩ 통찰력

- uncertain ⑩ 불확실한
- conviction ⑩ 확신
- easy-to-follow ⑩ 따르기 쉬운
- yearning ⑩ 갈망, 열망
- seemingly ⑩ 겉보기에
- pros and cons 장단점
- bear ⑩ 참다, (아이를) 낳다
- unknown ⑩ 미지의, 알려지지 않은

구문 풀이

3행 "We spend far more time and effort on trying to control the
「spend + 시간/노력 + on + 동명사: ~하는 데 시간/노력을 들이다」
world," (best-selling writer Yuval Noah Harari says), "than on trying
( ) : 삽입절 병렬구조(than 앞의 on trying과 연결됨)
to understand it."

★★ 문제 해결 꿀~팁 ★★

▶ 많이 틀린 이유는?
빈칸이 있는 문장 바로 앞의 'We look for ~'에서 우리는 쉽게 따라할 수 있는 것을 좇는 경향이 있다고 하므로, '어려운 문제를 풀며 영감을 얻는다'는 의미의 ④는 맥락상 상충한다.

▶ 문제 해결 방법은?
어두운 길가에서 열쇠를 잃어버렸음에도 빛이 있는 가로등 밑에서 열쇠를 찾아 헤매는 남자의 예는 '새롭고 위험할지라도 시도해봐야 하지만 안전한 현재 상태만 고수하고 있는' 우리의 모습을 비유한 것이다. 빈칸 문장은 이 상태가 지속되면 결국 우리가 '미지의 것을 살펴보는 능력 자체를 잃게 된다'는 전망을 제시하는 것이다.

---

09 인플레이션에 따르는 위험   정답률 62% | 정답 ④

다음 글에서 전체 흐름과 관계 없는 문장은?

[본문 해석]
인플레이션에 의한 위험성은 개인 투자의 미래 실질 가치에 대한 불확실성과 관련되어 있다. 예를 들어, 당신이 수수료가 없고 이자가 생기지 않는 은행 계좌에 100달러를 가지고 있다고 하자. 그대로 내버려 두면, 그 은행 계좌에는 항상 100달러가 있을 것이다. ① 만약 당신이 1년 동안 은행에 그 돈을 보관하고 그 기간에 인플레이션이 100퍼센트라면, 당신은 여전히 100달러만 가지고 있는 것이다. ② 이제, 만약 당신이 그 돈을 인출해서 지갑에 넣어둔다면, 당신은 1년 전에 당신이 살 수도 있었던 물건들의 반만 구매할 수 있게 될 것이다. ③ 다시 말하자면, 만약 인플레이션이 당신이 받고 있는 이자의 양보다 더 빨리 증가한다면, 이것은 시간이 지남에 따라 당신 투자의 구매력을 감소시킬 것이다. ④ 만약 당신이 상품의 가격을 올린다면 회사 총수입에 어떤 일이 일어날지를 미리 아는 것은 매우 유용할 것이다. ⑤ 그것이 우리가 명목 가치와 실질 가치를 구별하는 이유이다.

Why? 왜 정답일까?

인플레이션에 수반되는 위험에 관해 설명하는 글로, ①부터 예시를 소개한 뒤 마지막 문장에서 이러한 위험 때문에 명목 가치와 실질 가치가 구분되어야 한다는 결론을 도출하고 있다. 하지만 ④는 상품 가격을 올렸을 때 총수입에 어떤 영향이 있을 것인지 알면 좋다는 내용이므로 흐름상 어색하다. 따라서 전체 흐름과 관계 없는 문장은 ④이다.

- uncertainty ⑩ 불확실성
- account ⑩ 계좌, 계정
- differentiate ⑩ 구분하다, 구별하다

- investment ⑩ 투자
- total revenue 총수입

구문 풀이

4행 If (it is) left untouched there will always be $100 in that bank
생략 과거분사구 동사 주어
account.
접속사

★★★ 1등급 대비 고난도 3점 문제

10 과학에서의 획기적 발견   정답률 53% | 정답 ④

주어진 글 다음에 이어질 글의 순서로 가장 적절한 것을 고르시오. [3점]
① (A) − (C) − (B)   ② (B) − (A) − (C)
③ (B) − (C) − (A)   ✔ (C) − (A) − (B)
⑤ (C) − (B) − (A)

[본문 해석]
19세기 후반 생리학의 발견처럼, 오늘날 생물학의 획기적인 발견은 인간 유기체가 작동하는 방식에 대한 우리의 이해를 근본적으로 바꿔놓았고, 의료 행위를 본질적이면서도 철저하게 변화시킬 것이다.

(C) 그러나 '획기적인 발견'이라는 말은 많은 사람들의 마음속에서는 순식간에 모든 것을 명확하게 만드는 놀랍고 전례 없는 발견을 의미하는 것처럼 보인다. 사실 과학은 그런 방식으로 작동하지 않는다.

(A) 여러분이 대략 초등학교 때 아마 처음 배웠을 과학적 방법을 기억하는가? 그것은 관찰, 가설, 실험, 검증, 수정, 재검증, 그리고 재차 반복되는 재검증이라는 길고 어려운 과정을 지닌다.

(B) 그것이 과학이 작동하는 방식이고, 우리 유전자와 만성 질환 사이의 관계에 대한 획기적 이해도 수십 년, 심지어 수백 년 전으로부터의 과학자들의 연구를 기반으로 하여 바로 그러한 방식으로 일어났다. 사실, 그것은 여전히 일어나고 있으며 연구가 계속되는 한 그 이야기는 계속 펼쳐진다.

Why? 왜 정답일까?

오늘날 생물학의 획기적 발견을 화두로 제시하는 주어진 글 뒤에는, however로 흐름을 반전시키며 사실 과학에는 순식간에 모든 것을 정리해주는 '획기적 발견'이라는 것이 존재하지 않는다고 언급하는 (C)가 먼저 이어진다. 이어서 (A)는 과학이 관찰, 가설, 실험, 검증, 수정, 재검증 등의 길고 복잡한 과정을 통해 이루어진다는 점을 상기시키고, (B)는 그러한 긴 과정이 곧 과학의 진정한 작동 방식이라는 결론을 제시한다. 따라서 글의 순서로 가장 적절한 것은 ④ '(C) − (A) − (B)'이다.

- physiological ⑩ 생리학적인
- fundamentally ⑩ 근본적으로
- hypothesis ⑩ 가설
- chronic ⑩ 만성의
- unprecedented ⑩ 전례 없는

- breakthrough ⑩ 획기적 발견
- thoroughly ⑩ 철저히
- modify ⑩ 수정하다
- unfold ⑩ 펼쳐지다, 펴다
- revelation ⑩ 발견

구문 풀이

12행 That's how science works, and the breakthrough understanding
관계부사(~하는 방법) 주어
of the relationship between our genes and chronic disease happened
동사
in just that way, building on the work of scientists from decades
분사구문(~하면서)
— even centuries — ago.

★★ 문제 해결 꿀~팁 ★★

▶ 많이 틀린 이유는?
(C)와 (B)에 나오는 breakthrough만 보고 (C) − (B)를 곧장 연결시켜서는 안 된다. (C)는 'Science doesn't actually work that way.'로 끝나는데, 이 뒤에 (B)의 'That's how science works, ~'가 이어지면 '과학은 그런 식으로 작동하지 않는다. vs. 바로 그렇게 과학이 작동한다.'와 같이 상충되는 의미의 두 문장이 역접의 연결어 없이 이어져 버린다.

▶ 문제 해결 방법은?
맥락상 (C) 뒤에 관찰, 가설, 실험, 검증, 수정, 재검증 등을 언급하며 과학의 작동 원리를 설명하는 (A)가 먼저 나오고, 이것이 바로 과학의 작동 원리가 맞다고 확인해주는 (B)가 연결되어야 적절한 흐름이 완성된다.

11-12 도주와 공격을 결정짓는 거리

[본문 해석]

동물 연구는 동물들이 그들 자신과 다른 종의 구성원들 사이에 유지할 수도 있는 거리를 다루어 왔다. 「이러한 거리는 소위 '도주 또는 공격' 메커니즘의 기능을 결정짓는다.」 동물은 자기가 포식자라고 여기는 것이 자신의 '도주' 거리 내로 접근하는 것을 감지하면, 정말 그야말로 도망갈 것이다. 이러한 현상이 일어나는 거리는 놀라울 정도로 (a) 일관되며, 스위스 생물학자 Hediger는 자신이 연구하는 일부 종에 대해 그것을 놀라울 만큼 정확하게 측정했다고 주장했다. 당연히 그것은 종에 따라 다르며, 보통 동물이 더 클수록 그것의 도주 거리는 (b) 더 짧다(→ 더 길다). 「나는 기린의 사진을 찍기 위해서는 원거리 초점 렌즈를 사용해야만 했는데, 기린은 도주 거리가 매우 크기 때문이다. 대조적으로, 정원에서 다람쥐를 거의 밟을 뻔했을 때 다람쥐가 갑자기 도망쳐서 나의 주의를 끈 적이 몇 번 있었다!」 우리는 거리에서의 이러한 (c) 차이가 속력을 내서 달릴 수 있는 능력에 대한 동물 자신의 평가와 일치한다고 추정할 수 있을 뿐이다.

'공격' 거리는 항상 도주 거리보다 더 (d) 짧다. 인식된 포식자가 도주 거리 내로 접근하지만, 그 동물이 장애물이나 다른 포식자들에 의해 갇혀서 (e) 달아날 수 없다면, 그 동물은 (물러나지 않고) 버텨야 한다. 하지만, 결국에는 공격이 가장 좋은 형태의 방어 수단이 되므로, 그 갇힌 동물은 돌아서서 싸울 것이다.

- ● deal with ~을 다루다
- ● flight or fight 도주 또는 공격
- ● consistent ⓐ 일관적인
- ● remarkably ⓐⅾ 놀라울 만큼
- ● variation ⓝ 차이, 변화
- ● accelerate ⓥ 가속화하다
- ● flee ⓥ 달아나다, 도망가다
- ● migrate ⓥ 이주하다
- ● functioning ⓝ 기능
- ● predator ⓝ 포식자
- ● measure ⓥ 측정하다
- ● precisely ⓐⅾ 정확하게
- ● assessment ⓝ 평가
- ● obstacle ⓝ 장애물
- ● stand one's ground 버티다, 공격에 견디다
- ● determining ⓐ 결정적인

구문 풀이

7행 The distance [at which this happens] is amazingly consistent,
주어1 「전치사＋관·대」 동사1
and Hediger, a Swiss biologist, claimed to have measured it remarkably
주어2 동사2 목적어(완료부정사)
precisely for some of the species [that he studied].
선행사 목적격 관·대

11 제목 파악   정답률 61% | 정답 ④

윗글의 제목으로 가장 적절한 것은?

① How Animals Migrate Without Getting Lost
동물이 길을 잃지 않고 이동하는 방법
② Flight or Fight Mechanism: Still in Our Brain
도주 또는 공격 메커니즘: 아직도 우리 뇌 속에
③ Why the Size Matters in the Survival of Animals
동물의 생존에서 크기가 중요한 이유
④ Distances: A Determining Factor for Flight or Attack
거리: 도주나 공격의 결정 요인
⑤ Competition for Food Between Large and Small Animals
큰 동물과 작은 동물 간의 먹이 경쟁

Why? 왜 정답일까?

두 번째 문장인 'These distances determine the functioning of the so-called 'flight or fight' mechanism.'에서 도주 또는 공격 중 무엇을 택할지를 결정해주는 요인은 바로 거리라는 주제를 제시하므로, 글의 제목으로 가장 적절한 것은 ④ '거리: 도주나 공격의 결정 요인'이다.

★★★ 1등급 대비 고난도 2점 문제

12 어휘 추론   정답률 44% | 정답 ②

밑줄 친 (a) ~ (e) 중에서 문맥상 낱말의 쓰임이 적절하지 않은 것은?

① (a)   ② (b)   ③ (c)   ④ (d)   ⑤ (e)

Why? 왜 정답일까?

'I have had to use a long focus lens to take photographs of giraffes, which have very large flight distances. By contrast, I have several times nearly stepped on a squirrel in my garden before it drew attention to

---

itself by suddenly escaping!' 몸집이 큰 기린과 작은 다람쥐를 예로 들어 큰 동물은 도주 거리가 길다는 내용을 제시하고 있다. 따라서 (b)의 smaller를 반의어인 longer로 고쳐야 한다. 문맥상 낱말의 쓰임이 적절하지 않은 것은 ② '(b)'이다.

★★ 문제 해결 꿀~팁 ★★

▶ 많이 틀린 이유는?

첫 단락에서 '도주' 거리가 동물의 크기에 따라 달라진다는 내용이 나온 뒤, (d)가 포함된 문장은 '공격'의 거리를 언급하고 있다. 'If a perceived predator approaches ~'에서 도주 거리 안에 포식자가 들어왔으나 장애물이나 다른 포식자가 더 있어 '도주하기 어려운' 경우에 먹이 동물은 공격을 선택한다고 하므로, 공격 거리는 도주 거리보다 '더 짧을' 것임을 유추할 수 있다.

▶ 문제 해결 방법은?

밑줄 어휘 문제는 앞뒤 맥락이 주로 답의 근거를 제시한다. 여기서도 (b) 뒤의 두 문장이 기린과 다람쥐의 예를 통해 몸집의 크기에 따른 도주 거리 차이를 설명하고 있으므로 이 내용을 잘 읽어 (b)의 쓰임이 적합한지를 결정해야 한다.

DAY 20 — 20분 미니 모의고사

01 ④	02 ①	03 ②	04 ④	05 ②
06 ⑤	07 ①	08 ④	09 ①	10 ②
11 ⑤	12 ⑤			

---

01 큰 글자판 잡지가 있는지 문의하기　정답률 94% | 정답 ④

다음 글의 목적으로 가장 적절한 것은?
① 잡지 기삿거리를 제보하려고
② 구독 기간 변경을 신청하려고
③ 구독료 인상에 대해 항의하려고
✓④ 잡지의 큰 글자판이 있는지 문의하려고
⑤ 잡지 기사 내용에 대한 정정을 요구하려고

[본문 해석]

고객 서비스팀께,

저는 잡지 구독과 관련하여 글을 씁니다. 현재 저의 *Economy Tomorrow* 구독이 일 년 조금 넘게 남았는데, 저는 수년간 귀사의 잡지를 즐겨왔기 때문에 구독을 계속하고 싶습니다. 안타깝게도, 제 시력이 나빠서 귀사의 잡지를 읽는 데 어려움이 있습니다. 의사 선생님 말씀이 큰 글자판의 책과 잡지를 찾아봐야 할 필요가 있다고 합니다. 저는 귀사 잡지의 큰 글자판이 있는지 알고 싶습니다. 이를 제공한다면 저에게 연락 부탁드립니다. 시간 내주셔서 감사합니다. 조만간 소식을 들을 수 있기를 기대합니다.

Martin Gray 드림

Why? 왜 정답일까?

'I'd like to know whether there's a large print version of your magazine. Please contact me if this is something you offer.'에서 현재 구독하고 있는 잡지의 큰 글자판이 있는지 알고 싶다고 하므로, 글의 목적으로 가장 적절한 것은 ④ '잡지의 큰 글자판이 있는지 문의하려고'이다.

● in regard to ~에 관해서
● subscription ⓝ 구독
● have trouble ~ing ~하는 데 어려움이 있다
● currently ⓐⓓ 현재
● eyesight ⓝ 시력
● look forward to ~하기를 고대하다

구문 풀이

6행 Unfortunately, due to my bad eyesight, I have trouble reading
~ 때문에　「have trouble + 동명사 : ~하는 데 어려움이 있다」
your magazine.

★★★ **1등급 대비 고난도 2점 문제**

02 크라우드 펀딩과 기업 자금 조달　정답률 36% | 정답 ①

밑줄 친 the democratization of business financing이 다음 글에서 의미하는 바로 가장 적절한 것은?
✓① More people can be involved in funding a business.
더 많은 사람들이 사업 자금 조달에 관여할 수 있다.
② More people will participate in developing new products.
더 많은 사람들이 신제품 개발에 참여하게 된다.
③ Crowdfunding can reinforce the conventional way of financing.
크라우드 펀딩은 전통적 자금 조달 방식을 강화할 수 있다.
④ Crowdfunding keeps social networking from facilitating funding.
크라우드 펀딩은 소셜 네트워크가 펀딩을 용이하게 하지 못하게 만든다.
⑤ The Internet helps employees of a company interact with each other.
인터넷은 한 회사의 직원들이 서로 상호작용하는 것을 돕는다.

[본문 해석]

크라우드 펀딩은 프로젝트를 위한 자금을 확보하는 새롭고 더 협력적인 방법이다. 그것은 세계 어느 곳에서나 가치 있는 명분을 위한 기부를 요청하고, 이후에 프로젝트의 파트너가 되는 기부자들과 함께 프로젝트를 위한 자금을 조성하는 등 다양한 방식들로 사용될 수 있다. 본질적으로, 크라우드 펀딩은 소셜 네트워킹과 벤처 자본주의의 융합이다. 소셜 네트워킹이 사람들이 서로 의사소통하고 상호작용하는 방법에 대한 전통적인 규칙을 다시 쓴 것과 동일한 방식으로, 온갖 다양한 방식의 크라우드 펀딩은 미래에 기업과 다른 프로젝트가 자금을 얻는 방법에 대한 규칙을 다시 쓸 잠재력을 가진다. 크라우드 펀딩은 기업 자금 조달의 민주화로 여겨질 수 있다. 자본 조달과 할당을 비교적 소규모의 고정된 소수에 한정하는 대신에 크라우드 펀딩은 인터넷에 연결된 모든 사람이 인터넷에 접속하는 다른 모든 사람의 집단 지혜와 쌈짓돈 둘 다에 다가갈 수 있게 해준다.

Why? 왜 정답일까?

마지막 문장에서 크라우드 펀딩을 통해 기업들은 고정된 소수에게서 자본 조달과 할당을 받는 대신에 인터넷에 연결된 모든 사람들의 지혜와 돈에 접근할 수 있게 된다(~ crowdfunding empowers everyone connected to the Internet to access both the collective wisdom and the pocket money of everyone else ~.)고 설명한다. 따라서 밑줄 친 부분이 의미하는 바로 가장 적절한 것은 ① '더 많은 사람들이 사업 자금 조달에 관여할 수 있다.'이다.

● collaborative ⓐ 협력적인
● donation ⓝ 기부, 기증
● cause ⓝ 대의명분
● in essence 본질적으로
● venture ⓝ 벤처 (사업)
● conventional ⓐ 전통적인
● view ⓥ (…라고) 여기다, 보다
● restrict ⓥ 한정하다, 제한하다
● allocation ⓝ 할당
● empower ⓥ 권한을 주다
● pocket money 쌈짓돈, 용돈
● keep A from B A가 B하지 못하게 하다
● secure ⓥ 확보하다
● worthy ⓐ 가치 있는
● contributor ⓝ 기부자
● fusion ⓝ 융합, 혼합
● capitalism ⓝ 자본주의
● variation ⓝ 변주, 변형
● democratization ⓝ 민주화
● capital ⓝ 자본
● minority ⓝ 소수
● collective wisdom 집단 지혜
● reinforce ⓥ 강화하다
● facilitate ⓥ 용이하게 하다

구문 풀이

7행 In just the same way as social networks have rewritten the
딱 ~한 방식과 마찬가지로
conventional rules about [how people communicate and interact
전치사　관계부사(~하는 방법)
with each other], crowdfunding in all its variations has the potential
주어　동사
to rewrite the rules on [how businesses and other projects get funded
형용사적 용법　전치사 └관계부사(~하는 방법)
in the future].

★★ 문제 해결 꿀~팁 ★★

▶ **많이 틀린 이유는?**
밑줄 친 부분의 의미를 마지막 문장에서 풀어서 서술하고 있다. 즉 기존에는 기업 자금이 주로 소수의 정해진 이들에 의해 조달되었지만 이제는 '인터넷에 연결된 모든 이들로부터' 조달될 수 있게 되었다는 것이다. ④의 경우 크라우드 펀딩이 소셜 네트워크를 통한 자금 조달을 도리어 '막는다'는 의미를 나타내므로 주제와 상충한다.

▶ **문제 해결 방법은?**
글에 따르면 기업 자금 조달에 더 많은 사람들, 나아가 인터넷에 연결된 모든 사람들을 관여시킬 수 있는 수단이 바로 크라우드 펀딩이다. 이를 비유적으로 나타낸 표현이 바로 '민주화'임을 파악하도록 한다.

---

03 분명한 언어 사용의 중요성　정답률 64% | 정답 ②

다음 글의 제목으로 가장 적절한 것은?
① Earn Trust with Reliable Goods Rather Than with Words!
말보다는 믿을 수 있는 상품으로 신뢰를 얻으라!
✓② Linguistic Precision: A Key to Successful Economic Transactions
언어적 정확성: 성공적인 경제 거래의 열쇠
③ Difficulties in Overcoming Language Barriers and Distrust in Trade
무역에서 언어 장벽과 불신을 극복하는 데 있어서의 어려움
④ The More the Economy Grows, the More Complex the World Gets
경제가 성장할수록 세계는 더 복잡해진다
⑤ Excessive Confidence: The Biggest Reason for Miscommunication
지나친 신뢰: 잘못된 의사소통의 가장 큰 이유

[본문 해석]

정치 체제, 법, 문화, 그리고 가족 및 가까운 이웃을 넘어서는 일상적인 매일의 상호작용에서, 폭넓게 이해되고 확실하게 표현된 언어가 상호 신뢰에 굉장히 도움이 된다. 재산이나 계약서, 심지어 단순히 상품과 서비스의 일상적인 교환을 다룰 때 개념과 설명은 가능한 한 정확하고 모호하지 않아야 하며, 그렇지 않으면 오해가 생길 것이다. 만약 거래에서 잠재적 상대방과의 완전한 의사소통이 가능하지 않다면 불확실성과 아마 어느 정도의 불신이 남아있을 것이다. 경제 생활이 중세 시대 후반에 더 복잡해지면서 더욱 완전하고 더욱 정확한 의사소통에 대한 필요가 강조되었다. 공유된 언어는 해명과 아마도 어떤 분쟁의 해결을 용이하게 했다. 국제무역에서도 또한 정확하고 잘 표현된 언어의 사용

은 통역의 과정을 도왔다. 실크로드는 교환 지점에서 통역가들이 항상 이용 가능했기 때문에 그나마 기능할 수 있었다.

Why? 왜 정답일까?

첫 문장에서 명확한 언어 사용이 상호 신뢰를 구축하는 데 도움이 된다고 언급된 데 이어, 중반 이후로 특히 거래 등 경제 상황에서 명확하고 완전한 의사소통이 중요하게 여겨진다는 내용이 나온다. 따라서 글의 제목으로 가장 적절한 것은 ② '언어적 정확성: 성공적인 경제 거래의 열쇠'이다.

- interaction ⓝ 상호 작용
- formulate ⓥ 만들어내다, 표현하다
- mutual ⓐ 상호의
- contract ⓝ 계약서
- description ⓝ 설명, 묘사
- unambiguous ⓐ 모호하지 않은
- arise ⓥ 발생하다
- uncertainty ⓝ 불확실성
- distrust ⓝ 불신
- clarification ⓝ 해명, 설명
- dispute ⓝ 논쟁
- interchange ⓝ (특히 생각·정보의) 교환
- transaction ⓝ 거래, 매매

- immediate ⓐ 가까운, 당면한, 즉각적인
- aid ⓝ 도움, 원조
- property ⓝ 재산, 소유물
- exchange ⓝ 교환, 주고받음
- precise ⓐ 정확한, 정교한
- misunderstanding ⓝ 오해, 착오
- counterparty ⓝ 한쪽 당사자
- a measure of 어느 정도의, 꽤 많은 양의
- facilitate ⓥ 용이하게 하다
- settlement ⓝ 해결, 합의
- translation ⓝ 통역
- earn ⓥ 얻다, 받다

구문 풀이

4행 When dealing with property, with contracts, or even just
접속사 / 분사구문 / 전명구1 / 전명구2
with the routine exchange of goods and services, concepts and
전명구3 / 주어1
descriptions need to be as precise and unambiguous as possible,
동사구1 「as + 원급 + as possible : 가능한 한 ~한/하게」
otherwise misunderstandings will arise.
그렇지 않으면 / 주어2 / 동사구2(자동사)

---

04 딸기 축제 공지 정답률 87% | 정답 ④

2022 Strawberry Festival에 관한 다음 안내문의 내용과 일치하지 않는 것은?

① 올해는 대면 행사로 개최된다.
② 6세 이하의 어린이에게는 입장료를 받지 않는다.
③ 딸기파이 먹기 대회가 오후에 열린다.
✔ 매표소로 가는 트램 서비스는 주차비에 포함되지 않는다.
⑤ 자원봉사에 관심이 있다면 신청서를 이메일로 보내야 한다.

[본문 해석]

2022 딸기 축제

즐거운 가족 축제에 함께하세요. 『올해에는 Berry Square에서 대면 행사를 다시 개최하게 되었습니다!』┐:①의 근거 일치

□ **날짜:** 2022년 11월 26일(오전 11시–오후 5시)
□ **티켓:** 1인당 20달러 『6세 이하의 아이들은 무료입니다.』┐:②의 근거 일치

□ **특별행사**
• 오전 11시 : 아이들을 위한 베이킹 수업
• 『오후 1시 : 딸기파이 먹기 대회』┐:③의 근거 일치
• 오후 3시 : 딸기 의상 대회

□ **참고**
• 『주차비는 5달러이며, 매표소로 가는 트램 서비스가 포함됩니다.』┐:④의 근거 불일치
• 『자원봉사에 관심이 있으시다면, 신청서를 작성하여 manager@strawberryfestival. org로 이메일을 보내 주십시오.』┐:⑤의 근거 일치

Why? 왜 정답일까?

'The parking fee is $5 and includes tram service to the ticket booth.'에서 주차비 5달러에는 매표소까지 가는 트램 서비스가 포함되어 있다고 하므로, 안내문의 내용과 일치하지 않는 것은 ④ '매표소로 가는 트램 서비스는 주차비에 포함되지 않는다.'이다.

Why? 왜 오답일까?

① 'This year, we are back to hosting an in-person event in Berry Square!'의 내용과 일치한다.
② '(Children 6 and under are FREE.)'의 내용과 일치한다.
③ '1:00 p.m. : Strawberry Pie–Eating Contest'의 내용과 일치한다.

---

⑤ 'If you are interested in volunteering, complete an application form and email it to manager@strawberryfestival.org.'의 내용과 일치한다.

- be back to 다시 ~하게 되다
- square ⓝ 광장
- volunteer ⓥ 자원봉사하다

- in-person ⓐ 직접 하는, 대면의
- ticket booth 매표소
- application ⓝ 신청, 지원

★★★ 1등급 대비 고난도 3점 문제

05 이집트 예술의 기념비적 특성 정답률 31% | 정답 ②

다음 글의 밑줄 친 부분 중, 어법상 틀린 것은? [3점]

[본문 해석]

'기념비적'이라는 말은 이집트 예술의 기본적인 특징을 표현하는 데 매우 근접한 단어이다. 그 이전에도 이후에도 기념비성이라는 특성이 이집트에서 그랬듯 완전히 달성된 적은 한 번도 없었다. 이에 대한 이유는 그들 작품의 외적 크기와 거대함이 아닌데, 비록 이 점에서 이집트인들이 확실히 몇 가지 대단한 것들을 달성했다는 점에도 불구하고 그러하다. 많은 현대 구조물은 순전히 물리적인 크기 면에서는 이집트의 구조물들을 능가한다. 그러나 거대함은 기념비성과는 아무 관련이 없다. 예를 들어, 겨우 사람 손 크기의 이집트의 조각이 Leipzig의 전쟁 기념비를 구성하는 그 거대한 돌무더기보다 더 기념비적이다. 기념비성은 외적 무게의 문제가 아니라 '내적 무게'의 문제이다. 이 내적 무게가 이집트 예술이 지닌 특성인데, 이집트 예술은 그 안에 있는 모든 작품이 단지 폭이 몇 인치에 불과하거나 나무에 새겨져 있을지라도, 마치 산맥처럼 원시 시대의 돌로 만들어진 것처럼 보일 정도이다.

Why? 왜 정답일까?

비교 구문의 as 앞에 'be + 과거분사' 형태의 수동태 동사가 나오고, 이집트의 예술은 과거의 예술이므로, as 뒤의 대동사 자리에는 did 대신 was를 쓰는 것이 적절하다. 따라서 어법상 틀린 것은 ②이다.

Why? 왜 오답일까?

① 'close to(~에 근접한)'에서 to는 전치사이므로, 이 뒤에 목적어로서 동명사 expressing을 쓴 것은 적절하다.
③ structures를 받는 지시대명사로서 those를 쓴 것은 어법상 맞다.
④ 선행사 that gigantic pile를 꾸미는 주격 관계대명사로서 that을 쓴 것은 어법상 맞다.
⑤ 문맥상 even if절의 주어는 나무에 '새겨진' 예술 작품을 가리키므로, is 뒤에 수동태를 이루는 과거분사 carved를 쓴 것은 어법상 맞다.

- monumental ⓐ 기념비적인, 엄청난
- admittedly ⓐⓓ 인정컨대
- have nothing to do with ~와 관련이 없다
- carve ⓥ 새기다, 파다, 조각하다

- massiveness ⓝ 거대함, 육중함
- respect ⓝ 점, 측면, 사항
- possess ⓥ 지니다, 소유하다

구문 풀이

3행 Never before and never since has the quality of monumentality
「부정어구 + / have + / 주어 +
been achieved as fully as it was in Egypt.
과거분사」: 도치 구문 「as + 원급 + as(~만큼) : 원급 비교」

15행 This inner weight is the quality [which Egyptian art possesses
선행사 / 목·관·대
/ to such a degree that everything in it seems to be made of primeval
~할 정도로 / 주어 / 동사 / ~로 만들어지다
stone, like a mountain range, / even if it is only a few inches across
비록 ~일지라도 / 보어1
or carved in wood].
보어2(수동태)

★★ 문제 해결 꿀~팁 ★★

▶ **많이 틀린 이유는?**

최다 오답인 ⑤는 be동사 뒤에 보어처럼 나오는 분사의 태를 묻고 있는데, 문맥상 even if절의 주어인 it이 사물을 대신하는 대명사로서 예술 작품을 가리키므로, 이를 '새겨진' 행위의 객체로 보아 과거분사 carved를 쓴 것은 적절하다. 이 과거분사는 or 앞의 보어와도 병렬 관계를 이룬다.

▶ **문제 해결 방법은?**

비교 구문의 as, than 뒤에 do가 대동사로 나오려면 앞에 일반동사가 나와야 한다. 여기서는 앞에 현재완료 수동태인 has been achieved가 동사로 나오므로 do/does/did로 대신하기에 적절하지 않다.

DAY **20**

06 비행 조종에서 기술에 대한 의존이 낳는 역설   정답률 48% | 정답 ⑤

다음 글의 밑줄 친 부분 중, 문맥상 낱말의 쓰임이 적절하지 <u>않은</u> 것은?

[본문 해석]

가장 진보된 군사용 제트기는 전자식 비행 조종 장치이다. 그것들은 매우 불안정해서 계속 제어하려면 인간 조작자보다 더 빠르게 감지하고 행동할 수 있는 자동화된 시스템이 필요하다. 스마트 기술에 대한 우리의 의존은 ① 역설로 이어졌다. 기술이 향상될수록 그 기술은 신뢰성과 효율성이 더 높아지고, 인간 조작자들은 훨씬 더 그것에 의존한다. 결국, 그들은 집중력을 잃고, ② 산만해지며, 시스템이 스스로 작동하도록 내버려 둔 채로 떠난다. 가장 극단적인 경우, 대형 여객기를 조종하는 것은 TV를 보는 것과 같은 ③ 수동적인 직업이 될 수 있다. 이것은 예상치 못한 일이 일어나기 전까지는 괜찮다. 예상치 못한 일은 인간의 가치를 드러낸다. 우리가 제시하는 것은 새로운 상황에 대처할 수 있는 ④ 유연성이다. 기계는 공동의 목표를 추구하기 위해 협력하는 것이 아니라 단지 도구의 역할을 할 뿐이다. 따라서 인간 조작자가 관리를 포기하면 그 시스템이 심각한 사고를 겪을 가능성이 ⑤ 더 적을(→ 더 많을) 것이다.

Why? 왜 정답일까?

전자식 비행 조종 장치에 다양한 스마트 기술이 도입되면서 인간 조작자는 기술에 더 많이 의지하게 되었지만, 예기치 못한 상황이나 사고 속에서는 인간 조작자의 역할이 여전히 필요하고 중요하다는 내용의 글이다. ⑤가 포함된 문장 앞에서 기술 또는 기계는 인간의 협력자라기보다는 도구에 불과하다고 하므로, 인간 조작자가 관리 의무를 포기한 상황을 설명하는 ⑤는 심각한 사고가 일어날 가능성이 '더 커진다'는 의미여야 한다. 즉 **less**를 **more**로 고쳐야 문맥이 자연스럽다. 따라서 문맥상 낱말의 쓰임이 적절하지 않은 것은 ⑤이다.

- **advanced** ⓐ 진보된, 고급의
- **automate** ⓥ 자동화하다
- **dependence** ⓝ 의존
- **lose focus** 집중력을 잃다
- **occupation** ⓝ 직업, 일
- **bring to the table** 제시하다
- **in pursuit of** ~을 추구하여
- **unstable** ⓐ 불안정한
- **operator** ⓝ 조작자
- **reliable** ⓐ 믿을 만한
- **distracted** ⓐ 산만한, 주의가 분산된
- **unexpected** ⓐ 예상치 못한
- **flexibility** ⓝ 유연성
- **oversight** ⓝ 관리, 감독

구문 풀이

12행 The unexpected reveals the value of humans; {what we bring
주어1(the + 형용사: ~한 것) 동사1
to the table} is the flexibility to handle new situations.
{ }: 주어2(명사절) → 동사2(단수)

★★★ 1등급 대비 고난도 2점 문제

07 자부심과 연관된 신체적 표현의 보편성   정답률 36% | 정답 ①

다음 빈칸에 들어갈 말로 가장 적절한 것을 고르시오.

✓ innate – 선천적인   ② creative – 창의적인
③ unidentifiable – 확인 불가능한   ④ contradictory – 모순적인
⑤ offensive – 모욕적인

[본문 해석]

여러분은 자부심을 드러내는 신체적 표현이 생물학적 기반을 두고 있을 것으로 기대하는가, 아니면 문화적으로 특정할 것으로 기대하는가? 심리학자 Jessica Tracy는 어린아이들이 누군가가 언제 자부심을 느끼는지를 알아볼 수 있다는 것을 발견했다. 더욱이, 그녀는 서구와의 접촉이 아주 적은 고립된 인구 집단 또한 정확하게 그 신체 신호를 알아본다는 것을 발견했다. 이러한 신호에는 웃고 있는 얼굴, 들어 올린 두 팔, 펼친 가슴, 그리고 밖으로 내민 상체가 포함된다. Tracy와 David Matsumoto는 2004년 올림픽 대회와 장애인 올림픽 대회의 유도 경기에서 시합을 치르는 선수들에게서 자부심을 드러내는 반응들을 조사했다. 37개 국가 출신의 볼 수 있는 선수들과 시각 장애가 있는 선수들이 시합을 치렀다. 승리 후에, 앞을 볼 수 있는 선수들과 시각 장애가 있는 선수들이 보여준 행동은 매우 비슷했다. 이러한 연구 결과는 자부심을 드러내는 반응이 선천적이라는 것을 보여준다.

Why? 왜 정답일까?

첫 문장에서 자부심을 드러내는 신체 표현이 생물학적인 요소 혹은 문화적 요소 중 어느 것에 영향을 받는지 질문한 뒤 예시를 통해 답을 도출하는 글이다. 두 번째와 세 번째 문장에서 아이들 또는 서구 문화권과의 교류가 적은 고립된 인구 집단이 모두 자부심의 신체 신호를 정확히 인지할 수 있었다는 예가 제시된 뒤, 빈칸 앞의 문장에서는 시각 장애

가 있(기에 남의 신호를 눈으로 보고 학습할 수 없는 선수들 또한 비장애인 선수들과 비슷한 자부심의 신체 신호를 보였다는 예가 추가로 제시된다. 이는 자부심으로 인한 신체의 반응이 일종의 문화로서 후천적으로 학습된 것이 아니라 '타고났기에' 어느 정도 보편적임을 보여주는 것이므로, 빈칸에 들어갈 말로 가장 적절한 것은 ① '선천적인'이다.

- **pride** ⓝ 자랑스러움
- **specific** ⓐ 특정적인, 구체적인
- **isolated** ⓐ 고립된
- **minimal** ⓐ 최소의, 아주 적은
- **identify** ⓥ 알아보다, 확인하다
- **pushed-out** 밖으로 내밀어진
- **compete** ⓥ 경쟁하다
- **biologically** ⓐⓓ 생물학적으로
- **recognize** ⓥ 인식하다, 알아보다
- **population** ⓝ 인구
- **accurately** ⓐⓓ 정확하게
- **expanded** ⓐ 펼쳐진, 넓어진, 확대된
- **examine** ⓥ 조사하다, 검토하다
- **sighted** ⓐ 앞을 볼 수 있는

구문 풀이

1행 Would you expect the physical expression of pride to be
「expect + 목적어 + to부정사: ~이 …하리라고 기대하다」
보어1
biologically based or culturally specific?
보어2

★★ 문제 해결 꿀~팁 ★★

▶ 많이 틀린 이유는?
연구의 결론인 주제문을 완성하는 빈칸 문제로, 예시를 읽고 공통된 결론을 유추해야 한다. 어린 아이들, 문화적으로 고립된 인구 집단, 시각 장애가 있는 선수 집단 모두 나이, 문화, 장애 여부와 상관없이 자부심의 신체 표현을 이해하거나 보여주었다는 내용으로 보아, 자부심의 신체적 반응은 생물학적 기반을 두고 있다고 이해해야 옳다. ③은 자부심의 신체 표현이 어떤 것인지 알아보거나 확인할 수 없다는 뜻이므로 글의 내용과 다르다.

▶ 문제 해결 방법은?
연구 내용에 나오는 어린 아이들, 문화적으로 고립된 인구 집단, 시각 장애가 있는 선수들은 첫 문장의 **biologically based**의 예시이고, 이를 달리 표현한 말이 **innate**임에 유의한다.

---

08 창의성과 생산성의 관계   정답률 47% | 정답 ④

글의 흐름으로 보아, 주어진 문장이 들어가기에 가장 적절한 곳을 고르시오. [3점]

[본문 해석]

창의성은 생산성에 영향을 미칠 수 있다. 창의성은 어떤 이들이 남들은 보지 못하는 문제들을 인식하게 하지만, 이는 매우 어려울 수도 있다. ① 종 분화 문제에 대한 찰스 다윈의 접근이 이것의 좋은 예시인데, 그는 매우 어렵고 복잡한 문제인 종 분화를 선택했고, 이것은 그를 오랜 자료 수집과 심사숙고의 기간으로 이끌었다. ② 이러한 문제 선택은 빠른 착수나 간단한 실험을 허용하지 않았다. ③ 이 경우, 노력은 어려운 문제에 집중되기 때문에 창의성은 (출판물의 수로 측정되듯) 사실 생산성을 감소시킬 수 있다. ④ 창의성이 방법과 기술에 더 집중돼 있는 다른 이들의 경우, 창의성은 문제 해결에 필요한 작업을 극적으로 줄이는 해결책으로 이어질 수 있다. 우리는 작은 DNA 조각들을 짧은 시간에 증폭시켜 주는 중합 효소 연쇄 반응(PCR)의 개발에서 한 예를 볼 수 있다. ⑤ 이러한 유형의 창의성은 단계의 수를 줄이거나 실패할 가능성이 더 낮은 단계로 대체해주고, 그리하여 생산성을 높일 수도 있다.

Why? 왜 정답일까?

창의성이 생산성에 부정적 또는 긍정적 영향을 끼친다는 내용으로, ④ 앞에서는 창의성으로 인해 생산성이 떨어지는 예시를, ④ 뒤에서는 생산성이 오르는 사례를 보여주고 있다. 따라서 생산성의 긍정적 영향에 관한 설명으로 넘어가는 주어진 문장이 들어가기에 가장 적절한 곳은 ④이다.

- **lead to** ~로 이어지다
- **productivity** ⓝ 생산성
- **tangled** ⓐ 복잡한, 뒤엉킨
- **publication** ⓝ 출판(물)
- **polymerase chain reaction** 중합 효소 연쇄 반응
- **amplify** ⓥ 증폭하다
- **drastically** ⓐⓓ 극적으로
- **speciation** ⓝ 종(種) 분화
- **deliberation** ⓝ 숙고
- **development** ⓝ 개발, 발전, 전개
- **substitute** ⓥ 대체하다

구문 풀이

1행 For others, whose creativity is more focused on methods and
선행사 소유격 관계대명사
technique, creativity may lead to solutions [that drastically reduce
the work necessary to solve a problem]. [ ]: 형용사절(solutions 수식)
형용사구

09 학습에 영향을 미칠 수 있는 문화적 지식
정답률 66% | 정답 ①

다음 글의 내용을 한 문장으로 요약하고자 한다. 빈칸 (A), (B)에 들어갈 말로 가장 적절한 것은?

	(A)		(B)
✓①	cultural 문화적	……	learning 학습
②	cultural 문화적	……	responsibility 책임감
③	mathematical 수학적	……	imagination 상상력
④	mathematical 수학적	……	intelligence 지능
⑤	nutritional 영양적	……	development 발달

[본문 해석]
한 초등학교 선생님이 자신이 생각하기에 아주 흔히 언급되는 것을 사용해서 학생들이 분수 부분을 이해하도록 돕고 있는 중이다. "오늘, 우리는 추수감사절에 인기 있는 것인 호박 파이를 자르는 것에 대해 이야기할 거예요." 그녀는 분수 부분에 대한 설명을 이어간다. 그녀의 이야기에 열심히 몰두한 채로, 한 어린 아프리카계 미국인 소년이 의아해 보이는 모습으로 질문한다. "호박 파이가 뭐예요?" 대부분의 아프리카계 미국인들은 명절 만찬으로 고구마 파이를 내는 경향이 있다. 사실, 아프리카계 미국인 부모들이 그들의 자녀들에게 호박 파이를 설명하는 방식 중 하나는 그것이 고구마 파이와 비슷한 무언가라고 말하는 것이다. 그들에게 있어서는 고구마 파이가 흔하게 언급되는 것이다. 심지어 호박 파이에 대한 낯섦이라는 작은 차이도 그 학생에게는 간섭의 원인으로 작용할 수 있다. 그 수업에 적극적으로 참여하기보다는, 그는 호박 파이를 상상하기 위해 노력하는 데 사로잡혀 있었을지도 모른다. 그건 무슨 맛일까? 무슨 향이 날까? 그것의 질감은 사과나 체리 파이처럼 덩어리가 져 있을까? 한 아이의 마음속에서, 이러한 모든 질문들은 그 선생님이 가르치려 시도하는 분수라는 주제보다 더 초점이 될 수 있다.

➡ (A) <u>문화적</u> 지식에서의 작은 차이조차도 학생들의 (B) <u>학습</u>에 영향을 미칠 잠재성이 있다.

Why? 왜 정답일까?
'Even the slight difference of being unfamiliar with pumpkin pie can serve as a source of interference for the student.'에서 문화적 지식에서의 아주 작은 차이라도 학생이 지식을 습득하는 데 간섭할 수 있다는 내용이 나오므로, 요약문의 빈칸 (A), (B)에 들어갈 말로 가장 적절한 것은 ① '(A) cultural(문화적), (B) learning(학습)'이다.

- **commonplace** ⓐ 아주 흔한
- **slight** ⓐ 작은, 사소한
- **interference** ⓝ 간섭, 방해, 개입
- **chunky** ⓐ 덩어리가 진, 두툼한
- **referent** ⓝ 지시 대상
- **unfamiliar** ⓐ 낯선, 친숙하지 않은
- **preoccupied with** ~에 사로잡힌
- **nutritional** ⓐ 영양의, 영양상의

구문 풀이
1행 A primary school teacher is helping students to understand
　　　　준사역동사(현재진행) 　　목적어 　　목적격 보어
fractional parts by using what (she thinks) is a commonplace reference.
~함으로써　관계대명사　( ): 삽입절 └동사

10-12 위기를 기회로 바꾼 Victor

[본문 해석]

(A)
『Victor는 아주 큰 회사의 사무실 청소부 자리에 지원했다.』「┌:12번 ①의 근거 일치」 매니저는 그를 인터뷰한 뒤, 청소하기, 비품 정리하기, 지정된 부서에 비품 보급하기 등 그를 테스트해 보았다. (a) 그가 하는 일을 지켜본 후, 매니저는 말했다. "당신은 채용되었습니다. 이메일 주소를 알려 주세요, 그럼 작성하실 몇 가지 서류들을 보내드리겠습니다."

(C)
Victor는 대답했다. "저는 컴퓨터도 없고 이메일도 없습니다." "유감이네요,"라고 매니저가 말했다. 그리고 그는 덧붙였다. "만약 당신이 이메일이 없다면 이 일을 어떻게 하려고 합니까? 이 작업을 하려면 당신은 이메일 주소를 가지고 있어야 합니다. 당신을 채용할 수 없습니다." Victor는 아무 희망도 없이 떠났다. 주머니에 10달러만 가진 채, (d) 그는 어떻게 해야 할지 몰랐다. 『그리고 나서

그는 슈퍼마켓에 가기로 결심하고 10kg짜리 토마토 한 상자를 샀다.』
「┌:12번 ③의 근거 일치」

(B)
그 뒤 (b) 그는 집집마다 돌아다니며 토마토를 팔았다. 『2시간 만에, 그는 자본금을 두 배로 늘리는 데 성공했다.』「┌:12번 ②의 근거 일치」 그는 이 작업을 세 번 반복했고 60달러를 가지고 집으로 돌아왔다. Victor는 이런 방법으로 살아남을 수 있다는 것을 깨닫고, 매일 더 일찍 나가기 시작했고, 늦게 돌아왔다. 이런 식으로, (c) 그의 돈은 매일 두 배 또는 세 배로 불었다. 얼마 지나지 않아, 그는 카트를 사고, 트럭을 사고, 이후 자기 배달 차량을 여러 대 갖게 되었다.

(D)
『몇 년 후, Victor의 회사는 시에서 가장 큰 식품 회사가 되었다.』「┌:12번 ④의 근거 일치」 그는 가족의 미래를 계획하기 시작했고, 생명 보험에 가입하기로 결심했다. 그는 보험 중개인을 불렀다. 대화가 끝나자, (e) 그는 그에게 이메일을 물었다. 『Victor가 대답했다. "저는 이메일이 없어요."』「┌:12번 ⑤의 근거 불일치」 중개인은 의아해하며 대답했다. "당신은 이메일이 없는데도 성공적으로 제국을 건설했군요. 이메일이 있었다면 어땠을지 상상되나요?" 그는 잠시 생각한 뒤 대답했다. "사무실 청소부가 됐을 겁니다!"

- **apply for** ~에 지원하다
- **supply** ⓥ 보급하다, 제공하다
- **facility** ⓝ 시설
- **double** ⓥ 두 배로 만들다, 두 배가 되다
- **repeated** ⓐ 반복[되풀이]되는
- **triple** ⓥ 3배가 되다
- **intend** ⓥ 의도하다, 작정하다
- **several pron** 몇의
- **broker** ⓝ 중개인
- **curiously** ⓐⓓ 의아해하며, 신기한 듯이
- **stock** ⓥ (식품·책 등으로) 채우다
- **designate** ⓥ 지정하다
- **fill out** (서류 등을) 작성하다
- **capital** ⓝ 자본
- **operation** ⓝ (조직적인) 작업
- **reply** ⓥ 대답하다
- **require** ⓥ 필요하다, 필요로 하다
- **life insurance** 생명 보험
- **conclude** ⓥ 끝내다, 마치다
- **empire** ⓝ 거대 기업, 제국

구문 풀이
(A) 2행 The manager interviewed him, then gave him a test: cleaning,
stocking, and supplying designated facility areas.
　　　　　　　　　　　　　동격(= a test)

(B) 4행 Victor realized that he could survive by this way, and started
　　　　　　　동사1　접속사(~것)　　　　　　　　　　　　　동사2
to go every day earlier, and returned late.
　　　　　　　　　　　　　　동사3

10 글의 순서 파악
정답률 84% | 정답 ②

주어진 글 (A)에 이어질 내용을 순서에 맞게 배열한 것으로 가장 적절한 것은?

① (B) – (D) – (C)　　　✓② (C) – (B) – (D)
③ (C) – (D) – (B)　　　④ (D) – (B) – (C)
⑤ (D) – (C) – (B)

Why? 왜 정답일까?
Victor가 사무실 청소부 자리에 지원하여 합격 통보와 함께 이메일 주소를 요청받았다는 내용의 (A) 뒤로, Victor가 이메일이 없다고 답하여 입사를 취소당한 뒤 주머니에 있던 10달러로 토마토를 한 상자 샀다는 내용의 (C)가 연결된다. 이어 (B)에서는 Victor가 이 토마토를 팔아 2시간 만에 자본금을 두 배로 늘렸고, 같은 식으로 장사를 계속하여 배달 차량을 여러 개 사들일 정도로 돈을 벌었다는 내용을 전개한다. 마지막으로 (D)는 Victor가 몇 년 뒤 시에서 가장 큰 식품 회사를 갖게 되어 미래 대비 차원으로 보험을 알아보다가 이메일 주소를 다시금 요청받는 자신의 인생을 되돌아보았다는 내용으로 마무리된다. 따라서 글의 순서로 가장 적절한 것은 ② '(C) – (B) – (D)'이다.

11 지칭 추론
정답률 83% | 정답 ⑤

밑줄 친 (a) ~ (e) 중에서 가리키는 대상이 나머지 넷과 다른 것은?

① (a)　② (b)　③ (c)　④ (d)　✓⑤ (e)

Why? 왜 정답일까?
(a), (b), (c), (d)는 Victor, (e)는 앞 문장의 an insurance broker를 가리키므로, (a) ~ (e) 중에서 가리키는 대상이 다른 하나는 ⑤ '(e)'이다.

12 세부 내용 파악
정답률 87% | 정답 ⑤

윗글의 Victor에 관한 내용으로 적절하지 <u>않은</u> 것은?

① 사무실 청소부 자리에 지원하였다.
② 2시간 만에 자본금을 두 배로 만들었다.
③ 슈퍼마켓에 가서 토마토를 샀다.
④ 그의 회사는 도시에서 가장 큰 식품 회사가 되었다.
☑ 이메일이 있다고 보험 중개인에게 답했다.

Why? 왜 정답일까?

(D) 'Victor replied: "I don't have an email."'에서 알 수 있듯이 Victor는 이메일이 있느냐는 보험 중개인의 질문에 '이메일이 없다'고 답하였다. 따라서 내용과 일치하지 않는 것은 ⑤ '이메일이 있다고 보험 중개인에게 답했다.'이다.

Why? 왜 오답일까?

① (A) 'Victor applied for the position of office cleaner at a very big company.'의 내용과 일치한다.
② (B) 'In two hours, he succeeded to double his capital.'의 내용과 일치한다.
③ (C) 'He then decided to go to the supermarket and bought a 10kg box of tomatoes.'의 내용과 일치한다.
④ (D) 'Several years later, Victor's company became the biggest food company in his city.'의 내용과 일치한다.

DAY 21 〉 20분 미니 모의고사

01 ⑤	02 ①	03 ②	04 ③	05 ③
06 ①	07 ②	08 ④	09 ④	10 ③
11 ③	12 ④			

---

01 타인을 설득하는 방법에 관한 조언 　　　정답률 84% | 정답 ⑤

다음 글에서 필자가 주장하는 바로 가장 적절한 것은?
① 타인의 신뢰를 얻기 위해서는 일관된 행동을 보여 주어라.
② 협상을 잘하기 위해 질문에 담긴 상대방의 의도를 파악하라.
③ 논쟁을 잘하려면 자신의 가치관에서 벗어나려는 시도를 하라.
④ 원만한 대인 관계를 유지하려면 상대를 배려하는 태도를 갖춰라.
☑ 설득하고자 할 때 상대방이 스스로 관점을 돌아보게 하는 질문을 하라.

[본문 해석]

누군가를 그 마음을 바꾸도록 설득하고자 할 때 대부분의 사람들이 논리적 주장을 펼치거나 또는 왜 자신의 관점이 옳고 다른 사람의 의견이 틀린지에 대해 열정적으로 항변한다. 하지만 여러분이 그것에 대해 생각해 보면 여러분은 이것이 종종 효과가 없다는 것을 깨달을 것이다. 누군가가 여러분이 자신의 마음을 바꾸려는 임무를 띠고 있다는 것을 알아차리자마자 은유적인 (마음의) 셔터는 내려간다. 만약 여러분이 누군가에게 자기 자신의 가정을 의심하도록 하는 잘 선택된, 다양한 대답이 가능한 질문을 한다면 여러분은 더 좋은 운이 따를 것이다. 만약 우리가 어떤 견해를 먼저 생각해 냈거나 최소한 우리가 그것을 먼저 생각해 냈다고 *생각한다면*, 우리는 그 견해를 인정하려는 경향이 있다. 그러므로 누군가에게 자기 자신의 세계관에 의문을 갖도록 장려하는 것은 그들에게 여러분의 의견을 사실로 받아들이도록 강요하려고 하는 것보다 종종 더 나은 결과를 가져올 것이다. 누군가에게 그들 자신의 관점을 다른 각도에서 바라보도록 잘 선택된 질문을 하면, 이것은 새로운 통찰력을 유발할 것이다.

Why? 왜 정답일까?

'Therefore, encouraging someone to question their own worldview will often yield better results than trying to force them into accepting your opinion as fact. Ask someone well-chosen questions to look at their own views from another angle, ~'에서 상대방을 설득하려고 할 때 의견을 관철하기보다는 상대방이 스스로 자기 자신의 견해를 돌아보게 할 수 있는 잘 선택된 질문을 던지는 것이 좋다고 하므로, 필자가 주장하는 바로 가장 적절한 것은 ⑤ '설득하고자 할 때 상대방이 스스로 관점을 돌아보게 하는 질문을 하라.'이다.

- **convince** ⓥ 설득하다
- **make a plea** 항변하다, 간청하다
- **metaphorical** ⓐ 비유의, 은유의
- **assumption** ⓝ 가정
- **yield** ⓥ (결과를) 내다, 산출하다
- **lay out** 펼치다
- **passionate** ⓐ 열정적인
- **open-ended** ⓐ 정해진 답이 없는, 주관식의
- **approve of** ~을 인정하다
- **trigger** ⓥ 유발하다

구문 풀이

12행 Therefore, encouraging someone to question their own
동명사구 주어 「encourage + 목적어 + to부정사 : ~이 …하게 장려하다」
worldview will often yield better results than trying to force them
동사구　　　목적어　　　　　동명사구(주어와 병렬)
into accepting your opinion as fact.

---

02 고객의 브랜드 칭찬에 응답하기 　　　정답률 81% | 정답 ①

다음 글의 요지로 가장 적절한 것은?
☑ 고객과의 관계 증진을 위해 고객의 브랜드 칭찬에 응답하는 것은 중요하다.
② 고객의 피드백을 면밀히 분석함으로써 브랜드의 성공 가능성을 높일 수 있다.
③ 신속한 고객 응대를 통해서 고객의 긍정적인 반응을 이끌어 낼 수 있다.
④ 브랜드 매니저에게는 고객의 부정적인 의견을 수용하는 태도가 요구된다.
⑤ 고객의 의견을 경청하는 것은 브랜드의 새로운 이미지 창출에 도움이 된다.

[본문 해석]

여러분의 응답을 우선시할 수 있다는 것은 여러분이 고객들 개인과 더 깊은 관계를 맺을 수 있게 해 주는데, 특별히 즐겁거나 화가 나는 경험을 둘러싼 일회성 소통이든, 혹은 여러분의 고객 기반 내에서 상당히 영향력 있는 개인과의 장기적 관계를 쌓는 것이든 간에 그렇다. 만약 여러분이 어떤 브랜드, 제품 또는 서비스에 관해 호의적인 의견이나 혹은 그 문제에 대한 무슨 의견이든 올려 본 적이 있다면, 그 결과로 가령 그 브랜드 매니저한테 개인적으로 인정의 반응을 얻는다면 어떤 기분일지 생각해 보라. 일반적으로, 사람들은 할 말이 있어서, 그리고 그 말한 것에 대해 인정받기를 위해서 글을 올린다. 특히, 사람들이 긍정적인 의견을 게시할 때 그것은 그 게시물을 작성하게 만든 경험에 대한 감사의 표현이다. 여러분 옆에 서 있는 사람에 대한 칭찬은 보통 '감사합니다'와 같은 답을 받지만, 슬픈 사실은 대부분의 브랜드 칭찬은 답을 받지 못한다는 것이다. 이것은 무엇이 칭찬을 이끌어냈는지 이해하고, 그 칭찬을 바탕으로 하여 확고한 팬을 만들어 낼 수 있는 기회를 잃은 것이다.

Why? 왜 정답일까?

고객들의 코멘트에 대한 답변을 우선시하는 것이 고객과의 관계 형성에 도움이 된다(Being able to prioritize your responses allows you to connect more deeply with individual customers)는 내용으로, 마지막 두 문장에서 사실 많은 브랜드가 고객의 긍정적 의견에 제대로 응답하지 않아 확고한 팬층을 만들 기회를 놓치고 있다고 지적하고 있다. 따라서 글의 요지로 가장 적절한 것은 ① '고객과의 관계 증진을 위해 고객의 브랜드 칭찬에 응답하는 것은 중요하다.'이다.

- prioritize ⓥ 우선시하다
- one-off ⓐ 일회성의, 단 한 번의
- significantly ⓐⓓ 상당히
- customer base 고객층
- acknowledge ⓥ 감사하다, 인정하다
- appreciation ⓝ 감사
- go unanswered 대답이 없다
- connect with ~와 관계 맺다, 연결하다
- long-term ⓐ 장기의
- influential ⓐ 영향력 있는
- favorable ⓐ 호의적인
- recognize ⓥ 인정하다
- compliment ⓝ 칭찬
- solid ⓐ 확고한, 탄탄한

구문 풀이

6행 If you've ever posted a favorable comment — (or any comment, for that matter) — about a brand, product or service, think about what it would feel like if you were personally acknowledged by the

가정법 과거(주절 + 조동사 과거형 + 동사원형 ~, if + 주어 + were ~)

삽입구

brand manager, ~

---

03 학습에 도움을 주는 잠   정답률 78% | 정답 ②

다음 글의 주제로 가장 적절한 것은?

① how to get an adequate amount of sleep
적절한 양의 수면을 취하는 방법
② the role that sleep plays in the learning process
잠이 학습 과정에 수행하는 역할
③ a new method of stimulating engagement in learning
학습 참여를 촉진하는 새로운 방법
④ an effective way to keep your mind alert and active
정신을 초롱초롱하고 활동적으로 유지하는 효과적인 방법
⑤ the side effects of certain medications on brain function
특정 약물이 뇌 기능에 끼치는 부작용

[본문 해석]

우리는 학습이 규칙적인 간격으로 이뤄질 때 훨씬 더 효율적이라는 것을 이미 보았다. 즉, 모든 과업을 하루에 밀어 넣기보다 그 과업을 분산하는 것이 더 좋다. 그 이유는 간단한데, 매일 밤 우리의 뇌는 그날 학습한 것을 통합 정리하기 때문이다. 이것은 지난 30년 동안 이뤄진 가장 중요한 신경과학 발견들 중 하나로, 잠은 단순한 비활동이나 우리가 깨어있는 동안 뇌가 축적하는 쓸모없는 생산물들의 쓰레기 수집 기간이 아니라는 것이다. 정반대로, 우리가 자는 동안 우리의 뇌는 활동적인 상태를 유지하며, 전날 하루 동안 기록한 중요한 사건들을 재상영하고 그것을 우리 기억의 더 효율적인 구획으로 점진적으로 이동시키는 특별한 알고리즘을 가동한다.

Why? 왜 정답일까?

우리가 자는 동안 뇌가 오히려 활성화 상태를 유지하여 그날 배운 것을 정리하고 조직화하는 과정이 이뤄진다(Quite the contrary: while we sleep, our brain remains active; it runs a specific algorithm ~)는 마지막 문장 내용으로 보아, 글의 주제로 가장 적절한 것은 ② '잠이 학습 과정에 수행하는 역할'이다.

- interval ⓝ 간격
- well off 잘 사는, 사정이 좋은
- cram ⓥ 밀어 넣다, 벼락치기하다
- spread out 펼쳐놓다

- accumulate ⓥ 축적하다, 모으다
- gradually ⓐⓓ 점진적으로, 점차
- quite the contrary 그와는 정반대이다
- side effect 부작용

구문 풀이

1행 We have already seen that learning is much more efficient when (it is) done at regular intervals: ~

접속사 생략 과거분사   비교급 강조(훨씬)

---

04 공원 점심 행사   정답률 91% | 정답 ③

Out to Lunch에 관한 다음 안내문의 내용과 일치하는 것은?

① 일 년 내내 수요일마다 열리는 행사이다.
② 푸드 트럭에서는 가격을 20% 할인해 준다.
✓③ 라이브 음악 공연이 마련되어 있다.
④ 개인 의자와 담요를 가지고 올 수 없다.
⑤ 주류를 포함한 음료를 마실 수 있다.

[본문 해석]

Out to Lunch(점심을 위한 외출)

맛있는 음식, 좋은 음악과 함께 오후를 즐기고 싶으세요? 'Out to Lunch'는 당신의 요구를 충족시켜 주는 더할 나위 없는 행사입니다! 오셔서 Missoula 시내의 Caras 공원에서 열리는 이 행사를 즐기세요!

날짜 & 시간
- 「6월 매주 수요일, 오후 12시 – 오후 3시」── 「」: ①의 근거 불일치

주요 특징
- 「Diamond 아이스크림을 포함한 모든 푸드 트럭에서 10% 할인」── 「」: ②의 근거 불일치
- 「신인 그룹 Cello Brigade의 라이브 음악 공연」── 「」: ③의 근거 일치
- 아이들을 위한 페이스 페인팅과 물풍선 놀이

공지
- 「개인 접이식 의자와 담요를 가져오세요.」── 「」: ④의 근거 불일치
- 개인 쓰레기를 올바르게 처리해 주세요.
- 「주류를 마시는 것은 엄격하게 금지됩니다.」── 「」: ⑤의 근거 불일치

Why? 왜 정답일까?

'Live music performance of the new group Cello Brigade'에서 신인 그룹의 라이브 공연이 있을 것이라고 하므로, 안내문의 내용과 일치하는 것은 ③ '라이브 음악 공연이 마련되어 있다.'이다.

Why? 왜 오답일까?

① 'Every Wednesday in June, 12 p.m. – 3 p.m.'에서 6월 한 달간 열리는 행사라고 하였다.

② '10% discount at all food trucks including Diamond Ice Cream'에서 할인율은 10%라고 하였다.

④ 'Bring your own lawn chairs and blankets.'에서 개인 의자와 담요를 가지고 오라고 하였다.

⑤ 'Drinking alcoholic beverages is strictly banned.'에서 주류는 엄격히 금지된다고 하였다.

- dispose of ~을 처리하다, ~을 버리다
- ban ⓥ 금지하다
- strictly ⓐⓓ 엄히

---

05 초기 시계의 역사   정답률 56% | 정답 ③

다음 글의 밑줄 친 부분 중, 어법상 틀린 것은? [3점]

[본문 해석]

시간에 대해 생각하면 무엇이 떠오르는가? 몇몇 초기 시계들이 발명됐던 고대 중국의 기원전 4천 년으로 돌아가 보자. 사원의 제자들에게 시간의 개념을 설명하기 위해 중국의 사제들은 시각을 나타내는 매듭이 있는 밧줄을 사원 천장에 매달곤 했다. 그들은 밧줄이 시간의 경과를 보여주면서 균등하게 타버리도록 밧줄 아래부터 불을 붙였다. 많은 사원이 그 당시에 불에 다 타버렸다. 어떤 사람이 물 양동이로 만들어진 시계를 발명할 때까지 사제들은 분명히 그것이 썩 마음에 들지 않았다. 그것(물시계)은 시각을 나타내는 표시가 있고 물로 가득 찬 커다란 양동이에 물이 일정한 속도로 흘러나가도록 구멍들을 뚫음으로써 작동했다. 그리고 나서 사원 제자들은 얼마나 빠르게 양동이 물이 빠졌는지로 시간

을 측정했다. 그것은 확실히 밧줄을 태우는 것보다 훨씬 더 나았으나, 더 중요한 것은 그것이 일단 시간이 지나가고 나면 절대로 되돌릴 수 없다는 점을 제자들에게 가르쳐 주었다는 것이다.

Why? 왜 정답일까?

접속사 until 뒤로 동사가 invented인 완전한 절이 나오므로 was made라는 동사는 쓰일 수 없다. 따라서 앞에 나온 명사 clock을 수식할 수 있도록 was made를 과거분사 made로 고치는 것이 적절하다. 어법상 틀린 것은 ③이다.

Why? 왜 오답일까?

① '~하기 위해'란 뜻의 부사구가 필요하므로 to부정사의 쓰임은 어법상 맞다. 뒤에 나온 'Chinese priests used to dangle ~'는 완전한 절이다.
② 분사구문 'indicating ~'은 '~하면서'로 해석한다.
④ 명사 a large bucket을 꾸미는 말로 'full of ~' 이하의 형용사구가 나왔다.
⑤ 주어 it, 동사 taught, 간접목적어 the students 뒤로 명사절인 that절이 나와 직접목적어 역할을 하는 구조이다.

- **demonstrate** ⓥ 입증하다, 증명하다
- **represent** ⓥ 나타내다, 표현하다
- **obviously** ⓐⓓ 분명히, 명백히
- **rate** ⓝ 속도
- **dangle** ⓥ 매달다, 매달리다, 달랑거리다
- **passage** ⓝ 흐름, 경과
- **measure** ⓥ 재다, 측정하다
- **drain** ⓥ 물이 빠지다, 물을 빼내다

구문 풀이

15행 It was much better than burning ropes for sure, / but more
『비교급 강조부사+비교급+than』
importantly, it taught the students {that (once time was gone), it could
주어　　　동사　　　간접목적어　　　　일단 ~하면
never be recovered}. { }: 직접목적어

★★★ 1등급 대비 고난도 2점 문제

06 실수 효과의 개념 　　　　　정답률 34% | 정답 ①

(A), (B), (C)의 각 네모 안에서 문맥에 맞는 낱말로 가장 적절한 것은?

(A)	(B)	(C)
✓① perceived 인지된	creates 만들며	less 덜
② perceived 인지된	narrows 좁히다	more 더
③ perceived 인지된	creates 만들며	more 더
④ hidden 숨겨진	creates 만들며	less 덜
⑤ hidden 숨겨진	narrows 좁히다	less 덜

[본문 해석]

사회 심리학의 한 현상인 실수 효과는 한 개인의 인지된 매력도가 그 사람이 실수를 한 후에 (A) 인지된 그 사람의 능력에 따라 증가 또는 감소한다고 말한다. 유명 인사들은 일반적으로 능력 있는 사람들로 여겨지고 특정한 측면에서 종종 흠이 없고 완벽하다고도 보이기 때문에, 실수를 저지르는 것은 그 사람의 인간미가 다른 사람들에게 사랑을 받도록 만들 것이다. 기본적으로, 전혀 실수를 범하지 않는 사람들은 이따금 실수를 범하는 사람들에 비해 덜 매력적이거나 덜 호감을 주는 것으로 인지된다. 완벽성, 혹은 그 자질을 개인들에게 귀속하는 것은 일반 대중들이 공감할 수 없는 인지된 거리감을 (B) 만들며 실수를 전혀 범하지 않는 사람들을 덜 매력적이고 덜 호감이 가도록 만든다. 하지만 이것은 또한 정반대의 효과도 가지는데, 평균 혹은 그 이하의 인지된 능력을 가진 사람이 실수를 범한다면, 그 사람은 다른 사람들에게 (C) 덜 매력적이고 호감을 덜 주게 될 것이다.

Why? 왜 정답일까?

(A) 사회 심리학의 실수 효과란 어떤 사람의 '인지된' 능력과 매력도 사이의 관계에 관한 것임을 설명하는 문장이므로, (A)에는 perceived가 적절하다.
(B) 앞 문장에서 실수를 범하지 않는 사람은 '덜 매력적'이라고 여겨지는 경향이 있음을 말하는데, (B)가 있는 문장에서는 이를 '거리감이 생긴다'는 말로 바꾸고 있다. 따라서 (B)에는 creates가 적절하다.
(C) However 앞과는 대조되는 내용이 이어지는 맥락으로, 평균 또는 그 이하의 능력을 가졌다고 여겨지는 사람이 실수를 범하면 오히려 매력이 '떨어진다'는 의미를 나타낼 수 있도록 (C)에는 less가 들어가는 것이 적절하다. 따라서 각 네모 안에서 문맥에 맞는 낱말로 가장 적절한 것은 ① '(A) perceived(인지된) – (B) creates(만들며) – (C) less(덜)' 이다.

- **phenomenon** ⓝ 현상
- **competence** ⓝ 능력, 역량, 유능함
- **commit** ⓥ 범하다, 저지르다
- **attribution** ⓝ (원인의) 귀속
- **attractiveness** ⓝ 매력도, 매력
- **flawless** ⓐ 흠이 없는, 무결점의
- **endearing** ⓐ 사랑스러운
- **relate to** ~에 공감하다, ~에 관련 짓다

구문 풀이

11행 Perfection, or the attribution of that quality to individuals,
주어
creates a perceived distance [that the general public cannot relate to]
동사(단수)　　　　　목적격 관계대명사　　　　~에 공감하다
— making those [who never make mistakes] perceived as being less
분사구문　목적어　　　　　　　　　　　목적격 보어(~라고 여겨지는)
attractive or likable.

★★ 문제 해결 꿀~팁 ★★

▶ 많이 틀린 이유는?
(C)에 들어갈 말을 정확히 고르는 것이 풀이의 성패를 좌우한다. 앞에서 주로 유명인 사의 예를 들어 유능한 사람들이 실수를 하면 도리어 인간적이라고 느껴 호감을 더 느끼게 된다는 내용을 다룬 반면, (C)가 포함된 문장에서는 능력이 '평균 이하'라고 여겨지는 사람들의 예를 들어 이들의 경우 실수를 하면 '덜' 매력적으로 느껴지게 된다는 내용을 전개하고 있다.

▶ 문제 해결 방법은?
However과 'the opposite effect' 등이 답에 대한 결정적인 힌트를 제공하고 있다. 이 역접 표현 앞에서 실수가 많을수록 호감이 상승하는 경우를 언급하므로, 뒤에서는 실수가 많을수록 '호감이 줄어드는' 경우를 언급해야 논리적으로 자연스럽다.

★★★ 1등급 대비 고난도 3점 문제

07 타인을 보이는 대로 판단해서는 안 되는 이유 　　정답률 40% | 정답 ②

다음 빈칸에 들어갈 말로 가장 적절한 것을 고르시오. [3점]
① narrow down your network in social media – 소셜 미디어에서 네트워크를 좁힐
✓② go beyond a person's superficial qualities – 그들의 피상적인 특성을 넘어설
③ focus on intelligence rather than wealth – 부보다는 지능에 집중할
④ trust your first impressions of others – 타인의 첫인상을 믿을
⑤ take advantage of criminals – 범죄자들을 이용할

[본문 해석]

당신은 당신의 아이들에게 낯선 사람을 멀리 하라고 조언하는가? 그것은 어른들에게는 무리한 요구이다. 결국, 당신은 낯선 사람들을 만남으로써 친구 관계를 확장하고 잠재적인 사업 파트너를 만든다. 그러나 이 과정에서, 사람들의 성격을 이해하기 위해 그들을 분석하는 것은 잠재적인 경제적 또는 사회적 이익에 관한 것만은 아니다. 당신이 사랑하는 사람들의 안전뿐 아니라, 당신의 안전도 생각해봐야 한다. 그런 이유로, 은퇴한 FBI 프로파일러인 Mary Ellen O'Toole은 사람들을 이해하기 위해 그들의 피상적인 특성을 넘어설 필요성을 강조한다. 예를 들어, 단지 낯선 이들이 공손하다는 이유로 좋은 이웃이라고 가정하는 것은 안전하지 않다. 매일 아침 잘 차려 입고 외출하는 관행을 따르는 그들을 보는 것이 이야기의 전부인 것은 아니다(매일 아침 그들이 관행처럼 잘 차려입고 외출하는 모습을 본다고 그들의 사정 전부를 알 수는 없다). 사실, O'Toole은 당신이 범죄자를 다룰 때, 심지어 당신의 느낌도 당신을 틀리게 할 수 있다고 말한다. 그것은 범죄자들이 조작과 사기의 기술에 통달했기 때문이다.

Why? 왜 정답일까?

빈칸 뒤의 예시에서 보이는 모습이 공손하다고 하여 어떤 이웃이 좋은 이웃이라고 가정하는 것은 안전하지 않다는 이야기를 통해, 타인을 '보이는 대로 판단하지 않을' 필요성에 대해 언급하고 있다. 따라서 빈칸에 들어갈 말로 가장 적절한 것은 ② '그들의 피상적인 특성을 넘어설'이다.

- **keep away from** ~을 멀리하다
- **analyze** ⓥ 분석하다
- **retired** ⓐ 은퇴한, 퇴직한
- **well-dressed** 잘 차려입은, 복장이 훌륭한
- **manipulation** ⓝ 조작, 교묘한 처리
- **superficial** ⓐ 피상적인, 얄팍한
- **potential** ⓐ 가능성이 있는
- **personality** ⓝ 성격
- **emphasize** ⓥ (중요성을) 강조하다
- **criminal** ⓝ 범죄자 ⓐ 형사상의, 범죄의
- **deceit** ⓝ 사기, 기만, 속임수
- **take advantage of** ~을 이용하다

구문 풀이

13행 Seeing them follow a routine of going out every morning
명사구 주어　　　　원형부정사
well-dressed doesn't mean {that's the whole story}. { }: 목적어
동사(단수)

▶ 많이 틀린 이유는?

빈칸이 주제 부분에 있고 답의 근거는 예시에 주로 나오므로, 예시를 읽고 이해한 뒤 이 내용을 일반화하여 최종적으로 답을 골라야 하는 문제이다. 'Seeing ~ doesn't mean the whole story.'에서 '보기에' 공손하고 옷을 잘 차려입는다고 하여 모든 것을 판단할 수는 없다는 일반적인 내용을 추론하여, '피상적인' 특성을 넘어서야 한다는 말을 답으로 고르도록 한다. 오답 중 ①은 'social media'라는 단어가 주제와 무관하며, ④는 주로 보이는 데 의존하기 마련인 '첫인상을 믿으라'는 뜻이므로 주제와 반대되는 내용에 가깝다.

▶ 문제 해결 방법은?

빈칸이 글 중간 부분에 있다면 힌트는 주로 뒤에 있다. 따라서 이 글 또한 후반부를 중점적으로 읽도록 한다.

---

08 드라마 속 추상적인 세계
정답률 47% | 정답 ④

다음 빈칸에 들어갈 말로 가장 적절한 것을 고르시오. [3점]

① is separated from the dramatic contents
극적인 내용과 분리되어 있기

② is a reflection of our unrealistic desires
비현실적인 욕망의 반영이기

③ demonstrates our poor taste in TV shows
TV 쇼에 대한 우리의 형편없는 취향을 보여주기

✓④ is built on an extremely familiar framework
매우 친숙한 틀 위에서 만들어졌기

⑤ indicates that unnecessary details are hidden
불필요한 세부사항이 숨겨져 있다는 의미이기

[본문 해석]

전형적인 드라마는 추상적인 세계를 만들어내는데, 그 세계에서는 매우 복잡한 관계망이 프로그램 제작자들의 마음속에만 먼저 존재하다가 이후에 시청자의 마음속에 재현되는 허구의 캐릭터들을 연결한다. 만약 줄거리를 따라가고 그것에 대해 추측하려면 시청자가 얼마나 많은 인간 심리학, 법, 그리고 심지어 일상에서의 물리학을 알아야 하는지 생각해보면, 여러분은 그 양이 상당하다는 것을 알게 된다. 적어도 현대 수학의 한 부분을 따라가고 거기에 대해 추측하는 데 필요한 지식만큼, 나아가 대부분의 경우 훨씬 더 많다는 것을 알게 된다. 하지만 시청자들은 드라마를 쉽게 따라간다. 그들은 어떻게 그런 추상에 대처할 수 있을까? 왜냐면 당연하게도, 그 추상은 매우 친숙한 틀 위에서 만들어졌기 때문이다. 드라마 속 인물들과 그들 사이의 관계는 우리가 매일 경험하는 실제 사람들 및 관계와 매우 흡사하다. 드라마의 추상은 현실 세계에서 불과 한 걸음 떨어져 있다. 드라마를 따라가는 데 필요한 정신적 '훈련'은 우리의 일상생활에 의해 제공된다.

Why? 왜 정답일까?

빈칸 뒤 내용의 핵심은 드라마 속의 추상이 우리 일상과 가깝다는 것이다(The mental "training" required to follow a soap opera is provided by our everyday lives.). 따라서 빈칸에 들어갈 말로 가장 적절한 것은 ④ '매우 친숙한 틀 위에서 만들어졌기'이다.

- soap opera 드라마, 연속극
- complex ⓐ 복잡한
- recreate ⓥ 되살리다
- speculate ⓥ 추측하다
- cope with ~에 대처하다
- reflection ⓝ 반영
- framework ⓝ 틀, 뼈대
- abstract ⓐ 추상적인
- fictional ⓐ 허구의
- physics ⓝ 물리학
- considerable ⓐ 상당한
- abstraction ⓝ 추상
- demonstrate ⓥ 입증하다, 보여주다

구문 풀이

5행 If you were to think about {how much human psychology,
가정법 미래 종속절(if + 주어 + were to + 동사원형 ~) { } : 명사절
law, and even everyday physics the viewer must know in order to
follow and speculate about the plot}, you would discover it is
가정법 미래 주절(주어 + 조동사 과거형 + 동사원형 ~)
considerable — at least as much as the knowledge required to
과거분사
follow and speculate about a piece of modern mathematics, and in
most cases, much more.

---

09 질투가 까다로운 이유
정답률 52% | 정답 ④

다음 글에서 전체 흐름과 관계 없는 문장은?

[본문 해석]

인간의 모든 감정 중, 질투보다 더 까다롭거나 더 이해하기 어려운 것은 없다. 사람들의 행동을 자극하는 질투를 실제로 알아차리기는 매우 어렵다. ① 이러한 모호함의 이유는 간단한데, 우리는 우리가 느끼고 있는 질투를 대부분 절대 직접적으로 표현하지 않는다. ② 질투는 우리가 가치 있게 여기는 어떤 것에서 또 다른 사람보다 열등하다는, 자기 자신에 대한 인정을 수반한다. ③ 이 열등감을 인정하기가 고통스러울 뿐 아니라, 우리가 이것을 느끼고 있다는 것을 다른 사람들이 알게 되는 것은 훨씬 더 나쁘다. ④ 질투는 질병을 유발할 수도 있는데, 질투하는 사람이 무의식적으로라도 자신이 부러워하는 사람에게 '증오에 찬 눈초리'를 보낼 수도 있고, 질투심이 강한 사람이 그 감정으로 인해 몸이 아플 수 있기 때문이다. ⑤ 그래서 우리는 최초의 질투를 느끼는 거의 바로 그 순간 그것을 자신에게서 감추려고 한다. 즉, 우리는 질투를 느끼는 것이 아니라, 재산의 분배나 관심에 대한 불공평함, 이 불공평함에 대한 분개, 심지어 분노를 느끼는 것이다.

Why? 왜 정답일까?

질투의 모호함을 설명하는 글인데, ④는 질투가 신체적 질병을 야기할 수 있다는 내용이므로 흐름상 어색하다. 따라서 전체 흐름과 관계 없는 문장은 ④이다.

- tricky ⓐ 까다로운
- envy ⓝ 부러움, 질투
- motivate ⓥ 동기 부여하다, 자극하다
- entail ⓥ 수반하다
- inferior to ~보다 열등한
- inferiority ⓝ 열등함
- unwittingly ⓐⓓ 자기도 모르게
- unfairness ⓝ 불공평함
- elusive ⓐ 이해하기 어려운
- discern ⓥ 분간하다, 알아차리다
- elusiveness ⓝ 모호함, 이해하기 어려움
- admission ⓝ 인정
- painful ⓐ 고통스러운
- illness ⓝ 질병
- disguise ⓥ 속이다
- resentment ⓝ 분개

구문 풀이

1행 Of all the human emotions, none is trickier or more elusive
모든 ~ 중에서 「부정 주어 + 비교급 + than : ~보다 더 …한 것은
than envy. 없다(최상급 의미)」

---

10 이성적 판단 이면의 감정
정답률 65% | 정답 ③

주어진 글 다음에 이어질 글의 순서로 가장 적절한 것을 고르시오. [3점]

① (A) - (C) - (B) ② (B) - (A) - (C)
✓③ (B) - (C) - (A) ④ (C) - (A) - (B)
⑤ (C) - (B) - (A)

[본문 해석]

일반적이지만 잘못된 가정은 우리가 이성의 피조물이라는 것이지만, 사실 우리는 이성과 감정 둘 다의 피조물이다. 어떤 이성도 항상 결국 감정으로 이어지기 때문에 우리는 이성만으로 살아갈 수 없다. 내가 통곡물 시리얼을 선택해야 할까, 혹은 초콜릿 시리얼을 선택해야 할까?

(B) 나는 내가 원하는 모든 이유를 열거할 수 있지만, 그 이유는 뭔가에 근거해야 한다. 예를 들어 건강하게 먹는 것이 나의 목표라면 통곡물 시리얼을 선택할 수 있지만, 건강해지고 싶다는 것을 뒷받침하는 내 근거는 무엇일까?

(C) 나는 더 오래 살고 싶은 것, 사랑하는 사람들과 양질의 시간을 더 많이 보내고 싶은 것 등과 같은 더 많은 이유를 나열할 수 있지만, 그러한 이유를 뒷받침하는 이유는 무엇인가? 여러분은 이유가 궁극적으로 가치, 느낌, 또는 감정과 같은 비이성에 근거한다는 것을 이제 알 수 있을 것이다.

(A) 우리가 가진 이러한 뿌리 깊은 가치, 느낌, 감정은 추론의 산물인 경우가 거의 없지만, 물론 추론의 영향을 받을 수 있다. 우리는 추론을 시작하기 전에, (더 정확히는) 추론을 효과적으로 시작하기 훨씬 전에 가치, 느낌, 감정을 갖는다.

Why? 왜 정답일까?

주어진 글은 우리가 이성과 동시에 감정도 가진 존재임을 언급하며 선택의 상황을 예로 든다. 이어서 (B)는 주어진 글에서 언급된 선택 상황에 대해 근거를 생각해보자고 언급하고, (C)는 근거를 열거하다 보면 결국 그 이면에 '비이성'이 있다는 것을 알게 된다고 말한다. (A)는 (C) 후반부에서 언급된 비이성적 요소, 즉 가치관이나 느낌, 감정 등을 다시 언급하며 이런 것들이 우리가 이성적 추론을 시작하기 훨씬 앞서 자리잡고 있던 것임을 설명한다. 따라서 글의 순서로 가장 적절한 것은 ③ '(B) - (C) - (A)'이다.

- incorrect ⓐ 부정확한
- creature ⓝ 피조물, 창조물
- assumption ⓝ 가정
- reason ⓝ 이성, 근거 ⓥ 추론하다

- **emotion** ⓝ 감정, 정서
- **wholegrain** ⓝ 통곡물
- **long before** ~하기 훨씬 이전에
- **list** ⓥ 열거하다
- **live long** 장수하다

- **get by on** ~로 그럭저럭 살아가다
- **deep-seated** ⓐ 뿌리 깊은
- **effectively** ⓐ 효과적으로
- **eat healthy** 건강한 음식을 먹다
- **loved one** 사랑하는 사람

구문 풀이

1행 A common but incorrect assumption is <u>that</u> we are creatures
　　　　　　　　　　　　　　　　　　　접속사(~것)
of reason when, (in fact), we are creatures of both reason and emotion.
접속사(~할 때)　( ) : 삽입구

11-12 　신호와 이야기에 주의를 기울이도록 이루어진 진화

[본문 해석]

이야기는 우리 삶에 거주한다. 만약 여러분이 이야기를 좋아하지 않는다면, 여러분은 가장 좋은 세상이란 이야기 없이 우리가 우리 앞에 있는 사실들만 볼 수 있는 세상이라고 생각할지도 모른다. 그러나 이렇게 하는 것은 우리의 뇌가 어떻게 작동하는지, 즉 어떻게 그것들이 작동하도록 *설계되어* 있는지를 (a) <u>부인하는</u> 것이다. 수십만 년의 자연 선택을 거쳐, 이야기에 주의를 기울일 수 있는 사고방식이 그들 주인의 유전자를 물려주는 것에 더 (b) <u>성공해</u> 왔기 때문에, 진화는 우리에게 이야기와 암시에 주의를 기울이는 사고방식을 주었다.

예를 들어 동물들이 싸움에서 서로를 직면할 때 무슨 일이 일어나는지 생각해 보라. 그것들은 좀처럼 즉시 전투에 뛰어들지 않는다. 오히려, 그것들은 먼저 전투의 *결과가* 무엇이 될지 온갖 종류의 방법으로 (c) <u>신호를 보내려</u> 애를 쓴다. 그것들은 가슴을 잔뜩 부풀리고, 포효하며, 송곳니를 드러낸다. 「이야기와 신호가 세상을 항해하는 효율적인 방법이 되기 때문에, 동물들은 이것들에 주의를 기울이도록 진화했다.」 만약 여러분과 내가 세렝게티의 한 쌍의 사자이고 우리가 가장 강한 사자를 결정하려 한다면, 우리 둘 다 싸움에 곧바로 뛰어드는 것이 가장 (d) <u>분별 있는(→ 어리석은)</u> 일일 것이다. 「우리 각자가 힘을 과시하는 것, 즉 어떻게 자신의 승리가 불가피한지에 대한 *이야기를* 하는 것이 훨씬 낫다.」 그 이야기들 중 하나가 다른 쪽보다 훨씬 더 (e) <u>설득력이</u> 있다면, 우리는 실제로 싸우지 않고도 그 결과에 동의할 수 있을지도 모른다.

└『 』: 11번의 근거
└『 』: 12번의 근거

- **populate** ⓥ 거주하다
- **natural selection** 자연 선택
- **conflict** ⓝ 갈등
- **puff up** 부풀리다
- **bare** ⓥ (신체의 일부를) 드러내다
- **make a show of** ~을 과시하다, 자랑하다
- **convincing** ⓐ 설득력 있는

- **deny** ⓥ 부인하다
- **pass on** ~을 전해주다
- **plunge into** ~에 뛰어들다
- **roar** ⓥ 으르렁거리다
- **sensible** ⓐ 분별 있는
- **inevitable** ⓐ 불가피한

구문 풀이

18행 If you and I were a pair of lions on the Serengeti, and
　　　　　「if + 주어1 + 과거동사1 ~
we were trying to decide the strongest lion, it would be most sensible
주어2 + 과거동사2 ~　　　　　　　(가)주어 + 조동사 과거형 + 동사원형 : 가정법 과거」
— for both of us — to plunge straight into a conflict.
　　　　　　　　　　진주어

11　제목 파악　　　　　정답률 48% | 정답 ③

윗글의 제목으로 가장 적절한 것은?

① The Light and Dark Sides of Storytelling
　스토리텔링의 명암
② How to Interpret Various Signals of Animals
　동물의 다양한 신호를 해석하는 방법
☑ Why Are We Built to Pay Attention to Stories?
　왜 우리는 이야기에 집중하도록 만들어졌을까?
④ Story: A Game Changer for Overturning a Losing Battle
　이야기: 지는 전투를 뒤집기 위한 게임 체인저
⑤ Evolution: A History of Human's Coexistence with Animals
　진화: 인간과 동물의 공존의 역사

Why? 왜 정답일까?

'Animals evolved to attend to stories and signals because these turn out to be an efficient way to navigate the world.'에서 이야기와 신호가 세상을 살아가는 데 도움이 되기 때문에 동물은 이것들에 주의를 기울이도록 진화해왔다고 한다. 따라서 글의 제목으로 가장 적절한 것은 이러한 요지를 정답으로 유도할 수 있는 질문 형태인 ③ '왜 우리는 이야기에 집중하도록 만들어졌을까?'이다.

★★★ 1등급 대비 고난도 2점 문제

12　어휘 추론　　　　　정답률 45% | 정답 ④

밑줄 친 (a) ~ (e) 중에서 문맥상 낱말의 쓰임이 적절하지 않은 것은?

① (a)　　② (b)　　③ (c)　　☑ (d)　　⑤ (e)

Why? 왜 정답일까?

'It is far better for each of us ~'에서 누가 강한지를 결정할 때 곧바로 싸우는 것보다 서로의 힘에 관해 '이야기'하는 것이 더 효과적이라고 하므로, 바로 싸움에 뛰어드는 것이 '어리석다'는 지적의 의미를 나타낼 수 있도록 (d)의 sensible을 unwise로 고쳐야 한다. 따라서 문맥상 낱말의 쓰임이 적절하지 않은 것은 ④ '(d)'이다.

★★ 문제 해결 꿀~팁 ★★

▶ 많이 틀린 이유는?
가장 헷갈리는 ⑤ (e)가 포함된 문장은 싸움을 앞두고 신호로 이야기를 전달하고 있는 두 사자에 관한 내용이다. 두 사자의 이야기 중 어느 한쪽의 이야기가 '설득력이 있다면' 실제로 싸워보지 않고도 서열을 결정할 수 있게 되고, 이 점이 신호 또는 이야기를 통한 이득이라는 것이 글의 결론이다. 따라서 convincing은 앞뒤 문맥상 적절하다.

▶ 문제 해결 방법은?
정답인 ④ (d)는 이야기의 이득을 설명하기 위한 예시인데, 여기서 '이야기를 전달하기도 전에 싸움에 뛰어드는' 상황을 지지하면 부자연스럽다. 따라서 sensible은 문맥상 어색하다.

DAY 22 20분 미니 모의고사

01 ②	02 ③	03 ③	04 ②	05 ④
06 ④	07 ②	08 ④	09 ①	10 ⑤
11 ④	12 ②			

01 미술 작품 구매 가능 여부 묻기
정답률 88% | 정답 ②

다음 글의 목적으로 가장 적절한 것은?

① 좋아하는 화가와의 만남을 요청하려고
☑ 미술 작품의 구매 가능 여부를 문의하려고
③ 소장 중인 미술 작품의 감정을 의뢰하려고
④ 미술 작품의 소유자 변경 내역을 확인하려고
⑤ 기획 중인 전시회에 참여하는 화가를 홍보하려고

[본문 해석]

지난주에 귀하의 화랑에서 만나서 즐거웠습니다. 다양한 미술 작품을 선정하고 전시한 귀하의 노력에 감사드립니다. 제가 말씀드렸듯이, 저는 Robert D. Parker의 그림을 대단히 좋아하는데, 그의 그림은 자연의 아름다움을 강조합니다. 지난 며칠 동안, 저는 귀하의 화랑 웹사이트를 통해 Robert D. Parker의 온라인 전시 공간에 관해 조사하고 알아보았습니다. 저는 수평선을 묘사한 *Sunrise*라는 제목의 그림을 구매하는 데 특히 관심이 있습니다. 저는 그 작품을 아직 구매할 수 있는지를 알고 싶습니다. 이 훌륭한 미술 작품을 소장할 수 있다면 큰 기쁨이 될 것입니다. 이 문의에 대한 귀하의 답변을 손꼽아 기다립니다.

Why? 왜 정답일까?

관심 있는 미술 작품을 아직 구매할 수 있는지(I would like to know if the piece is still available for purchase.) 물어보는 글이므로, 글의 목적으로 가장 적절한 것은 ② '미술 작품의 구매 가능 여부를 문의하려고'이다.

- **appreciate** ⓥ 고마워하다
- **mention** ⓥ 언급하다
- **emphasize** ⓥ 강조하다
- **depict** ⓥ 그리다, 묘사하다
- **house** ⓥ 소장하다, 보관하다
- **exhibit** ⓥ 전시하다
- **admire** ⓥ 존경하다, 찬탄하다
- **purchase** ⓥ 구매하다 ⓝ 구매
- **available** ⓐ 이용 가능한
- **inquiry** ⓝ 문의

구문 풀이

9행 I would like to know if the piece is still available for purchase.
명사절 접속사(~인지 아닌지)

02 눈이 깜박이는 속도로 나타나는 두려움
정답률 80% | 정답 ③

다음 글의 주제로 가장 적절한 것은?

① eye contact as a way to frighten others
다른 사람들을 겁주기 위한 방법인 눈 맞춤
② fast blinking as a symptom of eye fatigue
눈 피로의 증상인 빠른 눈 깜박임
☑ blink speed as a significant indicator of fear
두려움의 중요한 척도인 눈 깜박임 속도
④ fast eye movement as proof of predatory instinct
포식자 본능의 증거인 빠른 눈 움직임
⑤ blink rate as a difference between humans and animals
인간과 동물의 차이점인 눈 깜박임 속도

[본문 해석]

셔터 속도는 카메라 셔터의 속도를 지칭한다. 행동 프로파일링에서는 그것은 눈꺼풀의 속도를 지칭한다. 우리가 눈을 깜박일 때 우리는 단지 눈을 깜박이는 속도보다 더 많은 것을 드러낸다. 눈꺼풀 속도의 변화는 중요한 정보를 나타내는데, 즉 셔터 속도가 두려움의 척도라는 것이다. 겁이 많다는 평판이 있는 동물을 생각해 보라. 치와와가 생각날지도 모른다. 포유동물의 경우 진화 때문에, 우리가 다가오는 포식자를 볼 수 없는 시간의 양을 최소로 하기 위하여 우리의 눈꺼풀은 속도를 높일 것이다. 동물이 경험하고 있는 두려움의 정도가 더 클수록 그 동물은 다가오는 포식자에 대해 더 걱정한다. 가능한 한 많이 눈을 뜨고 있으려는 시도로 눈꺼풀은 무의식적으로 속도를 높인다. 행동에 관한 속도는 거의 항상 두려움과 같다. 인간의 경우 만약 우리가 무언가에 대한 두려움을 경험한다면, 우리의 눈꺼풀은 치와와와 똑같아질 것이어서, 즉 더 빠르게 닫히고 열릴 것이다.

Why? 왜 정답일까?

'~ shutter speed is a measurement of fear.'에서 눈을 깜박이는 속도는 두려움의 척도라는 핵심 내용이 제시되므로, 글의 주제로 가장 적절한 것은 ③ '두려움의 중요한 척도인 눈 깜박임 속도'이다.

- **refer** ⓥ 가리켜 말하다
- **eyelid** ⓝ 눈꺼풀
- **reveal** ⓥ 드러내다
- **indicate** ⓥ 나타내다
- **fear** ⓝ 두려움
- **fearful** ⓐ 겁이 많은
- **predator** ⓝ 포식자
- **involuntarily** ⓐⓓ 모르는 사이에
- **fatigue** ⓝ 피로
- **indicator** ⓝ 지표, 표시
- **profiling** ⓝ 프로파일링, 자료 수집
- **blink** ⓝ 눈을 깜박거림 ⓥ 눈을 깜박이다
- **rate** ⓝ 속도, 비율
- **measurement** ⓝ 척도
- **reputation** ⓝ 평판, 명성
- **minimize** ⓥ 최소화하다
- **degree** ⓝ 정도
- **frighten** ⓥ 겁을 주다
- **significant** ⓐ 중요한, 유의미한
- **instinct** ⓝ 본능

구문 풀이

15행 In humans, if we experience fear about something, our eyelids
접속사(조건)　　동사(현재)
will do the same thing as the Chihuahua; they will close and open
동사1(미래)　　　　　　　　　　　　동사2(미래)
more quickly.

03 사려 깊은 소비로 기업에 영향을 주기
정답률 67% | 정답 ③

다음 글의 제목으로 가장 적절한 것은?

① Green Businesses: Are They Really Green?
친환경 기업: 그들은 정말로 친환경적일까?
② Fair Trade Does Not Always Appeal to Consumers
공정 무역이 항상 소비자들에게 어필하는 것은 아니다
☑ Buy Consciously, Make Companies Do the Right Things
양심 있게 구매하고, 회사들이 옳은 일을 하게 하라
④ Do Voters Have a Powerful Impact on Economic Policy?
유권자들은 경제 정책에 강력한 영향을 끼칠까?
⑤ The Secret to Saving Your Money: Record Your Spending
돈을 아끼는 비결: 소비를 기록하라

[본문 해석]

이미 알고 있겠지만, 당신이 무엇을 어떻게 구매하는지는 정치적일 수 있다. 당신의 돈을 누구에게 주고 싶은가? 어떤 회사와 기업을 가치 있게 여기고 존중하는가? 우리의 지원을 받을 자격이 있는지를 결정하기 위해 우리 돈을 가져가는 기업을 면밀히 조사해 모든 구매에 주의를 기울이라. 그들은 환경을 오염시킨 기록이 있는가, 아니면 그들이 만드는 제품에 대한 공정 거래 관행과 제품 수명 종료 계획이 있는가? 그들은 세상에 득이 되는 것에 헌신하고 있는가? 예를 들어, 우리 가족은 사회적 양심을 가지고 재활용되고 플라스틱 포장이 없는 화장지를 생산하는 회사를 발견했다. 그들은 수익의 50%를 전 세계 화장실 건설에 기부하고, 우리는 이 특별한 화장지에 매달 돈을 쓸 수 있어서 정말 기쁘다. 기업의 세계는 소비자를 기반으로 구축되므로, 소비자로서 당신은 지갑으로 투표하고 당신이 선택한 모든 구매를 통해 회사들이 더 건강하고 더 지속 가능한 관행을 받아들이도록 권할 힘이 있다는 것을 기억하라.

Why? 왜 정답일까?

회사들을 많이 알아보고 책임감 있게 물건을 구매하여, 회사들로 하여금 정말로 옳은 일을 할 수 있도록 영향력을 행사하라(~ vote with your wallet and encourage companies to embrace healthier and more sustainable practices with every purchase you choose to make.)는 내용의 글이다. 따라서 글의 제목으로 가장 적절한 것은 ③ '양심 있게 구매하고, 회사들이 옳은 일을 하게 하라'이다.

- **deserve** ⓥ ~을 받을 만하다
- **fair-trade** ⓐ 공정 무역의
- **end-of-life plan** 수명 종료 계획
- **bring about** ~을 초래하다
- **contribute** ⓥ 기부하다
- **vote** ⓥ 투표하다
- **pollute** ⓥ 오염시키다
- **practice** ⓝ 관행
- **be committed to** ~에 헌신하다, 전념하다
- **conscience** ⓝ 양심
- **genuinely** ⓐⓓ 진짜로
- **embrace** ⓥ 받아들이다, 수용하다

구문 풀이

15행 Remember {that the corporate world is built on consumers,
동사(명령문)　　　　　　주어1　　　　　동사1
so as a consumer you have the power to vote with your wallet and
~로서　　　주어2　　동사2　목적어　　형용사적 용법1
encourage companies to embrace healthier and more sustainable
형용사적 용법2(encourage + 목적어 + to부정사)
practices with every purchase [you choose to make]}.
선행사

04 타인의 자극에 반응하는 인간의 선천적 경향   정답률 54% | 정답 ②

다음 글의 밑줄 친 부분 중, 어법상 틀린 것은?

[본문 해석]

많은 연구가 사회적 자극에 차별적으로 반응하는 타고난 인간 성향에 대한 상당한 증거를 제시한다. 태어날 때부터, 아기들은 사람의 얼굴과 목소리 쪽으로 우선하여 향하게 되는데, 이러한 자극이 특히 자신들에게 의미가 있다는 것을 알고 있는 것 같다. 게다가, 아기들은 혀 내밀기, 입술 다물기, 입 벌리기와 같이 자신들에게 보여지는 다양한 얼굴 제스처를 모방하면서 이러한 연결을 적극적으로 마음속에 새긴다. 심지어 그들은 자신들이 다소 어려워하는 제스처에 맞추려고 노력하고, 성공할 때까지 자기 자신의 얼굴로 실험한다. 그들은 정말 성공하면 눈을 반짝이면서 기쁨을 보여주고, 실패하면 괴로움을 나타낸다. 다시 말해, 그들은 운동감각적으로 경험한 그들 자신의 신체적 움직임과 시각적으로 지각한 다른 사람의 신체적 움직임을 일치시키는 타고난 능력을 가지고 있을 뿐만 아니라, 그렇게 하려는 타고난 욕구도 가지고 있다. 즉, 그들은 자신들이 '나와 비슷하다'고 판단하는 타인을 모방하려는 타고난 욕구가 있는 것으로 보인다.

Why? 왜 정답일까?

② 뒤에 'They have some difficulty'라는 완전한 절이 나오는 것으로 보아 ② 자리에 관계대명사를 단독으로 쓸 수 없다. 이때 which 앞에 have difficulty with(~에 어려움을 겪다)의 with를 써주면, 「전치사+관계대명사(with which)」 형태가 되어 완전한 문장을 이끌 수 있다. 따라서 어법상 틀린 것은 ②이다.

Why? 왜 오답일까?

① 주절의 infants를 보충 설명하는 분사구문이다.
③ 동사를 강조하는 「do + 동사원형」의 do이다.
④ 앞에 나온 복수 명사(bodily movements)를 가리키는 복수 대명사이다.
⑤ 5형식 구문인 「judge + 목적어 + to부정사(~이 …하다고 판단하다)」의 to부정사이다. 즉 여기서 to be는 judge의 목적격 보어이고, judge의 목적어는 선행사인 others이다.

- **a number of** 많은, 여럿의
- **evidence** ⓝ 증거
- **disposition** ⓝ 성향
- **differentially** ⓐⓓ 차별적으로, 남달리
- **birth** ⓝ 출생
- **orient** ⓥ 향하다
- **register** ⓥ 새기다, 인식하다, 기억하다
- **facial** ⓐ 안면의
- **protrusion** ⓝ 내밀기, 돌출
- **brighten** ⓥ 밝아지다, 반짝이다
- **kinaesthetically** ⓐⓓ 운동감각적으로
- **perceive** ⓥ 지각하다
- **substantial** ⓐ 상당한, 많은
- **innate** ⓐ 타고난
- **respond** ⓥ 응답하다
- **stimulus** (*pl.* stimuli) ⓝ 자극
- **infant** ⓝ 아기, 유아
- **preferentially** ⓐⓓ 우선적으로
- **imitate** ⓥ 모방하다
- **present** ⓥ 제시하다
- **match** ⓥ 일치시키다
- **distress** ⓝ 괴로움
- **bodily movement** 신체 움직임
- **drive** ⓝ 욕구, 추진력

구문 풀이

13행 In other words, they not only have an innate capacity (for

matching their own kinaesthetically experienced bodily movements
　　　　「match + A + with + B : A와 B를 일치시키다」
with those of others [that are visually perceived]); they have an

innate drive to do so.

05 집단 평가 시 유의 사항   정답률 49% | 정답 ④

다음 글의 밑줄 친 부분 중, 문맥상 낱말의 쓰임이 적절하지 않은 것은?

[본문 해석]

사람들이 서로에게 영향을 미치도록 하는 것은 집단 평가의 ① 정확도를 낮춘다. 증거에 대한 다수의 출처로부터 가장 유용한 정보를 도출하기 위해서, 당신은 항상 이 출처들을 서로 ② 독립적인 상태로 만들도록 노력해야 한다. 이러한 원칙은 좋은 수사 절차의 한 부분이다. 한 사건에 대한 다수의 목격자들이 있을 때, 그들은 증언하기 전에 사건에 대해 ③ 의견을 나누는 것이 허락되지 않는다. 그 목적은 적대적인 목격자들에 의한 공모를 예방하는 것뿐만 아니라, 목격자들이 서로에게 영향을 미치는 것을 막기 위해서이기도 하다. 경험을 교환한 목격자들은 증언에서 비슷한 오류를 범하는 경향이 있을 것이고, 이것은 그들이 제공하는 정보의 전체 가치를 ④ 향상시킨다(→ 떨어뜨린다). ⑤ 개방적인

의견 교환의 일반적인 관행은 먼저 그리고 자신 있게 말하는 사람들의 의견에 너무 많은 무게를 실어주어서, 다른 사람들이 그들 뒤에 줄을 서도록 한다.

Why? 왜 정답일까?

다수 사람들로부터 증거나 정보를 취할 때 서로가 영향을 줄 수 있는 가능성을 통제하고 서로를 독립적인 상태로 유지시킬 필요가 있다는 내용을 다룬 글이다. ④가 있는 문장의 경우, 사건에 대해 진술을 해야 하는 목격자들이 서로 의견을 교환하게 두면 의견을 진술할 때 비슷한 오류를 범하게 될 가능성이 있고, 이 경우 정보의 가치가 '떨어질' 수밖에 없다는 내용을 다루고 있으므로, 선택지의 **improving**은 **reducing**으로 수정되어야 한다. 따라서 문맥상 낱말의 쓰임이 적절하지 않은 것은 ④이다.

- **influence** ⓥ 영향을 미치다 ⓝ 영향
- **precision** ⓝ 정확도, 정확성
- **derive** ⓥ 도출하다, 이끌어내다
- **independent** ⓐ 독립적인, 독자적인
- **witness** ⓝ 목격자
- **collusion** ⓝ 공모, 결탁
- **testimony** ⓝ 증언, 증거
- **confidently** ⓐⓓ 자신 있게, 확신을 갖고
- **reduce** ⓥ 감소시키다
- **estimate** ⓝ 평가, 추정, 추산
- **evidence** ⓝ 증거
- **procedure** ⓝ 절차, 방법, 수순
- **prevent** ⓥ 예방하다, 방지하다
- **similar** ⓐ 비슷한, 유사한
- **value** ⓝ 가치, 값어치

구문 풀이

　　　　　　┌ 부사적 용법
2행 To derive the most useful information from multiple sources
　　「derive + A + from + B : B에서 A를 도출하다, 끌어내다」
of evidence, you should always try to make these sources
independent of each other.
~와 독립적으로, ~와 상관없이

06 우연과 전문가가 만나 탄생한 과학적 발명의 예   정답률 44% | 정답 ④

다음 빈칸에 들어갈 말로 가장 적절한 것을 고르시오. [3점]

① trial and error - 시행착오
② idea and a critic - 생각과 비평가
③ risk and stability - 위험과 안정성
✓ chance and a researcher - 우연과 연구자
⑤ a professional and an amateur - 프로와 아마추어

[본문 해석]

우연히 만들어진 과학적 발명의 예는 셀 수 없이 많다. 하지만 종종 이러한 우연은 이를 해석할 수 있는, 해당 분야에서 평균 이상의 지식을 가진 사람을 필요로 해 왔다. 우연과 연구자의 협업에 대해 보다 잘 알려진 예 중 하나는 페니실린의 발명이다. 1928년, 스코틀랜드의 생물학자인 Alexander Fleming이 휴가를 떠났다. 다소 부주의한 사람이었던 Fleming은 책상 위에 몇몇 박테리아 배양균을 두고 갔다. 그는 돌아왔을 때 배양균들 중 하나에서 곰팡이를 발견했는데 그 주변에는 박테리아가 없었다. 그 곰팡이는 'penicillium notatum' 종에서 나온 것인데, 이것이 Petri 접시 위의 박테리아를 죽였던 것이다. 이는 운 좋은 우연의 일치였다. 전문적 지식이 없는 사람에게는 박테리아가 없는 부분이 그리 중요하지 않았겠지만, Fleming은 그 곰팡이의 마법 같은 작용을 이해했다. 그 결과는 지구의 수많은 사람들을 구한 약물인 페니실린이었다.

Why? 왜 정답일까?

'There are countless examples of scientific inventions that have been generated by accident. However, often this accident has required a person with above-average knowledge in the field to interpret it.'에서 과학적 발명이 만들어질 수 있는 우연은 그 우연의 의미를 헤아릴 수 있는, 해당 분야에서 평균 이상의 지식을 지닌 사람을 필요로 했다고 이야기하므로, 빈칸에 들어갈 말로 가장 적절한 것은 ④ '우연과 연구자'이다.

- **countless** ⓐ 셀 수 없이 많은
- **accident** ⓝ 우연
- **interpret** ⓥ 해석하다, 이해하다
- **slightly** ⓐⓓ 다소, 약간
- **notice** ⓥ 발견하다, 알아채다
- **coincidence** ⓝ 우연의 일치
- **medication** ⓝ 약물, 약
- **generate** ⓥ 만들어 내다, 발생시키다
- **above-average** 평균 이상의
- **cooperation** ⓝ 협업, 협력
- **careless** ⓐ 부주의한
- **species** ⓝ (생물의) 종
- **significance** ⓝ 중요성

구문 풀이

11행 The mold was from the *penicillium notatum* species, which
　　　　　　　　　　　　　　　　　　　　선행사　　　　계속적 용법
had killed the bacteria on the Petri dish.
└ 동사(대과거) : was보다 먼저 일어남

★★★ 1등급 대비 고난도 3점 문제

07 약간의 도약에서 출발한 위대한 수학적 발견   정답률 38% | 정답 ②

> 다음 빈칸에 들어갈 말로 가장 적절한 것을 고르시오. [3점]

① calculus was considered to be the study of geniuses
미적분학은 천재들의 학문이라고 여겨졌기
✓ it was not a huge leap from what was already known
그것은 이미 알려진 것으로부터의 큰 도약은 아니었기
③ it was impossible to make a list of the uses of calculus
미적분학의 용도를 목록으로 만드는 것은 불가능했기
④ they pioneered a breakthrough in mathematic calculations
그들은 수학적 계산에서 중대한 발견을 선도했기
⑤ other mathematicians didn't accept the discovery as it was
다른 수학자들은 그 발견을 있는 그대로 받아들이지 않았기

[본문 해석]

수학의 모든 역사는 그 순간의 가장 좋은 생각들을 취하여 새로운 확장, 변이, 그리고 적용을 찾아가는 하나의 긴 연속적인 사건들이다. 오늘날 우리의 삶은 주로 미적분학의 통찰을 요구하는 과학적이고 기술적인 혁신 때문에 300년 전 사람들의 삶과는 전적으로 다르다. Isaac Newton과 Gottfried von Leibniz는 17세기 후반에 각기 독자적으로 미적분학을 발견하였다. 하지만 역사 연구는 수학자들이 Newton 또는 Leibniz가 나타나기 전에 미적분학의 모든 주요한 요소들에 대해 생각했다는 것을 보여준다. Newton 스스로도 "만약 내가 다른 사람들보다 더 멀리 보았다면 그것은 내가 거인들의 어깨 위에 섰기 때문이다."라고 썼을 때 이러한 흘러가는 현실을 인정하였다. Newton과 Leibniz는 본질적으로 동시대에 그들의 뛰어난 통찰력을 내놓았는데 왜냐하면 <u>그것은 이미 알려진 것으로부터의 큰 도약은 아니었기</u> 때문이었다. 모든 창의적인 사람들은, 심지어 천재라고 여겨지는 사람들조차, 천재가 아닌 사람으로 시작하여 거기에서부터 아기 걸음마를 뗀다.

Why? 왜 정답일까?

Newton과 Leibniz는 흔히 미적분학을 발견한 사람들로 회자되지만, 실은 미적분학에 대한 논의가 이들이 나타나기 이전부터 있었다(~ mathematicians had thought of all the essential elements of calculus before Newton or Leibniz came along.)는 언급을 통해, 위대한 발견은 완전한 무에서 이룩되지 않으며 기존의 것을 크게 뛰어넘는 것이라기보다는 약간 더 멀리 보는 관점에서 비롯되는 것이라는 내용을 유추할 수 있다. 마지막 문장인 'All creative people, even ones who are considered geniuses, start as nongeniuses and take baby steps from there.'에서 심지어 후에 천재로 여겨진 사람들조차 처음에는 천재가 아닌 존재로서 작은 걸음, 즉 아기 걸음마를 떼는 것으로부터 시작하여 위대한 성과를 이룩하였다는 결론을 제시하고 있다. 따라서 빈칸에 들어갈 말로 가장 적절한 것은 ② '그것은 이미 알려진 것으로부터의 큰 도약은 아니었기'이다.

- sequence ⓝ 연속적인 사건들, 순서
- variation ⓝ 변이, 변화
- owing to ~ 때문에
- independently [ad] 독립적으로
- essential ⓐ 본질적인, 필수적인
- come along 나타나다
- come up with ~을 떠올리다
- leap ⓝ 도약, 뜀
- breakthrough ⓝ 돌파구, 획기적 발견
- extension ⓝ 확장
- application ⓝ 응용, 적용
- insight ⓝ 통찰력
- reveal ⓥ 보이다, 나타내다
- element ⓝ 요소
- acknowledge ⓥ 인정하다
- brilliant ⓐ 뛰어난, 훌륭한
- pioneer ⓥ 선도하다

구문 풀이

4행 Our lives today are totally different from the lives of people
   <u>주어</u>   <u>동사</u>   <u>~와 다른</u>
three hundred years ago, / mostly owing to scientific and
                   <u>전치사(~ 때문에)</u>   <u>목적어</u>
technological innovations [that required the insights of calculus].
                <u>주격 관계대명사</u>

★★ 문제 해결 꿀~팁 ★★

▶ 많이 틀린 이유는?
미적분학의 발견을 예로 들어 수학적 발견이 어떻게 이루어지는지에 관해 설명한 글로, 소재가 낯설어 이해하기 까다롭다. 최다 오답인 ④의 경우 calculation(계산)과 calculus(미적분학)가 형태상 유사하기 때문에 혼동을 유발했을 수 있다. 하지만 본문에서 '계산'과 관련된 내용은 언급되지 않았다.

▶ 문제 해결 방법은?
빈칸이 글의 중후반에 나오면 주로 답의 근거는 뒤에 있다. '~ start as nongeniuses and take baby steps from there.'에서 중요한 표현은 baby steps이고, 이는 ②의 'not a huge leap'에 대응된다.

★★★ 1등급 대비 고난도 3점 문제

08 중요한 요소와 중추적 요소의 차이   정답률 39% | 정답 ④

> 글의 흐름으로 보아, 주어진 문장이 들어가기에 가장 적절한 곳을 고르시오. [3점]

[본문 해석]

어떤 자원들, 결정들 또는 활동들은 중요한(평균적으로 매우 가치 있는) 반면 다른 것들은 중추적(작은 변화가 큰 차이를 만든다)이다. 자동차의 두 구성요소인 타이어와 내부 디자인이 어떻게 소비자의 구매 결정과 관련이 있는지 생각해보자. 어떤 것이 평균적으로 더 큰 가치를 부가시키는가? 타이어이다. ① 타이어는 차의 운행 능력에 필수적이고 안전과 성능 모두에 영향을 준다. ② 하지만 타이어는 일반적으로 구매 결정에 영향을 미치지 않는데, 그 이유는 안전기준들이 모든 타이어가 매우 안전하고 믿을 만하다고 보장해주기 때문이다. ③ 최적의 음향 시스템, 스마트기기 거치대, 컵홀더의 개수와 위치와 같은 내부 디자인 사양 차이가 아마도 소비자의 구매 결정에 훨씬 더 큰 영향을 미친다. ④ 자동차의 전반적인 가치 측면에서, 당신은 타이어 없이는 운전할 수 없지만 컵홀더나 스마트기기 거치대가 없어도 운전할 수 있다. 하지만 내부 디자인 사양들은 확실히 구매 결정에 더 큰 영향을 미친다. ⑤ 우리 표현으로 하자면, 타이어는 중요하지만 내부 디자인은 중추적이다.

Why? 왜 정답일까?

자동차 구매 결정에 영향을 미치는 두 가지 요소로서 타이어와 내부 디자인을 예로 들어 비교한 글이다. ④ 앞의 두 문장에서 타이어는 보통 안전기준상 안전함을 보장받기 때문에 구매 결정에 큰 영향을 미치지 않지만, 내부 디자인은 구매 결정에 큰 영향을 미친다고 설명한다. 이어서 주어진 문장은 전반적인 가치 측면으로 보자면 타이어가 훨씬 중요하다는 점을 서술한다. 여기에 however로 연결되는 ④ 뒤의 문장은 그럼에도 불구하고 내부 디자인 사양이 구매 결정에 큰 영향을 끼친다는 점을 다시 기술한다. 따라서 주어진 문장이 들어가기에 가장 적절한 곳은 ④이다.

- in terms of ~의 면에서
- dock ⓝ 거치대
- essential ⓐ 필수적인
- reliable ⓐ 믿을 만한
- optimal ⓐ 최적의
- portable ⓐ 휴대용의
- pivotal ⓐ 중추적인
- impact ⓥ 영향을 미치다 ⓝ 영향
- feature ⓝ 기능, 특징
- have (an) effect on ~에 영향을 미치다

구문 풀이

4행 Some resources, decisions, or activities are *important* (highly valuable on average) while others are *pivotal* (small changes
                      <u>접속사(~한 반면)</u> = other resources
make a big difference).

★★ 문제 해결 꿀~팁 ★★

▶ 많이 틀린 이유는?
③ 앞에서 타이어는 구매 결정에 큰 영향을 끼치지 않는다고 서술한 데 이어, ③ 뒤에서는 '타이어보다 더 큰' 영향을 끼칠 수 있는 요소로 내부 디자인 사양을 언급하고 있다. 즉 ③ 앞뒤는 타이어와 내부 디자인이 소비자의 구매 결정에 미치는 영향력의 크기를 비교하며 서로 자연스럽게 연결된다.

▶ 문제 해결 방법은?
④ 앞뒤는 똑같이 '내부 디자인 사양'에 관해 언급하는데, ④ 뒤의 문장에는 however가 있다. 즉 ④ 앞에서 내부 디자인을 언급했다가, 잠시 주어진 문장을 통해 타이어에 관해 언급한 후, ④ 뒤에서 다시 내부 디자인에 관해 설명하는 흐름임을 알 수 있다.

★★★ 1등급 대비 고난도 2점 문제

09 풍부한 천연자원에 대한 지나친 의존의 부작용   정답률 46% | 정답 ①

> 다음 글의 내용을 한 문장으로 요약하고자 한다. 빈칸 (A), (B)에 들어갈 말로 가장 적절한 것은?

	(A)		(B)		(A)		(B)
✓	varying 다양화하는 것	·····	barrier 장애	②	varying 다양화하는 것	·····	shortcut 지름길
③	limiting 제한하는 것	·····	challenge 도전	④	limiting 제한하는 것	·····	barrier 장애
⑤	connecting 연결시키는 것	·····	shortcut 지름길				

[본문 해석]

천연자원이 풍부한 일부 개발 도상국들은 자국의 천연자원에 대한 지나친 의존을 초래하는 경향이 있으며, (이로 인해) 더 낮은 생산적 다양화와 더 낮은

성장률을 초래한다. 자원의 풍요가 그 자체로 해가 되어야 하는 것은 아닌데, 많은 나라들이 풍부한 천연자원을 가지고 있고 자국의 경제 활동을 다양화함으로써 그것(풍부한 천연자원)에 대한 의존에서 그럭저럭 벗어났다. 가장 중요한 나라들을 꼽자면 캐나다, 호주, 또는 미국의 경우가 그러하다. 하지만 일부 개발 도상국들은 자국의 많은 천연자원에 대한 의존에 갇혀 있다. 자연 자본에 대한 과도한 의존은 다른 형태의 자본을 배제하고 그로 인해 경제 성장을 저해하는 경향이 있기 때문에 그들은 일련의 문제를 겪고 있다.

➡ 경제 활동을 (A) 다양화하지 않은 채 풍부한 천연자원에 의존하는 것은 경제 성장에 (B) 장애가 될 수 있다.

Why? 왜 정답일까?

첫 문장과 마지막 문장에서 개발도상국은 천연자원에 지나치게 의존한 나머지 (~ developing countries tend to create an excessive dependence on their natural resources ~) 다른 형태의 자본을 배제하고 있고 그로 인해 경제 성장에 방해를 받는다(~ a heavy dependence on natural capital tends to exclude other types of capital and thereby interfere with economic growth.)고 언급하는 것으로 볼 때, 요약문의 빈칸 (A), (B)에 들어갈 말로 가장 적절한 것은 ① '(A) varying(다양화하는 것), (B) barrier(장애)'이다.

● excessive ⓐ 지나친, 과도한
● generate ⓥ 만들어 내다
● diversification ⓝ 다양화
● in oneself 그 자체로는
● outgrow ⓥ ~에서 벗어나다
● thereby [ad] 그로 인해

● dependence ⓝ 의존
● productive ⓐ 생산적인
● abundance ⓝ 풍요, 풍부함
● do harm 해를 끼치다
● exclude ⓥ 배제하다
● interfere with ~을 방해하다

구문 풀이

1행 Some natural resource-rich developing countries tend to create an excessive dependence on their natural resources, which
선행사(단수) / 계속적 용법
generates a lower productive diversification and a lower rate of growth.
단수 동사 / 목적어1 / 목적어2

★★ 문제 해결 꿀~팁 ★★

▶ 많이 틀린 이유는?
첫 문장에서 천연자원에만 너무 의존하면 생산적 다양화와 경제 성장이 더뎌진다고 하였다. 즉 생산 수단이나 경제 활동을 '다양화'하지 않고 자원에만 의존하는 경우의 문제점을 지적하는 것이 글의 목적임을 알 수 있다. (A)에 limiting을 넣으면 경제 활동을 '제한하지' 않고 자원에 의존하는 경우를 언급하게 되므로 글의 내용과 맞지 않다.
▶ 문제 해결 방법은?
중간에 흐름이 반전되는 부분 없이 처음부터 끝까지 일관된 흐름으로 주제를 전개하는 글이다. 따라서 첫 문장과 마지막 문장을 주의 깊게 읽어 요약문을 완성토록 한다.

10-12 금화로 인해 불행을 알게 된 구두 만드는 사람

[본문 해석]

(A)
옛날 옛적에 가난하지만 쾌활한 구두 만드는 사람이 살았다. 그는 너무 행복해서 온종일 노래를 불렀다. 아이들은 그의 창문에 둘러서서 (a) 그의 노래를 듣기 좋아했다. 구두 만드는 사람 옆집에는 부자가 살았다. 그는 자신의 금화를 세기 위해 밤을 새곤 했다. 『아침에 그는 잠자리에 들었지만 구두 만드는 사람의 노랫소리 때문에 잠을 잘 수 없었다.』 ─「」: 12번 ①의 근거 일치

(D)
어느 날, (d) 그는 그 노래를 멈출 방법을 생각해냈다. 그는 구두 만드는 사람에게 방문해 달라고 요청하는 편지를 써 보냈다. 『구두 만드는 사람은 즉시 왔고, 놀랍게도 부자는 그에게 금화가 든 가방을 주었다.』 집에 다시 돌아왔을 때, 구두 만드는 사람은 그 가방을 열었다. (e) 그는 그때까지 그렇게 많은 금화를 본 적이 없었다! 『그가 의자에 앉아 조심스럽게 그것을 세기 시작했을 때, 아이들이 창문을 통해서 지켜보았다.』 ─「」: 12번 ⑤의 근거 일치

(C)
거기엔 금화가 너무 많아서 구두 만드는 사람은 그것을 자신에게 보이지 않는 곳에 두기 겁났다. 그래서 그는 그것을 잠자리에 가져갔다. 그러나 그는 그것에 대한 걱정으로 잠을 잘 수 없었다. 매우 이른 아침에, 그는 일어나서 금화를

침실에서 가지고 내려왔다. 대신에 그는 그것을 굴뚝에 숨기기로 결정했다. 『그러나 그는 여전히 불안했고, 잠시 후에 정원에 구멍을 파고 그 안에 금화가 든 가방을 묻었다.』 일을 해 보려고 해도 소용없었다. (c) 그는 자신의 금화의 안전이 너무나 걱정되었다. 그리고 노래에 관해서라면, 그는 너무 불행해서 한 음도 낼 수 없었다. ─「」: 12번 ③의 근거 일치

(B)
그는 잠을 잘 수도, 일을 할 수도, 노래를 부를 수도 없었고, 최악으로는 아이들이 더 이상 (b) 그를 보러 오지 않았다. 마침내, 구두 만드는 사람은 너무 불행해져서 그의 금화가 든 가방을 움켜쥐고 옆집 부자에게 달려갔다. "제발 당신의 금화를 다시 가져가세요."라고 그가 말했다. "그것에 대한 걱정이 저를 아프게 하고, 저는 제 친구들을 모두 잃었어요. 『저는 예전처럼 차라리 가난한 구두 만드는 사람이 되겠어요.』" 그래서 구두 만드는 사람은 다시 행복해졌고 일을 하면서 온종일 노래를 불렀다. ─「」: 12번 ②의 근거 불일치

● cheerful ⓐ 쾌활한
● sit up all night 밤을 꼴딱 새우다
● seize ⓥ 붙잡다
● out of one's sight 보이지 않는 곳에
● uneasy ⓐ 불안한
● bury ⓥ 묻다
● as for ~에 관해 말하자면
● utter ⓥ (입으로) 소리를 내다, 말하다
● at once 즉시, 당장

● shoemaker ⓝ 제화공, 구두장이
● worst of all 무엇보다 나쁜 것은
● ill ⓐ 아픈
● chimney ⓝ 굴뚝
● in a little while 잠시 후에
● it is no use -ing ~해도 소용없다
● miserable ⓐ 몹시 불행한, 비참한
● note ⓝ (음악의) 음

구문 풀이

(A) 4행 Next door to the shoemaker lived a rich man.
「부사구 + 동사 + 주어: 도치 구문」

(B) 3행 At last, the shoemaker felt so unhappy that he seized his
「so ~that …: 너무 ~해서 …하다」
bag of gold and ran next door to the rich man.

(C) 8행 It was no use trying to work.
「it is no use + 동명사: ~하는 것도 소용없다」

(D) 6행 When he sat down at his bench and began, (carefully),
접속사(~할 때) / 동사1 / 동사2 ( ): 삽입구
to count it, the children watched through the window.
목적어(begin + to부정사: ~하기 시작하다)

---

10 글의 순서 파악 | 정답률 73% | 정답 ⑤

주어진 글 (A)에 이어질 내용을 순서에 맞게 배열한 것으로 가장 적절한 것은?
① (B) - (D) - (C)   ② (C) - (B) - (D)
③ (C) - (D) - (B)   ④ (D) - (B) - (C)
✔ (D) - (C) - (B)

Why? 왜 정답일까?

쾌활한 성격으로 온종일 노래를 부르는 구두 만드는 사람과 금화를 밤새 세느라 아침에서야 잠자리에 들려고 하지만 구두 만드는 사람의 노랫소리 때문에 잠 못드는 옆집 부자의 상황을 제시한 (A) 뒤에는, 부자가 구두 만드는 사람의 노래를 멈추게 하기 위해 집으로 불러 금화를 맡겼다는 내용의 (D)가 먼저 연결된다. 이어서 (C)에서는 구두 만드는 사람이 금화가 너무 많은 것을 알고 내내 불안해하며 어쩔 줄 몰라 했다는 내용을 제시한다. 마지막으로 (B)는 잠도 못 이루고 노래도 못 부르고 친구까지 잃게 된 구두 만드는 사람이 다시 부자를 찾아가 금화를 돌려주고 이전의 가난한 생활로 돌아갔다는 결말을 제시한다. 따라서 글의 순서로 가장 적절한 것은 ⑤ '(D) - (C) - (B)'이다.

11 지칭 추론 | 정답률 73% | 정답 ④

다음 밑줄 친 (a) ~ (e) 중에서 가리키는 대상이 나머지 넷과 다른 것은?
① (a)   ② (b)   ③ (c)   ✔ (d)   ⑤ (e)

Why? 왜 정답일까?

(a), (b), (c), (e)는 the shoemaker를, (d)는 the rich man을 가리키므로, (a) ~ (e) 중에서 가리키는 대상이 다른 하나는 ④ '(d)'이다.

12 세부 내용 파악 | 정답률 72% | 정답 ②

윗글의 shoemaker에 관한 내용으로 적절하지 <u>않은</u> 것은?

① 그의 노래로 인해 옆집 사람이 잠을 잘 수 없었다.
☑ 예전처럼 가난하게 살고 싶지 않다고 말했다.
③ 정원에 구멍을 파고 금화가 든 가방을 묻었다.
④ 부자가 보낸 편지에 즉시 그를 만나러 갔다.
⑤ 금화를 셀 때 아이들이 그 모습을 봤다.

Why? 왜 정답일까?

(B) 'I would rather be a poor shoemaker, as I was before.'에서 구두 만드는 사람은 금화로 인해 너무 걱정하게 된 자신의 처지가 싫어 차라리 예전처럼 가난한 삶을 택하겠다고 말했음을 알 수 있다. 따라서 내용과 일치하지 않는 것은 ② '예전처럼 가난하게 살고 싶지 않다고 말했다.'이다.

Why? 왜 오답일까?

① (A) '~ he could not sleep because of the sound of the shoemaker's singing.'의 내용과 일치한다.
③ (C) '~ he dug a hole in the garden and buried his bag of gold in it.'의 내용과 일치한다.
④ (D) 'The shoemaker came at once, ~'의 내용과 일치한다.
⑤ (D) 'When he sat down at his bench and began, carefully, to count it, the children watched through the window.'의 내용과 일치한다.

DAY 23 | 20분 미니 모의고사

01 ②	02 ③	03 ⑤	04 ⑤	05 ③
06 ⑤	07 ①	08 ③	09 ③	10 ②
11 ①	12 ③			

01 글쓰기 과제로 칭찬을 받아 기뻐한 필자
정답률 83% | 정답 ②

다음 글에 나타난 'I'의 심경 변화로 가장 적절한 것은?

① relieved → scared
  안도한   겁에 질린
☑ nervous → delighted
  긴장한   기쁜
③ bored → confident
  지루한   자신 있는
④ satisfied → depressed
  만족한   우울한
⑤ confused → ashamed
  혼란스러운   수치스러운

[본문 해석]

다음 날 아침 Belleville에 대한 나의 개인적인 회상을 제출할 수밖에 없었다. Fleagle 선생님이 채점된 과제들을 돌려주기까지 이틀이 흘렀고, 그는 내 것을 제외하고 모든 사람들의 과제를 돌려주었다. 그가 책상에서 내 과제를 집어들고 책상을 두드려 학생들의 주의를 끄는 것을 보았을 때, 나는 학교 끝나고 즉시 벌을 받으러 Fleagle 선생님에게 오라는 지시를 초조하게 기다리고 있었다. 그가 말했다. "자, 여러분, 나는 여러분에게 글 한 편을 읽어주고 싶습니다. 이 글의 제목은 '스파게티를 먹는 기술'입니다." 그리고 그는 읽기 시작했다. 내 글을! 그는 *내* 글을 우리 반 모두에게 소리 내어 읽어주고 있었다. 더욱이, 온 학급이 주의 깊게 듣고 있었다. 그 후 누군가가 웃었고, 그러자 온 학급이 경멸이나 조소가 아니고, 숨김없는 즐거움으로 웃고 있었다. 나는 기쁨을 드러내지 않으려고 애를 썼지만, 내가 느낀 것은 내 글이 사람들을 웃게 만드는 힘을 가졌다는 이 놀라운 시연에 대한 순수한 환희였다.

Why? 왜 정답일까?

글쓰기 과제를 혼자 돌려받지 못해 초조하던 필자가(I was anxiously expecting for ~) 선생님이 읽어 주시는 자신의 글을 듣고 모두가 순수하게 웃자 기뻐했다(I did my best to avoid showing pleasure, but what I was feeling was pure ecstasy ~)는 내용의 글이다. 따라서 'I'의 심경 변화로 가장 적절한 것은 ② '긴장한 → 기쁜'이다.

- **there is no choice but** ~할 수밖에 없다
- **anxiously** [ad] 걱정스럽게, 불안하게
- **report to** ~에게 출두하다, 보고하다
- **lift** [v] 들어올리다
- **read out loud** 소리 내어 읽다
- **attentively** [ad] 주의 깊게
- **ridicule** [n] 조롱, 조소
- **ecstasy** [n] 황홀감
- **demonstration** [n] 시연, 증명
- **delighted** [a] 기쁜
- **private** [a] 개인적인, 사적인
- **command** [n] 지시, 명령
- **discipline** [n] 훈육, 징계
- **rap** [v] (빠르게) 톡톡 두드리다
- **what's more** 더구나, 게다가
- **contempt** [n] 경멸
- **openhearted** [a] 솔직한, 숨김없는
- **startling** [a] 놀라운
- **nervous** [a] 긴장한
- **depressed** [a] 우울한

구문 풀이

4행 I was anxiously expecting for a command to report to Mr. Fleagle immediately after school for discipline when I saw him
〔지각동사←┘ └목적어〕
lift my paper from his desk and rap for the class's attention.
└원형부정사1   원형부정사2

02 판매 시 희소성의 원칙 이용하기
정답률 80% | 정답 ③

다음 글에서 필자가 주장하는 바로 가장 적절한 것은?

① 상품 판매 시 실현 가능한 판매 목표를 설정해야 한다.
② 판매를 촉진하기 위해서는 가격 경쟁력을 갖추어야 한다.
☑ 효과적인 판매를 위해서는 상품의 희소성을 강조해야 한다.
④ 고객의 신뢰를 얻기 위해서는 일관된 태도를 유지해야 한다.
⑤ 고객의 특성에 맞춰 다양한 판매 전략을 수립하고 적용해야 한다.

[본문 해석]

2003년에 영국 항공은 더 이상 런던에서 뉴욕까지 가는 콩코드 항공편을 하루에 두 번 운항할 수 없을 것이라고 발표했는데 왜냐하면 그것이 경제성이 없다고 판명되기 시작하고 있었기 때문이었다. 그런데 바로 다음날 이 노선의 항공편 판매가 증가했다. 노선이나 항공사에 의해 제공되는 서비스에 있어서 달라진 것은 아무것도 없었다. 단지 그것이 부족한 자원이 되었기 때문에 그것에 대한 수요가 증가했다. 만약에 여러분이 사람들을 설득하는 데에 관심이 있다면, 희소성의 원리가 효과적으로 사용될 수 있다. 만약 여러분이 특정 상품의 판매를 증가시키려 노력하는 판매원이라면, 여러분은 단지 고객이 언급된 상품으로부터 얻을 수 있는 혜택을 강조할 뿐만이 아니라 그것의 유일함과 만약에 그들이 그 상품을 빨리 구매하지 않는다면 무엇을 놓치게 될 것인지를 또한 강조해야만 한다. 판매에 있어 여러분은 무언가가 더 한정적일수록 더 가치 있게 된다는 것을 명심해야 한다.

Why? 왜 정답일까?

'~ then the principle of scarcity can be effectively used.'에서 판매를 위해 설득할 때 희소성의 원리를 효과적으로 이용할 수 있다고 하므로, 필자가 주장하는 바로 가장 적절한 것은 ③ '효과적인 판매를 위해서는 상품의 희소성을 강조해야 한다.'이다.

- make an announcement 발표하다
- scarce ⓐ 부족한, 희소한
- derive A from B B로부터 A를 얻어내다
- miss out on ~을 놓치다
- uneconomical ⓐ 수익이 안 나는
- effectively ⓐd 효과적으로
- uniqueness ⓝ 유일함, 고유함
- desirable ⓐ 바람직한, 가치 있는

구문 풀이

15행 In selling, you should keep in mind that the more limited
「the + 비교급 ~, the + 비교급 … : ~할수록 더 …하다」
something is, the more desirable it becomes.

---

03 운동 계획을 작게 세워 시작하기 | 정답률 93% | 정답 ⑤

다음 글의 요지로 가장 적절한 것은?

① 상황에 따른 유연한 태도가 목표 달성에 효과적이다.
② 올바른 식습관과 규칙적인 운동이 건강 유지에 도움이 된다.
③ 나쁜 습관을 고치기 위해서는 장기적인 계획이 필수적이다.
④ 꿈을 이루기 위해서는 원대한 목표를 세우는 것이 중요하다.
✓⑤ 장기적인 성공을 위해 작은 습관부터 시작하는 것이 필요하다.

[본문 해석]

더 많이 운동을 하려는 결정에 관해 말하자면, 당신은 거의 훈련을 하지 않고 하프 마라톤을 하는 것과 비슷한 목표들을 세우고 있다! 당신은 헬스장 회원권을 사기로 결정하고 매일 헬스장에서 한 시간을 보내기로 결정한다. 글쎄, 당신은 하루나 이틀은 그것을 지킬 수도 있겠지만, 장기적으로 그 다짐을 계속 이행할 수 없을 가능성이 있다. 하지만, 만약 당신이 하루에 몇 분씩 조깅을 하거나 잠자리에 들기 전에 매일 루틴에 몇 번의 윗몸 일으키기를 더하기로 다짐한다면, 당신은 당신의 결정을 지키고 당신에게 장기적인 결과를 제공하는 습관을 만들 가능성이 훨씬 더 높다. 핵심은 작게 시작하는 것이다. 작은 습관들은 장기적인 성공으로 이어진다.

Why? 왜 정답일까?

운동의 목표를 거창하게 설정하기보다 하루 조깅 몇 분, 윗몸 일으키기 몇 번과 같은 식으로 작게 잡아 시작하는 것이 좋다(The key is to start small.)는 내용의 글로, 마지막 두 문장에서 핵심 내용을 잘 제시하고 있다. 따라서 글의 요지로 가장 적절한 것은 ⑤ '장기적인 성공을 위해 작은 습관부터 시작하는 것이 필요하다.'이다.

- when it comes to ~에 관하여
- commitment ⓝ 약속, 다짐, 헌신
- stick to ~을 지키다, 고수하다

구문 풀이

1행 When it comes to the decision to get more exercise, you are
「when it comes to + 명사 : ~에 관하여」
setting goals [that are similar to running a half marathon with very
선행사   주격 관계대명사   전치사   동명사
little training]!

---

04 영국 남녀별 스마트 TV 사용 비교 | 정답률 83% | 정답 ⑤

다음 도표의 내용과 일치하지 <u>않는</u> 것은?

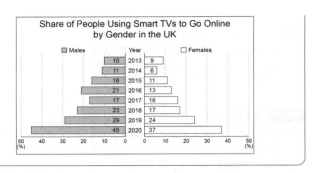

[본문 해석]

위 그래프는 2013년부터 2020년까지 영국에서 온라인 접속을 위한 스마트 TV 사용에 대한 설문 조사 결과를 성별에 따라 보여준다. ① 2013년부터 2020년까지 매년, 인터넷 접속을 위해 스마트 TV를 사용한 남성 응답자의 비율은 여성 응답자의 비율보다 더 높았다. ② 두 성별 간 비율의 차이는 2016년과 2020년에 가장 컸고, 두 해 모두 8퍼센트포인트 차이가 있었다. ③ 2020년에 온라인 접속을 위해 스마트 TV를 사용했다고 말한 응답자의 비율은 남성과 여성 둘 다 30%를 넘겼다. ④ 남성 응답자의 경우, 해당 기간 중 2017년은 전년도에 비해 스마트 TV를 통하여 인터넷에 접속한 사람의 비율이 감소한 유일한 해였다. ⑤ 2014년에 인터넷 접속을 위해 스마트 TV를 사용한 여성의 비율은 6%로 주어진 기간 중 가장 낮았고, 2015년에 여전히 10% 미만이었다.

Why? 왜 정답일까?

도표에 따르면 온라인에 접속하려고 스마트 TV를 사용한 영국 여성의 비율은 2015년에 10%를 넘겼다(11%). 따라서 도표와 일치하지 않는 것은 ⑤이다.

- survey ⓝ 설문 조사
- respondent ⓝ 응답자
- go online 온라인에 접속하다
- access ⓥ 접속하다

---

05 듣는 도중 질문하는 습관 갖기 | 정답률 55% | 정답 ③

(A), (B), (C)의 각 네모 안에서 어법에 맞는 표현으로 가장 적절한 것은? [3점]

	(A)	(B)	(C)
①	transform	what	interesting
②	transform	that	interested
✓③	transforms	what	interesting
④	transforms	that	interesting
⑤	transforms	what	interested

[본문 해석]

질문을 하는 습관을 갖는 것은 당신을 적극적인 청자로 바꾼다. 이러한 습관은 당신이 다른 내적 삶의 경험을 갖도록 하는데, 사실상 당신이 더욱 효과적으로 들을 것이기 때문이다. 때때로 당신이 어떤 이의 말을 듣기로 되어 있을 때, 당신의 마음은 산만해지기 시작한다는 것을 알고 있을 것이다. 모든 교사들은 이러한 것이 수업 중 학생들에게 빈번하게 발생한다는 것을 알고 있다. 당신이 듣는 것을 배우는 것으로 얼마나 잘 바꾸는가에 있어서 그 모든 차이를 만들어 내는 것은 바로 당신의 머릿속에서 일어나는 일이다. 듣는 것으로는 충분하지 않다. 만약 당신이 듣고 있는 것에 대하여 스스로에게 질문하는 데 구준히 몰입한다면, 당신은 심지어 따분한 강의자조차도 약간 더 흥미롭다고 생각할 것인데, 왜냐하면 그 흥미 중 많은 부분이 강의자가 제공하고 있는 것보다는 당신이 만들어내고 있는 것으로부터 오기 때문이다. 다른 누군가가 이야기를 할 때, 당신은 생각을 불러일으킬 필요가 있다!

Why? 왜 정답일까?

(A) 주어가 동명사구(Getting ~)이므로 단수 동사인 transforms를 쓰는 것이 적절하다.
(B) 동사 will convert의 목적어로서 선행사를 포함하는 관계대명사 what을 쓰는 것이 적절하다.
(C) 본래는 사람들을 지루하게 만들었던 강연자들도 '흥미를 주는' 사람이 될 수 있다는 뜻으로서, 현재분사 interesting을 쓰는 것이 적절하다. 과거분사 interested는 강연자들이 '흥미를 느끼는' 상태일 때 쓴다. 따라서 각 네모 안에서 어법에 맞는 표현으로 가장 적절한 것은 ③이다.

- get in the habit of ~하는 습관을 들이다
- effectively ⓐd 효과적으로, 실질적으로
- frequently ⓐd 빈번히, 자주, 흔히
- constantly ⓐd 끊임없이, 거듭
- provoke ⓥ 불러일으키다, 유발하다
- transform ⓥ 바꾸다, 탈바꿈시키다
- wander ⓥ 산만해지다
- convert ⓥ 전환시키다
- engaged in ~에 몰두한, 열심인

구문 풀이

8행 It's {what goes on inside your head} that {makes all the
`it is + (강조어구) + that + (나머지 문장) : 강조구문`
difference in [how well you will convert what you hear into something
의문부사   관계대명사
you learn]}.
[ ] : in의 목적어

---

06 인간에 맞춰 적응하는 기술　　정답률 52% | 정답 ⑤

다음 글의 밑줄 친 부분 중, 문맥상 낱말의 쓰임이 적절하지 않은 것은? [3점]

[본문 해석]

우리가 고개를 돌리는 곳 어디서든 우리는 전능하신 '사이버 공간'에 대해 듣는다! 과대광고는 우리가 지루한 삶을 떠나 고글과 보디슈트를 착용하고, 어떤 금속성의 3차원 멀티미디어 가상 세계로 들어갈 것이라고 약속한다. 산업 혁명이 위대한 혁신인 모터와 함께 도래했을 때 우리는 우리 세상을 떠나 ① 멀리 떨어진 어떤 모터의 세계로 들어가지 않았다! 반대로, 우리는 자동차, 냉장고, 드릴 프레스, 연필깎이와 같은 것들로 우리 삶에 모터를 가져왔다. 이 ② 흡수는 매우 완전해서 우리는 그것들을 '모터성'이 아니라 그것들의 사용을 분명하게 밝히는 이름으로 이 모든 도구를 지칭한다. 이러한 혁신품들은 정확히 우리의 일상생활에 들어와 깊은 ③ 영향을 미쳤기 때문에 주요한 사회경제적 운동으로 이어졌다. 사람들은 수천 년 동안 근본적으로 변하지 않았다. 기술은 끊임없이 변화한다. 그것(기술)이야말로 우리에게 ④ 적응해야 한다. 바로 이 일이 인간 중심의 컴퓨터 사용 하에서 정보 기술과 그 장치들에 일어날 것이다. 컴퓨터가 우리를 마법 같은 신세계로 데려다줄 것이라고 계속해서 더 오래 믿게 될수록, 컴퓨터와 우리 삶의 자연스러운 융합은 더 오래 ⑤ 유지될(→ 지체될) 것인데, 이는 사회경제적 혁명이라고 불리기를 열망하는 모든 주요 운동의 특징이다.

Why? 왜 정답일까?

우리는 기술을 통해 '다른 세계로 간다고' 여겨질 만큼 큰 변화를 맞이하리라 기대하지만, 실상은 그렇지 않다는 내용의 글이다. 글 전반부에서 산업혁명과 모터의 사례를 들며, 인간이 변하는 대신 기술이 인간 사회에 통합되고 맞춰졌음을 설명하고 있다. 이어서 'That's exactly ~'에서는 컴퓨터 및 정보 기술 또한 비슷한 과정을 겪을 것이라고 언급한다. 즉, 컴퓨터 기술이 우리를 지금과는 다른 세상으로 데려다줄 것이라고 믿으면 오히려 컴퓨터 기술과 우리 삶이 자연스럽게 융합되는 데 '지장이 생길' 것이라는 의미로, ⑤의 maintain 자리에는 delay를 써야 한다. 따라서 문맥상 낱말의 쓰임이 적절하지 않은 것은 ⑤이다.

- almighty ⓐ 전능한
- hype ⓝ 과대광고
- otherworld ⓝ 가상 세계
- innovation ⓝ 혁신
- automobile ⓝ 자동차
- drill press 드릴 프레스
- absorption ⓝ 흡수
- declare ⓥ 분명히 말하다, 선언하다
- precisely ⓐⓓ 바로, 정확하게
- fundamentally ⓐⓓ 근본적으로
- human-centric ⓐ 인간 중심의
- hallmark ⓝ 특징
- cyberspace ⓝ 사이버 공간
- metallic ⓐ 금속성의
- Industrial Revolution 산업혁명
- remote ⓐ 먼, 외딴
- refrigerator ⓝ 냉장고
- pencil sharpener 연필깎이
- complete ⓐ 완전한
- socioeconomic ⓐ 사회경제적인
- profoundly ⓐⓓ 깊이
- device ⓝ 장치, 장비
- magical ⓐ 마법 같은
- aspire ⓥ 열망하다

구문 풀이

10행 This absorption has been so complete that we refer to all
`so ~ that … : 너무 ~해서 …하다`
these tools with names [that declare their usage, not their "motorness."]

★★★ 1등급 대비 고난도 3점 문제

07 꿀벌의 집단 지성　　정답률 42% | 정답 ①

다음 빈칸에 들어갈 말로 가장 적절한 것을 고르시오. [3점]

✓① votes with their bodies – 몸으로 투표한다
② invades other bees' hives – 다른 벌들의 집에 쳐들어간다
③ searches for more flowers – 더 많은 꽃을 찾아 나선다
④ shows more concern for mates – 짝에 대한 걱정을 더 많이 보인다
⑤ improves their communication skills – 의사소통 기술을 향상시킨다

[본문 해석]

꿀벌은 한 군집 내 최대 5만 마리의 일벌이 함께 민주적인 결정을 내리기 위해 모여서 소위 "집단 지성"을 발전시켜 왔다. 봄철에 벌집이 너무 붐빌 때 군집들은 새로운 집을 찾기 위해 정찰병을 보낸다. 어느 정찰병이라도 어디에 다음 벌집을 지을지에 대해 동의하지 않으면, 그들은 문명화된 방법으로, 즉 춤을 통해 문제를 논의한다. 각 정찰병은 다른 정찰병들에게 자신이 찾은 장소의 장점을 납득시키기 위해 "waggle dance(8자 춤)"를 춘다. 춤이 더 열정적일수록 그 정찰병은 그 장소를 더 마음에 들어 하는 것이다. 군집의 나머지 벌들은 그들이 선호하는 장소로 날아가서 벌집이 될 가능성이 있는 한 장소가 주변의 모든 다른 춤들을 이길 때까지 춤에 합류하여 몸으로 투표한다. 의회가 의견 불일치를 똑같은 방법으로 해결한다면 멋질 것이다.

Why? 왜 정답일까?

'If any scouts disagree on where the colony should build its next hive, they argue their case the civilized way: through a dance-off.'에서 벌은 마음에 드는 벌집 장소를 결정함에 있어 '춤'이라는 수단을 이용한다고 이야기하는데, 이는 결국 춤이 벌들에게 있어 의사를 표현하는 중대한 수단임을 말하는 것이다. 따라서 빈칸에 들어갈 말로 가장 적절한 것은 '춤'을 간접적으로 풀어 쓴 ① '몸으로 투표한다'이다.

- evolve ⓥ 발전시키다, 진화하다
- up to ~까지
- democratic ⓐ 민주적인
- scout ⓝ 정찰병
- enthusiastic ⓐ 열정적인
- potential ⓐ ~일 가능성이 있는
- congress ⓝ 의회
- swarm ⓝ 떼
- colony ⓝ 군집
- hive ⓝ 벌집
- convince ⓥ 납득시키다, 설득하다
- remainder ⓝ 나머지
- overcome ⓥ 이기다, 극복하다
- settle ⓥ (혼란이나 갈등을) 해결하다

구문 풀이

1행 Honeybees have evolved what we call "swarm intelligence,"
동사(현재완료)　　관계대명사(~것)　　목적격 보어
with up to 50,000 workers in a single colony coming together
`with +`　　명사　　분사(~하면서)
to make democratic decisions.
부사적 용법(~하기 위해)

★★ 문제 해결 꿀~팁 ★★

▶ 많이 틀린 이유는?
'꿀벌이 춤으로 의사를 표현한다'는 주제를 파악했어도 정답 선택지에 '춤'이라는 단어가 직접 등장하지 않기에 한 번 더 생각을 요하는 문제였다. 최다 오답인 ②는 다른 선택지와는 달리 본문에 비교적 많이 나온 '벌집'이라는 단어를 포함하고 있지만 이 글은 '벌집 장소 결정'보다는 그 결정 방법인 '춤'에 더 무게중심을 두고 있다. 더구나 다른 벌집을 '침입'한다는 이야기는 글의 다른 부분에 나온 바 없다.

▶ 문제 해결 방법은?
주제를 잡는 데 어려움이 있었다면 글에서 가장 많이 반복된 단어가 무엇인지 먼저 파악해 본다('dance', 'hive'). 그리고 그 핵심 소재가 서로 어떤 연관성이 있는지 (dance → hive 장소 결정)에 중점을 두고 독해한다.

---

08 음악이 기억 회상에 미치는 영향　　정답률 56% | 정답 ③

다음 빈칸에 들어갈 말로 가장 적절한 것을 고르시오.

① analyzing memories of the event thoroughly
　사건에 대한 기억을 면밀히 분석하는 것
② increasing storage space for recalling the event
　사건을 기억하기 위한 저장 공간을 늘리는 것
✓③ re-hearing the same music associated with the event
　그 사건과 연관된 바로 그 음악을 다시 듣는 것
④ reconstructing the event in the absence of background music
　배경 음악 없이 사건을 재구성하는 것
⑤ enhancing musical competence to deliver emotional messages
　감정적인 메시지를 전달하는 음악적 능력을 향상시키는 것

[본문 해석]

음악이 우리의 내면세계에서 중요성을 가질 수 있는 주요한 방법 중 하나는 그것이 기억과 상호작용하는 방식에 의해서이다. 중요한 감정과 연관된 기억들은 다른 사건들보다 우리 기억 속에 더욱 깊이 박혀 있는 경향이 있다. 감정적인 기억들은 생생히 기억될 가능성이 더 크고 중립적인 기억들보다 시간이 지나도 기억될 가능성이 더 크다. 음악이 감정을 엄청나게 불러일으킬 수 있기 때문에 삶의 중요한 사건들은 음악의 존재에 의해 감정적으로 고조될 수 있고, 이는 그 사건에 대한 기억들이 확실히 깊이 부호화되도록 해 준다. 그리고 나서 그러한 기억들의 회복은 맥락 효과에 의해 강화되는데, 그 기억들이 부호화되었던 맥락과 비슷한 맥락의 재창조가 기억의 회복을 촉진시킬 수 있다. 따라

서 그 사건과 연관된 바로 그 음악을 다시 듣는 것이 그 사건에 대한 강렬하게 생생한 기억들을 활성화할 수 있다.

Why? 왜 정답일까?

음악은 듣는 이의 감정을 고조시키고, 감정적인 기억은 더 생생히 저장되게 하는 경향이 있기 때문에, 어떤 사건이 일어날 때 특정한 음악을 듣고 있었다면 나중에 그 음악을 다시 듣는 '맥락'이 조성될 때 관련된 사건을 기억해내기가 훨씬 쉬워진다(~ a recreation of a similar context to that in which the memories were encoded can facilitate their retrieval.)는 내용의 글이다. 따라서 빈칸에 들어갈 말로 가장 적절한 것은 ③ '그 사건과 연관된 바로 그 음악을 다시 듣는 것'이다.

- **primary** ⓐ 주요한
- **significance** ⓝ 중요성
- **associated** ⓐ 관련된
- **with the passing of time** 시간이 지남에 따라
- **neutral** ⓐ 중립적인
- **evocative** ⓐ ~을 환기시키는
- **presence** ⓝ 존재
- **enhance** ⓥ 강화하다
- **recreation** ⓝ 재창조
- **intensely** ⓐⓓ 강렬하게, 매우
- **storage** ⓝ 저장, 보관
- **in the absence of** ~이 없을 때
- **take on** (특징 등을) 띠다, (일을) 맡다
- **inner** ⓐ 내면의
- **be embedded in** ~에 박혀있다
- **extremely** ⓐⓓ 극도로
- **heighten** ⓥ 고조시키다
- **retrieval** ⓝ 회복, 회수
- **contextual** ⓐ 맥락과 관련된, 맥락의
- **activate** ⓥ 활성화하다
- **thoroughly** ⓐⓓ 면밀하게, 철저하게
- **reconstruct** ⓥ 재구성하다
- **competence** ⓝ 능력, 능숙함

구문 풀이

11행 Retrieval of those memories is then enhanced by
　　　　주어　　　　　　　　　　　　　　　동사구(수동태)
contextual effects, in which a recreation of a similar context to that
　　　　　　　　　선행사　= where　　주어　　　　　　　　　지시대명사= context ↵
[in which the memories were encoded] can facilitate their retrieval.
= where　　　　　　　　　　　　　　　　동사

09　아이들을 대상으로 한 제품 광고의 윤리적 타당성
정답률 62% | 정답 ③

다음 글에서 전체 흐름과 관계 없는 문장은?

[본문 해석]

지금까지 대학 교수, 정치인, 마케팅 담당자, 그리고 그 외의 사람들은 제품과 서비스를 어린 소비자들에게 직접 판촉하는 것이 윤리적으로 옳은지 그렇지 않은지를 논쟁해 왔다. ① 이것은 또한, 광고주들이 아이들을 조종해서 아이들이 광고되는 것을 본 더 많은 제품을 구매하게 만드는 것을 도와야 하는지 의문을 제기하는 심리학자들에게도 딜레마이다. ② 광고주들은 아이들이 그 '적절한' 제품을 소유하고 있지 않으면 자신이 패배자라고 느끼게 만드는 것이 쉽다는 사실을 이용한 것을 인정했다. ③ 제품이 더 인기 있어질 때 더 많은 경쟁자들이 시장에 진출하고 마케팅 담당자들은 경쟁력을 유지하기 위해 그들의 마케팅 비용을 줄인다. ④ 영리한 광고는 아이들에게 만약 그들이 광고되는 제품을 가지고 있지 않으면 자신의 또래 친구들에게 부정적으로 보일 것이라고 알려 주고, 그렇게 해서 아이들의 정서적인 취약성을 이용한다. ⑤ 광고가 만들어 내는, 끊임없이 부적절하다고 느끼는 감정은 아이들이 즉각적인 만족감과 물질적 소유물이 중요하다는 믿음에 집착하게 되는 데 기여한다고 언급되어 왔다.

Why? 왜 정답일까?

첫 문장에서 어린 소비자를 겨냥해 제품을 직접 판촉하고 광고하는 것이 윤리적으로 옳은가에 관한 논쟁이 있다고 언급한다. 이어서 ①, ②, ④, ⑤에서는 어린 소비자가 광고 속 제품을 자신만 갖고 있지 않을 때 또래로부터 느낄 소외감을 자극하여, 제품을 갖고 있지 않은 상황을 '부적절하다'고 여기게 만들고, 그리하여 제품 구매를 촉진한다는 내용을 일관되게 보충 설명하고 있다. 하지만 ③은 제품이 인기 있어질 때 마케팅 담당자들은 경쟁력을 유지하고자 마케팅 비용을 줄인다는 내용을 다루어 흐름에서 벗어난다. 따라서 전체 흐름과 관계없는 문장은 ③이다.

- **academic** ⓝ (대학) 교수
- **in the past** 지금까지
- **dilemma** ⓝ 딜레마
- **admit to** ~한 것을 인정하다
- **competitor** ⓝ 경쟁자
- **unfavorable** ⓐ 비판적인, 호의적이 아닌
- **play on** (감정 등을) 이용하다
- **vulnerability** ⓝ 취약성, 연약함
- **inadequateness** ⓝ 부적절성
- **material** ⓐ 물질적인
- **politician** ⓝ 정치인
- **ethically** ⓐⓓ 윤리적으로
- **psychologist** ⓝ 심리학자
- **take advantage of** ~을 이용하다
- **marketplace** ⓝ 시장
- **thereby** ⓐⓓ 그로 인해
- **emotional** ⓐ 정서적인
- **constant** ⓐ 끊임없는
- **contribute to** ~에 기여하다
- **possession** ⓝ 소유물

구문 풀이

7행 Advertisers have admitted to taking advantage of the fact
　　　　　　　　　　admit to + 동명사: ~하는 것을 인정하다
{that it is easy to make children feel that they are losers if they do
　　　가주어　　진주어(사역동사)　원형부정사 ↵ 접속사(~것)　접속사(~라면)
not own the 'right' products}.
〔 〕: 동격절(= the fact)

10　의도하지 않은 결과의 법칙
정답률 69% | 정답 ②

주어진 글 다음에 이어질 글의 순서로 가장 적절한 것을 고르시오.

① (A) – (C) – (B)
② (B) – (A) – (C) ✓
③ (B) – (C) – (A)
④ (C) – (A) – (B)
⑤ (C) – (B) – (A)

[본문 해석]

정책을 평가할 때, 사람들은 그것이 어떤 특정한 문제를 어떻게 해결할 것인가에 집중하는 경향이 있으며, 그 정책이 가질 수 있는 다른 효과는 무시하거나 경시한다. 경제학자들은 종종 이 상황을 *의도하지 않은 결과의 법칙*이라고 부른다.

(B) 예를 들어, 국내 철강 노동자들의 일자리를 보호하기 위해 수입된 철강에 관세를 부과한다고 가정해 보자. 만약 당신이 충분히 높은 관세를 부과한다면, 그들의 일자리는 실제로 외국 철강 회사들과의 경쟁으로부터 보호될 것이다.

(A) 그러나 한 가지 의도하지 않은 결과는 일부 자동차 노동자들의 일자리를 외국 경쟁사에 빼앗기게 된다는 것이다. 왜일까? 철강 노동자들을 보호하는 관세는 국내 자동차 제조업체들이 자동차를 만드는 데 필요한 철강의 가격을 높인다.

(C) 그 결과, 국내 자동차 제조업체들은 자동차 가격을 인상해야 하고, 국산차를 외제 차에 비해 상대적으로 덜 매력적이게 만든다. 가격을 올리는 것은 국산 차 판매를 줄이는 경향이 있어서, 일부 국내 자동차 노동자들은 일자리를 잃는다.

Why? 왜 정답일까?

'의도하지 않은 결과의 법칙'을 소개하는 주어진 글 뒤로, 국내 철강 회사를 보호하기 위한 무역 조치를 예로 드는 (B), 이 조치의 '의도하지 않은 결과'에 관해 언급하는 (A), 그 최종 영향을 설명하는 (C)가 차례로 연결되어야 한다. 따라서 글의 순서로 가장 적절한 것은 ② '(B) – (A) – (C)'이다.

- **evaluate** ⓥ 평가하다
- **downplay** ⓥ 경시하다
- **refer to A as B** A를 B라고 부르다
- **consequence** ⓝ 결과
- **tariff** ⓝ 관세
- **raise** ⓥ 올리다
- **attractive** ⓐ 매력적인
- **concentrate on** ~에 집중하다
- **economist** ⓝ 경제학자
- **unintended** ⓐ 의도되지 않은
- **autoworker** ⓝ 자동차 업체 근로자
- **steelworker** ⓝ 철강 노동자
- **import** ⓥ 수입하다

구문 풀이

1행 When evaluating a policy, people tend to concentrate on
　　分詞構文(= When they evaluate ~)　　　　　　　　　전치사
{how the policy will fix some particular problem} while ignoring or
〔 〕: 간접의문문　　　　　　　　　　　　　分詞構文(= while they ignore
downplaying other effects [it may have.]　　　　　　　　or downplay ~)

11-12　사람 관리에서 중요한 것

[본문 해석]

창의적인 사람들이 모두 같은 부류인 것은 아니다. 그들은 (a) 다양한 수준의 성숙도와 민감성을 지닌다. 그들은 일에 대한 접근법이 서로 다르다. 그리고 그들은 각자 서로 다른 것에 의해 동기 부여된다. 『사람 관리에서 중요한 것은 그들의 고유한 개성을 아는 것이다.』 또한 중요한 것은 공감과 적응성, 그리고 여러분이 하는 일과 하는 말이 어떻게 해석될지 알고 그에 따라 보조를 맞추는 것이다. 여러분이 누구인지와 무슨 말을 하는지는 사람마다 (b) 같지 않을 수 있다. 예를 들어, 여러분이 누군가에게 2주 연속 주말에 일하라고 요청하고 있다면, 또는 그들이 받아 마땅한 승진을 지금 당장은 받지 못할 것이라고 말하고

있다면, 그 (c) 집단(→ 개인)을 명심해야 한다. 「Vincent는 그 소식에 Emily와 매우 다른 반응을 보일 것이고, 그 소식이 서로 다른 것과 묶인다면 그들 각자는 더 잘 받아들일 것이다.」 ┌─「 ;:12번의 근거 아마 Vincent에게 명절에 며칠간의 추가적인 휴무일이 주어진다면 그 승진 소식은 (d) 더 쉽게 도달할(받아들여질) 것이고, 한편 Emily에게는 지금보다 1년 후에 더 큰 승진을 약속할 수도 있을 것이다. 무슨 말을 할지와 그 말을 어떻게 할지를 정할 때 사람 각각의 복잡한 긍정적 및 부정적인 개성의 특징, 그들의 인생 상황, 그 순간 그들의 사고방식을 고려하라. 개인적인 연관, 동감, 그리고 개별화된 관리 방식은 모든 사람으로부터 일관되고 록 스타 수준의(엄청난) 일을 끌어내는 (e) 핵심이다.

- cut from the same cloth 비슷한, 같은 부류인
- varying ⓐ 다양한
- sensitivity ⓝ 민감성
- personality ⓝ 개성, 성격
- adaptability ⓝ 적응력
- in a row 연달아
- promotion ⓝ 승진
- reaction ⓝ 반응
- bundle ⓥ 다발로 하다, 묶다
- trait ⓝ 특성
- individualize ⓥ 개별화하다
- appealing ⓐ 매력적인

- maturity ⓝ 성숙
- unique ⓐ 고유한
- empathy ⓝ 공감, 감정 이입
- accordingly ⓐⓓ 그에 따라
- deserve ⓥ (받을) 자격이 있다
- bear in mind ~을 유념하다
- receptive to ~을 잘 받아들이는
- land ⓥ 도달하다
- circumstance ⓝ 상황
- flexible hours 탄력 근로제, 유연 근무제

구문 풀이

17행 Perhaps that promotion news will land easier if Vincent is given a few extra vacation days for the holidays, while you can
4형식 수동태 ─── 직접목적어 ─── 접속사(~한 편)
promise Emily a bigger promotion a year from now.

★★★ 1등급 대비 고난도 2점 문제

11 제목 파악 | 정답률 42% | 정답 ①

윗글의 제목으로 가장 적절한 것은?

✓① Know Each Person to Guarantee Best Performance
최상의 수행을 보장하려면 사람 각각을 알라
② Flexible Hours: An Appealing Working Condition
탄력 근무제: 매력적인 근로 조건
③ Talk to Employees More Often in Hard Times
어려운 시기에는 직원들과 더 자주 이야기하라
④ How Empathy and Recognition Are Different
공감과 인정은 어떻게 다른가
⑤ Why Creativity Suffers in Competition
왜 창의성은 경쟁 속에서 악화되는가

Why? 왜 정답일까?

사람마다 개성이 다르기에 이 개성을 활용해야 사람들을 잘 관리할 수 있다(Managing people is about being aware of their unique personalities.)는 내용의 글이다. 따라서 글의 제목으로 가장 적절한 것은 ① '최상의 수행을 보장하려면 사람 각각을 알라'이다.

★★ 문제 해결 꿀~팁 ★★

▶ 많이 틀린 이유는?
사람 관리에 개성이 중요하다는 내용의 글로, empathy가 핵심 소재로 등장하므로 ④가 제목으로 그럴듯해 보일 수 있다. 하지만 '공감과 인정의 차이'를 설명하는 내용은 글에서 다루지 않았다.
▶ 문제 해결 방법은?
분량은 길지만, 명확한 주제문(Managing people is about being aware of their unique personalities.)이 있어 지엽적 소재와 관련된 함정에 주의하면 쉽게 답을 고를 수 있다. For instance 이하는 주제를 뒷받침하는 예시를 주로 다룬다.

★★★ 1등급 대비 고난도 2점 문제

12 어휘 추론 | 정답률 34% | 정답 ③

밑줄 친 (a) ~ (e) 중에서 문맥상 낱말의 쓰임이 적절하지 않은 것은?

① (a)   ② (b)   ✓③ (c)   ④ (d)   ⑤ (e)

Why? 왜 정답일까?

(c)가 포함된 문장 뒤를 보면, 사람마다 같은 소식에 대해 다른 반응을 보일 수도 있고,

그렇기 때문에 소식을 더 잘 받아들이게 하려면 각자 다른 것을 제시해야 한다는 내용이다. 이 예시에 앞서 일반적 내용을 정리하는 (c)가 포함된 문장은 집단보다 '개인'을 고려하라는 의미여야 하므로, group을 individual로 고쳐야 한다. 따라서 문맥상 낱말의 쓰임이 적절하지 않은 것은 ③ '(c)'이다.

★★ 문제 해결 꿀~팁 ★★

▶ 많이 틀린 이유는?
④가 예시를 다루고 있어 주제를 적용해야 하므로 다소 까다롭다. 내용을 살펴보면, Vincent와 Emily에게 똑같이 '승진 유예'라는 소식을 전하는 상황에서, Vincent 에게는 추가 휴가를 주고, Emily에게는 훗날 더 큰 승진을 약속해야 각자 소식을 '더 쉽게' 받아들일 것이라고 한다. 즉 ④가 포함된 문장은 '~ they will each be more receptive to the news if it's bundled with different things.'에 대한 적절한 예를 제시하고 있다.
▶ 문제 해결 방법은?
예시 앞의 unique personalities, empathy and adaptability, not be the same from one person to the next가 모두 한 논지를 가리키고 있다. 즉, '개인의 특징'을 고려해야 한다는 것이다.

DAY 24 20분 미니 모의고사

01 ⑤	02 ⑤	03 ③	04 ③	05 ②
06 ③	07 ②	08 ④	09 ①	10 ②
11 ②	12 ③			

---

01 직원의 '행동'에 관해 피드백하기 | 정답률 80% | 정답 ⑤

다음 글에서 필자가 주장하는 바로 가장 적절한 것은?

① 직원의 개인적 성향을 고려하여 업무를 배정하라.
② 업무 효율성 향상을 위해 직원의 자율성을 존중하라.
③ 조직의 안정을 위해 직원의 심리 상태를 수시로 확인하라.
④ 직원의 업무상 고충을 이해하기 위해 직원과 적극적으로 소통하라.
☑ 문제를 보이는 직원에게 인격적 특성보다는 행동 방식에 대해 제안하라.

[본문 해석]

관리자들은 직원이 왜 특정한 방식으로 행동했는지를 '알아낼' 목적으로 자주 심리학자 역할을 하려 한다. 직원들의 관점을 이해하려고 그들과 공감하는 것은 매우 도움이 될 수 있다. 하지만, 특히 문제 영역을 다룰 때, 나쁜 것은 사람이 아니라 근무 중에 나타나는 행동임을 기억하라. 직원들에게 그들이 바꿔야 할 인격적 특성에 대해 제안하기를 피하고, 대신 더 용인되는 수행 방법을 제안하라. 예를 들어, 관리자는 어떤 사람의 '미덥지 못함'에 집중하는 대신, 그 직원이 '이번 달에 회사에 일곱 번 지각했다'는 사실에 초점을 맞출 수도 있을 것이다. 직원들은 자신이 어떤 사람인지를 바꾸기는 어렵다. 일반적으로 자신이 행동하는 방식을 바꾸기가 훨씬 더 쉽다.

Why? 왜 정답일까?

직원이 문제를 보일 때 나쁜 것은 사람이 아니라 행동임을 명심하고, 인격적 특성보다는 수행 방법에 대해 피드백하라는(~ instead suggest more acceptable ways of performing.) 내용이다. 따라서 필자가 주장하는 바로 가장 적절한 것은 ⑤ '문제를 보이는 직원에게 인격적 특성보다는 행동 방식에 대해 제안하라.'이다.

- **certain** ⓐ 특정한, 어떤
- **point of view** 관점, 견해
- **make a suggestion** 제안하다
- **trait** ⓝ 특성
- **unreliability** ⓝ 미덥지 못함
- **empathize with** ~에 공감하다
- **deal with** ~을 다루다, ~에 대처하다
- **personal** ⓐ 개인적인, 인격의
- **acceptable** ⓐ 수용 가능한

구문 풀이

4행 However, when dealing with a problem area, in particular,
분사구문(= when you deal ~)
remember that it is not the person who is bad, but the actions exhibited
명령문(~하라) 'not+A+but+B : A가 아니라 B인' 과거분사
on the job.

★★★ 1등급 대비 고난도 2연 문제

02 문화적으로 이뤄지는 인종의 구별 | 정답률 37% | 정답 ⑤

다음 글의 주제로 가장 적절한 것은?

① causes of physical variations among different races
다른 인종 간 신체적 차이의 원인
② cultural differences between various races
다양한 인종 간의 문화 차이
③ social policies to overcome racism
인종 차별주의를 극복하기 위한 사회 정책
④ importance of environmental factors in evolution
진화에 있어서 환경적 요인의 중요성
☑ misconception about race as a biological construct
생물학적 구성물로서의 인종에 대한 오해

[본문 해석]

인간 개개인은 많은 가시적이고 비가시적인 면에서 신체적으로 서로 다르다. 대부분의 사람이 정의하듯이, 인종이 정말 생물학적 실체라면, 아프리카계 혈통인 사람들은 매우 다양한 특성을 공유하는 한편, 유럽계 혈통인 사람들은 (그것과) 다른 매우 다양한 특성을 공유할 것이다. 하지만 우리가 피부색, 머릿결 등 등보다 덜 가시적인 특성들을 추가해 보면, 우리가 '같은 인종'이라고 식별하는 사람들이 서로 점점 덜 닮았고 우리가 '다른 인종'이라고 식별하는 사람들과 더욱 더 닮았다는 것을 알게 된다. 어떤 사람을 어떤 인종의 전형이라고 식별하는

데 사용되는 신체적 특성(예를 들어, 피부색)이 지속적으로 변할 수 있어서 어디서 '갈색 피부'가 '흰 피부'가 되는지를 말할 수 없는 것을 이 점에 추가해 보라. 비록 신체적 차이 그 자체가 실재하더라도, 사람들을 별개의 인종으로 분류하기 위해 우리가 신체적 차이를 사용하는 방식은 문화적 구성이다.

Why? 왜 정답일까?

마지막 문장에서 비록 서로 다른 인종들 간의 생물학적 차이가 실제로 있다고 해도, 인종의 구별은 문화적으로 이루어진다(Although the physical differences themselves are real, the way we use physical differences to classify people into discrete races is a cultural construction.)는 내용이 제시된다. 따라서 글의 주제로 가장 적절한 것은 ⑤ '생물학적 구성물로서의 인종에 대한 오해'이다.

- **physically** ⓐⓓ 신체적으로
- **ancestry** ⓝ 혈통, 가계
- **coloration** ⓝ (생물의) 천연색
- **identify as** ~라고 식별하다
- **representative** ⓝ 전형, 대표
- **construction** ⓝ 구성
- **racism** ⓝ 인종 차별(주의)
- **multitude** ⓝ 다수
- **trait** ⓝ 특성
- **and the like** 기타 등등
- **feature** ⓝ 특징
- **variable** ⓐ 가변적인
- **overcome** ⓥ 극복하다
- **misconception** ⓝ 오해

구문 풀이

11행 Add to this point that the physical features used to identify
동사(명령문) 접속사(목적절 연결) 주어 과거분사구
a person as a representative of some race (e.g. skin coloration) are
동사(복수)
continuously variable, so that one cannot say {where "brown skin"
그래서 ~하다
becomes "white skin."} { } : 간접의문문

★★ 문제 해결 꿀~팁 ★★

▶ 많이 틀린 이유는?
difference, cultural, races 등 키워드만 보고 오답을 고르지 않도록 주의해야 한다. 먼저 ①은 서로 다른 인종 간 '신체적 차이'의 '원인'을 언급하는데, 글에서는 인종 간 '신체적' 차이가 실제적 개념이 아닐 수 있다고 했으며, 그 원인을 밝히지도 않았다. 이어서 ②는 서로 다른 인종 간 '문화적 차이'를 언급하는데, 글에서는 인종적 차이라는 개념이 문화적으로 구성된 개념일 수 있다고만 언급할 뿐, 인종들 간에 어떤 문화적 차이가 있는지는 구체적으로 다루지 않았다.

▶ 문제 해결 방법은?
인종이 생물학적 개념이라는 통념에 대해 사실은 이것이 문화적으로 구성된 개념임을 언급하며 반박하는 글이므로, 가리켜 '오해'라고 지적하는 선택지가 정답이다.

03 지역별 아동의 2차 홍역 백신 접종 비율 | 정답률 69% | 정답 ③

다음 도표의 내용과 일치하지 않는 것은?

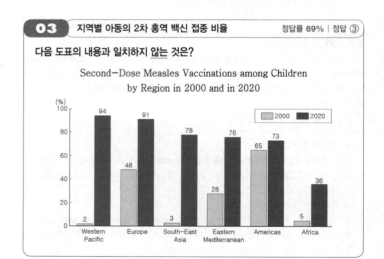

Second-Dose Measles Vaccinations among Children by Region in 2000 and in 2020

[본문 해석]

위 그래프는 2000년과 2020년에 6개 지역에서 2차 홍역 백신을 접종한 아이들의 비율을 보여 준다. ① 서태평양에서 백신을 접종한 아이들의 비율은 2000년에는 유럽에 비해 낮았지만 2020년 서태평양의 백신 접종율은 유럽을 3퍼센트 포인트 앞질렀다. ② 모든 지역들 중에서, 동남아시아는 백신 접종이 완료된 아이들의 비율에 있어 지난 20년간 두 번째로 큰 증가를 이뤘고, 이 지역은 2020년 백신 접종된 아이들의 비율에서 6개 지역 중 3위를 차지했다. ③ 동 지중해에서 백신을 접종한 아이들의 비율은 2000년에서 2020년까지 2배 이상 증가했지만, 두 해 모두 아메리카를 뛰어넘지는 못했다. ④ 아메리카에서 백신을 접종한 아이들의 비율은 2000년에 여섯 지역 중 가장 높았지만, 이는 지난 20

간 모든 지역 중 가장 적게 증가했다. ⑤ 아프리카에서 2020년에 백신을 접종한 아이들의 비율은 2000년보다 7배 이상 높았지만, 2020년에도 여전히 여섯 지역 중 최하였다.

Why? 왜 정답일까?

도표에 따르면 동 지중해 지역에서 2차 홍역 백신 접종을 완료한 아동의 비율은 2000 ~2020년 사이 28%에서 76%로 증가했고, 2020년의 경우 아메리카(73%)보다도 그 수치가 높았다. 따라서 도표와 일치하지 않는 것은 두 해 모두 아메리카보다 낮다고 잘못 기술한 ③이다.

- **dose** ⓝ (약의) 투여량, 복용량
- **vaccination** ⓝ 백신 접종
- **measles** ⓝ 홍역
- **Mediterranean** ⓐ 지중해의

04 외국인 학생 대상 한국어 말하기 대회 정답률 95% | 정답 ③

2022 Korean Speech Contest에 관한 다음 안내문의 내용과 일치하지 않는 것은?
① 한국에서 지내는 동안의 경험을 주제로 한다.
② 영상 제출 마감일은 9월 5일이다.
☑ 1등에게는 상금과 한국 전통 인형이 주어진다.
④ 영상 도입부에 이름이 언급되어야 한다.
⑤ 이메일로 영상 파일을 보내야 한다.

[본문 해석]

2022 한국어 말하기 대회

당신은 한국어를 뽐내고 싶은 외국인 학생인가요? 한국에서의 경험을 공유하는 자신만의 영상을 만들어 보세요.

- 『주제: "한국에서 지내는 동안의 경험"』—「」: ①의 근거 일치
- 『영상 제출 마감일: 9월 5일』—「」: ②의 근거 일치
- 상품
  - 『1등: $100 및 한국 전통차』—「」: ③의 근거 불일치
  - 2등: $50 및 한국 전통 인형
- 세부 사항
  - 『영상의 도입부에 이름이 언급되어야 합니다.』—「」: ④의 근거 일치
  - 영상은 3분에서 5분 길이여야 합니다.
  - 『영상 파일을 k-speech@kcontest.com에 이메일로 보내주십시오.』—「」: ⑤의 근거 일치

Why? 왜 정답일까?

'1st place: $100 and traditional Korean tea'에서 1등 수상자에게는 상금 100달러와 한국 전통차가 부상으로 주어진다고 하므로, 안내문의 내용과 일치하지 않는 것은 ③ '1등에게는 상금과 한국 전통 인형이 주어진다.'이다.

Why? 왜 오답일까?

① 'Theme: "My Experiences While Staying in Korea"'의 내용과 일치한다.
② 'Video Submission Deadline: September 5th'의 내용과 일치한다.
④ 'Your name must be mentioned at the beginning of the video.'의 내용과 일치한다.
⑤ 'Please email your video file to k-speech@kcontest.com.'의 내용과 일치한다.

- **show off** ~을 과시하다
- **mention** ⓥ 언급하다

★★★ 1등급 대비 고난도 3점 문제

05 두 가지 다른 기부 행위 비교 정답률 39% | 정답 ②

다음 글의 밑줄 친 부분 중, 어법상 틀린 것은? [3점]

[본문 해석]

기부 행위를 연구하는 심리학자들은, 어떤 사람들은 한두 자선단체에 상당한 액수를 기부하는 반면 어떤 사람들은 많은 자선단체에 적은 액수를 기부한다는 사실을 알게 되었다. 한두 자선단체에 기부하는 사람들은 그 자선단체가 무슨 일을 하고 있는지와 그것이 실제로 긍정적인 영향을 끼치고 있는지에 관한 증거를 찾는다. 증거에서 자선단체가 정말로 다른 사람들을 도와주고 있다는 것을 보여줄 경우 그들은 상당한 기부금을 낸다. 많은 자선단체에 적은 액수를 내는 사람들은 그들이 하는 일이 다른 사람들을 돕는지에는 그렇게 큰 관심을 두지 않는다. 심리학자들은 이들을 따뜻한 불빛 기부자라고 부른다. 기부금의 영향과 관계없이 자신들이 기부하고 있다는 사실을 아는 것이 이들을 기분 좋게

한다. 많은 경우 기부금은 10달러 이하의 매우 적은 금액이어서, 곰곰이 생각해 본다면, 그들은 기부금을 처리하는 비용이 기부금으로 인한 자선단체의 이득을 넘어서기 쉽다는 것을 알게 될 것이다.

Why? 왜 정답일까?

'it is really having a positive impact'가 3형식의 완전한 절이므로 what은 이 절을 이끌 수 없고, 앞에 나온 간접의문문 'what the charity is doing'과 병렬 구조를 이루도록 whether를 쓰는 것이 적절하다. 어법상 틀린 것은 ②이다.

Why? 왜 오답일까?

① 주어가 Psychologists라는 복수 명사이므로 have를 쓴 것은 적절하다.
③ whether절에서 helps의 주어로 what절이 나왔는데, what은 불완전한 절을 이끈다. 따라서 목적어가 없이 현재분사 doing을 쓴 것은 적절하다.
④ 앞에 나온 they와 마찬가지로 'warm glow givers'를 가리키는 복수대명사로서 them을 쓴 것은 적절하다.
⑤ 'stop + to부정사'는 '~하기 위해 멈추다'라는 뜻으로, 'stop + 동명사(~하는 것을 멈추다)'와 비교할 때 여기서 to think를 쓴 것은 적절하다.

- **behavior** ⓝ 행위, 행동
- **seek** ⓥ 찾다, 구하다, 추구하다
- **indicate** ⓥ 나타내다, 보여주다
- **regardless of** ~에 상관없이
- **exceed** ⓥ 초과하다, 능가하다
- **substantial** ⓐ (양·가치·중요성이) 상당한
- **evidence** ⓝ 증거
- **glow** ⓝ 불빛, 빛
- **process** ⓥ 처리하다

구문 풀이

1행 Psychologists [who study giving behavior] have noticed [that
주어(복수) 동사(현재완료)
some people give substantial amounts to one or two charities, /
부정대명사(어떤 사람들)
while others give small amounts to many charities].
부정대명사(some 다음에 나와 '어떤 사람들) [ ]: 목적어

★★ 문제 해결 꿀~팁 ★★

▶ 많이 틀린 이유는?
의문사 'what vs. whether'의 쓰임 구별, '인칭대명사 vs. 재귀대명사' 등 비교적 덜 출제되는 고난도 개념을 이용하여 난이도를 높인 문제였다. 최다 오답은 ⑤였는데 여기서 'stop + to부정사'는 '~하기 위해 멈추다, 곰곰이 ~하다'라는 뜻이다. to부정사 대신 동명사가 들어가면 'stop + 동명사'는 '~하는 것을 멈추다'란 뜻이 되는데 이는 맥락상 어색하다. 즉 이는 형태보다는 해석으로 풀어내는 문제임을 유의한다.
▶ 문제 해결 방법은?
②의 경우, 실전에서는 'it is really having a positive impact'가 완전한 구조이므로 앞에 what은 쓸 수 없다는 정도까지만 파악하고 바로 답을 고르도록 한다. 무엇으로 고쳐야 할지까지 고민하다가는 시간을 많이 뺏길 수 있다.

06 음식을 기다리는 중 되짚어본 원자 개념 정답률 57% | 정답 ③

다음 글의 밑줄 친 부분 중, 문맥상 낱말의 쓰임이 적절하지 않은 것은? [3점]

[본문 해석]

나는 어느 여름날 저녁 스페인에서 한 식당 밖에 앉아 저녁 식사를 기다리고 있었다. 주방의 향기가 나의 미뢰를 자극했다. 곧 먹게 될 내 음식은, 너무 작아 눈으로 볼 수는 없지만 코로는 ① 감지되는, 공중을 떠다니는 분자의 형태로 내게 오고 있었다. 고대 그리스인들은 이런 식으로 원자의 개념을 최초로 생각해 냈는데, 빵 굽는 냄새는 그들에게 작은 빵 입자가 눈에 보이지 않게 ② 존재한다는 생각이 들게 했다. 날씨의 순환은 이 생각을 ③ 뒤집었다(→ 강화했다). 지면 위 물웅덩이는 점차 말라 사라지고, 그런 다음 나중에 비가 되어 떨어진다. 그들은 수증기로 변하여 구름을 형성하고 땅으로 떨어지는 물 입자가 존재하는 게 틀림없고, 그래서 그 작은 입자들이 너무 작아 눈에 보이지 않더라도 그 물이 ④ 보존된다고 추론했다. 스페인에서 먹은 나의 파에야가 원자 이론에 대한 공로를 인정받기에는 4천 년이나 너무 ⑤ 늦게 내게 영감을 주었다.

Why? 왜 정답일까?

'They reasoned that there must be particles of water that turn into steam, form clouds, and fall to earth, so that the water is conserved even though the little particles are too small to see.'에서 물웅덩이가 수증기로 증발하여 구름을 이루고 나중에 비가 되어 떨어지는 것으로 볼 때 너무 작아 눈에 보이지 않더라도 항상 보존되는 물 입자가 있을 것으로 추론되었다는 설명이 나온다. 이에 비추어볼 때, ③이 포함된 문장은 날씨의 순환 과정이 항상 보존되는 입자가 있다는

DAY 24

생각을 '강화해 주었다'는 의미를 나타내야 한다. 따라서 ③의 disproved를 reinforced로 고쳐야 한다. 문맥상 낱말의 쓰임이 적절하지 않은 것은 ③이다.

- drift ⓥ 떠다니다
- ancient ⓐ 고대의
- atom ⓝ 원자
- gradually ⓐⓓ 점차
- disappear ⓥ 사라지다
- take the credit for ~의 공적을 인정받다
- detect ⓥ 감지하다
- come upon an idea 생각이 떠오르다
- disprove ⓥ 틀렸음을 입증하다
- dry out ⓥ 메마르다, 고갈되다
- conserve ⓥ 보존하다

구문 풀이

11행 They reasoned that there must be particles of water [that turn into steam, form clouds, and fall to earth], so that the water is conserved even though the little particles are too small to see.
접속사(~것) / 동사 / 주어(선행사) / 주격 관·대 / 복수 동사1 / 복수 동사2 / 복수 동사3 / (~해서) …하다 / 비록 ~일지라도 / 「too ~ to … : 너무 …해서 …할 수 없다」

★★★ 1등급 대비 고난도 2점 문제

07 화폐의 희소성 정답률 17% | 정답 ②

다음 빈칸에 들어갈 말로 가장 적절한 것을 고르시오.
① invested - 투자될
✓ scarce - 희소성이 있을
③ transferred - 이동될
④ divisible - 나뉠 수 있을
⑤ deposited - 예치될

[본문 해석]

가장 중요하게도, 돈은 예측 가능한 방식으로 희소성이 있을 필요가 있다. 귀금속은 내재적인 아름다움을 지니고 있을 뿐만 아니라 고정된 양으로 존재하기 때문에 수 천 년에 걸쳐 돈으로서 바람직했다. 금과 은은 발견되고 채굴되는 만큼 사회에 유입되는데, 추가적인 귀금속은 적어도 싸게는 생산될 수가 없다. 쌀과 담배와 같은 상품들은 재배할 수 있지만, 여전히 시간과 자원이 든다. Zimbabwe의 Robert Mugabe와 같은 독재자도 정부에 100조 톤의 쌀을 생산하라고 명령할 수 없었다. 그는 수조의 새로운 Zimbabwe 달러를 만들어 유통시킬 수 있었는데, 이것은 결국 그것이 통화(通貨)보다 휴지로서 더 가치가 있게 되었던 이유이다.

Why? 왜 정답일까?

빈칸 뒤에서 귀금속은 고정된 양으로 존재하기 때문에(~ they exist in fixed quantities.) 돈으로서 기능하기 바람직했다는 내용에 이어 추가적인 귀금속은 싸게 생산될 수 없다고 덧붙이고 있다. 이는 귀금속이 수요에 따라 무한정 늘어나지 못하고 늘 욕구에 비해 '희소한' 상태를 유지했기에 돈으로서의 가치를 지녔다는 뜻으로 이해할 수 있다. 따라서 빈칸에 들어갈 말로 가장 적절한 것은 ② '희소성이 있을'이다.

- predictable ⓐ 예측 가능한
- desirable ⓐ 바람직한
- intrinsic ⓐ 내재적인, 본질적인, 고유한
- quantity ⓝ 양
- dictator ⓝ 독재자
- distribute ⓥ 유통시키다, 배포하다
- precious ⓐ 귀중한, 소중한
- millennium ⓝ 1천 년
- fixed ⓐ 고정된
- commodity ⓝ 상품
- trillion ⓝ 1조의
- currency ⓝ 통화

구문 풀이

11행 He was able to produce and distribute trillions of new Zimbabwe dollars, which is (the reason) why they eventually became more valuable as toilet paper than currency.
「be able to+동사원형1 and 동사원형2 : ~하고 …할 수 있다」 / 계속적 용법(앞 문장 받음) / 생략된 선행사 / 관계부사 / 2형식 동사 / 보어

★★ 문제 해결 꿀~팁 ★★

▶ 많이 틀린 이유는?
지문의 다른 부분에 빈칸과 대응될 말이 없어 까다로운 문제였다. 귀금속은 애초에 양도 정해져 있고 추가로 만들어질 수도 없기에 '희소성'을 지니고 있고, 이로 인해 화폐로 쓰이기 적합했다는 내용상의 흐름을 이해하도록 한다. 오답으로 많이 꼽힌 ①, ③의 경우 지문의 내용보다는 상식을 근거로 할 때 답으로 고르기 쉬운 선택지였다.

▶ 문제 해결 방법은?
'not only ~ but also …'가 들어간 문장은 많은 경우 주제를 제시하며, 특히 but also 이하에는 핵심 소재가 나온다. 여기서도 but also 뒤에 나온 'exist in fixed quantities'가 정답에 대한 결정적인 힌트를 제공하고 있다.

---

08 카리스마의 학습과 단련 정답률 44% | 정답 ④

글의 흐름으로 보아, 주어진 문장이 들어가기에 가장 적절한 곳을 고르시오. [3점]

[본문 해석]

카리스마는 분명하게 배울 수 있고 가르칠 수 있으며, 그리고 여러 면에서 모든 작용에 대하여 같은 크기의 반작용이 존재한다는 뉴턴의 유명한 운동 법칙 중 하나를 따른다. ① 즉 모든 카리스마와 인간 상호 작용은 다른 신호와 단서들로 이어지는 일련의 신호와 단서들이며, 어떤 신호와 단서들이 자신에게 가장 유리하게 작용하는지를 판독하는 과학이 있다. ② 다시 말하면, 카리스마는 종종 어떤 때에 무엇을 해야 하는지의 체크리스트로 단순화될 수 있다. ③ 그러나 그것은 편안한 상태에서 벗어나려는 일시적 시도를 필요로 할 것이다. ④ 비록 논리적으로는 수월한 일련의 지켜야 할 절차들이 존재할 수 있지만, 습관을 바꾸고, 익숙하지 않은 새롭고 불편한 행동들을 시작하는 것은 여전히 감정적인 분투이다. 나는 이것이 단지 오랫동안 활동을 중단한 근육들을 사용하는 문제라고 말하는 것을 좋아한다. ⑤ 그것들을 준비시키는 데 시간이 좀 필요하겠지만, 원하는 목표를 성취하게 되는 것은 바로 오직 연습과 행동을 통해서이다.

Why? 왜 정답일까?

카리스마는 마치 운동으로 단련되는 근육과 같이 키워지고 학습될 수 있다는 점을 주장하는 글이다. ④ 앞의 두 문장에서 카리스마에는 일종의 과학이 있기 때문에 카리스마라는 개념은 언제 무엇을 해야할지의 체크리스트로 단순화될 수 있지만, 그렇게 하는 데에는 현재의 편안한 상태를 깨려는 도전적인 시도가 필요할 것임을 이야기한다. 여기에 이어 Even though로 시작하는 주어진 문장은 비록 따라야 할 절차가 단순하다고 하더라도 습관을 바꾸는 데에는 감정적인 분투가 따를 수밖에 없다는 점을 지적한다. ④ 뒤의 문장은 이것(it), 즉 습관을 바꾸어 카리스마를 연마하는 일이 그저 오랫동안 사용하지 않았던 근육을 다시 쓰는 문제와 비슷하다는 비유를 제시하며 연습의 중요성을 상기시킨다. 따라서 주어진 문장이 들어가기에 가장 적절한 곳은 ④이다.

- logically ⓐⓓ 논리적으로
- introduce ⓥ 도입하다, 들여오다
- learnable ⓐ 배울 수 있는, 학습 가능한
- reaction ⓝ 반작용, 반응
- cue ⓝ 단서
- in one's favor ~에 유리하게
- comfort zone 안전 지대
- procedure ⓝ 절차, 수순
- eminently ⓐⓓ 분명하게, 대단히
- teachable ⓐ 가르칠 수 있는
- interaction ⓝ 상호 작용
- work ⓥ 작동하다
- simplify ⓥ 단순화하다
- desired ⓐ 바랐던, 희망했던

구문 풀이

8행 That is to say that all of charisma and human interaction is a set of signals and cues [that lead to other signals and cues], and there is a science to deciphering {which signals and cues work the most in your favor}.
즉, 다시 말해서 / 주어1 / 동사1 / 선행사 / 주격 관계대명사 / 동사2 / 주어2 / 전치사 / 동명사 / 의문사(어떤)

09 취미에 들인 시간과 일에 대한 자기 효능감의 관계 정답률 52% | 정답 ①

다음 글의 내용을 한 문장으로 요약하고자 한다. 빈칸 (A), (B)에 들어갈 말로 가장 적절한 것은?

	(A)		(B)		(A)		(B)
✓	confidence 자신감	……	different 다른	②	productivity 생산성	……	connected 연결된
③	relationships 관계	……	balanced 균형 잡힌	④	creativity 창의성	……	separate 분리된
⑤	dedication 헌신	……	similar 비슷한				

[본문 해석]

Sheffield 대학교 몇몇 연구자들은 취미에 쓴 시간이 어떻게 직장 생활에 영향을 미치는지를 보기 위해 취미에 열정적인 사람들 129명을 모집했다. 먼저 연구팀은 '나는 이 (취미)활동을 위해 정기적으로 연습을 한다.'와 같은 진술에 동의하는 정도를 평가하도록 요청하며, 각 참가자가 가지고 있는 취미의 진지함을 측정하고, 또한 그들의 일과 취미를 하는 데 필요한 것들이 얼마나 비슷한지도 평가했다. 그 뒤, 7개월 동안 매월, 참가자들은 취미활동에 몇 시간을 투자했는지를 기록하고 그들의 직업을 효과적으로 수행하는 능력에 대한 믿음, 즉 '자기 효능감'을 측정하는 평가표를 작성했다. 연구자들은 참가자들이 보통 수준보다 취미활동에 더 긴 시간을 썼을 때 그들의 직업 수행능력에 대한 믿음이 증가하였다는 것을 발견했다. 하지만 이는 오로지 그들이 직업과 다른 진지한 취미를 가지고 있을 때만 그러했다. 그들의 취미가 진지하면서 직업과

유사할 때, 취미에 시간을 많이 보내는 것이 실제로 그들의 자기 효능감을 낮추었다.

➡ 연구에 따르면 취미와 직업이 충분히 **(B)** 다른 경우 진지한 취미에 더 많은 시간을 보내는 것이 일에서의 **(A)** 자신감을 높여줄 수 있다.

Why? 왜 정답일까?

마지막 세 문장에서 연구 참가자들은 직업과 다른 진지한 취미에 더 많은 시간을 들일 때 일에 대한 자기 효능감이 상승했으며, 직업과 취미가 비슷할 때에는 오히려 자기 효능감이 떨어지는 결과가 나타났다고 설명하고 있다. 따라서 요약문의 빈칸 **(A)**, **(B)**에 들어갈 말로 가장 적절한 것은 일에 대한 자신감이 일과 충분히 다른 취미에 종사할 때 높아질 수 있다는 의미를 완성하는 ① **(A) confidence**(자신감), **(B) different**(다른)이다.

- **seriousness** ⓝ 진지함
- **dedicate** ⓥ 바치다, 전념하다
- **self-efficacy** 자기 효능감
- **boost** ⓥ 높이다, 신장시키다
- **confidence** ⓝ 자신감
- **assess** ⓥ 평가하다
- **effectively** ⓐⓓ 효과적으로
- **dissimilar** ⓐ 다른, 같지 않은
- **sufficiently** ⓐⓓ 충분히

구문 풀이

1행 Some researchers at Sheffield University recruited 129 hobbyists to look at how the time spent on their hobbies shaped their work life.
~하기 위해 / 의문사 / 주어 / 과거분사 / 동사

10-12 크리스마스에 Martha 가족에게 생긴 일

[본문 해석]

(A)
"Emma, 올해 너는 참 착한 아이였어. 오늘밤, 산타 할아버지가 우리 집에 들러서 너에게 선물을 몇 개 두고 가실 거야." Martha가 (a) 자신의 귀여운 딸에게 웃으며 말했다. "Fred 너에게도." 그녀가 덧붙였다. 『그녀는 두 아이들에게 훨씬 더 많은 것을 주길 원했지만 올해는 Martha에게 특히 힘들었다.』 그녀는 두 아이들에게 크리스마스 선물을 사 주기 위해 밤낮으로 일했다.
└─『 』: 12번 ①의 근거 일치

(C)
그날 밤, 모두가 잠들고 난 후 Emma는 천천히 침대 밖으로 기어 나왔다. 『그녀는 산타 할아버지에게 편지를 쓰기 위해 공책 한 장을 찢어 냈다.』 그녀는 쓰면서 혼자 작은 소리로 속삭였다. "산타 할아버지께, 저희 엄마에게 미소와 웃음을 조금 보내주실 수 있나요? (c) 엄마는 별로 웃지 않아요. 그리고 Fred를 위한 장난감도 몇 개 보내주실 수 있나요? 고맙습니다." Emma는 그 편지를 두 번 접어 봉투에 넣고 붙였다. 그녀는 현관 밖에 그 봉투를 두고 나서 다시 잠자리에 들었다.
└─『 』: 12번 ④의 근거 일치

(B)
다음 날 아침 Emma가 엄마에게 뛰어왔다. "엄마, 어젯밤 정말로 산타 할아버지가 오셨어요!" 양말 속에서 (b) 딸이 틀림없이 발견했을 사탕과 쿠키를 떠올리며 Martha가 미소 지었다. "산타 할아버지가 주신 선물들이 마음에 들었니?" "네, 멋져요. 『Fred도 그분이 주신 장난감들이 마음에 든대요.』" Martha는 혼란스러웠다. 그녀는 사탕과 쿠키가 하룻밤 사이에 어떻게 장난감이 되었는지 궁금했다. 『Martha는 Emma의 방으로 뛰어 들어가서 반쯤 열려 있는 작은 빨간 상자를 보았다.』 그녀는 무릎을 꿇고 그 내용물을 보기 위해 안을 들여다보았다.
└─『 』: 12번 ②의 근거 일치
└─『 』: 12번 ③의 근거 불일치

(D)
그 상자는 장난감 몇 개, 그리고 셀 수 없이 많은 작은 사탕과 쿠키를 담고 있었다. 『"엄마, 이건 산타 할아버지가 엄마에게 주신 거예요." Emma가 Martha를 향해 카드 하나를 내밀며 말했다.』 당황한 채로, (d) 그녀는 그것을 열었다. 거기에는 이렇게 쓰여 있었다. "Emma 어머님께. 정말 메리 크리스마스입니다! 안녕하세요, 저는 Amelia입니다. 어젯밤 길 건너편에서 자녀분이 쓴 편지가 바람에 날아다니고 있는 걸 보았어요. 제가 감동 받아 답장을 하지 않을 수 없었습니다. 부디 이 선물을 크리스마스 인사로 받아주세요." Martha는 눈물이 (e) 자신의 볼을 타고 흘러내리는 것을 느꼈다. 그녀는 천천히 눈물을 닦고 딸을 껴안았다. "Emma, 메리 크리스마스. 엄마가 너에게 산타 할아버지가 오실 거라고 말했었지?"
└─『 』: 12번 ⑤의 근거 일치

- **drop by** ~에 들르다
- **overnight** ⓐⓓ 하룻밤 사이에

- **kneel down** 꿇어 앉다
- **whisper** ⓥ 속삭이다
- **envelope** ⓝ 봉투
- **glance** ⓥ 홀긋 보다
- **seal** ⓥ 봉인하다
- **countless** ⓐ 무수히 많은

구문 풀이

(A) 4행 She wanted to give her two children so much more, but
주어1 / 동사1
this year had been especially hard for Martha.
주어2 / 동사2(과거완료): wanted보다 이전

(B) 3행 Martha smiled, thinking of the candies and cookies [(that)
분사구문(~하면서) / 선행사 / 생략
she must have found in her socks].
「must have p.p.: ~했음에 틀림없다」

(D) 7행 I was touched and couldn't help but respond.
「cannot help but + 동사원형: ~하지 않을 수 없다」

---

10 글의 순서 파악   정답률 82% | 정답 ②

주어진 글 (A)에 이어질 내용을 순서에 맞게 배열한 것으로 가장 적절한 것은?

① (B) – (D) – (C)   ✓ (C) – (B) – (D)
③ (C) – (D) – (B)   ④ (D) – (B) – (C)
⑤ (D) – (C) – (B)

Why? 왜 정답일까?

시간적 단서를 잘 활용해야 하는 순서 문제이다. **(A)**에서 Martha가 크리스마스를 맞이해 아이들에게 선물을 사주기 위해 밤낮으로 일하고 있었다는 상황을 묘사한 데 이어, **(C)**에서는 산타클로스를 기다리던 '그날 밤(That night)' 딸인 Emma가 어머니에게 미소와 웃음을 달라는 편지를 쓰고 잠들었다는 내용을 제시한다. 이어서 **(B)**는 '다음 날 아침(the next morning)' 딸과 아들에게 자신이 준비한 쿠키 대신 장난감 선물이 주어졌다는 것을 안 Martha가 딸의 방에 들어가 상자를 확인해 보았다는 내용을 제시한다. 마지막으로 **(D)**는 Martha가 편지를 통해 Amelia라는 이웃이 Emma의 편지를 우연히 발견하고는 선물을 대신 준비해주었음을 알게 되었다는 결말을 제시한다. 따라서 글의 순서로 가장 적절한 것은 ② **(C) – (B) – (D)**이다.

---

11 지칭 추론   정답률 66% | 정답 ②

밑줄 친 (a) ~ (e) 중에서 가리키는 대상이 나머지 넷과 **다른** 것은?

① (a)   ✓ (b)   ③ (c)   ④ (d)   ⑤ (e)

Why? 왜 정답일까?

(a), (c), (d), (e)는 Martha를, (b)는 Emma를 가리키므로, (a) ~ (e) 중에서 가리키는 대상이 다른 하나는 ② **(b)**이다.

---

12 세부 내용 파악   정답률 77% | 정답 ③

윗글에 관한 내용으로 적절하지 않은 것은?

① 올해는 Martha에게 힘든 한 해였다.
② Fred가 선물받은 장난감을 마음에 들어 했다.
✓ Martha가 자신의 방에서 작은 빨간 상자를 보았다.
④ Emma가 산타에게 편지를 썼다.
⑤ Emma가 Martha에게 산타가 보냈다고 말하며 카드를 내밀었다.

Why? 왜 정답일까?

(B) 'Martha ran into Emma's room and saw a small red box that was half open.'에 따르면 Martha가 빨간 상자를 발견한 곳은 자신의 방이 아닌 딸 Emma의 방이다. 따라서 내용과 일치하지 않는 것은 ③ 'Martha가 자신의 방에서 작은 빨간 상자를 보았다.'이다.

Why? 왜 오답일까?

① **(A)** '~ but this year had been especially hard for Martha.'의 내용과 일치한다.
② **(B)** 'Fred loves his toys, too.'의 내용과 일치한다.
④ **(C)** 'She took out a page from a notebook to write a letter to Santa.'의 내용과 일치한다.
⑤ **(D)** '"Mommy, this is for you from Santa." Emma said holding out a card towards Martha.'의 내용과 일치한다.

DAY 25 ▷ 20분 미니 모의고사

01 ①	02 ②	03 ⑤	04 ④	05 ⑤
06 ⑤	07 ②	08 ③	09 ②	10 ②
11 ③	12 ④			

---

01 음식 기부 행사에 참여할 방법 안내   정답률 89% | 정답 ①

다음 글의 목적으로 가장 적절한 것은?
☑ ① 음식 기부에 참여하는 방법을 안내하려고
② 음식 배달 자원봉사 참여에 감사하려고
③ 도서관 이용 시간 변경을 공지하려고
④ 음식물 낭비의 심각성을 알려 주려고
⑤ 크리스마스 행사 일정을 문의하려고

[본문 해석]
후원자 여러분께,

즐거운 크리스마스를 보내기 바랍니다. 여러분 중 일부는 이미 알고 있듯이, 우리는 교내 음식 모으기 운동을 시작하고 있습니다. 참가 방법은 다음과 같습니다. 기부할 음식물을 우리 부스로 가져오면 됩니다. 우리 기부 부스는 교내 도서관 로비에 위치해 있습니다. 12월 4일부터 23일까지 도서관 정규 운영 시간에 그곳에 음식물을 갖다 놓기만 하면 됩니다. 기부되는 음식은 통조림 고기와 통조림 과일 같은 상하지 않는 음식이어야 합니다. 잼이나 땅콩버터 같은 포장 제품도 좋습니다. 우리는 그 음식을 크리스마스이브에 우리의 이웃들에게 나눠줄 겁니다. 여러분의 도움을 정말 고맙게 생각합니다.

축복을 기원하며,
Campus Food Bank의 Joanna 올림

Why? 왜 정답일까?
'As some of you already know, we are starting the campus food drive. This is how you participate.'에서 음식 기부 행사에 참여하는 방법을 알려주겠다고 언급한 후, 음식을 도서관 로비에 있는 기부 부스에 가져와야 한다는 등 구체적인 내용을 열거하고 있다. 따라서 글의 목적으로 가장 적절한 것은 ① '음식 기부에 참여하는 방법을 안내하려고'이다.

● food drive 음식 모으기 운동   ● drop off ~을 갖다 놓다
● non-perishable 상하지 않는   ● packaged ⓐ 포장된
● distribute ⓥ 나눠주다, 분배하다   ● blessing ⓝ 축복

구문 풀이

2행   As some of you already know, we are starting the campus
접속사(~듯이, ~대로)   현재진행(가까운 미래에 예정된 일)
food drive.

---

02 감정 지능(EI)의 중요성   정답률 62% | 정답 ②

다음 글의 요지로 가장 적절한 것은?
① 감성 지능의 결여는 직장 내 대인 관계 갈등을 심화시킨다.
☑ ② 미래의 직장에서는 감성 지능의 가치가 더욱 높아질 것이다.
③ 미래 사회에서는 감성 지능을 갖춘 기계가 보편화될 것이다.
④ 미래에는 대부분의 직장 업무를 인공 지능이 대신할 것이다.
⑤ 인간과 인공 지능 간의 상호 작용은 감성 지능의 발달을 저해한다.

[본문 해석]
아마도, 직장에서 인공 지능(AI)의 출현은 감성 지능(EI)에 좋은 징조가 될 수 있다. AI가 추진력을 받고 모든 수준의 일자리에서 사람들을 대신함에 따라, 높은 EI 능력을 가진 사람들에게 프리미엄이 주어질 것이라는 전망이 있다. 사람들이 상호 작용하는 동안 보내고 반응하는 감정적인 메시지들은 이런 점에서 AI 프로그램의 모방하는 능력을 훨씬 넘어선다. 우리가 스마트 기기의 시대로 접어들수록, 감정을 감지하고 관리하는 것은 AI를 당혹스럽게 하는 지능의 한 유형으로 남을 것이다. 이것은 EI와 관련된 사람들과 직업들이 기계에게 점령되는 것으로부터 안전하다는 것을 의미한다. 한 설문 조사에서, 일상적인 업무의 자동화가 정서적 기술이 필요한 활동에 효과적인 AI를 만드는 것이 불가

능하다는 점에 부딪히면서, 임원 네 명 중 세 명 가량이 EI를 향후 직장의 '필수' 기술로 보고 있다.

Why? 왜 정답일까?
스마트 기기 시대가 발전할수록 감정 지능에 관한 영역은 AI의 손이 닿을 수 없는 영역으로 남아 AI를 당혹스럽게 할 수 있으며, 이에 따라 감정 지능이 향후에 더 높은 가치를 지닐 것이라는(~ predictions are, there will be a premium placed on people who have high ability in EI.) 내용이다. 따라서 글의 요지로 가장 적절한 것은 ② '미래의 직장에서는 감성 지능의 가치가 더욱 높아질 것이다.'이다.

● advent ⓝ 출현   ● bode ⓥ ~의 징조가 되다
● momentum ⓝ 추진력, 기세   ● take over 장악하다, 탈취하다, 인수하다
● executive ⓝ 임원   ● bump up against ~에 부딪치다

구문 풀이

8행   As we get further into the age of the smart machine, it is
접속사(~함에 따라)   가주어
likely [that sensing and managing emotions will remain one type of
intelligence that puzzles AI]. [ ] : 진주어

---

03 Janaki Ammal의 생애   정답률 89% | 정답 ⑤

Janaki Ammal에 관한 다음 글의 내용과 일치하지 않는 것은?
① 관습을 따르지 않고 대학에 입학하기로 결심했다.
② 세계에서 가장 단 사탕수수 품종 개발에 기여했다.
③ *Chromosome Atlas of Cultivated Plants*를 공동 집필했다.
④ 식량 생산을 증가시키는 데 도움을 주기 위해 인도로 돌아갔다.
☑ ⑤ 수력 발전 댐의 건설로부터 Silent Valley를 지키는 데 실패했다.

[본문 해석]
인도의 가장 유명한 과학자 중 한 명인 Janaki Ammal은 1897년에 태어나 중매 결혼을 할 것으로 기대되었다. 「인도 여성들의 식자율이 1%보다 낮았던 시기에 살았음에도 불구하고, 그녀는 관습을 따르지 않고 대학에 입학하기로 결심했다.」 1924년에 그녀는 미국으로 갔고, 마침내 Michigan 대학교에서 식물학 박사 학위를 받았다. 「Ammal은 세계에서 가장 단 사탕수수 품종 개발에 기여했다.」 「그녀는 영국으로 건너가 그곳에서 *Chromosome Atlas of Cultivated Plants*를 공동 집필했다.」 「연이은 기근 이후, 그녀는 수상의 요청으로 식량 생산을 증가시키는 데 도움을 주기 위해 인도로 돌아갔다.」 그러나 Ammal은 더 많은 식량을 재배하려는 노력으로 삼림벌채가 일어나는 것에 반대하였다. 「그녀는 토종 식물 보존의 옹호자가 되었고, 수력 발전 댐의 건설로부터 Silent Valley를 성공적으로 지켰다.」 ── 「」: ⑤의 근거 불일치

Why? 왜 정답일까?
'~ successfully saved the Silent Valley from the construction of a hydroelectric dam.'에 따르면 Janaki Ammal은 수력 발전 댐의 건설로부터 Silent Valley를 성공적으로 지켜냈다고 하므로, 내용과 일치하지 않는 것은 ⑤ '수력 발전 댐의 건설로부터 Silent Valley를 지키는 데 실패했다.'이다.

Why? 왜 오답일까?
① '~ she decided to reject tradition and attend college.'의 내용과 일치한다.
② 'Ammal contributed to the development of the sweetest sugarcane variety in the world.'의 내용과 일치한다.
③ 'She moved to England where she co-authored the *Chromosome Atlas of Cultivated Plants*.'의 내용과 일치한다.
④ '~ she returned to India to help increase food production ~'의 내용과 일치한다.

● notable ⓐ 유명한, 저명한   ● arranged marriage 중매결혼
● literacy ⓝ 문해력, 식자율   ● doctorate ⓝ 박사 학위
● botany ⓝ 식물학   ● famine ⓝ 기근
● deforestation ⓝ 삼림벌채   ● hydroelectric ⓐ 수력 전기의

구문 풀이

3행   Despite living at a time [when literacy among women in
전치사 동명사   선행사(시간)   [ ] : 관계부사절
India was less than one percent], she decided to reject tradition and
decided의 목적어(~것)
attend college.

04 달리기와 쓰레기 줍기를 동시에 하는 행사 소개
정답률 84% | 정답 ④

Plogging Event에 관한 다음 안내문의 내용과 일치하는 것은?
① 2016년에 영국에서 시작되었다.
② 매달 첫 번째 일요일 오전 9시에 열린다.
③ 운동화를 포함한 장비들이 지급된다.
☑ 참가비는 무료이다.
⑤ 참가하려면 예약이 필요하다.

[본문 해석]

플로깅 행사

플로깅에 대해 들어본 적 있으신가요? 줍는다는 의미의 스웨덴어 단어인 'plocka upp'에서 왔으며 조깅과 쓰레기 줍기가 결합된 말입니다. 「2016년에 스웨덴에서 시작되었고 최근 영국으로 건너와 자연을 보호하기 위한 새로운 운동이 되었습니다.」—「」: ①의 근거 불일치

일시 및 장소
• 「매달 첫 번째 월요일 오전 9시」—「」: ②의 근거 불일치
• East Twickenham에 있는 ETNA 센터 밖

준비물
• 「운동화만 가져오시면 다른 모든 장비를 지급합니다.」—「」: ③의 근거 불일치
• 「참가비는 무료이나 우리의 자연보호 활동을 위한 기부는 기꺼이 받습니다.」—「」: ④의 근거 일치

「※ 참가하기 위해 예약은 필요하지 않습니다.」—「」: ⑤의 근거 불일치

더 많은 정보를 원하시면 www.environmenttrust.org를 방문하십시오.

Why? 왜 정답일까?

'There is no fee to participate. ~'에서 참가비는 없다고 하므로, 안내문의 내용과 일치하는 것은 ④ '참가비는 무료이다.'이다.

Why? 왜 오답일까?

① 'In 2016, it started in Sweden and has recently come to the UK. ~' 에서 플로깅 행사가 시작된 곳은 스웨덴이고 영국에는 최근 건너온 것임을 알 수 있다.
② '9 a.m. on the first Monday of each month'에서 매달 첫 월요일에 행사가 열린다고 하였다.
③ 'Just bring your running shoes, and we will provide all the other equipment.'에서 운동화는 참가자가 준비해야 한다고 하였다.
⑤ 'No reservations are necessary to participate.'에서 참가를 위해 예약할 필요는 없다고 하였다.

● combination ⓝ 조합
● movement ⓝ (조직적으로 벌이는) 운동
● conservation ⓝ (환경) 보호
● litter ⓝ 쓰레기
● equipment ⓝ 장비
● necessary ⓐ 필요한

05 조명 효과의 개념
정답률 45% | 정답 ⑤

다음 글의 밑줄 친 부분 중, 어법상 틀린 것은? [3점]

[본문 해석]

왜 우리는 종종 실제 그런 것보다 남들이 우리를 더 많이 주목하고 있다고 느끼는가? 조명 효과는 우리 자신이 무대 중앙에 있다고 보는 것이고, 그리하여 다른 사람들의 주목이 우리에게 향해 있는 정도를 직관적으로 과대평가하는 것이다. Timothy Lawson은 대학생들이 동료 집단을 만나기 전에 앞면에 커다란 유행 상표가 있는 운동복 상의로 갈아입도록 하여 조명 효과를 조사했다. 그들 중 거의 40퍼센트가 셔츠에 무엇이 쓰여 있는지를 다른 학생들이 기억할 거라 확신했지만, 실제로는 불과 10퍼센트만이 기억했다. 대개의 관찰자들은 학생들이 몇 분 동안 방을 떠난 뒤 운동복 상의를 갈아입은 것조차 알아차리지 못했다. 또 다른 실험에서는, 가수 Barry Manilow가 새겨진 티셔츠와 같이 매우 두드러지는 옷조차 오직 23퍼센트의 관찰자들만이 알아차렸는데, 이는 가슴에 1970년대 소프트록 가수 얼굴을 자랑스럽게 내보이고 있었던 학생들이 추정한 50퍼센트라는 수치보다 훨씬 적은 것이었다.

Why? 왜 정답일까?

⑤는 '준동사 vs. 동사'를 묻는 문제인데 이때 풀이의 관건은 문장의 다른 부분에 동사가 있는지 찾는 것이다. 여기서는 주어인 noticeable clothes 이후로 동사가 없으므로 ⑤의 분사 provoking이 과거형 동사인 provoked로 바뀌어 문장의 서술어 기능을 담당해야 한다. 따라서 어법상 틀린 것은 ⑤이다.

Why? 왜 오답일까?

① to which에서 to는 'to the extent(~한 정도로)'에서 나온 것이다. 이는 '전치사+관계대명사'이므로 뒤에 완전한 구조를 수반한다.
② having은 사역 동사 have의 동명사 형태로서 뒤에 원형부정사를 목적격 보어로 취할 수 있다. 따라서 change는 적절하다.
③ '부분 of 전체' 표현에서는 '전체'가 수를 결정하는데, 여기서는 them이 전체에 해당하는 말이다. 따라서 복수 동사인 were를 쓴 것은 적절하다.
④ 앞에 선행사가 없고 뒤에 완전한 구조가 나오므로 여기서 that은 접속사이다. 이때 that은 타동사 notice의 목적어 역할을 하는 명사절을 이끈다.

● intuitively ⓐ 직관적으로
● extent ⓝ 정도
● experiment ⓝ 실험
● estimate ⓥ 추정하다, 추산하다
● aim at ~을 겨냥하다, ~을 대상으로 하다
● sweatshirt ⓝ 운동복 상의
● noticeable ⓐ 두드러지는, 눈에 띄는
● sport ⓥ 자랑해 보이다

구문 풀이

2행 The spotlight effect means seeing ourselves at center stage,
주어 ▏ 동사 ▏ 목적어(~것)
thus intuitively overestimating the extent [to which others' attention
부사 ▏ 분사구문(그리고 ~하다) ▏ 전치사 + 관계대명사 ▏ 완전한 문장
is aimed at us].

06 아들에게 패배 경험을 가르치려한 Jack
정답률 78% | 정답 ⑤

밑줄 친 부분이 가리키는 대상이 나머지 넷과 다른 것은?

[본문 해석]

Jack은 ① 자신의 아들 Mark가 나타내고 있는 완벽주의의 순환을 멈추게 했다. Mark는 8살이 되자 시합에서 지는 것을 참지 못했다. Jack은 Mark가 체스 시합에서 항상 이기게 하여 Mark의 태도에 일조하고 있었는데 ② 그는 Mark가 화가 나서 우는 것을 보고 싶지 않았기 때문이었다. 어느 날, Jack은 Mark가 패배를 경험하게 하는 것이 중요하다는 것을 깨달았고, 그래서 ③ 그는 최소한 시합의 절반은 이기기 시작했다. Mark는 처음에는 화를 냈지만, 곧 더 흔쾌히 이기고 지기 시작했다. Jack은 ④ 자신이 Mark와 캐치볼 경기를 하다가 공을 잘못 던졌던 어느 날 중대한 시점에 이르렀음을 느꼈다. 공을 놓친 데 대하여 화를 내는 대신에, Mark는 ⑤ 자신(Mark)의 유머 감각을 사용할 수 있었고, "잘 던졌어요, 아빠. 잡는 게 엉망이네, Mark."라고 말했다.

Why? 왜 정답일까?

①, ②, ③, ④는 Jack, ⑤는 Mark를 가리키므로, 밑줄 친 부분이 가리키는 대상이 다른 하나는 ⑤이다.

● perfectionism ⓝ 완벽주의
● contribute to ~에 이바지하다
● at least 최소한, 적어도
● comment ⓥ 말하다, 논평하다
● develop ⓥ 나타내다, 드러나게 하다
● realize ⓥ 깨닫다
● with grace 흔쾌히, 선선히
● lousy ⓐ 엉망인, 서투른

구문 풀이

3행 Jack was contributing to Mark's attitude / by always letting
~에 일조하다(과거진행) ▏ 「by + 동명사(~함으로써)」
him win at chess / because he didn't like to see Mark get upset and
원형부정사 ▏ 지각동사 ▏ 원형부정사1
cry.
원형부정사2

★★★ 1등급 대비 고난도 2점 문제

07 생명체의 출현으로 인한 지구의 대기 변화
정답률 29% | 정답 ②

다음 빈칸에 들어갈 말로 가장 적절한 것을 고르시오.

① a barrier to evolution – 진화에 있어 장벽
☑ a consequence of life – 생명체의 결과
③ a record of primitive culture – 원시 문화의 기록
④ a sign of the constancy of nature – 자연의 불변성에 대한 신호
⑤ a reason for cooperation among species – 종들 간 협력의 이유

[본문 해석]

45억 년도 더 전에 지구의 원시 대기는 아마도 대부분 수증기, 이산화탄소, 이산화황과 질소였을 것이다. 극히 원시적인 생물체(박테리아 같은 미생물과 단순한 단세포 식물)의 출현과 연이은 진화는 산소를 유리(遊離)시키고 이산화탄소

DAY 25

와 이산화황을 분해하면서 대기를 변화시키기 시작했다. 이것은 더 상위 유기체가 발달하는 것을 가능하게 했다. 가장 최초라고 알려진 핵이 있는 식물 세포가 약 20억 년 전 진화했을 때, 대기에 현재 산소 함량의 고작 약 1%만이 있었던 것 같다. 약 5억 년 전에 최초의 육지 식물이 출현하면서 산소는 현재 농도의 약 3분의 1에 달했다. 그것은 약 3억 7천만 년 전까지 거의 현재 수준으로 증가했고, 그때 동물들이 처음 육지에 퍼졌다. 그러므로 오늘날의 대기는 우리가 알고 있듯이 생명체를 유지하기 위한 필요조건인 것만이 아니라, 생명체의 결과이기도 하다.

Why? 왜 정답일까?

첫 두 문장에서 지구의 원시 대기는 수증기, 이산화탄소, 이산화황, 질소 등으로 이루어져 있었을 것이나 생명체의 탄생 이후 산소가 유리되고 이산화탄소와 이산화황이 분해되는 등 그 변화를 맞이하게 되었다고 한다. 이어서 핵이 있는 최초의 식물 세포, 최초의 육지 식물 등이 출현하며 산소 농도 또한 점점 더 많은 생명체가 살기 적합하도록 높아졌다는 내용이 전개된다. 이러한 흐름으로 보아, 빈칸 문장은 대기가 생명체의 탄생으로 말미암아 '결과적으로' 변화해온 것이라는 결론을 적합하게 제시해야 한다. 따라서 빈칸에 들어갈 말로 가장 적절한 것은 ② '생명체의 결과'이다.

- billion ⓝ 10억
- subsequent ⓐ 연이은, 그다음의
- liberate ⓥ (화학) 유리시키다
- emergence ⓝ 출현
- requirement ⓝ 필요조건
- consequence ⓝ 결과
- nitrogen ⓝ 질소
- exceedingly ⓐⓓ 극히, 대단히
- nucleus ⓝ (생물) 핵, 세포핵 (pl. nuclei)
- concentration ⓝ 농도
- sustain ⓥ 유지하다, 지탱하다
- constancy ⓝ 불변성

구문 풀이

15행 It had risen to almost its present level by about 370 million
과거완료　　　　　　　　　　　　　시간 선행사
years ago, when animals first spread on to land.
관계부사(계속적 용법)

★★ 문제 해결 꿀~팁 ★★

▶ 많이 틀린 이유는?
지구의 대기가 생물체 출현에 따라 '변화해' 왔다는 것이 글의 주제이므로, ④의 constancy(불변성, 항구성)는 주제와 정반대되는 단어이다. 또한 글에서 '원시 문화'에 관해 언급하지 않으므로 ③도 답으로 부적절하다.

▶ 문제 해결 방법은?
첫 두 문장에서 초창기 대기는 오늘날과 많이 달랐으나 생물체의 진화에 따라 대기가 변화되기 시작했다는 내용을 파악하면 답이 ②임을 알 수 있다.

---

08 어떤 것을 선택하기 전에 먼저 작게 시도해보기 정답률 67% | 정답 ③

다음 빈칸에 들어갈 말로 가장 적절한 것을 고르시오.
① trying out what other people do – 다른 사람들이 하는 것을 시험 삼아 해보는
② erasing the least preferred options – 가장 선호하지 않는 선택권을 지우는
✓③ testing the option on a smaller scale – 선택을 좀 더 작은 규모로 시험해보는
④ sharing your plans with professionals – 전문가와 계획을 상의하는
⑤ collecting as many examples as possible – 가능한 한 많은 사례를 모으는

[본문 해석]

우리는 종종 높은 수준의 결정에 직면하는데, 거기에서 우리는 그 결정의 결과를 예측할 수 없다. 그런 경우에, 대부분의 사람들은 결국 선택권을 전적으로 포기하는데, 왜냐하면 위험성이 높고 결과가 매우 예측 불가능하기 때문이다. 그러나 여기에는 해결책이 있다. 당신은 선택을 좀 더 작은 규모로 시험해보는 과정을 활용해야 한다. 많은 경우에, 물속에 머리부터 뛰어들기보다는 발끝을 담그는 것이 현명하다. 최근에, 나는 비싼 코칭 프로그램에 등록하려고 했었다. 그러나 나는 그 결과가 어떠할지 완전히 확신하지 못했다. 그러므로 나는 똑같은 강사의 저렴한 미니 코스에 등록함으로써 이러한 과정을 활용했다. 이것은 내가 그의 방법론, 스타일, 그리고 교육 내용을 이해하도록 도왔고, 비싼 프로그램에 완전히 전념하기 전에 나는 그것을 더 적은 투자, 그리고 더 적은 시간과 노력으로 시험해 볼 수 있었다.

Why? 왜 정답일까?

빈칸 뒤의 'In many situations, it's wise to dip your toe in the water rather than dive in headfirst.'에서 물속에 머리부터 다 뛰어들기보다는 발끝을 담가보는게 현명하다는 비유적인 표현을 통해 어떤 것을 선택하기 앞서 작게 시도해보라는 조언을 제시하고 있다. 이어서 마지막 두 문장 또한 필자가 비싼 코칭 프로그램을 듣기로

결정하기 전에 먼저 미니 코스부터 들어 보아서 비교적 저렴한 비용과 노력으로 의사 결정에 참고할 만한 정보를 얻었다고 언급하고 있다. 따라서 빈칸에 들어갈 말로 가장 적절한 것은 ③ '선택을 좀 더 작은 규모로 시험해보는'이다.

- predict ⓥ 예측하다
- altogether ⓐⓓ 전적으로, 완전히
- enroll in ~에 등록하다
- outcome ⓝ 결과
- content ⓝ 내용
- end up 결국 ~하게 되다
- dip ⓥ 담그다, 적시다
- convinced ⓐ 확신하는
- methodology ⓝ 방법론
- investment ⓝ 투자

구문 풀이

1행 We are often faced with high-level decisions, where we
　　　　　　　　　　　　　선행사(추상적 공간)　　관계부사
are unable to predict the results of those decisions.
~할 수 없다

★★★ 1등급 대비 고난도 3점 문제

09 겸손을 길러주는 근거와 주장 정답률 46% | 정답 ②

주어진 글 다음에 이어질 글의 순서로 가장 적절한 것을 고르시오. [3점]
① (A) − (C) − (B)
✓② (B) − (A) − (C)
③ (B) − (C) − (A)
④ (C) − (A) − (B)
⑤ (C) − (B) − (A)

[본문 해석]

근거와 주장의 한 가지 이점은 겸손을 기를 수 있다는 점이다. 만약에 두 사람이 논쟁 없이 의견만 다르다면, 그들이 하는 것은 서로에게 고함을 지르는 것뿐이다. 어떠한 발전도 없다.

(B) 양측은 여전히 자신이 옳다고 생각한다. 대조적으로, 양측이 자신의 입장에 대한 이유를 분명하게 말하는 주장을 제시한다면, 새로운 가능성이 열린다. 이러한 주장 중 한쪽이 반박된다. 즉, 틀렸다는 것이 드러난다. 이런 경우에 반박된 주장에 의지했던 사람은 자신의 관점을 바꿀 필요가 있다는 것을 배운다.

(A) 이것은 적어도 한쪽에서는 겸손을 얻는 한 가지 방식이다. 또 다른 가능성은 어떤 주장도 반박되지 않는 것이다. 둘 다 자기 입장에 대해 어느 정도 근거가 있다. 두 대화자 모두 상대의 주장에 설득되지 않더라도, 양측은 그럼에도 불구하고 반대 견해를 이해하게 된다.

(C) 또한 그들은 자신이 약간의 진실은 몰라도 완전한 진실은 가지고 있지 않다는 점을 인식하게 된다. 그들은 자신의 견해에 반대되는 근거를 인식하고 이해할 때 겸손을 얻을 수 있다.

Why? 왜 정답일까?

근거와 주장은 겸손에 도움이 될 수 있다는 내용과 함께 서로 의견 차이를 좁히지 못하는 두 사람의 예를 드는 주어진 글 뒤에는, 양쪽이 적절한 근거를 들어 말하다가 한쪽의 결함이 드러나는 경우를 설명하는 (B)가 먼저 연결된다. 이어서 (A)는 두 주장에 모두 합당한 근거가 있는 '또 다른' 경우를 언급하고, (C)는 이들 또한 각자 주장이 '온전히' 맞지 않음을 수긍하며 겸손을 배울 수 있게 된다고 설명한다. 따라서 글의 순서로 가장 적절한 것은 ② '(B) − (A) − (C)'이다.

- yell at ~에게 소리 지르다
- refute ⓥ 반박하다
- appreciate ⓥ 제대로 이해하다
- whole ⓐ 온전한, 전체의
- progress ⓝ 진전, 진행
- a degree of 어느 정도의
- opposing ⓐ 반대되는, 상충하는

구문 풀이

14행 One of the arguments gets refuted — that is, it is shown
　　　　　　　　　　　　　　　　　　　　　　　　　　　　「be shown +
to fail.
to부정사 : ~함이 드러나다」

★★ 문제 해결 꿀~팁 ★★

▶ 많이 틀린 이유는?
(B)를 자세히 읽어보면, 견해가 다른 두 사람 중 한쪽의 주장이 반박당하는 경우를 설명하고 있다. 하지만 (C)는 '둘 중 아무도 온전한 진실을 갖고 있지 않은 경우'를 다루므로 (B)와 연결되지 않는다. 이때 (A)가 '둘 중 어느 주장도 반박되지 않는 경우'를 말하고 있으므로, 이 상황에 대한 보충 설명이 (C)임을 알 수 있다.

안도감을 주지만, 뇌는 세상에 대한 그것의 모형에 새로운 사실을 (e) 포함시키려 노력한다. 그것은 항상 새로움을 추구한다. ⌐┐ : 11번의 근거

- **endeavor** ⓝ 수고, 노력
- **appealing** ⓐ 매력적인
- **beg the question** 질문을 하게 만들다
- **put effort into** ~에 노력을 들이다
- **indifference** ⓝ 무관심
- **reassuring** ⓐ 안심시키는
- **novelty** ⓝ 새로움
- **expertise** ⓝ 전문성, 전문기술

- **edible** ⓐ 먹을 수 있는
- **predictability** ⓝ 예측 가능성
- **emit** ⓥ 내보내다, 방출하다
- **familiarity** ⓝ 익숙함
- **suppression** ⓝ 억제
- **incorporate** ⓥ 포함시키다, 통합시키다
- **rerun** ⓝ 재방송
- **at the expense of** ~을 희생하여

구문 풀이

13행 But if our brains are going to all this effort to make the
→지시대명사(= 앞의 if절)
world predictable, that begs the question: if we love predictability
질문을 하게 만들다
so much, why don't we, (for example), just replace our televisions
: 삽입구 「replace +A + with + B : A를 B로 대체하다」
with machines [that emit a rhythmic beep twenty-four hours a day],
동사(복수)
predictably?

---

10 창의력 지수 　정답률 52% | 정답 ②

글의 흐름으로 보아, 주어진 문장이 들어가기에 가장 적절한 곳을 고르시오.

[본문 해석]

창의성 연구의 첫 번째 급증의 궁극적 목표는 IQ가 전반적인 지능을 측정했던 것과 같은 방식으로 전반적인 창의력을 측정하기 위한 성격 검사였다. ① 한 사람의 창의성 점수는 IQ 점수가 물리학, 수학 또는 문학에 국한되지 않는 것과 마찬가지로, 그 사람이 노력하는 어떤 분야에서든 그 사람의 창의적 잠재력을 우리에게 알려줄 것이었다. ② 그러나 1970년대에, 심리학자들은 전반적인 '창의성 지수' 같은 것은 없음을 깨달았다. 창의적인 사람들은 전반적이고 보편적으로 창의적인 것은 아니어서, 이들은 활동의 특정 범위, 즉 특정 영역에서 창의적이다. ③ 우리는 창의적인 과학자가 재능 있는 화가도 되리라고 기대하지 않는다. ④ 창의적인 바이올린 연주자는 창의적인 지휘자가 아닐 수도 있고, 창의적인 지휘자는 새로운 곡을 작곡하는 데 매우 뛰어나지 않을 수도 있다. ⑤ 심리학자들은 이제 창의성이 특정 영역에만 한정된 것이라는 것을 안다.

Why? 왜 정답일까?

창의적 연구 초창기에는 전반적인 창의력을 측정하고자 했다는 내용이 ② 앞에 나오는데, 주어진 문장은 But으로 흐름을 전환시키며 1970년대부터 전반적인 창의력 지수라는 것은 없다는 인식이 생겨났다고 설명한다. ② 뒤에서는 창의적인 사람들이 전반적 또는 보편적으로 창의적인 것은 아니라는 보충 설명으로 주어진 문장 내용을 뒷받침한다. 따라서 주어진 문장이 들어가기에 가장 적절한 곳은 ②이다.

- **realize** ⓥ 깨닫다
- **personality test** 성격 검사
- **endeavor** ⓝ 노력
- **literature** ⓝ 문학
- **sphere** ⓝ 범위, 영역
- **conductor** ⓝ 지휘자

- **quotient** ⓝ 지수
- **intelligence** ⓝ 지능
- **physics** ⓝ 물리학
- **universal** ⓐ 보편적인
- **domain** ⓝ 영역
- **compose** ⓥ 작곡하다

구문 풀이

3행 The holy grail of the first wave of creativity research was
주어　　　　　　　　　　　　　　　　　　　　　　　　동사(단수)
a personality test to measure general creativity ability, in the same
주격 보어　　　　형용사적 용법　　　　　　　　　　~와 같은 방법으로
way that IQ measured general intelligence.

11-12 예측 가능성과 새로움의 균형을 필요로 하는 우리 뇌

[본문 해석]

우리는 우리의 몸 안에 쌓아온 에너지 저장량에 의해 살고 죽는 생명체이다. 세상을 항해하는 것은 여기저기로 이동하는 것과 많은 지력을 사용하는 것을 필요로 하는 어려운 일, 즉 에너지가 많이 드는 수고로움이다. 우리가 정확한 (a) 예측을 할 때, 그것은 에너지를 아껴준다. 여러분이 먹을 수 있는 곤충이 특정한 종류의 바위 아래에서 발견될 수 있다는 것을 알 때, 그것은 모든 바위를 뒤집어야 하는 일을 덜어준다. 우리가 더 잘 예측할수록, 그것은 우리에게 더 적은 에너지를 들게 한다. 반복은 우리의 예측에 있어서 우리를 더 자신 있게 만들고 우리의 행동에 있어서 더 효율적으로 만든다. 그래서 예측 가능성에 관해서는 (b) 매력적인 무언가가 있다.

하지만 만약 우리의 뇌가 세상을 예측 가능한 것으로 만들기 위해 이 모든 노력을 하고 있다면, 그것은 이 질문을 하게 만든다. 만약 우리가 예측 가능성을 이토록 좋아한다면, 예를 들어, 왜 우리는 예측 가능하도록 우리의 텔레비전을 하루 24시간 규칙적인 소리를 내보내는 기계로 교체하지 않을까? 그 대답은 놀라움의 (c) 결핍에는 문제가 있다는 것이다. 「우리가 어떤 것을 더 잘 이해할수록, 우리는 그것에 대해 생각하는 데 노력을 덜 기울인다.」 친숙함은 무관심을 ⌐┐ : 12번의 근거
(d) 줄인다(→ 키운다). 반복 억제(반복이 주는 억제)가 생겨나고 우리의 주의가 감소한다. 이것 때문에 여러분은 월드 시리즈 시청을 아무리 즐긴다 할지라도 같은 경기를 반복해서 시청하며 만족하지 않을 것이다. 「비록 예측 가능성이

---

11 제목 파악 　정답률 58% | 정답 ③

윗글의 제목으로 가장 적절한 것은?

① Why Are Television Reruns Still Popular?
무엇이 TV 재방송을 여전히 인기 있게 만드는가?
② Predictability Is Something Not to Be Feared!
예측 가능성은 두려워할 대상이 아니다!
③ What Really Satisfies Our Brain: Familiarity or Novelty
무엇이 우리 뇌를 정말로 만족시키는가: 익숙함인가 새로움인가
④ Repetition Gives Us Expertise at the Expense of Creativity
반복은 창의성을 희생시켜 우리에게 전문성을 준다
⑤ Our Hunter-Gatherer Ancestors Were Smart in Saving Energy
우리의 수렵채집인 조상들은 에너지를 똑똑하게 아꼈다

Why? 왜 정답일까?

글의 결론을 제시하는 마지막 두 문장에서 비록 예측 가능성이 우리를 안심시켜 주기는 하지만, 우리 뇌는 계속해서 새로움을 추구한다(Although predictability is reassuring, the brain strives to incorporate new facts into its model of the world. It always seeks novelty.)고 언급하고 있다. 따라서 글의 제목으로 가장 적절한 것은 이와 같은 핵심 내용을 답으로 유도할 수 있는 질문인 ③ '무엇이 우리 뇌를 정말로 만족시키는가: 익숙함인가 새로움인가'이다.

★★★ 1등급 대비 고난도 3점 문제

12 어휘 추론 　정답률 46% | 정답 ④

밑줄 친 (a) ~ (e) 중에서 문맥상 낱말의 쓰임이 적절하지 않은 것은? [3점]
① (a)　② (b)　③ (c)　④ (d)　⑤ (e)

Why? 왜 정답일까?

'The better we understand something, the less effort we put into thinking about it.'에서 우리는 어떤 대상을 더 잘 이해할수록 그 대상에 관해 덜 생각하게 된다고 하는 것으로 보아, (d)가 포함된 문장은 익숙함이 무관심을 '키운다'는 의미를 나타내야 한다. 따라서 (d)의 reduces를 반의어인 breeds로 고쳐야 한다. 문맥상 낱말의 쓰임이 적절하지 않은 것은 ④ '(d)'이다.

★★ 문제 해결 꿀~팁 ★★

▶ 많이 틀린 이유는?
맨 마지막 문장에서 우리 뇌는 새로움을 항상 추구한다고 언급하는 것으로 보아, 우리 뇌가 예측 가능성과 더불어 새로운 사실도 '통합시키기' 위해 애쓴다는 뜻의 (e)는 바르게 쓰였다.

▶ 문제 해결 방법은?
(d) 바로 뒤의 문장에서 어떤 것이 반복되어 익숙해지면 '주의력이 감소한다'고 언급하고 있다. 이는 다른 말로 바꾸면 익숙함이 무관심을 '키운다'는 것이다.

▶ 문제 해결 방법은?
단순히 지시어나 연결어 등 형태적인 힌트에만 의존하면 답을 찾기 어렵다. 다른 쉬운 문제(심경, 도표, 안내문 등)를 빨리 풀고 남은 시간을 투자해 단락별 내용을 깊이 파악해야 한다.

DAY 25

DAY 26 ▷ 20분 미니 모의고사

01 ①	02 ①	03 ②	04 ③	05 ③
06 ①	07 ①	08 ④	09 ①	10 ②
11 ③	12 ②			

01 아이의 사랑 가득한 선물에 기뻐진 필자 정답률 84% | 정답 ①

다음 글에 드러난 'I'의 심경 변화로 가장 적절한 것은?

☑ annoyed → delighted
　짜증 난　　기쁜
② ashamed → relieved
　수치스러운　안도한
③ excited → confused
　신난　　혼란스러운
④ scared → confident
　겁에 질린　자신 있는
⑤ indifferent → jealous
　무관심한　　질투하는

[본문 해석]

내 열 살짜리 아이가 와서 25센트 동전을 간절히 원했다. "25센트 동전? 도대체 25센트 동전이 왜 필요하지?" 나의 말투는 거의 짜증에 가까웠다. 나는 그런 사소한 요구에 방해받고 싶지 않았다. "거리 위쪽에서 중고 물품 판매 행사를 하는데, 꼭 사야 할 게 있어요! 25센트밖에 안 해요. 네?" 나는 아들의 손에 25센트 동전을 쥐어 주었다. 잠시 후 작은 목소리로 "여기요, 엄마, 엄마 주려고 산 거예요."라고 말했다. 나는 내 어린 아들의 손을 힐끗 내려다보았고, 두 어린아이가 서로 껴안고 있는 4인치짜리 크림색의 조각상을 보았다. 그들의 발밑에는 'L'로 시작하여 'E'로 끝나고, 사이에 'O'와 'V'가 있다는 말이 새겨져 있었다. 아이가 중고 물품 판매 행사로 서둘러 돌아가는 모습을 바라보며 나는 행복이 가득한 마음으로 미소를 지었다. 그 25센트짜리 중고 물품 판매 행사 구입품은 내게 큰 기쁨을 가져다 주었다.

Why? 왜 정답일까?

어린 아들이 느닷없이 동전을 달라고 하자 짜증이 났던(My tone bordered on irritation.) 필자가 아들의 사랑이 담긴 선물을 받고 행복해했다(~ I smiled with a heart full of happiness.)는 내용이다. 따라서 'I'의 심경 변화로 가장 적절한 것은 ① '짜증 난 → 기쁜'이다.

- in need of ~이 필요한, ~이 없는
- quarter ⓝ 25센트 동전
- irritation ⓝ 짜증
- trivial ⓐ 사소한
- inscribe ⓥ 새기다
- confused ⓐ 혼란스러운
- desperate ⓐ 간절한
- border on 거의 ~에 달하다
- be bothered with ~로 귀찮다
- glance ⓥ 흘깃 보다
- annoyed ⓐ 짜증 난
- jealous ⓐ 질투하는

구문 풀이

10행 Inscribed at their feet were words [that read *It starts with 'L'*
「도치 구문: p.p.+be+주어」　　주격 관·대
ends with 'E' and in between are 'O' and 'V.']

02 마케팅에서 중요한 균형 정답률 58% | 정답 ①

밑줄 친 'give away the house'가 다음 글에서 의미하는 바로 가장 적절한 것은? [3점]

☑ risk the company's profitability – 회사의 수익성을 위태롭게 해서는
② overlook a competitor's strengths – 경쟁자의 강점을 간과해서는
③ hurt the reputation of the company – 회사의 명성에 해를 끼쳐서는
④ generate more customer complaints – 고객 불만을 더 창출해서는
⑤ abandon customer-oriented marketing – 고객 중심 마케팅을 버려서는

[본문 해석]

고객들을 즐겁게 하는 데 관심이 있는 기업들에게, 뛰어난 가치와 서비스는 기업 문화 전반의 일부가 된다. 예를 들어, 고객 만족이라는 측면에서 Pazano는 해마다 서비스업 중 최상위 또는 상위권을 차지한다. 고객을 만족시키려는 그 기업의 열정은 그것의 신조에 요약되어 있는데, 그 기업의 고급 호텔이 진정으로 기억될 만한 경험을 제공할 것을 약속한다. 고객 중심 기업은 경쟁사 대비 높은 고객 만족을 제공하고자 하지만, 그것이 고객 만족을 *최대화*하려고 하지는 않는다. 기업은 가격을 낮추거나 서비스를 증진시켜 고객 만족을 항상 높일 수 있다. 하지만 이것은 더 낮은 이윤으로 이어질지도 모른다. 따라서, 마케팅

의 목적은 수익을 내면서 고객 가치를 창출하는 것이다. 이것은 매우 섬세한 균형을 필요로 하는데, 즉 마케팅 담당자는 더 많은 고객 가치와 만족을 계속해서 창출해야 하지만, '집을 거저나 다름없이 팔아서는' 안 된다.

Why? 왜 정답일까?

마케팅은 고객을 만족시키는 한편으로 수익 창출도 노려야 한다(Thus, the purpose of marketing is to generate customer value profitably.)는 내용으로 보아, 밑줄 친 부분은 고객 만족만을 신경 쓰다가 '수익을 놓쳐서는 안 된다'는 의미일 것이다. 따라서 밑줄 친 부분의 의미로 가장 적절한 것은 ① '회사의 수익성을 위태롭게 해서는' 이다.

- delight ⓥ (~을) 즐겁게 하다, 기쁘게 하다
- hospitality industry 서비스업
- relative to ~에 비해
- profitably ⓐ🇩 수익을 내며, 수익성 있게
- give away 거저 주다
- reputation ⓝ 명성
- exceptional ⓐ 뛰어난, 예외적인
- sum up 요약하다, 압축해서 보여주다
- result in ~로 이어지다, ~를 낳다
- delicate ⓐ 섬세한, 미묘한
- overlook ⓥ 간과하다

구문 풀이

5행 The company's passion for satisfying customers is summed
up in its credo, which promises {that its luxury hotels will deliver a
　　선행사　　계속적 용법　　　　　　　　　　　　　　　동사(미래)
truly memorable experience}.
{ }: 명사절(promises의 목적어)

03 생물 다양성 증가와 침입에 대한 방어력 강화 정답률 67% | 정답 ②

다음 글의 제목으로 가장 적절한 것은?

① Carve Out More Empty Ecological Spaces!
　비어 있는 더 많은 생태 공간을 개척하라!
☑ Guardian of Ecology: Diversity Resists Invasion
　생태계의 수호자: 다양성은 침입을 격퇴한다
③ Grasp All, Lose All: Necessity of Species-poor Ecology
　모든 것을 쥐면 모든 것을 잃는다: 종이 빈약한 생태계의 필요성
④ Challenges in Testing Biodiversity-Invasibility Hypothesis
　생물 다양성–침입성 가설 시험에서의 난제
⑤ Diversity Dilemma: The More Competitive, the Less Secure
　다양성의 딜레마: 더 경쟁력이 있을수록, 덜 안정적이다

[본문 해석]

비토착종에 의한 자연 군집 침입은 현재 가장 중요한 세계적 규모의 환경 문제 중 하나로 평가된다. 생물 다양성 상실은 생태계 기능에 대한 영향에 대한 염려를 불러일으켰고 그에 따라 둘 사이의 관계 이해는 지난 20년 동안의 생태계 연구에서 주요 초점이 되어왔다. Elton에 의한 '생물 다양성–침입성' 가설은 높은 다양성이 군집의 경쟁력 있는 환경을 증가시켜 그 군집에 침투하는 것을 더 어렵게 만든다고 제안한다. 수많은 생물 다양성 실험이 Elton의 시대 이후로 수행되어 왔고, 흔히 관찰되는 다양성과 침입성 사이의 부정적 관계를 설명하기 위해 여러 기제들이 제안되어 왔다. 빈 생태적 지위의 가능성은 감소하지만 침입 성공을 방지하는 경쟁자들의 가망성은 증가하는 것 이외에도, 다양한 군집은 자원을 더 완전하게 사용하여 침입자가 확고히 자리 잡는 능력을 제한하는 것으로 여겨진다. 나아가, 더 다양한 군집은 종이 빈약한 군집보다 더 광범위한 생태적 지위를 사용하기 때문에 더 안정적인 것으로 여겨진다.

Why? 왜 정답일까?

'생물 다양성–침입성' 가설에 관해 설명한 글로, '~ high diversity increases the competitive environment of communities and makes them more difficult to invade.'에서 생물 다양성이 증가하면 군집에 대한 침입이 더욱 어려워진다는 내용을 제시한 후 관련된 연구 결과를 들어 뒷받침하고 있다. 따라서 글의 제목으로 가장 적절한 것은 ② '생태계의 수호자: 다양성은 침입을 격퇴한다'이다.

- invasion ⓝ 침략
- ecological ⓐ 생태계의
- numerous ⓐ 많은
- broader ⓐ 넓은
- biodiversity ⓝ 생물의 다양성
- hypothesis ⓝ 가설
- assume ⓥ 사용하다
- guardian ⓝ 수호자

구문 풀이

15행 Beside the decreased chance of empty ecological niches
　　　전치사(~ 외에도)　　　　　　　목적어1
but the increased probability of competitors [that prevent invasion
　　　　　　　목적어2
success], diverse communities are assumed to use resources more
　　　주어　　　　　　동사(5형식 수동태)　　보어1
completely and, therefore, limit the ability of invaders to establish.
　　　　　　　　　보어2　　　　　　　　　　　형용사적 용법(ability 수식)

04 출판사의 원고 선별　　정답률 56% | 정답 ③

다음 글의 밑줄 친 부분 중, 어법상 틀린 것은? [3점]

[본문 해석]

출판사에 원고를 팔려는 경쟁은 치열하다. 내가 추산하기로는 출판사로 보내진 자료 중 1% 미만이 출판된다. 아주 많은 자료가 저술되고 있어, 출판사는 (어떤 것을 출판할지 정하는 데 있어) 매우 까다로울 수 있다. 그들이 출판하기로 하는 자료는 상업적 가치를 지니고 있어야 할 뿐만 아니라 매우 적절하게 집필되고 편집 및 사실 오류가 없어야 한다. 오류를 포함한 어떤 원고도 출판이 수락될 가능성이 거의 없다. 대부분의 출판사는 자료에 너무 많은 오류를 포함하고 있는 집필자와 시간을 낭비하려 하지 않을 것이다.

Why? 왜 정답일까?

'not only A but (also) B'의 상관접속사 구문에서 A 자리에 'must ~ have'라는 '조동사＋동사원형' 구조가 나오므로, B 자리에도 must와 연결되는 동사원형이 나와야 적절하다. 따라서 being은 be가 되어야 한다. 어법상 틀린 것은 ③이다.

Why? 왜 오답일까?

① 주어가 단수 명사인 The competition이므로 is를 쓴 것은 적절하다.
② material은 '보내지는' 대상이므로 수동의 의미를 나타내는 과거분사 sent를 써서 꾸민 것은 적절하다.
④ chance가 여기서는 '가능성'이라는 불가산 명사로 쓰여 뒤에 복수형 어미인 '-s'를 달고 있지 않으므로 few가 아닌 'little(거의 없는)'을 써서 꾸민 것은 적절하다.
⑤ 앞에 나온 선행사를 꾸미지만 뒤에 주어, 동사, 목적어가 갖추어진 완전한 3형식 구조가 나오므로 소유격 관계대명사 whose로 연결되어야 한다. whose는 '(선행사)의'라고 해석되므로 뒤에 관사가 없는 명사로 시작하는 완전한 절이 나온다.

- **manuscript** ⓝ 원고
- **estimate** ⓥ 추산하다, 추정하다
- **selective** ⓐ 까다로운, 조심해서 고르는
- **competently** ⓐⓓ 적절하게, 유능하게
- **factual** ⓐ 사실의
- **fierce** ⓐ (경쟁 등이) 치열한
- **material** ⓝ (책 등의) 소재
- **commercial** ⓐ 상업적인
- **free of** ~이 없는
- **accept** ⓥ 수락하다, 받아들이다

★★★ 1등급 대비 고난도 3점 문제

05 생물 다양성을 고려한 경작의 필요성　　정답률 39% | 정답 ③

다음 글의 밑줄 친 부분 중, 문맥상 낱말의 쓰임이 적절하지 않은 것은? [3점]

[본문 해석]

농업에서 인류의 혁신은 식물의 자연적 번식 주기를 통해서는 결코 실현할 수 없었을 사과, 튤립, 감자의 개량을 가능케 했다. 이러한 경작 과정은 소비자들이 식료품 가게에서 찾는 (여러분이) 알아볼 수 있는 몇몇 채소나 과일을 만들어냈다. 그러나 만약 추수가 망쳐지면 소수의 재배된 작물에만 의존하는 것은 인류를 기아나 농업의 손실에 ① 취약한 상태에 둘 수도 있다. 예를 들어, 아일랜드 감자 기근 동안 1백만 명의 사람들이 3년이라는 기간에 걸쳐 사망했는데, 아일랜드 사람들이 영양학적으로 균형 있는 식사를 마련하기 위해 ② 주로 감자와 우유에 의존했기 때문이다. 재배 식물과 공생 관계를 유지하려면, 인류는 생물의 다양성을 고려해야만 하고 식물의 단일 경작이 가져올 수 있는 잠재적 ③ 이점(→ 결점)에 대해서도 인식해야만 한다. 설령 그것들이 당장은 유용하고 이득이 되어 보이지는 않아도, 모든 종류의 씨앗을 심는 것은 다가올 세대들을 위해 그러한 식물들이 오래 지속되는 것을 ④ 보장해 줄 수 있다. 야생에 대한 자연의 능력과 통제에 대한 인간의 욕망 사이에서 ⑤ 균형이 유지되어야 한다.

Why? 왜 정답일까?

'However, relying on only a few varieties of cultivated crops ~'에서 몇 가지 작물에만 의존하는 것은 인류를 기아나 농업적 손실에게 취약하게 만들 수 있다고 언급하고, 이어서 아일랜드 감자 기근이 예로 제시된다. 이러한 맥락에서 볼 때, ③이 포함된 문장은 식물의 단일 경작이 낳을 수 있는 '결점'을 인지하고 식물의 다양성을 지킬 방법을 고민해야 한다는 의미여야 한다. 즉 ③의 **benefits**를 **drawbacks**로 바꾸어야 맥락이 자연스러워진다. 따라서 문맥상 낱말의 쓰임이 적절하지 않은 것은 ③이다.

- **agriculture** ⓝ 농업
- **reproductive** ⓐ 번식, 재생의
- **recognizable** ⓐ 알아보기 쉬운
- **starvation** ⓝ 기아, 굶주림
- **nutritionally** ⓐⓓ 영양학적으로
- **monoculture** ⓝ 단일 경작
- **longevity** ⓝ 오래 감, 장수
- **modification** ⓝ 개량, 수정
- **cultivation** ⓝ 재배, 경작
- **vulnerable** ⓐ 취약한
- **famine** ⓝ 기근
- **biodiversity** ⓝ 생물 다양성
- **profitable** ⓐ 수익성 있는
- **generations to come** 후대, 후세

구문 풀이

9행 For example, a million people died over the course of three
　　　　　　　　주어　　　　동사　　　　~라는 기간에 걸쳐
years during the Irish potato famine because the Irish relied primarily
전치사(~ 동안)　　　　　　　　접속사(이유)　'the + 형용사 : ~한 사람들'
on potatoes and milk to create a nutritionally balanced meal.
　　　　　　　　　　　　부사적 용법(목적)

★★ 문제 해결 꿀~팁 ★★

▶ 많이 틀린 이유는?
② 앞에서 소수 재배 작물에만 의지하면 인간이 기근 등의 위기에 '취약해진다'고 했다. 이에 대한 예시로 감자 기근 당시 아일랜드 사람들에 관한 내용이 제시되는 것이므로, 아일랜드 사람들이 '주로' 감자에만 의존했기에 감자 기근에 그토록 취약했다는 의미를 나타내는 ② primarily는 바르게 쓰였다. 또한 ④가 포함된 문장은 앞 내용과 마찬가지로 다양한 작물 재배를 옹호하기 위해, 여러 작물을 재배하는 것이 당장은 이득이 안 되어 보여도 결국 식물 다양성 유지를 '보장해준다'라고 설명하고 있다. 따라서 ④의 ensure 또한 맥락에 맞는 어휘이다.

▶ 문제 해결 방법은?
However 이후로 단일 경작보다는 식물의 다양성을 존중한 경작이 인류에 이롭다는 내용이 일관되게 제시된다. 주제에 비추어 각 어휘 선택을 판단하도록 한다.

06 맛 선호도의 발달　　정답률 54% | 정답 ①

다음 빈칸에 들어갈 말로 가장 적절한 것을 고르시오.

✓ ① Taste preferences – 맛 선호도
② Hunting strategies – 사냥 전략
③ Migration patterns – 이주 패턴
④ Protective instincts – 보호 본능
⑤ Periodic starvations – 주기적 굶주림

[본문 해석]

어떤 특정한 동물이 필요로 하는 요소들은 상대적으로 예측 가능하다. 그것들은 과거에 기반하여 예측 가능한데, 즉 어떤 동물의 조상들이 필요로 했던 것은 그 동물이 현재에도 필요로 하는 것일 가능성이 있다. 그러므로 맛 선호도는 타고나는 것일 수 있다. 나트륨(Na)을 생각해 보라. 포유동물의 몸을 포함하여 육생 척추동물의 몸은 육지의 주된 생산자인 식물보다 나트륨 농도가 거의 50배인 경향이 있다. 이는 부분적으로는 척추동물이 바다에서 진화했고, 따라서 나트륨을 포함하여 바다에서 흔했던 성분들에 의존한 세포를 진화시켰기 때문이다. 나트륨에 대한 욕구와 식물에서 얻을 수 있는 나트륨 사이의 격차를 해결하기 위해 초식 동물은 그렇지 않은 경우 필요로 하는 것보다 50배 더 많은 식물을 섭취할 수 있다(그리고 초과분을 배설한다). 또는 나트륨의 다른 공급원을 찾아다닐 수 있다. 짠맛 수용기는 후자의 행위, 즉 엄청난 욕구를 충족시키기 위해 소금을 찾아다니는 것에 대해 동물에게 보상을 한다.

Why? 왜 정답일까?

예시에 따르면 본래 바다에서 진화한 육생 동물들은 식물에 비해 체내 나트륨 비율이 훨씬 높아서, 필요한 만큼 나트륨을 먹으려면 식물을 아주 많이 먹어야 하거나 다른 나트륨 공급원을 찾아야 하는 상황이라고 한다. 그리고 마지막 문장에서는 이들의 짠맛 수용기가 나트륨을 더 찾아나서는 행위에 '보상'을 해준다고 한다. 이는 짠맛에 대한 선호로 이어지게 될 것이므로, 빈칸에 들어갈 말로 가장 적절한 것은 ① '맛 선호도'이다.

- **predictable** ⓐ 예측 가능한
- **concentration** ⓝ 농도
- **remedy** ⓥ 해결하다, 바로잡다
- **receptor** ⓝ (신체의) 수용기, 감각기
- **periodic** ⓐ 주기적인
- **hardwired** ⓐ 타고난, 내장된
- **dependent upon** ~에 의존하는
- **eliminate** ⓥ 배설하다, 제거하다
- **reward** ⓥ 보상하다

구문 풀이

12행 To remedy the difference between their needs for sodium
　　부사적 용법(~하기 위해)　　　　「between + A + and + B : A와 B 사이에」
and that available in plants, herbivores can eat fifty times more plant
　　　　　　　　　　　　　　　　　　「배수표현 + 비교급 + than : ~보다 …배 더 한」
material than they otherwise need (and eliminate the excess).

★★★ 1등급 대비 고난도 3점 문제

07 실제 보이는 것을 인식하기　　정답률 49% | 정답 ①

다음 빈칸에 들어갈 말로 가장 적절한 것을 고르시오. [3점]

[문제편 p.157]

☑ consciously acknowledge what you actually see
여러분이 실제로 보는 것을 의식적으로 인정하라
② accept different opinions with a broad mind
넓은 마음으로 다양한 의견을 받아들이라
③ reflect on what you've already learned
이미 배운 것을 반추해보라
④ personally experience even a small thing
작은 것이라도 직접 경험하라
⑤ analyze the answers from various perspectives
다양한 시각에서 답을 분석하라

[본문 해석]

학기 초, 우리 미술 교수는 보는 이를 등지고 바닷가에 서서 푸른 바다와 거대한 하늘을 바라보고 있는 수도승의 이미지를 제시했다. 교수는 반 학생들에게 물었다, "무엇이 보이나요?" 어두컴컴한 강당은 조용했다. 우리는 그 숨겨진 의미를 파헤치기 위해 가능한 한 열심히 보고 또 보고 생각하고 또 생각했지만, 아무것도 생각해 내지 못했다 — 우리는 그것을 놓쳤음에 틀림없다. 극도로 분노하며 그녀는 자신의 질문에 대답했다. "이것은 수도승의 그림이에요! 그는 우리를 등지고 있어요! 그는 해안 근처에 서 있죠! 푸른 바다와 거대한 하늘이 있네요!" 흠… 왜 우리는 그것을 보지 못했을까? 우리에게 편견을 주지 않기 위해, 그녀는 그 작품의 작가나 제목을 밝히지 않고 질문을 제시했다. 사실, 그것은 Caspar David Friedrich의 *The Monk by the Sea*였다. 여러분의 세상을 더 잘 이해하려면, 여러분이 생각하기에 봐야 한다고 기대되는 것을 추측하기보다는 여러분이 실제로 보는 것을 의식적으로 인정하라.

Why? 왜 정답일까?

제시된 예에 따르면 교수가 바닷가에 등을 보이고 서 있는 수도승의 이미지를 주었을 때, 학생들은 교수가 기대하는 답 또는 그림의 의미를 찾는 데 골몰하다가 그 이미지를 있는 그대로 감상하지 못했다. 이는 애초에 작가와 작품명도 주지 않고 이미지를 최대한 편견 없이 보기를 바랐던 교수의 기대와는 상반된 결과였다. 이 예시를 토대로 빈칸이 포함된 문장은 이미지를 볼 때 이미지 너머의 것을 추론하기보다는 '보이는 것을 보라'는 결론을 도출하고 있다. 따라서 빈칸에 들어갈 말로 가장 적절한 것은 ① '여러분이 실제로 보는 것을 의식적으로 인정하라'이다.

● project ⓥ 제시하다, 투사하다
● auditorium ⓝ 강당
● come up with ~을 떠올리다
● acknowledge ⓥ 인정하다
● analyze ⓥ 분석하다

● enormous ⓐ 거대한
● unearth ⓥ 파헤치다, 밝혀내다
● bias ⓥ 편견을 갖게 하다 ⓝ 편견
● reflect on ~을 반추하다, 되돌아 보다
● perspective ⓝ 시각, 관점

구문 풀이

1행 Early in the term, our art professor projected an image of a
주어 — 동사 — 목적어
monk, his back to the viewer, standing on the shore, looking off into
= the monk's — 현재분사1 — 현재분사2(a monk 보충 설명)
a blue sea and an enormousus sky.

★★ 문제 해결 꿀~팁 ★★

▶ 많이 틀린 이유는?
세상을 어떤 기대에 맞추어 바라보려고 하기보다 있는 그대로 이해하는 것이 중요하다는 글로, 일화가 생소하여 내용이 쉽게 와닿지 않을 수 있다. 오답 중 ②와 ⑤는 모두 의견의 '다양성'을 언급하고 있는데, 이는 글에서 언급되지 않은 소재이므로 답으로 적절하지 않다.

▶ 문제 해결 방법은?
교수의 말을 주의 깊게 읽도록 한다. 수도승 그림에 관해 교수가 언급한 내용은 필자가 첫 문장에서 그림 속 수도승을 '보이는 대로' 묘사한 내용과 일치한다.

08 문화적 세계화의 중심지를 지니고 있는 아시아   정답률 66% | 정답 ④

다음 글에서 전체 흐름과 관계 없는 문장은?

[본문 해석]

문화적 세계화는 인도에서 제작된 Bollywood 영화와 홍콩에서 제작된 Kung Fu 영화와 같이 아시아에 다수의 중심지가 있다. ① 그것들은 무려 17개 언어로 자막 처리가 되며 특정 디아스포라에 배급된다. ② 힌디 어, 만다린 어와 같은 언어들에 지배되는 이러한 문화적 장소들은 영어의 확산을 무시하고 이에 저항한다. ③ Vaish 교수는 싱가포르의 중국인 아이들과 인도인 아이들이 각각 중국 대중음악과 인도 영화에 대한 참여를 통해 범중국 문화와 범인도 문화로 어떻게 연결되는지를 보여주었다. ④ 전 세계에서 가장 인구가 많은 두 나라로서, 중국은 인도의 가장 큰 무역 파트너이며, 두 국가 사이의 무역 규모는 715억

달러의 가치에 이른다. ⑤ 그래서 그녀는 아시아 젊은이들이 문화적 세계화, 즉 서구로부터 퍼져 나온 '세계 문화'의 수동적 희생자라는 생각에 실증적으로 이의를 제기한다.

Why? 왜 정답일까?

아시아는 문화적 세계화에 수동적으로 희생되는 지역이 아니라 오히려 다수의 중심지를 두고 문화적 세계화에 참여하고 있는 곳이라는 내용의 글로, 인도 및 홍콩의 영화 또는 중국 대중음악의 예가 주제를 뒷받침하고 있다. 하지만 ④는 중국과 인도의 무역 규모 및 관계에 관해 언급하여 흐름에서 벗어난다. 따라서 전체 흐름과 관계없는 문장은 ④이다.

● globalization ⓝ 세계화
● subtitle ⓥ 자막 처리를 하다, 자막을 달다
● specific ⓐ 특정한
● challenge ⓥ 저항하다, 반박하다
● engagement ⓝ 참여, 관여
● populous ⓐ 인구가 많은
● empirically [ad] 실증적으로
● victim ⓝ 희생자

● multiple ⓐ 다수의, 많은
● distribute ⓥ 배급하다, 배포하다
● dominate ⓥ 지배하다
● spread ⓝ 확산 ⓥ 퍼뜨리다
● respectively [ad] 각각
● value ⓥ 값을 매기다
● passive ⓐ 수동적인, 소극적인

구문 풀이

14행 She thus empirically challenges the idea [that Asian youth
타동사 — 목적어 — 동격 접속사
are passive victims of cultural globalization, or "world culture"
선행사
{that comes out of the West}].
주격 관계대명사   (= cultural globalization)

★★★ 1등급 대비 고난도 3점 문제

09 권력 거리의 의미   정답률 38% | 정답 ①

다음 글의 내용을 한 문장으로 요약하고자 한다. 빈칸 (A), (B)에 들어갈 말로 가장 적절한 것은? [3점]

	(A)	(B)		(A)	(B)
☑①	willing 기꺼이 ~하는	mobility 이동	②	willing 기꺼이 ~하는	assistance 도움
③	reluctant 꺼리는	resistance 내성	④	reluctant 꺼리는	flexibility 유연성
⑤	afraid 두려워하는	openness 개방성			

[본문 해석]

*권력 거리*는 권력의 불평등한 분배가 한 문화의 구성원들에 의해 얼마나 널리 수용되는지를 나타내는 데 사용되는 용어이다. 그것은 권력이 더 적은 사회 구성원들이 권력에서의 불평등을 수용하고 그것을 규범으로 여기는 정도와 관계가 있다. 권력 거리에 대한 수용이 높은 문화들(예를 들어, 인도, 브라질, 그리스, 멕시코 그리고 필리핀)에서, 사람들은 평등한 것으로 여겨지지 않으며, 모든 사람이 사회 계층 내에서 명확하게 정해지거나 할당된 위치를 가진다. 권력 거리에 대한 수용이 낮은 문화들(예를 들어, 핀란드, 노르웨이, 뉴질랜드, 이스라엘)에서는, 사람들은 불평등이 최소여야만 한다고 믿으며, 계층적 구분은 오직 편의상 구분으로서만 여겨진다. 이러한 문화에서는 사회 계층 내에서의 더 많은 유동성이 있으며, 개인이 그들의 개인적 노력과 성취를 토대로 사회 계층을 상승시키는 것이 상대적으로 쉽다.

➡ 구성원들이 불평등을 더 (A) 기꺼이 수용하는 권력 거리에 대한 수용이 높은 문화들과는 다르게, 권력 거리에 대한 수용이 낮은 문화들은 사회 계층 내에서 더 많은 (B) 이동을 허용한다.

Why? 왜 정답일까?

이 글은 권력 거리의 개념을 소개하며, 권력 거리에 대한 수용 수준이 높은 문화와 낮은 문화의 특징을 대조하고 있다. 권력 거리에 대한 수용 수준이 높은 문화에서는 사람들이 사회에서 비교적 고정된 위치(In cultures with high acceptance of power distance ~ everyone has a clearly defined or allocated place in the social hierarchy.)를 가지는 반면, 권력 거리에 대한 수용 수준이 낮은 문화에서는 불평등은 최소여야 한다는 믿음을 바탕으로 개인의 노력과 성취에 근거한 계층 이동이 상대적으로 쉽게 일어난다(~ it is relatively easy for individuals to move up the social hierarchy based on their individual efforts and achievements.). 따라서 요약문의 빈칸 (A), (B)에 들어갈 말로 가장 적절한 것은 ① '(A) willing(기꺼이 ~하는), (B) mobility(이동)'이다.

● term ⓝ 용어
● relate to ~와 관련이 있다

● distribution ⓝ 분배, 분포
● inequality ⓝ 불평등

- **allocate** Ⓥ 할당하다, 배당하다
- **convenience** Ⓝ 편의, 편리
- **relatively** ad 상대적으로
- **hierarchical** ⓐ 위계의, 계층의
- **fluidity** Ⓝ 유동성
- **unlike** prep ~와는 다르게

구문 풀이

3행 It relates to the degree [to which the less powerful members
~와 관련이 있다   전치사+관계대명사
of a society accept their inequality in power and consider it the norm].
동사1   동사2 「consider+A+B : A를 B로 여기다」

★★ 문제 해결 꿀~팁 ★★

▶ 많이 틀린 이유는?

(A)에 들어갈 말을 제대로 파악하는 것이 풀이의 핵심이다. 지문의 'people are not viewed as equals'를 근거로 사람들이 불평등을 '더 기꺼이' 받아들인다는 의미를 추론해야 하기에 까다로운 문제이다.

▶ 문제 해결 방법은?

요약문에서 새로운 개념을 소개한 뒤 2가지 상반된 대상의 예를 대조하여 설명하는 경우는 비교적 흔하다. 이 글 또한, 우선 '권력 거리'라는 소재의 개념을 파악한 뒤, 권력 거리의 수용 수준이 높은 문화와 낮은 문화 간의 상반되는 특성에 관하여 정확히 이해해야 한다. 대의파악 문항에서 아낀 시간을 투자하여 글을 비교적 꼼꼼히 읽을 필요가 있다.

10-12 스위스 기차 여행 중 경험한 친절

[본문 해석]

(A)

나는 스위스에서 기차를 타고 있었다. 기차가 멈췄고 스피커를 통해 차장의 목소리가 독일어, 이탈리아어, 그다음 프랑스어로 메시지를 전했다. 나는 휴가를 떠나기 전에 이 언어 중에 어떠한 것도 배우지 않는 실수를 했다. 「안내방송 후, 모두가 기차에서 내리기 시작했고,」한 노부인이 내가 혼란스러워하고 스트레스를 받는 것을 보았다. (a) 그녀가 나에게 다가왔다.

(C)

「그녀는 영어를 조금 할 수 있었고, 나에게 선로에서 사고가 발생했다고 말했다.」「그녀는 나에게 어디로 가려고 하는지 물었으며, 그 후 기차에서 내려 티켓 부스에 있는 여자에게 갔다.」노부인은 (c) 그녀에게서 기차 노선표와 기차 시간표를 얻었고, 나에게 돌아와서 우리가 거기 가려면 서너 번 기차를 갈아타야 한다고 말했다. 나 혼자서는 그 사실을 알아낼 가망이 없었을 것이기 때문에, 나는 (d) 그녀가 나와 같은 방향으로 간다는 것이 정말로 기뻤다.

(B)

그래서 우리는 여러 기차역을 이동하였고, 그동안 서로에 대해 알아갔다. 총 2.5시간의 여행이었으며 마침내 목적지에 도착했을 때 우리는 기차에서 내렸고 작별의 인사를 했다. 「나는 로마로 가는 기차 시간에 딱 맞추어 도착했고, 그녀는 나에게 그녀 역시 기차를 타야 한다고 말했다.」나는 (b) 그녀에게 얼마나 더 가야 하는지 물었고, 알고 보니 그녀의 집은 반대 방향으로 두 시간 거리에 있었다.

(D)

그녀는 단지 내가 잘 도착하는지를 확인하기 위해 기차를 갈아타면서 끝까지 계속 이동했다. "당신은 내가 만난 사람 중에서 가장 친절한 사람이에요."라고 나는 말했다. 그녀는 부드럽게 미소 지었고 나를 안아주며 내가 서두르지 않으면 기차를 놓칠 것이라고 내게 말했다. 이 여성은 단지 자신의 나라를 방문한 혼란스러워하는 여행객을 돕기 위해 자신의 집에서 몇 시간이나 떨어진 곳으로 (e) 자신을 실어가는 기차에 앉아 하루 종일을 보냈다. 「아무리 많은 나라를 방문하거나 장소를 보더라도, 나는 세계에서 가장 아름다운 나라는 스위스라고 항상 말한다.」

- **come to a stop** 멈추다, 서다
- **destination** Ⓝ 목적지
- **hopeless** ⓐ 가망 없는, 절망적인
- **conductor** Ⓝ 차장, 안내원, 지휘자
- **in time** 때맞춰, 제시간에
- **gently** ad 부드럽게

구문 풀이

(A) 4행 I had made the mistake of not learning any of those
과거완료   전치사 「not+동명사 : 동명사 부정 표현」
languages before my vacation.

(B) 7행 I asked her {how much farther she had to go}, and it turned
4형식 동사   └ 간접 목적어 { } : 직접 목적어(간접의문문)   ~임이 판명되다
out (that) her home was two hours back the other way.

(C) 7행 I was really glad (that) she was headed the same way because
가주어   생략(접속사)   접속사(~ 때문에)
it would have been hopeless for me to figure it out on my own.
~했었을 것이다   의미상 주어   진주어(~것)

(D) 5행 This woman spent her entire day sitting on trains taking her
「spend+시간+동명사 : ~하는 데 ···을 들이다, 쓰다」
hours away from her home just to help out a confused tourist
목적(단지 ~하기 위해)
visiting her country.

---

10 글의 순서 파악   정답률 81% | 정답 ②

주어진 글 (A)에 이어질 내용을 순서에 맞게 배열한 것으로 가장 적절한 것은?

① (B) − (D) − (C)   ☑ (C) − (B) − (D)
③ (C) − (D) − (B)   ④ (D) − (B) − (C)
⑤ (D) − (C) − (B)

Why? 왜 정답일까?

스위스에서 기차 여행을 하던 도중 갑자기 방송이 나와 모두가 기차에서 내리는 모습을 보고 필자가 당황했다는 내용의 주어진 글 뒤에는, 필자에게 한 노부인이 다가와 상황을 설명해주고 기차 노선표와 시간표를 구해다 주었다는 내용의 (C), 약 2.5시간을 함께 간 끝에 필자가 로마로 가는 기차를 타기 위해 도착했을 때 사실은 노부인의 집이 반대 방향에 있었다는 사실을 알게 되었다는 내용의 (B), 필자가 노부인의 친절에 감동과 감사를 느꼈음을 서술하는 (D)가 차례로 이어져야 한다. 따라서 글의 순서로 가장 적절한 것은 ② '(C) − (B) − (D)'이다.

11 지칭 추론   정답률 72% | 정답 ③

밑줄 친 (a) ~ (e) 중에서 가리키는 대상이 나머지 넷과 다른 것은?

① (a)   ② (b)   ☑ (c)   ④ (d)   ⑤ (e)

Why? 왜 정답일까?

(a), (b), (d), (e)는 모두 필자를 도와준 the old woman을 가리키지만, (c)는 앞 문장의 a woman in the ticket booth를 가리키므로, (a) ~ (e) 중에서 가리키는 대상이 다른 하나는 ③ '(c)'이다.

12 세부 내용 파악   정답률 82% | 정답 ②

윗글에 관한 내용으로 적절하지 않은 것은?

① 안내 방송 후 모두가 기차에서 내리기 시작했다.
☑ 'I'는 로마로 가는 기차 시간에 맞춰 도착하지 못했다.
③ 노부인은 선로에서 사고가 발생했다고 말했다.
④ 노부인은 기차에서 내려 티켓 부스로 갔다.
⑤ 'I'는 세계에서 가장 아름다운 나라가 스위스라고 항상 말한다.

Why? 왜 정답일까?

(B) 'I had made it just in time to catch my train to Rome, ~'에서 나는 로마로 가는 기차 시간에 딱 맞추어 도착했다고 하므로, 내용과 일치하지 않는 것은 ② 'I'는 로마로 가는 기차 시간에 맞춰 도착하지 못했다.'이다.

Why? 왜 오답일까?

① (A) 'After the announcement, everyone started getting off the train, ~'의 내용과 일치한다.

③ (C) '~ she told me that an accident had happened on the tracks.'의 내용과 일치한다.

④ (C) '~ then she got off the train and went to a woman in the ticket booth.'의 내용과 일치한다.

⑤ (D) '~ I always say the most beautiful country in the world is Switzerland.'의 내용과 일치한다.

[문제편 p.160]

DAY 27 — 20분 미니 모의고사

01 ⑤	02 ②	03 ⑤	04 ④	05 ④
06 ⑤	07 ②	08 ①	09 ⑤	10 ⑤
11 ①	12 ⑤			

---

01 회사 가치를 담은 행동에 관한 지침의 필요성
정답률 69% | 정답 ⑤

다음 글에서 필자가 주장하는 바로 가장 적절한 것은?

① 조직 문화 혁신을 위해서 모든 구성원이 공유할 핵심 가치를 정립해야 한다.
② 조직 구성원의 행동을 변화시키려면 지도자는 명확한 가치관을 가져야 한다.
③ 조직 내 문화가 공유되기 위해서 구성원의 자발적 행동이 뒷받침되어야 한다.
④ 조직의 핵심 가치 실현을 위해 구성원 간의 지속적인 의사소통이 필수적이다.
☑ 조직의 문화 형성에는 가치를 반영한 행동의 공유를 위한 명시적 지침이 필요하다.

[본문 해석]

가치만으로는 문화가 창조되고 구축되지 않는다. 일부 시간에만 가치에 따라 생활하는 것은 문화의 창조와 유지에 기여하지 않는다. 가치를 행동으로 바꾸는 것은 전투의 절반에 불과하다. 물론, 이것은 올바른 방향으로 나아가는 단계이지만, 그다음에 그러한 행동은 기대되는 바에 대한 명확하고 간결한 설명과 함께 조직 전체에 널리 공유되고 배포되어야 한다. 단순히 그것에 관해 이야기하는 것만으로는 충분하지 않다. 리더와 모든 인력 관리자가 자기 팀을 지도하는 데 사용할 수 있는 특정 행동을 시각적으로 표현해 놓는 것이 중요하다. 스포츠 팀이 좋은 성과를 내고 승리하는 데 도움이 되도록 고안된 특정 플레이를 담고 있는 플레이 북을 갖고 있는 것과 마찬가지로, 회사는 문화를 행동으로 바꾸고 가치를 승리하는 행동으로 바꾸는 데 필요한 핵심적인 변화를 담은 플레이 북을 갖고 있어야 한다.

Why? 왜 정답일까?

회사의 가치를 그저 말하는 수준에 그치지 말고, 가치를 반영한 행동에 관해 구체적으로 지침을 만들어 공유하라(It is critical to have a visual representation of the specific behaviors that leaders and all people managers can use to coach their people.)는 내용이다. 따라서 필자의 주장으로 가장 적절한 것은 ⑤ '조직의 문화 형성에는 가치를 반영한 행동의 공유를 위한 명시적 지침이 필요하다.'이다.

- **contribute to** ~에 기여하다
- **distribute** ⓥ 배포하다
- **organization** ⓝ 조직
- **concise** ⓐ 간결한
- **critical** ⓐ 중요한, 결정적인
- **specific** ⓐ 특정한, 구체적인
- **playbook** ⓝ 플레이 북
- **shift** ⓝ 변화
- **maintenance** ⓝ 유지
- **throughout** prep ~의 구석구석까지
- **along with** ~와 함께
- **description** ⓝ 설명, 기술
- **representation** ⓝ 표현, 묘사
- **coach** ⓥ 지도하다
- **perform** ⓥ 경기하다, 수행하다
- **transform** ⓥ 바꾸다

구문 풀이

11행 Just like a sports team has a playbook with specific plays
~와 마찬가지로
designed to help them perform well and win, your company should
과거분사구
have a playbook with the key shifts needed to transform your culture
과거분사구
into action and turn your values into winning behaviors.

---

02 사람들이 원을 그리며 걷는 이유
정답률 70% | 정답 ②

다음 글의 주제로 가장 적절한 것은?

① abilities to construct a mental map for walking
걷기에 대한 정신적 지도를 구성하는 능력
☑ factors that result in people walking in a circle
사람이 원을 그리며 걷게 되는 원인
③ reasons why dominance exists in nature
자연에 우성이 존재하는 이유

④ instincts that help people return home
사람들이 집으로 돌아갈 수 있도록 도와주는 본능
⑤ solutions to finding the right direction
올바른 방향을 찾는 데 관한 해법

[본문 해석]

나는 만약 내가 넓은 숲에서 길을 잃었다면, 머지않아 내가 출발했던 곳으로 결국 올 것을 믿도록 길러졌다. 길을 잃은 사람들은 항상 원을 그리며 걷는데, 이를 알지 못한 채 그렇게 한다. *지도나 나침반 없이 길 찾기*라는 책에서 저자인 Harold Gatty는 이것이 사실임을 확인해 준다. 우리는 몇 가지 이유로 원을 그리며 걷는 경향이 있다. 가장 중요한 것은 실제로 어떤 사람도 두 다리 길이가 정확히 똑같지 않다는 점이다. 한쪽 다리는 항상 다른 쪽보다 조금 더 길고 이는 우리가 심지어 그것을 알아채지 못한 채 돌도록 한다. 게다가 만약 여러분이 배낭을 메고 도보 여행을 하는 중이라면, 그 배낭의 무게로 인해 여러분은 불가피하게 균형을 잃게될 것이다. 우리가 주로 쓰는 손도 이 조합의 한 요소가 된다. 만약 여러분이 오른손잡이라면 여러분은 오른쪽으로 돌려는 경향을 갖고 있을 것이다. 그리고 여러분이 장애물을 만났을 때 여러분은 무의식적으로 그것을 오른쪽으로 지나가겠다고 결정할 것이다.

Why? 왜 정답일까?

'We tend to walk in circles for several reasons.' 이후로 사람은 두 다리의 길이가 같지 않고 주로 쓰는 손 쪽으로 움직여가는 경향을 갖고 있어 원을 그리며 걷게 된다는 내용이 제시되고 있다. 따라서 글의 주제로 가장 적절한 것은 ② '사람이 원을 그리며 걷게 되는 원인'이다.

- **bring up** ~을 기르다[양육하다]
- **end up** 결국 ~이다
- **virtually** ⓐⓓ 거의, 사실상
- **weight** ⓝ 무게 ⓥ 무게가 ~이다
- **off balance** 균형을 잃고
- **factor into** ~을 요인으로 포함하다
- **subconsciously** ⓐⓓ 무의식적으로
- **instinct** ⓝ 본능
- **get lost** 길을 잃다, 헤매다
- **compass** ⓝ 나침반
- **slightly** ⓐⓓ 약간
- **inevitably** ⓐⓓ 불가피하게
- **dominant** ⓐ 우성의, 지배적인
- **obstacle** ⓝ 장애물
- **dominance** ⓝ (유전적) 우성, 우세함, 지배

구문 풀이

10행 In addition, if you are hiking with a backpack on, the weight
조건 접속사 · 현재시제(진행)
of that backpack will inevitably throw you off balance.
미래시제

---

03 요일별 풋볼 리그 경기 부상률
정답률 69% | 정답 ⑤

다음 도표의 내용과 일치하지 않는 것은?

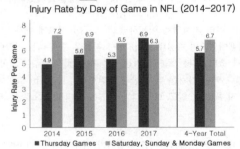

Injury Rate by Day of Game in NFL (2014–2017)

[본문 해석]

위 그래프는 2014년부터 2017년까지 내셔널 풋볼 리그(NFL) 경기의 요일별 부상률을 보여 준다. ① 목요일 경기 부상률은 2014년에 가장 낮았고 2017년에 가장 높았다. ② 토요일과 일요일과 월요일 경기 부상률은 2014년부터 2017년까지 꾸준히 감소하였다. ③ 2017년을 제외한 모든 해에 목요일 경기 부상률이 토요일, 일요일 그리고 월요일 경기 부상률보다 더 낮았다. ④ 목요일 경기 부상률과 토요일, 일요일 그리고 월요일 경기 부상률 간의 차이는 2014년에 가장 컸고 2017년에 가장 작았다. ⑤ 4년 중 두 해에, 목요일 경기 부상률이 4년 전체의 목요일 경기 부상률보다 더 높았다.

Why? 왜 정답일까?

도표에 따르면 한 해의 목요일 경기 부상률이 4년 합계 목요일 경기 부상률보다 높았던 해는 **2017년**뿐이다. 따라서 도표의 내용과 일치하지 않는 것은 ⑤이다.

- **injury** ⓝ 부상
- **steadily** ⓐⓓ 꾸준히
- **rate** ⓝ 비율
- **out of** ~ 중에서, ~로부터

---

04 John Ray의 생애

정답률 72% | 정답 ④

John Ray에 관한 다음 글의 내용과 일치하지 <u>않는</u> 것은?
① 마을 대장장이의 아들이었다.
② 성직자의 길로 들어서기 전 Cambridge 대학에 다녔다.
③ 병에서 회복하기 위해 자연을 산책하기 시작했다.
☑ Francis Willughby에게 후원받아 홀로 유럽을 여행하였다.
⑤ 동식물의 목록을 만들기 위해 표본을 연구하며 말년을 보냈다.

[본문 해석]
「1627년 잉글랜드 Essex주 Black Notley에서 태어난 John Ray는 마을 대장장이의 아들이었다.」「16세에 그는 Cambridge 대학교에 들어가서 폭넓게 공부하고 그리스어부터 수학까지 강의를 하다가 1660년에 성직자의 길로 들어섰다.」「1650년 병에서 회복하기 위해, 그는 자연을 산책하기 시작했고 식물학에 대한 관심을 키웠다.」①의 근거 일치「부유한 학생이자 후원자인 Francis Willughby와 함께 Ray는 1660년대에 영국과 유럽을 여행했고 식물과 동물을 연구하고 수집했다.」그는 1673년 Margaret Oakley와 결혼했고, Willughby 집안을 떠난 후에는 Black Notley에서 77세까지 조용히 살았다. 「그는 동식물 목록을 만들기 위해 표본을 연구하면서 말년을 보냈다.」⑤의 근거 일치 그는 식물과 그 형태, 기능뿐만 아니라 신학과 그의 여행에 관해 20편 이상의 저서를 썼다.

Why? 왜 정답일까?
'Accompanied by his wealthy student and supporter Francis Willughby, Ray toured Britain and Europe ~'에서 Ray는 영국 및 유럽 여행에 Francis Willughby의 후원을 받은 동시에 그와 동행도 했다고 하므로, 내용과 일치하지 않는 것은 ④ 'Francis Willughby에게 후원받아 홀로 유럽을 여행하였다.'이다.

Why? 왜 오답일까?
① '~ John Ray was the son of the village blacksmith.'의 내용과 일치한다.
② 'At 16, he went to Cambridge University, ~ before joining the priesthood in 1660.'의 내용과 일치한다.
③ 'To recover from an illness in 1650, he had taken to nature walks ~'의 내용과 일치한다.
⑤ 'He spent his later years studying samples in order to assemble plant and animal catalogues.'의 내용과 일치한다.

- **blacksmith** ⓝ 대장장이
- **lecture on** ~에 관해 강의하다
- **mathematics** ⓝ 수학
- **recover from** ~에서 회복하다
- **botany** ⓝ 식물학
- **wealthy** ⓐ 부유한
- **household** ⓝ 집, 가정
- **spend A ~ing** A를 ~하는 데 쓰다
- **theology** ⓝ 신학
- **widely** ⓐⓓ 널리
- **Greek** ⓝ 그리스어 ⓐ 그리스의
- **priesthood** ⓝ 성직, 사제직
- **illness** ⓝ 질병
- **accompany** ⓥ ~을 동반하다
- **supporter** ⓝ 후원자, 지지자
- **quietly** ⓐⓓ 조용히
- **assemble** ⓥ 모으다, 조립하다
- **function** ⓝ 기능

구문 풀이

2행 At 16, he went to Cambridge University, where he studied
　　　　　　　　　　　　　　　　　장소 선행사　　　관계부사
widely and lectured on topics from Greek to mathematics, before
　　　　　　　　　　　　　　　　　　　　　　　　　　　　~하기 전에
joining the priesthood in 1660.

★★★ 1등급 대비 고난도 3점 문제

05 비용 절감 대신 생산성 향상을 통한 수익성 향상

정답률 36% | 정답 ④

다음 글의 밑줄 친 부분 중, 어법상 틀린 것은? [3점]

[본문 해석]
비용 절감은 수익성을 향상시킬 수 있지만 어느 정도까지일 뿐이다. 만약 제조업자가 비용을 너무 많이 절감해서 그렇게 하는 것이 제품의 질을 손상시키게 된다면, 그 증가된 수익성은 단기적일 것이다. 더 나은 접근법은 생산성을 향상시키는 것이다. 만약 기업이 똑같은 수의 직원들로부터 더 많은 생산을 얻을 수 있다면 그들은 기본적으로 거저 얻게 되는 것이다. 그들은 판매할 상품을 더 많이 얻고, 각 상품의 가격은 떨어진다. 생산성 향상에 필요한 기계 또는 직원 연수가 생산성 향상으로 얻는 이윤의 가치보다 비용이 적게 든다면, 이는 어떤 기업이든 할 수 있는 쉬운 투자이다. 생산성 향상은 이를 이뤄 내는 각 기업에 중요한 만큼 경제에도 중요하다. 일반적으로 생산성 향상은 모두의 생활 수준을 올려 주고 건강한 경제의 좋은 지표가 된다.

Why? 왜 정답일까?
'as ~ as' 구문에서 두 비교 대상은 구조상 일치되어야 한다. 이 문장은 'Productivity improvements are important to the economy.'와 'They(= productivity improvements) are important to the individual business that's making them.'라는 두 문장을 원급 비교문 한 문장으로 바꾼 것이므로 동사는 do가 아닌 are가 되어야 한다.

Why? 왜 오답일까?
① 'so ~ that'은 '(너무 ~해서 …하다)' 구문이다.
② 'are tapping into'라는 동사를 꾸미기 위해 부사 basically가 쓰였다.
③ 꾸밈을 받는 명사 machinery와 employee training은 어떤 필요를 느낄 수 있는 주체라기보다는 '필요해지는' 대상이므로, 수동의 의미를 나타내는 과거분사 needed는 어법상 맞다.
⑤ and 앞의 복수 동사 raise와 병렬을 이루는 구조이므로 are는 적절하다.

- **improve** ⓥ 향상시키다
- **up to a point** 어느 정도까지
- **short-lived** 단기적인
- **basically** ⓐⓓ 기본적으로
- **generally** ⓐⓓ 일반적으로, 대개
- **profitability** ⓝ 수익성
- **harm** ⓥ 손상시키다, 해치다
- **approach** ⓝ 접근법
- **tap into** ~에 다가가다
- **indication** ⓝ 지표

구문 풀이

8행 As long as the machinery or employee training [needed for
　　　　　조건 접속사(~하는 한)　　　　주어　　　　　　과거분사
productivity improvements] costs less than the value of the productivity
　　　　　　　　　　　　　동사(단수)
gains, / it's an easy investment for any business to make.
　　　　　　　　　　　　　　　　to make의 의미상 주어　형용사적 용법

★★ 문제 해결 꿀~팁 ★★

▶ **많이 틀린 이유는?**
'현재분사 vs. 과거분사', '형용사 vs. 부사', 병렬구조 등의 전형적인 문법 사항과 함께 as 뒤 대동사 사용이라는 고난도 개념을 묻는 어려운 문제였다. 오답으로 ③이 많이 나왔는데, 명사를 꾸미는 분사의 태(현재분사 vs. 과거분사)는 꾸밈을 받는 명사 입장에서 명사가 '하는' 주체인지(현재분사), '당하는' 대상인지(과거분사)를 파악해야 한다.

▶ **문제 해결 방법은?**
'~처럼, ~대로, ~만큼' 등의 뜻으로 쓰인 접속사 as는 주절에 나온 동사를 그대로 뒤에서 반복하기보다 대동사를 많이 이용하여, 앞에 나온 동사가 be동사이면 as 뒤에도 be를, 앞에 나온 동사가 일반동사이면 do/does/did를 쓰게 된다. 이는 알면 맞고 모르면 틀리기 좋은 개념으로 보통 문법 문항의 난이도를 높일 때 출제된다. 기출에서 확인할 때마다 따로 정리해 두어 감각을 키우도록 한다.

★★★ 1등급 대비 고난도 3점 문제

06 카운터쉐이딩의 개념

정답률 29% | 정답 ⑤

다음 글의 밑줄 친 부분 중, 문맥상 낱말의 쓰임이 적절하지 <u>않은</u> 것은? [3점]

[본문 해석]
카운터쉐이딩(명암 역위형 보호색)은 시각적으로 평평하게 하는 과정으로 동물에게 위장을 제공한다. 햇빛이 물체를 위에서 비출 때, 그 물체는 맨 위가 가장 밝을 것이다. 물체의 색깔은 ① 맨 아래로 향할수록 점차 더 어두운색으로 음영이 생길 것이다. 이러한 음영은 물체에 ② 농도를 주고, 보는 사람이 그것의 모양을 식별하게 해 준다. 따라서 비록 동물이 밑바탕과 정확하게, 하지만 균일하게 같은 색일지라도 빛을 받을 때 쉽게 ③ 눈에 띌 것이다. 그러나 동물 대부분은 아랫부분보다 윗부분이 더 어둡다. 그들이 위에서 빛을 받을 때, 더 어두운 등은 밝아지고 더 밝은 복부에 음영이 진다. 따라서 동물은 ④ 하나의 색처럼 보이고 밑바탕과 쉽게 섞인다. 이런 형태의 배색, 즉 카운터쉐이딩은 생물체의 모양의 시각적 인상을 ⑤ 강화한다(→ 파괴한다). 그것은 동물이 자신의 배경에 섞여들게 해 준다.

Why? 왜 정답일까?
동물이 주변 색에 섞여들게 하는 장치인 카운터쉐이딩에 관해 설명한 글이다. 전반적으로 색이 균일한 물체를 향해 위에서 빛을 주면 아래로 갈수록 음영이 지면서 형태감이 생기는데, 동물 대부분은 몸 위쪽 색이 더 어둡기에 위에서 빛을 비추더라도 아래로 갈수록 색이 비슷해지게 되고 만다. 따라서 동물은 '하나의' 색깔처럼 보이고, 형태감이 오히려

DAY 27

[문제편 p.163]

'무너져' 배경에 섞여버리게 된다는 것이다. 이를 근거로 할 때, 시각적 인상은 '파괴된다'는 설명이 적절하므로 ⑤의 reinforces를 destroys로 고쳐야 한다. 따라서 문맥상 낱말의 쓰임이 적절하지 않은 것은 ⑤이다.

- optical ⓐ 시각적인
- gradually ⓐⓓ 점점
- uniformly ⓐⓓ 균일하게
- visible ⓐ 눈에 띄는
- reinforce ⓥ 강화하다
- camouflage ⓝ 위장
- distinguish ⓥ 구별하다
- substrate ⓝ 밑바탕, 기질(基質)
- blend in with ~에 섞여들다

구문 풀이

7행 Thus even if an animal is exactly, but uniformly, the same (설령 ~하더라도) color as the substrate, it will be easily visible when (it is) illuminated. (생략)

★★ 문제 해결 꿀~팁 ★★

▶ 많이 틀린 이유는?
몸이 햇빛을 받으면 대체로 위가 밝고 아래가 어두워지므로, 아예 위쪽 몸을 더 어둡게 해서 형태가 분간되지 않도록 보호하는 countershading에 관해 설명하는 글이다. ③의 전후 문맥을 보면, 몸 색깔이 전체적으로 균일하다면 빛을 받을 때 형태가 더 '잘 보일' 것이라고 한다. 이는 실제로 동물들이 countershading 전략을 취하는 이유를 적절히 설명한 것이다. 이어서 ④를 보면, 위쪽 몸의 색깔이 더 어두울 때 빛을 받으면 아래쪽 몸의 색상 톤과 비슷해지면서 '한 가지' 색깔로 보이게 된다고 설명한다. 색상이 '하나로' 보인다는 것은 입체 형태가 잘 분간되지 않는다는 의미이고, 그렇기에 countershading 전략과 잘 맞는 설명이다.

▶ 문제 해결 방법은?
어휘 문제는 항상 전후 문맥을 잘 봐야 한다. 특히 ⑤가 포함된 문장을 보충 설명하는 마지막 문장에 밑줄이 없으므로, 이 문장은 '맞는' 진술이다. 따라서 이를 근거로 ⑤를 판단한다.

---

07 산업의 집중화 경향   정답률 43% | 정답 ②

다음 빈칸에 들어갈 말로 가장 적절한 것을 고르시오.

① Automation - 자동화
✓ Concentration - 집중
③ Transportation - 교통
④ Globalization - 세계화
⑤ Liberalization - 자유화

[본문 해석]
거의 모든 산업의 회사들은 밀집되는 경향이 있다. 당신이 미국 지도에 무작위로 다트를 던진다고 가정해보라. 당신은 다트에 의해 남겨진 구멍들이 지도 전체에 다소 고르게 분포된 것을 보게 될 것이다. 하지만 어떤 특정 산업의 실제 지도는 전혀 그렇게 보이지 않고, 마치 어떤 사람이 모든 다트를 같은 지역에 던진 것처럼 보인다. 이것은 아마 부분적으로는 평판 때문일 것이다. 구매자들은 옥수수밭 한가운데 있는 소프트웨어 회사를 수상쩍게 여길 것이다. 당신이 새로운 직원을 필요로 할 때마다 근처에서 인력을 빼내기보다는 오히려 누군가로 하여금 나라를 가로질러 이주하도록 설득해야 한다면 직원을 채용하는 것이 또한 어려울 것이다. 또한 규제상의 이유도 있다. 토지 사용 제한법들은 종종 공해 유발 산업들을 한 지역에, 식당들과 술집들을 다른 지역에 집중시키려 노력한다. 마지막으로, 같은 산업에 종사하는 사람들은 종종 유사한 선호도를 보인다. (컴퓨터 엔지니어들은 커피를 좋아하고 금융업 종사자들은 비싼 와인을 가지고 뽐낸다.) 집중이 그들이 좋아하는 생활 편의시설을 제공하는 것을 더 쉽게 해준다.

Why? 왜 정답일까?
첫 문장인 'Firms in almost every industry tend to be clustered.'에서 어느 산업 부문에서건 회사들은 밀집되는 경향이 있다고 언급하는 것으로 볼 때, 빈칸에 들어갈 말로 가장 적절한 것은 '밀집'을 다른 말로 나타낸 ② '집중'이다.

- firm ⓝ 회사
- suppose ⓥ 가정하다, 추정하다
- evenly ⓐⓓ 고르게
- reputation ⓝ 평판, 명성
- cornfield ⓝ 옥수수밭
- persuade ⓥ 설득하다
- concentrate ⓥ 집중시키다
- financier ⓝ 금융업자, 자본가
- automation ⓝ 자동화
- cluster ⓥ 밀집하다, 모이다
- more or less 거의, 약
- distribute ⓥ 분포하다
- suspicious ⓐ 수상쩍어하는, 의심스러운
- recruit ⓥ 채용하다, 모집하다
- regulatory ⓐ 규제의, 단속력을 지닌
- preference ⓝ 선호(도)
- amenity ⓝ 편의시설
- liberalization ⓝ 자유화

구문 풀이

4행 But the real map of any given industry looks nothing like that; it looks more as if someone had thrown all the darts in the same place. 「as if + 주어 + had p.p. : 가정법 과거완료(마치 ~했던 것처럼)」

★★★ 1등급 대비 고난도 3점 문제

08 인간의 무의식적인 인지 과업 분담   정답률 37% | 정답 ①

다음 빈칸에 들어갈 말로 가장 적절한 것을 고르시오. [3점]

✓ divide up cognitive labor - 인지 노동을 나누는데
② try to avoid disagreements - 의견 불일치를 피하려고 노력하는데
③ seek people with similar tastes - 비슷한 취향을 가진 사람을 찾는데
④ like to share old wisdom - 옛 지혜를 공유하기 좋아하는데
⑤ balance work and leisure - 일과 여가의 균형을 맞추는데

[본문 해석]
심리학 연구에 따르면, 사람들은 자연스럽게 인지 노동을 나누는데, 흔히 그것에 대해서 별 생각 없이 그렇게 한다. 여러분이 친구와 함께 특별한 저녁식사를 요리하고 있다고 상상해 보라. 여러분은 요리를 잘하지만, 친구는 아마추어 소믈리에라고 할 수 있는 와인 전문가이다. 이웃이 들르더니 여러분 두 사람에게 거리를 따라가면 바로 있는 주류 가게에서 파는 기막히게 좋은 새로운 와인에 대해 말하기 시작한다. 많은 새로운 와인이 있어서 기억해야 할 것이 많다. 어떤 와인을 사야 하는지에 관해 이웃이 할 말을 기억하기 위해 여러분은 얼마나 열심히 노력할까? 여러분 옆에 앉아 있는 와인 전문가가 그 정보를 더 잘 기억하고 있는데 무엇 하러 그러겠는가? 여러분의 친구가 곁에 없다면 더 열심히 애쓸지도 모른다. 어쨌든 뭐가 저녁 만찬을 위해 좋은 와인일지 아는 것은 좋은 일일 것이다. 하지만, 와인 전문가인 여러분의 친구는 애쓰지도 않고 그 정보를 기억하기가 쉽다.

Why? 왜 정답일까?
첫 문장에서 주제를 제시하고 두 번째 문장부터 주제를 뒷받침하는 예를 소개한다. 예시에 따르면 와인 전문가인 친구와 함께 새로 들어온 와인에 관한 이야기를 들을 때, 친구가 그 정보를 큰 노력 없이 더 잘 기억할 것이기 때문에 우리는 무의식적으로 별 노력을 들이지 않게 된다고 한다. 이에 근거할 때, 우리는 무의식적으로 함께 있는 사람과 인지적인 노력을 '분담해서' 효율적으로 정보를 처리하려는 경향이 있다는 내용을 추론할 수 있다. 따라서 빈칸에 들어갈 말로 가장 적절한 것은 ① '인지 노동을 나누는데'이다.

- expert ⓝ 전문가
- terrific ⓐ 아주 멋진
- retain ⓥ 보유하다
- cognitive ⓐ 인지적인
- leisure ⓝ 여가
- sommelier ⓝ 소믈리에(와인 담당 웨이터)
- liquor ⓝ (독한) 술
- festivity ⓝ 축제 기분
- disagreement ⓝ 불일치

구문 풀이

9행 How hard are you going to try to remember what the neighbor has to say about which wines to buy? (관계대명사(~것)) 「which + 명 + to부정사 : 어떤 ~을 … 할지」

★★ 문제 해결 꿀~팁 ★★

▶ 많이 틀린 이유는?
어떤 정보를 더 잘 기억할 사람이 옆에 있다면 우리는 무의식적으로 그 정보를 기억하려는 노력을 덜 들일 것이라는 내용의 글이다. 의견 불일치를 피하거나 서로 비슷한 취향을 가진 사람을 찾는다는 내용은 언급되지 않으므로 ②, ③은 모두 답으로 부적절하다.

▶ 문제 해결 방법은?
빈칸 뒤의 예시를 읽고 그 전체적인 내용을 근거로 도출할 수 있는 논리적 결론을 추론해내는 문제이다. 와인에 대한 정보를 별로 애쓰지도 않고 쉽게 기억해낼 친구가 있다면, 이웃이 와인에 대한 정보를 이야기해줄 때 그 정보를 처리하기 위한 인지적 노력을 덜 기울일 것이라는 내용을 통해, 인간은 무의식 속에서도 '인지적 부담'을 나눌 수 있는지 살펴보고 행동한다는 내용이 빈칸에 들어가야 한다.

---

09 촉감 수용체의 분포   정답률 47% | 정답 ⑤

주어진 글 다음에 이어질 글의 순서로 가장 적절한 것을 고르시오.

① (A) - (C) - (B)　　　② (B) - (A) - (C)
③ (B) - (C) - (A)　　　④ (C) - (A) - (B)
✓⑤ (C) - (B) - (A)

[본문 해석]

촉감 수용체는 신체 곳곳에 퍼져 있지만 골고루 퍼져 있지는 않다. 대부분의 촉감 수용체는 손가락 끝, 혀, 그리고 입술에서 발견된다.

(C) 예를 들어, 각각의 손가락 끝에는 별개의 촉감 수용체가 약 5천 개있다. 몸의 다른 부분에는 훨씬 더 적다. 당신의 등 피부에는 촉감 수용체가 2인치만큼 떨어져 있을 수도 있다.

(B) 당신은 스스로 이것을 테스트해 볼 수 있다. 누군가에게 당신의 등을 한 손가락, 두 손가락, 또는 세 손가락으로 찌르게 하고 그 사람이 손가락을 몇 개 사용했는지 추측해 보라. 만약 손가락이 서로 가까이 붙어 있다면, 당신은 아마 그것이 한 개라고 생각할 것이다.

(A) 하지만 만약 손가락끼리 멀리 떨어져 있다면, 당신은 그것들을 각각 느낄 수 있다. 하지만 만약 그 사람이 당신의 손등에 똑같이 해보면(몇 개의 손가락이 사용되고 있는지 모르도록 눈을 감은 채로), 당신은 아마 손가락이 서로 가까이 있을 때조차도 쉽게 구별할 수 있을 것이다.

Why? 왜 정답일까?

촉감 수용체의 분포에 관해 언급하는 주어진 글 뒤로, 손가락 끝과 다른 부분을 예를 들어 비교하는 (C), 촉감 수용체를 테스트하는 과정에 대한 설명으로 넘어가는 (B), 설명을 이어 가는 (A)가 차례로 이어져야 자연스럽다. 따라서 글의 순서로 가장 적절한 것은 ⑤ '(C) - (B) - (A)'이다.

- **receptor** ⓝ 수용체
- **individually** [ad] 개별적으로
- **poke** ⓥ 쿡 찌르다
- **back** ⓝ 등, 허리
- **fingertip** ⓝ 손가락 끝
- **for oneself** 스스로, 혼자 힘으로
- **separate** ⓐ 각각의, 별개의 ⓥ 분리하다

구문 풀이

6행 Yet if the person does the same thing on the back of your
　　　 접속사(조건)　　　　　　　동사(현재)
hand (with your eyes closed, so that you don't see how many fingers
　　　 「with + 명사 + 분사: ~한 채로」 접속사(조건: ~하도록)
are being used), you probably will be able to tell easily, even when
　　 동사(미래)
the fingers are close together.

---

10 과학자들이 생각을 전달하는 수단의 변화　정답률 38% | 정답 ⑤

글의 흐름으로 보아, 주어진 문장이 들어가기에 가장 적절한 곳을 고르시오.

[본문 해석]

현대 과학의 초기 단계에서 과학자들은 주로 책을 출판하여 자신의 창의적인 생각을 전달했다. ① 이런 작업 방식은 뉴턴의 *Principia*뿐만 아니라 코페르니쿠스의 *On the Revolutions of the Heavenly Spheres*와 케플러의 *The Harmonies of the World*, 갈릴레오의 *Dialogues Concerning the Two New Sciences*로도 설명된다. ② *Transactions of the Royal Society of London* 같은 과학 정기 간행물의 출현과 함께, 책은 과학적 의사소통의 주요한 형식으로 전문 학술지 논문에 점차 자리를 내주었다. ③ 물론 다윈의 *Origin of Species*가 보여주듯이, 책이 완전히 버려진 것은 아니었다. ④ 그렇다고 하더라도, 과학자들은 자기 생각을 다른 책 한 권 길이의 출간물을 내지 않고도 자신이 창의적으로 기여한 바에 대한 명성을 세우는 것이 결국 가능해졌다. ⑤ 예를 들어, 아인슈타인에게 노벨상을 안겨 준, 특수 상대성 이론과 광전 효과에 관한 혁명적인 생각들은 *Annalen der Physik*에 논문으로 등장했다. 역사상 가장 위대한 과학자 중 한 명이라는 그의 지위는 단 한 권의 책의 출간에 달려 있지는 않다.

Why? 왜 정답일까?

현대 과학 초기에 과학자들은 책을 출판해 자신의 생각을 세상에 알렸지만, 시간이 흐르며 책보다 짧은 학술 논문의 형태로 생각을 발표하게 되었다는 내용의 글이다. ⑤ 앞에서 책 한 권 길이의 출간물 없이도 과학자들이 자신의 업적을 드러낼 수 있게 되었다고 설명한 데 이어, 주어진 문장에서는 책 대신 '논문'을 활용한 과학자의 예로 아인슈타인을 언급한다. 이어서 ⑤ 뒤에서는 아인슈타인을 **His**로 지칭하며, '그'의 입지가 책 출간 여부에 좌우되지는 않는다고 부연한다. 따라서 주어진 문장이 들어가기에 가장 적절한 곳은 ⑤이다.

- **revolutionary** ⓐ 혁명적인
- **special theory of relativity** 특수 상대성 이론
- **photoelectric effect** 광전 효과
- **communicate** ⓥ 전달하다
- **publish** ⓥ 출판하다
- **periodical** ⓝ 정기 간행물
- **yield ground to** ~에 자리를 내주다
- **abandon** ⓥ 버리다
- **establish** ⓥ 세우다, 확립하다
- **contribution** ⓝ 기여, 공헌
- **status** ⓝ 지위, 상태
- **concerning** [prep] ~에 관하여
- **paper** ⓝ 논문
- **largely** [ad] 주로, 대개
- **advent** ⓝ 출현
- **gradually** [ad] 점차로
- **journal** ⓝ 학술지
- **altogether** [ad] 완전히, 전적으로
- **reputation** ⓝ 명성
- **treatment** ⓝ 취급, 대우
- **depend on** ~에 달려 있다

구문 풀이

17행 Even so, it eventually became possible for scientists
　　　　　　　가주어　　　　　　2형식 동사　 보어　　의미상 주어
to establish a reputation for their creative contributions
진주어(~것)
without publishing a single book-length treatment of their ideas.
~하지 않은 채

11-12 나이에 대한 사회적 규범과 인식

[본문 해석]

1680년대 영국에서 50세까지 사는 것은 이례적인 일이었다. 이 시기는 지식이 (a) 널리 보급되지 않았고, 책이 거의 없었으며, 대부분의 사람들이 (글자를) 읽을 수 없었던 때였다. 결과적으로, 지식은 이야기와 공유된 경험이라는 구전 전통으로 전수되었다. 그리고 더 나이 든 사람들이 더 많은 지식을 축적했기 때문에, 사회적 규범은 50세가 넘으면 지혜롭다는 것이었다. 「나이에 대한 이런 사회적 인식은 인쇄기와 같은 새로운 기술의 출현으로 변화하기 시작했다.」 시간이 지나면서 더 많은 책이 인쇄됨에 따라 문해력이 (b) 증가했고, 지식 전달의 구전 전통이 사라지기 시작했다. 구전 전통이 사라지면서 노인들의 지혜는 덜 중요해졌고, 결과적으로 50세가 넘은 것은 더 이상 지혜로움을 (c) 의미하는 것으로 여겨지지 않았다. 「우리는 생활 연령과 생물학적 연령 사이의 격차가 빠르게 변화하고, 사회적 규범이 (d) 적용하기 위해 분투하는 시기에 살고 있다.」 AARP(이전의 American Association of Retired Persons)에 의해 제작된 영상에서 젊은이들은 다양한 활동을 '마치 꼭 노인처럼' 하도록 요청받았다. 영상에서 노인들이 그들에 합류했을 때, 고정관념과 노인들의 실제 행동 사이의 격차는 (e) 눈에 띄지 않았다 (→ 두드러졌다). 「오늘날의 세상에서 우리의 사회적 규범은 신속하게 갱신되어야 한다는 것이 분명하다.」

- **unusual** ⓐ 이례적인
- **as a consequence** 결과적으로
- **oral tradition** 구전
- **norm** ⓝ 규범
- **advent** ⓝ 출현, 도래
- **literacy** ⓝ 문해력, 읽고 쓰는 능력
- **fade** ⓥ 사라지다, 옅어지다
- **chronological age** 생활 연령
- **formerly** [ad] 이전에
- **unnoticeable** ⓐ 눈에 띄지 않는
- **spread** ⓥ 퍼뜨리다
- **pass down** 전해지다
- **accumulate** ⓥ 축적하다
- **perception** ⓝ 인식
- **printing press** 인쇄기
- **transfer** ⓝ 이동, 전파
- **signify** ⓥ 의미하다
- **biological age** 생물학적 연령
- **stereotype** ⓝ 고정관념

구문 풀이

6행 And since older people had accumulated more knowledge,
　　　 ~ 때문에　　　　　　　　 과거완료(was보다 이전 시점)
the social norm was {that to be over fifty was to be wise}.
　　　　　　　　　　　　　 주어　　　　　　 주격 보어　　{ }: 명사절

---

11 제목 파악　정답률 53% | 정답 ①

윗글의 제목으로 가장 적절한 것은?

✓① Our Social Norms on Aging: An Ongoing Evolution
　 노화에 대한 우리의 사회적 규범: 지속적 변화
② The Power of Oral Tradition in the Modern World
　 현대 세계에서의 구전의 힘
③ Generational Differences: Not As Big As You Think
　 세대별 차이: 생각보다 크지 않다
④ There's More to Aging than What the Media Shows
　 노화에는 미디어가 보여주는 것보다 더 많은 것이 있다
⑤ How Well You Age Depends on Your Views of Aging
　 나이를 얼마나 잘 먹는가는 나이를 보는 시각에 달려 있다

DAY 27

Why? 왜 정답일까?

과거에는 50세를 넘겨 살기도 힘들었고, 사람들의 문해력도 충분히 발달하지 못한 시기였기에 나이가 든다는 것이 지혜의 상징처럼 여겨졌지만, 오늘날에는 기술적 변화와 함께 노화에 대한 이러한 사회적 규범이 변하게 되었다(This social perception of age began to shift ~)는 내용이다. 따라서 글의 제목으로 가장 적절한 것은 ① '노화에 대한 우리의 사회적 규범: 지속적 변화'이다.

---

12 어휘 추론   정답률 55% | 정답 ⑤

밑줄 친 (a) ~ (e) 중에서 문맥상 낱말의 쓰임이 적절하지 <u>않은</u> 것은? [3점]

① (a)   ② (b)   ③ (c)   ④ (d)   ☑ (e)

Why? 왜 정답일까?

두 번째 단락의 핵심 내용은 실제 살아가는 나이와 먹은 나이 사이의 격차가 점점 벌어지고 있고 사회적 규범이 이 격차를 부지런히 따라가야 한다는 것이다. 즉 고정관념 속 노인과 실제 노인의 모습이 '다르고', 이에 맞춰 사회적 규범을 빨리 변화시켜야 한다는 결론이 되도록 (e)의 unnoticeable을 striking으로 고쳐야 한다. 따라서 낱말의 쓰임이 가장 적절하지 않은 것은 ⑤ '(e)'이다.

DAY 28 | 20분 미니 모의고사

01 ①	02 ①	03 ⑤	04 ①	05 ②
06 ①	07 ④	08 ③	09 ①	10 ②
11 ⑤	12 ④			

---

01 여름 방학을 삼촌과 숙모와 보내게 된 Ryan   정답률 91% | 정답 ①

다음 글에 드러난 Ryan의 심경 변화로 가장 적절한 것은?

☑ excited → disappointed
　신이 난　실망한
② furious → regretful
　분노한　후회하는
③ irritated → satisfied
　짜증 난　만족한
④ nervous → relaxed
　긴장한　여유로운
⑤ pleased → jealous
　기쁜　질투하는

[본문 해석]

11살 소년 Ryan은 가능한 한 빨리 집으로 달려갔다. 마침내, 여름 방학이 시작되었다! 그가 집으로 들어갔을 때 그의 엄마는 냉장고 앞에 서서 그를 기다리고 있었다. 그녀는 그에게 가방을 싸라고 말했다. Ryan의 심장이 풍선처럼 날아올랐다. *왜 가방을 싸지? 우리가 디즈니랜드에라도 가나?* 그는 마지막으로 부모님이 자신을 데리고 휴가를 갔던 때가 기억나지 않았다. 그의 두 눈이 반짝거렸다. "너는 Tim 삼촌과 Gina 숙모와 함께 여름을 보내게 될 거야." Ryan은 불만의 신음소리를 냈다. "여름 내내요?" "그렇단다. 여름 내내." 그가 느꼈던 기대감이 순식간에 사라졌다. 끔찍한 3주 내내, 그는 삼촌과 숙모의 농장에서 지내게 될 것이었다. 그는 한숨을 쉬었다.

Why? 왜 정답일까?

'Ryan's heart soared like a balloon.'와 'His eyes beamed.'에 따르면 방학이 시작된 날 어머니로부터 짐을 싸라는 이야기를 들은 Ryan은 기대감에 부풀었지만, 'The anticipation he had felt disappeared in a flash.' 이후에 따르면 방학 내내 삼촌과 숙모의 농장에서 지낼 것이라는 사실을 알고는 불만을 느꼈다. 따라서 Ryan의 심경 변화로 가장 적절한 것은 ① '신이 난 → 실망한'이다.

- **pack** ⓥ (가방이나 짐을) 싸다
- **beam** ⓥ 빛나다, 활짝 웃다
- **anticipation** ⓝ 기대감
- **in a flash** 순식간에
- **regretful** ⓐ 후회하는, 유감스러운
- **soar** ⓥ 날아오르다, 솟구치다
- **groan** ⓥ 신음소리를 내다
- **disappear** ⓥ 사라지다
- **miserable** ⓐ 끔찍한, 비참한
- **irritated** ⓐ 짜증 난

구문 풀이

10행 The anticipation [he had felt] disappeared in a flash.
　　　　　　　주어　　　　　　　　　자동사

---

02 미개척 영역에 대한 탐구의 중요성   정답률 71% | 정답 ①

다음 글의 제목으로 가장 적절한 것은?

☑ Researchers, Don't Be Afraid to Be Wrong
　연구자여, 틀리는 것을 두려워 말라
② Hypotheses Are Different from Wild Guesses
　가설은 터무니없는 추측과 다르다
③ Why Researchers Are Reluctant to Share Their Data
　연구자가 데이터를 공유하기 주저하는 이유
④ One Small Mistake Can Ruin Your Whole Research
　하나의 작은 실수가 여러분의 연구 전체를 망칠 수 있다
⑤ Why Hard Facts Don't Change Our Minds
　확실한 사실이 우리의 생각을 바꾸지 않는 이유

[본문 해석]

일부 처음 시작하는 연구자들은 좋은 가설은 옳다는 것이 보장된 것(예를 들면, *알코올은 반응 시간을 둔화시킬 것이다.*)이라고 잘못 믿는다. 하지만 여러분의 가설을 여러분이 검사해 보기 전에 그것이 사실이라고 이미 우리가 알고 있다면 여러분의 가설을 검사하는 것은 우리에게 아무런 새로운 것도 말해 주지 않을 것이다. 연구란 *새로운* 지식을 생산해야 한다는 것을 기억하라. 새로운 지식을 얻기 위해서 연구자이자 탐험가로서 여러분은 해변의 안전함(기정사실)을 떠나 미개척 영역으로 과감히 들어가 볼 필요가 있다(아인슈타인이 말했듯이, "우리가 무엇을 하고 있는지 안다면 그것은 연구라고 불리지 않을 것이다. 그렇지 않은가?"). 이런 미개척 영역에서 무엇이 일어날 것인지에 관한 여러분의 예측이 틀린다면 그것은 괜찮다. 과학자는 실수를 하는 것이 허용된다(Bates가 말

했듯이, "연구는 막다른 길인지 보려고 골목길을 올라가 보는 과정이다."). 정말로 과학자는 흔히 결과를 내는 예측들보다는 결과를 내지 않는 예측들로부터 더 많이 배운다.

Why? 왜 정답일까?

'To get new knowledge, you, as a researcher-explorer, need to leave the safety of the shore ~'에서 과학자들은 새로운 지식을 얻기 위해서는 기정사실, 즉 이미 사실로 밝혀진 것들의 영역을 넘어 아직 개척되지 않은 영역으로 들어가 볼 필요가 있다고 언급한다. 이어서 마지막 문장에서는 과학자들이 결과를 실제로 내지 못한 예측이나 가정을 통해 도리어 더 많이 배운다는 언급을 통해 '틀리는 것'을 두려워할 필요가 없다는 내용을 시사한다. 따라서 글의 제목으로 가장 적절한 것은 ① '연구자여, 틀리는 것을 두려워 말라'이다.

- mistakenly [ad] 잘못, 실수하여
- guarantee [v] 보장하다
- established [a] 확립된, 공고한
- prediction [n] 예측
- hard facts 확실한 정보, 엄격한 사실
- hypothesis [n] 가설
- be supposed to ~하기로 되어 있다
- venture into ~에 발을 들여놓다
- reluctant [a] 마지못해 하는, 꺼리는

구문 풀이

7행 To get new knowledge, you, (as a researcher-explorer),
목적(~하기 위해) 주어 ( ): 삽입구
need to leave the safety of the shore (established facts) and
동사구1
(need to) venture into uncharted waters (as Einstein said,
동사구2 접속사(~듯이, ~대로)
"If we knew what we were doing, it would not be called research,
「if + 주어 + 과거 동사 ~, 주어 + 조동사 과거형 + 동사원형:
would it?"). 가정법 과거(현재 사실의 반대 가정)

---

03 박물관 일일 캠프 정답률 95% | 정답 ⑤

One Day Camp at Seattle Children's Museum에 관한 다음 안내문의 내용과 일치하지 않는 것은?

① 7월 8일 목요일에 진행된다.
② 음악과 춤 활동이 있다.
③ 아이의 참가비는 30달러이다.
④ 모든 아이들은 어른과 동행해야 한다.
✓ ⑤ 점심 식사는 참가비에 포함되지 않는다.

[본문 해석]

Seattle 어린이 박물관에서의 일일 캠프

Seattle 어린이 박물관에서의 일일 캠프는 아이들에게 창의력을 불어넣을 것을 약속하는 체험입니다. 발견의 놀라운 여행에 함께 하세요!

- 「날짜: 2021년 7월 8일 목요일」—「: ①의 근거 일치
- 연령: 5 ~ 10세
- 일정

시간	활동
10:30 – 12:30	미술 & 공예
12:30 – 13:30	점심 식사
13:30 – 15:30	「음악 & 춤」—「: ②의 근거 일치

- 참가비
– 「아이: 30달러」—「: ③의 근거 일치
– 어른: 10달러
- 알림
– 「모든 아이들은 반드시 어른과 동행해야 합니다.」—「: ④의 근거 일치
– 「참가비에는 점심 식사와 프로그램 재료비가 포함됩니다.」—「: ⑤의 근거 불일치

Why? 왜 정답일까?

'The participation fee includes lunch and materials for the program.'에서 참가비에는 점심 식사와 재료비가 포함된다고 하므로, 안내문의 내용과 일치하지 않는 것은 ⑤ '점심 식사는 참가비에 포함되지 않는다.'이다.

Why? 왜 오답일까?

① 'Date: Thursday, July 8, 2021'의 내용과 일치한다.

② 'Activity / Music & Dance'의 내용과 일치한다.
③ 'Child: $30'의 내용과 일치한다.
④ 'All children must be accompanied by an adult.'의 내용과 일치한다.

- experience [n] 체험
- journey [n] 여행, 여정
- accompany [v] 동반하다, 동행하다
- promise [v] 약속하다
- discovery [n] 발견
- material [n] (특정 활동에 필요한) 재료

★★★ 1등급 대비 고난도 3점 문제

04 마음 챙김을 적용한 통증 관리법 정답률 21% | 정답 ①

다음 글의 밑줄 친 부분 중, 어법상 틀린 것은? [3점]

[본문 해석]

불교 방식의 마음 챙김을 서양 심리학에 적용하는 것은 원래 Massachusetts 대학교 의료 센터의 Jon Kabat-Zinn의 연구에서 비롯됐다. 그는 처음 만성 통증 환자들을 치료하는 힘든 일을 맡고 있었는데, 그들 중 다수는 전통적인 통증 관리 요법에는 잘 반응하지 않았었다. 여러 가지 면에서, 그러한 치료는 완전히 역설적인 것으로 보이는데, 사람들이 통증에 대해 더 많이 의식하도록 도와줌으로써 통증을 다루는 법을 그들에게 가르쳐 준다! 그러나, 그 핵심은 통증과의 싸움, 즉 통증에 대한 그들의 인식을 사실상 연장시키는 싸움에 동반되는 끊임없는 긴장감을 사람들이 놓을 수 있도록 도와주는 것이다. 마음 챙김 명상은 이 사람 중 많은 이들이 행복감을 높이고 더 나은 삶의 질을 경험하도록 했다. 어떻게 그럴 수 있었을까? 왜냐하면 그러한 명상은 우리가 불쾌한 생각이나 기분을 무시하거나 억누르려고 하면 결국 그것들의 강도를 더 증가시킬 뿐이라는 원리에 바탕을 두고 있기 때문이다.

Why? 왜 정답일까?

앞에 나오는 사람 선행사 chronic-pain patients를 꾸미면서 뒤에 절을 연결하는 구조이므로, 접속사와 대명사의 기능을 병행할 수 있는 관계대명사가 필요하다. 따라서 ①의 them을 목적격 관계대명사 whom으로 고쳐야 한다. 어법상 틀린 것은 ①이다.

Why? 왜 오답일까?

② 2형식 감각동사인 seem(~인 것처럼 보이다)의 보어로서 형용사 paradoxical은 어법상 맞다.
③ 단수 선행사 the constant tension을 꾸미는 주격 관계대명사 that 뒤로 단수 동사가 이어지는데, 뒤에 목적어인 their fighting of pain이 나오므로 타동사 accompanies를 능동태로 쓴 것은 어법상 맞다.
④ 등위접속사 and 앞에 to increase가 나오므로, 이와 병렬을 이루는 말로서 and 뒤에 to experience를 쓴 것은 어법상 맞다.
⑤ 'end up + 동명사(결국 ~하게 되다)' 구문을 완성하도록 increasing을 쓴 것은 어법상 맞다.

- mindfulness [n] 마음 챙김
- initially [ad] 처음에, 초기에
- paradoxical [a] 역설적인
- accompany [v] (~을) 동반하다
- meditation [n] 명상, 묵상
- intensity [n] 강도, 강렬함
- primarily [ad] 주로
- take on ~을 떠맡다
- tension [n] 긴장, 불안
- prolong [v] 연장하다
- repress [v] 참다, 억누르다

구문 풀이

4행 He initially took on the difficult task of treating chronic-pain
~을 떠맡다 동명사(task 설명) 선행사
patients, many of whom had not responded well to traditional
목적격 관계대명사(계속적 용법)
pain-management therapy.

9행 However, the key is to help people let go of the constant
준사역동사 목적어 원형부정사(~을 놓다)
tension [that accompanies their fighting of pain, a struggle {that
주격 관계대명사 동격
actually prolongs their awareness of pain}].
주격 관계대명사

★★ 문제 해결 꿀~팁 ★★

▶ 많이 틀린 이유는?
빈출 포인트 중심의 어법 문제로, ②는 '형용사 vs. 부사', ③은 '관계절 동사의 수와 태'를 묻고 있다. ②의 경우 바로 앞의 부사 completely의 수식을 받으면서 2형식 동사 seems의 보어 역할을 하도록 형용사 paradoxical이 바르게 쓰였다. ③의 경우, 관계절 동사의 수는 선행사에 일치시키므로 단수형이 올바르게 쓰였고, 뒤에 목적어가 나오므로 능동형 또한 올바르게 쓰였다.

▶ 문제 해결 방법은?
어법 문제에서 대명사에 밑줄이 있으면 관계대명사가 들어갈 자리는 아닌지 검토해야 한다. ①번과 같이 대명사 앞뒤로 접속사 없이 절이 나온다면 관계대명사가 쓰일 자리이다.

★★★ 1등급 대비 고난도 2점 문제

05 이윤 추구의 목적과 양립하기 어려운 고고학   정답률 39% | 정답 ②

다음 글의 밑줄 친 부분 중, 문맥상 낱말의 쓰임이 적절하지 않은 것은?

[본문 해석]
일부 저명한 언론인은 고고학자들이 보물 사냥꾼과 협력해야 한다고 말하는데 이들은 과거에 대해 많은 것을 드러낼 수 있는 가치 있는 역사적 유물을 축적해 왔기 때문이다. 하지만 고고학자는 마찬가지로 가치 있는 유물을 갖고 있는 도굴꾼과 협력하도록 요구받지는 않는다. 이윤 추구와 지식 탐구는 ① 시간이라는 요인 때문에 고고학에서 공존할 수 없다. 상당히 믿기 어렵지만, 보물 탐사 기업에 고용된 한 고고학자는 난파선의 유물이 판매되기 전에 이것들을 연구할 수 있도록 고고학자들에게 6개월이 주어지기만 하면, 그 어떤 역사적 지식도 ② 발견되지(→ 사라지지) 않는다고 말했다! 그와는 반대로, 해양고고학 연구소(INA)의 고고학자들과 조교들은 그들이 발굴한 서기 11세기 난파선의 모든 발굴물 ③ 목록을 만들 수 있기까지 10여 년 동안 상시 보존이 필요했다. 그러고 나서 그러한 발굴물을 해석하기 위해 그들은 러시아어, 불가리아어, 루마니아어를 ④ 배워야만 했는데, 그렇게 하지 않았다면 그들은 유적지의 본질을 결코 알지 못했을 것이다. '상업적인 고고학자'가 발굴물을 팔기 전에 10여년 정도의 기간을 ⑤ 기다릴 수 있었을까?

Why? 왜 정답일까?
On the contrary 뒤에서 모든 발굴물 목록을 만드는 데만 10년 이상이 걸렸던 해양 고고학 연구소의 사례를 들어, 앞에서 '6개월만 있으면 된다'고 말했던 예에 반박을 전개하고 있다. 이를 고려할 때, 6개월 있으면 역사적 지식이 '사라지지' 않는다는 말이 나와야 뒤에 나오는 사례와 반박 구도가 형성되므로, ②의 found를 lost로 고쳐야 한다. 문맥상 적절하지 않은 낱말은 ②이다.

- prominent ⓐ 저명한, 유명한
- accumulate ⓥ 축적하다, 모으다
- artifact ⓝ 인공 유물
- coexist ⓥ 공존하다
- shipwrecked ⓐ 난파한, 깨어진, 파괴된
- excavate ⓥ 발굴하다
- nature ⓝ 본질, 천성
- archaeologist ⓝ 고고학자
- valuable ⓐ 가치 있는
- a tomb robber 도굴범
- incredibly ⓐⒹ 믿기 힘들게도
- year-round 연중무휴의, 내내
- interpret ⓥ 해석하다, 이해하다
- site ⓝ 장소, 유적지

구문 풀이

17행 Then, to interpret those finds, / they had to learn Russian,
　　　　　　～하기 위해
Bulgarian, and Romanian, without which they would never have
　　　　　　선행사　　　　「전치사＋관계대명사」　　　　완전한 절
learned the true nature of the site.

★★ 문제 해결 꿀~팁 ★★

▶ 많이 틀린 이유는?
보통 어휘는 반의어 중심으로 출제되는데 정답인 ②의 경우 대응되는 반의어가 바로 떠오르기 어려웠다. 최다 오답인 ③ 또한 보통 '목록'이라는 명사로 쓰이지만 여기서는 '목록을 만들다'라는 동사로 쓰여 수험생들에게 혼동을 유발할 여지가 있었던 것으로 보인다.
▶ 문제 해결 방법은?
고고학적 유물 조사를 두고 '시간이 적게 걸린다 vs. 많이 걸린다'는 입장이 대립하고 있음을 이해하도록 한다. ②의 경우 6개월의 시간만 있어도 '손실되는' 역사적 지식이 없을 것이라는 뜻을 나타내며, ③의 경우에는 단순히 '목록만 정리하는 데도' 10년 가까운 시간이 걸렸던 예를 소개하며 고고학적 조사에는 시간이 오래 들 수밖에 없다는 내용을 뒷받침하고 있다.

★★★ 1등급 대비 고난도 3점 문제

06 반항 경향을 이용한 마케팅   정답률 45% | 정답 ①

다음 빈칸에 들어갈 말로 가장 적절한 것을 고르시오. [3점]

✔ ① reversal - 반전
③ repetition - 반복
⑤ collaboration - 협력
② imitation - 모방
④ conformity - 순응

[본문 해석]
반항자들은 자기가 반항자라고 생각할지도 모르지만, 영리한 마케터들은 나머지 우리에게 그러듯이 그들에게 영향을 준다. "모두가 그렇게 하고 있다."라고 말하는 것은 일부 사람들이 어떤 생각에 흥미를 잃게 할지도 모른다. 이 사람들은 대안을 찾을 것이고, 그것은 (만약 영리하게 계획된다면) 정확히 마케터나 설득자가 여러분이 믿기를 원하는 것일 수 있다. 만약 내가 여러분이 어떤 아이디어를 고려하길 바라는데, 여러분이 독립성과 고유성을 유지하기 위해서 대중적인 의견을 강하게 거부한다는 것을 안다면, 나는 대다수가 선택하는 것을 먼저 제시할 것이고, 여러분은 내 실제 선호에 따라 그것을 거부할 것이다. 우리는 반항의 입장을 유지하려 할 때 종종 속는다. 사람들은 우리가 그들의 목적에 맞는 선택지를 '독자적으로' 택하도록 만들기 위해 이러한 반전을 사용한다. 일부 브랜드들은 주류에 대한 우리의 반항을 온전히 활용해 반항자로 자리 잡았으며, 이는 훨씬 더 강력한 브랜드 충성도를 만들어 왔다.

Why? 왜 정답일까?
반항자들을 대상으로 한 마케팅 기법을 소개하고 있다. 반항자들은 스스로의 독립성과 고유성을 중시하기 때문에, 대중의 생각을 제시받으면 그에 반감을 보이고, 실은 그 '반감 형성'이 마케터들의 의도라는 것이다. (Some brands have taken full effect of our defiance towards the mainstream and positioned themselves as rebels; which has created even stronger brand loyalty.)따라서 반항적인 행동 경향을 '역이용'하여 본래의 마케팅 목적을 달성한다는 의미로, 빈칸에 들어갈 말로 가장 적절한 것은 ① '반전'이다.

- rebel ⓝ 반항아
- turn off ~을 지루하게 만들다
- reject ⓥ 거부하다
- independence ⓝ 독립
- majority ⓝ 대다수
- defiance ⓝ 반항
- mainstream ⓝ 주류
- repetition ⓝ 반복
- clever ⓐ 영리한
- alternative ⓝ 대안
- in favor of ~을 위해
- uniqueness ⓝ 고유성
- trick ⓥ 속이다
- suit ⓥ ~에 맞추다
- loyalty ⓝ 충성도
- conformity ⓝ 순응

구문 풀이

6행　　　접속사(~라면)
If I want you to consider an idea, and know {(that) you strongly
　　　동사1　　　　　　　　　　　동사2　　　접속사
reject popular opinion in favor of maintaining your independence
and uniqueness}, I would present the majority option first, which
　　　　　　선행사　　　　　　　　　　　　계속적 용법
you would reject in favor of my actual preference.

★★ 문제 해결 꿀~팁 ★★

▶ 많이 틀린 이유는?
'누구나 다 하고 있다'는 인용구만 보면 남들을 '따라 한다'는 의미의 ②를 고르기 쉽다. 하지만 글에서 언급된 반항자들은 대중의 의견을 따르기보다는 '반대하는' 사람들이므로 '모방'이라는 단어는 적절하지 않다.
▶ 문제 해결 방법은?
대중적인 의견에 반대하려는 성향을 '오히려 이용해서' 브랜드에 대한 강한 충성도를 형성한다는 내용을 요약하는 단어가 필요하다.

07 생태 환경에 대한 감정적 묘사에 신중하기   정답률 44% | 정답 ④

다음 빈칸에 들어갈 말로 가장 적절한 것을 고르시오. [3점]
① complex organisms are superior to simple ones
다세포 생물이 단세포보다 우월하다
② technologies help us survive extreme environments
기술은 우리가 극심한 환경에서 생존하도록 돕는다
③ ecological diversity is supported by extreme environments
생태적 다양성이 극심한 환경들에 의해 뒷받침된다
✔ ④ all other organisms sense the environment in the way we do
모든 다른 유기체가 우리가 느끼는 방식으로 환경을 느낀다
⑤ species adapt to environmental changes in predictable ways
생물 종들은 예측 가능한 방식으로 환경 변화에 적응한다

[본문 해석]
특정한 환경 조건을 '극심한', '혹독한', '온화한' 또는 '스트레스를 주는'이라고 묘사하는 것은 당연해 보인다. 사막 한낮의 열기, 남극 겨울의 추위, 그레이트 솔트호의 염도와 같이 상태가 '극심한' 경우에는 그것이 명백해 보일지도 모른다.

하지만 이것은 우리의 특정한 생리적 특징과 내성을 고려할 때 이러한 조건이 *우리에게* 극심하다는 것을 의미할 뿐이다. 선인장에게 선인장들이 진화해 온 사막의 환경 조건은 전혀 극심한 것이 아니며, 펭귄에게 남극의 얼음에 뒤덮인 땅은 극심한 환경이 아니다. 생태학자가 모든 다른 유기체가 우리가 느끼는 방식으로 환경을 느낀다고 추정하는 것은 나태하고 위험하다. 오히려 생태학자는 다른 유기체가 세계를 보는 방식으로 세계를 바라보기 위해 환경에 대한 벌레의 관점이나 식물의 관점을 취하려고 노력해야 한다. 혹독한, 그리고 온화한 같은 감정적 단어들, 심지어 덥고 추운 것과 같은 상대적인 단어들은 생태학자들에 의해 오로지 신중하게 사용되어야 한다.

Why? 왜 정답일까?

Rather로 시작하는 문장에서, 생태학자는 우리 자신의 시각으로 어떤 환경을 바라보기보다, 그 환경에 적응해 사는 다른 생물의 관점을 두루 취할 의무가 있다(~ the ecologist should try to gain a worm's-eye or plant's-eye view of the environment: to see the world as others see it.)고 한다. 즉 '모두가 우리와 같게 느낄 것이라고' 나태하게 가정하지 말아야 한다는 것이 글의 주제이다. 따라서 빈칸에 들어갈 말로 가장 적절한 것은 ④ '모든 다른 유기체가 우리가 느끼는 방식으로 환경을 느낀다'이다.

- extreme ⓐ 극심한, 극도의
- benign ⓐ 온화한
- Antarctic ⓐ 남극의
- physiological ⓐ 생리적인
- tolerance ⓝ 내성, 저항력, 인내
- lazy ⓐ 나태한, 게으른
- emotive ⓐ 감정적인, 감정을 나타내는
- complex organism 다세포 생물
- harsh ⓐ 혹독한
- obvious ⓐ 명백한
- salinity ⓝ 염도
- characteristic ⓝ 특성
- cactus (*pl.* cacti) ⓝ 선인장
- ecologist ⓝ 생태학자
- relativity ⓝ 상대성

구문 풀이

11행 It is lazy and dangerous for the ecologist to assume that all
가주어 / 의미상 주어 / 진주어
other organisms sense the environment in the way we do.
대동사(= sense)

---

08 목표에 따라 수요에 다양한 영향을 가하는 마케팅 정답률 65% | 정답 ③

다음 글에서 전체 흐름과 관계 없는 문장은?

[본문 해석]

마케팅 경영은 수요를 찾고 증가시키는 것뿐만 아니라 그것을 바꾸거나 심지어 줄이는 것과도 관련이 있다. 예를 들어, Uluru (Ayers Rock)에는 그것을 등반하기를 원하는 너무 많은 관광객이 있을지도 모르고, 그리고 North Queensland의 Daintree 국립공원은 관광 시즌에 과도하게 붐비게 될 수 있다. ① 전력 회사들은 때때로 최고 사용 기간 중 수요를 충족시키는 데 어려움이 있다. ② 과도한 수요의 이런저런 경우들에서, 요구되는 마케팅 과업, 즉 역 마케팅은 일시적 혹은 영구적으로 수요를 줄이는 것이다. ③ 공급 증가에 의해 유발된 손실들을 보상하기 위해서 노력해야 한다. ④ 역 마케팅의 목적은 수요를 완전히 없애는 것이 아니라, 단지 그것을 줄이거나 또는 다른 시기 또는 심지어 다른 제품으로 이동시키는 것이다. ⑤ 따라서, 마케팅 경영은 조직이 그것의 목표들을 달성하는 것을 돕는 방식으로 수요의 수준, 시기, 그리고 특성에 영향을 주는 것을 추구한다.

Why? 왜 정답일까?

마케팅은 수요를 창출하는 과정뿐 아니라 바꾸거나 줄이는 과정과도 연관되어 있다는 내용을 다룬 글로, 첫 문장과 마지막 문장에 주제가 일관되게 제시된다. 한편 ③은 공급의 증가로 나타난 손실을 보상하고자 노력해야 한다는 내용으로 글의 주제와 무관하다. 따라서 전체 흐름과 관계없는 문장은 ③이다.

- overcrowded ⓐ 과하게 붐비는
- excess ⓐ 초과한
- temporarily ⓐⓓ 일시적으로
- compensate for ~을 보상하다, 상쇄하다
- aim ⓝ 목적, 목표
- seek ⓥ 추구하다
- demand ⓝ 수요
- demarketing ⓝ 역 마케팅
- permanently ⓐⓓ 영구적으로
- supply ⓝ 공급
- shift ⓥ 이동시키다
- objective ⓝ 목표

구문 풀이

15행 Thus, marketing management seeks to affect the level,
~하기를 추구하다
timing, and nature of demand in a way [that helps the organisation
~한 방식으로 / 준사역 동사 / 목적어
achieve its objectives].
원형부정사

---

09 기대에 좌우되는 예측 정답률 63% | 정답 ①

다음 글의 내용을 한 문장으로 요약하고자 한다. 빈칸 (A), (B)에 들어갈 말로 가장 적절한 것은?

	(A)		(B)
✔	wish 희망	……	affected 영향을 미쳤다
②	wish 희망	……	contradicted 모순되었다
③	disregard 무시	……	restricted 제한했다
④	disregard 무시	……	changed 바꾸었다
⑤	assurance 확신	……	realized 실현시켰다

[본문 해석]

한 연구에서 행동 경제학자인 Guy Mayraz는 시간이 지나면서 오르내린 가격을 보여주는 도표들을 실험 대상자들에게 보여주었다. 그 도표들은 사실 주식 시장에서의 과거 변동에 관한 것이었으나 Mayraz는 사람들에게 그 도표들이 밀 가격의 최근 변동을 보여준다고 말했다. 그는 각각의 사람에게 가격이 다음에 어디로 움직일지를 예측하도록 요청했으며, 예측이 실현되면 그들에게 보상을 제공했다. 그러나 Mayraz는 또한 참가자들을 '농부'와 '제빵사'라는 두 개의 범주로 나누었다. 농부들은 밀 가격이 높으면 추가 보상을 받을 것이었다. 제빵사들은 밀이 저렴하면 보너스를 받을 것이었다. 따라서 실험 대상자들은 두 가지의 별개의 보상을 받았을지도 모르는데, 즉 정확한 예측에 대한 보상과 밀의 가격이 자기 (집단에 유리한) 쪽으로 움직이게 될 경우의 보너스였다. Mayraz는 보너스에 대한 기대가 예측 자체에 영향을 미쳤음을 발견했다. 농부들은 밀의 가격이 올라갈 것이라고 희망하고 *예측했다.* 제빵사들은 그 반대를 희망하고 예측했다. 그들은 자신들의 희망이 추론에 영향을 미치게 했다.

➡ 참가자들이 밀의 가격 변동을 예측하도록 요청받았을 때, 가격이 어디로 이동할 것인가에 대한 그들의 (A) 희망은 자신들이 속했던 집단에 의해 정해졌고 그들의 예측에 (B) 영향을 미쳤다.

Why? 왜 정답일까?

실험에 따르면 밀 가격이 높을 때 보상을 받기로 한 '농부' 집단은 밀 가격의 상승을 바라고 예측했으며, 반대로 가격이 낮을 때 보상을 받기로 한 '제빵사' 집단은 밀 가격의 하락을 바라고 예측했다. 이를 마지막 문장에서는 희망에 따라 추론이 영향을 받았다(They let their hopes influence their reasoning.)고 정리하므로, 요약문의 빈칸 (A), (B)에 들어갈 말로 가장 적절한 것은 ① '(A) wish(희망), (B) affected(영향을 미쳤다)'이다.

- stock market 주식 시장
- forecast ⓝ 예측, 예보
- accurate ⓐ 정확한
- reasoning ⓝ 추론
- disregard ⓝ 무시 ⓥ 무시하다
- wheat ⓝ 밀
- separate ⓐ 별개의
- prospect ⓝ 예상, 전망
- contradict ⓥ ~와 모순되다
- assurance ⓝ 확언, 장담, 자신감

구문 풀이

6행 He asked each person to predict {where the price would
동사1 / 목적어 / 목적격 보어 / { }: 간접의문문
move next} — and offered them a reward if their forecasts came
동사2 / 간접목적어 / 직접목적어 / 접속사(만일 ~라면)
true.

10-12 선행을 돌려받은 Bahati

[본문 해석]

(A)

Bahati는 작은 마을에 살았는데, 그곳에서는 어떤 사람이 누군가를 그리워할 때 배고픈 행인을 위해 빵을 굽는 것이 관습이다. 「그녀는 멀리 살고 있는 외아들이 있었고, 그를 몹시 그리워했기에」 (a) 그녀는 매일 여분의 빵을 구워 누구든 가져갈 수 있도록 창틀에 그것을 두었다. 매일 한 가난한 노파가 그 빵을 가져가면서 고마움을 표현하는 대신 "당신이 행하는 선한 일은 당신에게로 돌아옵니다!"라고 중얼거리기만 했다.
└ :12번①의 근거 일치

(C)

"감사의 말도 한마디 없어."라고 Bahati는 혼잣말을 했다. 「어느 날, 짜증이 나서 그녀는 여분의 빵 굽기를 그만두고 싶은 마음이 들었지만 곧 마음을 고쳐먹었다. 가난한 노파의 말이 계속 생각났기 때문에 그녀는 여분의 빵을 구웠고

선행을 계속했다.』 (d) 그녀는 그 빵을 창틀에 두었다. 가난한 노파는 같은 말을
『 』: 12번 ④의 근거 불일치
중얼거리며 평소처럼 빵 덩어리를 가져갔다.

(B)

이번에는 짜증을 내는 대신에, Bahati는 기도하기로 결심했다. 『몇 년 동안, 그녀
는 아들의 소식을 듣지 못했다.』 (b) 그녀는 그의 안전을 위해 기도했다. 그날
『 』: 12번 ②의 근거 일치
밤, 문을 두드리는 소리가 났다. 문을 열었을 때, (c) 그녀는 문간에 서 있는
아들을 발견하고 놀랐다. 그는 말랐고 야위어 있었다. 그의 옷은 찢겨 있었다.
『그녀는 울며 아들을 껴안은 후에 갈아입을 옷과 약간의 음식을 그에게 가져다
주었다.』 『 』: 12번 ③의 근거 일치

(D)

약간의 휴식을 취한 후에 Bahati의 아들은 말했다. "집에 오는 길에 저는 너무
배가 고파서 쓰러졌어요. 저는 빵 한 덩어리를 가진 한 노파를 봤어요. 저는 그
녀에게 작은 빵 한 조각을 구걸했어요. 그런데 (e) 그녀(an old woman)는 제
어려움이 자신의 어려움보다 더 크다고 말하며 그 빵 덩어리 전부를 저에게 주
었어요." 『바로 그때 Bahati는 마침내 그 가난한 노파의 말의 의미를 깨달았다.』
『 』: 12번 ⑤의 근거 일치
"당신이 행하는 선한 일은 당신에게로 돌아옵니다!"

- passerby ⓝ 행인
- loaf ⓝ (빵) 덩어리
- mutter ⓥ 중얼거리다
- irritated ⓐ 짜증 난
- starved ⓐ 굶주린
- custom ⓝ 관습
- sill ⓝ (문이나 창문의) 틀
- gratitude ⓝ 감사
- lean ⓐ 야윈
- collapse ⓥ 쓰러지다, 붕괴하다

구문 풀이

(A) 1행 Bahati lived in a small village, where baking bread for a
장소 선행사 관계부사 동명사구 주어
hungry passerby is a custom when one misses someone.
동사(단수) ~할 때

(A) 3행 She had an only son living far away and missed him a lot,
동사1 현재분사구 동사2
so she baked an extra loaf of bread and put it on the window sill
동사3 동사4
every day, for anyone to take away.
의미상 주어 부사적 용법(~하도록)

(C) 2행 One day, irritated, she was tempted to stop baking extra
수동분사구문(~된 채로) 동사1 ~하기를 멈추다
bread, but soon changed her mind.
동사2

(D) 6행 It was then that Bahati finally realized the meaning of the
「it is ~ that : 강조구문 : …한 것은 바로 ~이다」
words of the poor old woman: "The good you do, comes back to you!"
동격(윗줄의 the words ~)

---

10 글의 순서 파악
정답률 79% | 정답 ②

주어진 글 (A)에 이어질 내용을 순서에 맞게 배열한 것으로 가장 적절한 것은?

① (B) – (D) – (C)
✓② (C) – (B) – (D)
③ (C) – (D) – (B)
④ (D) – (B) – (C)
⑤ (D) – (C) – (B)

Why? 왜 정답일까?

아들이 그리워 여분의 빵을 구워 창틀에 놓아두던 Bahati와 그 빵을 가져가는 노파를
소개한 (A) 뒤에는, 노파가 감사의 말 한마디 하지 않는 데 불만이었던 Bahati가 빵 굽
기를 그만두려다가 계속해서 빵을 구웠다는 내용의 (C)가 먼저 연결된다. 이어서
Bahati가 몇 년간 소식도 없었던 아들과 재회하게 되었다는 내용의 (B), 집에 오던 중
배가 고파 쓰러졌던 아들이 노파에게서 빵 덩이를 얻었음이 밝혀지는 (D)가 차례로 뒤따
른다. 따라서 글의 순서로 가장 적절한 것은 ② '(C) – (B) – (D)'이다.

---

11 지칭 추론
정답률 81% | 정답 ⑤

밑줄 친 (a) ~ (e) 중에서 가리키는 대상이 나머지 넷과 다른 것은?

① (a) ② (b) ③ (c) ④ (d) ✓⑤ (e)

Why? 왜 정답일까?

(a), (b), (c), (d)는 Bahati를, (e)는 두 문장 앞의 an old woman을 가리키므로,
(a) ~ (e) 중에서 가리키는 대상이 다른 하나는 ⑤ '(e)'이다.

---

12 세부 내용 파악
정답률 80% | 정답 ④

윗글의 Bahati에 관한 내용으로 적절하지 않은 것은?

① 멀리 살고 있는 아들을 몹시 그리워했다.
② 수년간 아들의 소식을 듣지 못했다.
③ 아들에게 갈아입을 옷과 음식을 주었다.
✓④ 여분의 빵을 굽는 일을 그만두었다.
⑤ 결국은 노파의 말의 의미를 깨달았다.

Why? 왜 정답일까?

(C) 'One day, irritated, she was tempted to stop baking extra bread,
but soon changed her mind. She baked an extra loaf ~'에서 Bahati는
여분의 빵 굽기를 그만두려다가 곧 마음을 고쳐먹고 빵을 구웠다고 하므로, 내용과 일치
하지 않는 것은 ④ '여분의 빵을 굽는 일을 그만두었다.'이다.

Why? 왜 오답일까?

① (A) 'She had an only son living far away and missed him a lot, ~'의
내용과 일치한다.
② (B) 'For years, she had got no news of her son.'의 내용과 일치한다.
③ (B) 'Crying and hugging her son, she gave him clothes to change
into and some food.'의 내용과 일치한다.
⑤ (D) 'It was then that Bahati finally realized the meaning of the
words of the poor old woman: ~'의 내용과 일치한다.

DAY 29 | 20분 미니 모의고사

01 ①	02 ⑤	03 ①	04 ③	05 ⑤
06 ⑤	07 ③	08 ①	09 ⑤	10 ⑤
11 ①	12 ④			

---

01 축제 개막식 공연 부탁하기
정답률 93% | 정답 ①

다음 글의 목적으로 가장 적절한 것은?

☑ ① 개막 행사에서 연주를 요청하려고
② 공연 스케줄 변경을 공지하려고
③ 학교 행사 취소를 통보하려고
④ 모금 행사 참여를 독려하려고
⑤ 올해의 음악가 상 수상을 축하하려고

[본문 해석]

Stanton 씨에게,

저희 Future Music School에서는 십 년 동안 재능 있는 아이들에게 음악 교육을 제공해 오고 있습니다. 저희는 학생들에게 그들의 음악을 지역 사회와 나눌 기회를 주기 위해 매년 축제를 개최하며, 항상 개막 행사에서 연주할 유명한 음악가를 초청합니다. 세계적인 바이올린 연주자로서의 당신의 명성이 자자하고 학생들은 당신을 그들에게 가장 큰 영향을 준 음악가로 생각합니다. 그래서 저희는 당신이 축제 개막 행사에서 공연해 주시기를 요청합니다. 그들이 공연에서 역대 가장 유명한 바이올린 연주자 중 한 분의 연주를 본다는 것은 큰 영광일 것입니다. 당신의 연주는 축제를 더 다채롭고 훌륭하게 만들어 줄 것입니다. 긍정적인 답변을 받을 수 있기를 기대하겠습니다.

Steven Forman 드림

Why? 왜 정답일까?

'That's why we want to ask you to perform at the opening event of the festival.'에서 개막 행사에서 연주를 해주기를 요청한다는 내용이 언급되므로, 글의 목적으로 가장 적절한 것은 ① '개막 행사에서 연주를 요청하려고'이다.

- talented ⓐ 재능 있는
- reputation ⓝ 명성
- influence ⓥ 영향을 끼치다
- look forward to ~을 고대하다
- annual ⓐ 매년의
- precede ⓥ 앞서다, 선행하다
- splendid ⓐ 훌륭한

구문 풀이

7행 Your reputation as a world-class violinist precedes you and
주어1　전치사(~로서)　동사1

the students consider you the musician [who has influenced them
주어2　동사2　목적어　목적격 보어

the most].
부사 최상급

---

02 현대 과학 교과서의 법칙 기술 방법의 오류
정답률 51% | 정답 ⑤

밑줄 친 turns the life stories of these scientists from lead to gold 가 다음 글에서 의미하는 바로 가장 적절한 것은? [3점]

① discovers the valuable relationships between scientists
과학자들 간의 소중한 관계를 발견해낸다
② emphasizes difficulties in establishing new scientific theories
새로운 과학 이론을 세우는 것의 어려움을 강조한다
③ mixes the various stories of great scientists across the world
전 세계 위대한 과학자들의 다양한 이야기들을 섞는다
④ focuses more on the scientists' work than their personal lives
과학자들의 사생활보다 그들의 공적에 집중한다
☑ ⑤ reveals only the scientists' success ignoring their processes and errors
과학자들의 과정과 오류는 무시한 채 오로지 그들의 성공만을 드러내 보인다

[본문 해석]

학교에는 하나의 교육과정, 과학을 공부하는 하나의 올바른 방식, 표준화된 시험의 정답을 내어놓는 하나의 올바른 공식이 있다. 물리학의 원리와 같은 대단한 제목을 가진 교과서들은 300페이지에 걸쳐 '그 원리들'을 마법처럼 보여 준다. 그러고 나서 권위자가 우리에게 '진실'을 알려 주기 위해서 강의대로 다가간다. 이론 물리학자 David Gross가 자신의 노벨상 수상자 강연에서 설명했듯

이, 교과서들은 종종 사람들이 헤매고 다닌 그 많은 다른 경로들과 그들이 따랐던 그 많은 잘못된 단서들과 그들이 가졌던 그 많은 오해들을 묵살한다. 우리는 뉴턴의 '법칙들'에 대해 마치 그것들이 대단한 신의 방문이나 한 번의 천재성에 의해 도래하는 것처럼 배우지만, 그가 그것들을 탐구하고 수정하고 변경하는 데 들인 여러 해에 대해서는 배우지 않는다. 뉴턴이 확립하는 데 실패한 법칙들, 즉 가장 공공연하게는 납을 금으로 바꾸기 위해 시도했으나 엄청나게 실패했던 그의 연금술 실험은 물리학 수업에서 언급되는 일차원적인 이야기의 일부로 선택되지 못한다. 대신에, 우리의 교육 시스템은 이런 과학자들의 인생 이야기들을 납에서 금으로 바꿔 버린다.

Why? 왜 정답일까?

'~ textbooks often ignore the many alternate paths that people wandered down, the many false clues they followed, the many misconceptions they had.' 이후로 오늘날 과학 교과서는 과학적 법칙 이면에 있는 과학자들의 무수한 실패나 오류를 묵살한 채 과학자들이 마치 '납을 금으로 바꾸기라도 한 듯이' 천재적으로 그 법칙을 발견해 낸 것처럼 묘사한다는 내용이 이어진다. 이를 근거로 볼 때, 과학자들의 인생 이야기가 '납에서 금으로 바뀌어 버렸다'고 언급한 밑줄 친 부분이 의미하는 바로 가장 적절한 것은 ⑤ '과학자들의 과정과 오류는 무시한 채 오로지 그들의 성공만을 드러내 보인다'이다.

- formula ⓝ 공식, 제조법
- reveal ⓥ 드러내다
- alternate ⓐ 대안의
- visitation ⓝ (격식) 방문, 사찰
- establish ⓥ 확립하다
- make the cut 목표를 달성하다, 성공하다
- standardize ⓥ 표준화하다, 규격화하다
- authority figure 권위자
- misconception ⓝ 오해
- stroke of genius 천재성, 신의 한 수
- spectacularly ⓐⓓ 구경거리로, 볼 만하게
- emphasize ⓥ 강조하다

구문 풀이

7행 As theoretical physicist David Gross explained in his Nobel
접속사(~대로, ~듯이)

lecture, textbooks often ignore the many alternate paths [that people
주어　　　　　　동사　　　　　　　　목적어1

wandered down], the many false clues [they followed], the many
목적어2

misconceptions [they had].
목적어3

---

03 온라인 팔로워 수와 실제 삶에서의 성공
정답률 71% | 정답 ①

다음 글의 요지로 가장 적절한 것은?

☑ ① 성공하는 데 소셜 미디어에서의 인기가 중요하다.
② 코미디언에게 인기에 대한 지나친 집착은 독이 된다.
③ 온라인 상황과 실제 상황을 구별하는 것이 필요하다.
④ 소비자의 성향을 파악하는 것이 마케팅의 효과를 높인다.
⑤ 공연을 완성하기 위해서는 다양한 분야의 협조가 필요하다.

[본문 해석]

만약 당신이 전문가라면, 당신의 소셜 미디어 계정상에 많은 팔로워 수가 있는 것은 당신이 실제 생활에서 하고 있는 모든 일을 향상시킨다. 한 가지 좋은 예는 코미디언이다. 그녀는 매일 여러 시간을 그녀의 기술을 연마하는 데 보내지만, 그녀는 그녀의 Instagram 팔로잉에 대해 계속해서 질문을 받는다. 이는 비즈니스가 항상 그들의 상품을 홍보할 더 쉽고 더 값싼 방법들을 찾기 때문이다. 10만 명의 팔로워를 가진 코미디언은 그녀의 다가오는 쇼를 홍보할 수 있고, 사람들이 그녀를 보러 오기 위해 티켓을 구매할 가능성을 높일 수 있다. 이것은 코미디 클럽이 쇼를 홍보하는 데 써야 하는 비용을 줄이고 기획사가 다른 코미디언보다 그녀를 선택할 가능성을 더 높인다. 많은 사람들은 팔로워 수가 재능보다 더 중요한 것처럼 보이는 것에 언짢아하지만, 그것은 사실 전력을 다하고 있는가에 관한 것이다. 오늘날의 쇼 비즈니스에서 비즈니스 부분은 온라인상에서 일어난다. 당신은 적응할 필요가 있는데, 왜냐하면 적응하지 못하는 사람들은 그다지 크게 성공하지 못할 것이기 때문이다.

Why? 왜 정답일까?

'If you're an expert, having a high follower count on your social media accounts enhances all the work you are doing in real life.'에서 소셜 미디어 계정의 팔로워 수가 많으면 실제 하는 모든 일에서도 향상이 일어난다는 내용이 나온 데 이어, 마지막 세 문장에서는 비즈니스의 많은 부분이 온라인에서 일어나므로 팔로워 수를 관리할 필요가 있다는 논지를 다시 정리하고 있다. 따라서 글의 요지로 가장 적절한 것은 ① '성공하는 데 소셜 미디어에서의 인기가 중요하다.'이다.

DAY 29

[문제편 p.173]

- **expert** ⓝ 전문가
- **enhance** ⓥ 높이다, 향상시키다
- **promote** ⓥ 홍보하다
- **upset** ⓐ 속상한
- **adapt** ⓥ 적응하다
- **account** ⓝ 계정, 계좌
- **market** ⓥ 광고하다
- **upcoming** ⓐ 다가오는
- **firing on all cylinders** 전력을 다하는

구문 풀이

1행 If you're an expert, / having a high follower count on your
동명사구 주어
social media accounts enhances all the work [(that) you are doing in
동사(단수) 목적어 생략(목적격 관계대명사)
real life].

04 5개국 GDP에서 여행 및 관광의 비중 　정답률 75% | 정답 ③

다음 도표의 내용과 일치하지 않는 것은?

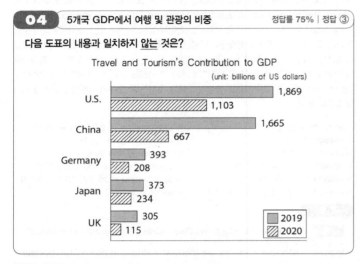

Travel and Tourism's Contribution to GDP
(unit: billions of US dollars)

국가	2019	2020
U.S.	1,869	1,103
China	1,665	667
Germany	393	208
Japan	373	234
UK	305	115

[본문 해석]

그래프는 2019년과 2020년 5개국 각각의 GDP에 대한 여행 및 관광의 기여를 보여 준다. ① 5개국 모두에서, 2020년에 GDP에 대한 여행 및 관광의 기여는 전년에 비해 감소하였다. ② 2019년과 2020년 모두에서, 5개국 중 미국이 GDP에 대한 여행 및 관광의 가장 큰 기여를 나타냈고, 중국이 그 뒤를 이었다. ③ 중국에서, 2020년에 GDP에 대한 여행 및 관광의 기여는 2019년 기여분의 3분의 1 미만이었다. ④ 2019년에, 독일은 GDP에 대한 여행 및 관광의 기여가 일본보다 더 큰 것으로 나타난 반면, 2020년에는 그 반대였다. ⑤ 2020년에는, 영국이 GDP에 대한 여행 및 관광의 기여가 2,000억 달러 미만인 유일한 국가였다.

Why? 왜 정답일까?

도표에 따르면 2020년 중국 GDP에서 여행 및 관광이 차지한 액수(6,670억)는 2019년 액수(1조 6,650억)의 3분의 1을 넘으므로, 도표와 일치하지 않는 것은 ③이다.

- **contribution** ⓝ 기여
- **previous** ⓐ 이전의
- **billion** ⓝ 10억
- **reverse** ⓝ 반대, 역

★★★ 1등급 대비 고난도 2점 문제

05 코알라의 특징 　정답률 24% | 정답 ⑤

다음 글의 밑줄 친 부분 중, 어법상 틀린 것은?

[본문 해석]

코알라가 잘하는 것이 한 가지 있다면, 그것은 자는 것이다. 오랫동안 많은 과학자들은 유칼립투스 잎 속의 화합물이 그 작고 귀여운 동물들을 몽롱한 상태로 만들어서 코알라들이 그렇게도 무기력한 상태에 있는 것이라고 의심했다. 그러나 더 최근의 연구는 그 잎들이 단순히 영양분이 너무나도 적기 때문에 코알라가 거의 에너지가 없는 것임을 보여 주었다. 그래서 코알라들은 가능한 한 적게 움직이는 경향이 있다. 그리고 그것들이 정말 움직일 때에는, 주로 마치 슬로 모션으로 움직이는 것처럼 보인다. 그것들은 하루에 16시간에서 18시간 동안 휴식을 취하는데, 의식이 없는 상태로 그 시간의 대부분을 보낸다. 사실 코알라는 생각을 하는 데에 시간을 거의 사용하지 않는데, 그것들의 뇌는 실제로 지난 몇 세기 동안 크기가 줄어든 것처럼 보인다. 코알라는 뇌가 겨우 두개골의 절반을 채운다고 알려진 유일한 동물이다.

Why? 왜 정답일까?

앞뒤로 절과 절을 연결하는 접속사의 기능을 하면서 동시에 선행사 **The koala**의 소유

격을 나타낼 수 있는 말이 필요하므로, ⑤의 대명사 **its**는 소유격 관계대명사 **whose**로 바뀌어야 한다. 어법상 틀린 것은 ⑤이다.

Why? 왜 오답일까?

① 뒤에 주어인 **the compounds**와 동사 **kept**가 나오는 완전한 절이 이어지므로, 전치사인 **because of**가 아닌 접속사 **because**를 사용하여 이유를 설명한 것은 적절하다.
② 앞에 「so + 원급」 형태의 **so low**가 나오므로, '~해서 …하다'의 부사절을 이끄는 **that**을 쓴 것은 적절하다.
③ 3인칭 복수 주어인 **they** 뒤로 현재시제의 동사 **move**를 강조하기 위해 「do + 동사원형」의 **do**를 쓴 것은 적절하다.
④ 뒤에 과거의 기간 표현인 **over the last few centuries**가 나와 '뇌가 줄어든' 일이 현재에 앞서 일어났음을 알 수 있으므로, 주절보다 먼저 일어난 사건을 묘사하는 완료부정사 **(to) have shrunk**를 쓴 것은 적절하다.

- **suspect** ⓥ 의심하다
- **state** ⓝ 상태
- **rest** ⓥ 쉬다
- **shrink** ⓥ 줄어들다, 수축하다
- **compound** ⓝ 화합물
- **nutrient** ⓝ 영양분
- **unconscious** ⓐ 의식이 없는, 무의식의
- **skull** ⓝ 두개골

구문 풀이

7행 Therefore they tend to move as little as possible — / and
주어1 동사1 「as + 원급 + as + possible : 최대한 ~한/하게」
when they do move, they often look as though they're in slow motion.
동사 강조 주어2 동사2 마치 ~인 것처럼

★★ 문제 해결 꿀~팁 ★★

▶ 많이 틀린 이유는?
'동사 강조', '완료부정사' 등 다소 지엽적이며 난이도가 높은 개념을 다루어 까다로운 어법 문제이다. ③의 경우, 동사를 강조하는 **do**의 형태를 결정하기 위해서는 앞에 나오는 **they**와 뒤에 나오는 동사 **look**을 봐야 한다. 수는 3인칭 복수이고 시제는 현재이므로 **do**로 **move**를 강조한 것은 어법상 적절하다. ④는 주절의 동사가 현재형인 **appear**로 쓰였고, 부정사구는 과거로부터의 기간 부사구인 **over the last few centuries**와 어울려 쓰였음을 감안할 때, 주절보다 앞선 시제임을 나타내는 「to have + 과거분사」 형태로 쓰인 것이 적절하다.

▶ 문제 해결 방법은?
문법 문제에서 대명사에 밑줄이 있으면 관계대명사와 쓰임을 비교해야 한다. 특히 대명사 앞뒤로 절이 이어지고 있다면 **whose**를 쓸 자리인지 유념하여 보도록 한다.

06 편승 효과의 예를 보여주는 빛의 속도 측정의 역사 　정답률 63% | 정답 ⑤

다음 글의 밑줄 친 부분 중, 문맥상 낱말의 쓰임이 적절하지 않은 것은?

[본문 해석]

편승 효과가 어떻게 발생하는지는 빛의 속도 측정의 역사로 입증된다. 이 속도는 상대성 이론의 기초이기 때문에, 과학에서 가장 자주 면밀하게 측정된 ① 물리량 중 하나이다. 우리가 아는 한, 그 속도는 시간이 흐르는 동안 변함이 없었다. 하지만 1870년부터 1900년까지 모든 실험에서 너무 빠른 속도를 발견했다. 그러고 나서, 1900년부터 1950년까지는 ② 반대되는 현상이 일어났다 — 모든 실험에서 너무 느린 속도를 발견했다! 결과가 항상 실제 값의 어느 한쪽에 있는 이런 오류는 '편향'이라 불린다. 그것은 아마 시간이 지나면서 실험자들이 자신들이 발견하리라 예상했던 것과 ③ 일치하도록 결과를 무의식적으로 조정했기 때문에 생겨났을 것이다. 결과가 그들이 예상한 것과 부합하면, 그들은 그것을 취했다. 결과가 부합하지 않으면, 그들은 그것을 버렸다. 그들은 고의로 부정직했던 것이 아니고, 그저 통념에 ④ 영향을 받았을 뿐이다. 그 패턴은 누군가가 예상된 것 대신에 실제로 측정된 것을 보고할 용기가 ⑤ 부족했을(→ 있었을) 때에야 바뀌었다.

Why? 왜 정답일까?

빛의 속도 측정 역사를 돌이켜 보았을 때 시기마다 너무 빠르거나 너무 느린 측정값이 연달아 보고되었던 이유는 실험자들이 자신도 모르는 사이에 통념에 따라 예상되는 결과에 맞추어 실험 결과를 채택했기 때문이라는 내용을 다룬 글이다. 마지막 문장에서는 이러한 '편승 효과'의 패턴이 깨질 수 있었던 것은 누군가 예상한 바와 달리 실제로 도출된 값을 보고할 용기를 '냈을' 때 비로소 가능했다는 결론을 제시하고 있다. 따라서 ⑤의 **lacked**를 **had**로 고쳐야 한다. 밑줄 친 낱말의 쓰임이 적절하지 않은 것은 ⑤이다.

- **demonstrate** ⓥ 입증하다
- **relativity** ⓝ 상대성
- **adjust** ⓥ 조정하다
- **measurement** ⓝ 측정, 치수, 크기
- **subconsciously** ⓐⓓ 무의식적으로
- **match** ⓥ 일치하다

- intentionally **ad** 고의로, 의도적으로
- conventional wisdom 일반 통념
- dishonest **ⓐ** 부정직한

구문 풀이

10행 This kind of error, where results are always on one side of
　　　주어　　　　　　관계부사(보충 설명)
the real value, is called "bias."
동사(5형식 수동태)　명사 보어

---

07 가짜 뉴스의 확산을 막는 방법　　정답률 67% | 정답 ③

다음 빈칸에 들어갈 말로 가장 적절한 것을 고르시오.

① political campaigns – 정치 운동
② irrational censorship – 불합리한 검열
✓③ irresponsible sharing – 무책임한 공유
④ overheated marketing – 과열된 마케팅
⑤ statistics manipulation – 통계 수치 조작

[본문 해석]

많은 가짜 뉴스 확산은 무책임한 공유를 통해 일어난다. 2016년 뉴욕에 위치한 Columbia University와 프랑스의 기술원인 Inria의 연구는 소셜 미디어에서 공유된 링크로부터의 뉴스 중 59퍼센트가 먼저 읽히지 않았음을 밝혀냈다. 사람들은 자신의 뉴스 피드나 다른 웹 사이트에 있는 흥미로운 제목이나 사진을 보고, 클릭해서 기사 전체를 살펴보지도 않은 채, 자신의 소셜 미디어 친구들을 대상으로 다시 게시하기 위해 '공유하기' 버튼을 클릭한다. 그러면 그들은 가짜 뉴스를 공유하고 있는지도 모른다. 가짜 뉴스의 확산을 막기 위해, 기사를 공유하기 전에 그것을 읽어보아라. 여러분이 그들에게 어떤 정보를 보내고 있는지 알 만큼 충분히 여러분의 소셜 미디어 친구들을 존중하라. 자세히 들여다보면, 여러분은 공유하려는 기사가 분명 속이는 것이라거나, 제목이 약속하는 것을 정말로 이야기하지 않는다거나, 또는 여러분이 실제로 그것에 동의하지 않는다는 것을 발견할지도 모른다.

Why? 왜 정답일까?

'People see an intriguing headline or photo in their news feed or on another website and then click the Share button to repost the item to their social media friends—without ever clicking through to the full article. Then they may be sharing fake news.'에서 뉴스를 공유하기 전에 그것을 제대로 읽어보지 않음으로 인해 가짜 뉴스가 확산되고 있다고 지적한 후, 이를 막기 위해서는 뉴스를 공유하기 앞서 전체 내용을 확인할 필요가 있음을 주장한 글이다. 따라서 빈칸에 들어갈 말로 가장 적절한 것은 ③ '무책임한 공유'이다.

- spread **ⓝ** 확산
- inspection **ⓝ** 검토, 조사
- irrational **ⓐ** 불합리한, 비이성적인
- overheated **ⓐ** 과열된
- intriguing **ⓐ** 흥미로운
- be about to ~하려고 하다
- censorship **ⓝ** 검열
- manipulation **ⓝ** 조작

구문 풀이

6행 People see an intriguing headline or photo in their news feed
　　　　　　　동사1
or on another website and then click the Share button to repost the
　　　　　　　　　　　　동사2　　　　　　　　　　~하기 위해
item to their social media friends — without ever clicking through to
　　　　　　　　　　　　　　　　「without + 동명사 : ~하지 않은 채」
the full article.

★★★ **1등급 대비 고난도 3점 문제**

08 우리가 고지방 음식을 찾는 이유　　정답률 35% | 정답 ①

다음 빈칸에 들어갈 말로 가장 적절한 것을 고르시오. [3점]

✓① actually be our body's attempt to stay healthy
　실제로 건강을 유지하려는 우리 몸의 시도일
② ultimately lead to harm to the ecosystem
　궁극적으로 생태계에 대한 피해를 낳을
③ dramatically reduce our overall appetite
　우리의 전반적 식욕을 극적으로 줄일
④ simply be the result of a modern lifestyle
　단지 현대 생활 방식의 결과일
⑤ partly strengthen our preference for fresh food
　신선 식품에 대한 우리의 선호를 부분적으로 강화할

[본문 해석]

기름에 튀긴 음식은 싱거운 음식보다 더 맛있고, 어린이와 어른들은 그런 음식

에 대한 취향을 발달시킨다. 지방이 많은 음식은 뇌로 하여금 진정, 항스트레스와 진정 효과를 가진 강한 호르몬인, 아드레날린의 반대로 알려진 옥시토신을 혈류에 분비하게 하고 그로 인해 '위안을 주는 음식'이란 용어가 있다. 심지어 우리는 너무 많이 먹도록 유전적으로 프로그램되어 있을지도 모른다. 수천년 동안, 음식은 매우 부족했다. 소금, 탄수화물, 지방이 있는 음식은 구하기 어려웠고, 더 많이 구할수록 더 좋았다. 이러한 모든 것은 인간의 식단에 필수적 영양소이고, 이용 가능성이 제한되었을 때, 아무리 많이 먹어도 지나침은 없었다. 사람들은 또한 음식을 위해 동물을 사냥하거나 식물을 채집해야 했고, 그것은 많은 칼로리를 필요로 했다. 오늘날은 이와 다르다. 많은 패스트푸드점의 음식과 식료품점의 포장음식과 같이 도처에 음식이 있다. 하지만 그 뿌리 깊은 '원시인 사고방식'은 우리가 너무 많아 못 먹는 만큼을 구할 수는 없다고 말한다. 그래서 '건강하지 않은' 음식에 대한 갈망은 실제로 건강을 유지하려는 우리 몸의 시도일 수 있다.

Why? 왜 정답일까?

'It's different these days.' 앞에서 아주 오랫동안 음식은 매우 부족했고, 어떤 영양소든 먹어두는 것이 다 필요하고 좋았기에 지나친 섭취라는 개념이 없었다고 언급한다. 오늘날에는 상황이 비록 달라졌지만, 'But that ingrained "caveman mentality" says that we can't ever get too much to eat.'에 따르면 우리의 사고방식은 여전히 음식이 부족하던 시대에 머물러 있다고 한다. 즉 우리가 고지방 음식을 찾는 것은 옛날 관점에서 생각하면 '필요하게' 여겨지는 행위일 수 있다는 것이다. 따라서 빈칸에 들어갈 말로 가장 적절한 것은 ① '실제로 건강을 유지하려는 우리 몸의 시도'일이다.

- bland **ⓐ** 싱거운, 담백한, 특징 없는
- calming **ⓐ** 진정시키는
- genetically **ad** 유전적으로
- carry-out food 포장음식
- ultimately **ad** 궁극적으로
- strengthen **ⓥ** 강화하다
- release **ⓥ** 분비하다
- comfort food 위안을 주는 음식
- scarce **ⓐ** 드문
- mentality **ⓝ** 사고방식
- dramatically **ad** 극적으로

구문 풀이

9행 Food, (along with salt, carbs, and fat), was hard to get, and
　　　주어　　（ ）: 삽입구　　　　　　　동사
the more you got, the better.
「the + 비교급 ~,　the + 비교급 ... : ~할수록 더 ...하다」

★★ 문제 해결 꿀~팁 ★★

▶ **많이 틀린 이유는?**

우리가 기름진 음식을 선호하는 이유로 우리 뇌가 아직 과거에 머물러 있기 때문(caveman mentality)이라는 내용을 다룬 글이다. 글에 따르면 과거에는 식량이 부족해서 음식을 구하는 대로 다 먹어두면 좋았지만, 오늘날에는 식량이 풍부해졌고, 따라서 기름진 음식이 '건강하지 않게' 여겨지게 되었음에도 우리의 몸은 계속해서 기름진 음식을 찾는다고 하였다. 최다 오답인 ④에서는 우리가 기름진 음식을 찾는 까닭이 현대적 생활 방식(a modern lifestyle)에 있다고 하는데, 이는 정답의 주요 근거인 'caveman mentality'라는 표현과 정반대다.

▶ **문제 해결 방법은?**

더 이상 건강하게 여겨지지 않는 기름진 음식이 과거에는 사람이 살아남고 건강을 유지하는 데 도움이 되는 것이었기에, 그 시절 사고방식이 아직 박혀 있는 인간으로서는 '건강을 유지하기 위해' 기름진 음식을 찾는 것이라는 내용을 완성시키는 말이 빈칸에 들어가야 한다.

★★★ **1등급 대비 고난도 2점 문제**

09 협상에서 근원적인 이해관계 살피기　　정답률 29% | 정답 ⑤

주어진 글 다음에 이어질 글의 순서로 가장 적절한 것을 고르시오.

① (A) - (C) - (B)　　　② (B) - (A) - (C)
③ (B) - (C) - (A)　　　④ (C) - (A) - (B)
✓⑤ (C) - (B) - (A)

[본문 해석]

두 사람이 도서관에서 싸우는 이야기를 생각해 보자. 한 사람은 창문을 열고 싶어 하고 다른 사람은 그것을 닫고 싶어 한다. 그들은 얼마나 많이, 즉 조금, 절반, 혹은 4분의 3 정도 중 얼마나 열어 둘지에 대해 옥신각신한다.

(C) 어떤 해결책도 둘 다를 만족시키지 못한다. 사서를 투입하라. 사서는 한 명에게 왜 창문을 열고 싶어 하는지 묻는다. "신선한 공기를 쐬기 위해서."(라는 답이 돌아온다.) 사서는 다른 사람에게도 왜 창문을 닫고 싶어

하는지 묻는다. "외풍을 피하기 위해서."(라는 답이 돌아온다.)

(B) 잠시 생각한 후, 사서는 옆방의 창문을 활짝 열고, 외풍 없이 신선한 공기를 들여온다. 이 이야기는 많은 협상의 전형이다. 당사자들의 문제가 입장 충돌로 보이기 때문에, 그들은 자연스레 (자신의) 입장을 말하는 경향이 있고, 흔히 막다른 상황에 이른다.

(A) 만약 창문을 열거나 닫기를 원하는, 말로 언급된 두 사람의 입장에만 집중했다면 사서는 자신이 생각해 낸 해결책을 생각해 낼 수 없었을 것이다. 대신에, 사서는 신선한 공기가 있고 외풍이 없어야 한다는 그들의 근본적인 이해관계를 살펴보았다.

Why? 왜 정답일까?

주어진 글은 도서관에 있는 두 사람 중 한 사람은 창문을 열고 싶어 하고 다른 사람은 창문을 닫고 싶어 하여 충돌이 일어나는 상황을 소개한다. 이어서 (C)는 주어진 글에서 언급되듯이 창문을 약간만 열든, 절반만 열든, 4분의 3을 열든 두 사람 모두를 만족시키기는 어렵기 때문에, 사서를 투입해서 이유를 들어본다고 언급한다. (B)에서는 두 사람의 이야기를 모두 들어본 사서가 잠시 생각한 뒤 옆방 창문을 열어 문제를 해결한다고 설명하고, (A)에서는 이것이 양쪽 입장의 근원적인 욕구에 집중하여 문제를 해결한 사례임을 정리한다. 따라서 글의 순서로 가장 적절한 것은 ⑤ '(C) – (B) – (A)'이다.

- **quarrel** ⓥ 싸우다
- **crack** ⓝ (좁은) 틈, (갈라진) 금
- **invent** ⓥ 발명하다, ~을 지어내다
- **underlying** ⓐ 근본적인, 기저에 있는
- **negotiation** ⓝ 협상
- **argue back and forth** 옥신각신하다
- **librarian** ⓝ (도서관의) 사서
- **state** ⓥ 언급하다, 말하다
- **typical** ⓝ 전형 ⓐ 전형적인
- **conflict** ⓝ 충돌, 갈등

구문 풀이

6행 The librarian could not have invented the solution she did
「주어 + 조동사 과거형 + have p.p. ~」
if she had focused only on the two men's stated positions of
「if + 주어 + had p.p. ~」: 가정법 과거완료(과거 사실의 반대 가정)
wanting the window open or closed.

★★ 문제 해결 꿀~팁 ★★

▶ 많이 틀린 이유는?
도서관에서 싸우는 두 사람을 중재시킨 사서의 예를 통해 협상의 기본 원칙을 보여주는 글로, (C) 이후 나머지 두 단락의 순서를 파악하는 것이 관건이다. (A)의 첫 문장을 살펴보면, 사서가 만일 두 사람이 말로 표현한 입장에만 치중했다면 '그 해결책(the solution)'을 고안할 수 없었을 것이라는 의미이다. 하지만 (C)에서는 아직 해결책이 언급되지 않으므로, (C) 뒤에 (A)를 연결하면 the solution으로 가리킬 내용이 앞에 없어 흐름이 어색해진다.

▶ 문제 해결 방법은?
(B)에서 사서가 옆방 창문을 열어 외풍 없이 신선한 공기를 들여왔다고 하는데, 바로 이 내용을 (A)에서 the solution으로 받았다.

---

10 고정 공급 일정
정답률 38% | 정답 ⑤

글의 흐름으로 보아, 주어진 문장이 들어가기에 가장 적절한 곳을 고르시오. [3점]

[본문 해석]
공급 일정은 소비자의 수요를 충족하기 위해 생산율을 바꿀 수 있는 업체의 능력을 말한다. 몇몇 업체는 증가한 수요를 맞추고자 조업도를 빠르게 늘릴 수 있다. 그러나, 스포츠 클럽은 고정된, 혹은 유연하지 못한(비탄력적인) 생산 능력을 가지고 있다. ① 그들은 소위 고정 공급 일정이라는 것을 가지고 있다. ② 이것이 의류, 장비, 회원권, 기념품 판매에는 해당하지 않는다는 것에 주목할 가치가 있다. ③ 그러나 클럽과 팀은 시즌 동안 일정 횟수만 경기할 수 있다. ④ 팬과 회원이 경기장에 들어갈 수 없으면, 그 수익은 영원히 손실된다. ⑤ 스포츠 클럽과 리그가 고정 공급 일정을 가지고 있을지라도, (경기를) 보는 소비자의 수를 늘리는 것이 가능하다. 예를 들어, 더 많은 좌석을 제공하거나, 경기장을 바꾸거나, 경기 시즌을 연장하거나, 심지어 새로운 텔레비전, 라디오, 혹은 인터넷 배급으로 스포츠 제품의 공급을 늘릴 수 있다.

Why? 왜 정답일까?

⑤ 앞에서는 고정 공급 일정으로 인해 수요에 빠르게 대응하기 어려운 스포츠 클럽의 상황을 설명한다. 한편 주어진 문장은 이렇게 고정 공급 일정일지라도 소비자의 수를 늘릴 수 있다는 내용으로 흐름을 반전시키고, ⑤ 뒤에서는 그 구체적인 방법을 열거한다. 따라서 주어진 문장이 들어가기에 가장 적절한 곳은 ⑤이다.

- **inflexible** ⓐ 유연하지 못한, 융통성 없는
- **note** ⓥ 알아차리다
- **revenue** ⓝ 수입, 수익
- **distribution** ⓝ 배급, 분배
- **inelastic** ⓐ 비탄력적인, 적응력이 없는
- **equipment** ⓝ 장비
- **extend** ⓥ 연장하다

구문 풀이

11행 It is worth noting that this is not the case for sales of clothing,
「be worth + 동명사 : ~할 가치가 있다」
equipment, memberships and memorabilia.

11-12 미국 민간 항공사의 오류 보고 시스템

미국 민항 사업에는 조종사들이 오류 보고서를 제출하도록 장려하는 매우 효과적인 시스템이 오랫동안 있어 왔다. 이 프로그램은 항공 안전에 있어 많은 개선점을 만들어 왔다. 그것을 정착시키기가 쉽지는 않았다. 조종사들은 오류를 (a) 인정하는 것에 대해 스스로 만들어낸 심한 사회적 압박감을 느꼈다. 더구나, 누구에게 그 오류들을 보고한단 말인가? 분명 그들의 고용주에게는 아닐 것이다. 처벌을 받을 수도 있기에 심지어 미국 연방 항공청(FAA)에게는 더욱 아닐 것이다. 『해결책은 항공 우주국(NASA)으로 하여금 조종사들이 그들이 저질렀거나 다른 조종사에게서 목격한 오류에 대해 반(半)익명의 오류 보고서를 제출할 수 있는 (b) 자발적인 사고 보고 체계를 만들도록 하는 것이었다.』 일단 NASA 인사부가 필요한 정보를 얻어내면, 보고서에 있던 연락처 정보를 (c) 떼어내어 조종사에게 돌려보냈다. 『이것은 NASA가 오류를 누가 보고했는지를 더 이상 알지 못한다는 것을 의미했고, 이는 (오류에 대해 제재를 가할 수 있는) 항공사나 FAA가 누가 보고서를 (d) 거절했는지(→ 제출했는지) 알아내는 것을 불가능하게 만들었다.』 만일 FAA가 독립적으로 오류를 발견하고 민사상 처벌 또는 면허정지를 실시하려고 하면, 자기 보고서의 접수가 자동으로 해당 조종사가 처벌을 면하게 해주었다. 유사한 오류가 충분히 수집되면, NASA는 그것들을 분석하여 보고서와 권고안을 항공사들과 FAA에 발송하곤 했다. 이러한 보고서는 또한 조종사들로 하여금 그들의 오류 보고서가 안정을 높이는 데 (e) 가치 있는 도구였다는 것을 깨닫게 하는 데 도움을 주었다.

- **aviation** ⓝ 항공
- **numerous** ⓐ 수많은
- **self-induced** 자기 유도의, 저절로 생긴
- **punish** ⓥ 처벌하다
- **acquire** ⓥ 얻다, 습득하다
- **enforce** ⓥ 집행하다, 실시하다
- **civil penalty** 민사상 처벌(주로 벌금형)
- **suspension** ⓝ 정지, 연기, 보류
- **exempt A from B** A로 하여금 B를 면하게 하다
- **sufficient** ⓐ 충분한
- **extremely** ⓐ 매우, 극도로
- **improvement** ⓝ 개선, 향상
- **admit to** ~을 인정하다
- **anonymous** ⓐ 익명의
- **detach** ⓥ 떼어내다, 분리시키다
- **invoke** ⓥ 적용하다, 들먹이다
- **certificate** ⓝ 자격(증)
- **automatically** ⓐ 자동으로, 저절로
- **controversy** ⓝ 논란

구문 풀이

18행 This meant that NASA no longer knew {who had reported
→ 계속적 용법(앞 문장 보충)
the error}, which made it impossible for the airline companies or the
가목적어   목적격 보어   의미상 주어
FAA (which enforced penalties against errors) to find out {who had
진목적어
submitted the report}.
{ } : 간접의문문(누가 ~했는지)

---

11 제목 파악
정답률 63% | 정답 ①

윗글의 제목으로 가장 적절한 것은?
☑ ① Aviation Safety Built on Anonymous Reports
익명 보고서로 구축된 항공 안전
② More Flexible Manuals Mean Ignored Safety
더 융통성 있는 매뉴얼은 안전 무시를 의미한다
③ Great Inventions from Unexpected Mistakes
예기치 못한 실수로부터 나온 위대한 발명품
④ Controversies over New Safety Regulations
새 안전 규정에 대한 논란
⑤ Who Is Innovating Technology in the Air?
누가 공중에서 기술을 혁신하고 있는가?

Why? 왜 정답일까?

첫 두 문장에서 미국 민간 항공사에 오류를 보고하는 효과적인 체계가 있음을 언급한 뒤, 'The solution was ~'에서는 이 체계가 반익명의 오류 보고서를 특징으로 한다는 점

을 제시한다. 따라서 글의 제목으로 가장 적절한 것은 ① '익명 보고서로 구축된 항공 안전'이다.

12 어휘 추론
정답률 48% | 정답 ④

밑줄 친 (a) ~ (e) 중에서 문맥상 낱말의 쓰임이 적절하지 <u>않은</u> 것은? [3점]

① (a) ② (b) ③ (c) ☑ (d) ⑤ (e)

Why? 왜 정답일까?

(c)가 포함된 문장과 'This meant that NASA no longer knew who had reported the error, ~'에 따르면 NASA에서는 오류 보고를 수렴한 후 보고자의 연락처를 지워서 다시 조종사들에게 돌려보냈고 누가 오류를 보고했었는지에 대한 정보를 더 이상 보관하지 않았다고 한다. 이에 근거할 때, (d)가 포함된 문장은 추후 항공사나 FAA에서 누가 오류 보고서를 '제출했는지' 알려 해도 알 수 없었다는 의미를 나타내야 한다. 따라서 (d)의 rejected를 submitted로 고쳐야 한다. 문맥상 낱말의 쓰임이 적절하지 않은 것은 ④ '(d)'이다.

DAY 30 ▸ 20분 미니 모의고사

01 ②	02 ④	03 ②	04 ⑤	05 ⑤
06 ①	07 ③	08 ②	09 ④	10 ③
11 ⑤	12 ④			

01 기억의 중요성
정답률 88% | 정답 ②

다음 글에서 필자가 주장하는 바로 가장 적절한 것은?

① 창의력 신장을 학습 활동의 목표로 삼아야 한다.
☑ 배운 것을 활용하기 위해서는 내용을 기억해야 한다.
③ 기억력 저하를 예방하기 위해 자신의 일상을 기록해야 한다.
④ 자연스러운 분위기를 만들 수 있는 농담을 알고 있어야 한다.
⑤ 학습 의욕을 유지하기 위해서는 실천 가능한 계획을 세워야 한다.

[본문 해석]

수년간 기억은 오명을 받아 왔다. 그것은 (기계적인) 암기 학습과 정보를 뇌 속으로 주입하는 것과 연관되어 왔다. 교육자들이 이해가 학습의 핵심이라고 말해 왔지만, 만약 여러분이 어떤 것을 기억해내지 못한다면 어떻게 그것을 이해할 수 있겠는가? 우리는 모두 우리가 정보를 인식하고 이해하지만, 우리가 그것을 필요로 할 때 그것을 기억해 내지 못하는 이러한 경험을 해본 적이 있다. 예를 들어, 여러분은 몇 개의 농담을 알고 있는가? 여러분은 아마도 수천 개를 들었겠지만 지금 당장은 대략 네 다섯 개만 겨우 기억해 낼 수 있다. 네 개의 농담을 기억해 내는 것과 수천 개를 인식하거나 이해하는 것 사이에는 큰 차이가 있다. 이해는 사용을 만들어 내지 않으며, 오직 여러분이 이해한 것을 즉각적으로 기억해 내고 여러분의 기억된 이해를 사용하는 것을 시행할 수 있을 때 여러분은 숙달에 이른다. 기억은 여러분이 배운 것을 저장하는 것을 의미하는데, 그렇지 않다면 애초에 우리는 왜 굳이 배우는가?

Why? 왜 정답일까?

'~ only when you can instantly recall what you understand, and practice using your remembered understanding, do you achieve mastery. Memory means storing what you have learned; otherwise, why would we bother learning in the first place?'에서 배운 것을 이해하더라도 우선 기억하고 사용해야 숙달의 경지에 이를 수 있다고 하므로, 필자의 주장으로 가장 적절한 것은 ② '배운 것을 활용하기 위해서는 내용을 기억해야 한다.'이다.

- be associated with ~와 연관되다
- cram into ~에 쑤셔 넣다
- mastery ⓝ 숙달
- bother ⓥ 굳이 ~하다
- rote learning (기계적인) 암기 학습
- instantly [ad] 즉각적으로
- otherwise [ad] 그렇지 않으면
- in the first place 애초에

구문 풀이

12행 Understanding doesn't create use: only when you can instantly ⌜only + 부사절 + recall what you understand, and practice using your remembered understanding, do you achieve mastery. 조동사 + 주어 + 동사원형 : 도치 구문⌟

★★★ 1등급 대비 고난도 3점 문제

02 통합 교육을 촉진하는 공통 용어 사용
정답률 35% | 정답 ④

다음 글의 주제로 가장 적절한 것은? [3점]

① difficulties in finding meaningful links between disciplines
  학문 분야 간 유의미한 연결고리를 찾는 것의 어려움
② drawbacks of applying a common language to various fields
  공통 언어를 다양한 분야에 적용하는 것의 단점
③ effects of diversifying the curriculum on students' creativity
  커리큘럼을 다양화하는 것이 학생들의 창의력에 미치는 효과
☑ necessity of using a common language to integrate the curriculum
  커리큘럼 통합을 위해 공통된 용어를 사용할 필요성
⑤ usefulness of turning abstract thoughts into concrete expressions
  추상적 사고를 구체적 표현으로 전환하는 것의 유용성

[본문 해석]

교육은 나뭇가지, 잔가지, 잎이 모두 공통의 핵심에서 나오는 방식을 밝히면서, 지식의 나무 줄기에 초점을 맞춰야 한다. 다양한 분야의 실무자들이 혁신

DAY 30

과정에 대한 경험을 공유하고 그들의 창의적 활동 사이의 연결 고리를 발견할 수 있는 공통 언어를 제공하면서, 사고를 위한 도구는 이 핵심에서 비롯된다. 교육과정 전반에 걸쳐 동일한 용어가 사용될 때, 학생들은 서로 다른 과목들과 수업들을 연결하기 시작한다. 글쓰기 수업에서 추상을 연습하고, 회화나 그림 그리기 수업에서 추상을 연습하고, 그리고 모든 경우에 그들이 그것을 추상이라고 일컫는다면, 그들은 학문의 경계를 넘어 사고하는 방법을 이해하기 시작한다. 그들은 자기 생각을 하나의 개념과 표현 방식에서 다른 방식으로 바꾸는 방법을 알게 된다. 용어들과 도구들이 보편적 상상력의 일부로 제시될 때 학문들을 연결하는 것은 자연스럽게 이루어진다.

Why? 왜 정답일까?

공통 용어 사용이 다양한 학문을 자연스럽게 연결할 수 있다(When the same terms are employed across the curriculum, students begin to link different subjects and classes.)는 내용이므로, 글의 주제로 가장 적절한 것은 ④ '커리큘럼 통합을 위해 공통된 용어를 사용할 필요성'이다.

- education ⓝ 교육
- reveal ⓥ 드러내다
- twig ⓝ 잔가지
- stem from ~에서 유래하다
- innovation ⓝ 혁신
- employ ⓥ 사용하다
- disciplinary ⓐ (학문) 분야의
- naturally ad 자연적으로
- drawback ⓝ 문제
- necessity ⓝ 필요성
- trunk ⓝ (나무) 줄기
- branch ⓝ (나무) 가지
- emerge from ~에서 생겨나다
- practitioner ⓝ 실무자
- term ⓝ 용어
- abstract ⓥ 추상하다, 요약하다
- conception ⓝ 개념
- as part of ~의 일환으로
- diversify ⓥ 다양화하다
- concrete ⓐ 구체적인

구문 풀이

3행 Tools for thinking stem from this core, providing a common language [with which practitioners (in different fields) may share their experience of the process of innovation and discover links (between their creative activities)].

★★ 문제 해결 꿀~팁 ★★

▶ 많이 틀린 이유는?
글 중반과 후반부에 다양한 학문 별로 공통된 용어를 사용해야 한다는 핵심 내용이 제시된다. ②는 주제와 정면으로 상충하며, ③은 '커리큘럼의 다양화', '창의력' 등 주제와 무관한 소재를 언급하므로 답으로 적절하지 않다.

▶ 문제 해결 방법은?
must가 포함된 첫 문장이 '지식의 나무 줄기'라는 비유로 주제를 제시하기 때문에 추상적으로 느껴진다. 하지만 주제는 반복 제시되기 마련이므로, 처음이 어렵다면 결론에 집중하면 된다.

03 Alice Coachman의 생애 정답률 92% | 정답 ②

Alice Coachman에 관한 다음 글의 내용과 일치하지 않는 것은?
① 집 근처에서 맨발로 달리며 훈련했다.
☑② 육상 경기에서의 재능을 고등학교 때부터 보였다.
③ 런던 올림픽에서 높이뛰기 올림픽 기록과 미국 기록을 세웠다.
④ 흑인 여성 최초로 올림픽 금메달리스트가 되었다.
⑤ 9개의 명예의 전당에 올랐다.

[본문 해석]

Alice Coachman은 1923년 미국 Georgia의 Albany에서 태어났다. 당시의 인종 차별 때문에 운동 훈련 시설을 이용할 수 없었기 때문에, 그녀는 자신에게 이용 가능한 것을 사용하여, 『자신의 집 근처 비포장도로를 따라 맨발로 달리고,』 점프를 연습하기 위해 집에서 만든 장비를 사용하면서 훈련했다. 『육상 경기에서의 그녀의 재능은 일찍이 초등학교 때 눈에 띄었다.』 Coachman은 계속 열심히 연습하여 고등학교와 대학교 시절 동안 여러 대회에서의 자신의 성취로 주목을 받았다. 『1948년 런던 올림픽에서 Coachman은 높이뛰기에 출전해 5피트 6.5 인치에 도달하여 올림픽과 미국 기록을 둘 다 세웠다.』 『이 성과로 그녀는 올림픽 금메달을 딴 최초의 흑인 여성이 되었다.』 『그녀는 미국 올림픽 명예의 전당을 포함하여, 9개의 각기 다른 명예의 전당에 올랐다.』 Coachman은 일생을 교육에 바친 후 2014년에 Georgia에서 90세의 나이로 사망했다.

Why? 왜 정답일까?

'Her talent in track and field was noticeable as early as elementary school.'에서 Alice Coachman은 초등학교 시절부터 육상 경기에 대한 재능을 보였다고 하므로, 내용과 일치하지 않는 것은 ② '육상 경기에서의 재능을 고등학교 때부터 보였다.'이다.

Why? 왜 오답일까?

① '~ she trained ~ running barefoot along the dirt roads near her home ~'의 내용과 일치한다.
③ 'In the 1948 London Olympics, Coachman competed in the high jump, reaching 5 feet, 6.5 inches, setting both an Olympic and an American record.'의 내용과 일치한다.
④ 'This accomplishment made her the first black woman to win an Olympic gold medal.'의 내용과 일치한다.
⑤ 'She is in nine different Halls of Fame, ~'의 내용과 일치한다.

- access ⓥ 접근하다, 이용하다
- facility ⓝ 시설
- of the time 그 당시의, 당대의
- dirt road 비포장도로, 흙길
- track and field 육상 경기
- competition ⓝ 대회
- accomplishment ⓝ 성취
- athletic ⓐ 운동의, 육상의
- racism ⓝ 인종 차별주의
- barefoot ad 맨발로
- equipment ⓝ 장비
- noticeable ⓐ 눈에 띄는, 두드러지는
- compete ⓥ 겨루다, (시합 등에) 참가하다
- dedicate A to B A를 B에 바치다

구문 풀이

2행 Since she was unable to access athletic training facilities because of the racism of the time, she trained using what was available to her, running barefoot along the dirt roads near her home and using homemade equipment to practice her jumping.

04 자기 자신을 대상으로 한 실험의 문제점 정답률 54% | 정답 ⑤

다음 글의 밑줄 친 부분 중, 어법상 틀린 것은? [3점]

[본문 해석]

인간 피험자에 대한 과학 실험을 다루는 규정은 엄격하다. 피험자는 충분한 설명에 입각한 서면 동의를 해야 하고, 실험자는 자신들의 실험 계획을 제출하여 감독 기관에 의해 철저한 검토를 받아야 한다. 자기 자신을 (대상으로) 실험하는 과학자들은 법률적으로는 아니더라도 기능적으로는 다른 사람을 실험하는 것과 관련된 규제를 피할 수 있다. 그들은 또한 관련된 윤리적인 문제도 대부분 피할 수 있는데, 실험을 고안한 과학자보다 그것의 잠재적인 위험을 더 잘 아는 사람은 아마 없을 것(이기 때문)이다. 그럼에도 불구하고, 자신을 대상으로 실험하는 것은 심각하게 문제가 있는 상태이다. 한 가지 분명한 문제점은 (실험에) 수반되는 위험인데, 위험이 존재함을 안다고 해서 위험이 줄어드는 것이 결코 아니다. 덜 분명한 문제점은 실험이 만들어낼 수 있는 데이터의 범위가 제한되어 있다는 것이다. 인체의 해부학적 구조와 생리적 현상은 성별, 나이, 생활 방식, 그리고 기타 요인에 따라 사소하지만 유의미하게 다르다. 따라서, 단 한 명의 피험자에게서 얻은 실험 결과는 가치가 제한적이며, 피험자의 반응이 집단으로서의 인간이 보이는 반응의 전형인지 혹은 이례적인 것인지 알 방법이 없다.

Why? 왜 정답일까?

앞에 선행사가 없고 뒤에 주어, 동사, 보어를 갖춘 완전한 2형식 구조가 연결되는 것으로 보아 관계대명사 what 대신 명사절 접속사 that을 써야 한다. 어법상 틀린 것은 ⑤이다.

Why? 왜 오답일까?

① 꾸밈을 받는 명사 the restrictions가 다른 사람을 대상으로 한 실험과 '연관지어진' 대상이므로 과거분사 associated를 쓴 것은 어법상 맞다.
② 맥락상 앞에 나온 an experiment를 받기 위해 단수대명사 it이 적절하게 쓰였다. 대명사에 밑줄이 있으면 기본적으로 수 일치를 살펴보도록 한다.
③ 앞에 나온 2형식 동사 remains의 보어가 형용사인 problematic이므로, 이 형용사 보어를 꾸미는 deeply가 적절하게 쓰였다.
④ 세미콜론(;) 뒤의 'knowing ~'은 동명사구 주어이므로 단수 취급해야 한다. 따라서 does를 쓴 것은 어법상 맞다. knowing과 does 사이의 that절은 knowing의 목적어인 명사절이다.

- regulation ⓝ 규정, 규제
- strict ⓐ 엄격한

- **informed** ⓐ 정보에 입각한
- **restriction** ⓝ 규제, 제한
- **sidestep** ⓥ 피하다
- **hazard** ⓝ 위험
- **drawback** ⓝ 문제점, 결점
- **atypical** ⓐ 이례적인
- **oversee** ⓥ 감독하다
- **associated** ⓐ 관련된
- **presumably** 〔ad〕 아마, 짐작건대
- **devise** ⓥ 고안하다, 생각해 내다
- **derive A from B** A를 B로부터 얻다

구문 풀이

4행 Scientists [who experiment on themselves] can, (functionally
주어(선행사)　　　재귀대명사(= Scientists)　조동사　( ): 삽입구
if not legally), avoid the restrictions associated with experimenting
동사원형　　목적어　　　　과거분사
on other people.

★★★ 1등급 대비 고난도 3점 문제

05　정상 과학의 특징　　정답률 34% | 정답 ⑤

다음 글의 밑줄 친 부분 중, 문맥상 낱말의 쓰임이 적절하지 않은 것은? [3점]

[본문 해석]

정상 과학은 정확히 무엇을 포함하는가? Thomas Kuhn에 따르면, 그것은 주로 *문제 해결*의 문제이다. 패러다임이 아무리 성공적이더라도, 그것은 항상 특정한 문제, 즉 그것이 쉽게 수용할 수 없는 현상이나, 이론의 예측과 실험적 사실 간의 불일치를 ① 마주할 것이다. 정상 과학자들의 일은 패러다임에 가능한 한 변화를 거의 주지 않으면서, 이러한 사소한 문제를 ② 제거하려고 노력하는 것이다. 그래서 정상 과학은 ③ 보수적인 활동으로, 그것을 실행하는 사람은 세상이 깜짝 놀랄 어떤 발견이라도 하고자 노력하고 있지 않고, 오히려 단지 현존하는 패러다임을 발전시키고 확장하려는 것이다. Kuhn의 말로 하자면, '정상 과학은 사실이나 이론의 참신함을 목표로 하지 않으며, 성공적일 때에는 아무 것도 못 찾아낸다.' 무엇보다도, Kuhn은 정상 과학자들이 패러다임을 *시험하려* 노력하지 않는다는 것을 강조했다. 오히려 그들은 패러다임을 ④ 의심하지 않고 받아들이고, 그것이 설정한 한계 안에서 자신의 연구를 수행한다. 만약 정상 과학자가 패러다임과 ⑤ 상응하는(→ 상충하는) 실험 결과를 얻는다면, 그들은 보통 자신의 실험 기술에 결함이 있고, 패러다임이 틀린 것은 아니라고 여긴다.

Why? 왜 정답일까?

④가 포함된 문장에서 정상 과학자들은 패러다임을 시험하려 하기보다는 의심 없이 받아들인다고 하므로, 흐름상 마지막 문장은 심지어 패러다임과 '맞지 않는' 실험 결과가 나오더라도 과학자들이 패러다임에 의문을 갖기보다는 실험 기술에 문제가 있다고 본다는 의미여야 한다. 즉 ⑤의 corresponds를 conflicts로 고쳐야 문맥이 자연스럽다. 따라서 문맥상 낱말의 쓰임이 가장 어색한 것은 ⑤이다.

- **primarily** 〔ad〕 주로
- **phenomenon** ⓝ 현상
- **mismatch** ⓝ 부조화
- **eliminate** ⓥ 제거하다
- **earth-shattering** ⓐ 세상이 깜짝 놀랄
- **novelty** ⓝ 참신함, 새로움
- **correspond with** ~와 부합하다, 일치하다
- **encounter** ⓥ 마주하다
- **accommodate** ⓥ 수용하다
- **experimental** ⓐ 실험에 근거한
- **conservative** ⓐ 보수적인
- **extend** ⓥ 확장하다
- **unquestioningly** 〔ad〕 의심 없이

구문 풀이

3행 However successful a paradigm is, it will always encounter
「however + 형/부 + 주어 + 동사 : 아무리 ~하더라도」
certain problems — phenomena [which it cannot easily accommodate],
　　　　　　　　선행사　　　목적격 관·대
or mismatches (between the theory's predictions and the experimental
　　　　　　　　　　　　　　　　　　( ): 전치사구(수식)
facts.)

★★ 문제 해결 꿀~팁 ★★

▶ 많이 틀린 이유는?

정상 과학자들은 기존의 패러다임을 수용하고 이를 유지보수하는 선에서 연구를 진행한다는 내용의 글이므로, 이들이 패러다임을 '의심 없이' 받아들인다는 의미의 ④는 문맥상 적합하다.

▶ 문제 해결 방법은?

정답인 ⑤의 주변 문맥을 보면, 정상 과학자들이 패러다임을 의심하는 대신 자기 실험이 잘못됐다고 느끼는 상황을 언급하고 있다. 이는 패러다임과 실험 결과가 '맞지 않아서' 사고 체계에 의문을 제기해볼 법한데도 그렇게 하지 않는 경우를 설명하는 것이므로, ⑤의 corresponds가 부적절함을 알 수 있다.

06　생물학적인 경쟁과 경제학적 경쟁의 유사성　　정답률 58% | 정답 ①

다음 빈칸에 들어갈 말로 가장 적절한 것을 고르시오. [3점]

✓① similar – 비슷한
② confusing – 혼란스러운
③ unrealistic – 비현실적인
④ conventional – 전통적인
⑤ complex – 복잡한

[본문 해석]

Charles Darwin이 자연 선택 이론을 전개했을 때, 그는 유기체의 적응이 결국 생존과 번식을 위한 경쟁에 의해 야기되는 진화 과정을 묘사했다. 이 생물학상의 '생존 경쟁'은 경쟁 시장에서 경제적 성공을 얻기 위해 애쓰는 사업자들 간에 일어나는 인간의 분투와 상당히 닮았다. Darwin이 연구를 발표하기 오래 전에, 사회 과학자 Adam Smith는 이미 사업에서 경쟁이 경제적 효율과 적응 이면에 있는 추진력이라고 생각했다. 진화 생물학과 경제학의 근대 이론 창시자들이 주된 견해의 근거로 둔 사상이 얼마나 *비슷한*가는 정말 매우 놀랍다.

Why? 왜 정답일까?

'This biological "struggle for existence" bears considerable resemblance to the human struggle between businessmen who are striving for economic success in competitive markets.'에서 생물학의 생존 경쟁 개념은 시장에서 일어나는 인간끼리의 경쟁과 그 양태가 '닮아있다'고 이야기하므로, 빈칸에 들어갈 말로 가장 적절한 것은 ① '비슷한'이다.

- **natural selection** 자연 선택
- **adaptation** ⓝ 적응
- **struggle** ⓥ 투쟁하다
- **publish** ⓥ 발표하다, 출시하다
- **efficiency** ⓝ 효율(성)
- **organismic** ⓐ 유기체의, 생물의
- **reproduction** ⓝ 번식, 재생
- **strive** ⓥ 분투하다
- **driving force** 추진력
- **evolutionary** ⓐ 진화의

구문 풀이

4행 This biological "struggle for existence" bears considerable
　　　　　　　　　　　　　　　　　　　　　~을 닮다　동반 생략 가능
resemblance to the human struggle between businessmen [who are
　　　　　　　　　　　　　　　　　　　　　　　주격 관계대명사
striving for economic success in competitive markets].

07　대양의 연결성과 유동성　　정답률 56% | 정답 ③

다음 글에서 전체 흐름과 관계 없는 문장은?

[본문 해석]

주요 대양은 모두 서로 연결되어 있어, 그것들의 지리적 경계가 대륙의 경계보다 덜 명확하다. 결과적으로 그들의 생물 군집은 육지에서의 생물 군집보다 명확한 차이를 덜 보여준다. ① 각 해저분지 안의 물이 천천히 회전하기 때문에 대양 자체가 끊임없이 움직인다. ② 이 이동하는 물은 해양 생물을 여기저기로 운반하며, 또한 그들의 새끼나 유충의 분산을 돕는다. ③ 즉 연안 해류는 예상보다 훨씬 덜 동물들을 이동시킬 뿐 아니라 근해 지역 내로 동물을 가두기도 한다. ④ 더욱이 다양한 지역의 대양 해수 덩어리 환경 사이의 변화도는 매우 점진적이며, 종종 생태적 내성이 다른 매우 다양한 유기체가 서식하는 넓은 지역으로 확장된다. ⑤ 유기체의 이동에 방해물이 있을 수 있지만, 넓은 대양에 확실한 경계는 없다.

Why? 왜 정답일까?

주요 대양은 서로 연결되어 있으며 그 경계가 대륙보다 불명확하므로 대양 안의 생물은 아주 넓은 지역까지 이동하고 퍼져나갈 수 있다는 내용의 글이다. ①, ②, ④, ⑤는 주제를 적절히 뒷받침하지만, ③은 연안 해류가 동물을 예상보다 덜 이동시키고 동물을 가두기도 한다는 내용을 다루며 흐름에서 벗어난다. 따라서 전체 흐름과 관계없는 문장은 ③이다.

- **interconnected** ⓐ 상호 연결된
- **continually** 〔ad〕 계속해서
- **rotate** ⓥ 회전하다
- **larva** ⓝ 유충, 애벌레
- **inhabit** ⓥ ~에 거주하다
- **geographical** ⓐ 지리적인
- **basin** ⓝ 분지, (큰 강의) 유역
- **dispersal** ⓝ 분산
- **gradual** ⓐ 점진적인
- **tolerance** ⓝ 내성, 관용

구문 풀이

1행 The major oceans are all interconnected, so that their
　　　　　　　　　　　　　　　　　접속사(~해서 …하다)
geographical boundaries are less clear than those of the continents.
　　　　　　　　　　「less + 원급 + than : ~보다 덜 …한」　　= boundaries

DAY 30

★★★ 1등급 대비 고난도 2점 문제

08 움직임에 대한 착각
정답률 19% | 정답 ②

글의 흐름으로 보아, 주어진 문장이 들어가기에 가장 적절한 곳을 고르시오.

[본문 해석]
당신은 어떤 역에서 다른 기차 옆에 서 있는 어느 기차 안에 있다. 갑자기 당신은 움직이기 시작하는 것 같다. 하지만 그때 당신은 당신이 사실상 전혀 움직이지 않고 있다는 것을 깨닫는다. ① 반대 방향으로 움직이고 있는 것은 바로 그 두 번째 기차이다. ② 상대적인 움직임에 대한 착각이 다른 방식으로도 작동한다. 당신은 다른 기차가 움직였다고 생각하지만, 결국 움직이고 있는 것은 바로 당신 자신의 기차라는 것을 발견하게 된다. ③ 외견상의 움직임과 실제 움직임 사이에 차이를 구별하는 것은 어려울 수 있다. ④ 물론, 당신의 기차가 덜컥하고 움직이기 시작한다면 이는 쉽지만, 만약 당신의 기차가 매우 부드럽게 움직인다면 쉽지 않다. ⑤ 당신의 기차가 약간 더 느린 기차를 따라잡을 때, 당신은 때때로 속아서 당신의 기차가 정지해 있고 다른 기차가 천천히 뒤쪽으로 움직이고 있다고 생각할 수 있다.

Why? 왜 정답일까?

② 앞의 두 문장에서 우리가 타고 있는 기차가 움직이고 있다는 느낌을 받을 때 실제로 움직이는 차는 맞은편에 있는 차일 수도 있다는 내용을 제시한 데 이어, 주어진 문장은 같은 착각이 '다른 방식'으로 일어날 수도 있음을 지적한다. ② 뒤에서는 이 '다른 방식'을 구체화하는 진술로서 다른 기차가 움직였다고 여겨질 때 실제로는 우리가 타고 있는 기차가 움직인 것일 수도 있다고 설명한다. 따라서 주어진 문장이 들어가기에 가장 적절한 곳은 ②이다.

- illusion ⓝ 착각
- opposite ⓐ 정반대의, 맞은편의
- smoothly ⓐⓓ 부드럽게
- slightly ⓐⓓ 약간
- still ⓐ 가만히 있는, 고요한
- relative ⓐ 상대적인
- tell ⓥ 구별하다
- overtake ⓥ 앞지르다, 추월하다
- fool oneself into ~ 속아서 ~하다

구문 풀이

7행 You think (that) the other train has moved, only to discover that it is your own train that is moving.
생략(접속사) / 「only+to부정사 : 결국 ~하다」 / 「it is ~ that … : 강조 구문」

★★ 문제 해결 꿀~팁 ★★

▶ 많이 틀린 이유는?
구문이 쉽고 예시 또한 친숙한 편이지만 논리적 공백을 확실히 파악하지 못한다면 오답을 고르기 쉽다. ②를 기점으로 '직접 탄 기차가 움직인다고 착각하는 경우 vs. 맞은편 기차가 움직인다고 착각하는 경우'가 대조를 이루고 있는데 사이에 역접을 나타내는 말이 없어 논리의 흐름이 깨진다. ③과 ④는 예시 이후에 일반적인 설명을 제시하는 부분으로서 앞뒤가 서로 맞물려 이어진다.

▶ 문제 해결 방법은?
지문에 앞서 주어진 문장을 먼저 읽고 논리의 흐름을 예측해보도록 한다. 주어진 문장의 illusion과 the other way로 볼 때, 앞에 일단 움직임의 '착각'을 보여주는 예가 언급된 뒤, 이 예와 반대되는 다른 경우가 뒤에서 언급될 것임을 예측할 수 있다.

09 이야기 반복을 통한 부정적 감정의 극복 유도
정답률 54% | 정답 ④

다음 글의 내용을 한 문장으로 요약하고자 한다. 빈칸 (A), (B)에 들어갈 말로 가장 적절한 것은?

	(A)	(B)
①	recall 기억해 내다	adapt 각색하다
②	recall 기억해 내다	repeat 반복하다
③	overcome 극복하다	erase 지우다
④✓	overcome 극복하다	repeat 반복하다
⑤	prevent 예방하다	erase 지우다

[본문 해석]
아이가 고통스럽거나 실망스럽거나 무서운 순간을 경험할 때, 격렬한 감정과 신체적인 느낌이 우뇌에 들이닥쳐 감당하기 힘들 수 있다. 이런 일이 일어날 때, 우리는 부모로서 아이가 무슨 일이 벌어지고 있는지 이해하기 시작할 수 있게 그 상황에 좌뇌를 불러들이도록 도와줄 수 있다. 이런 종류의 통합을 증진할 수 있는 가장 좋은 방법 중 하나는 무섭거나 고통스러운 경험의 이야기를 되풀이하도록 돕는 것이다. 예를 들어, Bella가 아홉 살 때 변기의 물을 내리자 변기가 넘쳤는데, 물이 불어나서 바닥으로 쏟아지는 것을 본 경험은 이후로 그녀가 변기의 물을 내리고 싶어 하지 않게 했다. Bella의 아버지 Doug이 '말해서 길들이기' 기법에 대해 배웠을 때, 그는 딸과 함께 앉아서 변기가 넘쳐흘렀을 때의 이야기를 되풀이했다. 그는 그녀가 할 수 있는 한 그 이야기를 최대한 많이 하게 해 주었고, 세부적인 내용을 채우는 데 도움을 주었다. 그 이야기를 여러 차례 되풀이하고 난 후 Bella의 두려움은 줄어들었고 결국 사라졌다.

➡ 우리는 아이로 하여금 고통스런 이야기를 가능한 한 많이 (B) 반복하게 하여서 아이가 고통스럽고 무서운 경험을 (A) 극복하게 할 수 있을지도 모른다.

Why? 왜 정답일까?

서두에서 주제를 제시하고 이어서 예시를 든 뒤 예시의 결론 형태로 주제를 반복하며 마무리되는 글이다. for instance 앞에서 격한 감정이 우뇌로 들이닥쳐 아이가 힘들어할 경우 좌뇌를 쓰게 해야 하는데, 이러한 좌뇌와 우뇌의 통합을 촉진하기 위해서는 감정의 원인이 되는 이야기를 반복시키는 것이 좋다(One of the best ways to promote this type of integration is to help retell the story of the frightening or painful experience.)는 내용이 나온다. 또한 글의 마지막 두 문장에서도 변기 물을 내리는 데 두려움을 느끼는 아이에게 왜 무서워하는지에 대한 이야기를 되풀이시키자 아이의 두려움이 감소되었다는 결론이 제시되고 있다. 따라서 요약문의 빈칸 (A), (B)에 들어갈 말로 가장 적절한 것은 부정적인 감정을 유발하는 이야기를 반복시킬 때 그 감정을 극복하도록 도울 수 있다는 뜻을 완성하는 ④ '(A) overcome(극복하다), (B) repeat(반복하다)'이다.

- disappointing ⓐ 실망스러운
- intense ⓐ 강렬한, 극심한
- hemisphere ⓝ 반구
- integration ⓝ 통합
- overflow ⓥ (가득 담겨) 넘쳐흐르다
- pour ⓥ 쏟아지다, 붓다
- tame ⓥ 길들이다, 다스리다
- overcome ⓥ 극복하다
- overwhelming ⓐ 압도하는, 저항하기 힘든
- sensation ⓝ 감각, 기분, 느낌
- promote ⓥ 장려하다, 진작하다
- frightening ⓐ 무서운, 겁에 질리게 하는
- flush ⓥ (변기의) 물을 내리다, 물이 쏟아지다
- unwilling ⓐ 꺼리는, 싫어하는
- lessen ⓥ 줄어들다, 감소하다

구문 풀이

1행 When a child experiences painful, disappointing, or scary moments, / it can be overwhelming, with intense emotions and bodily sensations flooding the right brain.
「with+명사+현재분사 : 분사구문(~하면서, ~한 채로)」

10-12 딸과 함께 Karen 가족의 크리스마스 선물을 마련한 Maria

[본문 해석]

(A)

「Maria Sutton은 평균 소득이 매우 낮은 지역의 사회복지사였다.」 Maria의 많은 고객들은 근처 마을의 석탄 산업이 붕괴되었을 때 일자리를 잃었다. 아이들이 크리스마스에 얼마나 선물을 좋아하는지 알았기 때문에, 크리스마스 시즌마다 Maria는 한 가족을 위해 산타클로스의 특별 방문을 계획하려 했다. Maria의 7살 된 딸 Alice는 (a) 자기 엄마의 크리스마스 이벤트를 돕는 것에 매우 열성적이었다.

(C)

「올해 행운의 가족은 Karen이라는 이름의 25살 된 엄마와 그녀의 3살 된 아들이었고, 그를 그녀는 혼자서 키우고 있었다.」 그러나, 상황이 나빠졌다. 「크리스마스 2주 전, 지역 단체의 대표가 Maria에게 전화해서 그녀가 Karen을 위해 요청했던 지원이 성사되지 않았다고 말했다.」 산타클로스는 없었다. 선물도 없었다. Maria는 그 소식에 Alice의 얼굴에서 생기가 사라지는 것을 보았다. 이 말을 듣고 난 뒤, (c) 그녀는 자기 방으로 달려갔다.

(D)

Alice가 돌아왔을 때, 그녀의 얼굴은 결의에 차 있었다. 그녀는 그녀의 돼지 저금통에서 동전들을 세면서 꺼냈고, $4.30였다. "엄마," 그녀는 Maria에게 "(d) 전 이것이 얼마 되지 않는다는 것을 알아요. 그러나 아마도 이것으로 그 아이를 위한 선물은 살 수 있을 거예요."라고 말했다. Maria는 그녀의 딸을 사랑스럽게 안아주었다. 그다음 날, Maria는 그녀의 동료들에게 딸의 최근 프로

젝트에 대해 말했다. (e) 그녀로서는 놀랍게도, 직원들은 그들의 지갑을 열기 시작했다. Alice의 선물 이야기는 Maria의 사무실을 넘어 퍼졌고, 「Maria는 300달러를 모금할 수 있었는데,」 이것은 Karen과 아들의 크리스마스 선물을 위해 충분했다.

└── : 12번 ⑤의 근거 일치

(B)

크리스마스 전날, Maria와 Alice는 크리스마스 선물들을 가지고 Karen의 집을 방문했다. Karen이 문을 열었을 때, Maria와 Alice는 그 깜짝 놀란 여성에게 즐거운 크리스마스를 빌어주었다. 「그런 다음 Alice는 차에서 선물들을 내리기 시작했고, 그것들을 하나씩 Karen에게 건넸다.」 Karen은 믿기지 않는다는 듯 웃었고, 자신이 언젠가 어려운 다른 사람을 위해 비슷한 어떤 일을 할 수 있기를 바란다고 말했다. 집으로 돌아가는 길에, Maria는 Alice에게, "신이 (b) 네 선물을 늘렸구나."라고 말했다.

└── : 12번 ②의 근거 일치

- **social worker** 사회 복지사
- **enthusiastic** ⓐ 열성적인
- **unload** ⓥ (짐을) 내리다
- **in need** 어려운, 도움이 필요한
- **representative** ⓝ 대표 ⓐ 대표하는
- **determination** ⓝ 결의
- **collapse** ⓥ 붕괴하다
- **astonished** ⓐ 깜짝 놀란
- **disbelief** ⓝ 믿기지 않음, 불신
- **multiply** ⓥ 배가시키다
- **fall through** 성사되지 않다

구문 풀이

[A] 4행 Every Christmas season, knowing how much children loved
분사구문(~하면서) 의문부사(얼마나)
presents at Christmas, Maria tried to arrange a special visit from
~하려고 노력하다
Santa Claus for one family.

[B] 6행 Karen laughed in disbelief, and said (that) she hoped (that)
동사1 동사2 접속사(~것)
she would one day be able to do something similar for someone
주어 동사구(~할 수 있다)
else in need.

[C] 4행 Two weeks before Christmas Day, a representative from a
주어
local organization called Maria to say that the aid [she had requested
동사 부사적 용법(~하기 위해) 주어
for Karen] had fallen through.
동사(과거완료)

---

10 글의 순서 파악　　　정답률 68% | 정답 ③

주어진 글 (A)에 이어질 내용을 순서에 맞게 배열한 것으로 가장 적절한 것은?

① (B) − (D) − (C)　　　② (C) − (B) − (D)
✓③ (C) − (D) − (B)　　　④ (D) − (B) − (C)
⑤ (D) − (C) − (B)

Why? 왜 정답일까?

가난한 지역에서 사회복지사로 일하는 Maria가 매년 크리스마스 시즌에 한 가정을 상대로 특별 방문 행사를 준비하곤 했다는 배경을 설명하는 (A) 뒤에는, 올해에는 Karen과 그 아들이 선정되었지만 이들을 위한 지원 준비가 원활히 이루어지지 않았다는 내용의 (C), Maria의 딸 Alice가 자신의 저금통을 깨 Karen의 아들에게 선물을 사주겠다는 결의를 보였고 이 이야기를 알리자 Maria의 동료들이 모금에 참여했다는 내용의 (D), Maria와 Alice가 마침내 크리스마스 선물을 잘 전달했다는 내용의 (B)가 차례로 이어져야 한다. 따라서 글의 순서로 가장 적절한 것은 ③ '(C) − (D) − (B)'이다.

---

11 지칭 추론　　　정답률 55% | 정답 ⑤

밑줄 친 (a)~(e) 중에서 가리키는 대상이 나머지 넷과 다른 것은?

① (a)　　② (b)　　③ (c)　　④ (d)　　✓⑤ (e)

Why? 왜 정답일까?

(a), (b), (c), (d)는 Alice를, (e)는 앞 문장의 Maria를 가리키므로, (a)~(e) 중에서 가리키는 대상이 다른 하나는 ⑤ '(e)'이다.

---

12 세부 내용 파악　　　정답률 78% | 정답 ④

윗글에 관한 내용으로 적절하지 <u>않은</u> 것은?

① Maria는 평균 소득이 매우 낮은 지역의 사회복지사였다.

---

② 크리스마스 전날 Karen은 선물을 받았다.
③ Karen은 세 살 된 아들을 키우고 있었다.
✓④ Maria는 지역 단체 대표의 연락을 받지 못했다.
⑤ Maria는 300달러를 모금할 수 있었다.

Why? 왜 정답일까?

(C) 'Two weeks before Christmas Day, a representative from a local organization called Maria to say that the aid she had requested for Karenz had fallen through.'에서 크리스마스 2주 전 지역 단체 대표가 Maria에게 연락하여 Karen을 위해 요청한 지원이 성사되지 않았음을 알려주었다고 하므로, 내용과 일치하지 않는 것은 ④ 'Maria는 지역 단체 대표의 연락을 받지 못했다.'이다.

Why? 왜 오답일까?

① (A) 'Maria Sutton was a social worker in a place where the average income was very low.'의 내용과 일치한다.
② (B) 'On Christmas Eve, ~ Alice began to unload the gifts from the car, handing them to Karen one by one.'의 내용과 일치한다.
③ (C) 'This year's lucky family was a 25-year-old mother named Karen and her 3-year-old son, who she was raising by herself.'의 내용과 일치한다.
⑤ (D) '~ Maria was able to raise $300 ~'의 내용과 일치한다.

MEMO

수능기출 전국연합 학력평가

하루 20분 30일 완성

미니모의고사

고2
영어

The Real series ipsifly provide
questions in previous real test and you can
practice as real college scholastic ability test.

하루 20분! 30일 완성!

고1 국어　　고2 국어　　고1 영어　　고2 영어　　고3 영어

Believe in yourself and show us what you can do!
자신을 믿고 자신의 능력을 당당히 보여주자.

리얼 오리지널 하루 20분 30일 완성 | 미니 모의고사 [고2 영어]

발행처 수능 모의고사 전문 출판 입시플라이　**발행일** 2024년 10월 15일　**등록번호** 제 2017-22호
홈페이지 www.ipsifly.com　**대표전화** 02-433-9979　**구입문의** 02-433-9975　**팩스** 02-6305-9907
발행인 조용규　**편집책임** 양창열 김유 이혜민 임명선 김선영　**물류관리** 김소희 이혜리　**주소** 서울특별시 중랑구 용마산로 615 정민빌딩 3층

※ 페이지가 누락되었거나 파손된 교재는 구입하신 곳에서 교환해 드립니다.　※ 발간 이후 발견되는 오류는 입시플라이 홈페이지 정오표를 통해서 알려드립니다.